SACRED MATTER

Animacy and Authority in the Americas

DUMBARTON OAKS PRE-COLUMBIAN SYMPOSIA AND COLLOQUIA

Series Editor
Colin McEwan

Editorial Board
Thomas B. F. Cummins
Kenneth G. Hirth

SACRED MATTER
Animacy and Authority in the Americas

STEVE KOSIBA, JOHN WAYNE JANUSEK,
AND THOMAS B. F. CUMMINS

Editors

DUMBARTON OAKS RESEARCH LIBRARY AND COLLECTION
WASHINGTON, D.C.

LIBRARY OF CONGRESS CATALOGING-IN-PUBLICATION DATA

NAMES: Kosiba, Steve, editor. | Janusek, John Wayne, 1963– editor. | Cummins, Tom, 1949– editor.
TITLE: Sacred matter : animacy and authority in the Americas / Steve Kosiba, John Wayne Janusek, and
    Thomas B. F. Cummins, editors.
OTHER TITLES: Sacred matter (2020) | Dumbarton Oaks Pre-Columbian symposia and colloquia.
DESCRIPTION: Washington, D.C. : Dumbarton Oaks Research Library and Collection, [2020] | Series: Dumbarton
    Oaks Pre-Columbian symposia and colloquia | Includes bibliographical references and index. | Summary:
    "Sacred Matter: Animacy and Authority in the Americas examines animism in Pre-Columbian America,
    focusing on how objects and places played central social roles in practices that expressed and sanctified political
    authority in the Andes, Amazon, and Mesoamerica. Pre-Columbian peoples staked claims to their authority
    when they animated matter by giving life to grandiose buildings, speaking with deified boulders, and killing
    valued objects. Likewise, things and places often animated people by demanding labor, care, and nourishment.
    In these practices of animation, things were cast as active subjects, agents of political change, and representatives
    of communities. People were positioned according to specific social roles and stations: workers, worshippers,
    revolutionaries, tribute payers, or authorities. Such practices manifested political visions of social order by
    defining relationships between people, things, and the environment. Contributors to this volume present a
    range of perspectives (archaeological, art historical, ethnohistorical, and linguistic) to shed light on how Pre-
    Columbian social authority was claimed and sanctified in practices of transformation and transubstantiation—
    that is, practices that birthed, converted, or destroyed certain objects and places, as well as the social and natural
    order from which these things were said to emerge"—Provided by publisher.
IDENTIFIERS: LCCN 2019030734 | ISBN 9780884024668 (hardcover)
SUBJECTS: LCSH: Animism—Latin America. | Authority. | Indians of Mexico—Religion. | Indians of Central
    America—Religion. | Indians of South America—Religion. | Indians of Mexico—Politics and government. |
    Indians of Central America—Politics and government. | Indians of South America—Politics and government.
    | Mexico—Politics and government—To 1519. | Central America—Politics and government—To 1821. | South
    America—Politics and government.
CLASSIFICATION: LCC GN471 .S24 2020 | DDC 299.8—dc23
LC record available at https://lccn.loc.gov/2019030734

GENERAL EDITOR: Colin McEwan
ART DIRECTOR: Kathleen Sparkes
DESIGN AND COMPOSITION: Melissa Tandysh
MANAGING EDITOR: Sara Taylor

Volume based on papers presented at the Pre-Columbian Studies symposium "Sacred Matter: Animism and Authority
in Pre-Columbian America," held at the Naval Heritage Center, Washington, D.C., on October 7–8, 2016.

www.doaks.org/publications

We dedicate this volume to coeditor, colleague, and longtime friend

John Wayne Janusek,

who passed away in October 2019.

John's archaeological studies of Tiwanaku and sites farther afield
greatly advanced our knowledge and understanding of ancient South America,
specifically by directing our attention to the role and value
of the material environment in native Andean social life.

We will always carry him with us,
remembering him for his warmth, humor, and brilliance.

John Wayne Janusek (1963–2019) voyaging across Lake Titicaca, Bolivia
(photograph by Anna Guengerich).

CONTENTS

PREFACE

THE PREPARATION AND PUBLICATION OF this volume coincide with a particularly fractious and polarized period in the body politic of the United States. Tribal rivalries loom large and, increasingly, one side of the political spectrum disavows any common ground with the other. Credible, objective accounts of controversial issues attract visceral, adversarial responses, and conventional reporting of unfolding events is undermined by claims of "fake news." Divergent narratives are deployed to make sense of the stream of apparently inchoate current events. When such narratives are structured and informed by religious ideologies, they often stand in stark contrast to countervailing historical narratives. Religious paradigms generally have readily identifiable tenets and well-articulated underlying beliefs, while the "secular" narratives that have emerged with the rise of the social sciences are themselves ideologically freighted. To take just one example, should we "believe" the mythological accounts of human origins and the creation of social order as furnished by religion, or should we "believe" documented history and archaeological evidence? Each perspective is often presented within an explanatory framework that excludes or dismisses any consideration of the other. We are frequently faced with seemingly irreconcilable points of view on how to understand our place in the world and interpret our experiences of it.

What is being played out in contemporary political life between competing ideologies finds striking antecedents in other historical confrontations that inform many of the contributions to this volume. In his introduction, Steve Kosiba deftly positions us as witnesses to a dramatic episode involving the execution of the Inka emperor Thupa Amaru that epitomizes the clash of radically different worldviews and perceptions. From the Spanish invaders' perspective, the "idolatry" of Native Americans pivoted on what the Spaniards perceived as misguided beliefs regarding nature and reality. Kosiba underlines how this perception resonates with current materialist explanations of indigenous politics, which hold that native practices of animacy reflect a "false consciousness" ideology. The Spanish perspective quickly led to the conviction that autochthonous Andeans worshiped "false idols" instead of a "true god." Paradoxically, the Spanish held faithfully to the absolute conviction that the efficacy of their own wooden sculptures of the saints would assure the favorable intervention of supernatural agency. Thus, each "side" engaged in the same kind of idol veneration to the evident incomprehension and condemnation of the other. Similar kinds of misapprehensions are also documented in analogous case studies for the Caribbean (not covered in this volume). José Oliver's treatment, in *Caciques and Cemí Idols: The Web Spun by Taíno Rulers between Hispaniola and Puerto Rico* (2009), of the fluctuating relationships between both Taíno wooden sculptures and Spanish wooden icons of the saints reveals how animacy and personhood are multimodal and situationally activated (see also Joyce, this volume).

The core question that we confront time and again in the vexatious history of human affairs is whether we are condemned to forever repeat these misunderstandings. If religious belief is materialized and "factualized," while at the same time documented history is "mythologized," we face a conundrum. Moreover, if as often appears, "history" and "myth" are inextricably entwined, how do we define "reality" and arrive at a satisfactory resolution of this dilemma? The nub of the debate seems to lie in the adoption of animacy as "disposition," expressed in the different kinds and degrees of multi-animating forces that can be but are not necessarily an inherent property of the places and objects being engaged (Allen, this volume; Kosiba, this volume; see also Stephen D. Houston, *The Life Within: Classic Maya and the Matter of Permanence*, 2014). Posed against this are claims to alternate and parallel "worlds" (Fausto, this volume) that meet with skepticism on the part of other authors (Giraldo, this volume). Nevertheless, all contributors, whatever their adopted position on animism, take it seriously as a valid orientation to the world. None, however, resolve the underlying issue of whether this is an objective spiritual "reality" and, if so, how this may be universally understood. Kosiba's introduction is nicely complemented by Catherine Allen's coda, which takes us on an imagined but very real personal journey that reprises the trajectory traced by successive chapters. The attentive reader will quickly realize that the dialogue that developed en vivo in the symposium is echoed in these reflections and commentaries and further enriched by an active postconference conversational engagement between archaeologist and ethnographer. Both authors might declaim such a rigid binary categorization and justifiably suggest that if any labels are to be applied at all, then "ethnographic archaeologist" and "archaeological ethnographer" might go some way toward doing justice to their respective approaches.

What scholars have called animism is deeply rooted in preconceived assumptions about the relationship between the human consciousness and the natural world. These oblige us to revisit our own personal experiences and perspectives, together with our unexamined biases. If I were to be asked whether animacy enjoys potent and productive agency in the technologized twenty-first century, I would need only point to the seventh inning of the almost endless third game in the 2018 World Series between the Los Angeles Dodgers and the Boston Red Sox. A mighty blow to center field by Dodgers slugger Yasiel Puig just failed to clear the wall for a decisive home run. Instead of castigating himself, Puig addressed his (named) bat to encourage it to greater effort and to work with him to make it better next time. Cradling his bat fondly in his arms, he speaks with it, then proffers a tender kiss! For the skeptical, suffice it to say that the encouragement appeared to reap dividends when he subsequently struck a three-run homer to break open the fourth game. The joy, however, was short-lived, as the Red Sox bit back to eventually win the series. Moreover, the Fenway Park faithful will testify to the agentive power of place in the form of the "Green Monster" lurking in left field with the refrain "the Green Wall giveth and the Green Wall taketh away" (Anthony Burrows, personal communication, 2019). Further afield in March 2017, the Whanganui River (North Island, New Zealand) became the world's second natural resource to be accorded personhood, with the rights, duties, and liabilities of a legal person. Giving a river rights raises all kinds of practical legal issues. What kind of legal entity is the river, and who speaks for Whanganui in courts of law? Maori ritual specialists may know how to communicate with the river in contexts incommensurable with legal proceedings (for a discussion of these issues in an Andean context, see Catherine J. Allen, "Righting Imbalance: Striving for Well-Being in the Andes," *Science, Religion, and Culture* 6[1]:6–14).

How then do we understand our intellectual consciousness in relation to broader notions of animacy? We appear to have arrived at some kind of impasse in terms of human cognition and our ability to penetrate the threshold between visible and invisible worlds, also conceived of as a dichotomy of material versus spirit and body versus mind. The chapters in this volume chart progress in a paradigm shift that the field is experiencing and pose fundamental questions about the nature of cognition. What, for example, is the relationship between "percept" and "concept," and how do we wed our perceptual experience to our conceptual constructs? To ask such a question takes us to the roots of human consciousness and how we think about our thinking. What, in fact, are the implications of the thinker observing his or her own thinking? Where are thinking, feeling, and willing located in relation to the human body? We are accustomed to observing and thinking about our feelings, but can we also observe and think about what we "will"?

A fundamental issue is whether the nature of human consciousness is something that is universal and timeless—that is, static and unchanging—or whether cognitive capacities are in some sense historically contingent and capable of change. What is the historical relationship between a participatory consciousness and an intellectual consciousness? Is there a demonstrable contrast or shift from a participatory consciousness (culture in nature) to a Cartesian separation of culture and nature? Is animacy simply an ascribed quality or attribute, and if so, what relation does this bear to imagination, inspiration, and intuition? An exploration of the varied contributions to this compilation invites the reader to reflect upon his or her own path toward the boundaries of human consciousness.

I thank Catherine Allen and Steve Houston for valued conversations and feedback. Responsibility for the final content is mine alone.

Colin McEwan
Director, Pre-Columbian Studies
Dumbarton Oaks Research Library and
    Collection, Washington, D.C.

The Nature of the World, the Stuff of Politics

Exploring Animacy and Authority in the Indigenous Americas

STEVE KOSIBA

An Inka's Confession

IN MARCH 1572, A COMPANY OF ARMED SPANIARDS and their native Cañari allies marched the last Inka emperor, Thupa Amaru, to his execution. An immense crowd gathered in the plaza of Cuzco, the former capital of the Inka empire, to witness this previously unimaginable event. The Inka ruler, whom most of the audience had never seen, was shackled in golden chains and was to be beheaded in public by a common Cañari. Though a deified sovereign, Thupa Amaru had only briefly reigned over a fragment of the empire from his stronghold in the Vilcabamba forests near Cuzco, where the Spaniards and their native confederates had finally run him down (Hemming 1970; Maúrtua 1906:3–70). In that raid, Thupa Amaru was captured, as were the most esteemed members of the Inka court—the mummies of two previous rulers and a gold figure named Punchao, who personified both the sun and the Inka nobility. The mummies were burned and

Punchao was lost, but Thupa Amaru was quickly catechized, baptized, then sentenced to death.

Spanish eyewitnesses wrote of the incidents that unfolded on the day of the Inka's execution.[1] They told of how throngs of Andeans wailed with sorrow and shouted in anguish when they saw Thupa Amaru ascend the black scaffold built for his death. Some writers suggested ominous signs, reporting that the clouds thundered in unison with the crowd (Murúa [1590] 1962–1964:271). All related that the Inka delivered a surprising confession.

Eyewitnesses reported that, atop the scaffold, Thupa Amaru silenced the crowd by raising his hand. He baldly proclaimed that the Inka faith, the backbone of their vast empire, was nothing but a lie. He then suggested that Inka nobles had deceived their subjects by ordering them to revere stones, to feed person-places (wak'as), and to follow the dictates of figures such as Punchao (Salazar, in Bauer, Halac-Higashimori, and Cantarutti 2016:188). According to one spectator, Thupa Amaru said,

And when we told you that we entered to speak with the Sun, and that he said that you should do as we said and that he spoke, this was a lie, because it did not speak, rather we [did], because it is a piece of gold and cannot speak. And my brother Titu Cusi told me that, when I wished to say something to the Indians, I should enter alone to the said idol Punchao, and that no one should enter with me, and that the said idol Punchao would not speak to me, because it was [just] a small piece of gold. Afterward, I should go out and tell the Indians that it had spoken to me and that it said whatever I wanted to tell them, so that the Indians would more willingly do what I would order them, and so that they would venerate what was inside the sun, Punchao, which is made from the hearts of the Incas, my ancestors. (Salazar [1596] 1867, in Bauer, Halac-Higashimori, and Cantarutti 2016:188; compare Oviedo [1573] 1908:407)

The audience was stunned by the Inka's words. Noble Inkas in the crowd had heard the ruler dismantle the ideological and sacramental framework of their empire. Spaniards, such as the viceroy Francisco de Toledo, expressed delight that the Inka's admission of a "false religion" would further their objectives to convert the Andean laity to the Christian faith (Levillier [1572] 1924:345).

After the confession, the Cañari executioner beheaded Thupa Amaru with a single stroke of a cutlass, then held aloft the severed head for all to see. Amid renewed roars from the crowd, the Inka's body was removed to a nearby house, while his head was mounted on a wooden pike in the plaza near the scaffold. According to one priest, Thupa Amaru's "ugly" face became "beautiful" when placed on this pike, suggesting that his baptized soul had ascended to heaven (Bauer, Halac-Higashimori, and Cantarutti 2016:131). Some Andeans rushed to the head and honored it with the kissing gestures (much'ay) by which they typically venerated and talked with mummies or stones. After two days, Spanish authorities removed the head, fearing that Andeans would continue to ignore the Inka's words and revere his body.

The tale of Thupa Amaru and its various iterations provide insights into the political roles and social perceptions of materials and bodies in the Pre-Columbian, indigenous, and colonial Americas. We may never know the intentions behind Thupa Amaru's confession—whether he spoke in this way only to save his own skin, whether his statement was coerced, whether he really spoke these words, or whether the story of the confession was a Spanish invention and political ploy. But what is certain is that the publication of Thupa Amaru's confession had political ramifications during early colonial times, when diverse arrays and coalitions of Andeans and Europeans struggled to define which things could embody authority: a cross, a saint, a head, a gold figure. In historical terms, the incidents in Cuzco's plaza and the published words of the Inka depict a nascent colonial European viewpoint that the "idolatry" of Andeans and other Native Americans pivoted on "misguided" beliefs regarding nature and reality (Albornoz [1584] 1988, 1990; Arriaga [1621] 1968; Calancha [1638] 1974–1981:1589–1590; Oviedo [1573] 1908:407; Toledo, in Levillier [1572] 1924:341–348, 503–505; outside the Andes, see Durán 1971; Tozzer 1941; Las Casas 1974). Though far from uniform and constantly under negotiation, this viewpoint played a large part in shaping European imperialism in the Americas, as well as later academic discourses that branded Native American practices as "animism" or "fetishism."

Indeed, elements of Thupa Amaru's story reverberate far beyond the historical process of colonization, and the tale contains several tropes that are still common in scholarly and literary accounts of the Pre-Columbian and indigenous Americas. First, Thupa Amaru's ability to effortlessly and immediately silence the crowd points to the absolute divine authority that is often central to accounts of ancient American states and empires. Second, multiple aspects of the story—the figure of Punchao, the venerable corpses of the royal court, and the concerted roar of thunder and crowd—invoke the material beings and nonhuman forces that have long been thought to lie at the base of Pre-Columbian and indigenous authority. Third, the Inka's confession about Punchao resonates with a pervasive materialist explanation of indigenous politics, which holds that native practices of animacy reflect a false-consciousness ideology meant to mask the brute and all-too-human machinations of power. Finally, the differing perceptions of Thupa Amaru—a priest sees a head mutate, a crowd venerates it—call to mind current theories that suggest vast differences in European Christian and Native American ontologies of nature and causality.

What is clear in these tropes is a widespread notion that politics in the Pre-Columbian Americas hinged on the animacy of nonhuman beings, whether materials, artifacts, or environmental forces. But far less clear are the terms by which scholars working in Western traditions of the humanities and social sciences understand a kind of politics that foregrounds the authority and social efficacy of things. Scholars have interpreted Pre-Columbian and indigenous American politics in two major ways. First is the aforementioned materialist interpretation, which holds sway in part because most current theories of politics do not adequately account for the authority or social efficacy of things (cf. Bauer and Kosiba 2016; Bennett 2010; Braun and Whatmore 2010). As the archaeologist Adam Smith (2015:4) notes, philosophical theorists from Hobbes to Habermas too often define politics as solely a human affair of consensus building and conflict. Matter and infrastructure are crucial to politics in some of these theories (e.g., Marx's commodity), but such things are most often treated as mystifications of a true reality, mere symbols of power or props and stages necessary for political action (e.g., DeMarrais, Castillo, and Earle 1996; Earle 1997; Kertzer 1988; Lincoln 1994; Wolf 1999). Such theories, therefore, have difficulty characterizing political life in some Native American or other societies, where things or nonhuman beings could be actors who not only symbolize, but also support or subvert, claims to authority.

Second, anthropologists have argued that Native Americans recognize the animacy and authority of things because they act in accordance with distinct worldviews and ideologies (e.g., Arnold 1999a, 1999b; Dean 2010; López Austin 1988) or ontological dispositions (e.g., Descola

2013; Viveiros de Castro 2004). Though productive in charting diversity in social categories for living and nonliving beings, these arguments offer rather blunt tools for understanding politics—the practices whereby people work to change or maintain their social environment and the social differences that can create cracks or coalitions in that environment. It would neither be satisfying nor wholly accurate to assert that the actions and perceptions that occurred during Thupa Amaru's execution simply reflect fundamental differences in systemic Western and indigenous worldviews or ontologies. Such an assertion overly generalizes both "West" and "indigenous" while silencing the voices and flattening the agency of the diverse people—Inka noble, non-Inka Andean, Cañari, Spanish administrator, Spanish scribe, Catholic priest, and so forth—who participated in, or creatively sought to redirect, the events of the execution and the crisis of authority that it introduced.

Hence, key questions remain regarding politics in Pre-Columbian and indigenous American societies. The current approaches, with their foci on regional political power or systemic ontological categories, seem to shed little light on the variable and contextual practices that constituted the authority of things in such societies. *Animacy* denotes practices that acknowledge the personhood or vitality of another being. This term is distinct from *animism*, which suggests a problematic scholarly attempt to generalize non-Western animacy in terms of a "primitive" religion (Bird-David 1999; Harvey 2006; Ingold 2006; Wilkinson 2016).[2] *Authority* refers to a fluid relationship in which one person acknowledges or acquiesces to the leadership position or decision-making capacity of another person (e.g., Arendt 1958, 2006).[3] Consequently, we are left wondering: How is authority claimed and constituted in social contexts where things and places are persons who can explicitly play social roles, have voices, influence decisions, demand recognition, and instill order? In such settings, how do humans of different social stations, subject positions, or backgrounds (e.g., woman, man, noble, commoner, insider, outsider, shaman, layperson, etc.)[4] perceive or engage with these things in distinctive ways?

This volume addresses these questions by examining the political roles of materials, artifacts, and nonhuman beings in Pre-Columbian and indigenous American social life. It suggests that to inquire into the significance of these politically charged things is to account for the roles that they played and the differences that they marked in particular social situations and struggles—to identify *how* and *when* people recognized the authority of things, *how* such recognition could impel political change, and *how* these things could come to animate people and compel them to act. In this regard, the volume follows the anthropologist Catherine Allen (2002a, 2002b, 2016, 2017b), who emphasizes that the things and nonhuman beings now recognized as animate persons in the Andes did not passively emerge from an enduring native worldview or ontology. She writes, "Over the centuries, as the people of Sonqo [near Cuzco] held out against the encroachments of landlords, tax collectors, and missionaries, their bond with the land developed into a paramount religious focus—more so than during the Incaic period. . . . The landscape became the last indestructible religious icon . . . the *ayllu* [e.g., community] itself" (2002a:31; see comparable conclusions in Gose 2006; Ramírez 2005; and in Mexico, Sandstrom [1991] 2012). Thus, the land came to hold authority and have social efficacy in this context because of *both* long-standing dispositions regarding its ontological status as a sentient being *and* a particular community's historical position within an unfolding colonial process.

Contributors to the volume build on this insight by applying archaeological, art historical, ethnographic, and linguistic methods to examine the politics of human-thing relationships in diverse regions—the Andes, Amazon, and Mesoamerica—from Pre-Columbian to contemporary times. They vary in their perspectives, from skepticism regarding animacy (Giraldo, this volume) to accounts of the deep-seated ontological dispositions in language (Mannheim, this volume) to warnings against radical relativism or interpretations of broad continuities across regions (Allen, this volume). Here, I offer a prelude to these perspectives by critically reviewing the literature on animacy and authority

in the Americas.[5] I acknowledge the limitations of concepts imported from Western philosophy and social science—sacred and material, animate and inert, authority and subject, nature and culture—to describe indigenous contexts in which such terms may have no place (see especially Atalay 2006; de la Cadena 2015; Deloria 1992, 1995; Laluk 2017; Viveiros de Castro 2014; see also Descola 2005, 2013; Evans-Pritchard 1965; Fowles 2013; Inomata 2016a, 2016b). I suggest that a closer attention to the situations in which things acted or marked social differences can yield new insights into the constitution of authority in Native American worlds. Such attention can also offer a critical perspective on and reevaluation of politics in so-called Western or modern societies, where things such as flags, crosses, and statues remain unrecognized as social actors even as they so stubbornly stand at the center of political debates and struggles.

The Nature of the World

Tales of animate things and forces have long been central to scholarly and popular accounts of the Americas. In fact, "animism" has come to stand in for Native American "culture," much like the way in which the Pacific world is largely known via accounts of mana or South Asia is seen through the lens of caste hierarchies (Appadurai 1988). For instance, Mesoamerica has been characterized through reference to its animistic ceremonies, such as those of Aztec Tenochtitlan, which scholars have interpreted as enactments of the world's violent origins or displays of links between warfare and agriculture (e.g., Boone 1987; Broda 1970; Broda, Carrasco, and Matos Moctezuma 1987; Carrasco 1995a, 1995b, 1999; Keen 1971; Matos Moctezuma 1987; Torquemada 1969:167–168). Several other examples—Amazonian predatory hunting and shamanism, Maya myth and house dedication, Andean mummy veneration—have provided similar lenses through which Western scholars see Native American landscapes or peoples south of the Rio Grande (e.g., Boteler Mock 1998; Bricker 1981; Carlsen and Prechtel 1991; Duviols 1986; Freidel, Schele, and Parker 1993; Gose

1993; Houston and Stuart 1998; Isbell 1997; Lau 2013; MacCormack 1993; Taube 1998, 2003; Viveiros de Castro 2004; Vogt 1964, 1969, 1976, 1998). These examples have over time shaped academic knowledge regarding Native American landscapes, while also cementing a host of colonialist ideas about the "indigenous" and the "West" (Atalay 2006; Trouillot 2003). In an attempt to decolonize these ideas by exposing their roots, I argue that what scholars have called "animism" is deeply rooted in their own assumptions about "nature."

The Colonial Roots of Animism

During the first decades of the Spanish invasion of the Americas, European writers depicted native practices of animacy in terms of idolatry. Both an interpretation and an accusation, the term *idolatry* linked the New and Old Worlds by likening American animate things to pagan idols, such as the golden calf of biblical lore (Cummins 2009; Mannheim and Salas Carreño 2015). For many Spanish authors, these idols revealed that Native Americans "mistakenly" attributed primary natural causes or divine power to artificial things.[6] Such authors emphasized that idols were everywhere (see Durán 1971:54), suggesting demonic influence (Cervantes 1994). After living among the Yucatec Maya in the mid-sixteenth century, for example, the Franciscan priest Diego de Landa Calderón wrote,

> There was not an animal or insect of which they did not make a statue, and they made all of these in the image of their gods and goddesses. . . . They knew well that the idols were the works of their hands, dead and without divine nature; but they held them in reverence on account of what they represented, and because they had made them with so many ceremonies, especially the wooden ones. (Landa 1566, in Tozzer 1941:111)

According to Landa, the Maya erroneously saw natural power in artificial matter, in the materials or practices by which things were made. Likewise, Portuguese traders stressed the artificiality of things, using the term *feitiço* (Latin *facticius*,

"artificial") to describe the things and materials that Africans and Brazilians saw as persons (Iacono 2016; Morris 2017; Müller 1891:117; Pietz 1985, 1987). These descriptions—"idol," "artificial," and "fetish"—reveal, in part, the inability of European writers to explain the novel situations they encountered in the New World (Pietz 1985). But these terms also came to shape an enduring image of Native Americans (and other non-Europeans), attributing to them a "childlike" or "primitive" character because they "misrecognized" primary causes such as the Christian god and his creation, "nature."

Other early Spanish writers added to this colonial image, suggesting that artifice was at the heart of idolatry. In 1538, the conquistador Miguel de Estete ([1535] 1918:325) told of how he and his companions burst into the inner temple at Pachacamac, a widely revered sanctuary in coastal Peru, and found only a "filthy wooden pole" bearing a "poorly carved" human image (see Bray 2009:357). Estete surmised a diabolical trick, stating that in this temple the Devil himself must have spoken to an Andean priest, who then voiced the idol's words to an unsuspecting audience. He aired his disgust that so many people could be fooled by, and offer precious gold and silver to, such a "dirty and stupid" (*sucio y torpe*) thing (Estete [1535] 1918:325). Others similarly described the Maya oracle of Cozumel, certain that native notions of animate things stemmed from deceit:

> This idol . . . was very singular and different from the others; its material was baked clay; it was a large hollow figure joined to the wall with mortar. At its back was something like a sacristy, in which the priests had a small hidden door opening into the back of the idol. Into this one of the priests entered, and from there he replied to the requests which were made. The unhappy dupes believed that the idol spoke to them and credited what was said to them; and so they venerated it more than the others with various offerings; sacrifices of blood, birds, dogs, and sometimes even men. Since, as they believed, it always spoke to them, they came together from everywhere in such great numbers to consult it and to beg for help

in their troubles. (López de Cogolludo 1688, in Tozzer 1941:109n)

Eerily evoking Thupa Amaru's final words, this passage emphasizes an essential colonial interpretation of the Americas that endures to this day—a contention that the artificiality of the idols and the artifice of their use obstructed native visions of reality and nature.[7]

For many writers of this time, idolatry revealed the inherent nature of Native Americans. Famously, in Valladolid, Spain (1550–1551), Bartolomé de las Casas contended with Juan Ginés de Sepúlveda about the meaning of American idolatry and sacrifice. Sepúlveda argued that accounts of cannibalism and human sacrifice demonstrated that natives violated divine law in irreparable ways, proving that they could be nothing more than inhuman beasts (*bestias despiadadas*) and "natural slaves" (sensu Aristotle; Hanke 1974:42, 85–86). Las Casas (1974:241–242) countered with an argument about the legitimacy of native regimes: "Offering sacrifice to the true god or to the one thought to be god comes from natural law, while the things offered to god are a matter of human law and legislation." Las Casas, therefore, contended that Native Americans were in accord with the dictates of law, though they were oriented toward the "wrong gods." He concluded that this required rectification through religious instruction (e.g., Hanke 1974:93–95; for the basis of these arguments, see also Las Casas 1966, 1967).

Despite the debate, these Spaniards and their contemporaries agreed on one thing: Native Americans misrecognized the nature of the world, whether because of their idolatry or their lack of knowledge of the Christian god. Colonial regimes in the Americas would endeavor to "civilize" natives in part by seeking to destroy their idols and replace them with new ones. But in Europe these tales of idols and fetishes would influence new philosophies, from skepticism about universal morality (Montaigne) to global histories of religion (de Brosses, Comte) to critiques of economics (Marx), colonialism (Voltaire), and the self (Freud) (for general sources on these categories, see Böhme 2014; Iacono 2016; Morris 2017; Pals 2006:10–11). In

particular, colonial ideas regarding "misrecognition" would give rise to anthropology and its theories of "animism."

Animism and the Misrecognition of Nature

Anthropology emerged from these colonial roots, often equating animacy with a "primitive" stage of human reason that misrecognized "nature." Edward Burnett Tylor ([1871] 1920) contended that the miscomprehension of nature and the anthropomorphism of nonhumans was at the root of all religions.[8] In studying contemporary spiritualism, he suggested that modern religion was a problematic and unnecessary relic of archaic human beliefs regarding souls, spirits, and the supernatural (Stocking 1971, 1987). Tylor explained that "primitives" saw the dead in their dreams and visions, mistaking them for real beings. He then argued that these perceptions underlay a duality of body and spirit that has structured all subsequent religious thought. To characterize this primordial misperception, Tylor ([1871] 1920:285) coined the term *animism*,[9] which described what he called a "childlike" stage in which "primitives" believed in "universal vitality" and considered "sun and stars, trees and rivers, winds and clouds, [to be] personal animate creatures."

Other early anthropologists followed suit, typically by seeking to explain "primitive" beliefs in supernatural forces. Anthropologists disagreed about fine points, such as whether religion stemmed from visions or sensory perceptions (Müller 1891:124–125) and whether there was a preanimistic phase defined by impersonal forces such as mana (Codrington 1891; Hocart 1914, 1922; Marett 1914). But most research began and ended with the assumption that "primitive" humans shared similar animistic beliefs. In circular fashion, it proceeded by identifying animistic sensibilities among living "primitive" people, then using terms such as *animism* and *mana* to both portray others' social interactions *and* to make inferences about early human development (e.g., Frazer 1890; Müller 1891). In the Americas, this trend led researchers to search for likenesses to Polynesian mana, such as Native American concepts of *orenda*, *wakan*, *manitou*, or *teotl* (e.g., Hvidtfeldt 1958; Jones 1905; Mauss [1904]

1972). These studies apply and impose general terms such as *animism* or *mana* in an effort to understand Native American practices that simply did not fit mechanical Western and Newtonian conceptualizations of "nature." At the time, the anthropologist Paul Radin (1914:340) maintained that when considering such accounts, "we are at a loss to know whether it is the Indian's viewpoint that is given, or an ethnologist's conception of that viewpoint" (see also Radin [1937] 1957).

Some critics stridently argued against theories that defined animism as primitive misrecognition and suggested that kinds of animacy are essential to all social life. Émile Durkheim ([1912] 1995) pointed to empirical fallacies of animism theories, arguing that people en masse are likely not misguided by dreams (66, 77); that visions of the dead cannot be the bases of religious thought (54); and that the idea of a "childlike" stage is erroneous because both "primitives" and children differentiate between living and nonliving things (63). He argued that "totemistic" notions, which identify things and animals as the progenitors of human clans, were the means by which people saw relationships with others. Durkheim focused on the totem as a representation that emerged simultaneously with the clan itself—hence, the totem was not merely a metaphor for something real; it was essential to the constitution of the clan inasmuch as it *was* the clan and its expression (cf. "representation₂" in Mannheim, this volume). Other scholars more sharply rebuked Tylor's evolutionism, stating that there is no evidence that animistic beliefs correspond to simpler ways of life (Evans-Pritchard 1965:25). They also argued that studies of animism too often proceed by smuggling in concepts (e.g., supernatural, soul, and mana) that distort the practices of the people they study (Firth 1940:487; Hogbin 1936). In light of these critiques, many scholars discarded the term *animism* and began to examine the cultural concepts and percepts by which people represented nature.

Worldviews and Representations of Nature

More recent approaches to American animacy tend to focus on the frameworks through which indigenous people experience and perceive nature—often

called "worldviews." The anthropologist Robert Redfield (1953:87) wrote that "worldview" refers to "an arrangement of things looked out upon, things in the first instance conceived of as existing. It is the way the limits or 'illimits,' the things to be lived with, in, or on, are characteristically known." This insight in part stemmed from the writings of Latin American scholars—such as Redfield's coauthor Alfonso Villa Rojas in Mexico or Julio Cesar Tello in Peru—who joined Franz Boas's more general charge to study native traditions on their own terms, rather than casting them as "primitive" (e.g., Redfield and Villa Rojas 1934, 1939). For instance, Tello (1921, 1930, 1937; see also Burger 2009) laid the foundations for an indigenous archaeology in Peru, arguing that ancient social phenomena such as the Chavín religion could only be understood relative to Andean concepts and technologies, not imported concepts.

Following this line of thought, many scholars of the Americas began to see native notions of animacy as *ways of thinking with* or *representing* nature—that is, frameworks by which people bring "culture to nature and back again" (Isbell 1985:285; see also López Austin 1988:259; Vogt 1998). Defined in different ways, this approach has yielded groundbreaking research on indigenous systems of semiotics (e.g., Freidel, Schele, and Parker 1993; Houston and Stuart 1989; Marcus 1992; Stuart 1996; Urton 2003), ontology (e.g., Hallowell 1960), timekeeping (e.g., Florescano 1987; Rice 2007; Zuidema 2010), kinship and resources (e.g., Murra [1956] 1980; Zuidema 1964, 1983), materiality (e.g., Dean 2010), numerology (e.g., Urton 1991), astronomy (e.g., Aveni 1986; Dowd and Milbraith 2015; León-Portilla 1986; Urton 1981), and ideology (e.g., Brumfiel 1996, 1998; Gose 1996, 2000; López Austin 1980, 1988). Far from simple descriptions of "native cultures," many of these anthropological accounts sought to undermine racist Western claims to intellectual exceptionalism by uncovering the complex and sophisticated manners by which indigenous people engage with and derive knowledge from the world.

Most commonly, scholars sought to understand Pre-Columbian worldviews by focusing on "mana-like" indigenous forces and concepts, such as Maya *ch'ulel* or *k'uh*, Nahuatl *tonalli* or *teotl*, and Quechua *cama*, *camaquen*, and *upani*.[10] Such studies broke apart prior contentions that all Native Americans practiced a similar kind of "animism." For instance, the Maya term *ch'ulel* is understood to mean the life essence of humans and things, such as houses or pots (Freidel and Schele 1989; Freidel, Schele, and Parker 1993; Taube 2004; Vogt 1969, 1976, 1998). The anthropologist Evon Vogt (1969:371) observed that among the Tzotzil Maya–speaking Zincantecos, everything significant (but not all things; see Hutson et al., this volume) has *ch'ulel*, including corn, wood crosses, houses, candles, and people. For Zincantecos, he added, most social life is only a facade for a deeper reality, and the most important and profound relationships are between the *ch'ulel* of humans and the *ch'ulel* of other beings, not between humans (Vogt 1976:18–19). In practice, Zincanteco Maya houses are given[11] *ch'ulel* by feeding them with sacrifices of black chickens and blood to repay the earth beings who control materials for the house (Vogt 1976, 1998). Also, children are protected against the loss of their *ch'ulel* (Vogt 1998). These insights suggest that *ch'ulel* is distinct from the body or material it inhabits, leading some scholars to describe it as a "soul-like quality" (e.g., Stuart 1996:157; see also Freidel, Schele, and Parker 1993). Epigraphers reveal long-term continuity in this force by demonstrating that the Classic Maya glyph for *k'uh* or *ch'ul*, meaning "holiness," is an analog of contemporary *ch'ulel* (Houston and Stuart 1996; Stuart 1996:157, 164; see also McAnany, this volume).

Nahuatl speakers of central and southern Mexico refer to more particular and partible forces called *tonalli*, *teyolia*, and *ihiyotl* (López Austin 1980, 1988; Ortiz de Montellano 1990; Sandstrom [1991] 2012; see also Furst 1995). Each of these vital forces has its own function and location: *tonalli* is the power of growth and is found in the head, *teyolia* is an animating vitality that is found in the heart, and *ihiyotl* is a destructive force that can attack humans and is nested in the liver (López Austin 1988:211–228, 234–236). These forces can be amplified or lost. A warrior can gain *teyolia* in battle, but he can also lose it due to sexual misconduct (López Austin 1988:180). Thus, like *ch'ulel*, these forces

can enter into and become separate from physical bodies. Beyond these, Nahuatl speakers recognize a concept called *teotl*, which denotes the consubstantiality of entities (cf. Houston and Stuart 1989). That is, entities that may be physically distinct are said to be identical if they share *teotl*. This bond is often established in ceremony. During the height of Aztec rule, likenesses were drawn between warriors and captives, a flayed skin and a god (Xipe Totec), a femur and a sacrificed body, or amaranth dough and a human body (Hvidtfeldt 1958:82, 90, 123–124, 140; see also Carrasco 1999:145–156; Cummins, this volume; Durán 1971:172–176).

Finally, Quechua speakers in the Andes use the terms *cama*, *camay*, and *camaquen* to refer to processes of growth and creation. *Camay* has a different connotation than these other frameworks and is commonly translated as the force that gives form or order to matter (Salomon and Urioste 1991:16, 45; Taylor 1974; see also Cummins 2005, this volume; Cummins and Mannheim 2011). It is not something that enters into matter, as with *ch'ulel* and *tonalli*, nor is it a force that connects essences of apparently distinct things, as with *teotl*. Rather, *camay* is a potential that lies in matter,[12] and it is often activated in a relationship with a human person (Taylor 1987:24–27, 2000:29). As the archaeologist Tamara Bray (2009:358) put it, "Unlike the simple act of creation, which once done is over, *camay* intends something of continuity in sustaining the being, a condition that involves an ongoing relationship between the *camac* and . . . *camasca* (e.g., its tangible instantiation)." In other words, the *camac* and the *camasca* come into being at the same time, in their intrarelationship (sensu de la Cadena 2015). Some have concentrated on how specific things, such as mummies (*mallquis*) were the source of *camay* (*camaquen*) for a community of Andean people, animals, and crops (Duviols 1978a, 1978b, 1986:68, 77, 280). In other instances, *camay* may imply a close, embodied knowledge of materials—the *camayoq* in this regard being the person who could find form in matter, as well as the person who had an obligation to that material (cf. DeLeonardis 2011).

Many scholars suggest that these frameworks operated as root metaphors for broader and enduring—Maya, Mesoamerican, or Andean—ways of being. They note that many of these concepts have persisted in some way from Pre-Columbian times to the present, suggesting remarkable continuities in worldviews. We might consider the well-published examples of consubstantial beings or "co-essences" in Classic and contemporary Maya worlds (Houston and Stuart 1989; Stuart 1996, 1998; see also Freidel, Schele, and Parker 1993:244–246; Harrison-Buck 2016; Houston and Stuart 1989, 1996; Taube 1998). The epigraphers Stephen Houston and David Stuart (1989) first suggested that the Classic Maya hieroglyph *way* (T539) was a reference to the co-essence or companion-being of a ruler. Corroborating this finding, Stuart (1996, 1998) argued that Classic Maya built structures, such as stone altars and stelae, bear inscriptions and symbols that indicate the monuments themselves operated as extensions of a ruler's self (McAnany, this volume). Like the ruler's body, the monuments were bundled in cloth, a practice by which the Maya invested things with *ch'ulel* and protected the interior essence of people and things (Stuart 1996:157–160; see also Benson 1976; Houston and Stuart 1989). This argument resonates with Arild Hvidtfeldt's (1958:90–96) earlier study of *teotl*, which showed that among the Aztecs, figures (*tzoalli*) made of amaranth dough were consubstantial with, and treated the same as, sacrificial victims (Durán 1971:70–80; Sahagún 1950:21–22; see also Hamann, this volume).

Archaeological research lends support to the epigraphic argument for Maya co-essences. Several studies reveal that the Classic Maya and their earlier Olmec neighbors methodically mutilated portrait statues of their leaders, often through decapitation, defacement, and the erasure of identifying features such as name glyphs or headdress motifs (Boteler Mock 1998; Coe 1977:186; Coe and Diehl 1980; Freidel and Schele 1989:237–241; Grove 1981:64–65; Spencer 2015; Sugiyama 1998:152; for later examples, see Wren, Nygard, and Spencer 2015). These data reveal focused acts to terminate and inter only certain monuments of select people. Hence, this was not a widespread process of iconoclasm or revolution. In sites with evidence for mutilation, only specific portrait monuments were

defaced, and they were defaced in systematic ways (targeting neck, head, and name glyphs) and at different times (Freidel and Schele 1989; Grove 1981). In one striking instance at Chalcatzingo (Morelos, Mexico), the head of a decapitated monument was placed in an elite crypt, which indicates that the monument was defaced at the time of the person's death and suggests the consubstantiality of the human and stone bodies (Grove 1981:63). As David Grove (1981:66–67) contends, it appears as though these monuments *had to be* destroyed because their essential power could no longer be controlled after the death of the person with whom they were connected in a consubstantial manner.

There are parallels among the contemporary Maya, ranging from animal companion-beings to god-pots (Houston and Stuart 1989). Ethnographic accounts of Tzeltal Maya–speakers of Chiapas and their neighbors have revealed a type of co-essence or companion-being called a *nagual* (e.g., Brinton 1894; Foster 1944; López Austin 1988:366–374; Klein et al. 2002; Martínez González 2006, 2010a, 2010b; Romero López 2008; Saler 1964; Villa Rojas 1947). Particular leaders or elders have *naguals*, which can be animals such as a dog or hawk, dwarves, or balls of fire (Villa Rojas 1947:583). *Naguals* are directly connected to their humans, and if a *nagual* is harmed or killed, then its human will become sick or die (Houston and Stuart 1989; Thompson 1958:273–277). At night, the *nagual* does its owner's bidding, punishing people for transgressions or ridding others of invasive *naguals* (Martínez González 2010a, 2010b; Villa Rojas 1947). Similar practices can be found in sources regarding "god-pots" (*u-läk-il k'uh*) among the Lacandon Maya (Perera and Bruce 1982:30–32; Tozzer 1941:160–161). These are braziers meant to burn copal for specific gods. They are birthed in complicated rites of renewal, during which the old pots must be washed with fire (killed) and then wrapped in palm leaves (entombed) within a limestone cave (McGee 1998). At the same time, new pots are fed with *balché* (a mead made from *Lonchocarpus violaceous* bark), tobacco, incense, beans, and tamales (McGee 1990:44, 1998:45).

Such cases emphasize potential similarities in past and present concepts of animacy, focusing on terms used within Pre-Columbian and indigenous societies, rather than imposing ideas such as "animism," "fetishism," and "mana." But these cases also elicit further questions about whether and how such resemblances in materials or beliefs suggest lasting worldviews or principles. Some researchers suggest that we proceed with caution when claiming continuity in cultural frameworks, lest we create new kinds of black boxes with assumptions about essentialized subjects (cf. Smith 2004)—in this case, general definitions of "Mayas," "Andeans," "Mesoamericans," or "Amazonians." In the past, anthropologists assumed continuity in core traditions within closed and isolated "little" communities (sensu Redfield 1955) detached from broader social forces. But even in cases of supposed isolation, appearances of continuity spur questions about *how, why*, and *when* particular people have retained particular practices. As the ethnographer Alan Sandstrom ([1991] 2012:5, 34–45) argues, "traditions" observed among indigenous groups are not always "quaint survivals" of ancient worldviews but can also be "subtle and powerful political instruments wielded by a people who wish to endure and survive" (see also Bricker 1981; cf. Boone and Cummins 1998).

In this light, it is worthwhile to recall Catherine Allen's insight about supposed continuities in some Andean frameworks and manners of being. Her research shows that over time highland Andeans focused their social attention on chiefly mountains (*apus*), seeing these peaks as anchors of social identities and members, if not leaders, of local communities (cf. de la Cadena 2010, 2015; Gose 2006; Ramírez 2005:130–131; Salas Carreño 2014, 2016, 2017). In her ethnographic research, Allen (2016) traces changes in how Andeans use miniatures in rites directed to mountains surrounding a shrine called Qoyllur Rit'i. She calls attention to how, in the past, people used stones to embody their kin and herd when asking the adjoining mountains of Ausangate and Qolquepunku to care for the community. Now they use mass-produced miniature models to ask for commodities they desire (e.g., cars, ovens, and storefronts). With this, Allen subtly points to a key distinction in how people have called on nonhuman forces and beings. Highland

Andeans continue to recognize these mountains as persons, as well as the being housed within the stone and shrine of Qoyllur Rit'i, suggesting an enduring attitude and disposition with regard to these beings, despite different social positions or aims (see also Salas Carreño 2014; cf. Gose 2018). But the changes in materials suggest that people now also do so as individuals rooted in and creatively responding to the logic of the market, not solely as a community of human and nonhuman persons. The subject—a mountain or a stone—may remain the same, but its connections to people have changed. To explain this requires a discussion of ontological theories regarding human relationships to "nature."

Ontologies of Nature

The anthropologist A. Irving Hallowell's (1960:34) writings on the Ojibwe (Anishaabe) first suggested a shift in focus for studies of animate things, concentrating less on representations or worldviews and more on the attitudes and bodily habits by which humans relate to other beings (see recent discussions of Hallowell in Harvey 2006; Ingold 2000). Hallowell revealed that the Ojibwe attributed personhood, action, or speech to things (e.g., shells, stones, or thunderstorms). For example, he told of an errant rock:

> A white trader, digging in his potato patch, unearthed a large stone. . . . He sent for John Duck, an Indian who was the leader of the *wabano*, a contemporary ceremony that is held in a structure something like that used for the Midewiwin [Ojibwe ritual]. The trader called his attention to the stone, saying that it must belong to his pavilion. John Duck did not seem pleased at this. He bent down and spoke to the boulder in a low voice, inquiring whether it had ever been in his pavilion. According to John, the stone replied in the negative. (Hallowell 1960:25)

John Duck gave a typical Ojibwe response to such a situation, simply asking the stone its history. In other examples, Hallowell argued that among the Ojibwe, stones have a *potential* to be animate and, thus, can have social agency *when treated as persons.* This argument reframes anthropological notions of animacy, moving beyond studies concentrating on cultural definitions of "life" or "personhood" to inquire into the often unspoken dispositions by which people relate and respond to other persons, whether human or not (cf. Bird-David 1999; Gell 1998; Harvey 2006; Kohn 2013:17).

Lately, anthropologists and other scholars have taken these insights one step further, suggesting that Native American animacy reveals a distinct *ontological* disposition (e.g., Descola 1996:98–99, 2005, 2013, 2014a; Ingold 2000; Viveiros de Castro [1986] 1992, 1996; 1998:473, 2004, [2002] 2013; see also Alberti and Bray 2009; Århem 1993:124; Bray 2015; Costa and Fausto 2010; de la Cadena 2015; Kohn 2013, 2015; Sillar 2004, 2009). Here, *ontology* does not mean discourses about reality or being,[13] as defined in most philosophy (Graeber 2015:15). Instead, it refers to tacitly understood, but not always consciously acknowledged, *dispositions toward reality* or, put simply, those "things that go without saying" (Bloch, paraphrased in Descola 2014b:274). These dispositions are not worldviews or knowledge systems through which people represent and cognize the natural world. Rather, they are modes of engagement and action. Scholars who follow such an ontological approach often examine how "the social" (or the possibility for social relationships in general) is constituted through enduring interactions and socioecological commitments between humans, nonhuman beings, and things—that is, bundles of relationships called "machines" or "assemblages" (e.g., Deleuze and Guattari 1983, 1987; Latour 1993; also DeLanda 2006; Henare, Holbraad, and Wastell 2007; Smith 2015). Such approaches see nonhumans and things as equally influential kinds of actors who play key roles in broader assemblages and, as such, come to shape different environments and condition social actions or outcomes.[14] The literature on ontologies is varied and vast, so I focus on its Americanist roots in the writings of Amazonian scholars—Eduardo Viveiros de Castro and Philippe Descola—who recently redefined "animism" to describe indigenous "natures."

The revival of "animism" often stems from a critique of Western science (Bird-David 1999;

Descola 1996:86, 2013; Viveiros de Castro 2004). Scholars describe a modern or scientific ontological mode that distinguishes culture and nature—a Cartesian conceptual schema that separates *res cogitans* and *res extensa* (or *corporea*), mind and body, human and other beings (see Hamann, this volume). Descola (2005, 2013) uses the term *naturalism* to refer to this ontological mode.[15] *Scientism* is often substituted for *naturalism*, and both terms refer to a tacit understanding that the world is knowable via natural science and that the findings of natural science exhaust what is to be known about the world. Though not using these terms, some authors claim that this "naturalistic" mode is the inversion of "animism," a disposition in which humans and nonhumans relate to one another as persons (Bird-David 1999; Viveiros de Castro 2004:468, 474; cf. Ingold 1999). Many scholars seek to define and explore such animistic ontologies in an effort to destabilize and challenge Western scientific views regarding the nature of the world (e.g., Alberti and Marshall 2009; Viveiros de Castro 2004:483). They contend that non-Western perspectives on nature are not merely beliefs about a singular reality; rather, they are dispositions that are consistent with other realities or "worlds."

Empirically, many new approaches to animism draw from ethnographic studies of Amazonian peoples. Attending to the Achuar and Araweté, Descola and Viveiros de Castro note that native Amazonians see and treat nonhumans as human-like persons. This view is evident in myths regarding a primordial world in which all living beings were indistinguishable and shared a human-like culture (Descola 2005:183; Viveiros de Castro 2004:464). For native Amazonians, it follows that all living beings use the same concepts, because they were all once human. Nonhuman beings are, thus, fully cultural subjects who live in societies and communicate with other persons. For example, the Achuar say that river otters have kinship systems, cement houses, cars, and police (Taylor 2013:99). But bodies differentiate beings. Amazonians hold that living beings experience and perceive their environments in diverse ways because of their bodies, which are, in fact, clothes that can be put on or taken off (Viveiros de Castro 1996, 1998; cf. Turner 2009). Beings with the same kinds of bodies have the same perspectives. This is to say, conspecifics (the same "species") live in the same "nature," but their "nature" is different than that of a being from another species. Hence, mud is an obstacle to a human, while it is a hammock to a tapir (Viveiros de Castro 2004:472–473). As Viveiros de Castro (2004:471) remarks, "As far as humans are concerned, the Makuna [Amazonian people, cf. Århem 1993] would say that there is indeed only one correct and true [human] representation of the world. If *you* start seeing, for instance, the maggots in rotten meat as grilled fish, you may be sure you are in deep trouble, but grilled fish they are from the *vulture's* point of view."

Hence, in these Amazonian societies, perspectives define social positions—not just the kind of species but also the kind of subject one is (e.g., predator, owner, master, etc.; Viveiros de Castro 1998:476; see also Kohn 2013:17). In one moment a human can be a predator tracking a peccary. In the next, that human can be the prey of another person, such as a stalking jaguar or a police officer. Such relational perspectives structure many Amazonians' social lives, commonly through relationships of the predator/prey and owner/pet (Costa and Fausto 2010; Fausto 1999, 2007a, 2007b; Grotti and Brightman 2016:95). Viveiros de Castro (1992) demonstrates that Arawaté identity is constituted in practices of "ontological predation," whereby humans capture, kill, ingest, and hence incorporate the essences and selves of enemy humans. Arawaté gods also play roles of predators who feast on the human dead and, in so doing, render them immortal (Viveiros de Castro 1992; see also Descola 1996:94; Grotti and Brightman 2012; Vilaça 2000, 2002, 2005). Within human communities, Amazonian animistic relationships take on an idiom of nurturing or mastery, relationships similar to those between an owner and a pet (Costa and Fausto 2010:99–100; Fausto 2012, this volume). In this relationship, the chief is an owner-master whose body contains and provides for followers (Costa and Fausto 2010:100). Only shamans hold a fixed position that can adopt the point of view of myriad other beings, and hence

Amazonian idioms of power are rooted in the ability to assume the perspective or affect of a predator that consumes another self (Viveiros de Castro 1992:xiv).

For many researchers, these insights from Amazonian "perspectivism" can explain broader Native American notions of animacy.[16] The first line of evidence comes from myths, which for Viveiros de Castro (2004:464) suggest a "virtually universal Amerindian notion" of an original state of nature with "beings whose form, name, and behavior inextricably mix human and animal attributes in a common context of intercommunicability, identical to that which defines the present-day intrahuman world."[17] Second, many claim that examples from the Amazon are applicable to other regions. Anthropologists suggest that Amazonian ornaments of bodily enhancement, such as jaguar pelts or bird costumes, share a common ontological root with the eagle or jaguar dresses that constituted Aztec warriors as fearsome predators (Martínez González 2010b). Archaeologists such as George Lau (2013) point to similarities between Amazonian idioms of predation and ownership and the ethos of Pre-Columbian Andean societies, especially the warrior communities who took and displayed the heads of human prey (cf. Arnold and Hastorf 2008). Lau (2013) presents evidence of the authoritative persons who stood at the center of society—Recuay clay pots with people, houses, and environmental features suggesting a composite being who provided for and nurtured the community.

But such apparent similarities can hide subtle differences. When uncritically applied to other contexts and ecologies, Amazonian models of animism can too easily lead us back to the same kinds of generalized interpretations and black boxes that so worried Radin and Evans-Pritchard (see also Allen 2017b:22, 35). There is a danger in slipping between "Amazonian" and "Amerindian" descriptions of cultures or ontologies, as if evidence from the former is sufficient for a definition of the latter. Such descriptions can too easily suggest a "primitivism," casting the peoples of the Amazon as living fossils of both past and present Native Americans. There is evidence to the contrary. For example, some scholars suggest that Amazonian perspectivism may be rooted in the ecologies and hunting practices of the forest, which require the predator-hunter to understand or take on the viewpoint of the prey (e.g., Descola 2013; Kohn 2013:17; Willerslev 2007). Others argue that perspectivism should be seen more as a cultural idiom of power (Costa and Fausto 2010:97; Fausto 2007). Most importantly, we have ample evidence that even in remote areas of the Amazon, notions of animacy, such as the recognition of "invisible" personified forces, have been amplified or revived because of historical changes, especially colonialism and other Western intrusions (Grotti and Brightman 2016:103–104).

In brief, the ontological approach leaves us with the same questions that troubled studies of worldviews. That is, we are left asking how and why there appears to be continuity in ontological dispositions among some Native American societies and whether such apparent similarities have the same social and political implications. Ontological approaches, with their tendency to generalization, seem to lead toward renderings of essentialized subjects—Amerindians who share the same dispositions (see also Graeber 2015:5). But we might ask whether, how, and if the talking Ojibwe stone described in the tale of John Duck played the same or even a similar political role as, for example, the talking stones or gold figures of the ancient Inka. As in all anthropological studies of human social actors or persons, a *political* understanding of such person-things requires an examination of their subject roles, their histories, and the situations in which they acted or had a voice. Perhaps the newly revived "animism" works best as a heuristic category that describes non-Western ways of being and not as a catchall adjective for Native American perspectives (see Taylor 2013:201–202). Some critics of ontological approaches argue for a more historical approach that attends to how animate things may (and may not) play roles in particular social settings (Sahlins 2014; see also Allen 2017b). This critique brings politics into view by changing the focus from an investigation into categories of being (e.g., human and nonhuman) to an inquiry into how and when animate things come into being and when they matter.

The Stuff of Politics

Worldview and ontological theories regarding animacy are largely about the representations or dispositions through which people, in their actions, contribute to "the nature of the world." Researchers who follow such theories organize their inquiries at a systemic scale to understand how *the* Andeans or *the* Araweté engage with nonhumans and things, whether through cultural frameworks that codify and represent "nature" or via ontological dispositions and ecological commitments that constitute distinct "natural worlds." But these accounts often overlook politics, in particular the variable social distinctions and practices that can differentially define people and things as subjects or objects, as well as the disparities in how people and things can contribute to or shape social life. Hence, they often provide only a faint rendering of the situations in which people constitute the authority of things, in which places affect and shape people, or in which things authorize the actions and decisions of people.

Still, in the stories and data discussed previously, things and nonhuman beings are essential to political differences and social transformations. The tale of Thupa Amaru depicts a struggle over how a royal body part should be defined, as an authoritative subject or a muted object. Maya monument defacement exemplifies how transitions in authority can be realized through the destruction, desecration, or decommissioning of the built structures that once tied people to a ruling regime or a vision of the world. The examples of Mesoamerican *nagual* owners and Amazonian shamans alike reveal how only select people can relate to animal persons and adjudicate social disputes. Cases of *nagualismo*, in particular, also suggest historical situations in which indigenous people creatively developed traditions to oppose the spread of Catholicism (Villa Rojas 1947:585–587).[18] Finally, the account of John Duck and the errant stone exposes a situation in which an Ojibwe leader faces down a white trader's accusation and creates a distinction between self and other by referring to his own ability to hear a rock's speech. These stories indicate that these animate things are not only about the nature of the world. They are also the "stuff of politics" (a phrase best explained by Braun and Whatmore 2010).

Scholarly discussions of Pre-Columbian politics have long suggested that Native American notions of animacy are traditions recast in political terms or reflections of a dominant political ideology. From the writings of James Frazer (1890) onward, scholars of the Americas have argued that politics in the Pre-Columbian world was deeply embedded in religious foundations or cultural principles, such that the "cosmic kings" of Maya or Andean realms expressed an enduring authority that was seemingly unquestioned and unquestionable (e.g., Freidel, Schele, and Parker 1993). These arguments suggest that authority simply emanated from ancestral traditions or ideologies of divine mandate, largely echoing the claims of authoritative regimes rather than examining their social histories. Another long-standing interpretation assumes that Native American animistic concepts of authority were not only appropriations of cultural values, but also political inventions mobilized in the service of more earthly and exploitative motives. Such interpretations might suggest that people who speak to or engage with things in public ceremonies are "faking it" or simply "acting" their status while, in reality, they seek to fool the masses by implanting ideas that things or deities are the "true" rulers (see Cummins, this volume; Weismantel, this volume). In so doing, these interpretations often debase American animacy, treating it less as a framework for politics and more as a culturally structured "metaphor" for "real" political and economic processes.

An example from the early days of the Spanish invasion of the Andes greatly complicates this view of politics. In particular, it points to how the authority of things is largely constituted in particular situations and not spontaneously derived from enduring ontologies or ideological frameworks. The conquistador Pedro Pizarro wrote about how he agreed to help convince an Inka lord to approve the marriage of an Inka and a woman:

I, who believed that I was going to speak to some living Indian, was taken to a bundle [a mummy], [like] those of these dead folk, which was seated in a litter, which held him, and on one side was the Indian who spoke for him, and on the other was the Indian woman [the potential bride], both sitting close to the dead man. Then, when we arrived before the dead one, the interpreter gave the message, and being thus for a short while in suspense and silence, the Indian man looked at the Indian woman as I understand it, to find out her wish. Then, after having been thus as I relate it for some time, both the Indians replied to me that it was the will of the lord dead one that she go, and so the captain already mentioned carried off the Indian woman. (Pizarro [1571] 1921:204–205)

Pizarro did not believe that the mummy spoke. But he acted as if it did. For those present, he affirmed that things such as corpses could and did hold authority. This was not simply a matter of contrasting world views or ontological dispositions. *It was a matter of authority.*

Authority is difficult to define in general terms. Colloquially, it is often seen as if it were a fixed quality of a person (e.g., "respect *my* authority"). But most scholarly definitions see authority more as a fluid relationship in which one person acknowledges the decision or direction of another person (Gauthier 1986; Habermas 1975; Hardin 2009; Löschke 2015). Authority is distinct from power, and to be authoritative is to direct social action without resorting to force, deceit, or even persuasion (Arendt 1958, 2006; cf. Lukes 2005). As such, authority is constituted, performed, and reproduced in interpersonal situations, like the marriage proposal that Pizarro and a corpse together authorized. These situations are often mediated by or presided over by things or nonhuman beings, whether the stone *wak'as* that were critical to Inka politics (Curatola, this volume; see also Chase 2015; Dean 2010; Kosiba 2015) or the flag lapel-pins that are now essential and constitutive parts of the U.S. president's body (Smith 2015; on the things that signal authority in the ancient Americas, see Martínez Cereceda 1995; Ramírez 2005).

Despite their apparent ubiquity, such things have been largely left out of academic discourses and interpretations of authority.[19] This is, in part, because of a long tradition of Western philosophy that downplays or disregards the roles of materials or nonhumans in political life (cf. Bauer and Kosiba 2016; Bennett 2010; Braun and Whatmore 2010; Latour 1993; Smith 2015). Arguably, this tradition emerged during the shift from Catholicism to Protestantism and the replacement of Roman models of authority with those derived from "rational" principles. This is not to say that Western models of authority cannot be applied or compared to other contexts, but it is to argue that these models' assumptions and expectations should be exposed rather than assumed to be commensurate with Native American ones (Mannheim 2015, this volume). Such an approach would seek to expose and annul the anthropological tradition of imposing Western concepts on contexts where they may have little relevance (Atalay 2006; Deloria 1988, 1992; Laluk 2017; Watkins 2000).

To explore problems with the assumption of commensurability of Western and indigenous American concepts is to critically excavate the roots of authority as we know it. First, it is important to note the historical and cultural specificity of many points of view regarding politics that are often put forth as if they were natural or transhistorical. For instance, the notion that authority is grounded in the ancestors and deities has firm footing in Roman soils. The term *authority* comes from the Latin *auctoritas*, which refers to the *auctor*, a revered source or foundational act (Hammer 2008:190; Park 2003:51–52). As Carlos Fausto (this volume) points out, the term *auctor* is linked to the verb *augere*, which denotes a person's or collective's ability to improve or grow society (Arendt 1958; Friedrich 1958:30–32; Waldron 2000). This ability, though, was checked by the *auctoritas* of the ancestors, a kind of moral authority seen as the quintessential Romanness (*mos maioirum*) of deified forebears (*maiores*; Takács 2009:46).

The Roman model persisted for centuries after the fall of the Western empire, as Catholic monarchs began to claim their legitimacy through reference to a moral authority personified by classical ancestors or the Christian god (Hardin

2009:239–240). Slightly before the conquest of the Americas, European monarchs began to sponsor a new genre of tightly controlled "official histories" to both recount their heroism and link it to classical myths (Burke 1969; Linehan 1993; Von Ostenfeld-Suske 2012; see also Kosiba 2017). That which was old demanded authority in early modern Europe, and accordingly, these monarchs found ancient lineages for their courts—the Tudors claimed to rise from Arthur, the Habsburgs from Jason and Noah, the French dynasties from the Trojans, the Scots from the Egyptians, and the Spanish monarchy from Noah's grandson Tubal (Burke 2012; Kosiba 2017). Unsurprisingly, early histories of the Americas uncritically described the authority of indigenous civilizations in terms of these Roman-style lineages and ancestral origins, a trend and a mistranslation that continues to this day (see critique in MacCormack 2007:49–50; see also Mannheim, this volume).

Consistent with the goals of the Reformation and then the Enlightenment, later Western models of politics instead claimed that authority should be established without reference to extra-human moral sources such as animate forces, ancestors, or deities. These theories explicitly sought to demystify politics, rejecting Roman and Catholic notions that a deity conferred the right to rule or Platonic and Aristotelian ideas that select people had a "natural" ability to lead. In Enlightenment treatises, "rule upheld solely by right of birth, by divine right, by charisma, by physical force—these are all denied legitimacy" (Forsyth 1994:38). Such theories were a shattering blow to earlier political doctrines that rested on sacred matter and divine mandate, replacing them with arguments regarding how the only appropriate and reasonable government is that which rests on the consent of the people (Locke) and that which is structured according to reason (Kant).[20]

Somewhat ironically, many of the theories that modern scholars employ to understand the "animated" politics of the Pre-Columbian and indigenous Americas arise from this Enlightenment attempt to demystify politics, to expel the things and animate beings that had so heavily influenced social life—a process often referred to as the "disenchantment of the world" (Gauchet 1999). Perhaps the most pervasive and influential theories of authority come from Max Weber ([1922] 1978), who invented ideal types of social organization and authority in an attempt to understand the historical process of demystification (or disenchantment) from the Catholic to the Protestant state and the transition from patrimonial to bureaucratic authority. Weber defined authority as legitimate domination, a definition that has reverberated throughout the social sciences despite a lack of clarity. The problem is that Weber's definition turns on a kind of Lockean consent. Hence, its measure of whether a ruling regime is "legitimate" rests on whether that regime stays in power—a regime is deemed to be legitimate and authoritative if enough people believe or behave as if it is (Weber [1922] 1978:213–214; also Hardin 2009:248–249).[21] This tautological definition is neither verifiable nor very compelling. It provides a superficial account of *when* authority works, rather than inquiring into *how*—the conditions or circumstances under which a person may succeed or fail in claiming authority.

Nonetheless, archaeologists frequently apply Weberian categories of authority to Native American societies. Most commonly, they liken types of authority to stages of social development, finding something akin to patrimonial authority among smaller-scale societies such as chiefdoms and seeing bureaucratic authority in expansionistic states (see critique in Inomata 2016a, 2016b). In employing these categories, some archaeologists seek to trace diverse cultural expressions of patrimonial or bureaucratic governance—applying Weber's types as guides to understand social organization in non-Western worlds. But more often they simply map administration by charting the distribution of materials (e.g., artifact styles, architectural forms, and iconography) that likely represented claims to rule, or evidence of the capacity to stay in power, and then analyzing whether and how these materials and signs are linked to a hierarchy of administrative sites and economic resources (e.g., Billman 2002; Claessen 1984; Claessen and Skalník 1978; Wright and Johnson 1975). What is rendered is a sharply political economic picture that conceptualizes authority in terms of a managerial web spread over territory.

These models suggest that authority is derived from the bureaucracy, the monuments, or the aesthetic of a ruling regime. Such a critical appraisal could also be levied at more current approaches that draw on philosophers such as Michel Foucault or Giorgio Agamben, which argue that archaeology or history can best shed light on indigenous and colonial American politics by identifying the institutions or apparatuses through which ideology or power flowed—that is, the spaces, materials, disciplinary measures, or bodily gestures that form the basis of everyday social life and condition which actions are possible or thinkable. These approaches sharply focus on the systemic parameters of social life and the general contours of politics within general social entities (e.g., Inka, Moche, Aztec, or Amazonian idioms of power). Hence, they perform a kind of sociological analysis similar to a study of a modern nation's laws, an analysis that cannot account for the situations in which those laws are recognized or rejected.[22] They concentrate on the authoritative apparatuses or institutions of a ruling regime, but they rarely examine the *constitution of authority*, an interpersonal relationship in a community of persons, human and nonhuman, mediated through things.

Critics have suggested that such systemic accounts of politics can only describe the apparatus of rule at a given time but that they cannot adequately explain transformations in that apparatus (Inomata 2016a:91–92; Yoffee 2004). Shifts from local to regional political organization (chiefdoms to states) are often explained through political economic models about power and resource control, leaving questions regarding how people established or recognized things of authority (Kosiba 2011). As the archaeologist Takeshi Inomata (2016b:42) argued, the problem is that such models often assume that the mere *presence* of a kind of material (e.g., Inka pottery) indicates the *acceptance* of a kind of authority (e.g., state rule). Such assumptions appear to misunderstand the relational concept of authority, which refers to the intersubjective situations in which a person acknowledges another person's leadership. This relational concept becomes especially complicated when it is constituted within a community of persons, of which only some are human (sensu Harvey 2006).

Hence, an understanding of most Native American principles of authority might move beyond theories that are based in demystification and disenchantment. If we agree that many Pre-Columbian and indigenous American peoples attributed personhood or vitality to nonhuman beings and things, we might ask a series of questions meant to clarify how politics worked: *who* had the ability to communicate or engage with these persons, *when* did these persons enter into and participate in politics, and *how* were explanations about the animacy of things granted authority or not?

Plan of the Book

This book examines politics in the Pre-Columbian and indigenous Americas, focusing on how things played central social roles in situations that supported, sanctified, or subverted political authority in the Amazon, Andes, and Mesoamerica. The goal is to consider how politics worked in societies and cultural settings where things and nonhuman actors were defined as persons who could watch over communities, prompt political conflicts, adjudicate disputes, participate in social decisions, and authorize both people and their actions. One of the book's principal assumptions is that notions of animacy in the indigenous Americas and elsewhere are not solely representations of worldviews or artifacts of deep-seated ontological dispositions. Rather, they are the stuff of politics, the magic and the mana that can build or break political authority (cf. Taussig 1997). Exploring this theme, the book brings together scholars from multiple disciplines to creatively rethink how they might examine the constitution of authority in Pre-Columbian and indigenous American societies whose political practices have long been understood only through generalizing academic categories—"animism" or "political economy"—that may obscure more

than they explain due to their lack of fit in many American settings.

Herein, we do not advocate any single perspective on Pre-Columbian and indigenous American animacy and authority. Chapters within this volume only start from the premise that many people in these societies acknowledged the personhood and authority of things. These chapters seek to understand how politics worked in such societies. American societies are not the only ones that recognize the authority of things, but given the association of "animism" and the Americas, they provide a fertile ground for a reconsideration of authority or animacy in archaeological and ethnographic contexts, as well as an inquiry into broader concerns regarding how colonization and anthropological discourses have shaped or distorted knowledge of Native American political life. More generally, the volume offers insights into topics of current concern, including the political roles of things and the relative influence of both ideological and ontological structures on social interactions.

Contributors to this volume provide diverse accounts of animacy and authority in the Americas. Many critique essentializing notions of worldviews or ontologies, underscoring the historicity or situatedness of these frameworks (see essays by Conklin, Fausto, Giraldo, Hamann, Hutson et al., Joyce, and McAnany). Such chapters shift our attention from static *assemblages* of a period (e.g., Inka) or a cultural tradition (e.g., Andes) to an inquiry into the fluid process of *assembly*—the circumstances that brought together people, places, and things in novel ways and, in so doing, framed their political decisions and actions. Others concentrate on case studies that demonstrate diversity in Native American dispositions toward other beings, a diversity grounded in particular ecologies, material landscapes, frames of reference, and rhythms of human-thing interaction (see essays by Cummins, Curatola, Fausto, Janusek, Mannheim, and Weismantel). Many of these chapters reflect the Durkheimian injunction to consider what might be called "ritual" practices as the principal means by which people manifest community or authority (see essays by Conklin, Fausto, Janusek, Joyce, and

McAnany). These chapters resonate with Edward Swenson's (2015a) compelling proposition that to hold authority in the ancient Americas was perhaps to not only be in charge of persons, human or not, but to also demonstrate an uncommon and uncanny ability to assemble and bundle those persons, or to reassemble them in radically new ways.

Overall, chapters in the volume are organized to emphasize complementary and contrasting views, rather than region or chronology. In the first three chapters, the reader will find different accounts of how Native American people have attributed personhood or authority to deceased chiefs or relatives, from a rendering of the stages of transformation from living body to mute wooden object that signal changes in Kuikuro chieftainship (Fausto), to an examination of deep continuities in Maya notions of the soul (McAnany), to a description of the Wari' practice of transforming the dead and their things into the generative soils of their immediate environment (Conklin). The chapters that follow concentrate on the nonrepresentational aesthetic of Pre-Columbian things, pointing to how particular American ontological dispositions and mediational frameworks lie in the practices of transubstantiation by which matter is brought to life (Cummins) or to the very process of unfolding or "unbundling" a Mesoamerican manuscript (Hamann). Subsequent chapters delve into ecologies and "eco-regimes" that might constitute a framework for political action, by mapping the stone outcrops and beings that interpellated people as objects in Tiwanaku (Janusek), by creatively imagining how the central stone of Chavín de Huantar affected human perceptions and emotions (Weismantel), or by identifying the myriad voices and aural experiences that were embedded in Andean landscapes (Curatola). These chapters are followed by analyses that more closely attend to practices of making buildings and bodies by documenting the interlinked feeding and construction events that gave life to Maya and Mesoamerican structures (Hutson et al. and Joyce) or to the mixtures of things that constituted bodies in colonial Mexico (Loren).

The final chapters see animacy and authority in markedly different ways—from skepticism regarding the political instrumentality of claims regarding animism (Giraldo) to a linguistic approach regarding the spatial orientations and conceptual distinctions through which people constitute and experience their environments (Mannheim). The anchor of this final section, a review chapter from Catherine Allen, discusses this book in light of her inimitable forty-year career, during which she greatly advanced our knowledge of Native American animacy and animacy in general (Allen 1982, 1998, 2002a, 2011, 2017a, 2017b). This volume grows directly from the foundations that she established. It is the product of the persons—Basilia, Luis, Erasmo, Ausangate, Pascual the Fox—who have taught her and who will continue to teach us.

Acknowledgments

I dedicate this chapter to Ambrosio Ariza, Adrián Huarco, Leonardo Huaman, Markusa Quintasi, Leonardo Quispe, and Mario Hermosa (Kirkas, Peru), who have taught me much more about authoritative things than I could ever learn in a classroom or a library. I express my deep gratitude to Colin McEwan and Sara Taylor at Dumbarton Oaks, who have provided consistent support for this volume. I am indebted to Sarah Newman, Kitty Allen, Rebecca Bria, B. Scot Rousse, Bruce Mannheim, Tom Cummins, John Janusek, and two anonymous peer reviewers, who provided helpful comments on this paper as I worked through seemingly endless drafts. Finally, I thank the Dumbarton Oaks Research Library and El Albergue (Ollantaytambo, Peru), both of which provided much-needed institutional and intellectual support.

1 Here, I provide citations when only one writer noted an incident that occurred during the execution. All other details are found in at least two eyewitness sources: Antonio Bautista de Salazar, Friar Gabriel de Oviedo, and Baltasar de Ocampo Conejeros (Bauer and Halac-Higashimori 2013; Bauer, Halac-Higashimori, and Cantarutti 2016:148, 177; Hemming 1970:587; Oviedo [1573] 1908; Salazar [1596] 1867). Viceroy Francisco de Toledo was not at the execution, but soon after he wrote two letters that described its importance (Toledo, in Levillier [1572] 1924).

2 Scholars have emphasized Native American "animism" while obscuring or overlooking the sacred things of the Spanish invaders, who revered saints' images and personified "nature" even as they sought to destroy American animate things (Hahn and Klein 2015; Lamana 2007; Park 2003). The term *animacy* positions indigenous American and European practices on similar ground. Such practices may not be ontologically commensurate, but they are comparable if we first recognize the ways that European ideas regarding "nature" have obscured and silenced Native American notions of animacy (see Mannheim 2015).

3 Though scholars distinguish between *power* (the ability to accomplish tasks given resources and infrastructure) and *authority* (the recognized ability to make decisions or direct action), they debate the extent to which authority implies the willful acquiescence, voluntary obedience, or conscious recognition of subjects (Scott 1985; cf. Lukes 2005). Some readers may object to the use of the Roman-Latin concept "authority" to describe social contexts and linguistic settings in which the term itself was not present or prevalent. On this, the philosopher Andrés Rosler (2005:88) writes: "The problem with this type of objection is that it seems to mistake the existence of the word for the existence of the concept itself and that it also seems to claim that for a concept to exist it must be conveyed by a single word or expression." In other words, it appears obvious that people in non-Roman societies tacitly or explicitly acknowledged that "authoritative" people and things (e.g., the Inka, Punchao) had the ability to direct social action and make social decisions.

4 As Eric Wolf (1999:592) stated, this issue "continues to echo in many quarters: in feminist anthropology that questions the assumption that men and women share the same cultural understandings; in ethnography from various areas, where 'rubbishmen' in Melanesia and 'no-account people' on the Northwest Coast do not seem to abide by the norms and ideals of Big Men and chiefs; in studies of hierarchical systems in which different strata and segments exhibit different and contending models of logico-aesthetic integration (India furnishes a telling case). We have been told that such divergences are ultimately kept in check and on track by cultural logic, pure and simple. This seems to me unconvincing."

5 This is not a review of "animism" in general (for such a review, see Harvey 2006; also Bird-David 1999; Descola 2005, 2013; Viveiros de Castro 2004; Wilkinson 2016).

6 Friars such as Landa recognized the animacy of things, such as the relics of saints. Indeed, at the same time as Thupa Amaru's execution, Spaniards endeavored to rescue the body of the Augustinian Diego Ortiz from Vilcabamba. Some Inkas had buried Ortiz's body face down in a deep hole containing saltpeter. When the Spaniards recovered the body a year later, they referred to several "miracles": the body had not deteriorated, roses had grown from Ortiz's face, and when the body was in Vilcabamba, mosquitoes left this tropical area (Bauer, Halac-Higashimori, and Cantarutti 2016:13–14, 202–212; see also Bauer et al. 2014). Hence, Spaniards too attributed animacy to things and bodies. But they often saw them as extensions of the Christian god and his will (e.g., the "true cross"; a martyr's body), *not* as artificial things (Hahn and Klein 2015). For many, native idols were abominations because they were powerful *on their own*, as *artificial beings*.

7 Reports about idolatry were themselves political, and many Spanish writers overstressed it to further colonial aims (DiCesare 2009:4–17; Thompson 1970:457).

8 David Hume ([1757] 1957) also argued that all humans anthropomorphize the natural world and that this is the foundation of religion (Holley 2002).

9 Tylor drew from the German physician and chemist Georg Stahl's 1708 proposal that all living things contain *anima* (Harvey 2006:3).

10 Terms such as *ch'ulel*, *teotl*, or *camay* are best seen as linguistically and culturally specific mediational frameworks, *not* translations of supposed "universals" such as mana or "the supernatural." Mediational frameworks are those that hold true in a social setting because they mediate experience of the world, even if such experience cannot be pithily explained (cf. Dreyfus and Taylor 2015). As David Graeber (2017:266) notes with regard to the Malagasy force called *hasina*, such concepts are often "first and foremost a way of talking about powers that no one understands." Hence, such frameworks are not beliefs, but incomplete descriptions of a state of affairs—just as someone can claim that a recent fortune is due to "luck," even if they do not believe in it (see also Apter 2017). In this sense, these mediational frameworks do not refer to *super*natural forces. They refer to the way nature worked in a certain setting, similar to how Evans-Pritchard (1937) emphasized that, among the Azande, witchcraft is a normal explanation for a normal state of affairs.

11 The passive voice is intentional here because it is not just the human actors who provide for the emergence and materialization of *ch'ulel*.

12 Later Spanish historical sources suggest that, in the Andes, things could contain a kind of spiritual essence. For instance, Cristóbal de Molina (el Cusqueño) describes the tumultuous time of Taqui Onqoy, when many Andeans sought to join the *huacas* in a rebellion against the Christian god. He notes that the *huacas*, at this time, no longer entered stones or springs to speak; rather, they came to lodge themselves within humans (Molina [1573] 1947:147), suggesting that the *huacas* came to be detached from their material moorings during early colonial times. This may reflect Christian ideas that separate body and spirit, and not Inka ideas that often see matter itself as the root of the sacred.

13 For theories and concepts regarding ontological anthropology and its relatives, see the work of key theorists such as Jane Bennett (2010); Manuel DeLanda (2006); Tim Ingold (2007, 2012); Amiria Henare, Martin Holbraad, and Sari Wastell (2007); Martin Holbraad (2007); Bruno Latour (1993, 1996, 1999); and Marilyn Strathern (1988, 1999). See reviews in Alberti 2016; Alberti, Jones, and Pollard 2013; Kohn 2015; and Paleček and Risjord 2012. Finally, see critiques of the "ontological turn" in Bessire and Bond 2014; Cepek 2016; Graeber 2015; and Swenson 2015b.

14 The ontological literature is replete with metaphors to describe the interplay of humans, nonhuman beings, environmental forces, and things—terms include *assemblage, bundle, machine, meshwork, mixture, network,* and *rhizome* (e.g., Deleuze and Guattari 1983, 1987; Ingold 2000; Pauketat 2013). *Assemblage* is a particularly popular term that emerged from the philosophy of Gilles Deleuze and Félix Guattari. Jane Bennett (2010:25), for example, refers to the electrical power grid in the United States as an assemblage made up of "a volatile mix of coal, sweat, electromagnetic fields, computer programs, electron streams, profit motives, heat, lifestyles, nuclear fuel, plastic, fantasies of mastery, static, legislation, water, economic theory, wire, and wood." With this, she divests action and agency from humans alone, arguing that the people and things of the grid together cause phenomena such as blackouts. Some archaeologists attempt to impose concepts from the philosophy of Deleuze and Guattari on the social practices of the ancient Maya or Moche. This chapter, and many others in this volume, contends that such an imposition is a radical reinterpretation. In other words, continental philosophy and ancient American metaphysics may share some common ground, but to locate it, one must first detail the process of commensuration on which comparisons may be built. As Tim Pauketat (2013) notes, the term *bundle* may be more appropriate to ancient America.

15 Descola (2005, 2013) envisions four ontological frameworks through which people engage with other beings: animism, totemism, analogism, and naturalism. The point of this typology is to resituate modern and scientific ontological dispositions—what he terms *naturalism*—seeing them less as an objective rendering of reality (as typically claimed) and more as one possible ontological framework among others (Mannheim, this volume).

16 Outside of America, scholars have drawn on theories of Amazonian perspectivism, especially for Siberia and Inner Asia (e.g., Brightman, Grotti, and Ulturgasheva 2012; Hill 2011; Pederson 2001;

Pederson, Empson, and Humphrey 2007; Pederson and Willerslev 2012; Willerslev 2007).

17 Viveiros de Castro's (2004) arguments appear to be equally rooted in Paris and the Amazon (cf. Costa and Fausto 2010). On one hand, his comment on a common conceptual framework reflects Lévi-Strauss's monumental work, *Mythologiques*, which sought to uncover common threads or structural elements among Native American myths and their descriptions of the natural world. It also resonates with research on common Native American myths, such as the emphasis on things (e.g., pots and spindle whorls) that come to life and prey on humans in the Maya *Popol Vuh*, Moche iconography, and modern tales (see Gose 1994; Quilter 1990, 1997). On the other hand, Viveiros de Castro's insistence on the link between perspective and embodiment almost perfectly echoes the philosophy of Maurice Merleau-Ponty. It is troubling, especially from the perspective of decolonizing anthropology (e.g., Atalay 2006), that scholars so often find Native American worlds in continental philosophy.

18 Early accounts stress *nagualismo*'s historical and political roots, suggesting it was born of "detestation of the Spaniards and hatred of the Christian religion" (Brinton 1894:35).

19 The philosopher Hannah Arendt (1958:52, 2006; Villa 2000) came close to defining things as social actors. She described the things that are needed for social life, referring to "furnishings," such as a house or a table, as structures that at once bring people together into a situation of consensus-building while also separating them according to their position. Despite this compelling metaphor, Arendt stops short of arguing that things in themselves are essential to politics or that broader assemblages can contribute to politics. Rather, she follows a traditional Western view that the structures of political life and the bases of authority are norms, boundaries, and laws converted into durable, objective forms (Arendt 1963:157). Likewise, the writings of the historian-philosophers Michel Foucault, Louis Althusser, or Giorgio Agamben may be perceived as attempts to envision political life in terms that decenter human intention and emphasize the roles of nonhumans and things. In particular, they see power in the modern world's streets, clinics, schools, bodies, and mechanisms of discipline. But their writings are explicitly focused on understanding the historical changes that yielded modern capitalist-industrial societies and their characteristic apparatuses and institutions (though, for an exception, see Foucault 2014). It is difficult to see how they can be uncritically applied to contexts such as the Pre-Columbian and indigenous Americas. This is not to say that such theories cannot be applied. It is to argue that their application requires a critical exploration of the concepts and assumptions that they may carry.

20 John Locke was particularly concerned with dispelling the fantasies of divine favor or magical growth that could too easily emerge along with the body politic, its institutions, and its ideologies. Philosopher Jeremy Waldron (1994:53) suggests that for Locke this process of mystification was part of a necessary political evolution: "Because the development of government was gradual and discernible, men could easily be mystified about its nature and justification. . . . The course of human development . . . has left men bewildered and mystified and it is now the task of true philosophy—the task Locke takes upon himself—to dispel some of that mystification." There are echoes of other Enlightenment thinkers, especially Karl Marx, in this statement regarding the need to dispel the mystification of things, fantasies, or nonhuman beings in political life.

21 The category of charismatic authority is particularly puzzling in Weber's theory, in part because it is unclear whether charisma is the characteristic or radiance of a person (*Ausstrahlung*) or an attribute given by a crowd. This term is also intriguing because Weber himself, for all of his concerns regarding demystification, equates charisma to a kind of mana or orenda, suggesting that animacy or animate forces are essential to notions of authority.

22 Researchers of the Pre-Columbian Americas might do well to draw from such theories in terms of their underlying methodologies and logics, rather than their conceptual frameworks and expectations. For example, it may be logically unsound to expect that "power" or "institutions" in Pre-Columbian societies operated via the appendages of a state and its economic apparatus—and a concomitant notion of a "society" that "must be defended"—as Foucault famously noted in his studies of the social transformations in the eighteenth and nineteenth centuries that yielded "modern" Europe (e.g., Foucault 1979a, 1979b, 1980, 2003). But it certainly would be fruitful

for researchers to learn from Foucault's methods, to approach politics in the Pre-Columbian world by seeking to isolate and identify the key sites or practices of political representation or conflict according to the cultural or ontological frameworks of those societies, and then to understand how these sites or practices came to channel a kind of power or manifest a kind of authority.

REFERENCES CITED

Alberti, Benjamin

2016   Archaeologies of Ontology. *Annual Review of Anthropology* 45:163–179.

Alberti, Benjamin, and Tamara L. Bray

2009   Introduction to Special Section, Animating Archaeology: Of Subjects, Objects, and Alternative Ontologies. *Cambridge Archaeological Journal* 19(3):337–343.

Alberti, Benjamin, Andrew Meirion Jones, and Joshua Pollard (editors)

2013   *Archaeology after Interpretation: Returning Materials to Archaeological Theory.* Left Coast Press, Walnut Creek, Calif.

Alberti, Benjamin, and Yvonne Marshall

2009   Animating Archaeology: Local Theories and Conceptually Open-Ended Methodologies. *Cambridge Archaeological Journal* 19(3):344–356.

Albornoz, Cristóbal de

[1584] 1988   Instrucción para descubrir todas las guacas del Pirú y sus camayos y haziendas. In *Fábulas y mitos de los incas,* edited by Henrique Urbano and Pierre Duviols, pp. 161–198. Historia 16, Madrid.

1990   *El retorno de las huacas: Estudios y documentos sobre el Taki Onqoy, siglo XVI.* Instituto de Estudios Peruanos, Lima.

Allen, Catherine J.

1982   Body and Soul in Quechua Thought. *Journal of Latin American Lore* 8(2):179–196.

1998   When Utensils Revolt: Mind, Matter, and Modes of Being in the Pre-Columbian Andes. *RES: Anthropology and Aesthetics* 33:18–27.

2002a   *The Hold Life Has: Coca and Cultural Identity in an Andean Community.*

Smithsonian Institution Press, Washington, D.C.

2002b   The Incas Have Gone Inside: Pattern and Persistence in Andean Iconography. *RES: Anthropology and Aesthetics* 42:180–203.

2011   *Foxboy: Intimacy and Aesthetics in Andean Stories.* University of Texas Press, Austin.

2016   The Living Ones: Miniatures and Animation in the Andes. *Journal of Anthropological Research* 72(4):416–441.

2017a   Connections and Disconnections: A Response to Marisol de la Cadena. *HAU: Journal of Ethnographic Theory* 7(2):11–13.

2017b   Pensamientos de una etnógrafa acerca de la interpretación en la arqueología andina. *Mundo de antes* 11:13–68.

Appadurai, Arjun

1988   Putting Hierarchy in Its Place. *Cultural Anthropology* 3(1):36–49.

Apter, Andrew

2017   Ethnographic X-Files and Holbraad's Double-Bind: Reflections on an Ontological Turn of Events. *HAU: Journal of Ethnographic Theory* 7(1):287–302.

Arendt, Hannah

1958   *The Human Condition.* 2nd ed. University of Chicago Press, Chicago.

1963   *On Revolution.* Viking Press, New York.

2006   "What Is Freedom?" and "What Is Authority?" In *Between Past and Future: Eight Exercises in Political Thought,* edited by Jerome Kohn. Penguin, London.

Århem, Kaj

1993   *Makuna—An Amazonian People.* Socialantropologiska institutionen, Göteborg.

Arnold, Denise Y., and Christine A. Hastorf

2008 *Heads of State: Icons, Power, and Politics in the Ancient and Modern Andes.* Left Coast Press, Walnut Creek, Calif.

Arnold, Philip P.

1999a *Eating Landscape: Aztec and European Occupations of Tlalocan.* University Press of Colorado, Niwot.

1999b Eating Landscape: Human Sacrifice and Sustenance in Aztec Mexico. In *Aztec Ceremonial Landscapes*, edited by David Carrasco, pp. 219–232. University Press of Colorado, Niwot.

Arriaga, Pablo José de

[1621] 1968 Extirpacion de la idolatria del Piru. In *Biblioteca de autores españoles*, pp. 191–277. Crónicas Peruanas de Interés Indigena 209. Ediciones Atlas, Madrid.

Atalay, Sonya

2006 Indigenous Archaeology as Decolonizing Practice. *American Indian Quarterly* 30(3–4):280–310.

Aveni, Anthony F.

1986 *World Archaeoastronomy: Selected Papers from the 2nd Oxford International Conference on Archaeoastronomy.* Cambridge University Press, Cambridge.

Bauer, Andrew, and Steve Kosiba

2016 How Things Act: An Archaeology of Materials in Political Life. *Journal of Social Archaeology* 14(2):1–27.

Bauer, Brian S., Teófilo Aparicio López, Jesús Galiano Blanco, Madeleine Halac-Higashimori, and Gabriel Cantarutti.

2014 *Muerte, entierros y milagros de Fray Diego Ortiz: Política y religión en Vilcabamba, S. VXI.* Ceques editors, Cuzco.

Bauer, Brian S., and Madeleine Halac-Higashimori

2013 *Baltasar de Ocampo Conejeros y la Provincia de Vilcabamba.* Ceques editors, Cuzco.

Bauer, Brian S., Madeleine Halac-Higashimori, and Gabriel Cantarutti

2016 *Voices from Vilcabamba: Accounts Chronicling the Fall of the Inca Empire.* University Press of Colorado, Boulder.

Benett, Jane

2010 *Vibrant Matter: A Political Ecology of Things.* Duke University Press, Durham, N.C.

Benson, Elizabeth P.

1976 Ritual Cloth and Palenque Kings. In *The Art, Iconography, and Dynastic History of Palenque, Part III*, edited by Merle Green Robertson, pp. 45–58. Robert Louis Stevenson School, Pebble Beach, Calif.

Bessire, Lucas, and David Bond

2014 Ontological Anthropology and the Deferral of Critique. *American Ethnologist* 41(3):440–456.

Billman, Brian R.

2002 Irrigation and the Origins of the Southern Moche State on the North Coast of Peru. *Latin American Antiquity* 13:371–400.

Bird-David, Nurit

1999 "Animism" Revisited: Personhood, Environment, and Relational Epistemology. *Current Anthropology* 40:S67–S91.

Böhme, Hartmut

2014 *Fetishism and Culture: A Different Theory of Modernity.* De Gruyter, Berlin.

Boone, Elizabeth Hill (editor)

1987 *The Aztec Templo Mayor.* Dumbarton Oaks Research Library and Collection, Washington, D.C.

Boone, Elizabeth Hill, and Thomas B. F. Cummins (editors)

1998 *Native Traditions in the Postconquest World.* Dumbarton Oaks Research Library and Collection, Washington, D.C.

Boteler Mock, Shirley (editor)

1998 *The Sowing and the Dawning: Termination, Dedication, and Transformation in the Archaeological and Ethnographic Record of Mesoamerica.* University of New Mexico Press, Albuquerque.

Boucher, David, and Paul Kelly

1994 *The Social Contract from Hobbes to Rawls.* Routledge, London.

Braun, Bruce, and Sarah J. Whatmore

2010   The Stuff of Politics: An Introduction. In *Political Matter: Technoscience, Democracy, and Public Life*, edited by Bruce Braun, Sarah Whatmore, Isabelle Stengers, and Jane Bennett, pp. ix–xl. University of Minnesota Press, Minneapolis.

Bray, Tamara L.

2009   An Archaeological Perspective on the Andean Concept of *Camaquen*: Thinking through Late Pre-Columbian *Ofrendas* and *Huacas*. *Cambridge Archaeological Journal* 19(3):357–366.

Bray, Tamara L. (editor)

2015   *The Archaeology of Wak'as: Explorations of the Sacred in the Pre-Columbian Andes.* University Press of Colorado, Boulder.

Bricker, Victoria Reifler

1981   *The Indian Christ, The Indian King: The Historical Substrate of Maya Myth and Ritual.* University of Texas Press, Austin.

Brightman, Marc, Vanessa Elisa Grotti, and Olga Ulturgasheva

2012   *Animism in Rainforest and Tundra: Personhood, Animals, Plants and Things in Contemporary Amazonia and Siberia.* Berghahn Books, New York.

Brinton, Daniel G.

1894   Nagualism: A Study of Native American Folk-Lore and History. *Proceedings of the American Philosophical Society* 33(144):11–73.

Broda de Casas, Johanna

1970   Tlacaxipehualiztli: A Reconstruction of an Aztec Calendar Festival from 16th Century Sources. *Revista española de antropología americana* 5:197–273.

Broda de Casas, Johanna, David Carrasco, and Eduardo Matos Moctezuma

1987   *The Great Temple of Tenochtitlan.* Thames and Hudson, London.

Brumfiel, Elizabeth M.

1996   Figurines and the Aztec State: Testing the Effectiveness of Ideological Domination. In *Gender in Archaeology: Research in Gender and Practice*, edited by R. P. Wright, pp. 143–166. University of Pennsylvania Press, Philadelphia.

1998   Huitzilopotchli's Conquest: Aztec Ideology in the Archaeological Record. *Cambridge Archaeological Journal* 8:3–13.

Burger, Richard L.

2009   The Intellectual Legacy of Julio C. Tello. In *The Life and Writings of Julio C. Tello: America's First Indigenous Archaeologist*, edited by Richard L. Burger, pp. 65–90. University of Iowa Press, Iowa City.

Burke, Peter

1969   *The Renaissance Sense of the Past.* Edward Arnold, New York.

2012   History, Myth, and Fiction: Doubts and Debates. In *Oxford History of Historical Writing: Volume 3, 1400–1800*, edited by José Rabassa, Masayuki Sato, Edoardo Tortarolo, and Daniel Woolf, pp. 261–281. Oxford University Press, Oxford.

Calancha, Antonio de la

[1638]   *Corónica moralizada del Orden de San*
1974–1981   *Agustín en el Perú, con sucesos egenplares en esta monarquia.* Edited by Ignacio Prado Pastor. Lima.

Carlsen, Robert T. S., and Martin Prechtel

1991   The Flowing of the Dead: An Interpretation of Highland Maya Culture. *Man* 26(1):23–42.

Carrasco, David

1995a   Cosmic Jaws: We Eat the Gods and the Gods Eat Us. *Journal of the American Academy of Religion* 63(3):429–463.

1995b   Give Me Some Skin: The Charisma of the Aztec Warrior. *History of Religions* 35(1):1–26.

1999   *City of Sacrifice: The Aztec Empire and the Role of Violence in Civilization.* Beacon Press, Boston.

Cepek, Michael

2016   There Might Be Blood: Oil, Humility, and the Cosmopolitics of a Cofán Petro-Being. *American Ethnologist* 43(4):623–635.

Cervantes, Fernando

1994   *The Devil in the New World: The Impact of Diabolism in New Spain.* Yale University Press, New Haven.

Chase, Zachary

    2015   What Is a Wak'a? When Is a Wak'a? In *The Archaeology of Wak'as: Explorations of the Sacred in the Pre-Columbian Andes*, edited by Tamara Bray, pp. 75–126. University Press of Colorado, Boulder.

Claessen, H. J. M.

    1984   The Internal Dynamics of the Early State. *Current Anthropology* 25:365–379.

Claessen, H. J. M., and P. Skalník (editors)

    1978   *The Early State*. Mouton, The Hague.

Codrington, Robert Henry

    1891   *The Melanesians: Studies in Their Anthropology and Folk-Lore*. Clarendon Press, New York.

Coe, Michael D.

    1977   Olmec and Maya: A Study in Relationships. In *The Origins of Maya Civilization*, edited by Richard E. W. Adams, pp. 183–195. University of New Mexico Press, Albuquerque.

Coe, Michael D., and Richard A. Diehl

    1980   *In the Land of the Olmec: The Archaeology of San Lorenzo Tenochtitlan*. University of Texas Press, Austin.

Costa, Luiz, and Carlos Fausto

    2010   The Return of the Animists: Recent Studies in Amazonian Ontologies. *Religion and Society: Advances in Research* 1:89–109.

Cummins, Thomas B. F.

    2005   *Toasts with the Inca*. University of Michigan Press, Ann Arbor.

    2009   The Golden Calf in America. In *The Idol in the Age of Art: Objects, Devotions, and the Early Modern World*, edited by Michael W. Cole and Rebecca Zorach, pp. 77–104. Routledge, London.

Cummins, Thomas B. F., and Bruce Mannheim

    2011   The River around Us, the Stream within Us: The Traces of the Sun and Inka Kinetics. *Res* 59/60:5–21.

Dean, Carolyn

    2010   *A Culture of Stone: Inka Perspectives on Rock*. Duke University Press, Durham, N.C.

de la Cadena, Marisol

    2010   Indigenous Cosmopolitics in the Andes. *Cultural Anthropology* 25(2):334–370.

    2015   *Earth Beings: Ecologies of Practice across Andean Worlds*. Duke University Press, Durham, N.C.

DeLanda, Manuel

    2006   *A New Philosophy of Society: Assemblage Theory and Social Complexity*. Continuum, London.

DeLeonardis, Lisa

    2011   Itinerant Experts, Alternative Harvests: *Kamayuq* in the Service of the *Qhapaq* and Crown. *Ethnohistory* 58(3):445–489.

Deleuze, Gilles, and Félix Guattari

    1983   *Anti-Oedipus: Capitalism and Schizophrenia*. Translated by R. Hurley, M. Seem, and H. R. Lane. University of Minnesota Press, Minneapolis.

    1987   *A Thousand Plateaus: Capitalism and Schizophrenia*. Translated by B. Massumi. University of Minnesota Press, Minneapolis.

Deloria, Vine, Jr.

    1988   *Custer Died for Your Sins: An Indian Manifesto*. University of Oklahoma Press, Norman.

    1992   Indians, Archaeologists, and the Future. *American Antiquity* 57:595–598.

    1995   *Red Earth, White Lies: Native Americans and the Myth of Scientific Fact*. Scribner, New York.

DeMarrais, Elizabeth, Luis Jaime Castillo, and Timothy Earle

    1996   Ideology, Materialization, and Power Strategies. *Current Anthropology* 37(1):15–31.

Descola, Philippe

    1996   *In the Society of Nature: A Native Ecology in Amazonia*. Cambridge University Press, Cambridge.

    2005   *Par-delà nature et culture*. Gallimard, Paris.

    2013   *Beyond Nature and Culture*. University of Chicago Press, Chicago.

    2014a   The Grid and the Tree: Reply to Marshall Sahlins's Comment. *HAU: Journal of Ethnographic Theory* 4(1):295–300.

    2014b   Modes of Being and Forms of Predication. *HAU: Journal of Ethnographic Theory* 4(1):271–280.

DiCesare, Catherine R.

2009   *Sweeping the Way: Divine Transformation in the Aztec Festival of Ochpaniztli.* University Press of Colorado, Boulder.

Dowd, Anne S., and Susan Milbrath

2015   *Cosmology, Calendars, and Horizon-Based Astronomy in Ancient Mesoamerica.* University Press of Colorado, Boulder.

Dreyfus, Hubert, and Charles Taylor

2015   *Retrieving Realism.* Harvard University Press, Cambridge, Mass.

Durán, Diego

1971   *Book of Rites and the Ancient Calendar.* Translated and edited by Fernando Horcasitas and Doris Heyden. University of Oklahoma Press, Norman.

Durkheim, Émile

[1912] 1995   *Elementary Forms of Religious Life.* Translated by Karen E. Fields. Free Press, New York.

Duviols, Pierre

1978a   Camaquen, Upani: Un concept animiste des anciens péruviens. In *Estudios americanistas*, edited by R. Hartmann and U. Oberam, pp. 132–144. Collectanea Institui Anthropos, Bonn.

1978b   Un symbolisme andin du double: La lithomorphose de l'ancêtre. *Actes du XLIIe Congrès International des Américanistes* 4:359–364.

1986   *Cultura andina y represión: Procesos y visitas de idolatrías y hechicerías Cajatambo, siglo XVII.* Centro de Estudios Rurales Andinos, Bartolomé de las Casas, Cuzco.

Earle, Timothy K.

1997   *How Chiefs Come to Power: The Political Economy in Prehistory.* Stanford University Press, Stanford.

Estete, Miguel de

[1535] 1918   Noticia del Perú. *Boletín de la Sociedad Ecuatoriana de Estudios Históricos Americanos* 1(3):312–335. Quito.

Evans-Pritchard, E. E.

1937   *Witchcraft, Oracles, and Magic among the Azande.* Clarendon Press, Oxford.

1965   *Theories of Primitive Religion.* Oxford University Press, Oxford.

Fausto, Carlos

1999   Of Enemies and Pets: Warfare and Shamanism in Amazonia. *American Ethnologist* 26(4):933–956.

2007a   Feasting on People: Eating Animals and Humans in Amazonia. *Current Anthropology* 48(4):497–530.

2007b   If God Were a Jaguar: Cannibalism and Christianity among the Guarani (Sixteenth–Twentieth Centuries). In *Time and Memory in Indigenous Amazonia: Anthropological Perspectives*, edited by Carlos Fausto and Michael Heckenberger, pp. 74–105. University Press of Florida, Gainesville.

Firth, Raymond

1940   The Analysis of *Mana*: An Empirical Approach. *Journal of the Polynesian Society* 49(4):483–510.

Forsyth, Murray

1994   Hobbes's Contractarianism: A Comparative Analysis. In *The Social Contract from Hobbes to Rawls*, edited by David Boucher and Paul Kelly, pp. 35–50. Routledge, London.

Foster, George

1944   Nagualism in Mexico and Guatemala. *Acta americana* 2:85–103.

Foucault, Michel

1979a   *Discipline and Punish.* Random House, New York.

1979b   On Governmentality. *Ideology and Consciousness* 6:5–21.

1980   *Power/Knowledge: Selected Interviews and Other Writings, 1972–1977.* Pantheon, New York.

2003   *Society Must Be Defended: Lectures at the Collège de France.* Picador, New York.

2014   *On the Government of the Living: Lectures at the Collège de France, 1979-1980.* Palgrave Macmillan, Hampshire.

Fowles, Severin

2013   *An Archaeology of Doings: Secularism and the Study of Pueblo Religion.* School for Advanced Research Press, Santa Fe, N.Mex.

Frazer, James George

1890   *The Golden Bough: A Study in Comparative Religion.* Macmillan, London.

Freidel, David A., and Linda Schele

1989   Dead Kings and Living Temples: Dedication and Termination Rituals among the Ancient Maya. In *Word and Image in Maya Culture: Explanations in Language, Writing, and Representation,* edited by William F. Hanks and Don S. Rice, pp. 233–243. University of Utah Press, Salt Lake City.

Freidel, David A., Linda Schele, and Joy Parker

1993   *Maya Cosmos: Three Thousand Years on the Shaman's Path.* William Morrow, New York.

Friedrich, Carl (editor)

1958   *Authority.* Harvard University Press, Cambridge, Mass.

Furst, Jill

1995   *The Natural History of the Soul in Ancient Mexico.* Yale University Press, New Haven.

Gauchet, Michel

1999   *The Disenchantment of the World: A Political History of Religion.* Translated by Oscar Burge. Princeton University Press, Princeton.

Gauthier, David

1986   *Morals by Agreement.* Clarendon Press, Oxford.

Gell, Alfred

1998   *Art and Agency: An Anthropological Theory.* Clarendon Press, Oxford.

Gose, Peter

1993   Segmentary State Formation and the Ritual Control of Water under the Incas. *Comparative Studies in Society and History* 35(3):480–514.

1996   Past Is a Lower Moiety: Diarchy, History, and Divine Kingship in the Inka Empire. *History and Anthropology* 9:383–414.

2000   The State as a Chosen Woman: Brideservice and the Feeding of Tributaries in the Inka Empire. *American Anthropologist* 102:84–97.

2006   Mountains Historicized: Ancestors and Landscape in the Colonial Andes. In *Kay Pacha: Cultivating Earth and Water in the Andes,* edited by Penelope Dransart, pp. 29–38. British Archaeological Reports International Series 1478. Archaeopress, Oxford.

2018   The Semi-Social Mountain: Meta-personhood and Political Ontology in the Andes. *HAU: Journal of Ethnographic Theory* 8(3):488–505.

Graeber, David

2015   Radical Alterity Is Just Another Way of Saying "Reality": A Reply to Eduardo Viveiros de Castro. *HAU: Journal of Ethnographic Theory* 5(2):1–41.

2017   The People as Nursemaids of the King: Notes on Monarchs as Children, Women's Uprisings, and the Return of the Ancestral Dean in Central Madagascar. In *On Kings,* by David Graeber and Marshall Sahlins, pp. 249–344. Hau Books, Chicago.

Grotti, Vanessa E., and Marc Brightman

2012   Humanity, Personhood, and Trans-formability in Northern Amazonia. In *Animism in Rainforest and Tundra: Personhood, Animals, Plants and Things in Contemporary Amazonia and Siberia,* edited by M. Brightman, V. Grotti, and O. Ulturgasheva. Berghahn Books, New York.

2016   Narratives of the Invisible: Auto-biography, Kinship, and Alterity in Native Amazonia. *Social Analysis* 60(1):92–109.

Grove, David C.

1981   Olmec Monuments: Mutilation as a Clue to Meaning. In *The Olmec and Their Neighbors: Essays in Memory of Matthew W. Stirling,* edited by Elizabeth P. Benson, pp. 49–78. Dumbarton Oaks, Washington, D.C.

Habermas, Jürgen

1975   *Legitimation Crisis.* Beacon, Boston.

Hahn, Cynthia, and Holger Klein (editors)

2015   *Saints and Sacred Matter: The Cult of Relics in Byzantium and Beyond.* Dumbarton Oaks Research Library and Collection, Washington, D.C.

Hallowell, A. Irving

1960   Ojibwa Ontology, Behavior, and World View. In *Culture in History: Essays in Honor of Paul Radin*, edited by Stanley Diamond, pp. 19–52. Columbia University Press, New York.

Hammer, Dean

2008   *Roman Political Thought and the Modern Theoretical Imagination.* University of Oklahoma Press, Norman.

Hanke, Lewis

1974   *All Mankind Is One: A Study of the Disputation between Bartolomé de Las Casas and Juan Ginés de Sepúlveda in 1550 on the Intellectual and Religious Capacity of the American Indians.* Northern Illinois University Press, DeKalb.

Hardin, Russell

2009   *The Oxford Handbook of Comparative Politics.* Edited by Carl Boix and Susan C. Stokes. Oxford University Press, Oxford.

Harrison-Buck, Eleanor

2016   Killing the "Kings of Stone": The Defacement of Classic Maya Monuments. In *Ritual, Violence, and the Fall of Classic Maya Kings*, edited by Gyles Iannone, Brett A. Houk, and Sonja A. Schwake, pp. 61–88. University Press of Florida, Gainesville.

Harvey, Graham

2006   *Animism: Respecting the Living World.* Columbia University Press, New York.

Hemming, John

1970   *The Conquest of the Incas.* Harcourt, San Diego, Calif.

Henare, Amiria, Martin Holbraad, and Sari Wastell

2007   Introduction: Thinking through Things. In *Thinking through Things: Theorising Artefacts Ethnographically*, edited by Amiria Henare, Martin Holbraad, and Sari Wastell, pp. 1–31. Routledge, London.

Hill, Erica

2011   Animals as Agents: Hunting Ritual and Relational Ontologies in Prehistoric Alaska and Chukotka. *Cambridge Archaeological Journal* 21(3):407–426.

Hocart, A. M.

1914   Mana. *Man* 14:97–101.

1922   Mana Again. *Man* 22:139–141.

Hogbin, H. Ian

1936   Mana. *Oceania* 6(3):241–274.

Holbraad, Martin

2007   The Power of Powder: Multiplicity and Motion in the Divinatory Cosmology of Cuban Ifá (or Mana, Again). In *Thinking through Things: Theorising Artefacts Ethnographically*, edited by Amiria Henare, Martin Holbraad, and Sari Wastell, pp. 189–225. Routledge, London.

Holley, David M.

2002   The Role of Anthropomorphism in Hume's Critique of Theism. *International Journal for Philosophy of Religion* 51(2):83–99.

Houston, Stephen, and David Stuart

1989   *The Way Glyph: Evidence for "Co-essences" among the Classic Maya.* Research on Ancient Maya Writing 30. Center for Maya Research, Washington D.C.

1996   Of Gods, Glyphs, and Kings: Divinity and Rulership among the Classic Maya. *Antiquity* 70:289–312.

1998   Ancient Maya Self: Personhood and Portraiture in the Classic Period. *RES: Anthropology and Aesthetics* 33:72–101.

Hume, David

[1757] 1957   *The Natural History of Religion.* Stanford University Press, Palo Alto, Calif.

Hvidtfeldt, Arild

1958   *Teotl and Ixiptlatli: Some Central Conceptions in Ancient Mexican Religion.* Munksgaard, Copenhagen.

Iacono, Alfonso Maurizio

2016   *The History and Theory of Fetishism.* Translated by V. Tchernichova and M. Boria, with the collaboration of E. MacDonald. Palgrave MacMillan, New York.

Ingold, Timothy

1999   Comment on Nurit Bird-David's
         "Animism Revisited." *Current
         Anthropology* 40:S81–S82.

2000   *The Perception of the Environment:
         Essays in Livelihood, Dwelling, and Skill.*
         Routledge, London.

2006   Rethinking the Animate, Re-animating
         Thought. *Ethnos* 71(1):9–20.

2007   Materials against Materiality.
         Archaeological Dialogues 14(1):1–16.

2012   Toward an Ecology of Materials. *Annual
         Review of Anthropology* 41:427–442.

Inomata, Takeshi

2016a   Concepts of Legitimacy and Social
         Dynamics: Termination Ritual and
         the Last King of Aguateca, Guatemala.
         In *Ritual, Violence, and the Fall of the
         Classic Maya Kings*, edited by Gyles
         Iannone, Brett A. Houk, and Sonja A.
         Schwake, pp. 89–107. University Press
         of Florida, Gainesville.

2016b   Theories of Power and Legitimacy in
         Archaeological Contexts: The Emergent
         Regime of Power at the Formative Maya
         Community of Ceibal, Guatemala. In
         *Political Strategies in Pre-Columbian
         Mesoamerica*, edited by Sarah Kurnick
         and Joanne Baron, pp. 37–60. University
         Press of Colorado, Boulder.

Isbell, Billie Jean

1985   The Metaphoric Process: "From Culture
         to Nature and Back Again." In *Animal
         Myths and Metaphors in South America*,
         edited by Gary Urton, pp. 285–313.
         University of Utah Press, Salt Lake City.

Isbell, Willliam H.

1997   *Mummies and Mortuary Monuments:
         A Post-Processual Prehistory of Andean
         Social Organization.* University of Texas
         Press, Austin.

Jones, William

1905   The Algonkin Manitou. *Journal of
         American Folklore* 18(70):183–190.

Keen, Benjamin

1971   *The Aztec Image in Western Thought.*
         Rutgers University Press, New
         Brunswick, N.J.

Kertzer, David

1988   *Ritual, Politics, and Power.* Yale
         University Press, New Haven.

Klein, Cecelia F., Eulogio Guzmán, Elisa C. Mandell,
and Maya Stanfield-Mazzi

2002   The Role of Shamanism in Mesoameri-
         can Art: A Reassessment. *Current
         Anthropology* 43(3):383–419.

Kohn, Eduardo

2013   *How Forests Think: Toward an Anthro-
         pology Beyond the Human.* University of
         California Press, Berkeley.

2015   Anthropology of Ontologies. *Annual
         Review of Anthropology* 44:311–327.

Kosiba, Steve

2011   The Politics of Locality: Pre-Inka Social
         Landscapes of the Cusco Region. In *The
         Archaeology of Politics: The Materiality
         of Political Practice in the Past*, edited
         by Peter Johansen and Andrew Bauer,
         pp. 114–150. Cambridge Scholars,
         Newcastle upon Tyne.

2015   Of Blood and Soil: Tombs, Wak'as,
         and the Naturalization of Social
         Difference in the Inka Heartland. In *The
         Archaeology of Wak'as: Explorations of
         the Sacred in the Pre-Columbian Andes*,
         edited by Tamara L. Bray, pp. 167–212.
         University Press of Colorado, Boulder.

2017   Ancient Artifice: The Production of
         Antiquity and the Social Roles of Ruins
         in the Heartland of the Inca Empire.
         In *Antiquarianisms: Contact, Conflict,
         Comparison*, edited by Benjamin
         Anderson and Felipe Rojas, pp. 72–108.
         Oxbow Books, Oxford.

Laluk, Nicholas

2017   The Indivisibility of Land and
         Mind: Indigenous Knowledge and
         Collaborative Archaeology within
         Apache Contexts. *Journal of Social
         Archaeology* 17(1):92–112.

Lamana, Gonzalo

2007   *Domination without Dominance:
         Inca-Spanish Encounters in Early
         Colonial Peru.* Duke University Press,
         Durham, N.C.

Las Casas, Bartolomé de

 1966   *Tratados.* Translated by A. Millares
        Carlo and R. Moreno. Fondo de Cultura
        Económica, Mexico City.

 1967   *Apologética historia sumaria.* Edited
        by Edmundo O'Gorman. Universidad
        Autónoma Nacional de México,
        Mexico City.

 1974   *In Defense of the Indians.* Translated
        and edited by Stafford Poole. Northern
        Illinois University Press, DeKalb.

Latour, Bruno

 1993   *We Have Never Been Modern.* Harvard
        University Press, Cambridge, Mass.

Lau, George

 2013   *Ancient Alterity in the Andes: A
        Recognition of Others.* Routledge,
        New York.

León-Portilla, Miguel

 1986   A Reflection of the Ancient
        Mesoamerican Ethos. In *World
        Archaeoastronomy: Selected Papers
        from the 2nd Oxford International
        Conference on Archaeoastronomy,*
        edited by Anthony F. Aveni, pp. 219–227.
        Cambridge University Press, Cambridge.

Levillier, Roberto

 [1572] 1924 *Gobernantes del Perú: Cartas y pape-
        les, siglo XVI.* Vol. 4. Sucesores de
        Rivadeneira, Madrid.

Lincoln, Bruce

 1994   *Authority: Construction and Corrosion.*
        University of Chicago Press, Chicago.

Linehan, Peter

 1993   *History and Historians of Medieval
        Spain.* Clarendon Press, Oxford.

López Austin, Alfredo

 1980   *Cuerpo humano e ideología: Las
        concepciones de los antiguos nahuas.*
        Universidad Nacional Autónoma de
        México, Mexico City.

 1988   *The Human Body and Ideology: Concepts
        of the Ancient Nahuas.* Translated by
        T. Ortiz de Montellano and B. Ortiz de
        Montellano. University of Utah Press,
        Salt Lake City.

López de Cogolludo, Diego

 1688   *Historia de Yucathan.* Juan García
        Infanzón, Madrid.

Löschke, Jörg

 2015   Authority in Relationships. *Interna-
        tional Journal of Philosophical Studies*
        23(2):187–204.

Lukes, Stephen

 2005   *Power: A Radical View.* 2nd ed. Palgrave
        Macmillan, Hampshire.

MacCormack, Sabine

 1993   *Religion in the Andes: Vision and
        Imagination in Early Colonial Peru.*
        Princeton University Press, Princeton.

 2007   *On the Wings of Time: Rome, the Incas,
        Spain, and Peru.* Princeton University
        Press, Princeton.

Mannheim, Bruce

 2015   All Translation Is Radical Translation.
        In *Translating Worlds: The Epistemo-
        logical Space of Translation,* edited by
        Carlo Severi and William F. Hanks,
        pp. 199–219. University of Chicago Press,
        Chicago.

Mannheim, Bruce, and Guillermo Salas Carreño

 2015   Wak'a: Entifications of the Andean
        Sacred. In *The Archaeology of Wak'as:
        Explorations of the Sacred in the Pre-
        Columbian Andes,* edited by Tamara L.
        Bray, pp. 46–72. University of Colorado
        Press, Boulder.

Marcus, Joyce

 1992   *Ancient Mesoamerican Writing Systems:
        History, Myth, and Propaganda.*
        Princeton University Press, Princeton.

Marett, R. R.

 1914   *The Threshold of Religion.* Macmillan,
        New York.

Martínez Cereceda, José Luis

 1995   *Autoridades en los Andes: Los atributos
        del señor.* Pontificia Universidad Católica
        del Perú, Fondo Editorial, Lima.

Martínez González, Roberto

 2006   Le nahualli-tlahuipuchtli dans le
        monde nahuatl. *Journal de la Société des
        Américanistes* 92(2):111–136.

 2010a *El nahualismo.* Instituto de Investiga-
        ciones Antropológicas, Universidad
        Nacional Autónoma de México,
        Mexico City.

2010b La animalidad compartida: El nahual-ismo a la luz del animismo. *Revista española de antropología americana* 40(2):256–263.

Matos Moctezuma, Eduardo

1987 Symbolism of the Templo Mayor. In *The Aztec Templo Mayor*, edited by Elizabeth Hill Boone, pp. 185–209. Dumbarton Oaks Research Library, Washington, D.C.

Maúrtua, Victor M. (editor)

1906 *Vilcabamba.* Vol. 7 of *Juicio de límites entre el Perú y Bolivia.* Henrich y Comp, Barcelona.

Mauss, Marcel

[1904] 1972 *A General Theory of Magic.* Routledge and K. Paul, London.

McGee, R. Jon

1990 *Life, Ritual, and Religion among the Lacandon Maya.* Wadsworth, Belmont, Calif.

1998 The Lacandon Incense Burner Renewal Ceremony: Termination and Dedication Ritual among the Contemporary Maya. In *The Sowing and the Dawning: Termination, Dedication, and Transformation in the Archaeological and Ethnographic Record of Mesoamerica*, edited by S. Boteler Mock, pp. 41–46. University of New Mexico Press, Albuquerque.

Molina, Cristóbal de

[1573] 1947 *Ritos y fabulas de los Incas.* Colección Eurindia 12. Editorial Futuro, Buenos Aires.

Morris, Rosalind C.

2017 After de Brosses: Fetishism, Translation, Comparativism, Critique. In *The Returns of Fetishism: Charles de Brosses and the Afterlives of an Indea*, edited by Rosalind C. Morris and Daniel H. Leonard, pp. 133–320. University of Chicago Press, Chicago.

Müller, Max F.

1891 *Physical Religion (The Gifford Lectures Delivered before the University of Glasgow in 1890).* Longmans, Green, London.

Murra, John V.

[1956] 1980 *The Economic Organization of the Inka State.* JAI Press, Greenwich.

Murúa, Martín de

[1590] 1962–1964 *Historia general del Perú, origen y descendencia de los Incas.* Colección joyas bibliográficas, Biblioteca Americana Vetus, 1 and 2. Instituto Gonzalo Fernandez de Oviedo, Madrid.

Ortiz de Montellano, Bernard R.

1990 *Aztec Medicine, Health, and Nutrition.* Rutgers University Press, New Brunswick, N.J.

Oviedo, Gabriel de

[1573] 1908 *A Narrative of the Vice-Regal Embassy to Vilcabamba, 1571, and the Execution of Tupac Amaru, December 1571.* The Hakluyt Society, London.

Paleček, Martin, and Mark Risjord

2012 Relativism and the Ontological Turn within Anthropology. *Philosophy of the Social Sciences* 43(1):3–23.

Pals, Daniel

2006 *Eight Theories of Religion.* Oxford University Press, Oxford.

Park, Katharine

2003 Nature in Person: Medieval and Renaissance Allegories and Emblems. In *The Moral Authority of Nature*, edited by Lorraine Daston and Fernando Vidal, pp. 50–74. University of Chicago Press, Chicago.

Pauketat, Timothy R.

2013 *An Archaeology of the Cosmos: Rethinking Agency and Religion in Ancient America.* Routledge, London.

Pederson, Morten A.

2001 Totemism, Animism, and North Asian Indigenous Ontologies. *Journal of the Royal Anthropological Institute* 7(3):411–427.

Pederson, Morten A., Rebecca Empson, and Caroline Humphrey

2007 Editorial Introduction: Inner Asian Perspectivisms. *Inner Asia* 9(2):141–152.

Pederson, Morten A., and Rane Willerslev

2012 "The Soul of the Soul Is the Body": Rethinking the Concept of the Soul through North Asian Ethnography. *Common Knowledge* 18(3):464–486.

Perera, Victor, and Robert D. Bruce

  1982   *The Last Lords of Palenque: The Lacandon Mayas of the Mexican Rain Forest.* University of California Press, Berkeley.

Pietz, William

  1985   The Problem of the Fetish, I. *RES: Anthropology and Aesthetics* 9(1):5–17.

  1987   The Problem of the Fetish, II: The Origin of the Fetish. *RES: Anthropology and Aesthetics* 13(1):23–45.

Pizarro, Pedro

  [1571] 1921   *Relation of the Discovery and Conquest of the Kingdoms of Peru.* Translated and annotated by P. Means. New York Cortes Society, New York.

Quilter, Jeffrey

  1990   The Moche Revolt of the Objects. *Latin American Antiquity* 1(1):42–65.

  1997   The Narrative Approach to Moche Iconography. *Latin American Antiquity* 8(2):113–133.

Radin, Paul

  1914   Religion of the North American Indians. *Journal of American Folklore* 27(106):335–373.

  [1937] 1957   *Primitive Religion: Its Nature and Origin.* Dover, New York.

Ramírez, Susan E.

  2005   *To Feed and Be Fed: The Cosmological Bases of Authority and Identity in the Andes.* Stanford University Press, Stanford.

Redfield, Robert

  1953   *The Primitive World and Its Transformations.* Cornell University Press, Ithaca.

  1955   *The Little Community: Viewpoints for the Study of a Human Whole.* University of Chicago Press, Chicago.

Redfield, Robert, and Alfonso Villa Rojas

  1934   *Chan Kom: A Maya Village.* Publication 448. Carnegie Institution, Washington, D.C.

  1939   *Notes on the Ethnography of Tzeltal Communities of Chiapas.* Publication 509, Contribution 28. Carnegie Institution, Washington, D.C.

Rice, Prudence M.

  2007   *Maya Calendar Origins: Monuments, Mythohistory, and the Materialization of Time.* University of Texas Press, Austin.

Romero López, Laura Elena

  2008   La noción de persona: La cosmovisión de los nahuas de la Sierra Negra de Pueblo. *Arqueología mexicana* 15:62–66.

Rosler, Andrés

  2005   *Political Authority and Obligation in Aristotle.* Clarendon Press, Oxford.

Sahagún, Bernardino de

  1950   *Florentine Codex: General History of the Things of New Spain.* Translated by Arthur J. O. Anderson and Charles E. Dribble. School of American Research Press, Santa Fe, N.Mex., and University of Utah, Salt Lake City.

Sahlins, Marshall

  2014   On the Ontological Scheme of *Beyond Nature and Culture.* HAU: Journal of Ethnographic Theory 4(1):281–290.

Salas Carreño, Guillermo

  2014   The Glacier, the Rock, the Image: Emotional Experience and Semiotic Diversity at the Quyllurit'I Pilgrimage (Cuzco, Peru). *Signs and Society* 2(S1): S188-S124.

  2016   Places Are Kin. *Anthropological Quarterly* 89:813–838.

  2017   *Lugares parientes: Comida y cohabitación en la emergencia de mundos andinos.* Unpublished manuscript, Pontificia Universidad Católica del Perú, Lima.

Salazar, Antonio Baptista de

  [1596] 1867   De virreyes y gobernadores del Perú. In *Colección de documentos inéditos, relativos al descubrimiento, conquista y organizacíon de las antiguas posesiones españolas,* vol. 8, pp. 212–293. Transcribed by Luis Torres de Mendoza. Imprenta de Frías y Compañía, Madrid.

Saler, Benson

  1964   Nagual, Witch, and Sorcerer in a Quiché Village. *Ethnology* 3(3):305–328.

Salomon, Frank L., and Jorge Urioste (editors)

  1991   *The Huarochirí Manuscript: A Testament of Ancient and Colonial Andean Religion (of Francisco de Ávila).* University of Texas Press, Austin.

Sandstrom, Alan R.

[1991] 2012   *Corn Is Our Blood: Culture and Ethnic Identity in a Contemporary Aztec Indian Village.* University of Oklahoma Press, Norman.

Scott, James C.

1985   *Weapons of the Weak: Everyday Forms of Peasant Resistance.* Yale University Press, New Haven.

Sillar, Bill

2004   Acts of God and Active Material Culture: Agency and Commitment in the Andes. In *Agency Uncovered*, edited by A. Gardner, pp. 153–209. UCL Press, London.

2009   The Social Agency of Things? Animism and Materiality in the Andes. *Cambridge Archaeological Journal* 19(3):367–377.

Smith, Adam T.

2004   The End of the Essential Archaeological Subject. *Archaeological Dialogues* 11(1):1–20.

2015   *The Political Machine: Assembling Sovereignty in the Bronze Age Caucasus.* Princeton University Press, Princeton.

Spencer, Kaylee R.

2015   Locating Palenque's Captive Portraits: Space, Identity, and Spectatorship in Classic Maya Art. In *Maya Imagery, Architecture, and Activity: Space and Spatial Analysis in Art History*, edited by M. Werness-Rude and K. Spencer, pp. 229–279. University of New Mexico Press, Albuquerque.

Stocking, George

1971   *Race, Culture, and Evolution: Essays in the History of Anthropology.* Free Press, New York.

1987   *Victorian Anthropology.* Free Press, New York.

Strathern, Marilyn

1988   *The Gender of the Gift.* University of California Press, Berkeley.

1999   *Property, Substance and Effect: Anthropological Essays on Persons and Things.* Athlone Press, London.

Stuart, David

1996   Kings of Stone: A Consideration of Stelae in Ancient Maya Ritual and Representations. *RES: Anthropology and Aesthetics* 29/30:148–171.

1998   "The Fire Enters His House": Architecture and Ritual in Classic Maya Texts. In *Function and Meaning in Classic Maya Architecture*, edited by Stephen D. Houston, pp. 373–426. Dumbarton Oaks Research Library, Washington, D.C.

Sugiyama, Saburo

1998   Termination Programs and Prehispanic Looting at the Feathered Serpent Pyramid in Teotihuacan, Mexico. In *The Sowing and the Dawning: Termination, Dedication, and Transformation in the Archaeological and Ethnographic Record of Mesoamerica*, edited by Shirley Boteler Mock, pp. 147–164. University of New Mexico Press, Albuquerque.

Swenson, Edward

2015a   The Archaeology of Ritual. *Annual Review of Anthropology* 44:329–345.

2015b   The Materialities of Place Making in the Ancient Andes: A Critical Appraisal of the Ontological Turn in Archaeological Interpretation. *Journal of Archaeological Method and Theory* 22:677–712.

Takács, Sarolta A.

2009   *The Construction of Authority in Ancient Rome and Byzantium: The Rhetoric of Empire.* Cambridge University Press, Cambridge.

Taube, Karl A.

1998   The Jade Hearth: Centrality, Rulership, and the Classic Maya Temple. In *Function and Meaning in Classic Maya Architecture*, edited by Stephen D. Houston, pp. 427–478. Dumbarton Oaks Research Library and Collection, Washington, D.C.

2003   Maws of Heaven and Hell: The Symbolism of the Centipede and Serpent in Classic Maya Religion. In *Antropología de la eternidad: La muerte en la cultura maya*, edited by A. Ciudad Ruíz, M. Humberto Ruíz, and M. J. I. Ponce de León, pp. 405–442. Sociedad Española de Estudios Mayas, Madrid.

2004 Flower Mountain: Concepts of Life, Beauty, and Paradise among the Classic Maya. *RES: Anthropology and Aesthetics* 45:69–98.

Taussig, Michael

1998 *The Magic of the State*. Routledge, London.

Taylor, Anne-Christine

2013 Distinguishing Ontologies. *HAU: Journal of Ethnographic Theory* 3(1):201–204.

Taylor, Gerald

1974 *Camay, camac* et *camasca* dans le manuscrit Quechua de Huarochirí. *Journal de la Société des Américanistes* 63:231–244.

Tello, Julio C.

1921 *Introducción a la historia antigua del Perú*. Editorial Euforión, Lima.

1930 Andean Civilization: Some Problems of Peruvian Archaeology. In *Proceedings of the XXIII International Congress of Americanists*, pp. 259–290. New York.

1937 La civilización de los Incas. *Letras* 3(6): 5–37.

Thompson, J. Eric S.

1958 *Thomas Gage's Travels in the New World*. University of Oklahoma Press, Norman.

1970 *Maya History and Religion*. University of Oklahoma Press, Norman.

Torquemada, Juan de

1969 *Monarquía indiana*. 4th ed. Editorial Porrua, Mexico City.

Tozzer, Alfred M.

1941 *Landa's Relación de las Cosas de Yucatan: A Translation*. Papers of the Peabody Museum of American Archaeology and Ethnology 18. Harvard University, Cambridge, Mass.

Trouillot, Michel-Rolph

2003 *Global Transformations: Anthropology and the Modern World*. Palgrave Macmillan, New York.

Turner, Terry S.

2009 The Crisis of Late Structuralism. Perspectivism and Animism: Rethinking Culture, Nature, Spirit, and Bodiliness. *Tipití: Journal of the Society for the Anthropology of Lowland South America* 7(1):3–40.

Tylor, Edward B.

[1871] 1920 *Primitive Culture: Researches into the Development of Mythology, Philosophy, Religion, Language, Art, and Custom*. John Murray, London.

Urton, Gary

1981 *At the Crossroads of Earth and Sky: An Andean Cosmology*. University of Texas Press, Austin.

1985 *Animal Myths and Metaphors in South America*. University of Utah Press, Salt Lake City.

1991 *The Social Life of Numbers: A Quechua Ontology of Numbers and Philosophy of Arithmetic*. University of Texas Press, Austin.

2003 *Signs of the Inka Khipu: Binary Coding in the Andean Knotted-String Records*. University of Texas Press, Austin.

Vilaça, Aparecida

2000 Relations between Funerary Cannibalism and Warfare Cannibalism: The Question of Predation. *Ethnos* 65(1):83–106.

2002 Making Kin Out of Others in Amazonia. *Journal of the Royal Anthropological Institute* 8:347–365.

2005 Chronically Unstable Bodies: Reflections on Amazonian Corporalities. *Journal of the Royal Anthropological Institute* 11:445–464.

Villa, Dana Richard

2000 *The Cambridge Companion to Hannah Arendt*. Cambridge University Press, Cambridge.

Villa Rojas, Alfonso

1947 Kinship and Nagualism in a Tzeltal Community, Southeastern Mexico. *American Anthropologist* 49:578–587.

Viveiros de Castro, Eduardo

[1986] 1992 *From the Enemy's Point of View: Humanity and Divinity in an Amazonian Society*. University of Chicago Press, Chicago.

1996 Os pronomes cosmológicos e o perspectivismo ameríndio. *Mana* 2(2):115–144.

1998 Cosmological Deixis and Amerindian Perspectivism. *Journal of the Royal Anthropological Institute* 4:469–488.

2004   Exchanging Perspectives: The Transformation of Objects into Subjects in Amerindian Ontologies. *Common Knowledge* 10:463–485.

[2002] 2013   The Relative Native. *HAU: Journal of Ethnographic Theory* 3(3):473–502.

2014   *Cannibal Metaphysics: For a Post-structural Anthropology.* Translated by Peter Skafish. Univocal, Minneapolis, Minn.

Vogt, Evon Z.

1964   The Genetic Model and Maya Cultural Development. In *Desarollo cultural de los mayas,* edited by E. Vogt and A. Ruz, pp. 9–48. Universidad Nacional Autónoma de México, Mexico City.

1969   *Zinacantán: A Maya Community in the Highlands of Chiapas.* Harvard University Press, Cambridge, Mass.

1976   *Tortillas for the Gods: A Symbolic Analysis of Zinacanteco Rituals.* Harvard University Press, Cambridge, Mass.

1998   Zinacanteco Dedication and Termination Rituals. In *The Sowing and the Dawning: Termination, Dedication, and Transformation in the Archaeological and Ethnographic Record of Meso-america,* edited by S. Boteler Mock, pp. 21–30. University of New Mexico Press, Albuquerque.

Waldron, Jeremy

1994   John Locke: Social Contract versus Political Anthropology. In *The Social Contract from Hobbes to Rawls,* edited by David Boucher and Paul Kelly, pp. 51–72. Routledge, London.

2000   Arendt's Constitutional Politics. In *The Cambridge Companion to Hannah Arendt,* edited by Dana Villa, pp. 201–219. Cambridge University Press, Cambridge.

Watkins, Joe

2000   *Indigenous Archaeology: American Indian Values and Scientific Practice.* AltaMira Press, Walnut Creek, Calif.

Weber, Max

[1922] 1978   *Economy and Society: An Outline of Interpretative Sociology.* University of California Press, Berkeley.

Wilkinson, Darryl

2016   Is There Such a Thing as Animism? *Journal of the American Academy of Religion* 85(2):289–311.

Willerslev, Rane

2007   *Soul Hunters: Hunting, Animism, and Personhood among the Siberian Yukaghirs.* University of California Press, Berkeley.

Wolf, Eric R.

1999   *Envisioning Power: Ideologies of Dominance and Crisis.* University of California Press, Los Angeles.

Wren, Linnea, Travis Nygard, and Kaylee Spencer

2015   Establishing and Translating Maya Spaces at Tonina and Ocosingo: How Indigenous Portraits Were Moved, Mutilated, and Made Christian in New Spain. In *Memory Traces: Analyzing Sacred Space at Five Mesoamerican Sites,* edited by C. Kristan-Graham and L. M. Amrhein, pp. 169–202. University Press of Colorado, Boulder.

Wright, H. T., and G. A. Johnson

1975   Population, Exchange, and Early State Formation in Southwestern Iran. *American Anthropologist* 77:267–289.

Yoffee, Norman

2004   *Myths of the Archaic State: Evolution of the Earliest Cities, States, and Civilizations.* Cambridge University Press, Cambridge.

Zuidema, R. Tom

1964   *The Ceque System of Cuzco: The Social Organization of the Capital of the Inca.* E. J. Brill, Leiden.

1983   Hierarchy and Space in Incaic Social Organization. *Ethnohistory* 30:49–75.

2010   *El calendario inca: Tiempo y espacio en la organización ritual del Cuzco, la idea del pasado.* Fondo Editorial de la Pontificia Universidad Católica del Perú, Lima.

2

Chiefly Jaguar, Chiefly Tree

Mastery and Authority in the Upper Xingu

CARLOS FAUSTO

IT WAS JUNE 2015. AFTER TWO DAYS OF SAILING UP the Xingu River from the city of Altamira, we were about to harbor at the Apyterewa-Parakanã's village port. We were beginning a workshop among the Tupi-speaking Parakanã on audio-video production, and I was traveling with two long-standing friends and partners in filmmaking: the brothers Takumã and Mahajugi, of the Kuikuro people, who live in the upper part of the same river, about one thousand kilometers to the south. Takumã had traveled extensively, both in Brazil and abroad, and is quite attentive to cultural differences, always trying to avoid possible gaffes. Just before the pilot turned off the engines, he turned to me and asked in Portuguese:

> Carlos, what's the name of the chief who's going to welcome us?
> Taku, there's no chief here.
> What do you mean? There's no chief?
> Yeah, no chief.
> But, then, who's going to welcome us?

Takumã's perplexity at the absence of chiefs among the Parakanã has nothing to do with European expectations about indigenous political power. It is not one of these *cherchez le chef* kind of anecdotes that appears in colonial documents. Rather, it expresses an objective contrast between a world in which chiefs are nonviable and one in which chiefs are the very condition for a world to exist.[1] This same contrast also surprised me when I first went to the Kuikuro in 1998, after a ten-year research experience with the Parakanã.[2] It was a genuine cultural shock that led me to revise my assumptions about Amazonia in the past and the present and to recognize more variability within so-called tropical forest cultures.

If I had been invited to write about the key topics of this volume before my research among the Kuikuro, I would have considered the enterprise doomed to fail. Moreover, two decades ago, there existed a consensus that matter did not much matter in the region due to the low level of objectification of social relations—the only important

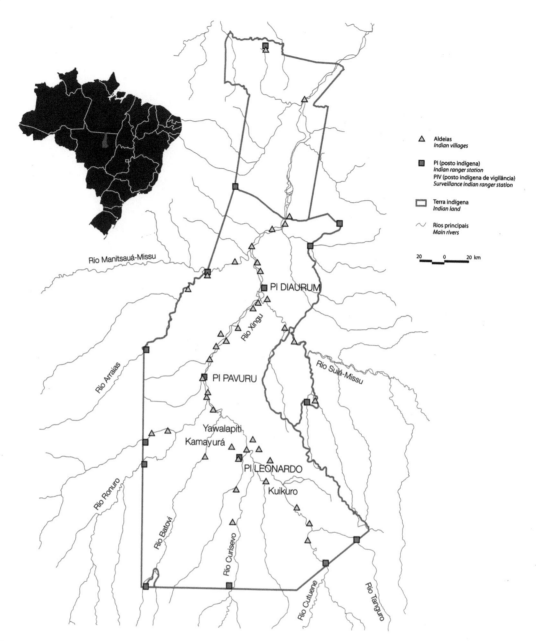

figure 2.1

A map of the Upper Xingu. Map reproduced from Guran and Fausto 2008.

Amazonian artifact would be the body. As for animism, it still had a bad reputation at the time, and few people would have employed the word before Philippe Descola's 1992 article on animistic systems. Whereas less problematic than power, authority would also be hair-raising for many people, since one of the dominant approaches to Amazonian sociopolitical regimes depicted the region as averse to all forms of power, veering instead toward autonomy and liberty (Clastres 1974; Overing 1993).

Today the situation is quite different. First, a number of works on indigenous art and materiality, as well as on exchange networks, have shown that artifacts did (and do) strongly mediate social and political relations in many areas of Amazonia (Barbosa 2007; Barcelos 2008; Hugh-Jones 2013; Lea 2012; Santos-Granero 2009). Second, although used in different senses (and somewhat abused), the concept of animism has served to instigate studies not only on the mediatory role of artifacts but also on their proper agency and efficacy (Fausto 2011a; Fausto and Penoni 2014; Guerreiro 2015; Lagrou 2007; Velthem 2003). Such efficacy has also been correlated to the construction of authority and to the way power relations are made visible in Amazonia, especially in ritual situations.

In this chapter, I try to articulate the issues of matter, animation, and authority within a specific ethnographic context, that of the Upper Xingu multiethnic and plurilingual system in southeastern Amazonia (Figure 2.1). I draw on my own research among the Carib-speaking Kuikuro, who number some seven hundred individuals. I start with an overview of the emergence of the Upper Xingu society from Pre-Columbian times to the present. I intend to show how its constitution and functioning depend on an intimate articulation between shamanism and political power through ritual. I then analyze the meaning of chiefly status among the Kuikuro, pointing to the dynamics of hereditariness and acquisition, expressed through the double image of a tree (the *humiria*) and an animal (the jaguar). Subsequently, I explore the substantial association between chiefs and the *humiria* tree, showing how it is expressed through artifacts and mythical narratives. From this point on, I focus on the Quarup funerary ritual, revealing how the chief's two bodies are decomposed through ritual actions so that at the end, the chief can stand for a vegetal image of continuity.[3] I also address the status of the main ritual artifact—the dead chief's effigy—and explore the issue of its animation and the presence of the commemorated deceased in the ritual scene. Finally, through an exploration of the etymology of *auctor*, I briefly suggest how we should understand the authority of a Xinguano chief.

Upper Xingu Prehistory

The Upper Xingu is a transitional zone between the central Brazilian savanna and the Amazonian rain forest that presents unique ecological characteristics.[4] The predominant tropical forest is interspersed with open flood plains, gallery forests, and lacustrine formations (Figure 2.2). In this bountiful and diverse region, a unique sociocultural system emerged, one that became known as the Upper Xingu constellation. The first evidences of Xinguano occupation in the region date back at least to the ninth century CE with the appearance of circular settlements and a distinctive pottery industry (a variant of the Amazonian Barrancoid macrotradition). Given the similarity between the Pre-Columbian and contemporary ceramics, today produced by only Arawak-speaking groups in the region, it seems likely that the initial colonists were their forebears (Heckenberger 2005:60–61, 209–215). Cultural continuity is noticeable not only in ceramics but also in distinctive landscape transformations, such as road networks interlinking major and minor circular plaza villages, some of which are encircled by moats and present other earthen features (Heckenberger et al. 2003). The first colonizers arrived in the region with a well-established cultural grammar of which the most conspicuous expression is the circular villages with their politico-ritual center: the plaza (Heckenberger 2005:293–295). These colonizers represent the southeasternmost tip of an Arawak diaspora that began in central Amazonia many centuries before (Heckenberger 2002). This hypothesis is supported by the distribution of other Arawak-speaking peoples in the southern Amazonian periphery from Llanos de Mojos in Bolivia to the Upper Xingu. Across this vast area are historical and ethnographic evidences of similar spatial configurations and landscape modifications.

Once settled in the Upper Xingu, the colonizing population greatly increased in number in the subsequent centuries. The rich environment, with its unique aquatic resources and its manioc cultivation, certainly played a decisive role in this process (Carneiro 1957). New arrivals may have also promoted growth and diversity, including the possible early incorporation of non-Arawakan peoples. Although still lacking paleobotanical data, we suspect that the management and cultivation of *pequi* fruit trees was also significant here

figure 2.2
An aerial view of contemporary Lahatuá village and its lake, Xingu Indigenous Park, MT, Brazil, February 2007.
Photograph by Carlos Fausto.

(Smith and Fausto 2016). Be that as it may, by the mid-thirteenth century, a demographic threshold was crossed: the villages expanded not only in number but also in size. Around 1250 CE, we see a great change happening across the whole region. Large villages up to 40 ha (about ten times larger than the contemporary ones) dominate the scenery. Some of these villages were surrounded by large defensive structures—ditches up to 15 m wide and 4 m deep and extending up to 2.5 km around the inhabited area. These fortified villages were linked to others, forming a network of clustered villages. Well-defined pathways and roads, up to 20 m wide and 5 km long, connected these sites, indicating contemporaneous occupation and intense social interaction (Heckenberger et al. 2003).[5] Current archaeological work suggests a recurrent structuring pattern organizing the villages in clusters. The thirty prehistoric residential sites identified in the

Kuikuro study area are associated with two main clusters that integrate large (≥30 ha) and medium-sized (<30 ha) plaza towns and smaller (<10 ha) plaza villages, as well as small hamlets (Figure 2.3). Each cluster of villages possibly configured an internally hierarchical territorial polity that existed within a multicentric regional constellation of peer polities (Heckenberger et al. 2008).

In the mid-seventeenth century, this galactic system collapsed due to diseases introduced by the conquest that, even without direct contact with Europeans, were already spreading throughout Amazonia and may have violently impacted the dense and sedentary regional population (Heckenberger 2005:144–147). The collapse of the large villages is marked by the abandonment of collective structures and the appearance of smaller sites similar to those observed at the end of the nineteenth century by the German explorer Karl

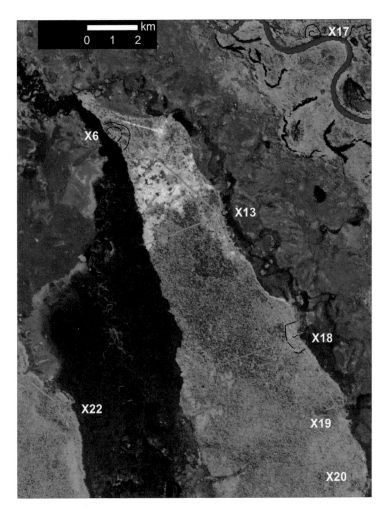

figure 2.3
The distribution of late Pre-Columbian settlement sites in the northern cluster, showing GPS-mapped earthworks (overlaid on Landsat TM 7 satellite scene, 5-4-3), including road berms (red line) and settlement peripheral ditches (black line). These include first-order walled towns (X6 and X18), second-order walled towns (X17 and X22), a central nonwalled "hub" site (X13), and nonwalled satellite plaza villages (X19, X20, and X21). Image by Michael J. Heckenberger, the Xingu Ethnoarchaeological Project.

von den Steinen, the first to leave written records of the Upper Xingu system. At the moment of Steinen's arrival, the Xingu was already a single multiethnic and plurilingual sociocultural system, composed of peoples speaking Tupi, Carib, and Arawak languages and a language isolate, Trumai. How did this cultural complex take shape?

The Upper Xingu Multiethnic Constellation

All Upper Xinguano peoples share a common historical explanation for the regional system's formation. Today those peoples identified as autochthonous are the Wauja and Mehinaku (Arawak), along with the Kuikuro, Kalapalo, Nahukwá, and Matipu (Carib). The remainders are deemed to be newcomers who entered the region

in historical times and adopted Xinguano cultural values and ways of living. Those arriving after the eighteenth century include Tupi peoples (Kamayurá and Aweti), an Arawak people (Yawalapiti), and the Trumai. The archaeological version of this history partially coincides with local narratives, the main difference being the time of arrival of Carib-speaking peoples in the region.[6]

Nowadays, Upper Xinguano peoples conceive of the incorporation of newcomers into their constellation as the voluntary adoption of a cultural package that includes a diet prohibiting game meat, a specific house and village structure, a certain body decoration, a generous and pacific behavior, the acknowledgment of chiefs, and the participation in a common mytho-ritual complex. Both peoples held to be autochthonous and those held to be newcomers recognize the preeminence of an Arawak cultural matrix. At the same time, they also recognize that the production of their present culture was far from a one-way process of adaptation to this matrix (Fausto, Franchetto, and Heckenberger 2008:139–141). The arrival of new groups led to an enrichment of the Upper Xinguano tradition: many of the contemporary ritual manifestations result from the appropriation of rituals or parts of rituals of Xinguano-ized peoples. Even the most important of them all, the Quarup, displays evidences of the historical process of hybridization, and its songs are in Arawak, Carib, and Tupi languages (Fausto, Franchetto, and Montagnani 2011).

If the flow of ideas led to a similar sociocultural morphology, which local people identify as a common regional culture, linguistic differences together with craft specialties functioned as diacritics in the system. Thus, Arawak peoples have the monopoly on producing pottery, whereas Carib peoples possess exclusive rights over the manufacture of shell necklaces and belts. These crafts (along with vegetal salt and black bows) play a central role in ritual payments. The main diacritical mark, however, is language, including at the dialectical level.[7] Xinguano diacritical plurilingualism contrasts with language homogenization characteristic of imperial expansion from a center outward. Unlike the spread of Aymara and Quíchua in the Andes, no lingua franca emerged in the Upper Xingu (until the spread of Portuguese). Rather than involving the creation of a linguistic community, the overall process of incorporating, transforming, and creating the Upper Xingu constellation involved the construction of a moral community through the common participation in a politico-ritual economy (Fausto, Franchetto, and Heckenberger 2008:144). As Menezes Bastos (1983) aptly proposed, ritual was, and still is, Xinguano's lingua franca.

Shamanic and Political Articulations

Ceremonial life is where Upper Xinguanos objectify their own culture for themselves. If you ask a Kuikuro person about their *ügühütu* (way of living/ doing), she or he will most certainly point to ritual life (Fausto 2011a). Ritual is the key mechanism in producing the identity of the whole, while simultaneously displaying the autonomy of each group as a political unity. Such autonomy is marked by the right of sponsoring intertribal rituals and, reciprocally, of receiving invitations from other peoples to participate in their rituals. Ritual autonomy, therefore, defines political autonomy: a village remains a satellite of the one from which it split until it receives invitations from and sends invitations to other peoples. There is no one-to-one correlation between speaking a language, inhabiting a village, and counting as an independent polity. Politically autonomous people acquire this status through the sponsoring of rituals, and their capacity to do so depends on many factors, including acceptance from other peoples within the system. This politico-ritual dynamic offers us a clue for understanding the clustered configuration of villages during the galactic period.

Upper Xinguanos celebrate about fifteen different festivals. All are structured around a set of songs, one or more mythic narratives, and a precise choreographic routine (Fausto, Franchetto, and Montagnani 2011). Some of these rituals are intertribal, reuniting different peoples; others are internal to the same people. All intertribal rituals include wrestling contests between hosts and guests. In the past, racing competitions and ball games also took place. All rituals share the same organizational structure: each possesses an "owner-master" responsible for its performance, helped by three to six "requesters."[8] The latter are those people who ask the master-to-be to hold a particular ritual. Nobody can propose him- or herself to sponsor a ritual. There must always be an invitation from respected members of the community, usually chiefly persons and ritual specialists.

Upper Xingu rituals can be roughly divided into two major types: those that are linked to chiefly status (i.e., the ear-piercing ceremony, the Quarup funerary ritual, and the Javari), and those that are closely related to shamanism or, more exactly, to the process of illness and cure. One may become the owner-master of a ritual after being attacked by spirits, who steal one's soul/double. During the therapy, the shamans identify the spirits responsible

figure 2.4
Kamaluhé, the owner of the Hyperwomen's Festival, feeds the people and the spirits at the end of the ritual, Ipatse Village, Xingu Indigenous Park, MT, Brazil, September 2010. Photograph by Carlos Fausto.

for the disease. They then promote a shamanic séance in which many people stage the spirits in a mimetic way, thus attracting them to the village. After the patient's recovery, he or she is summoned to the plaza, where ritual specialists tell him or her that they are willing to "copy/duplicate" (*akuapüte*) the pathogenic spirits.[9] On fulfilling this wish, the patient becomes the owner-master of the ritual related to this class of spirits. The pathogenic relation is redefined: the predatory spirits become the patient's pets and protect him or her as long as they are fed through the sponsoring of ritual events.[10] Rituals, thus, mediate sociopolitically between humans and cosmopolitically between humans and nonhumans, transforming a private sickness into a productive public affair.[11]

Although ritual ownership depends on the vicissitudes of illness (and on shamans' diagnoses), most, if not all, people who actually become an owner-master have chiefly status and acquire further respect through the sponsoring of rituals, especially large ones. In other words, though not mandatorily ascribed to people with chiefly status, the ownership of rituals is attributed to them.[12] Some minor chiefs are particularly eager to sponsor a festival and to aggrandize their image in the community's eyes. To sponsor a ritual means to provide food not only to the community and the human invitees but also to nonhuman ones (Figure 2.4). This position of feeder is typically one of authority and is strongly associated with mastery over others: the one who feeds creates an asymmetrical bond with the one who is fed, a relationship that is recurrently characterized in Amazonia as that between an owner and a wild pet. Feeding produces a relation of dependency.[13] Hence, every ritual performance publicly marks and produces a chiefly status, actualizing and aggrandizing it. Now, what counts as a chiefly status in the Upper Xingu?

Being Born and Becoming a Chief

All Upper Xinguano languages have a term designating a particular social condition, usually translated in the literature as that of a "chief," although it would be probably better translated as that of a "noble." These are *anetü* (Carib), *amulaw* (Arawak), *morerekwat* (Tupi), and *aek* (Trumai). These categories imply a condition that is given by birth: *anetão* are sons and daughters of other *anetão*.[14] But there are some gradations. First, someone's nobility or chieftainship is said to be "heavier" (*titeninhü*) when it comes from both sides (maternal and paternal). Second, first-born children are, in principle, more chiefly than their younger siblings, a fact that is marked by a series of acts, such as a longer couvade and puberty seclusion, the sponsoring of an ear-piercing ceremony, or the bestowal of the most valued grandparents' names to them.[15]

Other gradations result from the actualization of the genealogically given condition during one's life (Heckenberger 2005:296). This depends both on personality and on the randomness of any biography. Thus, a firstborn son who is prone to anger is set aside in favor of his younger brother. A chiefly person must be trusted by his or her community, and this confidence is built upon acts of generosity and cordiality. Such qualities define the *kuge* condition—a term that means "human" and "moral person" but also "chief," depending on the context (Guerreiro 2016:158). A chiefly person who is overly shy, though, will never occupy an executive position, since true leaders must also be jaguars.

Men and women have an equally legitimate chiefly status. But men have more opportunities to actualize and aggrandize this condition, starting with the fact that women can neither take part in the meetings in the central plaza nor enter the flute's house. Moreover, among the Kuikuro, there is no female equivalent to the all-male ear-piercing ceremony, in which many youngsters participate in accordance with a precise hierarchical order. Six of them occupy internally ranked positions, at the summit of which is the chiefly son for whom the ritual is said to be made. Being the leader of an ear-piercing ceremony confers an indelible mark of chieftainship, especially if a jaguar bone is used as the piercing tool (Mehinako 2010:136).

Chiefs are considered assets of their community, the reason why people live together in the same village and do not split into a multitude of family places. They are said to be "the ones we miss" (*tuhüninhü*), and one can only be a chief to his or her own people. Nonetheless, in order to become an influential chief, one must be known beyond one's own community. Personal magnification depends on the circulation of one's name throughout the region. A great chief is said to be much "talked about" (*tikaginhü*)—his or her name endures over time and expands across space.[16] One of the first acts that serves to mark a person as potentially having a leading regional position consists in designating him or her as a "chief of the guests" (*hagito anetügü*) in an intertribal festival. On these occasions, three internally ranked individuals, who will be formally

figure 2.5
A young chiefly woman is formally received by a chief from the host village during a Quarup, Ipatse Village, Xingu Indigenous Park, MT, Brazil, August 2005. Photograph by Carlos Fausto.

greeted by the hosts, are chosen to lead their own people attending the festival (Figure 2.5).[17] It is their responsibility to take care of their people and feed them with the food they receive from the hosts. During the ritual performance, they must stay on stools—a passive act signaling their chiefly status. This is why they are commonly referred to as "the ones on stools" (*tahaguhongo*).

Another venue to become much talked about in the regional system is the wrestling contests that occur in intertribal rituals (Figure 2.6). These competitions bring together the ten best wrestlers from the hosts and the ten best wrestlers of each invited people. A true champion, known as *kindoto* (master of the wrestling), acquires remarkable prestige. Even with no genealogical chiefly ascendency, a *kindoto* is allowed to don the jaguar adornments exclusive to high-ranking chiefs and is usually honored in a Quarup funerary ceremony upon his death.[18] Neither ritual singers nor shamans have this privilege, unless they already descend from chiefly lines. It is not by chance that the majority of executive chiefs of the last quarter of the twentieth century were wrestling champions in their youth.

The main Kuikuro chief, now almost a septuagenarian, is genealogically half chief (*heinongo*), since only his mother had a chiefly ascendancy. This fact was balanced by a fortuitous fate: he is the firstborn grandson of a former executive chief and consequently received an already well-known name.[19] Although only ranked as fifth in the ear-piercing ceremony, thanks to his personality and his ability as a wrestler, he finished becoming the main executive chief, the one said to be the "owner-master of the central plaza" (*hugogo oto*). This "title" stems from his role as the one who delivers the formal speech of reception to messengers coming from other villages, which only true chiefs have the right to learn and deliver (Franchetto 2000; Figure 2.7). Additionally, it points to the fact that he has the first word in initiating a deliberation among adult men in the central plaza. On such occasions, he always addresses his own people as "children" (*kangamuke*), regardless of age (Heckenberger 2005:259).[20] On this occasion, the chief appears as the owner-master-father (*oto*) of his entire community.

Chiefs can also become owners of other collective structures, such as the men's house, the main ritual path, the fishing dam, and so on.[21] These structures are collective in the sense of being bestowed on a person by the community and not in the sense of *res publica*. For the Kuikuro, that which is *tatutolo engü* (everybody's thing) is nobody's responsibility and is, thus, left in a state of disregard (Fausto 2012a). The community has to attribute it to an owner, who will become its caretaker.

figure 2.6
Wrestling between hosts and invitees during a Quarup, Ipatse Village, Xingu Indigenous Park, MT, Brazil, August 2005. Photograph by Carlos Fausto.

figure 2.7
Chief Afukaká delivers the chiefly discourse to receive messengers from another Upper Xinguano people, Ipatse Village, Xingu Indigenous Park, MT, Brazil, July 2007. Photograph by Carlos Fausto.

Owners must be capable of mobilizing collective work to build and conserve the structures they are taking care of, which always implies providing food for those doing the work. In most cases, this is closely associated with a spirit ritual. For instance, the construction of the men's house (*kuakutu*) is necessarily accompanied by the continuous playing of the sacred flutes. These flutes have their own owners—both a spirit and a human one. In all public affairs, a number of ownership and feeding relations, between humans and between humans and spirits, intersect. Ritual life is the axis around which political authority and shamanism spin together as inseparable phenomena. And this also applies to the chiefly house, the *tajühe*, to which I turn now.

The Chiefly House and the Sacred Tree

One of the greatest distinctions that a community can grant to a chief is to build a house for him or her. This is no ordinary house. First of all, the community at large must construct it under the coordination of six "requesters" (*tajope*), who ask the chief's permission for building the *tajühe*. If the chief and his family give their consent, they also accept the feeding of the people during the whole construction. As happens in any ritual, this requires the previous production of a surplus of manioc flour and the mobilization of a workforce for fishing. The second distinctive aspect of the *tajühe* is that it is built in association with one of three intratribal rituals (Nduhé, Aga, or Hugagü). Here again, the construction of a collective structure is closely linked to a ritual ownership articulating the human and the nonhuman worlds.

The third distinctive feature concerns the material and aesthetic singularity of the *tajühe*. It is larger than ordinary houses, and it also receives a series of enhancements, inside and outside. Community members apply graphic designs to a panel that is secured on the roof gable and attach similar panels to the internal wall facing the front door. Less often, but more impressively, three figures (a jaguar, a constrictor, and a toad) are sculpted with clay at its center place (Figures 2.8 and 2.9). The whole set is meant

to make the *tajühe* respected-feared (*itsanginhü*), that is, redoubtable.[22] An important chief is said to be *itsanginhü*, a qualification that also applies, for instance, to the flutes that women must never see. The *tajühe* is also *itsanginhü*—no one should talk loudly or make jokes inside of it. At the same time, the *tajühe* is of the community who builds it. Former owners of a chiefly house recount how difficult it is to correspond to people's expectations: the doors should always stay open, and food should invariably be offered, as anyone could walk in at any time. Conversely, most people say they would not even dare to go inside it. Respect-fear is, thus, a double mechanism of control: of chiefs who must correspond to the expectation of generosity and of their people who must show deference to them.

The jaguar and the anaconda are also by definition *itsanginhü*: they are beautiful, having pelts covered with designs, and fierce, inspiring awe and respect. This association of beauty and ferocity is quite common across Amazonia (and probably across the whole continent).[23] As Van Velthem's (2003) apt phrase goes: the beauty is the beast. In the Upper Xingu, however, one must add a vegetal image of chieftainship to this jaguarized one.

Another distinctive feature of the *tajühe*—and this is the fourth one—is that it is built using a special kind of wood, the trunk of the *humiria* tree (*uēgühi* in Kuikuro).[24] All Xinguano peoples consider this tree as the chief of all trees. It is one of the densest and heaviest woods in the region, but it cannot be used as a construction material in an ordinary house. It can only be used in a *tajühe*, which receives trunks of *humiria* in two parts: the front and rear doorjambs; and the two main pillars that sustain the house and to which the hammocks are fastened. On these pillars a special square motif is painted, a motif that cannot be applied to human bodies, only to *humiria* trunks, as we will see later.[25]

The *humiria* pillars index a number of facts: they point to the enormous collective effort required to bring 5 to 8 m high posts from the forest, which people carry for about 3 to 5 km. Until recently, when there were no camions or tractors in the villages, some twenty young men were needed to carry each of them. It was a huge effort that made tangible

figure 2.8
The flute's or men's house (*kuakutu*), Ipatse, 1995. Photograph by J. B. Petersen, the Xingu Ethnoarchaeological Project.

figure 2.9
Two men finishing the painting of the toad and the jaguar inside the chiefly house, Ipatse Village, Xingu Indigenous Park, MT, Brazil, June 2004. Photograph by Carlos Fausto.

the chief's authority and the community's trust in him or her. The very matter of the *humiria* tree also makes tangible the quality of a person's chieftainship: this tree is as heavy as a chieftainship is expected to be. Another important material dimension is its rectilinear trunk, which functions as an apt image of intergenerational continuity. Finally, the tree also recalls a myth to which I turn now.

The Wooden Women and the Jaguar Husband

This story is the master myth of the Upper Xingu (Carneiro 1989) and a version of the Pan-American saga of the twins. The myth explains many features of today's world and reveals the origin of mortality and the Quarup ritual. A good storyteller would recount it in no less than two hours, but here I abridge it to its very essentials.[26] Among the Kuikuro, the story starts with the mythic character Kuãtüngü collecting a vegetal fiber in the outskirts of the village of the jaguars.[27] The jaguar chief, Nitsuegü (a name meaning "hyper-enemy"), spots and captures Kuãtüngü. In order to avoid being devoured, Kuãtüngü offers his daughters in marriage, but upon his arrival home, he decides not to send his own children to marry Nitsuegü. Instead, he fabricates multiple pairs of women employing different kinds of wood. Depending on the version, the number of women varies. In all of them, though, Kuãtüngü utilizes at least two kinds of wood: one lighter called *hata*, the other heavier, the *humiria*.

The story recounts in all details how Kuãtüngü fabricates the bodies of these wooden women— their hair, teeth, ears, vaginas—and experiments with different materials. Once ready, he animates them with his blowing spells and sends them to the village of the jaguars. The pairs of women depart for a long and adventurous journey on which they copulate with various animals. Most of them get lost, and only the *humiria* women arrive at their final destination. Their names are Tanumakalu (an Arawakan name) and Itsangitsegu (a Carib name that seems to contain the stem for "respect-fear"). As agreed, they become Nitsuegü's spouses, and

Itsangitsegu soon becomes pregnant with twins. However, she is killed by her mother-in-law while her husband is away in the company of her sister.

As in other Amerindian versions of this myth, the birth of the twins follows their mother's death. Sun is the elder brother and is known as Tãugi, a name related to *tãuginhü* (liar)—he is indeed the trickster. Moon is the younger brother and is known as Aulukumã, an Arawak word meaning "bush dog."[28] They are both born with a jaguar tail, just like their father, but Tanumakalu hastens to cut them before anyone notices, thus defabricating their jaguar bodies. The twins grow up rapidly, unaware of their mother's death, believing themselves to be Tanumakalu's sons. One day, they go to the garden of Intihi (a Tinamidae bird) to pick up peanuts on the sly. Intihi discovers them and, in a burst of anger, reveals that their true mother is dead. Sun and Moon go out looking for her corpse and find it on the ceiling of the house.

The mother is not really dead but in a liminal state between life and death—too feeble, too emaciated, too difficult to take care of. The twins decide not to revive her, causing her to die definitely. They do not know what to do with the corpse, and the giant armadillo convinces them to bury it. The first burial in history takes place, the script of which is still followed today whenever a chief dies. A year later, Sun and Moon hold a big festival in which they pay tribute to their mother, representing her as an effigy confected of *humiria* wood, the same wood from which her father Kuãtüngü had fabricated her. The myth, thus, narrates not only the origin of mortality, but also a weak form of immortality, which consists of being remembered in a ritual at the center of which is an artifact: the effigy. Henceforth, whenever a chief dies an effigy is made in his or her homage. The whole ritual cycle, however, begins much earlier, as we shall see in the next section.

Gutting the Jaguar

The opening move of any Quarup is the request made to the family for permission to bury the corpse at the center of the village. The family has

figure 2.10
Chiefs Afukaká and Jakalu ready to "attack" the latter's grandson, who is about to have his ears pierced, Ipatse Village, Xingu Indigenous Park, MT, Brazil, August 2005. Photograph by Carlos Fausto.

figure 2.11
Chief Afukaká, a former *kindoto*, gives practical advice to the youngsters before a wrestling competition, Ipatse Village, Xingu Indigenous Park, MT, Brazil, August 2015. Photograph by Carlos Fausto.

to grant this right, and through this act they accept sponsorship of a festival a year later. The place of burial (the plaza) as well as the form of the grave is distinctive. Among the Kuikuro, it is composed of two holes connected by a tunnel, within which the painted and decorated chief, wrapped in a hammock, is suspended from two poles.[29] The dead chief's decoration contrasts with that of the living, who cannot adorn themselves throughout the mourning period.[30]

Five days after the burial, villagers leave mourning by means of a "washing ceremony."[31] Until then, nobody goes to the plaza, talks loudly, or makes jokes. A respectful silence, along with a wailing coming from the deceased's house, dominates the soundscape. The washing ceremony commences with a risky rite called the "gutting of the jaguar" (*ekege tehukipügü*), in which specialists execute five songs in an Arawakan language, incomprehensible to the Kuikuro. The origin of these songs is recounted in a myth that, in a nutshell, runs like this: A couple once adopted a jaguar as their pet, but when it grew up, it devoured their daughter. It then fled and started eating all possible artifacts—hammocks, pots, weapons—and terrorizing a whole region. The people of Magakani village raised four boys as bow masters. After being fully trained, they went in search of the jaguar and succeeded in killing it. They brought the corpse to the village, and while gutting it, they performed the songs that are now used to close the mourning period. As they sang, they extracted and washed all the artifacts that the jaguar had eaten in life, in the same way that the community is washed today at the end of the mourning ceremony.

The gutting of the jaguar is a ritual for extracting a people from their dead chief's body.[32] From this point on, the chief does not contain his artifact-people anymore. He was gutted and will be progressively transformed into a vegetal ancestor, the last stage of which is the fabrication of the *humiria* effigy. A good part of a male chief's biography is marked by the production of a jaguar's body (and, paradoxically, of an antijaguar moral disposition).[33] Through his ritual history, he is fabricated in the image of the feline: as a novice, his ears are pierced by other chiefs attacking him with a sharpened jaguar bone; as a young wrestler, he acts and sounds like a jaguar; as a ritual owner, he dons a jaguar claw necklace and a belt and hat made of its pelt; as an executive chief, he receives from the community a house containing a jaguar sculpted out of the soil clay; as a master of the plaza, he delivers chiefly discourses in the early morning and late afternoon, respectively known as "eagle" and "jaguar" (Figures 2.10 and 2.11). If Tanumakalu had not

cut the tails of Sun and Moon, perhaps it would be easier to fabricate chiefs as jaguars today.[34]

In this sense, Xinguano chiefs are just like other Amazonian owner-masters, who are also associated with jaguars. They are, as well, Janus-faced beings: in the eyes of their children-pets, they are protective fathers; in the eyes of others, they are predatory affines (Fausto 2012a). These are ambivalent and volatile faces, though, not stable sides of the same coin. Xinguano people are well aware of this changeability; otherwise, they would not be so picky in evaluating the moral character of their chiefs. What is less frequent in Amazonia is the way this double-faced dynamic resolves into an image of vegetal continuity after the chief's death. The Quarup ritual cycle is geared exactly toward that goal: it defabricates the jaguar and disassembles the chief, so that he can sustain an image of intergenerational continuity. Affinity relinquishes space to ancestrality or, more exactly, to the memory of commemorated names and lines.

The Chief as an Effigy

About ten days after the death and five days after the washing ceremony, the community builds an hourglass-shaped sepulture, named *tahiti*, on top of the grave. It is said to be the dead one's chiefly house (*tajühe*) and is mostly made of small trunks of two woods: the omnipresent *humiria* and another one called *tahaku* (*Xylopia* sp.).[35] The ritual cycle continues at a slow pace during the following months. The *humiria* tree only returns to the main scene on the eve of the festival, when adult men go into the forest to cut a tree. Usually one tree is enough to confect at least three effigies—a chief is never commemorated alone and must be accompanied by his or her followers (*isandagü*). The lowest trunk section is reserved for the main chief (the one to whom the Quarup is being celebrated), and the upper sections to his or her followers. Cutting a *humiria* tree involves dangers since it has a powerful owner-master, who must be appeased. Shamans placate the owner by pouring pepper porridge and blowing tobacco on the cut ends of the trunk. The ritual

figure 2.12
Ekehijo blesses with tobacco the recently cut *humiria* trunk, Xingu Indigenous Park, MT, Brazil, August 2002.
Photograph by Carlos Fausto.

owner also addresses a formulaic speech, asking the spirit-owner to be nice (Figure 2.12).

Young men carry the 1.5 m trunk sections to the village and lay them down at its outskirts. They apply wads of cotton to the sap that exudes from the cut extremities. The flow of the sap is the cry of the spirit-owner, which is a bad omen for the living. It is, thus, imperative to continue managing the relationship with the *humiria* owner, who is consubstantial with the dead chief. From the wood of this tree, the chief's effigy will be confected and commemorated during the following Quarup. The connection between the spirit and the tree has to be loosened so that a new connection can be created between the deceased and the effigy. However, this off-on process does not happen once and for all, producing a zone of indeterminacy between the dead chief and the *humiria* spirit. During the whole

figure 2.13
Two friends decorated for the Quarup. In the background are the three standing chiefs sponsoring the ritual, Ipatse Village, Xingu Indigenous Park, MT, Brazil, August 2000. Photograph by Carlos Fausto.

ritual, shamans will remain watchful of the presence of the tree-owner, asking it "to not cry on us."

After the cutting of the trunks, the ritual speeds up. At long last, the final stage of the Quarup begins. In the early morning, the deceased's closest kinsfolk and owners of the ritual are taken to the central plaza, where their hair is cut and their bodies are painted. Mourning finally comes to an end. Three of them, all men, will preside over the ritual, maintaining an erect and static posture, just like that of a rectilinear trunk. They present themselves as images of their own destiny: as effigies (Figure 2.13).

The trunks are carried to the center of the plaza, accompanied by two ritual specialists who chant the same prayers that served to bury the corpse. There is a temporal compression between the burial and the feast: the trunks are carried like corpses, but instead of being interred in a supine position, they

are stood up on the earth, reversing—if only for a limited span of time—human mortality. Once fixed in an upright position, a part of the rugged bark is stripped off and painted: first, a base of white clay is uniformly applied on the cortex; next, two vertical strips of annatto paste (known as "red navel") are painted on the trunk's front and back, dividing the white area in two halves; finally, a graphic motif is painted in black. Different patterns are used for male and female effigies. The latter are decorated with body-painting motifs, whereas the former receive an exclusive design that is only applied to artifacts made of *humiria*. Composed of a black square circumscribed by other squares, this is one of the rare squared motifs in the region (Figure 2.14). It is named *tihigu angagu*, "black painting of the *tihigu liana*." *Tihigu* is the raw material for weaving fishing traps, whose transverse fibers form a squared grid.[36] As we shall see, the effigy is, indeed, a kind

figure 2.14
A Quarup post painted with the *tihigu angagu* motif, Ipatse Village, Xingu Indigenous Park, MT, Brazil, August 2015. Photograph by Carlos Fausto.

figure 2.15
The ritual wailing takes place while the trunk is dressed in Xinguano ritual attire, Ipatse Village, Xingu Indigenous Park, MT, Brazil, August 2005. Photograph by Carlos Fausto.

of trap whose agency lies in its passive capacity to mimetically attract the deceased's soul double.

After being painted, the effigies stay put in the plaza until a pair of song masters start intoning the *auguhi* songs.[37] The effigies' kinsfolk come out of their houses, carrying cotton belts, shell necklaces, and feather crowns, with which they adorn the poles. At this moment, many people squat down and wail, as they have done during the burial (Figure 2.15). In fact, from the families' perspective, the effigy is the deceased and will be grieved as a dead person until the next morning. From the perspective of ritual specialists, though, the effigy is being animated and coming to embody a living chief.

The Double's Double

I have never heard anyone say that the deceased's ex-soul double (*akuãpe*) comes to inhabit the Quarup effigy. What most Kuikuro say is that the ex-double comes down from the sky and stays beside the trunk throughout the ritual. We, thus, have two doubles—one tangible, the other intangible—standing side by side. In this sense, the *akuãpe* is the invisible fold of a visible double rather than a principle of animation—a fact that should make us more cautious when attributing subjectivity to artifacts or explicating it as form of "ensoulment" (Santos-Granero 2009; see Kosiba, this volume). After death, the *akuã* becomes the double of a body that no longer exists. This is why it is called, henceforth, *akuãpe*, where the suffix -*pe* marks a disjunction: the double, the soul, the image, briefly the *akuã*, continues to exist, but the body of which it was the invisible fold does not exist anymore. What the Quarup ritual allows is the simultaneous presence of the *akuãpe* and its artifactual body.[38] The effigy replaces the nonexisting body in a pragmatically well-defined context, becoming temporarily the anchor of the *akuãpe*, which is attracted down from the sky and temporarily trapped on earth. But how does an image made of wood attract the deceased's freestanding soul?

An effigy is usually referred to as X-*hutoho*, where X is the deceased's name. *Hutoho* designates any figurative visual expression with mimetic evocation in two or three dimensions. It applies to sculptures and effigies, as well as to figurative drawings and photography (but not to film, nor to sound). In the Upper Xingu, visual resemblance strongly convokes presence, a fact that would delight Hans Belting (1994) and David Freedberg (1989), whose theories of art are based on the power of likeness to evoke presence and obtain an emotional response from the beholder. The Kuikuro notion of *hutoho* implies a likeness that attracts what it is like—it acts as bait and as trap. Thus, for instance, witches know how to make a peccary figurine and bury it in their foe's garden in order to attract a herd of pigs to eat the manioc. Some people of a more benevolent disposition shape a small fish out of clay and leave it inside a fishing trap to attract a good catch. At the *pequi* fruit festival, people sculpt the bird-owners of *pequi* groves and give them food. In these contexts, the mimetic artifacts—all of them called *hutoho*—do not work by themselves but need to be activated by human words in the form of songs and spells.

Another interesting figurative artifact in the Upper Xingu is a doll made by shamans to attract a patient's soul that has been stolen by a spirit (Figure 2.16). Despite being a perfectly anthropomorphic representation, this doll is not called *kuge hutoho*, "the figurative image of a human person." Rather, it is plainly referred to as *akuã* (soul, shadow, double, image). During the curing séance, shamans manufacture the doll and insufflate it with the breath of prayers and the smoke of tobacco. One of them gets intoxicated and travels to the spirits' home, where he tries to convince the hosts to liberate the *akuã*, which is then transferred to the doll and later back to the patient. This transference, however, should not be understood as the moving of a substantial unity back from the spirit world to the human patient. Illness distributes the person so that he or she will exist in both worlds at the same time. Even if the patient recovers the soul, he or she will be forever linked to his or her captors, living a sort of double existence here and there (actually, the person gets distributed as many times as he or she gets seriously ill). The spirits' predatory action

figure 2.16
The shaman Kalusi finishes the manufacturing of the *akuã* and prepares himself to animate it, Ipatse Village, Xingu Indigenous Park, MT, Brazil, July 2002. Photograph by Carlos Fausto.

produces a duplication of the double. Nevertheless, until the person's death there remains a vital link between the embodied person and his or her multiple replicas.[39]

The name of this shamanic therapy expresses well this idea: it is called *akuãte-*, a verbalized form of *akuã* that can be translated as "making a double."[40] The act of fabricating the Quarup's effigy, especially in ritual discourse, is also referred to by

a similar term: *akuãpüte-*, where *-pü-* connotes a disjunction or a past condition, indicating that this is a double of something that does not exist anymore (i.e., the living body).[41] Thus, manufacturing the effigy is like making a new double. The effigy is a copy that attracts the dead chief's *akuãpe* because it has a likeness to him or her. From an image without an existing prototype, the *akuãpe* becomes the prototype of an artifact and vice versa. There is a working misunderstanding in this play of duplications, one that is necessary for obtaining ritual efficacy. From the ex-soul's point of view, the effigy is its embodied prototype, but this is a lure the living build in order to attract it from the sky. Inversely, from the living's point of view, the ex-soul is the intangible prototype of the effigy, but only if the artifact becomes somehow alive. This very possibility is what the shamans' point of view offers to laypeople, as we shall see in the next section.

The Animation of the Effigy

The two shamans with whom I discussed this issue told me that the effigy "becomes human" (*kuge*) during the ritual. The verbal form they employed was *sukugeti-*, which can also be used to say that an animal or a spirit acquired human form or that a child acquired the morally correct dispositions of an adult person.[42] I asked the shamans to identify the moment in which this transformation occurs. They pointed to various moments in a crescendo: in the morning, when the trunks are painted; in the beginning of the afternoon, when the families adorn them and reunite around them to wail; in midafternoon, while the *auguhi* songs are chanted; and during the night, when these same songs are performed. *Auguhi* songs are said to be *tita egi-kaginetoho*, "that which awakens the pole's top" (Figure 2.17).[43] During the night, a pair of singers from each invited people comes to the plaza to sing for the effigies. This is the climax of the first phase of the ritual, after which most people go to sleep. Only close kinsfolk, old people, ritual specialists, and the anthropologist remain beside the effigies, which are still illuminated by the slow-burning fire of *tahaku* wood. Before dawn, the complete set of twenty-eight *auguhi* songs are chanted for the last time. This is the most dangerous and solemn moment of the Quarup. It is said that one may actually see the deceased as a real person, beautifully adorned as the effigy. A shaman's wife told me how this once happened in a Kalapalo village. A man saw his dead sister, who had been made into an effigy, as a real person. He saw her neither as an artifact nor as an immaterial double, but as a true *kuge*. Seeing what one is not supposed to see is considered *ahintsa*—that is, an omen, a presage that one who is alive will soon be dead. On that day, the festival was aborted and no wrestling occurred. By early morning, the invitees had already departed. Five days later, the man who had seen his dead sister was no longer alive.

In most cases, the rules of the ritual and the shamans' protective acts guarantee the smooth development of the Quarup. The ritual does not aim at conflating the dead person and the effigy—this happens only when it goes wrong. The aim is to create a zone of indeterminacy, to produce an asymptotic identity between the artefact and the prototype, to flirt with the possibility of animation, but not to revive the dead.[44] It is about invoking a living presence without canceling the distance—even if infinitesimal—between presence and representation. Total conflation is fatal. The whole point is to create a space-time in which it is possible to produce presence within a subjunctive (as if) state (Seligman et al. 2008). It is not a question of choosing between literal or metaphorical meanings. A ritual is indeed a very serious play (Bateson 1972), which means not only that it is to be taken seriously but also that it is to be taken as a play with its own constitutive rules. Such rules produce a state of uncertainty (Fausto 2011b:50–52) and a suspension of disbelief (Severi 2007:241; Seligman et al. 2008:89), making it possible for a double (the effigy) to index another double (a soul), but not to become one and the same.

One should also remember that the spirit-owner of the *humiria* tree is also part of this equation, such that during the very last *auguhi* song, there is still the risk of the effigy "crying on us." If everything goes well—and most of the time it does—the singers and shamans will tell the deceased (and the *humiria* owner) to go away in peace, to leave and to not come back. The fire will be extinguished, the effigies will be left aside—nobody will care about them anymore. It is time to awaken the living. As the first morning lights come out, the hosts and guests reunite in the plaza. Wrestling begins. For most people, this is the apex of the festival and the reason

figure 2.17
Singing the *auguhi* songs to the effigies, Ipatse Village, Xingu Indigenous Park, MT, Brazil, August 2015. Photograph by Carlos Fausto.

figure 2.18
Chief Afukaká accompanies a secluded girl who gives *pequi* nuts to the chiefs of the invitees during the final stage of the Quarup, Ipatse Village, Xingu Indigenous Park, MT, Brazil, August 2002. Photograph by Carlos Fausto.

for attending it. The three masters of ceremony preside over the wrestling, maintaining their trunklike posture and guaranteeing that no conflict ensues from the strictly ruled combats. The wrestlers must exhibit their jaguarlike bodies and their capacity for violence, but once the combat ends, they must evince a peaceful disposition. In fact, experienced wrestlers change their facial expression in a blink, opening a wide smile and hugging their opponents. Just before noon, the ritual owners, accompanied by girls leaving seclusion, formally bid farewell to the invited chiefs (Figure 2.18). Everyone departs, the plaza empties, and the effigies are carelessly laid down, later to be discarded in the lake.

A Name to Remember

The Quarup effigy does not depict a generic human condition, but a chiefly one. The mimetic evocation is built on several levels: the trunk is dressed with chiefly ritual attire, it is erect and immobile as the posture of a chief presiding over a ritual, and it is made of chiefly matter: the *humiria* wood. The Xinguano axial myth explains this substantial unity, which is reaffirmed whenever a chief's house, a chief's sepulture, and a chief's effigy are built. Effigies figure the body of past, present, and future chiefs, conveying a vegetal image of the continuity of chiefly lines. The body of a chief is not, though, a monolithic entity, but two, as Ernst Kantorowicz (1981) would phrase it. As we saw, chiefs are not only homologous to a *humiria* trunk, they are also jaguars tamed by their own people, whom they contain within their magnified bodies. Rather than a representative, an executive chief is the form through which a plurality is constituted as a singular image to others (in the case, to other Xinguano peoples invited to the festivals).

In interethnic encounters, chiefs often wear their exclusive jaguar adornments, with one single exception: in a Quarup, neither they nor the effigies can be decorated with them. The father-as-effigy and the son-as-ritual-owner must appear as a pure image of vegetal continuity, as upstanding supports of their own people.[45] If the effigy and the ritual owner come into view in vegetal form, then the jaguar part of this chiefly line is also made visible through the wrestling grandson, who, ideally, is one of the village champions. Not by chance, when ritual owners summon the wrestlers to come to the arena, they address them as "grandsons of a redoubtable person."[46] In a Quarup, then, we have the synchronous image of a chiefly line comprised of the grandparent-effigy, the father-owner, and the grandson-wrestler.

What is this chiefly line made of? Institutions, norms, rights, or properties? Although in the Upper Xingu there is a loose set of transmissible ritual rights and properties and a certain institutionalization of the House form (sensu Lévi-Strauss 1984), the continuity of a chiefly line is mostly made of mnemonic traces produced through ritual events and circulated by means of ritually magnified names passed from grandparents to grandchildren.[47] There is a general expectation that children will succeed their parents in chiefly functions, and this tends to occur whenever biographical hazards do not prevent it. After all, great chiefs are in a privileged condition to "make" (*-üi*) their children in the proper way.[48] Chiefs can sponsor ear-piercing ceremonies for their firstborn sons, take care of them during seclusion, teach them the chiefly discourse (*anetü itaginhu*), accompany them whenever they go "on the stool" (*tagahuhongo*), and so on. A son is the "substitute" (*itakongo*) of his father, as is the daughter of her mother. It is so common to see a son replacing his father in ritual activities that we could claim that "when you see the son, you see the father."

If the child is the parent's ritual substitute, then the grandchild is the grandparent's nominal substitute. The latter may refer to the former as "my name" (*uititü*): "Come and see my name," said to me a friend, whose grandson had just been born (Figure 2.19). Among the Kuikuro, names have an existence that precedes and succeeds the person who carries them at a certain moment. They are signs attached to different individuals over time, functioning as connecting nodes between alternate generations. Every time the current Kuikuro main chief told me of his rise to leadership, he recalled that, in addition to having made a name as a wrestler, the community relied on him thanks to his grandfather's name—not any of the latter's names, but the most prestigious one of his name-set, Afukaká, which is presently carried by the chief's oldest grandson. Magnified names thus link more than one life history, extending back into the past and forward into the future. And this also holds true of the effigy's name (the X in the expression X-*hutoho*). Hardly ever is it the name the deceased held at the moment of his or her death. Rather, it is

figure 2.19
Tsaná presents his grandson and namesake to us, Ipatse Village, Xingu Indigenous Park, MT, Brazil, August 2002. Photograph by Carlos Fausto.

his or her most celebrated name as a young adult, the one by which he or she became "much talked about." At the occasion of his or her Quarup, this name will have already been passed on to the oldest grandchild, who, in the case of a grandson, will be wrestling in the plaza. Thus, a chiefly line results from the substitution of genitors by their offspring as ritual equivalents and grandparents by grandchildren as namesakes.

I hope it is clear by now that the Quarup effigy depicts more than a one-to-one relation between an artifact and a prototype. If we take the whole ritual cycle, then the deceased appears at first as a jaguar that contains a people and later as an overdecorated trunk that stands for a line of past, present, and future chiefs of the same name—or more accurately, for names whose history has been inscribed in the bodies of people fabricated as chiefs and planted in the soil of collective memory as wooden effigies.

Conclusions

I started this chapter with a view to Upper Xingu prehistory and the formation of its multiethnic and plurilingual society. I suggested that its development was anchored on a politico-ritual system that came to constitute the region's lingua franca. Next, I showed how this ritual system articulates shamanism to political authority, not because chiefs are necessarily shamans but because ritual life articulates mastery relations between humans with those between humans and nonhumans. Subsequently, I described who is a chief and how one becomes a chief in the Upper Xingu, showing how genealogy turns into prestige through acts of feeding and the ritual construction of a jaguar body. I turned then to another aspect of the chiefly condition, namely its substantial association with the material qualities of a tree, which is explained in the axial myth

figure 2.20
The shaman Lümbu carrying fish to his kinfolk camped at the outskirts of Ipatse village for the Quarup, Xingu Indigenous Park, MT, Brazil, August 2002. Photograph by Carlos Fausto.

of the Upper Xingu. In the second half of the chapter, I turned to the Quarup ritual, focusing on the defabrication of the dead chief as a jaguar and his or her transformation into a wooden effigy. I analyzed this process as a movement toward ancestrality, which highlights the intergenerational continuity of chiefly lines. Then, I examined the effigy as an artifact and asked how it comes to (re)present the dead chief during the ritual performance. I suggested that merely drawing on an animistic ontology does not explain much of what happens in the ritual, nor does it allow us to understand the "secret of animation" (Gell 1998:148).[49] Finally, I turned to the issue of memory and ancestrality, asking what a chiefly line is made of in the Upper Xingu and how the Quarup ritual offers an instant image of it.

Now let me conclude by asking what the authority of a Xinguano chief may consist of.

Etymologically, authority comes from the Latin *auctor*, which we normally gloss as the one who makes or creates something, a prime mover or an originator.[50] This overly active understanding of *auctor* is not easily applicable to Xinguano chiefs, whose acts depend on previous requests from the community: their followers are the ones who initiate a course of action, ask a chief to sponsor a ritual, let them build the chiefly house, allow them to bury the chief in the plaza, and so on. In other words, the chief's authority depends on the ability to extract actions from others rather than acting by him or herself. This is the coercion: to make people act with the chief always in mind (Strathern 1988:272).

There is another etymological thread of *auctor* that may be interesting to follow: its association with *augere* (to augment).[51] In this sense, the author would be the one who makes something grow, and his or her authority would derive from this incremental capacity. Upper Xinguano chiefs are imagined as nurturing their people and making them increase, instantiating this growth not only in their own names and physical bodies but also in all the other material bodies assigned to them: their houses, their plazas, their villages, and nowadays, their tractors, trucks, radios, and other nonindigenous goods. This is clearly a case of an Amazonian ritual-economy of grandeur (Sahlins 1990), which proved to be strikingly functional at very different scales. Scaling it down (as happened in the twentieth century) or up (as happened in the thirteenth century) does not seem to change the basic working pattern of the system (Heckenberger 2005). Hence, with some methodological flexibility, try to imagine what was going on in the dawn of the galactic period. Magnify the scale ten times or more. Travel along one of the roads connecting the fortified villages with hundreds, maybe thousands, of fellow people beautifully adorned to attend a ritual. From afar you start to discern the palisade and hear the sound of flutes coming from the plaza. Welcome to the Upper Xingu (Figure 2.20).

Acknowledgments

I thank Steve Kosiba, John Janusek, and Tom Cummins for their invitation to participate in this volume. My thanks also go to Bruna Franchetto, Takumã Kuikuro, Mutuá Mehinako, and Sergio Meira for helping me with linguistic questions. I am grateful to Aparecida Vilaça, Luiz Costa, Kleyton Rattes, and Messias Basques for reading and commenting on earlier versions of this text. Since 1992, I have been learning a lot with Michael Heckenberger. Finishing this chapter is a way of starting to reciprocate his generosity. In the name of Chief Afukaká, I heartily acknowledge the Kuikuro people for all their help and friendship. Field research was mostly supported by two Brazilian agencies for the development of science (CNPq and Faperj).

NOTES

1 See Conklin (this volume) for another ethnographic example of an Amazonian people where the possibility of having a chief is hardly imaginable.

2 I conducted research among the Parakanã from 1988 to 1996. I started working with the Kuikuro in 1998.

3 *Quarup* or *Kwarup* is a corruption of the Kamayurá (Tupi) designation for this ritual: *Kwaryp*, meaning the "Sun's Tree." The Xinguano Arawaks call it Kayumai, whereas the Kuikuro (Carib) do not have an exclusive name for it. They call it *egitsü*, a word that applies to all intertribal rituals, of which the Quarup is the prototype. It is considered the most important ritual by all the Upper Xingu peoples, who share the same ritual procedures with minor differences.

4 This section is based on the Upper Xingu Archaeological Project, coordinated by Michael J. Heckenberger.

5 Heckenberger calls this period, spanning from about 1250 to 1650 CE, the "galactic period" in order to highlight the difference between the kind of sociopolitical intensification happening at the time in the Upper Xingu and the classic centralized urban model associated with state formation in the Levant. He borrows the adjective *galactic* from Tambiah's (1985) work on the nature of polity in Southeast Asia.

6 Some evidence points to the sixteenth century as the time of arrival, being more or less contemporaneous with the decline of the galactic system, but they may have arrived earlier. Another issue concerns the Arawak-speaking Yawalapiti, who are considered to be newcomers by the Xinguanos.

However, they may have been part of the prehistoric system. Inhabiting the region north of Morená (the place where the upper tributaries join together to form the Xingu River), they could have become isolated with the demise of the galactic system (Heckenberger 2005:103–107, 152–153).

7　For a general panorama, see Franchetto and Heckenberger 2001 and Franchetto 2011. For a prosodic analysis of dialectical variation, see Franchetto and Silva 2011.

8　The Kuikuro usually render the person who plays this role, in Portuguese, as *pedidor* (requester), as he or she is the one who asks someone to accept the ownership of a ritual. The requester is also the coordinator, who mediates between the community and the owner. In Kuikuro language, this person is called *tajope* (in the case of chiefs' rituals) and *ihü* (in the case of spirits' rituals) (Fausto and Penoni 2014:31).

9　See the following discussion of this notion of copying or doubling.

10　One of the more productive relational modes in Amazonia is that between masters and pets. Indigenous peoples have a passion for pet-keeping, normally the young of hunting prey. This practical activity furnishes the language to describe many other relationships, such as that between the shaman and an auxiliary spirit, the warrior and a victim, the ritual specialist and a ceremonial artifact, the cultivator and plants, and so forth (Fausto 1999, 2012a, 2012b; Fausto and Neves 2018).

11　For a description of this process among the Arawak-speaking Wáuja, see Barcelos Neto (2008:163–178). Here, I employ the term *cosmopolitics* in a loose sense, in order to include other-than-human beings in the picture. The concept comes mainly from Stenger's multivolume *Cosmopolitics*, published in the 1990s, being contemporaneous with political ecology, the resurgence of animism, and ontological perspectivism. Stengers uses it in order to put science and our political concepts at risk through the consideration of multiple, divergent worlds. For a synthethic take on it, see Stengers 2005; for the distinction between cosmopolitanism and cosmopolitics, see Latour 2004.

12　For a similar observation, see Viveiros de Castro (1977:221) for the Yawalapiti, and Barcelos Neto (2008:261–271) for the Wáuja. The latter suggests

that shamans' diagnoses are both conditioned by the patient's status and a means to actualize it.

13　On feeding and dependency in Amazonia, see Costa 2016 and Fausto and Costa 2013.

14　*Anetão* is the plural form of *anetü*.

15　In fact, this involves not only siblings but also cousins of the first degree, since it is the firstborn grandson and granddaughter who receive the most important names. Additionally, in the former's case, this also implies a bet on who will lead an ear-piercing ritual in the future.

16　In the literature, we commonly find qualifications such as *anetü hekugu* (true chief) or *anetü indzonho* (small chief). To my knowledge, these qualifications occur mostly as a response to an anthropologist's question, rather than in ordinary conversation. Gradations are mainly manifested by means of ritual acts, body postures, and the ownership of places and artifacts—not as a verbalized ranking typology.

17　All ceremonial functions, except for ritual ownership, imply a strict ordinal sequence: there is always a first, second, and third organizer, a messenger, chiefs, and so forth. Whenever there are three terms, they can be spatially organized as a vertical, sequential line (an "Indian queue") or as a horizontal, simultaneous line with the first at the center, the second to the right, and the third to the left.

18　Notice, though, that this condition is not transmissible to his children.

19　On his genealogy and personal history, see Heckenberger 2005:273–275.

20　See also Barcelos Neto (2008:266) on the Wáuja: "A 'chief' is always the one who takes 'care' of, and that is the reason why a *putakanaku owekeho* [master of the village] calls his people 'children' in their ceremonial discourses." On the subject of mastery and care, see Fausto 2012a.

21　Actually, the "owner of the center" may or may not be the same person as the "owner of the village" (*ete oto*), who is the person responsible for its foundation. On the relation between these two positions, see Heckenberger 2005:275–276, 308–310. For the Kalapalo, see Guerreiro 2015:242–243.

22　The stem *itsangi* implies danger and calls for deference. It is the closest Kuikuro translation I can think of for our notion of "sacred."

23　See Cummins, this volume, on the large snake (*amaru*) and the jaguar (*otorongo*) as symbols of Inka royalty. See also Weismantel, this volume.

24 *Humiria balsamifera* var. floribunda (Emmerich, Emmerich, and Sena Valle 1987), a tree from the Humiriaceae family, which occurs almost exclusively in the neotropics and comprises eight genera and fifty-six known species (Christenhusz and Byng 2016). The fourteen botanical varieties of *H. balsamifera* present great morphological variation. All *H. balsamifera* are evergreen trees with rounded crowns. Some can be as high as 25–30 m, unbranched up to 15–20 m, and 70 cm in diameter. The wood is heavy and hard (density 0.95 g/cm³; Lorenzi 1998:108). *H. balsamifera* is less dense than some species of the *Handroanthus* genus. The *H. serratifolius*, known in Portuguese as *ipê-amarelo* (yellow trumpet tree or *ipe*) or *pau-d'arco* (bow tree) has a density of 1.08 g/cm³. Not by chance, it is also an important tree in Kuikuro mythology.

25 The Kuikuro "wrap" the base of these pillars with earth to make them resemble a buriti palm tree (*Mauritia flexuosa*). It is apposite to remember that palms are strongly associated with ancestrality in western and northwestern Amazonia.

26 I summarize it from two recordings I made among the Kuikuro. For another Kuikuro version, see Carneiro 1989. For two Kalapalo versions, see Basso 1987:29–33 and Guerreiro 2015:183–227.

27 Kuantüngü is the grandson of Jukuku (the Yellow Trumpet tree), who was the chief of the tree people. See note 24.

28 Aulukumã is the supporting character in a story in which Tãugi is the leading actor. In this version, Carib peoples assume the regional primogeniture. This is probably not how Arawakan people narrate the same myth.

29 According to Guerreiro (2015:263), these poles must be also made of *humiria* wood. There are references to two other kinds of chiefly burial in the Upper Xingu: one with the corpse standing up attached to a sort of wooden ladder, the other with the corpse sitting down on a stool (Agostinho 1974:45–49). Oberg (1953:68) writes that the latter is reserved for a mature chief's son. This is what happened when the Kuikuro main chief's firstborn son died in 1993 at seventeen years of age (Heckenberger, personal communication).

30 The dead must arrive beautifully adorned in the sky, where their kinsfolk put them in seclusion, during which Itsangitsegu breastfeeds them. The celestial seclusion lasts until the eve of the Quarup festival.

31 Unlike the Wari' people (Conklin, this volume), the Kuikuro do not try to erase all visual and auditory traces of the dead person. The family does not keep his or her personal belongings, and his or her name is hardly ever pronounced during mourning. But that is all. When it comes to chiefs, as we will see, the effort is to generalize him or her as a collective person to be remembered by the community and, at the same time, to be forgotten by the family at the end of the Quarup festival.

32 I could not find any other reference to the gutting of the jaguar in the literature on Xinguano peoples. It remains to be seen if this ritual occurs among Arawak peoples or if it is a Kuikuro innovation (or a solitary retention of an archaic tradition).

33 Chiefly women are scarcely jaguarized during their lives. They stay more like *humiria* trees, whose original model is Itsangitsegu, the wooden twins' mother. Unlike the twins, the mother continues to play a part in people's lives (or better, deaths), since she breastfeeds them in the sky. For an interpretation of Itsangitsegu's chiefly role in the village of the dead, see Guerreiro 2015:271.

34 On jaguarization and de-jaguarization, see Fausto 2007. On its moral ambivalence, see Fausto 2012a:169–172.

35 The *humiria* trunks are posited at the straight sides of the hourglass, marking the sepulture "ears" and the "top of its head" (the fontanel).

36 I could not obtain any indigenous confirmation on this visual link.

37 There are twenty-eight different songs, divided into two suites, one accompanied by dance, the other not. These songs may be in an Arawak, Carib, or Tupi language, which makes most of them incomprehensible for a Kuikuro person.

38 For an analysis of the effigy as a body, see Guerreiro 2011.

39 On this issue, see Barcelos Neto 2008:77–87; Piedade 2004:52–54.

40 According to Santos (2007:141), the verbalizer *-te* has the following semantics: "to cause X to have/be Y." Here, it is the shamans who do something to the patient. I could have translated it as "to give a soul," as in the case of *embuta-te*, "to administer a medicine to someone" (*embuta* means "medicine"). However, here it involves the idea of replication, of making a replica to bestow on the patient, a fact also

confirmed by Mutuá Mehinaku (personal communication, 2012).

41 According to Sergio Meira (personal communication, 2016), the affix -*pü* is probably derived from the Proto-Carib *tüpë* / *tüpü*, which marked the nominal past in possessed forms ("my ex-something"). In Kuikuro, it still occurs in the perfective aspect -*pügü*, but most of its semantics correspond to the suffix -*pe* (Meira and Franchetto 2005). *Akuãpüte*- is, thus, possibly a lexicalized retention of an archaic form. For a discussion of the suffix -*pe* in Kuikuro, see Santos 2007.

42 It is composed of the third-person pronoun + *kuge* (person) + verbalizer -*ti*, which has an inchoative semantics, indicating a passage from one state to another (Santos 2007:140).

43 The expression contains the verb *kagine*, meaning "to scare." I here translate it as "to awaken" because it points to the act of rapidly breathing in through the mouth, becoming alive once again.

44 On the notion of asymptotic identity, see Fausto n.d.

45 The Kuikuro refer to their main chiefs as *kukiho* (our support, our stay) or as *kiküpo* (our seat). The former conveys a vertical image, whereas the latter a horizontal one. In addition to these two terms, the Kalapalo also refer to their chiefs as *katote ihüko* (everybody's body-trunk). Although the Kuikuro do not call their chiefs "our body," this idea is implicated in my argument about the chiefs' magnified bodies. On this topic, see Costa 2010; Guerreiro 2015:169–170.

46 *Itsanginhü higü*. As we saw previously, the stem *itsangi*- connotes respect and fear.

47 For an innovative use of the notion of House in the Upper Xingu, in tandem with Wagner's (1991) concept of the fractal person, see Heckenberger 2005.

48 The translation of the stem *üi* as "to make" needs some clarification. It has a wide field of application, either in the sense of "to make" or "to put on." *Üi* applies to the making of both things and persons and, thus, differs from another verb (*ha*) that only applies to the making of concrete things (such as stools, houses, instruments, etc.). *Ha* cannot be used to refer to people, whereas *üi* is used to express the "making-transformation" of a person. Some examples: parents *üi* their children by means of seclusion, the family *üi* its forebear by sponsoring a ritual for him or her, a person *üi* the other by applying body painting on him or her (Fausto and Penoni 2014:32–34). On the *üi*-making of chiefs, see Guerreiro 2015:154–156.

49 On the recent resurgence of animism as an anthropological category, see Costa and Fausto 2018. For a discussion of the uses of animism and analogism in the context of this book, see Kosiba, this volume. The Upper Xingu sits somewhere between animist and analogist ontologies as defined by Descola (2005). This also holds true for the Upper Río Negro region, where we also encounter hierarchical forms. We might recall here, as does Allen (this volume), Sahlins's (2014:281) definition of analogism as animism with a hierarchical emphasis.

50 Oxford Latin Dictionary 1968:204–206.

51 In his dictionary, Valpy (1828:40–41) quotes Forcellini's *Lexicon totius latinitatis*: "Auctor is from *augeo, auctum*; and properly means one who (*auget*) increases, i.e., generates and produces." The Online Etymological Dictionary makes the same derivation: "*auctor* 'enlarger, founder, master, leader,' literally 'one who causes to grow.'" See https://www.etymonline.com/search?q=Auctor, consulted on April 14, 2019.

Agostinho, Pedro
1974   *Kwarìp: Mito e ritual no Alto Xingu.* EPU-EDUSP, São Paulo.

Barbosa Coutinho, Gabriel
2007   Os Aparai e Wayana e suas redes de intercâmbio. PhD dissertation, Universidade de São Paulo, São Paulo.

Barcelos Neto, Aristóteles
2008   *Apapaatai: Rituais de máscaras no Alto Xingu.* EDUSP, FAPESP, São Paulo.

Basso, Ellen B.
1987   *In Favor of Deceit: A Study of Tricksters in an Amazonian Society.* University of Arizona Press, Tucson.

Bateson, Gregory
1972   *Steps to an Ecology of Mind: Collected Essays in Anthropology, Psychiatry, Evolution, and Epistemology.* Chandler, San Francisco.

Belting, Hans
1994   *Likeness and Presence: A History of the Image before the Era of Art.* University of Chicago Press, Chicago.

Carneiro, Robert L.
1957   Subsistence and Social Structure: An Ecological Study of the Kuikúru Indians. PhD dissertation, University of Michigan, Ann Arbor.
1989   To the Village of the Jaguars: The Master Myth of the Upper Xingú. *Antropologica* 72:3–40.

Christenhusz, Maarten J. M., and James W. Byng
2016   The Number of Known Plants Species in the World and Its Annual Increase. *Phytotaxa* 261(3):201–217.

Clastres, Pierre
1974   *La société contre l'état: Recherches d'anthropologie politique.* Les Éditions de Minuit, Paris.

Costa, Luiz
2010   The Kanamari Body-Owner: Predation and Feeding in Western Amazonia. *Journal de la Société des Américanistes* 96(1):169–192.
2016   Fabricating Necessity: Feeding and Commensality in Western Amazonia. In *Ownership and Nurture: Studies in Native Amazonian Property Relations*, edited by Marc Brightman, Carlos Fausto, and Vanessa Grotti, pp. 81–109. Berghahn, New York.

Costa, Luiz, and Carlos Fausto
2018.   Animism. In *The International Encyclopedia of Anthropology*, edited by Hilary Callan. Wiley-Wiley, Malden, Mass. Electronic document, https://doi.org/10.1002/9781118924396.wbiea1722.

Descola, Philippe
1992   Societies of Nature and the Nature of Society. In *Conceptualizing Society*, edited by A. Kuper, pp. 197–126. Routledge, London.
2005   *Par-delà nature et culture.* Gallimard, Paris.

Emmerich, Margarete, Charlotte Emmerich, and Luci de Sena Valle
1987   O Kuarupe: Árvore do sol. *Bradea—Boletim do Herbarium Bradeanum* 4(49):388–391.

Fausto, Carlos
1999   Of Enemies and Pets: Warfare and Shamanism in Amazonia. *American Ethnologist* 26(4):933–956.
2007   If God Were a Jaguar: Cannibalism and Christianity among the Guarani (16th–20th Centuries). In *Time and Memory in Indigenous Amazonia: Anthropological Perspectives*, edited by Carlos Fausto and Michael J. Heckenberger, pp. 74–105. University Press of Florida, Gainesville.
2011a   Le masque de l'animiste: Chimères et poupées russes en Amérique indigène. *Gradhiva* 13:49–67.
2011b   Mil años de transformación: La cultura de la tradición entre los del Alto Xingú. In *Por donde hay soplo: Estudios amazónicos en los países andinos*, edited by Jean-Pierre Chaumeil, Oscar Espinosa, and Manuel Cornejo, pp. 185–216. IFEA-CAAP-PUCP, Lima.

2012a   Too Many Owners: Ownership and
         Mastery in Amazonia. In *Shamanism in
         Rainforest and Tundra: Personhood in
         the Shamanic Ecologies of Contemporary
         Amazonia and Siberia*, edited by Marc
         Brightman, Vanessa Grotti, and Olga
         Ulturgasheva, pp. 85–105. Berghahn,
         Oxford.

2012b   *Warfare and Shamanism in Amazonia.*
         Cambridge University Press, Cambridge.

n.d.   *Art Effects: Image, Agency, and Ritual in
         Amazonia.* University of Nebraska Press,
         Lincoln. In press.

Fausto, Carlos, and Luiz Costa
2013   Feeding (and Eating): Reflections on
         Strathern's "Eating (and Feeding)."
         Cambridge Anthropology 31:156–162.

Fausto, Carlos, Bruna Franchetto, and Michael J.
Heckenberger
2008   Ritual Language and Historical
         Reconstruction: Towards a Linguistic,
         Ethnographical, and Archaeological
         Account of Upper Xingu Society. In
         *Lessons from Documented Endangered
         Languages*, edited by Arienne Dwyer,
         David Harrison, and David Rood,
         pp. 129–158. John Benjamins, Amsterdam.

Fausto, Carlos, Bruna Franchetto, and Tommaso
Montagnani
2011   Les formes de la mémoire: Art verbal
         et musique chez les Kuikuro du Haut
         Xingu (Brésil). *L'homme* 197:1–69.

Fausto, Carlos, and Eduardo Góes Neves
2018   Was There Ever a Neolithic in the
         Neotropics? Plant Familiarization and
         Biodiversity in the Amazon. *Antiquity*
         92(366):1604–1618.

Fausto, Carlos, and Isabel R. Penoni
2014   L'effigie, le cousin et le mort: Un essai sur
         le rituel du Javari (Haut Xingu, Brésil).
         Cahiers d'anthropologie sociale 10:14–37.

Franchetto, Bruna
2000   Rencontres rituelles dans le Haut
         Xingu: La parole du chef. In *Les rituels
         du dialogue: Promenades ethnolin-
         guistiques en terres amérindiennes*,
         edited by Aurore Monod-Bequelin and
         Philippe Erikson, pp. 481–510. Societé
         d'Ethnologie, Nanterre.

Franchetto, Bruna (editor)
2011   *Alto Xingu: Uma sociedade multilíngue.*
         Museu do Índio, Funai, Rio de Janeiro.

Franchetto, Bruna, and Michael J. Heckenberger
(editors)
2001   *Os povos do Alto Xingu: História e cul-
         tura.* Editora UFRJ, Rio de Janeiro.

Franchetto, Bruna, and Glauco R. Silva
2011   Prosodic Distinctions between the
         Varieties of the Upper-Xingu Carib
         Language: Results of an Acoustic
         Analysis. *Amérindia* 35:41–52.

Freedberg, David
1989   *The Power of Images: Studies in the
         History and Theory of Response.* Univer-
         sity of Chicago Press, Chicago.

Gell, Alfred
1998   *Art and Agency: An Anthropological
         Theory.* Clarendon Press, Oxford.

Guerreiro, Antonio
2011   Refazendo corpos para os mortos: As
         efígies mortuárias kalapalo (Alto Xingu,
         Brasil). *Tipití: Journal of the Society
         for the Anthropology of Lowland South
         America* 9(1):1–29.

2015   *Ancestrais e suas sombras: Uma etno-
         grafia da chefia Kalapalo e seu ritual
         mortuário.* Editora Unicamp, Campinas.

Guran, M., and Carlos Fausto
2008   *A casa xinguana.* Museu da Casa
         Brasileira, São Paulo.

Heckenberger, Michael J.
2002   Rethinking the Arawakan Diaspora:
         Hierarchy, Regionality, and the
         Amazonian Formative. In *Comparative
         Arawakan Histories: Rethinking
         Language Family and Culture Area in
         Amazonia*, edited by Jonathan D. Hill
         and Fernando Santos-Granero, pp.
         99–122. University of Illinois Press,
         Urbana.

2005   *The Ecology of Power: Culture, Place, and
         Personhood in the Southern Amazon,
         A.D. 1000–2000.* Routledge, New York.

Heckenberger, Michael J., Afukaká Kuikuro, Urissapá Tabata Kuikuro, Christian Russel, Morgan J. Schmidt, Carlos Fausto, and Bruna Franchetto

2003   Amazonia 1492: Pristine Forest or Cultural Parkland? *Science* 301(5640):1710–1714.

Heckenberger, Michael J., Christian Russell, Carlos Fausto, Joshua R. Toney, Morgan J. Schmidt, Edithe Pereira, Bruna Franchetto, and Afukaka Kuikuro

2008   Pre-Columbian Urbanism, Anthropogenic Landscapes, and the Future of the Amazon. *Science* 321:1214–1217.

Hugh-Jones, Stephen

2013   Bride-Service and the Absent Gift. *Journal of the Royal Anthropological Institute* 19(2):356–377.

Kantorowicz, Ernst H.

1981   *The King's Two Bodies: A Study in Mediaeval Political Theology.* Princeton University Press, Princeton.

Lagrou, Els

2007   *A fluidez da forma: Arte, alteridade e agência em uma sociedade amazônica (Kaxinawa, Acre).* Topbooks, Rio de Janeiro.

Latour, Bruno

2004   Whose Cosmos? Which Cosmopolitics? A Commentary on Ulrich Beck's Peace Proposal. *Common Knowledge* 10(3):450–462.

Lea, Vanessa

2012   *Riquezas intangíveis de pessoas partíveis: Os Mebêngôkre (Kayapó) do Brasil Central.* EDUSP, FAPESP, São Paulo.

Lévi-Strauss, Claude

1984   La notion de maison (année 1976–1977). In *Paroles données*, pp. 189–194. Plon, Paris.

Lorenzi, Henri

1998   *Árvores brasileiras.* Vol. 2. Instituto Plantarum, Nova Odessa.

Mehinako, Makaulaka

2010   A hereditariedade tradicional da função de cacique entre os Mehinako. In *Pesquisas indígenas na universidade*, edited by Bruna Franchetto, pp. 117–148. Museu do Índio, Funai, Rio de Janeiro.

Meira, Sérgio, and Bruna Franchetto

2005   The Southern Cariban Languages and the Cariban Family. *International Journal of American Linguistics* 71(2):127–192.

Menezes Bastos, Rafael José de

1983   Sistemas políticos, de comunicação e articulação social no Alto Xingu. *Anuário antropológico* 81:3–58.

Oberg, Kalervo

1953   *Indian Tribes of Northern Matto Grosso, Brazil.* Institute of Social Anthropology Publications 15. Smithsonian Institution, Washington, D.C.

Overing, Joanna

1993   The Anarchy and Collectivism of the "Primitive Other": Marx and Sahlins in the Amazon. In *Socialism: Ideals, Ideologies, and Local Practice*, edited by C. M. Hann, pp. 43–58. Routledge, London.

Oxford Latin Dictionary

1968   *Oxford Latin Dictionary.* Clarendon Press, Oxford.

Piedade, Acácio Tadeu de Camargo

2004   O canto do Kawoká: Música, cosmologia e filosofia entre os Wauja do Alto Xingu. PhD dissertation, Universidade Federeal de Santa Catarina, Florianópolis.

Sahlins, Marshall

1990   The Political Economy of Grandeur in Hawai'i from 1810 to 1830. In *Culture through Time: Anthropological Approaches*, edited by E. Ohnuki-Tierney, pp. 26–56. Stanford University Press, Stanford.

2014   On the Ontological Scheme of *Beyond Nature and Culture*. *HAU: Journal of Ethnographic Theory* 4(1):281–290.

Santos, Gelsama Mara Ferreira dos

2007   Morfologia Kuikuro: Gerando nomes e verbos. PhD dissertation, Universidade Federal do Rio de Janeiro, Rio de Janeiro.

Santos-Granero, Fernando

2009   *The Occult Life of Things: Native Amazonian Theories of Materiality and Personhood.* University of Arizona Press, Tucson.

Seligman, Adam B., Robert P. Weller, J. Puett Michael, and Bennett Simon

    2008   *Ritual and Its Consequences: An Essay on the Limits of Sincerity.* Oxford University Press, Oxford.

Severi, Carlo

    2007   *Le principe de la chimère: Une anthropologie de la mémoire.* Éditions Rue d'Ulm-ENS and Musée du quai Branly, Paris.

Smith, Maira, and Carlos Fausto

    2016   Socialidade e diversidade de pequis (*Caryocar* sp., Caryocaraceae) entre os Kuikuro do Alto Xingu (Brasil). *Boletim do Museu Paraense Emilio Goeldi: Antropologia* 11:87–113.

Stengers, Isabelle

    2005   The Cosmopolitical Proposal. In *Making Things Public*, edited by Bruno Latour and Peter Weibel, pp. 994–1003. MIT Press, Boston.

Strathern, Marilyn

    1988   *The Gender of the Gift: Problems with Women and Problems with Society in Melanesia.* University of California Press, Berkeley.

Tambiah, Stanley Jeyaraja

    1985   The Galactic Polity in Southeast Asia. In *Culture, Thought, and Social Action: An Anthropological Perspective*, pp. 252–286. Harvard University Press, Cambridge, Mass.

Valpy, Francis E. J.

    1828   *Etymological Dictionary of the Latin Language.* Baldwin, London.

Van Velthem, Lucia Hussak

    2003   *O belo é a fera: A estética da produção e da predação entre os Wayana, Colecção Coisas de índios.* Assírio and Alvim, Museu Nacional de Etnologia, Lisbon.

Viveiros de Castro, Eduardo B.

    1977   Indivíduo e sociedade no Alto Xingu: Os Yawalapití. MA thesis, Museu Nacional, Universidade Federal do Rio de Janeiro, Rio de Janeiro.

Wagner, Roy

    1991   The Fractal Person. In *Big Men and Great Men: Personifications of Power in Melanesia*, edited by M. Godelier and M. Strathern, pp. 159–173. Cambridge University Press, Cambridge.

3

Soul Proprietors

Durable Ontologies of Maya Deep Time

PATRICIA A. MCANANY

H OW CAN WE THINK ABOUT SACRED MAT-
ters in a way that diverges from the Western
duality of body and soul? Many of us are comfortable with the idea that the body refers to the mundane and finite experience of life while the soul
links us to a realm of sacred infinity. In Western
ontologies, animation—in the sense of sacrality—
emanates from the soul and leaves the body upon
death. But what if a soul could be reanimated in
the body of a descendant or easily slip away from
a living body to inhabit nonhuman bodies? How
would these ideas influence daily life and mortuary practices? I address such questions in light of
Mesoamerican and particularly Pre-Columbian
Maya beliefs and practices related to both body
and soul. Since the seminal work of Robert Hertz
(originally published in 1907 with an English
translation provided in 1960), the anthropological
investigation of death, the soul, mortuary ritual,
and the impact of death on survivors has steadily
intensified (Metcalf and Huntington 1991; Tiesler
and Scherer 2018; among others). More recently,

and evident in the chapters of this book, greater
attention has been given to the ontological and culturally distinctive framing of life and its passing.
Here, body and soul are not conceived as a duality;
rather, I focus on the relationship between qualities of soul and organic material—such as bone—
that index transformative phases of vitalization,
devitalization, and rejuvenation.

In a book focused on sacred matters, it is hard
to ignore a near-cognate term—*vibrant matter*—
invoked by philosopher Jane Bennett (2010:xiii) "to
theorize a vitality intrinsic to materiality ... and
to detach materiality from the figures of passive,
mechanistic, or divinely infused substance." Is
Bennett, along with other philosophers of materiality, reinventing the web of vital materialities
long ago conceived by Mesoamerican peoples of
Pre-Columbian times, as some (Vosters 2014)
have claimed? Or are the similarities more apparent than real? After reviewing ethnographic and
archaeological evidence relevant to materialities of
the soul, we will return to this question.

a

b

figure 3.1
Classic-period representations of
k'uh: a) a glyph for *k'uh* (adapted
by Ashley Peles, from Coe and Van
Stone 2001:109); b) Yaxchilan Stela
31 carved from a speleothem; and
c) a closeup drawing of a portion of
Stela 31 showing *k'uh* flowing into a
basket (Houston 2014:fig. 50).

c

Anthropologists turned to a study of ontology as an alternative to the constructed dualities foundational to Western thought (Bird-David 1999; Hornborg 2006; cf. Argyrou 2017). As Johannes Neurath (2015:58) and others have noted, this attempt to recast the frame of anthropological inquiry is not "just a matter of translating 'their [indigenous peoples'] beliefs' into scientific language," but an attempt to understand what Philippe Descola (2013:91–92) termed "schemas of practice" (Kosiba, this volume). Such terms move beyond the structuralism of our forefathers while not tumbling into the abyss of nonstructured chaos. In other words, cultural practices are studied as part of a larger schema—an outline, script, cultural logic, or reality—that can be improvised or transformed but that nonetheless provides a baseline of expected action and meaning in a given setting.

Particularly salient schemas of practice surround beliefs about the soul. As anthropologists have followed the trail of these durable spiritual entities into non-Western contexts, such vital entities are seen to behave in different, dangerous, and unpredictable ways; to exhibit strong agency; and to inhabit a wide range of entities beyond *Homo sapiens*. After issuing a caveat, most cultural anthropologists employ the term *soul*, but advisedly (e.g., Pitarch 2010; Vogt 1970; Watanabe 1989). I follow their lead, while keeping in mind that much is lost in translating indigenous concepts into English-language words (for further discussion of terms that can be lost in translation, see the essays by Fausto, Kosiba, and Mannheim, this volume). This chapter considers the challenges and uncertainties of a reality in which many entities are ensouled and soul loss represents an existential threat.

Ensouled, animated, sacred—all three terms carry heavy freight and do not translate well across ontological chasms. Within Western discourse, the terms *ensouled* and *sacred* are reserved for the religious realm, whereas *animated* refers to the movement of drawn or digitally produced images (and not those that move of their own intentionality). For the Classic Maya, we gloss the term *k'uh* (Figure 3.1) as "holy" or "sacred": a radiance that is godlike, differentially present, and exhibited by humans and nonhumans alike. *K'uh* was recognized, harnessed, and managed by humans. Stephen Houston (2014:83) interprets the enigmatic substance that flows from royal hands on Yaxchilan Stela 31 as *k'uh*. Fabricated from a speleothem extracted from the charged environment of a cave, Stela 31 provides a telling example of royal entanglement with *k'uh*. During the Classic period, ruling families intensively interacted with materials that indexed these godlike qualities, including ancestor relics, tomb contexts, and patron deity effigies (Baron 2016). Stabilizing the powerful transformations surrounding *k'uh* promoted social order and balance as well as provided supernatural sanction for those who ruled.

On the other hand, ordinary families possessed the authority or proprietary privilege to manage affairs involving body/soul transformations—particularly human death. Both ethnohistorical and archaeological data are brought to bear on the idea that this authority was not restricted to the kingly realm. The practice of residential burial across status distinctions among Pre-Columbian Maya peoples is pertinent to the idea of proprietary claims over the body and soul of deceased family members. In the English language, the term *proprietary* invokes the concept of possessing or holding exclusive rights to something, albeit couched within capitalistic notions of ownership and alienability. The latter are not relevant here, but notions of possessing and holding rights are highly relevant. Although soul proprietorship—possessing and holding rights to the soul of a deceased person—may seem overly esoteric, this construct can be grounded by indexing the soul to material properties—including bones—of a deceased person. Who had the authority to manage the separation of the soul from bodily remains and its later regeneration, perhaps within the body of an infant? The cycle of birth/renewal and death/decay is experienced by everyone, and royal iconography indicates its centrality within Classic Maya ontology of life and death. While authority over life processes—the power to control them—may have been an aspiration of Classic Maya royalty, "supernaturals" were acknowledged to be the ultimate authority in this realm. In a book about animacy and authority, it is important to note that authority surrounding death and ensoulment—because of its ubiquity and emotional freight—is perceived to have been widely distributed and not to conform to the types of circumscribed authority modeled by Michael Mann (1986).

From an anthropological perspective, *ensouled* and *animated* may seem to form rough cognates, but as noted earlier, these terms bump up against the limits of the English lexicon. With taproots going back to Edward B. Tylor, the concept of animism has proved to be fertile ground for generations of anthropologists interested in relational worlds and what Alf Hornborg (2006:21) calls "universal semiotic anxieties about where or how to draw boundaries between persons and things." Importantly, the approach taken here—as in other chapters of this book—adopts Tim Ingold's (2011:67–68) preferred term *animacy*, which prioritizes the experience of living in a world rather than a way of believing about a world.

In the pages to come, I explore how authority over durable spiritual entities—glossed as souls and embodied in both persons and things—was distributed across sectors of Maya society in a highly differentiated but surprisingly equalized manner. Through this discussion, I recast mortuary practices as intimately related to concepts of soul. To begin, ideas about ensoulment and soul loss gleaned from ethnographic and ethnohistoric accounts are critically examined, after which archaeological evidence from the Maya region is presented. The final section returns to contemporary theories of "vibrant matter" and examines why and how this body of contemporary theory fails to explain archaeological and ethnographically attested ontologies of vital matter.

Ensoulment—Ethnographically and Ethnohistorically Understood

Any discussion of Mesoamerican concepts of body and soul must begin with the pioneering ethnohistorical work of Alfredo López Austin (1980). In his trailblazing study of Nahua body concepts, López Austin noted that souls are elusive vital forces that can detach, travel, and reattach to other-than-human entities in unpredictable and often dangerous ways. The head, heart, and liver embody places where souls reside (Figure 3.2). Thus, managing and balancing this vibrant matter (and nonmatter) constituted the stuff of local ecological knowledge and of skillful participation in a universe of spirits, gods, and ancestors. López Austin—as well as ethnographers of Tzeltal and Tzotzil Maya ontologies of soul, such as Pedro Pitarch (2010) and Evon Z. Vogt (1970)—emphasizes that the authority to manage vital forces was seated within the family (Figure 3.3). For the most part, this was the case during Pre-Columbian times as well.

Within the realm of ethnographic reporting, Pitarch's (2010) study of Tzeltal Maya souls most directly approaches the metaphysics of body/soul correspondence. In Cancuc (the locale of his study), an individual human person is thought to possess a group of souls (*ch'uleltik*) that reside within the heart. Although *ch'ul* is generally translated as "holy" or "sacred," Pitarch (2010:122) maintains that when applied to personhood *ch'ul* more strictly means the body's "other." These nonhuman beings/souls that compose a body's other include a small bird called *mutil o'tan*; a *bats'il ch'ulel* (which is responsible for dreams, memories, feelings, and emotions); and a third life force called *lab* (which can take the form of an animal, meteor, or human figure and is often hostile, dangerous, and prone to causing illness). Soul loss (in which these nonhuman beings desert a body) is triggered by many forces and states of being, including sleeping, dreaming, and illness.

Pitarch (2010:56) further describes the settling in of a *lab*, which is transferred from a dying person to a "child that is still inside its mother's womb." Robert Carlsen and Martin Prechtel (1991:27–28) write of a Tz'utujil Maya belief that a grandchild embodies the soul of a grandparent in a transformative renewal process called *jaloj-k'exoj*. In reference to the K'iche' language, James Mondloch (1980) describes *k'e?š* naming practices in which a grandchild is named after a grandparent. Evon Vogt (1970:1155) likewise reports a belief among Tzotzil Maya that a "*ch'ulel* is placed in the body

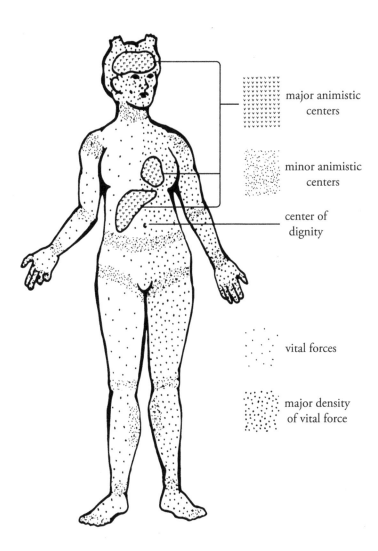

major animistic
centers

minor animistic
centers

center of
dignity

vital forces

major density
of vital force

figure 3.2
Vital forces and animistic
centers. Adapted by Ashley
Peles, from López Austin
1988:200.

of an unborn embryo by the ancestral deities." Archaeological evidence indicates that this concept has deep roots.

Tzeltal people of Cancuc amplify the idea of history encoded in the embodied soul of a descendant. Pitarch (2010:3) uses the term *folded* to describe the process that occurs when an unborn infant receives a soul and suggests that "human beings carry the other [and earlier] world[s]" within them. Souls enfold the violent history of encounters with the "other," primarily *kaxlan*, or Spanish-speaking persons (Pitarch 2010:3). This historical dimension of ensoulment indicates an embodied complexity and brings into question the idea of a person as a discrete individual (see Fowler 2004 for extended discussion of relational personhood). Rather, Tzeltales might think "of a person as composed of heterogeneous

fragments, a heteroclite conjunction of beings, places, and times" (Pitarch 2010:70). Intriguingly, by enfolding a historical dimension into the soul of a person, Tzeltales create a construct that parallels the historical trauma that is now thought to be encoded epigenetically within the human genome. Such compositionality and partible notions of personhood also resonate with the discussion of Andean ontologies presented by Tom Cummins (this volume) and with Classic Maya epigraphy (cf. Houston, Stuart, and Taube 2006). The concept of enfolding, moreover, is relevant to nonroyal ontologies of the soul in Maya deep time.

Enfolding implies a temporal and a spatial expansiveness. Personal destiny is not divorced from events external to Cancuc, or as Pitarch (2010:78) expresses it: "What happens to the

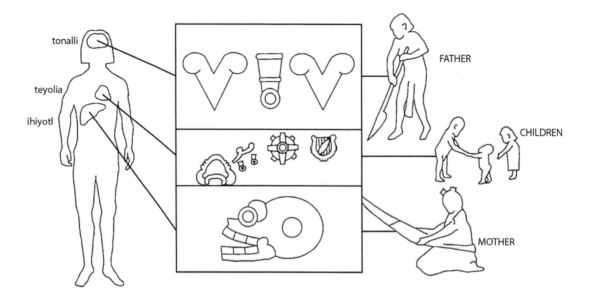

figure 3.3

Managing vital forces within the family. Adapted by Ashley Peles, from López Austin 1988:348.

jaguar in the jungle will affect the human body in the village." The relational implications of this ontology—also expressed by Evon Vogt and John Watanabe for Tzotzil- and Mam-speaking Maya peoples, respectively—to local ecological knowledge are particularly significant and divergent from Western ontology. In reference to the separation of the soul from the body after death, Vogt (1993:18) reports that Zinacanteco souls stay associated with a grave for the same number of years in which the soul had inhabited the living person. Vogt (1993), as well as Carlsen and Prechtel (1991:27–28), sees a correspondence between the renewal and regeneration of souls and agricultural cycles. In short, death and regeneration are perceived as temporary states along a continuum of soul immortality.

Many similarities existed between Nahua and Maya concepts of soul, but there also are key distinctions in both beliefs and practices. For instance, according to López Austin, the hazardous wandering of Nahua *teyolia* (soul) was particularly critical upon the death of a person. At this point, Nahua mortuary practices emphasized fire as an effective and transformative agent employed to separate the body from the soul and to hasten the soul upon its journey (Figure 3.4). Postmortem, fire kick-starts

and augments the separation of a soul from a corpse. During Pre-Columbian times, fire was employed in the Mexican Highlands and—to a lesser extent—in the Maya Lowlands to promote both this separation and the later conjoining via conjuring (see Scherer 2015; Tiesler and Scherer 2018). In this chapter, I suggest that people in the lowlands put more emphasis on the *materiality of human remains* as a substance that indexed durable soul. This difference helps to explain the preference for *inhumation* in the Maya Lowlands in contradistinction to the practice of *cremation*—which was more popular in the highlands. Both practices contrast sharply with the South American Wari' treatment of the dead (see Conklin, this volume), for example, which emphasizes the separation of the living from the dead, the distribution of the belongings of a deceased person, and the political and economic equality that is maintained through these kinds of mortuary practices.

Among both Nahua and Maya peoples, however, the desire of surviving family members appears to be similar: to facilitate the separation of the soul from the body, to hasten the journey of the soul, and to encourage the process of regeneration through the reattachment of a soul to a new body. Significantly, López Austin (1988:322) writes that

figure 3.4
Book 12 of the *Florentine
Codex*, showing the
reverential burning of
the body of Itzquauhtzin
(after Anderson and
Dibble 1975:pl. 88).

regeneration was thought to be ensured "if fore-fathers' names were repeated in the descendants." Vogt (1970) discusses Tzotzil ideas about soul loss resulting from witchcraft conducted in a cave (Figure 3.5). During this practice, parts of a person's *ch'ulel*, or soul, could be sold to the earth "owner," Yahval Balamil, who would "use the victim as a serpent" (Vogt 1970:1155–1156). Significantly, the association of caves (or cenotes) with menacing serpents is widespread. In eastern Yucatan today, stories about a large and dangerous serpent that lives in a cenote are frequently invoked. Regarding soul loss in El Peten, Guatemala, William Duncan and Charles Hofling (2011:204) report that pregnant women and newborn infants traditionally are thought to be extremely vulnerable to soul loss. High rates of morbidity in childbearing women and neonates during Pre-Columbian and colonial times may provide the logical substrate for this idea. I will also address the possibility that soul loss from witchcraft was encoded hieroglyphically in the form of the *way* glyph.

Due to the possibility of soul loss, death and even sleeping can be fraught with peril for family members. A "bad death"—in which a soul lingers due to violent circumstances, the performance of witchcraft, or simply the inability of the family to conduct mortuary practices—can have implications for surviving family members. Alan Sandstrom (1991:252) notes that the principal reason why Nahua peoples of Amatlan summon a ritual specialist is to manage restless *ejecatl* (wind) spirits of the dead.

Linguist Paul Kockelman (2009) notes that a grammatical category indicating inalienable possession of souls and spirits exists among Q'eqchi', Jacaltec, and Tzeltal Mayan speakers. Although marked by immateriality and, thus, distinct from a house, heirloom jewelry, or a piece of land, souls of the deceased count among the inalienable possessions of a family or—writ large—a community. Such unequivocal linguistic evidence of soul proprietorship among Mayan speakers who have been subjected to five hundred years of Christian missionization suggests that this linguistic marker has deep antiquity.

Among Tzotzil Mayan speakers, ensoulment (*ch'ulel*) goes beyond the properties of humans. Vogt states:

figure 3.5
The Tzotzil
conceptualization
of a cave inhabited
by an earth "owner,"
wife, and serpent
who are visited by a
Tzotzil man. Drawn by
Marian López Calixto,
from Gossen 2002:356.

Virtually everything that is important and valuable to Zinacantecos also possesses a *ch'ulel*: domesticated plants . . . salt . . . houses, and the fires at the hearths inside the houses; [and] the wooden crosses erected on sacred mountains, inside caves, and beside waterholes. . . . The ethnographer in Zinacantan soon learns that the *most important interaction* [emphasis added] going on in the universe is not between persons, nor between persons and material objects, as we think of these relationships, but rather between *ch'uleletik* inside these persons and [those inside] material objects. (Vogt 1970:1156)

In light of this statement, it is not surprising that Linda Brown and Kitty Emery (2008) found that hunting shrines around Lake Atitlan were concerned primarily with managing the spirits of hunted animals, ensuring their regeneration through the return of bones from butchered animals, and pleasing the spirit guardians of the forest.

This intensely relational ontology includes the weapons and dogs used in the hunt. Significantly, Brown and Emery (2008:331) do not ascribe the hunting shrines (often created in rock shelters) to a fear of untamed forests but rather to the danger of crossing a threshold between the domesticated landscape of settlements and fields to the less or nondomesticated forested places. The shrines show respect for this threshold, and returning the bones of hunted animals is thought to encourage regeneration of new animals. Thus, the *depositional place* of the bones is linked to the ease and speed of regeneration of the spirit of an animal. The value in which wild animals are held provides the subtext for human efforts to ensure their regeneration.

Anthropologist Didier Boremanse (2000) provides a final example of enlivened objects that can become the focus of ritual propitiation. Upon request of the Qeqchi' community of San Lucas, sewing machines were supplied by the anthropologist and his students from Universidad del Valle de

Guatemala. As the machines became entangled in the social life of the community, a *kwatesink* ritual was performed. Incense, candles, and food were offered to the spirit of each machine in order to nourish it and to ensure that no harm came to the users of the sewing machine. Importantly, these spirits were not created by the people of San Lucas, they simply were acknowledged and nurtured within the community. (See Allen 2002 for a comparable example of a radio in an Andean context.) Given the rich corpus of ethnographic and ethnohistorical information about ensoulment in Mesoamerica, these concepts likely provided salient schemas of practice during earlier times, to which we now turn.

Managing Spiritual Entities in Deep Time

The review of ethnographic sources suggests that since the sixteenth century, managing spiritual entities in the Maya region focused on four concerns: *protecting and nourishing* spiritual entities and the well-being of those who come in contact with them; *promoting rejuvenation*; *ensuring access* to spiritual beings by descendent populations; and *managing errant vital forces* that can manifest as witchcraft or other kinds of damaging spirit possession. Maintaining access to souls of the deceased was demonized by Spanish clergy and harshly suppressed, although one can argue that through skillful integration with the Catholic celebration of All Saints' Day, El Día de los Muertos effectively kept the souls of the dead accessible (Figure 3.6).

A concern with souls of the deceased suggests that Pre-Columbian Maya burial practices may have encoded metaphysical beliefs beyond a desire to inherit land, rights, and privileges of forebears (McAnany 2013). If curation of bodily remains was linked to an ontology of souls, then mortuary practices that cannot be explained by ancestor veneration alone would become comprehensible to Maya archaeologists. This idea is consonant with many contemporary Maya beliefs about soul revitalization and has been discussed by several archaeologists, including James Fitzsimmons (2009), Susan Gillespie (2002), Stephen Houston (2014), Anna Novotny (2013), and Andrew Scherer (2015), who propose that ontologies of the soul are significant for understanding Maya mortuary practices from deep time. In a similar vein, Christopher Carr and Robert McCord (2015) have reinterpreted North American Hopewell mortuary practices as referring to the journey of the soul after death. From this perspective, evidence from archaeological sites in the Maya Lowlands (Figure 3.7) is examined for fit with the concerns about spiritual entities noted in post-sixteenth-century sources. Importantly, archaeological examples are drawn from royal courts (such as Copan, Tikal, Palenque, Yaxchilan, Piedras Negras, and Motul de San José) and from decidedly nonroyal communities (such as K'axob, Pakal Na, Hershey, and Tahcabo). Since the sample crosscuts social differentiation and temporal sequence, evidence of soul proprietorship in both contexts would provide support for an equitable distribution of authority over matters of ensoulment.

figure 3.6
All Saints' Day altar, Amatlan, Veracruz (Sandstrom 1991:pl. 14).

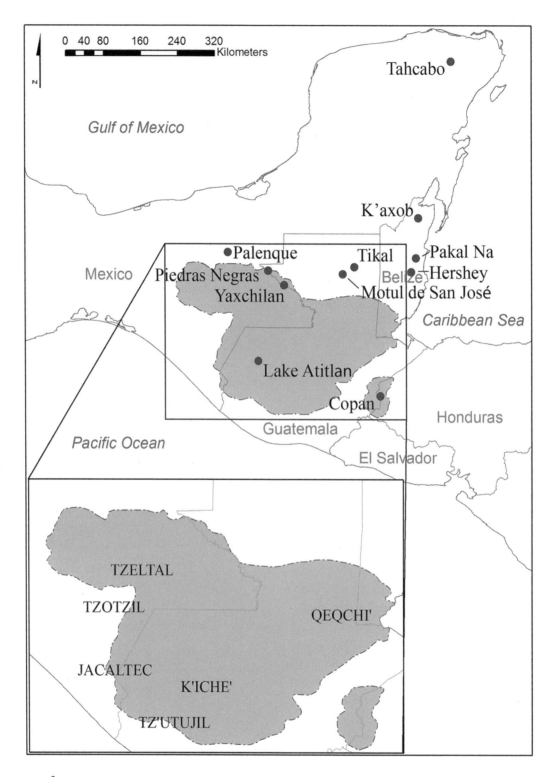

figure 3.7

The Maya region, highlighting the archaeological sites and ethnolinguistic groups mentioned in the text. Elaborated by Ashley Peles, from an electronic atlas by Witschey and Brown 2002.

Protecting and Nourishing the Soul

In reference to residential burials within the Pre-Columbian Maya region, Julia Hendon (2010) stresses the curational aspect of this practice and likens it to the storage of sacred, inalienable family possessions. There is a hidden quality to many residential burials (which are largely unmarked), and even those interred in tombs within pyramidal shrines are secreted away, often protected by layers of sharp obsidian and chert debris.

With these thoughts in mind, a cross-sectional drawing from Operation 1 at the Preclassic/Classic site of K'axob in northern Belize takes on new meaning (Figure 3.8; see McAnany 2004 for more details on excavations at K'axob; see McAnany, Storey, and Lockard 1999 and Storey 2004 for details of burial contexts). The stratigraphic sequence is no longer a "neutral" container for temporally sensitive artifacts or a context for the display of status, but a medium for curation of potentially revitalized souls. Interred within deeply intrusive pits that penetrate the Middle Preclassic houses of this ancient community, these Terminal Preclassic Burials (1-1, 1-2, and 1-45) were protected from despoiling by the overburden of an Early Classic pyramidal shrine (Structure 18). Associated ceramics (spouted jars and "buckets"—local precursors to the Classic-period vase form) and large bowls decorated with the quadripartite motif suggest that physical nourishment was provided for the journey of souls whose well-being may have been considered integral to the continued vitality of the community.

In a manner that is parallel to the "work" (*meyah* in Yucatec Mayan) discussed by Scott Hutson and colleagues (this volume), the practices that surround curational storage encode social memory as well as the exclusionary knowledge of exactly where ancestral remains are curated. Recall the statement by López Austin (1988:198, 200) that vital energies were prone to dangerous dissipation and reattachment or Sandstrom's (1991:252) observation that cleansing ceremonies among the Nahua of Amatlan were conducted to alleviate the dangerous *ejecatl* spirits that linger in the aftermath of a bad or neglected death. By curating the physical remains

of an ancestor, members of a residential community maintain surveillance over corporeal remains, which could be despoiled if deposited elsewhere, with deleterious results for lingering souls and the community as a whole. From this perspective, residential burial can be understood as a practice that attempts to manage the ambiguity of body-soul separation upon death. Furthermore, unlike the social context described by Beth Conklin (this volume), in which connections between the living and the dead are intentionally severed, Maya practices of residential burial emphasize and hyperextend the connection.

Stephen Houston, David Stuart, and Karl Taube (2006:143) discuss Classic Maya concepts of life and death gleaned from royal iconography and texts. Of particular interest is the concept of a "breath soul" and its representation as a white four-petaled flower (unusual in nature), as wind or smoke, or as a single jade bead in front of the nose or mouth (Figure 3.9). The final—a single jade bead—is sometimes found in the mouth of a buried person. This practice may have "served to capture and store the breath soul of [the] deceased" (Houston, Stuart, and Taube 2006:147), thus easing the separation of the soul from the body. At K'axob during the Late Preclassic period (400 BCE–250 CE), a large jade bead was placed in the mouth of an older male who was buried in a tightly flexed position along with a tetrapodal vessel (Figure 3.10). This finding (and there are many others from nonroyal contexts) suggests a concern with body-soul separation within nonroyal sectors of Pre-Columbian Maya society.

Difficult-to-access burial pits and tombs provide a setting of secure curation for the deceased, particularly within an unstable political environment in which tomb despoilment was a real possibility. Inaccessibility also could reflect the desire of survivors to distance themselves from the potency/danger of the spirit of a deceased person. During the politically tumultuous times of the Late to Terminal Classic period (600–950 CE), we have considerable evidence of tomb despoilment along with violent structure termination, so difficult-to-access burial contexts might be expected. Such was the case with

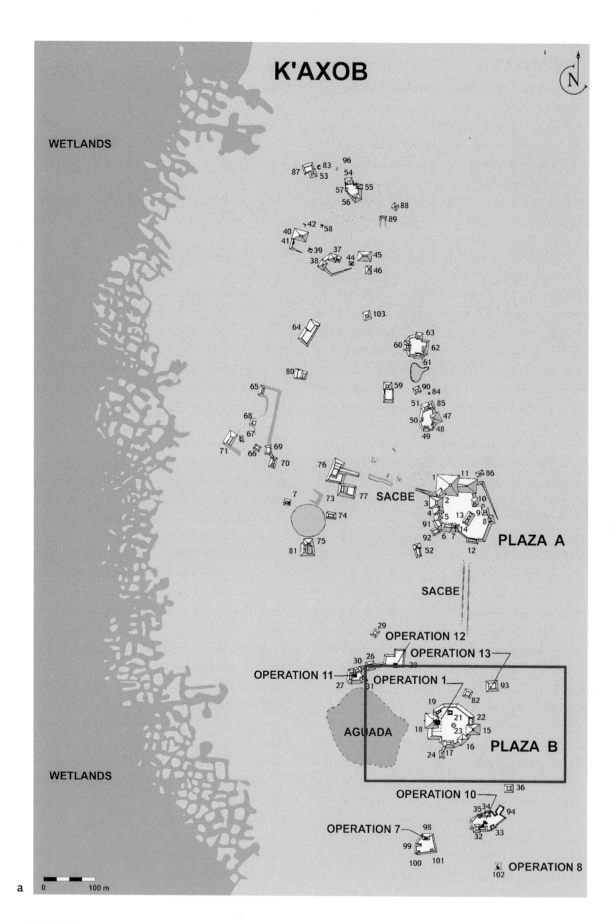

K'AXOB

WETLANDS

WETLANDS

SACBE

SACBE

PLAZA A

OPERATION 12

OPERATION 13

OPERATION 11

OPERATION 1

AGUADA

PLAZA B

OPERATION 10

OPERATION 7

OPERATION 8

0   100 m

a

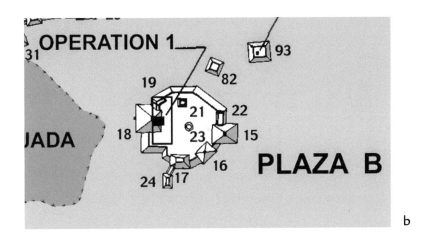

b

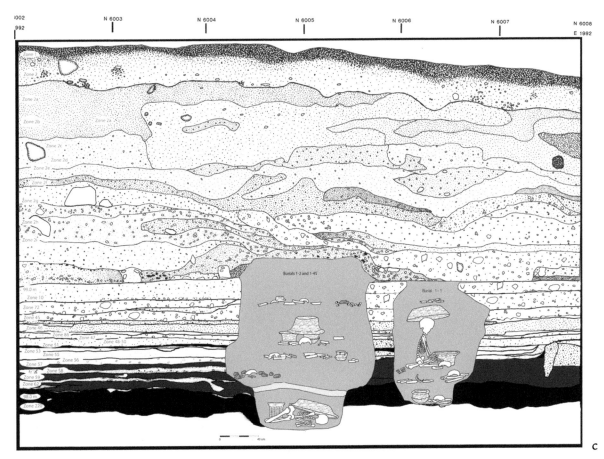

c

figure 3.8

K'axob, showing a) a plan view of the site; b) the location of Operation 1; and c) a cross section of the West Wall.
Archives of the K'axob Archaeological Project, composite image by Ashley Peles.

a

b

figure 3.9
a) Quatrefoil flowers as representations of the soul;
and b) nose beads that indicate breath or the soul
(Houston, Stuart, and Taube 2006:figs. 4.8 and 4.3).

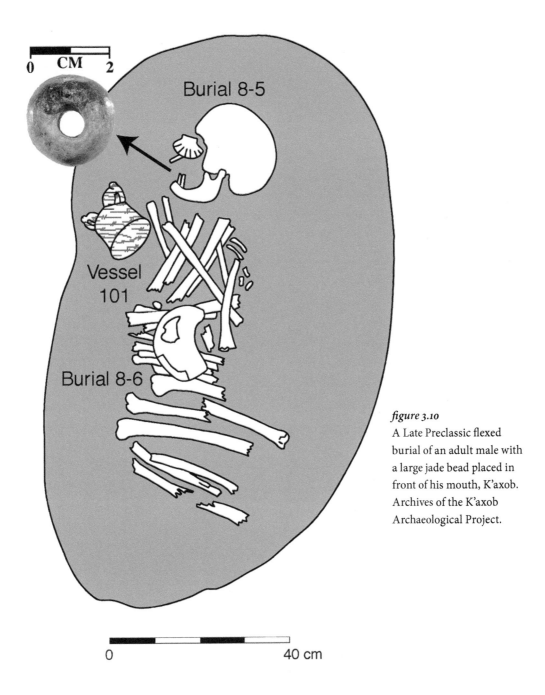

0   CM   2

Burial 8-5

Vessel
101

Burial 8-6

0   40 cm

figure 3.10
A Late Preclassic flexed
burial of an adult male with
a large jade bead placed in
front of his mouth, K'axob.
Archives of the K'axob
Archaeological Project.

an interment encountered in the Sibun Valley of
central Belize, where I conducted multiple seasons
of survey and excavation (see McAnany 2012 for
additional background).

   At a site called Pakal Na, located proximate to
the Sibun River, a local leader was buried within a
very deep pit that had been excavated into the central axis of a long platform built during the Terminal
Classic period (Figure 3.11). According to Rebecca
Storey, the principal interment within the large pit

was an older male (sixty years plus or a four-*k'atun*
lord) whose skeleton bore evidence of an active life
and periods of martial activity (Figure 3.12; see
also Harrison-Buck, McAnany, and Storey 2007).
Significantly, an *och k'ahk'*, or fire-entry ritual, had
taken place immediately after his interment. This
practice (hieroglyphically attested elsewhere) was
first deciphered by David Stuart (1998) and refers
to the introduction of fire or smoky incense into
a tomb chamber either upon interment or on the

a

b

figure 3.11
a) An oblique aerial view of Structure 130; and b) the axial trench in which the burial pit was discovered. XARP Archives.

anniversary of an interment. Although this ritual practice may have been perceived as a way to hasten body-soul separation, cremation does not appear to have been the goal. Nonetheless, the bones of this four-*k'atun* male were singed and the ample charcoal around the lower portion of his body yielded a radiocarbon date of 687–959 CE (2-sigma calibrated age range; sample no. AA55938). On a shelf to the east of his body, portions of a trophy skull— a carved mandible and cranial fragments—were found (Figure 3.12b). A prominent *k'ahk'* logograph (standing for "fire") carved on the forehead of the trophy skull suggests the possibility that this person was a *yajawk'ahk'*, or priestly warrior, as Marc Zender (2004) translates this title. The cranium of the principal interment also was placed on the shelf. Additional bundled burials were placed around his body, but we have no evidence that the grave was reentered for additional smoking, visitation, or offerings. In summary, bioarchaeological evidence, together with glyphic markings on a closely associated cranium, indicates that the principal interment was a person perceived as powerful during his lifetime.

Was this person also perceived to possess a dangerous spiritual force that was harmful to others, and thus was his burial place accorded great ceremony but definitively and deeply sealed? Since he embodied martial prowess and was buried with a trophy skull and a pyriform vessel that likely contained cacao (Figure 3.12c), this possibility cannot be discounted. Alternatively, was his Terminal Classic burial place dug deeply because it was vulnerable to predation? A site called Hershey that is located farther up the Sibun Valley contains at least two deposits that are indicative of violent structure termination and probable desecration of ancestral burials. The desire to protect and provide nourishment for departing souls would have been acutely frustrated during times of political instability.

During the Classic period, human remains were not the only entities linked to indestructible spiritual forces. Built landscapes—especially the shrines of founding dynasts—were something to be protected and nourished so as to perpetuate a dynastic line and the good fortunes of an entire

kingdom. Such was the case with the shrine of the Early Classic–period (250–600 CE) founder of the Copan dynasty: K'inich Yax K'uk' Mo'. His shrine, called the Rosalila structure, was buried intact within Temple 16 (Figure 3.13; Agurcia Fasquelle, Sheets, and Taube 2016). An extraordinary cache of nine eccentrics (elaborately flint-knapped forms), three bifaces, assorted fauna, and a jade bead was interred within the shrine (Figure 3.14a). The eccentrics feature flint-knapped images of the lineage deity, K'awiil (Figure 3.14b), a supernatural protector of royalty during the Classic period. Taube (2016:33) likens the eccentrics to supernatural weapons placed to safeguard the shrine and, thus, the royal line. After conducting a technological analysis of the eccentrics, Payson Sheets (2016:67) notes that while some of the eccentrics represent masterpieces of flint knapping (such as Figure 3.14b), others clearly were created by apprentices. Nonetheless, all were incorporated into the offering, which indicates that the act of crafting these guardians took precedence over the quality of the crafted images.

Caches are more often interpreted as nourishing rather than protecting the soul of an architectural space, but the latter interpretation deserves additional consideration—both desires may have been enacted through the practice that archaeologists refer to as "caching." This broader interpretation accords well with an Early Classic cache from K'axob. As at Copan, the cache was related to the entombment or termination of earlier structures. At K'axob, the cache sealed a series of closely laminated floors and burials that characterized Operation 1 during the Preclassic period (Figure 3.15). Overlying basket-load stratigraphy indicates the construction of a pyramidal shrine (Figure 3.15a). Before the shrine was built, a deposit of two vessels ringed by seven *yúuntun* was placed within the construction fill (Harrison-Buck 2004). (One of the *yúuntun* is visible in Figure 3.15b.) The balls were formed from pecked limestone. The function of the *yúuntun* stones was not clear until Señor Concepción Campos, landowner of K'axob, explained that *yúuntun* provided an excellent deterrent against birds in the cornfield when launched from a slingshot.

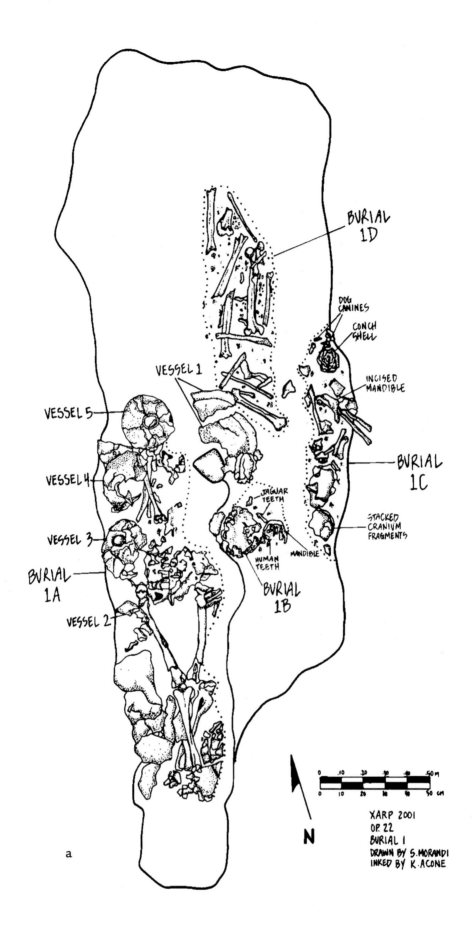

BURIAL
1D

DOG
CANINES

CONCH
SHELL

VESSEL 1

INCISED
MANDIBLE

VESSEL 5

VESSEL 4

BURIAL
1C

JAGUAR
TEETH

STACKED
CRANIUM
FRAGMENTS

VESSEL 3

MANDIBLE

BURIAL
1A

HUMAN
TEETH

BURIAL
1B

VESSEL 2

0 .10 .20 .30 .40 .50 m

0 10 20 30 40 50 cm

N

XARP 2001
OP. 22
BURIAL 1
DRAWN BY S. MORANDI
INKED BY K. ACONE

a

figure 3.12
The Pakal Na deep burial:
a plan view of the Terminal
Classic burial context, with
associated accoutrements (a),
including pieces of a trophy
skull (b) and a pyriform
vessel (c). XARP Archives.

b

c

figure 3.13
Copan Structure 16, showing the Early Classic entombed shrine (called Rosalila) of K'inich Yax K'uk' Mo'. Courtesy of the National Geographic Society.

Yúuntun may have been perceived as protecting not only a general locus of proprietary concern to Early Classic residents of K'axob, but also the specific contents of the lower cylindrical vessel, the top of which is barely visible in Figure 3.15. This vessel contained carefully selected and color-coded elements in triadic composition (Figure 3.16), including miniature figurines shaped from shell and jadeite (elsewhere called "Charlie Chaplin" figurines; Scherer 2015:111–112), as well as unshaped but perforated shell. One unique figurine, crafted from white marine shell, features a drilled hole in area of the heart (often noted as a place where a soul resides).

This deposit lacks the über-regal overtones of the Rosalila cache but seems to be performing the same kind of protective role. Like the Rosalila cache, the triadic cache of K'axob was buried deeply with massive overburden. Neither was meant to be revisited, but even "unseen," the cache elements may have been perceived as providing protection for ancestral bones buried at this locale. As Megan O'Neil (2009:119) has noted, the "unseen" character of many sculptures and other deposits at Maya sites suggests that they continued to have meaning outside the "mode of the visible" and likely were perceived as immanent regardless of their buried state. The exclusionary knowledge of what was buried where not only protected vulnerable spiritual entities but also likely cultivated a sense of proprietorship over buried remains.

a

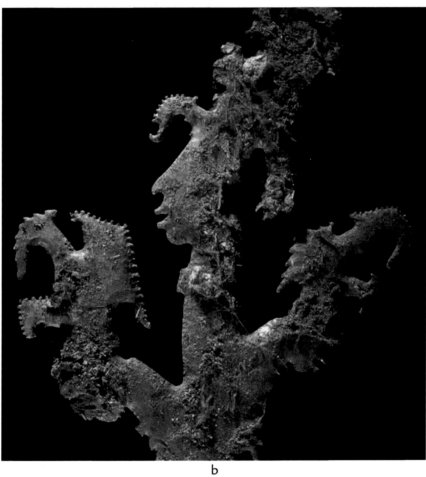

b

figure 3.14
Eccentrics placed within Rosalila upon structure entombment: a) an intrusive stone-lined pit containing eccentrics; and b) profile of the deity K'awiil on one of the eccentrics (Agurcia Fasquelle, Sheets, and Taube 2016:52 and 6, respectively).

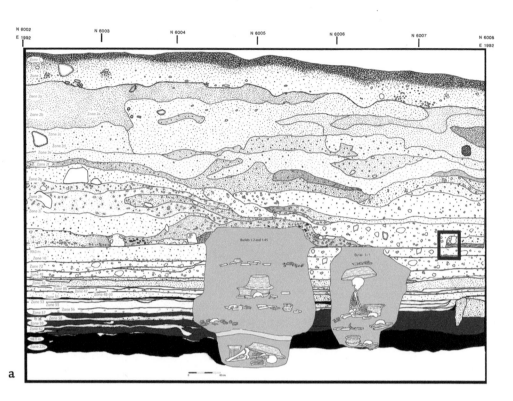

figure 3.15
K'axob Operation 1, showing the stratigraphic placement of a triadic cache (a) and a closeup (while under excavation) of the cache with one of the *yúuntun* (b). Archives of the K'axob Archaeological Project.

a

b

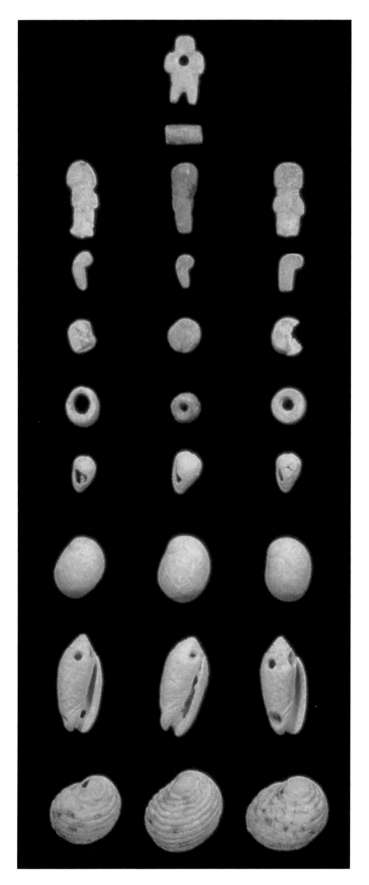

figure 3.16
Contents of the Zone 17 cache: a color-coded (red, green, and white) and triadic composition of miniature figurines and other shapes. Archives of the K'axob Archaeological Project.

Soul Rejuvenation

During the Late Classic period, royal texts and iconography indicate that the anniversary of the death of a ruler often spurred feasting and commemorative monuments. One well-known example comes from the royal court of Piedras Negras, where Ruler 7 commemorated the earlier reign of Ruler 4 on the masterfully carved Panel 3 (see Martin and Grube 2008:149). The elaborate ceremony included nighttime cacao drinking and a descending macaw dance (Houston, Stuart, and Taube 2006). This retrospective celebration seems to have been focused on accessing the spiritual force of the former ruler and conjuring his presence. The event represented time folding back on itself.

As Stuart (2011:280) has shown, royal naming conventions throughout the lowlands support the idea that rulers (and probably local leaders as well) served as a fulcrum around which time was folded and memories constructed. At Palenque in particular, royal names were repeated over a three-hundred-year cycle in a manner that foreshadows ethnographic naming conventions. This was not memory in the abstract but memory indexed to the bones and monuments of historical persons. The pairing of ancestors and descendants was anchored in the physical spaces of residences (writ large and small) in a manner that is similar to that discussed by Bruce Mannheim (this volume) among Quechua speakers.

Bones provide a powerful medium for communication with ancestors in the manner that Miguel Astor-Aguilera (2010) has documented. The familiar image of Altar 5 from Tikal (which shows the carefully stacked, exhumed bones of a royal woman) provides a relevant example of the care with which corporeal remains were handled in order to

figure 3.17
The ruins of the seventeenth-century *ramada* church at Tahcabo, Yucatan, Mexico. Photograph by Patricia McAnany.

a

b

figure 3.18
The restored statue of San Bartolomé (a), with a closeup of his knife and halo (b). Photographs by Patricia McAnany.

communicate with spirit souls and to nurture their regeneration. This image emphasizes recurrence and a folding back of time. But rather than a temporal cycle that is circular with endless repetition, this schema is more like a spiral of enlivened spirits that can be carefully tapped into at strategic moments.

In Mesoamerica prior to the sixteenth century, the journey of a soul after its separation from the body was differentiated based upon the role and status of a person while alive. Taube (2004) maintains that spirit-souls of Classic Maya royalty embarked upon a journey to a fragrant paradise called Flower Mountain. For instance, the well-known sarcophagus lid of K'inich Janaab' Pakal I of Palenque likely represents the soul of the ruler en route to Flower Mountain. Oswaldo Chinchilla Mazariegos proposes a more circuitous route for the soul of Pakal

based upon a close reading of the iconography and hieroglyphs of the sarcophagus. Briefly, the soul of the king first transformed into the maize deity and then into the sun god to assume an exalted position in the heavenly constellation (Chinchilla Mazariegos 2006:51–52). Needless to say, Flower Mountain was replaced by a Christian heaven (theoretically accessible to all) after the sixteenth century.

The rejuvenation of souls could be closely connected to the refounding of communities—a link that persists through colonial times and beyond. After the violence of the nineteenth-century Caste War receded in eastern Yucatan, people refounded many colonial towns, drawing upon an undocumented source of social memory to revitalize places and associated patron saints. For instance, in eastern Yucatan at Tahcabo (see Figure 3.7 for location), census data show that the town was virtually depopulated during the decades following the 1838 Rebellion of Santiago Imán (a precursor to the Caste War; see Batun Alpuche, McAnany, and Dedrick 2017). Yet half a century later (in 1892), the town was refounded around the colonial mission church at Tahcabo (Figure 3.17). The statue of San Bartolomé (the patron saint of Tahcabo since 1612) was refurbished and given a new halo and knife crafted by Juan B. Chan (Figure 3.18). The artist adorned the knife and halo with a foliated vine and four-petaled red flowers with white centers—an intriguing variation on the four-petaled white flower (*sak' nicte*) thought to represent the soul in Classic-period iconography.

Access to Souls

In contrast to the finality of the aforementioned interment at Pakal Na, plenty of burial contexts provided direct access to descendants, thus emphasizing the permeability between the realms of embodied and disembodied souls. Such access could be maintained for decades and even centuries after initial interment, as happened with the tomb of Pakal I at Palenque and with the tomb of an early queen of Copan who was buried beneath the acropolis within a structure that archaeologists named Margarita (Bell 2002). The vaulted roof of the tomb was extended twice in order to maintain access to her tomb for visitation and for gendered offerings of sewing needles and textiles (Bell 2002:96–97). Likewise, Diane Chase and Arlen Chase (1996) report repeated reentry events in the family crypts of Caracol. The deep burial pit at K'axob (shown in cross section in Figure 3.8) was also reopened and resealed several times, indicating that reentry of mortuary contexts was a widespread practice and not solely tomb related.

Piedras Negras Stela 40 shows an iconographic depiction of access to a royal female progenitor (Figure 3.19). A descendant kneels to communicate with a female in a subterranean tomb that is connected via rope to the surface. A substance (perhaps *k'uh*?) flows from the hands of

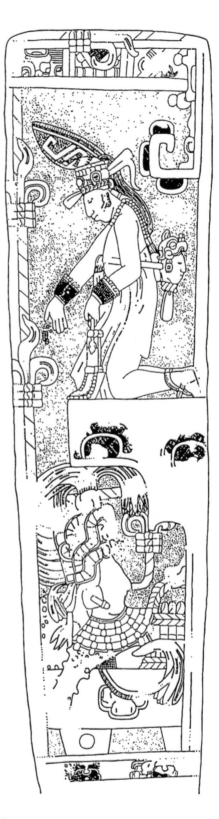

figure 3.19
Piedras Negras Stela 40, showing the accessibility of progenitors to descendants. Drawing courtesy of John Montgomery.

the living to the abode of the ancestor. In reference to Piedras Negras Stela 40, Scherer (2015:82) notes that although the ancestor is shown enlivened, her bone bundle also is depicted, which indicates the complexities of an ontology of the soul in which enlivened spirits could be conjured and represented in a corporeal form alongside the reality of bundled bones.

The aforementioned *och k'ahk'* ceremonies provide another example of maintaining access. *Och k'ahk'* expressions often refer to burial contexts as a house or *naah* (Stuart 1998). Fire could enter the "house" of a deceased person upon initial interment—as happened at Pakal Na—but often was associated with tomb reentry, a visit to make offerings and to smoke the chamber so that the soul of the departed and spirit guardians might take note of the attention being paid to their remains and make their presence immanent, perhaps through corporeal regeneration.

Dangers Presented by Errant Vital Forces: The *Way* Glyph

A fourth concern was expressed visually and hieroglyphically by a subset of Classic Maya royal artists: what to do about the dangers presented by errant vital forces that represented social order gone awry? These inversions of the moral order—including sickness, disease, and witchcraft—are reported ethnographically as linked to soul loss. Much has been written about Maya royalty as iconic of social order, but what about social disorder? Much less has been written about disorder, likely because hieroglyphic texts, in and of themselves, were an expression of royal male ideas about beauty and order (Houston 2018). However, Lisa Lucero and Sherry Gibbs (2007) argue that human remains found on floors deep within cave chambers may indicate the "destiny" of those accused of witchcraft. Late Classic royal artists and calligraphers living in the Mirador Basin, around El Zotz', and in the vicinity of Motul de San José (Ik' polity) also were particularly concerned with forms of otherness (errant souls?) that were linked to sickness, death, disorder, and

possibly witchcraft. Scribes referenced these forms with a logogram of a split face that is part *ajaw* and part jaguar pelt and is read as *way* (pronounced "why"; Figure 3.20).

Initially, Houston and Stuart (1989) suggested that the *way* glyph referred to a spirit co-essence. In 1994, Nikolai Grube and Werner Nahm contributed a "census" of the characters associated with the *way* glyph, separating hybrid human/animal forms from purely animal. Both forms show a kind of dynamism and movement that is not common in Classic Maya royal painting. Further accenting their dissimilarity, *way* figures are scantily clad, often with exposed genitalia. They embody the inverse of the orderly poses struck by heavily costumed royalty, in which a slight lifting of the heel is termed "dancing."

More recently, Stuart (1999, 2002:411) suggests that *way* figures may represent animated diseases, witchcraft, or other uncontrollable forces (the Classic-period equivalent of a Tzeltal *lab*). Epigraphers note that a *way* does not exist by itself but as a kingly possession, as are so many people and objects. Houston (personal communication, 2017) notes the etymology of the word, linked to states of dreaming and slumber, which are associated with sickness and with the Tzeltal idea discussed earlier that dreaming and slumber are dangerous states in which soul loss can occur.

Erik Velásquez García (2009) suggests that necromancy may well be what the scribes were concerned about and intended to represent. Just as the Salem witch trials of the late seventeenth century took place within a highly circumscribed area, the known pattern of *way* representation is highly restricted geographically and temporally; intriguingly, many *way* vessels belonged to young men, suggesting that the specters of disorder and disease may have played a pedagogical function (Houston, personal communication, 2017). Most recently, Brian Just (2012:208) reviewed the corpus and agreed with Stuart's interpretation of *way* as uncontrollable forces, such as death and disease. The glyph could represent the Classic-period equivalent of a Tzeltal *lab*, which can take the form of an animal and is prone to causing sickness. The

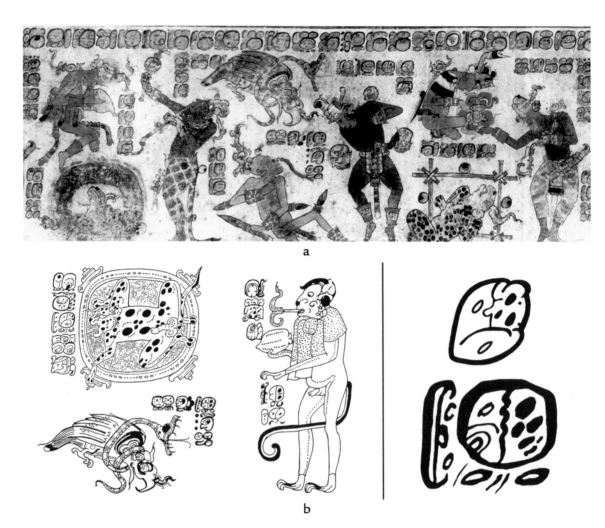

figure 3.20
Way glyphs, showing examples of associated iconography from Late Classic Maya vessels (a: Just 2012:131, 225; and b: Grube and Nahm 1994:690, 696, 705, adapted by Ashley Peles).

restricted geographical extent of this representation could indicate the ensoulment of a malaise about which only certain Late Classic royal courtiers were concerned.

Discussion

By framing these Maya ideas regarding souls with an eye to proprietorship, I situate animacy and authority within a schema of practice (Descola 2013): managing souls, spiritual entities, and their material embodiments. Along with protection and nourishment, proprietary concerns with exclusive knowledge, access, and rejuvenation loom large in terms of structuring principles of archaeological materials from the Pre-Columbian Maya region. Many but not all of these principles are ethnographically salient and represent an ontological durability that is notable.

Proprietorship per se suggests the authority to manage important transformations, such as the separation of the soul from the body and its potential rejuvenation in a new body. Safeguarding the physical spaces in which bodies were interred also required concerted political action. As Steve Kosiba (this volume) suggests, such closely situated political action provides a frame in which authority and order can be sustained (reinforcing the importance of the ancestors) or challenged (by despoiling ancestral burial places). Reviewing a range of archaeological contexts from royal courts and nonroyal communities, I suggest that families, residential groups, and communities retained authority over the disposition of the body and souls of their members.

Such proprietorship—including protection, nourishment, access, and regeneration—helps to explain much of what archaeologists document in burials, tombs, caches, and other structured deposits. This assertion does not negate the importance of ancestors, but ancestralizing practices alone cannot explain the age and gender inclusiveness of many residential burial contexts, particularly those of Preclassic times. Invoking ancestors does not explain why burial locales—whether monumental or modest—can take on the appearance of secretive, curational storage. Moreover, ancestralizing practices alone cannot explain how the immortality of the soul—as it separates from the materiality of a decomposing corpse—engenders "mortuary practice." A concern with the management and transmission of souls provides a schema of practice that renders the deposition and disposition of corporeal remains more comprehensible.

The existential questions surrounding death and the soul turn out to be highly determinative of how the dead are handled and how survivors move on. The mortuary practices detailed by Carlos Fausto (this volume) among Kuikuro peoples of the Upper Xingu and by Beth Conklin (this volume) among the Wari' of the southwestern Amazon Basin provide vividly contrastive examples of handling and remembering the dead. The highly mobile and egalitarian Wari' make every effort to erase the memory of the dead, including their names. Every belonging and field plot is either burned or given away; no inheritance is permitted and all connections with the dead are severed. Considering the key role of inheritance in promoting inequality (Bowles, Smith, and Mulder 2010), the Wari' have effectively institutionalized equality and decided that remembering ancestors is not good for egalitarianism. Conklin

(this volume) notes that by having no gravesites or monuments to defend, the Wari' are free to move when threatened.

In contrast, when a chiefly person dies among Kuikuro peoples, he is remembered for a time. An elaborate ceremony of remembrance—which features a carved effigy of the chief—is placed in the central plaza. But after the period of mourning is ended, the effigy is thrown into a nearby lake and life resumes as usual. There is no attempt to communicate with the deceased leader and if a vision of the chief occurs during the funeral ceremony, Fausto (this volume) emphasizes that it is not a welcome sight. However, grandchildren may be named after a grandparent—a practice that shows parallels to the Maya region.

Life is fleeting. This concept is embraced by Wari' mourners and to an extent by peoples of the Upper Xingu, but in the Maya region, great emphasis is placed on the durability of the soul and how it could be regenerated within the body of a descendant. This recursive ontology materializes in special places for the interment of human remains and extended access to those locales. Ancestral souls are expected to return and are provided nourishment. Generally, but not always, emblematic of social order, some souls were linked to errant forces that were difficult or impossible to control. Just as the acceptance of death and the erasure of the deceased among Wari' peoples provides a central strut of their egalitarianism, so acceptance of the durability of the soul and its potential regeneration became a central part of inheritance practices among socially differentiated Maya peoples.

Conclusions

The pragmatism of Mesoamerican ontologies of soul can be juxtaposed with the concrete abstraction of New Materialism with an eye to goodness of fit. Does the framework espoused by twenty-first-century philosopher Jane Bennett and others—in which vibrant matter pulsates with energy but no intentionality and is devoid of divine infusion—resonate with Maya ontologies? Bennett (2010) proposes a kind of vitality that is neither socially nor divinely constructed. In a very real and ontological sense, it simply *is*. Bennett further elaborates this proposition with the idea that humans create distinctive social worlds by interacting with such matter. In this chapter, a similar kind of interaction is under consideration for the Maya region, with an emphasis on Pre-Columbian times.

Contemporary acknowledgment of the web of connectivity that relates humans to "other-than-human persons" (as Hallowell [1960:30–34] phrased it), as well as to inorganic entities, aspires to restructure contemporary Western political ecology, decenter humans (Latour 2005), and encourage interentity reciprocity or at least respect for alterity, as Bjørnar Olsen (2012) and others propose by way of symmetrical archaeology. The manner in which this conceptual framework converges with many "first principles" of Mesoamerican ontologies in which nonhumans could be animated—or "enlivened" (as per Houston 2014:101)—certainly invites comparison.

But thinkers within the paradigm of New Materialism stop short of attributing sentience and spirituality to nonhuman entities (Bennett 2010:xvii). Within Mesoamerica and the Maya region, in particular, nonpersons and objects were perceived as agentive and could hold a charge that greatly enhanced both their value and their danger. Additionally, proponents of New Materialism and its many incarnations share in common a desire to flatten a hierarchy of life forms in which humans have been perceived as sitting on top. In reference to nonhuman agency and human hierarchy in the Maya region, however, the two coexisted. Living in a world in which many entities could be enlivened meant that humans both incurred responsibilities and accrued authority by managing relationships with those entities.

On the surface, the two ontologies appear to be similar, but as we drill deeper into the sacred matter of ensoulment, differences come into focus and similarities dissolve. The contemporary project of decentering humans in the great network of intermeshing actors bears only superficial similarity to the enlivened world of Pre-Columbian Maya society, in which human respect for nonhuman entities coexisted with the centrality of humans within a highly differentiated social order.

Acknowledgments

The scholarly rapport of this Dumbarton Oaks conference was exceptionally rich, and I wish to thank the symposium organizers—Steve Kosiba, Tom Cummins, and John Janusek—for making it so. I especially relished the opportunity to think with colleagues who work in South America. Such interaction provides an opportunity for cross-fertilization that is too rare in Pre-Columbian studies. Several scholars shared their thoughts about souls and materiality with me; I particularly would like to thank Stephen Houston for his generosity in this respect. This chapter is enriched by case studies from my field research at K'axob, in the Sibun Valley, and at Tahcabo. All three programs of research were supported by the National Science Foundation (K'axob, award SBR-9112310; Sibun, award BCS-0096603; Tahcabo, award 1134331 from OISE). This chapter benefited greatly from the comments of external reviewers, as well as a close reading by conference organizers. To both groups, I extend my heartfelt gratitude.

Agurcia Fasquelle, Ricardo, Payson Sheets, and
Karl A. Taube

2016   *Protecting Sacred Space: Rosalila's
        Eccentric Chert Cache at Copan and
        Eccentrics among the Classic Maya.*
        Precolumbia Mesoweb Press, San
        Francisco.

Allen, Catherine J.

2002   *The Hold Life Has: Coca and Cultural
        Identity in an Andean Community.*
        2nd ed. Smithsonian Institution Press,
        Washington, D.C.

Anderson, Arthur J. O., and Charles E. Dibble

1975   *The Conquest of Mexico.* Book 12 of
        *Florentine Codex: General History
        of Things of New Spain.* School of
        American Research, Santa Fe, N.Mex.

Argyrou, Vassos

2017   Ontology, "Hauntology," and the
        "Turn" that Keeps Anthropology
        Turning. *History of the Human Sciences*
        30(1):50–65.

Astor-Aguilera, Miguel Angel

2010   *The Maya World of Communicating
        Objects: Quadripartite Crosses, Trees,
        and Stones.* University of New Mexico
        Press, Albuquerque.

Baron, Joanne P.

2016   *Patron Gods and Patron Lords: The
        Semiotics of Classic Maya Community
        Cults.* University Press of Colorado,
        Boulder.

Batun Alpuche, Adolfo Ivan, Patricia A. McAnany,
and Maia Dedrick

2017   Tiempo y paisaje en Tahcabo, Yucatán.
        Arqueología mexicana 25(145):66–71.

Bell, Ellen E.

2002   Engendering a Dynasty: A Royal
        Woman in the Margarita Tomb, Copan.
        In *Ancient Maya Women*, edited by Traci
        Ardren, pp. 89–104. AltaMira Press,
        Walnut Creek, Calif.

Bennett, Jane

2010   *Vibrant Matter: A Political Ecology
        of Things.* Duke University Press,
        Durham, N.C.

Bird-David, Nurit

1999   "Animism" Revisited: Personhood,
        Environment, and Relational Epistemol-
        ogy. *Current Anthropology* 40S:S67–S91.

Boremanse, Didier

2000   Sewing Machines and Q'eqchi' Maya
        Worldview. *Anthropology Today*
        16(1):11–18.

Bowles, Samuel, Eric Alden Smith, and Monique
Borgerhoff Mulder

2010   The Emergence and Persistence of
        Inequality in Premodern Societies.
        Current Anthropology 51(1):7–17.

Brown, Linda A., and Kitty F. Emery

2008   Negotiations with the Animate Forest:
        Hunting Shrines in the Guatemalan
        Highlands. *Journal of Archaeological
        Method and Theory* 15(4):300–337.

Carlsen, Robert S., and Martin Prechtel

1991   The Flowering of the Dead: An Interpre-
        tation of Highland Maya Culture. *Man,*
        n.s., 26(1):23–42.

Carr, Christopher, and Robert McCord

2015   Ohio Hopewell Depictions of Composite
        Creatures: Part II—Archaeological
        Context and a Journey to an Afterlife.
        Midcontinental Journal of Archaeology
        40(1):18–47.

Chase, Diane Z., and Arlen F. Chase

1996   Maya Multiples: Individuals, Entries,
        and Tombs in Structure A34 of Caracol,
        Belize. *Latin American Antiquity*
        7(1):61–79.

Chinchilla Mazariegos, Oswaldo

2006   The Stars of the Palenque Sarcophagus.
        RES: Anthropology and Aesthetics
        49–50:40–58.

Coe, Michael D., and Mark Van Stone

2001   *Reading the Maya Glyphs.* Thames and
        Hudson, London.

Descola, Philippe

2013   *Beyond Nature and Culture.* University
        of Chicago Press, Chicago.

Duncan, William N., and Charles Andrew Hofling

2011   Why the Head? Cranial Modification as Protection and Ensoulment among the Maya. *Ancient Mesoamerica* 22:199–210.

Fitzsimmons, James L.

2009   *Death and the Classic Maya Kings.* University of Texas Press, Austin.

Fowler, Chris

2004   *The Archaeology of Personhood: An Anthropological Approach.* Routledge, London.

Gillespie, Susan D.

2002   Body and Soul among the Maya: Keeping the Spirits in Place. In *The Space and Place of Death,* edited by H. Silverman and D. B. Small, pp. 67–78. Archaeological Papers of the American Anthropological Association 11. American Anthropological Association, Arlington, Va.

Gossen, Gary H.

2002   *Four Creations: An Epic Story of the Chiapas Mayas.* University of Oklahoma Press, Norman.

Grube, Nikolai, and Werner Nahm

1994   A Census of Xibalba: A Complete Inventory of *Way* Characters on Maya Ceramics. In *The Maya Vase Book: A Corpus of Rollout Photographs of Maya Vases,* vol. 4, edited by Barbara Kerr and Justin Kerr, pp. 686–715. Kerr Associates, New York.

Hallowell, A. Irving

1960   Ojibwa Ontology, Behavior, and World View. In *Culture in History,* edited by Stanley Diamond, pp. 19–52. Columbia University Press, New York.

Harrison-Buck, Eleanor

2004   Nourishing the Animus of Lived Space through Ritual Caching. In *K'axob: Ritual, Work, and Family in an Ancient Maya Village,* edited by Patricia A. McAnany, pp. 65–85. The Cotsen Institute of Archaeology, University of California, Los Angeles.

Hendon, Julia A.

2010   *Houses in a Landscape: Memory and Everyday Life in Mesoamerica.* Duke University Press, Durham, N.C.

Hertz, Robert

[1907] 1960   *Death and the Right Hand: A Contribution to the Study of the Collective Representation of Death.* Translated by R. and C. Needham. Free Press, Glencoe, Ill.

Hornborg, Alf

2006   Animism, Fetishism, and Objectivism as Strategies for Knowing (or not Knowing) the World. *Ethnos* 71(1):21–32.

Houston, Stephen D.

2014   *The Life Within: Classic Maya and the Matter of Permanence.* Yale University Press, New Haven.

2018   *The Gifted Passage: Young Men in Classic Maya Art and Text.* Yale University Press, New Haven.

Houston, Stephen D., and David Stuart

1989   *The Way Glyph: Evidence for "Co-essences" among the Classic Maya.* Research Reports on Ancient Maya Writing 30. Center for Maya Research, Washington, D.C.

Houston, Stephen D., David Stuart, and Karl A. Taube

2006   *The Memory of Bones: Body, Being, and Experience among the Classic Maya.* University of Texas Press, Austin.

Ingold, Tim

2011   *Being Alive: Essays on Movement, Knowledge, and Description.* Routledge, New York.

Just, Brian

2012   *Dancing into Dreams: Maya Vase Painting of the Ik' Kingdom.* Princeton University Art Museum, Princeton.

Kockelman, Paul

2009   Inalienable Possession as Grammatical Category and Discourse Pattern. *Studies in Language* 33(1):25–68.

Latour, Bruno

2005   *Reassembling the Social: An Introduction to Actor-Network Theory.* Oxford University Press, Oxford.

López Austin, Alfredo

1980   *Cuerpo humano e ideología: Las concepciones de los antiguos Nahuas.* 2 vols. Universidad Nacional Autónoma de México, Mexico City.

1988   *The Human Body and Ideology: Concepts of the Ancient Nahuas.* Vols. 1 and 2. Translated by Thelma O. de Montellano and Bernard O. de Montellano. University of Utah Press, Salt Lake City.

Lucero, Lisa J., and Sherry A. Gibbs

2007   The Creation and Sacrifice of Witches in Classic Maya Society. In *New Perspectives on Human Sacrifice and Ritual Body Treatments in Ancient Maya Society,* edited by Vera Tiesler and Andrea Cucina, pp. 45–73. Springer Science Media, New York.

Mann, Michael

1986   *The Sources of Social Power: A History of Power from the Beginning to AD 1760.* Vol. 1. Cambridge University Press, Cambridge.

Martin, Simon, and Nikolai Grube

2008   *Chronicle of the Maya Kings and Queens: Deciphering the Dynasties of the Ancient Maya.* 2nd ed. Thames and Hudson, London.

McAnany, Patricia A.

2012   Classic Maya Heterodoxy and Shrine Vernacularism in the Sibun Valley of Belize. *Cambridge Archaeological Journal* 22(1):115–134.

2013   *Living with the Ancestors: Kinship and Kingship in Ancient Maya Society.* Rev. ed. Cambridge University Press, New York.

McAnany, Patricia A. (editor)

2004   *K'axob: Ritual, Work and Family in an Ancient Maya Village.* Monumenta Archaeologica 22. Cotsen Institute of Archaeology, University of California, Los Angeles.

McAnany, Patricia A., Rebecca Storey, and Angela K. Lockard

1999   Mortuary Ritual and Family Politics at Formative and Early Classic K'axob, Belize. *Ancient Mesoamerica* 10:129–146.

Metcalf, Peter, and Richard Huntington

1991   *Celebrations of Death: The Anthropology of Mortuary Ritual.* 2nd ed. Cambridge University Press, Cambridge.

Mondloch, James L.

1980   K'eʔš: Quiché Naming. *Journal of Mayan Linguistics* 1(2):9–25.

Neurath, Johannes

2015   Shifting Ontologies in Huichol Ritual and Art. *Anthropology and Humanism* 40(1):58–71.

Novotny, Anna

2013   The Bones of the Ancestors as Inalienable Possessions: A Bioarchaeological Perspective. In *The Inalienable in the Archaeology of Mesoamerica,* edited by Brigette Kovacevich and Michael G. Callahan, pp. 54–65. Archaeological Papers of the American Anthropological Association 23. Wiley, Hoboken.

Olsen, Bjørnar

2012   Symmetrical Archaeology. In *Archaeological Theory Today,* edited by Ian Hodder, pp. 208–228. 2nd ed. Polity Press, Cambridge.

O'Neil, Megan E.

2009   Ancient Maya Sculptures of Tikal, Seen and Unseen. *RES: Anthropology and Aesthetics* 55–56:119–134.

Pitarch, Pedro

2010   *The Jaguar and the Priest: An Ethnography of Tzeltal Souls.* University of Texas Press, Austin.

Sandstrom, Alan R.

1991   *Corn Is Our Blood: Culture and Ethnic Identity in a Contemporary Aztec Indian Village.* University of Oklahoma Press, Norman.

Scherer, Andrew K.

2015   *Mortuary Landscapes of the Classic Maya: Rituals of Body and Soul.* University of Texas Press, Austin.

Sheets, Payson

2016   Lithic Technology. In *Protecting Sacred Space: Rosalila's Eccentric Chert Cache at Copan and Eccentrics among the Classic Maya,* by Ricardo Agurcia Fasquelle, Payson Sheets, and Karl A. Taube, pp. 61–68. Precolumbia Mesoweb Press, San Francisco.

Storey, Rebecca

  2004   Ancestors: Bioarchaeology of the Human Remains of K'axob. In *K'axob: Ritual, Work, and Family in an Ancient Maya Village*, edited by Patricia A. McAnany, pp. 109–138. Monumenta Archaeologica 22. Cotsen Institute of Archaeology, University of California, Los Angeles.

Stuart, David

  1998   "The Fire Enters His House": Architecture and Ritual in Classic Maya Texts. In *Function and Meaning in Classic Maya Architecture*, edited by Stephen D. Houston, pp. 373–425. Dumbarton Oaks Research Library and Collection, Washington, D.C.

  1999   The Meaning of Sacrifice and Bloodletting among the Classic Maya. Paper presented at the Sixth Annual UCLA Maya Weekend, "Communicating with the Gods: Ancient Maya Ritual," Los Angeles.

  2002   Comment on Klein et al. *Current Anthropology* 43(3):410–411.

  2011   *The Order of Days: The Maya World and the Truth about 2012.* Harmony Books, New York.

Taube, Karl A.

  2004   Flower Mountain: Concepts of Life, Beauty, and Paradise among the Classic Maya. *RES: Anthropology and Aesthetics* 45:69–98.

  2016   Symbolism of Eccentrics in Classic Maya Religion. In *Protecting Sacred Space: Rosalila's Eccentric Chert Cache at Copan and Eccentrics among the Classic Maya*, by Ricardo Agurcia Fasquelle, Payson Sheets, and Karl A. Taube, pp. 9–37. Precolumbia Mesoweb Press, San Francisco.

Tiesler, Vera, and Andrew K. Scherer (editors)

  2018   *Smoke, Flames, and the Human Body in Mesoamerican Ritual Practice.* Dumbarton Oaks Research Library and Collection, Washington, D.C.

Velásquez García, Erik

  2009   Los vasos de la entidad política de "Ik": Una aproximación histórico-artística; Estudio sobre las entidades anímicas y el lenguaje gestual y corporal en el arte maya clásico. PhD dissertation, Universidad Nacional Autónoma de México, Mexico City.

Vogt, Evon Z.

  1970   Human Souls and Animal Spirits in Zinacantan. In *Échanges et communications: Mélanges offerts à Claude Lévi-Strauss à l'occasion de son 60ème anniversaire*, edited by J. Pouillon and P. Maranda, pp. 1148–1167. Mouton, The Hague.

  1993   *Tortillas for the Gods: A Symbolic Analysis of Zinacanteco Rituals.* University of Oklahoma Press, Norman.

Vosters, Helene

  2014   Military Memorialization and Its Object(s) of Period Purification. In *Performing Objects and Theatrical Things*, edited by Marlis Schweitzer and Joanne Zerdy, pp. 104–117. Palgrave Macmillan, New York.

Watanabe, John

  1989   Elusive Essences: Souls and Social Identity in Two Highland Maya Communities. In *Ethnographic Encounters in Southern Mesoamerica: Essays in Honor of Evon Zartman Vogt*, edited by Victoria Bricker and Gary Gossen, pp. 263–274. Institute for Mesoamerican Studies, State University of New York, Albany.

Witschey, Walter, and Clifford Brown

  2002   The Electronic Atlas of Ancient Maya Sites. Paper presented at the Annual Meeting of the Society for American Archaeology, Denver.

Zender, Marc U.

  2004   A Study of Classic Maya Priesthood. PhD dissertation, University of Calgary, Alberta.

Burning Sorrow

Engaging the Animacy of Social-Ecological Life Processes in Native Amazonian Death Rituals

BETH A. CONKLIN

I don't know if you can understand this, because you have never had a child die. But for a parent, when your child dies, it's a sad thing to put his body in the earth. It's cold in the earth. We keep remembering our child lying there, cold. We remember, and we are sad. It was better in the old days when the others ate the body. Then we did not think about our child's body much. We did not remember our child as much, and we were not so sad.

—Jimon Maram Oro Nao',
Posto Indígena Santo André, 1987

IN THE WAKE OF THE LOSS OF A LOVED ONE, THE Wari' of western Rondônia, Brazil,[1] experience certain material things, including the body of the deceased, to be charged with affects that have tangible effects on bereaved kin. In 1987, at the time Jimon Maram told me this, it was two years since he and his wife, Kimoin, had buried their two-year-old son. They were trying to explain why they and many other older people in their community felt

that something meaningful and helpful had been lost after 1956, when government agents and missionaries arrived in their community and forced them to bury their dead instead of roasting and consuming them (Figure 4.1).

Wari' death rituals are probably the most thoroughly documented case of funerary cannibalism in the ethnographic record. The cosmology and ideas expressed in these practices exemplify and expand upon classic principles of "animism" and lowland South American perspectivism, and my colleague Aparecida Vilaça and I have written extensively about Wari' funeral and mourning practices in relation to their values and ideas, kinship and social relations, and notions of body and spirit in different kinds of humans, animals, and cosmological forces.[2] But the body's consumption was just one step in a series of ritual acts of material erasure and transformation that unfolded over the course of about a year after a death. And animistic relations with spirits were just one kind of animate relationship with which these ritual processes

figure 4.1
A Wari' mother and her children during the "first contact" in June 1956, near Tanajura in the Dois Irmãos region. Photograph by Etta Becker Donner, courtesy of the Weltmuseum Wien, Vienna, Austria.

engaged. This chapter explores how Wari' experience the animacy of their tropical lifeworld after the death of a kinsperson and how the ritual practices with which they respond to these perceptions have shaped social and ecological dynamics in their people's history.

Today, as in the past, Wari' burn a dead person's house, possessions, crops, and household food stores soon after their death. Anything that carries traces of the former presence of the deceased goes into the fire or is excluded from daily life in other ways.[3] In the past, this began with

eliminating the body itself, which was roasted and eaten or cremated and pulverized. In the late 1950s and 1960s, government agents and missionaries intervened to coerce and persuade Wari' to stop consuming their dead. Burial has been the universal practice ever since, but Wari' still burn the deceased person's home, possessions, and other things associated with their life history and relationships. Objects that cannot be burned, such as the large grinding stones that belong to individual women, are discarded or given away to nonrelatives (Figure 4.2). Today, manufactured goods that

figure 4.2
A woman grinding maize
with a rocker stone on a
wooden slab. In the past,
such stones were one of the
only durable possessions that
could outlast death-ritual
destruction. Photograph by
Beth A. Conklin, 2011.

are too rare or expensive to destroy also are given away. Wari' see the removal of tangible traces of the dead as a practice of care that helps ease the sorrow that reminders of lost loved ones provoke for bereaved kin. They explain their practices of material destruction and transformation as a remaking of the sensory-phenomenal world that is intended to help the close relatives eventually achieve some tranquility and return to productive engagement in social life (Conklin 2001a:157–177).

In the weeks and months after a funeral, the focus of material transformation moves progressively outward into the built environment and forest. In the village, neighbors reroute paths and change the positions of their homes' doors and windows. In their agricultural fields, the bereaved family burns or uproots and discards crops with which the dead person worked. Later, senior kin go into the forest alone to visit places that evoke memories of the deceased. This culminates in a solitary ritual called *ton ho'*, which is like a kind of walking meditation. This is a discipline of focusing memory-emotions on plant materials, then burning the vegetation and sweeping over the ashes and char in order to let go of one's memories and "finish" the affective power the place has.

This is not about spirits, soul, or life-energy located in objects, nor is this about ghosts (compare with Fausto, this volume; McAnany, this volume). Wari' do encounter ghosts sometimes, and dead people's spirits can be dangerous. But those dangers and modes of action are different from and more limited than the pervasive effects of objects, places, and tangible reminders of the deceased. The potencies that Wari' experience in such things are *non-vitalistic*, relational, and contingent: they arise in encounters between a bereaved person and the specific things that evoke personal meanings and memories.

In the subjectivity of deep mourning, the world reverberates with the past. The objects and places that relatives associate with lost loved ones evoke past presences and present absences in ways that Wari' describe as tangibly visceral. They destroy things associated with their dead not because these things contain spirits, energies, or other elements that must be controlled, but because they resonate with traces of past relations that must be set aside and transformed to clear the way for other, future-oriented, revitalizing relations.

The visceral perceptions, ideas, and practices that frame Wari' bereavement engage experiences of animacy that are broader than "animistic" concerns with spirits or infusions of agency into material things. Hence, in focusing on *animacy* rather than "animism" (Kosiba, this volume), I follow Tim Ingold's (2011:67–68) distinction that "we are dealing here not with a way of believing *about* the world, but with a condition of being *in* it." Animacy is "a condition of being alive to the world, characterized by a heightened sensitivity and responsiveness, in perception and action, to an environment that is always in flux." Growth and movement, dynamic interactions with other beings and materials, and continual transformations of the capacities and configurations of things that comprise the world and human being-in-the-world are hallmarks of animacy.

In Amazonia, animacy is hypersalient. It is evident in the lively responsiveness of tropical ecosystems comprising multitudes of organisms and materials that are constantly in motion: growing, changing, dying, and decaying. Wari' are acutely attuned to how people's activities affect vegetation and animal behavior and how changes in surroundings and sensations affect people's consciousness and emotions. They talk about how human activities leave visible traces in the landscape. And they are highly sensitive to how sensory exposures influence an individual's affective experiences, the mesh of consciousness, emotions, and bodily conditions that constitute subjectivity. Their death rites recognize and work with this mutual responsiveness between persons and their lifeworlds.

This ritual remaking of the surrounding world in response to a death takes place in engagement with the specific historical, political, and environmental contexts of Wari' community life, and the unfolding over time of these ritual actions shapes collective social and material existence, as well as individual emotions and bodily states. The cognitive-symbolic schematics of Amerindian ontology and cosmology so richly developed in the work of Philippe Descola, Eduardo Viveiros de Castro, and other Amazonian ethnologists have highlighted systemic orienting frameworks of cultural constructs that shape indigenous thought and perception. But the transformations at play in Wari' death rituals also encompass affective, sensory, and material experiences, and engagements with more-than-just-human entities, affordances, and dynamics. Exploring these multifaceted processes offers an opportunity to historicize the workings of a system in an integrated ecological interpretation that shows how cultural principles participate in shaping, and responding to, the intimate, lived animacy of human experience as it unfolds in particular social-political-environmental contexts.

Throughout much of native lowland South America, the concern to promote individual and collective vitality is an organizing principle (Santos-Granero 2015). For Wari', the central value and objective of social life is to cultivate the conditions of health, safety, and sociality that foster productivity, fecundity, cooperation, and spiritual empowerment, which produce groups with many children, elders, and strong adults. The biosocial vitalities they seek to foster have taken shape in particular historical environments in which promoting the fertility of food plants and food animals and managing the risks of the infectious diseases and violence that came with contacts with other humans have been the primary parameters of concern in politics and ritual activities.

Wari' are staunchly egalitarian, and political power in their society is not power over (i.e., the capacity to control other people). It is power with: the agentive ability to move, motivate, orient, and shape people, materials, and more-than-just-human forces to produce life-supporting, security-enhancing vitality and social well-being. Men and women acquire authority and prestige by demonstrating knowledge, good judgment, and efficacy in providing food, protection, and care for others. This means coordinating relations with a variety of kinds of Wari' persons, non-Wari' outsiders and enemies, and spiritual forces. And it means caring for the emotional, as well as physical, well-being of one's kin and coresidents (see Overing and Passes 2000 on similar concerns in other native Amazonian societies). Performing the acts of death-ritual transformation is a practice of care for the emotions of others and oneself. As in the death rites that Patricia McAnany (this volume) describes for the Maya, among Wari' the authority to manage the social and spiritual vitalities disrupted by a death was seated in the family, and the care and ritual competence mobilized by senior kin was directed to revivifying relations after a death.

The quest to promote biosocial vitality and to vanquish forces of antivitality is at the center of Wari' ritual life. The rites of warfare they practiced in the past aimed to master the forces of physical and spiritual aggression and to cultivate resilience against disease and debility (Conklin 2015:78–81). The rituals with which they manage death and bereavement focus on intimate concerns with individual healing and the rebuilding of individual vitality, but the practices of material destruction and transformation also have pragmatic effects that affect broader human and more-than-human life processes.

This chapter focuses primarily on the precontact period (before 1956), when Wari' still lived outside the control of the Brazilian state. Since the 1960s, many aspects of their lives have changed with the introduction of new diseases, foods, crops, technologies, and ideas. Some aspects of their death and mourning practices have changed as well, most notably with the switch from cannibalism to burial. Other rituals and conventions for behavior in bereavement continue in more or less traditional form, though the scope and public display of postmortem destruction has lessened to some degree. Almost all families still burn the house where a dead person lived and burn, discard, or give away their possessions. Some elders continue to perform the *ton ho'* and burn places in the forest, although this is done less extensively than in the past. In this chapter, I use the past tense to describe former practices and conditions that are no longer part of contemporary Wari' life. I use the present tense to describe things that continue today.

In the precontact situation, when they lived as an independent, nearly self-sufficient people, the Wari' population's survival depended on their ability to avoid and contain the lethal risks of disease and violence that came from encounters with non-Indians. Geosocial flexibility—the capacity to avoid outsiders and move away when necessary—was the single most effective strategy for staying alive, and the destruction of houses and possessions that followed each death facilitated such mobility. Their ability to relocate elsewhere depended, in turn, on the availability of sites with soil fertile enough to grow maize (*Zea mays*), the staple crop that is central to Wari' subsistence and ritual life. Maize grows only in soil of relatively high fertility, and in this area it is found in relatively small patches of dark friable earth that contrast markedly with the denser, lighter-colored, less fertile soils that dominate the rest of the landscape. Wari' call places with the dark fertile soil that is suitable for growing maize *iri' makan*, "real earth." As I will discuss, these dark-earth sites are associated with complexes of trees and artifacts that suggest anthropogenic influences from earlier pre-Wari' native populations.

Iri' makan are foci of Wari' food production and family life: these are places where people plant their most productive gardens; harvest fruits, nuts, fiber, and wood; and wait for game to appear, attracted by fallen fruit. Many of these sites are named and remembered as places where prior generations lived. After a loved one's death, when elders go into the forest to seek out emotionally resonant things to transform with the *ton ho'* ritual of burning and clearing, they commonly focus on food-producing groves and gardens around fertile, black-earth sites.

Every act of material transformation is an ecological act. Displacing, assembling, fragmenting, destroying, and bringing things together are actions that reconfigure conditions for biological life at some level. The interventions performed in Wari' death rites—burning, clearing, and discarding materials, especially vegetative biomatter, and relocating people's movements and activities—are prime channels for human influences on tropical plants and soil. In remaking the phenomenal world in order to reshape mourners' subjective experiences, Wari' remake microconditions for microbes, plants, and animals, and the new growth that follows reconfigures conditions for people's subsequent activities. Tracing the multiple kinds of life processes that Wari' death rituals set in motion opens into thinking about how ritual actions oriented by cultural values participate in shaping historically situated lifeworlds in which symbolic, biological, sociopolitical, and ecological dynamics are thoroughly entwined, responsive, and coconstitutive.

Historical Contexts

The Wari' homeland in western Rondônia, Brazil, is a region of lowland rain forest located on the southwest periphery of the Amazon River basin, between the highlands of the Serra dos Pakaas Novos and the Guaporé and Mamoré Rivers, which are tributaries of the Madeira River, which forms the national border between Brazil and Bolivia. Today, more than four thousand Wari' live in eight primary villages and many smaller settlements near the blackwater streams that drain the Serra's western slope and alluvial basin: the Pakaas Novos, Dois Irmãos, Novo, Ocaia, Negro, Lage, and Ribeirão Rivers. The Wari' are the last remaining major group of people who speak a language in the Txapakuran (Chapakuran) family, which in past was spoken by a number of other native populations in eastern Bolivia and west-central Rondônia.

Archaeological and ethnobotanical research increasingly recognizes the upper Madeira Basin, together with the adjacent Llanos de Mojos in Bolivia, as a center of domestication for a number of important crops, including manioc, peanut, peach palm, coca, and tobacco (Clement et al. 2016), as well as now-extinct species of rice (Hilbert et al. 2017). The region has a long history of human habitation, and studies by William Denevan, Clark Erickson, John Walker in Bolivia, and Eduardo Neves and colleagues in Brazil near the Guaporé River have documented extensive networks of ancient earthworks, shell middens, and other features that indicate intensive occupation and modification of the landscape. Wari' territory lies nearby, but the only archaeological work that has been done was a small survey of a single site by Maria Dulce Gaspar of the Museu Nacional in Rio de Janeiro. Gaspar surveyed the site that Wari' call Kit (Knife), which was the only source of stone for stone axes in the area they controlled before contact. Radiocarbon dating of a single sample from Gaspar's excavations indicates this site has been used by native people for at least twenty-five hundred years (Conklin 2015).

The Wari' came to occupy this region a few centuries ago. Myths and oral history locate their origin in the mountainous Serra dos Pakaas Novos and recount how their ancestors moved down from the Serra and spread into the lowlands, probably during the eighteenth and early nineteenth centuries, or perhaps earlier. The region into which they moved seems to have been mostly empty of other indigenous inhabitants, probably because diseases introduced by colonizers had wiped out earlier native occupants.

In the nineteenth and first half of the twentieth century, Wari' were a fiercely independent people committed to an isolationist foreign policy.

They had no trade, no intermarriage, and no sustained, peaceful relations with any other non-Wari' human beings. By the 1930s, most other native groups in western Rondônia had been devastated by epidemics, enslavement, massacres, and dispossession inflicted by the settlers, traders, rubber tappers, and prospectors who pushed the frontier of the expanding market economy into the region. Wari' held out considerably longer, until the mid-1950s, when interethnic tensions escalated with a series of massacres perpetrated by gunmen whom local rubber businessmen hired to go into the forest and kill Indians. Under pressure to make the region safe for rubber extraction and protect the investments of the rubber bosses and the banks that were backing them, the national government sent teams of backwoodsmen to pacify the hostile Indians. The years 1961–1962 were the tipping point, when the great majority of Wari' were swept into the contact process; the last holdouts succumbed in 1969. In each "first contact" situation, wave after wave of measles, mumps, whooping cough, influenza, colds, malaria, and other diseases followed. Within two or three years, about 60 percent of the local population—three out of every five people—were dead.

This story of demographic devastation is a story that has been repeated in every case in which a formerly immunologically isolated or semi-isolated population has been infected with the pathogens that circulate in larger cosmopolitan populations where most people are infected during childhood and, thus, acquire immunity. What was unusual about the Wari' is that they managed to hold out for so long, avoiding much of the epidemic disease and violence that wiped out neighboring indigenous groups. Wari' survived into the second half of the twentieth century as an intact, independent society, in large part because of their adherence to two key social principles: a radical ethnic alterity that defined non-Wari' outsiders as likely enemies (Conklin 2001b, 2008; Vilaça 2010) and the geosocial flexibility that their egalitarianism and material nonaccumulation facilitated (Conklin 2001a:115–120, 2008, 2015).

Before contact, Wari' regarded all non-Wari' humans as *wijam*, "enemies," whom they treated with categorical mistrust and, in most cases, hostility. They avoided encounters with outsiders when they could and attacked them strategically when they needed to. Wari' warriors were famously effective at discouraging outsiders from settling or even venturing into large parts of their territory, and a complex of ideational, pragmatic, and ritual ways of dealing with non-Wari' humans helped put distance between themselves and potentially dangerous outsiders (Conklin 1997, 2008). When disease or attacks by Brazilians did strike, the flexibility of their social organization allowed families and communities to respond quickly by moving, relocating, splitting up, and regrouping as needed.

Individual Wari' biographies and oral histories testify to frequent changes of residence and shifts in the composition of residential groupings. Families moved and communities relocated, split up, and came together in response to events such as death or sickness, interpersonal tensions, attacks by enemies, and the expanding presence of Brazilian and Bolivian settlers, especially in the rubber-rich region around the Ouro Preto River. Not being tied to leaders or fixed group affiliations, and with few material possessions and no gravesites or monuments to defend, Wari' could move when necessary. Their ability to join other communities was facilitated by a model of human biology that sees kinship and body-based identities as mutable and contingent, created by transfers of body substances that can create new affiliations among previously unrelated people and between people and animal spirits (Conklin 2001a:111–131; Conklin and Morgan 1996).

Before the Brazilian government imposed new community leadership structures (which developed mostly in the 1990s–2000s), Wari' social organization was fluid and egalitarian. The precontact society was comprised of small residential groups that were loosely affiliated with several named, kin-based, territorial subgroups that had no formal political structure or leadership.[4] Individuals could foreground ties to their mother's or father's kin as they chose, and they shifted their identities and reframed their social affiliations to fit changing life circumstances (Conklin 2001a:115–140; Conklin and Morgan 1996; Vilaça 2002).

figure 4.3
Wari' leadership is fluid and contextual; individuals take the lead in activities in which others recognize their special expertise or good judgment. Here, a respected elder directs the visitors' performance in a *hŭroroin* festival ritual at Santo André. Photograph by Beth A. Conklin, 1986.

Wari' are strongly resistant to asymmetrical relations. Leadership was, and to a large extent still is, situational and ephemeral: they traditionally had no chiefs, no nobility, and no age grades or other internal social groupings. Men and women gain authority by demonstrating their capacities to procure, produce, and share food (especially maize, meat, and fish), raise healthy children, protect their kin and coresidents from harm, and cultivate amity, social cooperation, and loyalty. Authority is contextual; a man or a woman who takes the lead in organizing or directing one activity (such as a musical performance, festival, collective hunt, war expedition, or move to a new site) often purposefully fades into the background in other contexts (Conklin 2015; Figure 4.3). Like the Xinguano chiefs described by Carlos Fausto (this volume), whose authority is based on trust built by fostering their people's growth and well-being, individual Wari' acquire authority through cumulative acts of generosity and cordiality that demonstrate competence, good judgment, and responsibility in caring for others.

The destruction of houses and crops and the destruction or dispersal of possessions after each death reinforces egalitarianism. This practice negates intergenerational inheritance of material goods, which some archaeologists identify as a major factor in social inequality in "premodern" societies (Smith et al. 2010). Death-related destruction essentially presses the material reset button, taking households back to zero again and again. Since death happens to every family sometime, this is an impressively effective mechanism to dampen economic inequality.

Real hardship ensues with the loss of crops and food stores. Maize is the one food that Wari' traditionally stored in quantity, in carefully stacked golden pyramids elevated on platforms shielded by palm thatch. Wari' treat maize differently than other foods. Whereas norms for sharing allow people to ask for, and expect to be given, almost any other thing (except essential tools) that they can see in someone's home (which inevitably leads to much strategic hiding of possessions), maize is off-limits to routine begging and borrowing. Special protocols surround its handling, reinforced by myths about its humanlike spirit. In view of the care with which Wari' treat maize, it seems contradictory that they burned so much of it in response to a death, thus wasting its food value. However, this ritual depletion was countered somewhat by the surplus production of maize in anticipation of celebrations. Wari' parties and intergroup festivals require the hosts to provide large amounts of fermented maize drink (*tokwa*, called *chicha* in Portuguese and also contemporary Spanish). Socially ambitious families plant extra crops each year in anticipation of brewing large quantities of drink when the community hosts a party. However, death imposes a hiatus in party-giving: it is disrespectful to sing and celebrate while people in the community are in mourning,

and this pause in partying is supposed to last about a year. Thus, at the level of a community's food supplies, maize that would have gone into making extra maize beer (*chicha*) is freed for dietary consumption, which helps to compensate for the maize that is destroyed in the death-burning.

Missionaries and Brazilian government employees have criticized Wari' for their irrational waste of the food and scarce material goods that are burned or discarded in these rituals. The Wari' system does not fit the capitalist logic of investing in material possessions as a source of security. Nor does this system fit the logic of the native Northwest Coast potlatch, in which destroying or giving away goods was a form of status competition, a performance that asserted prestige by demonstrating wealth abundance (cf. Barnett 1938). Wari' destruction is also performative; what it performs is not material wealth, but the morality of bonds of affection and proper care for one's kin.

Wari' are well aware of how disruptive their bereavement practices are for individuals and families. For members of the household in which the dead person lived, the loss of their home, possessions, and crops throws them into radical dependency on others. The immediate family usually goes to live with relatives elsewhere, which often means moving to another village. For months, the bereaved family is expected to do little or no work: they do not farm, hunt, fish, or forage, and they eat little. People in deep mourning look terrible; they grow gaunt and haggard and spend large parts of every day indoors, crying, keening, or lying in silence (Figure 4.4). Others treat them gently and deferentially, but the crowding and extra mouths to feed strain the host household. Difficult as this is, caring for bereaved kin is one of the strongest and most valued commitments among Wari', and this prolonged dependency incurs debts of future reciprocity that strengthen familial bonds.

In his introduction to this volume, Kosiba calls attention to Catherine Allen's (1988:16–17) point that what we may think of as a classic indigenous cultural feature—namely, Andean religious relations to the land—is also part of a political history of holding out against landlords and tax commissions and

figure 4.4
After disassembling and burning their home and chopping down the huge mango tree his wife had loved, the widower Oro Iram spent his days sitting in silence by the remains, mourning her passing. Photograph by Beth A. Conklin, 2010.

missionaries. In the Wari' case, their acephalous egalitarianism and relative freedom from permanent ties to possessions, places, gravesites, and leaders helped them hold out as an intact, almost entirely self-sufficient society in the face of the biopolitical threats of diseases, enslavement, interethnic killings, and impoverishment that afflicted native people on the frontiers of the expanding Brazilian market economy. Their ability to avoid these threats by relocating when necessary depended, in turn, on local environmental affordances.

Anthropogenic Traces in the Landscape

When Wari' moved down from the Serra dos Pakaas Novos into the lowlands, they were fortunate to find the forested landscape dotted with small areas of *iri' makan*, the dark fertile soil that is good for growing maize. Generations of Wari' settled and farmed at these sites, but since the 1970s, government policies have forced them to live in bigger villages at locations that have poor soil but are more accessible by boat or truck from the administrative center in the city of Guajará-Mirim. Wari' continue to grow their maize at *iri' makan*, and most families have a second house near these distant maize fields. The palm fruits, nuts, and other useful materials from trees that grow near these sites draw people to return often.

The data on which this study is based come primarily from the community of Santo André and its environs, south and west of the Pakaas Novos River, where I have done ethnographic fieldwork since the mid-1980s. In this specific area, dark-earth *iri' makan* are found almost exclusively on interfluvial terra firma along small rivers and streams, away from the larger waterways of the Pakaas Novos and Mamoré Rivers.[5] In the past, non-Indians (rubber trappers, traders, prospectors, and military personnel) traveled and settled mostly via the bigger rivers, so the agroecological pattern that oriented Wari' to farm and live in the interior terra firma helped reduce the risk of encounters with hostile outsiders and the diseases and violence they brought.

When Wari' farmers are looking for places to plant a new field of maize, they look for a characteristic complex of fruit-bearing palm trees, especially aricury (Syagrus sp.) and buriti (Mauritia flexuosa). Groves of Brazil nuts (Bertholletia excelsa) sometimes occur in the vicinity as well. Wari' often find these sites littered with ceramic shards whose styles and designs they recognize as having been made by other, non-Wari' native people. To date, no soil analyses have been done, but the combination of dark fertile soil, indicator tree species, and concentrations of indigenous artifacts suggests that the sites Wari' call iri' makan are probably what ecologists call Amazonian dark earth (ADE), or terra preta. ADEs are anthropogenic, created by a variety of human activities and the waste and by-products of human habitation in interaction with microbial populations in the soil. Discarded animal and fish bones, shells, and scales; human feces; and the remains of household cooking fires, ceramic pots, and burned wattle and daub and roof thatch are potential contributors to the formation of ADEs (Erickson 2003:479–481). In Brazil, ADEs are often called terra preta do índio, "the Indian's black earth," because they tend to be full of broken pottery, stone axe heads, and other evidence that native people occupied these sites intensively in the past.[6]

If the sites that Wari' call iri' makan are indeed ADEs, then these were created by other native populations who came before them. Wari' have not lived in this region long enough, nor have they occupied these sites intensively enough, to be the originators of anthropogenic soil formation. Rather, they took advantage of the fortuitous existence of these fertile soils to support their maize-centered pattern of subsistence and a system of ritual life in which

tokwa, maize chicha, is a central element in every festival and celebration (Conklin 2001a:41–45).

As the most important places where Wari' farm, harvest tree products, and, in the past, located their villages, the dark-earth iri' makan are foci of family life and personal histories. Feeding others and eating together are prime values in Wari' social relations, and when people talk about dead relatives, many of their most pleasurable and poignant recollections coalesce around these sites: eating fruit, planting or harvesting, camping in the woods while breaking Brazil nuts, or visiting old garden sites. These fertile, food-rich places are affectively resonant, layered with personal meanings and memories of emotional bonds among kin. In a society that in the past had no written records, monuments, memorials, or inherited property, large trees are one of the more durable markers of past events and the passage of time. Trees are geographic markers in Wari' stories of events such as hunting trips and family excursions in the forest, and elders often measure the length of their lives and recall the growth of children against the size of certain trees, especially Brazil-nut trees and food-producing palms. Not surprisingly, these are some of the most common places where bereaved kin perform ton ho'. Since Wari' gardens and groves tend to be located at or near fertile black-earth sites, the death-ritual acts of clearing and burning forest vegetation may have interesting ecological implications.

Elsewhere in Amazonia, pioneering research by ethnobiologists and archaeologists, including Darryl Posey (Posey and Balick 2006), William Balée (1998, 2013), Eduardo Neves (Neves et al. 2003), Clark Erickson (2003, 2008), John Walker (2008), Michael Heckenberger (Heckenberger et al. 2003, 2008), Glenn Shepard (Shepard and Ramirez 2011), and others, has transformed understandings of the region's ecology by showing that many "natural" features, such as ADEs and the distribution of certain tree species, are partially the product of human activities. Key questions that are under debate involve how much and which parts of the forest are anthropogenic, the biochemical mechanisms that mediate human effects on the environment, and how much intentionality was involved in the human actions that shaped these "cultural forests" (Balée 2013). Most research and thinking about human inputs into the formation of ADEs has focused on agricultural practices and domestic routines whose effects accumulate over the long run with repetitive patterns of using fire, preparing food, and disposing of waste. The episodic but patterned environmental interventions that Wari' carry out in their ritual responses to an individual death suggest another possible mode of anthropogenic contributions to shaping forest ecology: they call attention to how cultural values and symbolic systems orient human actions to focus on places and things where social meanings coalesce.

These dark-earth sites tend to have characteristic microecological conditions, especially concentrations of useful trees and fertile soil, that respond to fire, clearing, and fallowing in ways that change and even intensify their productivity. The following analysis traces the interplay between social-symbolic and material-ecological dynamics in the multifaceted life processes with which Wari' death rites interact. Like the temporal-spatial trajectory in which this year-long ritual process unfolds, I begin in the immediacy of bereavement, with a sensory ethnography of Wari' mourners' intimate affective experiences. I then move progressively outward, examining how the conventional practices through which Wari' manage death and bereavement affect relations of care, dependency, and reciprocity within families. I end by considering how these ritual practices fit into the multispecies matrix of life in this tropical forest.

This is an ecological perspective on Wari' ritual, but it is not the kind of "ecosystem" model that Roy Rappaport (1968), for example, developed in his famous analysis of a Melanesian ceremonial system. Rather than serving as a "homeostat" regulating mechanism to maintain environmental factors within a viable range (Rappaport 1968:229), Wari' death rites change the microecology of places in the forest in ways that, in turn, change how people dwell in relation to these places. In this open-ended dynamic of mutual responsiveness between humans and their lifeworld, animacy—the "heightened sensitivity and responsiveness, in perception and action, to an environment that is always in flux" (Ingold 2011:67–68)—is the intimate, experiential driver of individual ritual actions.

Affective Assemblages in Bereavement

Wari' say that the explicit intent of their postmortem practices of material transformation is to eliminate all perceptible reminders of the dead person's former presence and life history, in order to help bereaved kin eventually come to terms with their grief and reengage in productive social life. They are highly sensitive to the ways that visceral responses affect emotions and bodily vitality, and they have a well-developed medical model of how sensory experiences affect memory, emotion, and physiology in ways that make prolonged mourning dangerous to individual health and social productivity (Conklin 2001a:142). Wari' say that intense, unrelieved sadness constricts the heart and slows and weakens the blood, making people grow thin and vulnerable to sickness and even death. To ease suffering and lessen the potential pathology of obsessive grieving, they consider it imperative to transform mourners' sensory environments by eliminating or changing things that remind them of the deceased.

When Wari' talk about how they experience places and things associated with lost loved ones, they describe the sense of things exerting a pull, compelling responses that are mixes of memories, emotions, and bodily sensations. They do not name this force, nor even consider it to be an independent force in itself. Rather, these felt potencies emerge in real-time encounters between an individual and specific objects, places, and sensory stimuli of sounds, smells, sights, and tactile feelings.

This experience comes close to contemporary theoretical notions of affective assemblages (Bertelson and Murphie 2010:148). A key point is that objects and places acquire affective power from their histories of involvement in events and social relations (Ahmed 2010:33). Affective assemblages coalesce in-between, in encounters between individuals and the many social and material contexts in which they engage. Drawing on the work of Félix Guattari (1996:158), Lone Bertelson and Andrew Murphie (2010:140) identify three aspects of "affect" that offer a framework for thinking about different dimensions of Wari' interactions with material things associated with dead kin: the human's inclusion in *matter* (the materiality of existence as a living being); the enfolding *register* of feelings and representations; and the body's power of *acting* and being acted upon, the capacity to affect and be affected.

The materiality of human existence begins with the body and its sensory-emotional-agentive capacities. Eduardo Viveiros de Castro (2005:54) has defined the Amerindian body itself as "a bundle of affects and capacities." "What I call a body," he writes, "is not a synonym for distinctive substance or characteristic anatomy; it is an assemblage of affects or ways of being that constitute a habitus." Wari' understand this bodily assemblage as an integrated whole that comprises what we call physiology, mind, emotion, and spirit. The human being is open to and interactive with the world: permeable, mutable, and constantly created and re-created as elements move among people, spirits, and material things.

The work of healing in Wari' bereavement is primarily memory work, carried out by acting on tangible things in order to influence the sensations and emotions they stimulate. To help people gradually detach from memories that provoke sadness and impossible longing, they eradicate or transform features of the social and physical environments that remind them of the dead. Wari' recognize the power of sensory experience to shape subjectivity in the many ways that tangible reminders affect sensations, emotions, and behavior in multiple registers. In the verbal/aural register, linguistic distancing operates: everyone stops speaking the dead person's name and kin terms, and they avoid referring to the dead except by using oblique, depersonalized, and usually plural terms. Visually, what people see around them changes in the village space and parts of the forest. Kinesthetically, the burning of houses, rerouting of pathways, and abandoning and avoiding of particular places change their spatial patterns of

movement, dwelling, and food-getting activities (Conklin 2001a:84–85). Altering material conditions (the idea of "matter" as one aspect of affect) changes bereaved individuals' subjective experience of the world ("feelings and representations").

In each phase of Wari' death rites, destruction and transformation is a prelude to generating a new situation comprised of different images, sensations, meanings, and relationships. In the precontact past, this began at the funeral with the transformation and erasure of the body, which is the most direct reminder of who the dead person was while alive. After the funeral, the process of ritual material transformation moves progressively outward in space and spiritual proximity. At each stage, affect-saturated foci are wiped out, removed, or transformed and then replaced or overlain with something new. Wari' act upon the register of feelings and representations in a symbolic trajectory in which representations of the dead person are gradually depersonalized and the individual human death is assimilated and encompassed in a vision of the person's metaphysical transformation into an ancestor-animal, with corresponding changes in their relations with living kin. Wari' say that the eventual letting go of old ties and the affirmation of a new, more distant but continuing relationship with the loved one in a new form helps bereaved kin regain their will to engage in social life and productivity ("agency").

Distancing and Destruction in Amazonian Death Practices

The emphasis that Wari' place on erasing and transforming tangible traces of the dead has parallels in some other native Amazonian societies. Many groups burn or abandon the houses of the dead, and sometimes this extends to burning and abandoning entire villages. Some groups also burn or disperse material possessions of the deceased. Much scholarship on the cultural management of death and bereavement in native Amazonia has explored how such acts of postmortem distancing are often associated with emphases on "forgetting" the dead and "genealogical amnesia" in which memories of ancestors extend back only two or three generations.[7] However, there is a great deal of variation across Amazonia, as Carlos Fausto's account (in this volume) of ancestrality in Brazil's Upper Xingu shows. Jean-Pierre Chaumeil's (2013) comprehensive survey of lowland South American death practices documents a broad array of distinct mortuary complexes and practices that range from wiping out and forgetting to memorializing ancestors. The distancing-and-forgetting complex seems to be especially common in small, relatively egalitarian communities in western Amazonia, such as the Jivaroans in eastern Ecuador described by Anne Christine Taylor. Summarizing key features of this pattern, Taylor writes:

> It has become a commonplace of Amazonian ethnology to point out the absence in lowland societies of anything resembling ancestor cults, the shallowness of genealogical memory as well as the paucity and apparent simplicity of most funerary rituals, and the general scarcity of tombs or indeed of any marked spaces durably associated with the dead. Far from stressing continuity with their ancestors and enshrining their memory in names, epics or monuments, lowland Amerindians expend considerable time and ingenuity in losing their dead, forgetting their names and deeds and emphasizing their remoteness from the world of the living. (Taylor 1993:653)

Wari' exemplify this orientation to respond to death with practices of erasure, distancing, and nonmemorialization. They are unusual only in the thoroughness with which they carry this out: in addition to avoiding the names of the dead and destroying their homes and possessions, they used to eliminate the dead person's physical body, and they continue to destroy crops and food stores and transform places in the forest associated with their memory. The specific techniques they use—burning, discarding, avoiding, and changing patterns of human activity and movement—do not just delete prior forms. They also contribute to the emergence of new social and ecological conditions.

Orienting Affects: Food, Feeding, and Biosocial Vitality

Affectively charged places and things emerge from intimate, idiosyncratic interpersonal histories. But social values influence which places and things Wari' tend to experience as significant and as foci for intervention. Feeding and being fed is a core value that organizes trust and affection in many domains of their social relations. Kinship and family life revolve around acts of care and nurturance, and extended families are the primary horizon within which food, materials, and social labor circulate.

Wari' are deeply concerned with promoting and protecting the biosocial vitality of their kin and communities—the conditions of growth, security, and thriving that foster the fecundity, productivity, social integration, and spiritual empowerment that produce groups with many healthy children, strong adults, and elders. Food-relations link Wari' with each other and with the animals, spirits, plants, and places that participate in the many relations of feeding and being fed that make up a human life. Individuals gain status, respect, and authority by demonstrating their ability to coordinate relations with a variety of Wari' persons, non-Wari' enemies and other outsiders, and spiritual forces in order to avoid harm (especially attacks by enemies and spirits) and to promote relations that increase food abundance. Meat obtained by hunting is the most highly valued food, and white-lipped peccary, a kind of wild boar, is the most highly valued kind of meat (see Conklin 2001a).

The meanings of food and feeding in social life and in cosmological relations between Wari' and animal spirits form a nexus of symbolism and practice as these unfold over the trajectory of Wari' death rites. In the past, the traditional yearlong ritual process began with the funeral at which the body was eaten collectively, then continued in various individual acts of ritual remembrance and material transformation, concluding with an extended family hunt and community feast. Food relations are central in the cosmology and imagery through which Wari' imagine the fate of the dead and their transformed relations with their living kin.

figure 4.5
A white-lipped peccary
killed by Torein Oro Nao'.
Photograph by Beth A.
Conklin, 1985.

Wari' believe that when someone dies, the human spirit goes to live in an underworld society that is located beneath the deep waters of rivers and lakes. In an arrangement whose origins are told in myth, the Wari' ancestors dwell underwater in a society that is led by a giant master of animals–like figure named Towira Towira. *Towira* means "testicle," and the doubling of the term highlights the size of his genitals, which hang below his knees. Fertility imagery surrounds this underworld, which is called *paxikom*, the word for "womb." In

everyday life, animal fertility manifests in the productivity of hunting and fishing, and this is the primary relation at stake in Wari' dealings with the denizens of the underworld. Towira Towira controls the movements of certain game animals, fish, and the Wari' ancestor-animals (Conklin 2001a).

As the master of the underworld, Towira Towira occupies a position of permanent, asymmetric leadership that is markedly different from the contingent, acephalous fluidity that has been the dominant pattern of authority in recent Wari' history. Stories of Towira Towira and other mythic leaders (who often appear in animal form) serve as repositories of knowledge of other possible forms of social organization and ways of dealing with hierarchical authority.

For Wari', the prime significance of their relations with the denizens of Towira Towira's underwater society is that these relations are essential to food security. When the ancestors who are the spirits of deceased Wari' decide to leave the water to visit their living kin back on the surface of the earth, they take on the bodies of white-lipped peccaries, a kind of wild boar that historically was the single most important source of meat in Wari' diets. Individual ancestor-peccaries look for hunters who are their own kin and offer themselves to be shot, to ensure that their meat will go to feed the relatives they love and remember (Figure 4.5). The ancestors can also send their allies, *jami kom*, the water spirits from Towira Towira's tribe. When these (non-Wari') water spirits emerge from the underworld, they manifest as dense schools of fish that are easy to kill. The special relationship that Wari' have with dead loved ones who have joined the world of animal spirits empowers them to call peccaries or fish in times of need, by singing songs from the myth that recalls the origin of this cosmic arrangement (Conklin 2001a:214–223).

In traditional funerals, the cooking and consumption of the body marked the beginning of this sociometaphysical transition: no longer part of the community of living meat-eaters, the dead person's spirit was moving into the otherworld of animal spirits, from which they eventually would return as meat to feed their living kin. Relations with the deceased shift outward, from dwelling on loss to accepting the death as part of ongoing exchanges between the living and the dead, Wari' and animal spirits. The ritual hunt and feast that mark the official end of the period of public mourning ostensibly mark the bereaved family's recognition of this change in their relations with the relative who is now part of the animal world (Conklin 2001a).

Memory and affection fuel this flow of nourishment from the underworld spirits. But memories fade in the afterlife just as they do in the minds of living people. It is mostly the spirits of recently deceased individuals who remember the kin they left behind and miss them most acutely, and it is these recently dead spirits who motivate the peccary herd to visit. Each death, thus, renews and strengthens the food-giving commitments in which the ancestor-animal spirits come to sing, dance, and bring meat and fish to feed their living relatives.

Places and Trees

The last phase of material destruction in Wari' death rituals is *ton ho'*, the "sweeping" ritual in which senior relatives cut and burn vegetation at places in the forest that are sedimented with traces and recollections of the dead person's former presence and events that took place there. This comes after several months of mourning have passed, when an individual begins to feel emotionally ready to move beyond the most intense period of grieving. The cultural model of personhood that locates food and feeding at the center of Wari' notions of social value orients them to seek out gardens and fields, fruit and nut trees, and other specific places that are linked to memories of times when they and the dead person connected around the food that they cultivated, gathered, fished, hunted, or ate together. Places saturated with food-related memories are not randomly distributed across the landscape; rather, they coalesce especially at the sites of fertile dark earth and fruit-bearing palms that Wari' call *iri' makan*, as well as the Brazil-nut groves (often found nearby) where families spend weeks camping together while breaking nuts.

At each memory-rich site, the kinsperson clears a wide circle, cutting small trees and brush with slow, deliberate movements. As they cut the vegetation, they think intensely, bringing specific images and memories of their relative's life into focus in their mind. They walk very slowly around the circular space, eyes on the ground, thinking about their loved one. They move with a bent posture and gestures that are specific to this ritual, coordinating the kinesthesia of bodily movements with deliberate memory practices. Using a hand or foot, they slowly turn over an individual leaf or plant and stare intently at its underside as they bring specific memories of the deceased into focus, silently thinking, "Koromikat," "I remember." Then they cut the small trees and brushy vegetation in a wide circle and go home, leaving it to dry. Sometime later, they return and set fire to the circular clearing. After the ashes have cooled, they perform the final act of sweeping (*ton ho'*). Walking slowly through the blackened clearing, staring at the ashes and char, they summon memories of the deceased one last time, then brush over the space and purposefully set aside each memory, thinking, "They are gone."

Afterward, Wari' say, the place "looks completely different." Young plants soon sprout among the cinders and verdant green spreads over the space, interrupted by the blackened remains of partially burned logs. Each small burned-over site with its new vegetation stands as a marker of the bereaved kinsperson's depth of feeling, an affirmation of human agency expressed in a commitment to do the right thing: to honor the deceased but also to reengage with productive social life.

Acts of destruction do not simply erase memories. As Elizabeth Hallam and Jenny Hockey (2001:92) observe, "The deliberate destruction, burning or locking away of such objects [material possessions of the dead] can further embed them within memory." What *ton ho'* and the acts of ritual destruction do is to attach new meanings and sensory experiences that add new layers to the original memories that the thing or place evoked, including new memories and narratives of the kinsperson's performance of the acts of remembering, crying, cutting, burning, and sweeping. The progressive complexification of material elements, meanings, and memories comprises new affective assemblages, bundles of potential experience that are not only cognitive and visual but also kinesthetic (with movements, postures, and gestures), aural (with the distinct melodies of death keening and crying), olfactory (with burning and new growth), and tactile, as the feel of the place changes over time as new vegetation emerges in newly sunlit spaces.

Microecological Transformations

Burning and clearing change the conditions of microzones, releasing nutrients into the soil, exposing lower levels to sunlight, and altering microbial populations and vegetative growth. After performing *ton ho'*, Wari' avoid those sites for some time, which effects a kind of fallowing. Clearing, burning, and fallowing echo processes of slash-and-burn (swidden) horticulture, but the idiosyncratic timing of death rituals diverges from the ordinary spatial-seasonal routines of Wari' horticulture. The spatial extent and intensity of a single ritual event is quite small, but it may be worth considering whether the repetition of such acts over time in concentrated areas with particular vegetative complexes might have anthropogenic effects. Research in Amazonian ecology increasingly recognizes the roles of what geographer Suzanna Hecht and ethnobotanist Darryl Posey (1989:17) have called "soft technology": agricultural practices such as cultivation, crop rotation, and uses of fertilizer and fire that do not have long-lasting effects on the landscape and, thus, are difficult to detect archaeologically (Denevan 2001:34). Geographer Antoinette M. G. A. WinklerPrins (2009) has highlighted the widespread practice of "sweep and char" in contemporary Amazonian households and villages where garden debris, tree litter and weeds, and household refuse are swept into piles and burned, often on a daily basis. Studies of the technologies and ideologies that have shaped anthropogenic influences on Amazonian landscapes have highlighted the effects of patterns and routines of producing, processing, consuming, and discarding food and resources, as well as patterns of settling, dwelling, and moving.

This Wari' case study points to ritual as another potential form of anthropogenic "soft" technology that is more episodic but also culturally, socially, and ecologically patterned. Burning a house, which is the most common form of death destruction in Amazonia, deposits carbon in a concentrated area that also typically contains the remains of cooking fires, human waste, discarded ceramics, fish and animal bones, and other

figure 4.6
Palm fronds assembled for roofing a house. Photograph by Beth A. Conklin, 2006.

remnants of human habitation. Amazonian house construction relocates significant amounts of bio-matter, especially to make the thick thatch used to cover roofs and often walls as well. Wari' traditionally lived mostly in individual nuclear family homes with lean-to roofs made of dozens or hundreds of long heavy palm fronds (Figure 4.6). In other native groups, large multifamily "maloca" dwellings are even more vegetation intensive: Steve Beckerman (1977) estimated that among the Barí in Venezuela, thatching a single multifamily communal house required 750,000 fronds collected from 125,000 palms spread over a region of 40 km². As Erickson (2003:480) points out, thatch is replaced every few years, making houses significant concentrators of biomatter and of char and ash when they burn (Figure 4.7).

At the forest sites where Wari' perform *ton ho'*, the immediate effects are visible in changes in light,

soil, and vegetation. Burning and clearing affect the propagation of certain fruit and nut trees that typically grow at or near dark-earth sites. Removing vegetative cover that blocks light facilitates the growth of tree seedlings that require significant amounts of sunlight to grow (Scoles, Gribel, and Klein 2011). The *burití* palm tree (*Mauritia flexuosa*), whose fruit is an important attractant of animals and fish, flourishes when fire removes leaf litter, vines, and brush. Fire stimulates the emergence of *babaçu* (*Orbignea phalerata*) seedlings, which germinate underground and grow downward into the earth until the ground above is cleared by fire; then, the seedling makes a U-turn and grows up out of the earth (Balée 2013:19).

Nutrient-rich char and ash support the growth of seedlings and young, tender plants, and some, like *Inajá* palms (*Maximiliana* sp.), are resistant to fire. Across Amazonia, many indigenous and

figure 4.7
The thick thatch of a Wari' house roof. Photograph by Beth A. Conklin, 1987.

nonindigenous rural people use fire to maintain landscapes of fire-resistant (pyrophilic) palm species that are useful as food, artisanal materials, and game animal attractants. After a low-intensity fire, many palms resprout from underground tissue, producing seedlings that grow more rapidly than seedlings that sprout from seeds (Kauffman 1991). The Kayapó of central Brazil, for example, use fire to promote the growth of *tucumá* (*Astrocayum* sp.) close to villages, which attracts collared peccaries to be killed (Hecht 2008:152; see also Beck 2006).

Brazil-nut trees are a "gap-loving" species: to regenerate, they depend on light reaching the forest floor. Burning kills Brazil-nut seedlings, but sprouts regrow from stumps of various sizes. In a field study of Brazil-nut ecology, Paulo Paiva, Marcelino Guedes, and Claudia Funi (2011:512–513) found that the more times a site had been cut and burned, the denser the seedlings: "Resprouts from

slash-and-burn events enjoy several advantages when competing against most plants started from seed. . . . The BN [Brazil nut] resprouts possess a deep and well-developed root system that favors water and nutrient intake. . . . Their above-ground growth in full-light conditions helps them cope with the dense and tangled understory of early forest succession. This ability to resprout renders the tree particularly resilient to SC [shifting cultivation] disturbances."

The only ethnobotanical study that has been done among the Wari' was carried out by Glenn Shepard, an ethnographer and ethnobotanist at the Museu Goeldi Amazonian research center in Belém, Brazil. Shepard studied Brazil-nut groves in Wari' territory as part of a project that demonstrated the likelihood that humans were responsible for the diffusion of Brazil nuts across the Amazon Basin (Shepard and Ramirez 2011). Archaeological evidence increasingly supports the hypothesis that the distribution of Brazil-nut groves, which are often associated with ADEs, resulted from indigenous management in the past (Neves 2016:230–234). "The juxtaposition of black earth and a Brazil nut grove is not unusual, and is no doubt repeated in many other parts of Amazonia," observes William Balée (2013:28). "A series of connections between nature, culture, and history make it logical. Brazil nut trees help keep people in the vicinity, because the seeds are good to eat, and long-term human occupation helps form black earth. Later generations of people can appreciate the concentration of resources, of which black soils and Brazil nuts are only two, afforded by ancient agriculturalists in the Amazon Basin."

In his field study of the Wari', Shepard recognized the ecological implications of their practice of death-ritual burning. In an article coauthored with Henri Ramirez (Shepard and Ramirez 2011:48), he observed: "When Wari' families return to their customary Brazil nut groves after a death in the family, they burn the underbrush and discarded fruit capsules from the previous years' collecting seasons, altering the appearance of the grove and eliminating physical reminders of past moments shared with the deceased. By generating localized disturbance and fertilizing soil with ash, this practice certainly facilitates Brazil nut sapling recruitment." If (and this remains to be tested in the field) other useful plant species also respond to the ecological interventions enacted in Wari' death rituals by propagating new growth, then this represents an elegant social-symbolic-ecological synergy: the cultural values that cause Wari' to transform particular forest places that are linked to the social meanings of food change microecological conditions in ways that may enhance concentrations of socially significant food plants, especially trees that produce fruit and nuts. There may be effects on animal behavior and hunting as well, since palm fruits attract peccary, deer, tapir, paca, agouti, and other game.

Despite—or perhaps because of—the lengths to which Wari' go to destroy tangible remains of their dead, the dead are not really forgotten. Rather, they come to be felt in different nonhuman forms. After the year of formal mourning ends, when most tangible traces have been erased, Wari' encounter their ancestors in peccary spirits that offer themselves to be hunted. And they recognize traces of past presences and events in the human-inflected landscape, inscribed in the patterning of plants that grow up out of the ashes of the rituals performed by caring kin.

The transformative practices through which Wari' shift their relations with the dead into more diffuse vitalities of plant growth and game populations resonate with Fausto's account of how the Quarup ritual among Xinguano villagers creates "vegetal continuity" after the chief's death. Wari' displace their relations with their dead, relocating affective foci away from static objects and sites and into generative, future-oriented relationships with aspects of the food-giving forest that have sustained generations of people living, caring, losing, and grieving in this particular place.

In this vision of Wari' death rites, the ecological intensification of food-fertility resonates with the symbolic trajectory of the ritual process that assimilates each individual death into the cosmological flow of vitality and renews and reinforces the ongoing, life-supporting relations between living people and the ancestor-animal spirits. In the historical context of precontact Wari' life, the material destruction enacted in their death rites also reinforced the egalitarian, geosocial flexibility that was essential to the population's health and biopolitical survival.

The affectively potent assemblages of ecological features, cultural meanings, personal histories, and emotions that coalesce around gardens and groves to make these focal sites for ritual work reflect the centrality of food, feeding, and commensality in Wari' notions of value, in which kinship, sociality, and authority are inextricably interwoven with material pragmatics of care and conditions for thriving. Wari' perceptions of animacy—the bundles of shifting meanings, materials, symbols, sensations, and sentiments that comprise their experience of the world's liveliness—form the bridge that links culture, environment, and biosocial vitality in generative meshworks of more-than-human being-in-the-world.

NOTES

1 Wari' is pronounced wah-REE, ending in a glottal stop. The data on which this study is based come primarily from the people who live in the contemporary Wari' village of Santo André.

2 On Wari' history and ethnography, see Conklin 2001a, 2001b, 2008, 2015; Vilaça 2002, 2005, 2010.

3 These days, postmortem burning includes photographs and personal papers. When a schoolchild dies, relatives go to the schoolhouse and ask the teacher to turn over the child's papers and drawings, to be thrown into the ritual fire.

4 This pattern of having no official leaders or formal political structure began to change in the 1990s, when the Brazilian government forced Wari' communities to appoint village "chiefs." (See Conklin 2015:74–77 on Wari' resistance to hierarchy and the trials and tribulations of those who try to take on leadership roles.) In the 2000s, the relative material equality that had prevailed began to erode when the government's expansion of cash payments to the poor gave every household substantial access to consumer goods for the first time, creating new bases for economic differentiation (Conklin 2015:81–83).

5 The territory inhabited by the people whose present-day descendants live in the community of Santo André is a region of relatively flat alluvial soil in which the sites with fertile soil suitable for growing maize are located on slightly higher terra firma, in interfluvial zones near small rivers (the Dois Irmãos and Rio Novo) and streams, away from the larger Pakaas Novos and Guaporé Rivers. The ecological pattern and distribution of farming and settlement sites described in this chapter is specific to this area; whether this applies in other parts of Wari' territory remains to be determined. As one moves east, toward the Serra dos Pakaas Novos and the forests drained by the Rio Negro and Rio Ocaia, the topography becomes hillier and the soil at old garden and settlement sites tends to be more reddish in color. As in the Santo André area, these sites often are littered with ceramic shards. Elsewhere in Amazonia, variant forms of anthrosols are lighter brown or red; these are less fertile than dark terra preta but more fertile than other soils in the surrounding forest. Called terra mulata in parts of Brazil, these lighter-colored soils contain few potsherds and human artifacts (Neves et al. 2003:46). Expanses of terra mulata often are located adjacent to more concentrated terra preta sites. Some archaeologists speculate that lower-fertility terra mulata formed in slash-and-burn swidden fields, while terra preta developed from intensive occupation at house and village sites (Rostain 2013:48), though this interpretation is a subject of ongoing debate.

6 In a study of Southeast Asian societies on the periphery of the state, Janet Carsten (1995:317) describes a similar combination of geosocial mobility, flexible identity, and a "politics of forgetting." Among Malay and Indonesian islanders who historically experienced a great deal of migration and mixing of peoples, she found a pattern of genealogical amnesia in which few people recall their ancestors beyond two or three generations and new kin relations can be created through sharing food, living together, marrying, and birthing and fostering children. She suggests that since identity is created in the present, the past has no special value or authority and there is a general lack of interest in memorializing ancestors or remembering details about the past.

7 Subjective perceptions of ancestors as presences in the landscape are one dimension of the entwining of "nature" and "culture" in native lowland South America. Fernando Santos-Granero (1998) and Jonathan Hill (1993) describe how salient events in Amazonian myths and history are inscribed in landscapes, especially sacred sites that are mnemonic markers of history and ritual processes. Peter Gow's (1991) work in Peru's Bajo Urubamba shows how kinship and relations with ancestors are deeply implicated in relations to land and landscape, especially through relations involving food and the sharing of food. Neil Whitehead (2003:60) highlights how landscape is formed in interactions among Abiota and topography, as well as in the dynamic activities of humans, fauna, flora, and the spirit world and historical consciousness that is reflected in the recounting and memory of the way that those interrelationships have developed through time. Laura Rival's (2002, 2016:37–90) work with the Huaorani of eastern Ecuador reveals a forested landscape inscribed with human activity, in which the former presence of ancestors is experienced at every turn, at sites associated with memories of dead individuals. Human presence is experienced also in

the natural abundance of forest trees and plants that are the ancestors' legacy. Huaorani recognize that chonta and other palms and fruit trees, and useful food and medicinal plants, exist in abundance and grow at convenient places along trekking paths and at former house sites because these are sites where past generations discarded seeds, planted seedlings, or tended wild plants to encourage the proliferation of useful species. By remaining in close association with forest groves, where they live, reproduce, and die along with fruit-bearing trees, birds, monkeys, and other species, people can forge long-term intergenerational relationships beyond so-called genealogical amnesia (Rival 2012:137).

REFERENCES CITED

Ahmed, Sara

2010   Happy Objects. In *The Affect Theory Reader*, edited by Melissa Gregg and Gregory J. Seigworth, pp. 29–51. Duke University Press, Durham, N.C.

Allen, Catherine

1988   *The Hold Life Has: Coca and Cultural Identity in an Andean Community*. 2nd ed. Smithsonian Books, Washington, D.C.

Balée, William

1998   Historical Ecology: Premises and Postulates. In *Advances in Historical Ecology*, edited by William Balée, pp. 13–29. Columbia University Press, New York.

2013   *Cultural Forests of the Amazon: A Historical Ecology of People and their Landscapes*. University of Alabama Press, Tuscaloosa.

Barnett, H. G.

1938   The Nature of the Potlatch. *American Anthropologist* 40(3):348–358.

Beck, Harald

2006   A Review of Peccary-Palm Interactions and Their Ecological Ramifications across the Neotropics. *Journal of Mammalogy* 87:519–530.

Beckerman, Steve

1977   The Use of Palms by the Barí Indians of the Maracaibo Basin. *Principes* 21:143–154.

Bertelson, Lone, and Andrew Murphie

2010   An Ethics of Everyday Infinities and Powers: Félix Guattari on Affect and the Refrain. In *The Affect Theory Reader*, edited by Melissa Gregg and Gregory J. Seigworth, pp. 138–160. Duke University Press, Durham, N.C.

Carsten, Janet

1995   The Politics of Forgetting: Migration, Kinship, and Memory on the Periphery of the Southeast Asian State. *Journal of the Royal Anthropological Institute*, n.s., 1:317–335.

Chaumeil, Jean-Pierre

2013   Bones, Flutes, and the Dead: Memory and Funerary Treatments in Amazonia. In *Time and Memory in Indigenous Amazonia: Anthropological Perspectives*, edited by Carlos Fausto and Michael Heckenberger, pp. 243–283. University Press of Florida, Gainesville.

Clement, Charles Roland, Dorian Picanço Rodrigues, Alessandro Alves-Pereiro, Gilda Santos Muhlen, Michelly de Cristo-Araujo, Priscila Ambrósio Moreira, Juliana Lins, and Vanessa Maciel Reis

2016   Crop Domestication in the Upper Madeira Basin. *Boletim do Museu Paraense Emílio Goeldi* 11(1):193–205.

Conklin, Beth A.

1997   Consuming Images: Representations of Cannibalism on the Amazonian Frontier. *Anthropological Quarterly* 702:68–78.

2001a   *Consuming Grief: Compassionate Cannibalism in an Amazonian Society*. University of Texas Press, Austin.

2001b   Women's Blood, Warriors' Blood, and the Conquest of Vitality in Amazonia and Melanesia. In *Gender in Amazonia and Melanesia: An Exploration of the Comparative Method*, edited by Thomas Gregor and Donald Tuzin, pp. 141–174. University of California Press, Berkeley.

2008   Revenge and Reproduction: The Biopolitics of Caring and Killing in Native Amazonia. In *Revenge in the Cultures of Lowland South America*, edited by Stephen Beckerman and Paul Valentine, pp. 10–21. University Press of Florida, Gainesville.

2015   Biopolitics of Health as Wealth in the Original Risk Society. In *Images of Public Wealth or the Anatomy of Well-Being in Indigenous Amazonia*, edited by Fernando Santos-Granero, pp. 60–88. University of Arizona Press, Tucson.

Conklin, Beth A., and Lynn M. Morgan

1996   Babies, Bodies, and the Production of Personhood in North America and a Native Amazonian Society. *Ethos* 244:657–694.

Denevan, William M.

2001   *Cultivated Landscapes of Native Amazonia and the Andes.* Oxford University Press, Oxford.

Erickson, Clark

2003   Historical Ecology and Future Explorations. In *Amazonian Dark Earths: Wim Sombrock's Vision*, edited by W. I. Woods, W. G. Teixeira, J. Lehmann, C. Steiner, A. M. G. A. WinklerPrins, and L. Rebellato, pp. 455–500. Springer, New York.

2008   Amazonia: The Historical Ecology of a Domesticated Landscape. In *Handbook of South American Archaeology*, edited by Helaine Silverman and William H. Isbell, pp. 157–183. Springer, New York.

Gow, Peter

1991   *Of Mixed Blood: Kinship and History in Peruvian Amazonia.* Clarendon Press, Oxford.

Guattari, Félix

1996   *The Guattari Reader.* Edited by Gary Genosko. Blackwell, London.

Hallam, Elizabeth, and Jenny Hockey

2001   *Death, Memory, and Material Culture.* Bloomsbury Academic, London.

Hecht, Susanna B.

2008   Kayapó Savanna Management: Fire, Soils, and Forest Islands in a Threatened Biome. In *Amazonian Dark Earths: Wim Sombrock's Vision*, edited by W. I. Woods, W. G. Teixeira, J. Lehmann, C. Steiner, A. M. G. A. WinklerPrins, and L. Rebellato, pp. 143–162. Springer, New York.

Hecht, Susanna B., and Darrel A. Posey

1989   Preliminary Results on Soil Management Techniques of the Kayapó Indians. *Advances in Economic Botany* 7:174–188.

Heckenberger, Michael J., Afukaka Kuikuro, Urissapá Tabata Kuikuro, J. Christian Russell, Morgan Schmidt, Carlos Fausto, and Bruna Franchetto

2003   Amazonia 1492: Pristine Forest or Cultural Parkland? *Science* 301:1710–1713.

Heckenberger, Michael J., J. Christian Russell, Carlos Fausto, Joshua R. Toney, Morgan Schmidt, Edithe Pereira, Bruna Franchetto, and Afukaka Kuikuro

2008   Pre-Columbian Urbanism, Anthropogenic Landscapes, and the Future of the Amazon. *Science* 321:1214–1217.

Hilbert, Lautaro, Eduardo Góes Neves, Francisco Pugliese, Bronwen S. Whitney, Myrtle Shock, Elizabeth Veasey, Carlos Augusto Zimpel, and José Iriarte

2017   Evidence for Mid-Holocene Rice Domestication in the Americas. *Nature, Ecology and Evolution* 1(11):1693–1698.

Hill, Jonathan

1993   *Keepers of the Sacred Chants: The Poetics of Ritual Power in an Amazonian Society.* University of Arizona Press, Tucson.

Ingold, Tim

2011   *Being Alive: Essays on Movement, Knowledge and Description.* Routledge, New York.

Kauffman, J. Boone

1991   Survival by Sprouting Following Fire in Tropical Forests of the Eastern Amazon. *Biotropica* 23(3):219–224.

Neves, Eduardo G.

2016   A Tale of Three Species or the Ancient Soul of Tropical Forests. In *Tropical Forest Conservation: Long-Term Processes of Human Evolution, Cultural*

Adaptations, and Consumption Patterns, edited by Nuria Sanz, pp. 228–245. UNESCO, Mexico City.

Neves, Eduardo Galvão, J. B. Petersen, R. N. Bartone, and C. A. Da Silva

2003   Historical and Socio-Cultural Origins of Amazonian Dark Earths. In *Amazonian Dark Earths: Origin, Properties, Management,* edited by Johannes Lehmann, Dirse C. Kern, Bruno Glaser, and William I. Woods, pp. 51–75. Kluwer Academic, Boston.

Overing, Joanna, and Alan Passes

2000   *Anthropology of Love and Anger: The Aesthetics of Conviviality in Native Amazonia.* Routledge, New York.

Paiva, Paulo Marcelo, Marcelino Carneiro Guedes, and Claudia Funi

2011   Brazil Nut Conservation through Shifting Cultivation. *Forest Ecology and Management* 261:508–514.

Posey, Darrel A., and M. J. Balick (editors)

2006   *Human Impacts on Amazonia: The Role of Traditional Ecological Knowledge in Conservation and Development.* Columbia University Press, New York.

Rappaport, Roy

1968   *Pigs for the Ancestors.* Yale University Press, New Haven.

Rival, Laura

2002   *Trekking through History: The Huaorani of Amazonian Ecuador.* Columbia University Press, New York.

2012   The Materiality of Life: Revisiting the Anthropology of Nature in Amazonia. *Indiana* 29:127–143.

2016   *Huaorani Transformations in Twenty-First-Century Ecuador.* University of Arizona Press, Tucson.

Rostain, Stéphen

2013   *Islands in the Rainforest: Landscape Management in Pre-Columbian Amazonia.* Left Coast Press, Walnut Creek, Calif.

Santos-Granero, Fernando

1998   Writing History into the Landscape: Space, Myth, and Ritual in Contemporary Amazonia. *American Ethnologist* 25(2):128–148.

2015   Introduction: Images of Public Wealth. In *Images of Public Wealth or the Anatomy of Well-Being in Indigenous Amazonia,* edited by Fernando Santos-Granero, pp. 3–34. University of Arizona Press, Tucson.

Scoles, R., R. Gribel, and N. Klein

2011   Crescimento e sobrevivência de castanheira (*Bertholletia excelsa* Bonpl.) em diferentes condições ambientais na região do Rio Trombetas, Oriximiná, Pará. *Boletim do Museu Paraemse Emílio Goeldi, Ciências Naturais* 6(3):273–293.

Shepard, Glenn H., and Henri Ramirez

2011   "Made in Brazil": Human Dispersal of the Brazil Nut (*Bertholletia excelsa,* Lecythidaceae) in Ancient Amazonia. *Economic Botany* 65(1):44–65.

Smith, Eric Alden, Monique Borgerhoff Mulder, Samuel Bowles, Michael Gurven, Tom Hertz, and Mary K. Shenk

2010   Production Systems, Inheritance, and Inequality in Premodern Societies. *Current Anthropology* 51(1):85–94.

Taylor, Anne Christine

1993   Remembering to Forget: Identity, Memory, and Mourning among the Jívaro. *Man* 28(4):653–678.

Vilaça, Aparecida

2002   Making Kin Out of Others in Amazonia. *Journal of the Royal Anthropological Institute* 8(2):347–365.

2005   Chronically Unstable Bodies: Reflections on Amazonian Coporalities. *Journal of the Royal Anthropological Institute* 11(3):445–464.

2010   *Strange Enemies: Indigenous Agency and Scenes of Encounter in Amazonia.* Duke University Press, Durham, N.C.

Viveiros de Castro, Eduardo B.

2005   Perspectivism and Multinaturalism in Indigenous America. In *The Land Within,* edited by Alexandre Surrallés and Pedro García Hierro, pp. 36–74. International Work Group for Indigenous Affairs, Copenhagen.

Walker, John

    2008   The Llanos de Mojos. In *Handbook of South American Archaeology*, edited by Helaine Silverman and William H. Isbell, pp. 927–939. Springer, New York.

Whitehead, Neil

    2003   *Histories and Historicities in Amazonia*. University of Nebraska Press, Lincoln.

WinklerPrins, Antoinette M. G. A.

    2009   Sweep and Char and the Creation of Amazonian Dark Earths in Homegardens. In *Amazonian Dark Earths: Wim Sombrock's Vision*, edited by W. I. Woods, W. G. Teixeira, J. Lehmann, C. Steiner, Antoinette M. G. A. WinklerPrins, and L. Rebellato, pp. 205–211. Springer, New York.

5

Descartes, Jesus, and Huitzilopochtli

Ontologies

BYRON ELLSWORTH HAMANN

If this discourse seems too long to be read at one time, you may divide it into six parts. In the first you will find introduced two circa-1540 sources on the sacred bundle of Huitzilopochtli, one telling of its origins & the other of its disappearance. In the second part, an argument for how animacy can be achieved through movement, illustrated by the entourage-accompanied, mirror-image travels of Huitzilopochtli's bundle from the two sources just introduced. In the third, an explanation for the strikingly parallel images—in which Humans & Nonhumans are linked by a flow of painted lines—from inheritance claims & inquisitorial evidence in sixteenth-century New Spain. In the fourth, an analysis of the physical-visual structure of Huitzilopochtli's early history in the Codex Boturini, & what this reveals about the ontological status of that screenfolded book as an object. In the fifth, a revisionist interpretation of the connections linking our inquisitorial investigations, a 1539 featherwork of the Mass of Saint Gregory, and a set of papal bulls from 1537

supposedly establishing Native Americans as Humans, not Animals. And in the last, a historical Constellation linking 1537 and 1539 and 1637 and explaining why René Descartes has never been modern.[1]

I'LL BEGIN WITH A LÉVI-STRAUSSIAN ANECDOTE I'm sure you have read before. It's impossible to avoid in today's anthropological ontological turn:[2] "In the Greater Antilles, some years after the discovery of America, whilst the Spanish were dispatching inquisitional commissions to investigate whether the natives had a soul or not, these very natives were busy drowning the white people they had captured in order to find out, after lengthy observation, whether or not the corpses were subject to putrefaction."[3] First recounted by Claude Lévi-Strauss in his *Race et histoire* (1952), this tale has been told over and over again: by Eduardo Viveiros de Castro (1998:475, 2004b:8–9, 2009:14–15), Bruno Latour (2004:451–452, 2009:1), Philippe Descola (2005:386–387), G. E. R. Lloyd (2011:831),

Indi volentes experiri immortalitatem Hifpano-   V.
rum Salfedum Hifpanum in mari fuffocant.

BORICHEN *Insulæ incolæ, Hifpanos eam fubigere adgreffos, immortales
effe credebant: eius rei periculum vnus è Primatibus eius Insulæ, cui no-
men Vraioan, Dominus Prouinciæ Iaguaca facere volens, Hifpanum
quendam Salfedo nomine iftac iter facientem comiter excipit, difcedenti
comites addit è fuis fubditis qui eius impedimenta ferant, cum mandatis,
vt in flumine, quod tranfeundum, mergant & fuffocent. Illi mandata fui Domini ftrenue
exequuntur: Salfedum fuffocatum ad fuum herum ferunt. Ex eo primùm intel-
lexerunt incolæ, Hifpanos perinde mortales effe ac
reliquos homines.*

B 2   Colum-

figure 5.1

A Native American experiment designed to test the immortality of the Spaniards. Plate 5, *Indi volentes experiri immortalitatem Hispanorum Salsedum Hispanum in mari suffocant* (Bry 1594). Image courtesy of the John Carter Brown Library, Brown University.

and Paolo Heywood (2012:144) (Figure 5.1). It also outlines the topography of the following pages. Like Lévi-Strauss's parable, my chapter centers on the first half of the sixteenth century, and on multiple perspectives and sites throughout the transatlantic Holy Roman Empire—Native American and Catholic, as well as Protestant; in Mexico City and Rome, as well as in Azcapotzalco, Culhuacan, Zurich, and Leiden. I draw on several types of documents, including "inquisitional commissions." And of course, like Lévi-Strauss I consider differing and debated ontologies: the understandings of being that distinguished or blurred the boundaries of humans and divinities and animals and houses and books and bundles and wafers. Following the manifesto for *Sacred Matter* (Kosiba, this volume), I won't simply describe ontological distinctions as given, but rather pay attention to the ways in which such distinctions were actively produced—or violently rejected (see also Lynch 2013; Woolgar and Lezaun 2013:336).

Most of what you are about to read takes place in the years surrounding 1537, when Pope Paul III issued three decrees outlining a whole host of ontological decisions in regard to Native Americans. My final comments, however, take place a century later, in 1637. This was when René Descartes published (in Leiden) his *Discourse on Method*. If the heroic triumvirate for ontology studies today is composed of Eduardo Viveiros de Castro, Philippe Descola, and Bruno Latour (Bessire and Bond 2014:440; Kohn 2015:316–322), then Descartes—and his nefarious "Cartesian dualisms"—provides the villain (Alberti and Bray 2009:341; Bassett 2015:184, 194; Bird-David 1999:79; Bray 2009:358; Brown and Emery 2008:327–328; Sillar 2009:368, 370; Viveiros de Castro 2004a:482; Zedeño 2009:408–409).[4] Yet many of the themes explored by Descartes in the *Discourse*—the comparative ontologies of humans, animals, and machines; the potentially violent politics of difference; the relations linking philosophy, cosmology, religion, and the sciences—are also themes central to recent ontological literature. The *Discourse* is (in)famous for Descartes's claim that "I knew that I was a substance the whole essence or nature of which is simply to think, and which,

in order to exist, has no need of any place nor depends on any material thing...this 'I,' that is to say, the soul through which I am what I am, is entirely distinct from the body."[5] Yet Descartes's goals were anything but disembodied and abstract. The *Discourse* was his attempt to provide a solution for horrific global conflicts over differences that had been burning for more than a hundred years. In other words, persecutions in New Spain and Europe in the 1530s illuminate why, a century later, Descartes attempted to create an applied anthropology that would better his war-ravaged world.[6]

The Life History of a Sacred Bundle

My story begins in Central Mexico, in the volcano-ringed valley surrounding the part-saltwater, part-freshwater Lake Texcoco. The Mexica capital of Tenochtitlan was built on an island in this lake, and starting in the 1440s it became the center of an ever-expanding empire that conquered much of Mesoamerica. Much, but not all, and in 1521 Tenochtitlan was itself conquered by an alliance of indigenous and European warriors.

According to Mexica histories, Tenochtitlan had been founded on a site revealed by their patron deity, Huitzilopochtli. His sacred bundle (made of layers of cloth wrapped around an unseen, but potent, sacred object) guided the Mexica ancestors to their future home during a long migration from Aztlan, another island-city. After many years of hardship, warfare, vassalage, and pulque-making (about which more later), the Mexica at last received a sign that they could end their wanderings: an eagle on a prickly pear cactus, facing the dawn with wings outstretched. On that site, the Mexica built a temple to house Huitzilopochtli's bundle. The city of Tenochtitlan slowly expanded around this sacred center.

Pre-Columbian sources on Huitzilopochtli are surprisingly elusive (Boone 1989:10–19), and so our earliest surviving information on his sacred bundle (and the Mexica migrations as well) dates to the years around 1540.[7] Two groups of documents are involved. The first consists of various copies of a now lost manuscript, which told how Huitzilopochtli commanded the Mexica ancestors to leave Aztlan, journey through the wilderness, and finally build a new city—and a new temple for Huitzilopochtli's bundle—on the island of Tenochtitlan. Key descendants of this vanished text include the *Codex Boturini* (in screenfold format) and the *Codex Aubin* and other derivative manuscripts (in Western spine-bound book format). The second group of documents comprises inquisitorial investigations that took place from June 1539 to May 1540, investigations that tried to find out what happened to the sacred bundle of Huitzilopochtli after the fall of Tenochtitlan in August 1521. At least two inquisitorial case files are involved: one connecting Mexico City and Azcapotzalco (a town on the western shores of Lake Texcoco) and the other focused on Culhuacan (a town on the lake's southern shores).[8]

With the pictorial documents, we have narratives of the early history of Huitzilopochtli's bundle, starting in the year 1 Flint. With the inquisitorial documents, we have narratives about the disappearance of Huitzilopochtli's bundle around 1521—at least as that disappearance was remembered in 1539. What is crucial to note here is that tales of the bundle's early history and tales of its final disappearance were both being written down *at the same time*, about a generation after the fall of Tenochtitlan. The migration histories were copied by indigenous artists, and the disappearance histories were recorded by European clerics in response to indigenous testimonies. It is, therefore, important to read these two seemingly separate archives (of origins and disappearances) as not simply contemporary, but as possibly linked—at least linked in the same horizon of remembrance. Indeed, it is striking that in the *Codex Boturini* the actual bundle of Huitzilopochtli is only depicted on the first four pages of the narrative. He is not actually shown during the later events of the Mexica migrations, even though we know from other sources that he was with the Mexica the whole time (and was finally installed in his own temple at what would become the center of Tenochtitlan). In other words, the *Codex Boturini* visualizes Huitzilopochtli only in its most ancient moments. In more recent events,

his bundle has disappeared, just as it had disappeared from the lives of the artists' present.

Documents of early history, documents of disappearance: the next three sections will explore different aspects of this two-part archive. I first consider the archive as a whole, and then focus on visual evidence from each of its halves: a painted diagram included in one of the inquisitorial investigations, and the page-spanning compositional structures of the *Codex Boturini*.

Migration and Inquisition

One of the basic methods that Irving Hallowell (1960), Catherine J. Allen (1998), and Nurit Bird-David (1999) propose for thinking about how humans forge social relations with persons-other-than-human is to look at patterns of practices, especially practices that reveal the ways in which human-nonhuman social relations parallel more familiar (to us) human-human ones (Kosiba, this volume). And so if we look at how humans treated the bundle of Huitzilopochtli in these twin archives of migration and inquisition, a number of parallel animating practices are revealed.

Most obvious is that, in a very literal sense, Huitzilopochtli's bundle is animated by being carried from place to place: a very Ingoldian strategy of movement (Ingold 2012). In migration narratives like the *Codex Boturini*, Huitzilopochtli is carried from Aztlan to Tenochtitlan. In the inquisition documents, he is carried from Tenochtitlan to hiding place after hiding place throughout the valley of Mexico. This strategy of animation-through-movement is deeply hierarchical. The carrying of persons was a way to honor them: it was a sign of *prestige*, not of helplessness or inanimacy. Indeed, the ways physical motion can generate both animation and inequality are explored by several authors in this volume: Tom Cummins on the spectacle of movement-enhancing elite costume, John Janusek on the animating power of "witnessed actions and engagements," and Marco Curatola Petrocchi on the connections of motion, sound, and revealed knowledge.

1 2 3 4 5 6 7 8 9 10 11 12 13 14 15 16 17 18 19 20 21 22 23 24 25 26

1   22

figure 5.2

Pages 1 and 22 of the *Tira de la Peregrinación / Codex Boturini*. Biblioteca Nacional de Antropología, Mexico City. Reproduction authorized by the Instituto Nacional de Antropología e Historia, Mexico.

The *Codex Boturini* is fundamentally a story of movement, a theme visualized by the footprints that walk from left to right across the entire document. Figure 5.2 includes the *Boturini*'s first page. Four footprints link the island and lake at Aztlan (on the left) to a cave inside the curved mountain of Teoculhacan. There, the bundle of Huitzilopochtli awaits the Mexica ancestors, commanding them with speech scrolls rising above his hummingbird helmet. To the right, in front of Huitzilopochtli's face and leading out of the cave, more footprints indicate that the Mexica take their patron with them on their journey.

Similarly, inquisitorial testimonies from 1539 are filled with accounts of sacred bundles being moved from one place to another, constantly on the go:

He said, that what he knows, is that when the Christians conquered this City of Mexico, this witness remembers that his father, who was called Tlatolatl, fled from this City with an idol which they said was the god of the Mexicans, extremely old, and he took this idol to Azcapotzalco, and the lords of that place, who were called Ocuitzin and Tlilantzin, received it very willingly, and they brought it to a house in which the idol could remain and be guarded, and they gave him four other idols to guard, which were called Tezcatlipoca and Cihuacoatl and Telpuchtli and Tepehua, and they told him to guard all of them; and that this witness saw that his father worshipped and made offerings to the said idols, and he decorated them with ornaments, as had been the custom. (Testimony of Pedro, resident of the City of Mexico, June 21, 1539)[9]

The Indians brought two bundles to Culhuacan, large and heavy, the one black and the other

2

figure 5.3
Page 2 of the *Tira de la
Peregrinación / Codex
Boturini*. Biblioteca
Nacional de Antropología,
Mexico City. Reproduction
authorized by the Instituto
Nacional de Antropología e
Historia, Mexico.

blue, and they were there four or five days, and
the Mexicans guarded them, and they took them
away in a canoe; and that when the said don
Baltasar asked about them [the bundles], some
told him that they had taken them to Xilotepec,
and others said to Xaltocan, and others to Peñol,
and to other places they named; and that the
said bundles were of the great idol of Mexico,
Huitzilopochtli. (Testimony of don Baltasar,
ruler of Culhuacan, December [?], 1539)[10]

We might be tempted to think that the post-1521
carryings of Huitzilopochtli's bundle from place to
place were mere functionalism: keeping the bundle
on the move kept it hidden from the Europeans.
But Huitzilopochtli's escape was more complicated than that, especially if we look to the details
of *where* his bundle was carried. Many of his stopping places were sites visited by the Mexica on
their ancient migration *to* Tenochtitlan. A number of the towns named by inquisitorial witnesses

are, therefore, depicted in the *Codex Boturini*,
including Tula (page 12), Azcapotzalco (page 16),
Xaltocan (page 19), and Culhuacan (pages 20–21)
(Castañeda de la Paz 2005:2–3, 2007:200–203,
2008:160).[11] In other words, hiding Huitzilopochtli
involved *retracing in reverse* his earlier travels.
Many of his stopping points were not accidental,
but meaningful.

Furthermore, in both migration and sequestration Huitzilopochtli never traveled alone. He
was always accompanied by a retinue of social
others. This is no surprise: cross-culturally, political figures manifest their power through a distributed entourage (Gell 1998:52). In both the
year 1 Flint of the *Codex Boturini*, and as remembered in Anno Domini 1539 by inquisitorial witnesses, Huitzilopochtli's entourage included both
human and other-than-human members. On
page 2 of the *Codex Boturini*, a line of four figures—three men and one woman—walk from left
to right (Figure 5.3). A path of footprints beneath

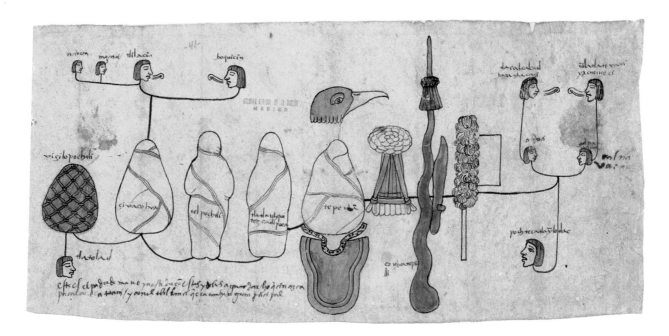

figure 5.4

The sacred bundles of Tenochtitlan and their human guardians, 1539. Archivo General de la Nación, Mexico City, Mapa 4848; original location AGN, Inquisición, volumen 37, fol. 41.

their feet indicates their movement away from the place signs of Aztlan and Teoculhacan. The man in front carries the hummingbird-helmeted bundle of Huitzilopochtli on his back. But humans are not the only persons traveling with Huitzilopochtli: he is accompanied by three other sacred bundles, carried on the backs of three human companions who walk behind him. This task was clearly an honor: the prestige of these bundle-bearers is indicated by the fact that all are named, with hieroglyphic signs floating above their heads.

Similarly, Figure 5.4 reproduces a painting submitted as evidence before inquisitors in the summer of 1539. Its surface is dominated by the rounded forms of cloth-wrapped sacred bundles. Each is carefully named in alphabetic script. Huitzilopochtli is on the far left; his four bundled companions are the same as those named in witness testimonies ("they gave him four other idols to guard, which were called Tezcatlipoca and Cihuacoatl and Telpuchtli and Tepehua"). But, as on page 2 of the *Codex Boturini*, sacred bundles are not the only persons being depicted. Above, below, and to the right, ten human

heads are painted in profile, connected to each other and to the bundles by thin black lines. These are the various men accused of helping to guard or carry the bundles during their perilous escape from Tenochtitlan. Like the bundle-bearers in the *Boturini*, all of these human companions are carefully named, with labels floating above their heads. Strategically, however, all but one of these men (Miguel Pochtecatl Tlaylotla) *had already died*: their painted eyes are closed. The strategy of accusing *deceased* bundle-chaperones appears in the spoken testimonies as well: "He said, that it could have been seventeen years ago, a little more or less, that they brought from this City [of Mexico] to the said town of Culhuacan the Huitzilopochtli and many other idols, and they were brought by Tehuachichilayo, an Indian who is dead, and they put them in a cave called Telatzin, and they were there six days" (Testimony of don Baltasar, ruler of Culhuacan, December 2, 1539).[12]

Animating practices: in both migration and sequestration, Huitzilopochtli was carried by his worshippers, visited many of the same places, and was surrounded by a retinue composed of humans as well as other sacred bundles. Huitzilopochtli's entourage, thus, echoes John Janusek's arguments (this volume) for the sacred images of Tiwanaku, where presentation monoliths were themselves surrounded by a host of attendants both stone and flesh—attendants whose presence enhanced the fame and authority of the being they accompanied.

Much more can be said about Huitzilopochtli's retinue, and the entanglements of humans and nonhumans in sixteenth-century Nahua thought.

Tlacamecayotl

Consider again the painted page of evidence submitted to inquisitors in the summer of 1539 (Boone 1989:26–28) (Figure 5.4). In the lower left-hand corner, a man's head is drawn in profile, facing to the right. A single black line connects the top of his head to the dark bundle of Huitzilopochtli, wrapped up in a net of green stones. A long note explains that this man is Tlatolatl, former adviser to Moctezuma and father to witnesses Mateo and Pedro (the young men whose June 1539 testimonies prompted this investigation). Just before Tenochtitlan was conquered, Moctezuma commanded Tlatolatl to take the bundle of Huitzilopochtli out of the capital and across the lake to the town of Azcapotzalco. There the bundle was welcomed; indeed, the ruler of Azcapotzalco (Ocuitzin) commanded another noble (Tlilantzin) to entrust four additional sacred bundles to Tlatolatl's care. These bundles are all depicted and labeled on the painting: Cihuacoatl, Telpochtli and Tlatlauhqui Tezcatlipoca (two aspects of Tezcatlipoca), and Tepehua. Visually speaking, their joint stewardship is represented by a black line that runs under all five bundles, connecting them to each other and back to their caretaker, Tlatolatl. Above, however, another black line rises up from the top of Cihuacoatl's bundle and connects to a line linking the ruler (Ocuitzin, on the right) and his nobleman (Tlilantzin, on the left). Another line then connects Tlilantzin to two other, smaller heads on the left: Nahueca and Maznal. The latter's identity is unclear, but Nahueca

is mentioned by Mateo and Pedro as "an old principal lord . . . in charge of the things of Tlilantzin."[13]

Mateo's inquisitorial testimony does not end with the gathering of idols at Azcapotzalco. When Tlatolatl, Ocuitzin, and Tlilantzin were all killed on an expedition with Hernán Cortés (down in "Gueymula"), the lord of Mexico (Tlacochcalcatl Nanahuatzin) and the lord of Tula (Ixcuecuetzin) sent two messengers (Coyotzin and Calnahuacatl) to Azcapotzalco to reclaim the bundled gods. These four men are depicted in the upper-right corner of the painting. The lord of Mexico is on the left, connected by a line to Coyotzin, below. The lord of Tula is on the right, connected by a line to Calnahuacatl, below. From Azcapotzalco, the two messengers then carried the bundles back to Mexico City, which is why the line connecting Coyotzin and Calnahuacatl is itself extended by another line to the bundles and their paraphernalia. Once in Mexico City, the bundles were first taken to the house of Tlacochcalcatl Nanahuatzin and then to the house of Pochtecatl Tlaylotla. He is the last man depicted in the painting (on the lower right-hand side; his eye is open), and a black line joins him to the meeting point of the ligatures connecting Coyotzin, Calnahuacatl, and the five sacred bundles.

The painting presents a literal web of suspects, human and nonhuman. In many ways, this image is unique. It is an extremely early example of post-Hispanic Nahua writing and has no equivalent anywhere else in the inquisitorial archive. At the same time, however, its complexly visualized relations are echoed in a noninquisitorial corpus of sixteenth-century legal paintings from Central Mexico. In those images, relations between humans and nonhumans are also roped together on the page.

We don't know who created the inquisitorial image, but it was probably made by the very first witness to give testimony in June 1539: "Mateo, indio, natural e vecino de la Cibdad de Mexico, de la colocacion de San Juan."[14] Mateo is said to be a painter. Given that his father, Tlatolatl, was "very close to Moctezuma and a person with which the said Moctezuma shared some of his secrets,"[15] we can imagine that Tlatolatl had been a *tlacuilo* and

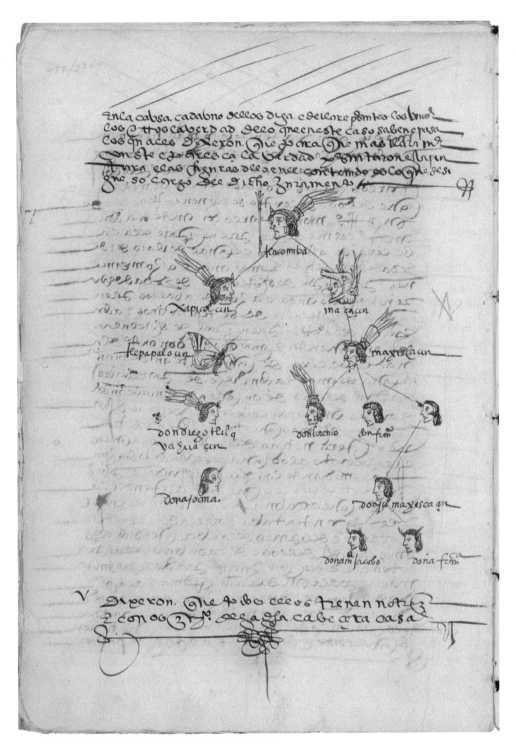

figure 5.5
Diego López de
Ayala, Genealogy
of Maxixcatzin,
Ocotelulco,
Tlaxcala, 1562.
Archivo General de
la Nación, Mexico
City, Mapa 551;
original location
AGN, Tierras,
volumen 20, 1a.
parte, expediente 1,
fol. 63v.

tlamatini, a pre-Hispanic scribe and wise man— and that Tlatolatl's sons were being trained to follow in his footsteps (Boone 2000:24–27). This was certainly true for don Andrés of Culhuacan, one of the other witnesses involved in the hunt for the sacred bundles. Like Mateo and Pedro, don

Andrés's father (Papalotecatl) was an adviser to Moctezuma. Don Andrés remembers his father bringing the emperor a codex to consult, and don Andrés himself was (like Mateo) a painter. He even mentions being commanded to paint an unnamed lord's genealogy, which apparently (like the *Codex*

Boturini) included a migration account ("cuando vinieron sus abuelos á México").[16]

Don Andrés's painting (of kinship relations and their deep history) brings us to our comparative visual corpus for the inquisitorial image of bundles and humans. During the sixteenth century, a number of genealogies were painted for indigenous inheritance lawsuits. Occasionally, they depict only humans, connected by a network of black lines (Figure 5.5) (Rojas Rabiela, Rea López, and Medina Lima 1999:53). But more often, their black lines entangle humans and nonhumans together: men, women, houses, fields, granaries. Inheritance lawsuits were seldom about human relationships alone: they were also about the rights to property enabled by those relationships. At first glance, the formal similarities between the inquisitorial painting in Figure 5.4 and the inheritance paintings in Figures 5.6 and 5.7 are quite striking. And if we consider the Nahua concepts that shaped the appearance of the genealogies, we can better understand why Mateo may have drawn on genealogical conventions to visualize a history of connections linking humans to sacred bundles. One Nahuatl term is especially important: *tlacamecayotl.*

Tlacamecayotl is not a common word in Nahuatl documents. Literally, it means "rope of people," and the first attempts to understand its meaning—and its implications for our understanding of Nahua kinship systems—focused on its use in the *Florentine Codex* and in Alonso de Molina's Nahuatl dictionaries (Kellogg 1995:174–180, 184–186; Lockhart 1992). Archival research has provided additional information. At least one Nahua genealogy is quite literal in its depiction of genealogical connections as ropelike: a painting from 1567 Moyotlan uses a twisted white cord to connect husband Martín Lázaro Pantecatl (deceased: his eye is closed) to his widowed wife, Ana Tepi (Figure 5.8). A cross is attached to the cord, perhaps indicating that the couple was married in the church. But human connections are not the only subject matter on this page. The couple is shown inside their (carefully measured) house, beyond which appears the house's lot and four fields. From the accompanying will, we know that Martín did indeed leave his wife

a house and four fields when he died in 1551. But his will also lists many other heirs and many other properties, which is probably why it became necessary for his widow to visualize her claims in litigation (Rojas Rabiela, Rea López, and Medina Lima 1999:35–36, 51).

In this image, genealogical lines connect human to human within a frame of heritable property; the term *tlacamecayotl* is not used in the accompanying alphabetic text. That word is used, however, in the text accompanying a very similar, if more complicated, painting (Figure 5.9). Once again, genealogical connections among humans are placed within a visual framework of heritable property: house, house lot, canal. From the use of *tlacamecayotl* in this and other lawsuits, Susan Kellogg argued that the word was used by litigants in reference to the genealogical connections (through both male and female ancestors) that allowed them to assert rights of inheritance. Thus the "rope of people" concept was used to link people not simply to other humans, but to heritable property as well. A literalization of these human-nonhuman relations probably explains the very curious images held by the Newberry Library (see Figure 5.6) and the Bibliothèque nationale de France (see Figure 5.7) in which black lines not only connect humans to each other, but entangle humans and property in a complex web (Kellogg 1980:145–146; Rojas Rabiela, Rea López, and Medina Lima 1999:40–44, 55–57).

Given this conceptual landscape of ropes, relations, and houses, we can better understand the striking format of our inquisitorial painting. The artist drew on a visual language of inheritance to explain how a set of objects—sacred bundles, in this case—was passed down over time from one person to another. The sacred bundle of Huitzilopochtli, having been entrusted by the Aztec emperor to Tlatolatl, was then "married," as it were, to four other bundles held by the noble Tlilantzin for the lord of Azcapotzalco. When all those men died, their consolidated patrimony was claimed—inherited—by two other nobles, the lords of Mexico and Tula. Those two lords then entrusted their sacred wealth (part of which, remember, could be traced back to a previous lord of Mexico) to yet another

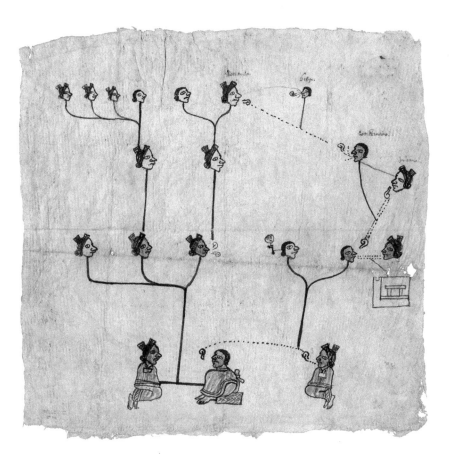

figure 5.6
The genealogy of Pedronilla Francisca Teuche and her mother-in-law, Juliana Tlaco, 1575. Pedronilla is named in the upper center and is connected to her deceased husband, Constantino, by a dotted line. A solid line connects Constantino to his mother, Juliana. A double dotted line connects Juliana to her parents; a solid line connects them to their house. Newberry Library, Chicago.

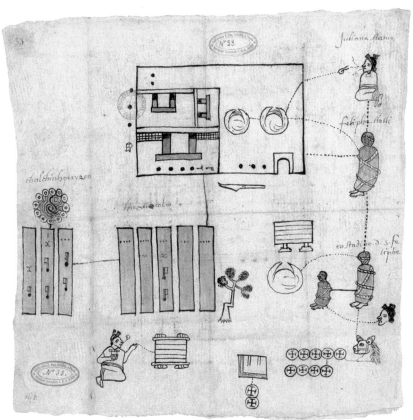

figure 5.7
The property claims of Juliana Tlaco, 1576. Juliana is named in the upper right, connected by dotted lines to her deceased husband, son, grandson, and properties inherited from her parents. Image courtesy of the Bibliothèque nationale de France, Paris, BNF Mexicain 33.

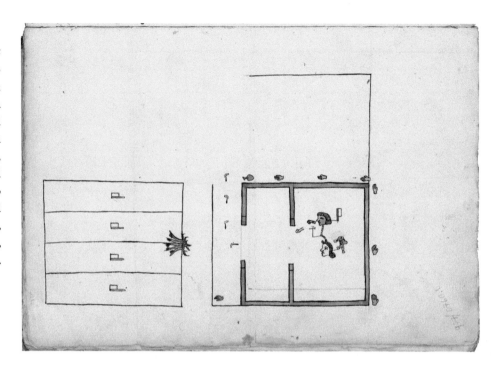

figure 5.8
Martín Lázaro Pantecatl (deceased); his widowed wife, Ana Tepi; their house; and their maguey fields in San Juan Moyotlan, 1567. Archivo General de la Nación, Mexico City, Mapa 552; original location AGN, Tierras, volumen 20, 1a. parte, expediente 3, fol. 256v.

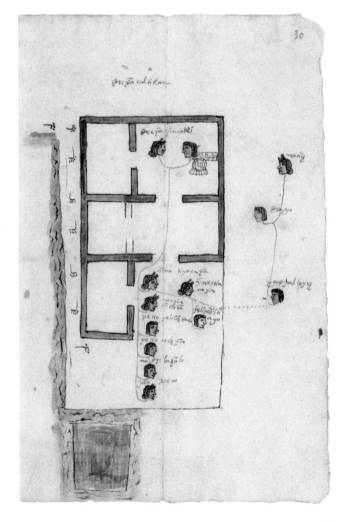

figure 5.9
The genealogy and property claims of Diego Francisco in San Juan Tecpancaltitlan, 1593. Image courtesy of the Bibliothèque nationale de France, Paris, BNF Mexicain 112.

representative: Pochtecatl Tlaylotla. Depicted near the lower right corner, eye open and thus still alive, he was the ultimate inheriting ego of this divinely connected *tlacamecayotl*.

But if in lawsuits over succession the end point of a genealogy was usually the person who commissioned that genealogy, and stood to gain by its claims, with our inquisitorial image the orienting ego was *not* the image's patron. He was the image's targeted victim. The connections this image visualized between humans and nonhumans led to his capture, torture, and finally house arrest within Mexico City's Franciscan monastery.

The Ontology of a Screenfold

The previous two sections have explored relations between humans and other-than-human persons in the valley of Mexico circa 1539. Now, however, I want to briefly leave humans behind and think about the blurring of ontological boundaries in the nonhuman world. I return to the *Codex Boturini* and ask a seemingly strange question: what kind of object is it?

On the surface (literally on the surface, for it is a thing covered with painted signs) the *Boturini* is an *amoxtli*, a Nahuatl word that literally means "glued sheets of bark paper" (Boone 2000:23). As it currently exists, it has 21.5 folded "pages." But it is obviously incomplete. The final 1.5 pages are only partially painted (Figure 5.10).

As mentioned previously, the *Boturini* is one of a number of copies made in sixteenth-century Mexico of a now-lost manuscript that María Castañeda de la Paz refers to as *Codex Y*. From other descendant manuscripts, especially the *Codex Aubin* and *Codex Azcatitlan*, we know that the *Boturini* was supposed to end with Huitzilopochtli's eagle-on-a-cactus, the sign that the Mexica could at last end their wanderings and start to build Tenochtitlan (Figure 5.11). Although we don't know how long the *Boturini* manuscript was originally designed to be, based on scenes from the *Codex Aubin* we can imagine a full length of twenty-six pages: two times thirteen, and half of fifty-two, all symbolically charged numbers in Mesoamerica.[17]

Despite being incomplete, the manuscript preserves a number of striking compositional structures (Brilliant 1991; Hamann 2004, 2013). The first five pages (in which the Mexica and Huitzilopochtli travel from Aztlan to Coatepec) feature a great deal of unpainted surface area, an emptiness that makes the large-format place signs stand out all the more (Figure 5.12). In contrast, pages 6–19 are packed with images. Year glyphs in square boxes alternate with small-format place signs indicating the various locations the Mexica ancestors stop during their journey from Aztlan. Those ancestors are abbreviated into a visually repetitive grid of four men, two above and two below (Figure 5.13). Dates, place sign, four men; dates, place sign, four men: these—connected by a twisting path of footprints—take up the majority of the *Boturini*'s visual real estate. But then, on page 20—after the Mexica have been driven from Chapultepec on page 19 and become mercenaries for the rulers of Culhuacan—the style of the screenfold returns to that of its opening pages. There is a lot of empty space, year glyphs are minimal, and varied compositions of human forms replace the schematic grid of four men.

The visual symmetry of composition—a work that begins and ends with relatively open spaces framing a dense, calendar glyph–filled band of migration history—would have been further enhanced by a symmetry of place signs (see Figure 5.12). The full narrative would have begun, and ended, at an island on a lake: Aztlan on page 1 and Tenochtitlan on the (hypothetical) page 26. Further visual symmetry is provided by other place signs. The curved hill of Teoculhacan appears right after the Mexica leave Aztlan on page 1; another curved hill for Culhuacan appears near the end of their journey, on page 20. The large-format place sign for Coatepec on page 5 (where the Mexica settle for twenty-three years) is paralleled by the large-format place sign for Chapultepec on page 18 (where the Mexica settle for twenty years).

Additional visual structures are provided by the spacing of glyphs for the New Fire ceremony (Figure 5.13). Held every fifty-two years (during the year 2 Reed), this ceremony marked the alignment

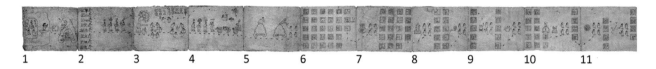

The overall visual structure of the *Tira de la Peregrinación / Codex Boturini*. Biblioteca Nacional de Antropología, Mexico City. Reproduction authorized by the Instituto Nacional de Antropología e Historia, Mexico.

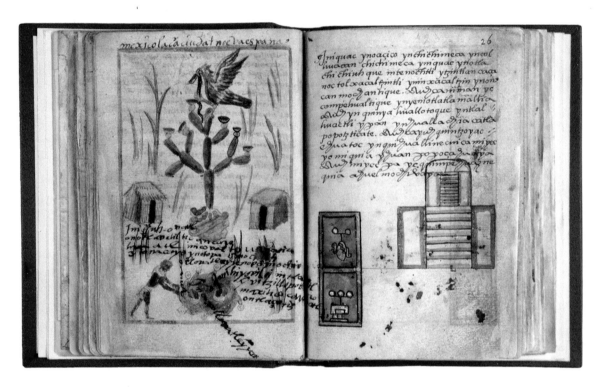

figure 5.11
The foundation of Tenochtitlan in the *Codex Aubin*, 1576. British Museum, London, Am2006,Drg.31219 © Trustees of the British Museum.

of cycles in the 260-day ritual calendar and the 365-day solar calendar (52 × 365 = 18,890 days, equal to seventy-three cycles of the 260-day calendar). All of a community's fires would be extinguished and then relit from a single sacred flame (see Hamann 2008:803–808; Tena 2009:123–127). This event (marked, appropriately, by a smoking fire drill glyph) appears every four to five pages in the *Boturini*: on the right edge of page 6, near the middle of page 10, on the left edge of page 15, and toward the right edge of page 19. Pages 6 and 19, as I mentioned, are where the *Boturini*'s dense presentation

of year glyphs and place signs begin and end. In other words, New Fire ceremonies frame the fourteen central pages of the screenfold. These first and last ceremonies are also equally spaced relative to the *Boturini*'s first and last pages: six pages in from its start and seven pages away from its (hypothetical) conclusion.

Symmetry and centrality were important compositional features of a number of Mesoamerican manuscripts. At the center of the fifty-two-page *Codex Vienna*, on pages 27 and 26, is a depiction of the covenants with earth and rain that made

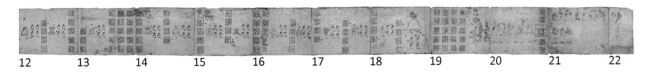

12 13 14 15 16 17 18 19 20 21 22

figure 5.10 (continued)

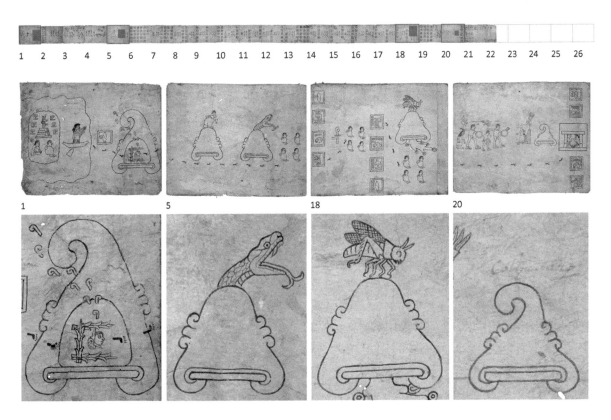

1 2 3 4 5 6 7 8 9 10 11 12 13 14 15 16 17 18 19 20 21 22 23 24 25 26

1 5 18 20

figure 5.12
The location of large-format place signs on pages 1, 5, 18, and 20 of the *Tira de la Peregrinación / Codex Boturini*. Biblioteca Nacional de Antropología, Mexico City. Reproduction authorized by the Instituto Nacional de Antropología e Historia, Mexico.

possible the agricultural foundation of Ñudzavui society (Hamann 2004). The two centers of the *Lienzo de Tlaxcala* contain images of two rival capitals: a First Sunrise at Tlaxcala itself and then a circular cosmogram of about-to-be-conquered Tenochtitlan (Figure 5.14) (Hamann 2013). The central pages of the *Codex Badianus* abandon alphabetic explanations of medicinal plants to depict a paradisiacal garden somewhere between Eden and Tollan (Rojas Silva 2018). I have just argued that the

Codex Boturini has a broadly symmetrical structure on a number of levels: changing glyphic density, opening and closing place signs, the spacing of the New Fire commemorations. Was this screenfold also meant (like the *Codex Vienna*, *Lienzo de Tlaxcala*, and *Codex Badianus*) to have a symbolically charged center?

If we turn to where this hypothetical center would fall, pages 13 and 14, a small but significant micronarrative emerges: the story of the origins of

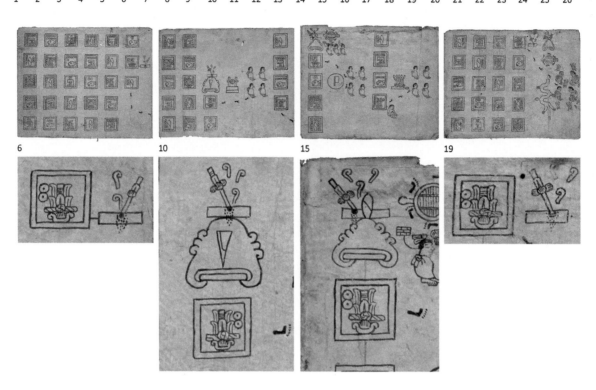

1 2 3 4 5 6 7 8 9 10 11 12 13 14 15 16 17 18 19 20 21 22 23 24 25 26

6   10   15   19

figure 5.13
The location of New Fire commemorations on pages 6, 10, 15, and 19 of the *Tira de la Peregrinación / Codex Boturini*. Biblioteca Nacional de Antropología, Mexico City. Reproduction authorized by the Instituto Nacional de Antropología e Historia, Mexico.

pulque (Figure 5.15). On page 13—hardly an accidental number—after the four representative Mexica ancestors have stopped at the Place of the Serpent, a maguey cactus is shown growing in a field. Sixteen years pass (from 5 Flint to 7 Reed) and end with two small vignettes.[18] Below is a man sucking sap from the heart of a maguey cactus. Above is a man holding a cup of foaming liquid before a larger jar of the same. The round handles on the jar confirm its contents as pulque (compare Hamann 2018:645).

Another account of the origins of pulque during the Mexica migrations appears in the *Florentine Codex*, so we shouldn't dismiss these pulque scenes in the *Boturini* as random scribal whimsy (Sahagún 1950–1982:11:193–194). Indeed, there are many reasons why a story about pulque is appropriate for the exact center of a story about Huitzilopochtli. Karl Taube points out several connections linking

pulque to the Four Hundred Southerners—the half brothers whom Huitzilopochtli destroyed en masse when he was born fully grown at the top of Serpent Mountain. South is the direction of the Rabbit Year Bearer, and the Four Hundred Southerners echo in their name the Four Hundred Rabbits who were gods of pulque. Once Huitzilopochtli defeated his half brothers, he appropriated them as part of his being: "And when he had slain them, when he had spent his wrath, he took from them their vestments, their adornment, their paper crowns ornamented with feathers. He arrayed himself with these and took [them] for himself; he assumed [them] as his due, as if taking the insignia to himself" (Sahagún 1950–1982:4:5). In turn, excavations at the Templo Mayor (a symbolic re-creation of Serpent Mountain) uncovered a greenstone statue of the pulque goddess in the company of the Coyolxauhqui carving (sister

figure 5.14

The First Sunrise at the physical center of the *Lienzo de Tlaxcala*, ca. 1552. The *Lienzo*'s second center (at the center of the 7 × 13 grid) is located two cells below: a circular representation of Lake Texcoco and Tenochtitlan surrounded by the place signs of four lakeside towns. Digital re-creation courtesy of www.mesolore.org.

to the Four Hundred Southerners and half sister to Huitzilopochtli). The greenstone pulque goddess had a 2 Rabbit glyph carved on her chest, which was the general name (Ome Tochtli) for the four hundred pulque gods. Nearby, Cache 6 contained a stone statue of pulque's male personification, as well as pulque-related costume elements (Taube 1993:3).

Given these complex associations, perhaps a story about the origins of pulque appears at the center of a book about the sacred bundle of Huitzilopochtli in order to commemorate the conquest of the Four Hundred Southerners and because drinking pulque involves the absorption of one body by another, like the regalia of Huitzilopochtli's defeated foes ("he assumed them as his due, as if taking the insignia to himself"). Returning to the themes of this volume, we know pulque was for the Mexica a kind of "sacred matter," its consumption carefully

regulated (Taylor 1979:28–45). And it was of course a literally animating substance as well. An animating substance at the center of the *Codex Boturini*.

All of which suggests that the symmetrical and centered compositional structure of the *Codex Boturini* makes it not simply a story *about* a sacred bundle. The *Codex Boturini* is itself a sacred bundle, with a key narrative at its exact center. It thus parallels other book-bundles created elsewhere in Mesoamerica. The *Codex Boturini* dramatizes the tension between interpretation and ontology that is of great current interest in anthropology (Boellstorff 2016:397; Viveiros de Castro 2004a:460–470, 2004b:5, 9, 14). As a text-artifact, its surface covered with signs, this screenfold is clearly an object created for interpretation. But the structure created by the document's combination of black-and-red imagery on folded bark paper

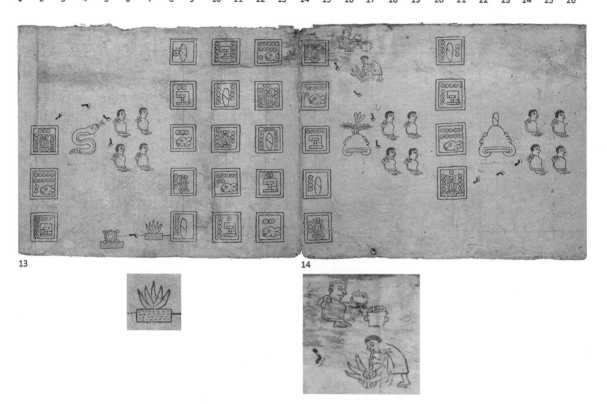

1 2 3 4 5 6 7 8 9 10 11 12 13 14 15 16 17 18 19 20 21 22 23 24 25 26

13

14

figure 5.15
The cultivation of maguey and the creation of pulque on pages 13 and 14 of the *Tira de la Peregrinación / Codex Boturini*. Biblioteca Nacional de Antropología, Mexico City. Reproduction authorized by the Instituto Nacional de Antropología e Historia, Mexico.

points in another direction: this is a structure that does not simply "symbolize" a sacred bundle. It actually creates a sacred bundle, to be unfolded and unwrapped in the reader's hands.

∴

Huitzilopochtli incorporated the insignia of his defeated half brothers into his own person. He was also, in turn, incorporated into the being of his devotees. On the feast day of Panquetzaliztli, an edible image of Huitzilopochtli was made of amaranth. This body was then killed:

> And when he died, thereupon they broke up his body, the amaranth seed dough. His heart

was Moctezuma's portion. And the rest of his members, which were made like his bones, were disseminated among the people; there was a distribution. . . . And when they divided among themselves his body of amaranth seed dough, it was only in very small [pieces]: only very small, tiny. The youths ate them. And of this which they ate, it was said: "The god is eaten." And of those who ate it, it was said: "They keep the god." (Sahagún 1950–1982:4:6; see also Durán 1964:95)

In 1539, Huitzilopochtli was not the only edible divinity being attacked and persecuted within the Holy Roman Empire of Emperor Charles V.

Huanitzin's Choices

In the middle of October 1539, a second group of depositions was gathered by inquisitors trying to uncover what happened to the sacred bundle of Huitzilopochtli after it was spirited from Tenochtitlan in 1521. On October 24, testimony was taken from Culhua Tapisque, a resident of the Mexico City barrio of Santa María. After telling inquisitors his name, where he lived, whether or not he was baptized (no), and his age (fifty-six, more or less), he was asked what he knew about Huitzilopochtli's whereabouts. His answer was politically shocking:

> Asked, if he knows where there are or who has the idols of Huitzilopochtli, he said: that this witness was a prophet, and kept the count of the demons and the duty of doing the things which were necessary for them, and that he heard tell from Tomolo, deceased, who held the same office as this witness, that Palacatl and Cuzcasuchatl and Yzcuen and Cocacal, the indigenous residents of Mexico who go about with don Diego, lord of Mexico, keep and guard the said idols, because their fathers had once kept them and guarded them, and they, after the death of their fathers, succeeded in the guard of the said idols, and they bring them and have them near to Tula, and that he who is testifying believes and knows for certain that they have them and know of them, because they are descendants of those who had once held the same post.

> And he adds that it might have been eight or ten years ago, more or less, that being in the town of Azcapotzalco this witness and don Diego, current lord of Mexico, and Achacatl, principal lord, and other three principal lords, talking about how the [Franciscan] fathers had arrested a principal lord so that he would give them Huitzilopochtli, the said don Diego said that it seemed to him that they should give Huitzilopochtli to the friars, and how did this sound to them; and Achacatl, principal lord, said that they should not hand him over, and that in no manner should they hand him over, and so they determined that they should not give him to them nor hand him over, and so they did not hand him over to them.[19]

This 1539 testimony is scandalous because it accuses don Diego de Alvarado Huanitzin of protecting idolatry, of not surrendering Huitzilopochtli's bundle to European authorities. A grandson of Emperor Axayacatl and nephew and son-in-law of Moctezuma, Huanitzin served as *gobernador* (ruler of indigenous Mexico City) from around 1538 to 1541. He was one of the most important figures in the viceregal capital. Along with Viceroy Antonio de Mendoza and Franciscan friar Pedro de Gante, he formed "the holy trinity of the emergent, post-Cortés city" (Mundy 2015:118). He was also the patron behind yet another object from 1539 that engages with questions of ontology. Figure 5.16 shows a featherwork mosaic of the Mass of Saint Gregory. It was commissioned—according to the Latin inscription around its border—by don Diego Huanitzin himself: "Fashioned for Pope Paul III in the great city of Mexico of the Indies by the governor don Diego under the care of Friar Pedro de Gante of the Minorites, A.D. 1539."

Why was this spectacular image created as a gift for Pope Paul III? Since the early 1990s, the work has been explained by reference to papal decrees on Native Americans that Paul III had given two years before, in 1537: "In 1537 Paul III issued a bull proclaiming the rationality of the Indians and the right of the mendicant orders to administer the sacraments to them. This decision was announced in New Spain in 1538 and in 1539, perhaps promoting the new Christians to show their appreciation" (Martínez del Río de Redo and Estrada de Gerlero 1990:260). Two details are important here. First is the idea that Paul III proclaimed "the rationality of the Indians," which in academic literature has been argued to be the key moment in which Europeans finally accepted Native Americans as true men, and not animals. This "rationality" argument is linked to a second: as "rational" beings, Native Americans could be given the sacraments. Since Communion is one of the sacraments, it has been argued that an image of Saint Gregory's vision of Christ as bodily

figure 5.16
The Mass of Saint
Gregory in featherwork,
1539 © Rmn-Grand
Palais (Musée des
Jacobins–Auch) /
Philippe Fuzeau.

present during Communion made an appropriate gift to thank the pope for his confirmation of both indigenous rationality and sacramental access.[20] I agree that Huanitzin's featherwork was created in response to papal decrees on the New World. But the full complexity of this story has not been explored.

Paul III issued three main rulings on Native Americans in 1537. But none of them, in fact, presented the humanity of Native Americans as ever in doubt. And none of them involved granting Native Americans access to the sacraments: that access was assumed as a given.[21] These twin myths (of

doubted rationality and sacramental access) seem to have been invented in the late eighteenth century, as part of the Americas-attacking, Black Legend–reviving "Dispute of the New World."[22] In the first volume of his bestselling (and multiply reprinted) *Philosophical Researches on the Americans* (1768), Cornelis de Pauw (1768–1769:35–36) wrote that the Spaniards initially claimed Native Americans were orangutans, until "a Pope issued an original bull" declaring that the Americans were "true men" (see also page 67 on "the opinion that the Americans were monkeys"). Perhaps not by chance (given the impact of de Pauw's work), the following year Francisco Antonio Lorenzana provided this misleading title (in Spanish) to introduce his reprinting of the (Latin) text of *Veritas ipsa*: "Another bull of Lord Paul III, which declares the Indians able to receive the Holy Sacraments of the Church, against the opinion of those who held them to be unable to receive them."[23] But access was not at issue in *Veritas ipsa*—or indeed its two companion decrees.

The first of these three rulings, *Altitudo divini concilii*, was issued on June 1, 1537. It focuses on the sacrament of baptism, although it also devotes a few lines to the sacrament of marriage. But it is not at all concerned with the question of *whether* these should be performed for Native Americans. That is taken for granted. Instead, most of the decree is concerned with the less-than-by-the-book mass baptisms conducted by the Franciscans in the Americas (something that deeply annoyed their Dominican rivals). The issue being decided by the pope was *not* whether those baptisms had been efficacious. The issue was whether the Europeans performing those baptisms had sinned in their haste to create converts. The baptizing clerics had not sinned, the pope decreed, but he went on to specify four minimal requirements with which all future baptisms must comply, including the use of holy water and the performance of exorcism and catechistical instruction. The decree concludes with instructions for dealing with the polygamous marriages of converts (ideally, a Catholic marriage ceremony was to be performed for the husband and his first wife), the days of fasting required of Native Americans, and the powers of absolution extended to New World bishops.

The two papal decrees issued the next day, on June 2, are far more famous: *Sublimis deus* and *Veritas ipsa*. Neither talks about the sacraments. Instead, both are responses to arguments made by American slave traders. Inspired by Satan, these flesh merchants claimed that Native Americans should be treated as brute animals (*bruta animalia*) incapable of conversion to the Catholic faith. In response, Paul III confirmed that Native Americans were true men (*veritas omnes*) and should not be enslaved or have their property taken from them.

In other words, although none of these three decrees is about allowing Native Americans to partake in the sacraments, they all are deeply engaged with questions of ontology. First, consider baptism from *Altitudo divini concilii*. In early modern Catholicism, baptism was not a superficially symbolic act. It was ontologically transformative, imagined to literally brand the soul with the mark of Christ (Camille 1989:45; Covarrubias Orozco 1611:198r; Didi-Huberman 1995:40; Park 1998). This brand could never be removed. Once someone had been baptized, he or she was irrevocably a Christian. Henceforth, the question was not whether or not a baptized person would live as a Christian. The question was whether he or she would live as a "good Christian" or a "bad Christian"—Catholic categories of being constantly referred to in early modern texts (Acosta 1954:366; Feria 1567:46v; Hamann 2020:268–274). Baptism brought about a change of state—a transformation so powerful that it was effective even if not performed with all of the steps recommended by the Catholic Church. Hence, less-than-by-the-book baptisms were valid, if undesirable.

Sublimis deus and *Veritas ipsa* engage with three additional categories of being: true men, brute animals, and slaves. Slavery, as Bill Brown (2006:179–181) famously described it, presents an "ontological scandal": the idea that a human being could be a mere piece of property. *Sublimis deus* and *Veritas ipsa* are often cited as evidence that Europeans *in general* thought of Native Americans as animals that could be bought and sold with no more thought than one would buy or sell a horse (Seed 1993:645). But things are more complicated. First, Paul III makes clear that claims about Native Americans being brute beasts had a specific origin and particular supporters. These claims were invented by Satan and promulgated by slave traders for their own benefit. Paul III does not present these ideas as widely held assumptions, but as strategic, self-serving assertions made by cynical businessmen. Twenty-first-century arguments about a general ontological confusion of humans and animals in the sixteenth-century New World misinterpret the evidence.

That said, it is also true that rhetorical bestialization was a common practice in Europe for denigrating social others (Kosiba, this volume). Claims that peasants and non-Christians were subhuman, animal-like beings had a very long history—and future—in the Old World.[24] Since the Middle Ages, Europe's upper classes had viewed rural laborers as "ferocious animals," "alien beings of a lower order" (Freedman 1999:1–2).[25] In 1480, the bishops of Toledo had this to say about Castile's peasantry: "Because of the defects of the teachers, neither children nor adults understand or learn what a Christian needs to know, and some of them are so ignorant that they are hardly worthy of being called Christians or human beings" (Dedieu 1991:1). Discourses of rural bestialization continued in the sixteenth and seventeenth centuries, when the peasant was portrayed as "a brutish being of monstrous appearance" (Prosperi 1995:178). Franciscan bishop Antonio de Guevara describes as "some animal in human form" one of the peasant characters in his *Clock of Princes* (1528).[26]

Peasants were not the only European subordinates to be described as animals. Muslims, too, were targets. In the words of Juan López de Palacios Rubios ([1514] 1954:81): "As oxen and other animals of the field we view the infidels, especially the Muslims, who like animals lacking in reason adore idols, disdaining the true God. That the Muslims are like animals is proved by the Master of the Sentences [Peter Lombard], in his Scholastic History." This harsh commentary, as it happens, appears in a text about the New World: the 1514 *Book of the Oceanic Islands*. Such anti-Islamic comparisons continued for at least another century. José María Pérez de Perceval (1992) has compiled a veritable bestiary of insults made between 1550 and 1650: Muslims are described as wolves, dogs, leeches, crows, rats, and rabbits.

The transatlantic applicability (and indeed banality) of early modern bestiality was nicely summarized by Sebastian de Covarrubias in 1611: "Ordinarily, we are in the habit of calling animal a man of little wisdom."[27] In other words, when slave traders in the Americas tried to claim that indigenous people were "brute animals," they were simply engaging in a practice of equal-opportunity denigration. They were extending to the New World strategies of subordination long established in the Old.[28]

But since situations of cultural difference often put established categories to the test, forcing them to be reevaluated, the use in the Americas of hierarchical rhetoric quite commonplace Europe became, in this new context, unacceptable (Sahlins 1981). Hence, the pope felt a need to formally intervene.

All of this returns us to Huanitzin's featherwork mosaic. Why was an image of the Mass of Saint Gregory chosen as a gift for Paul III, if his recent bulls were not, in fact, about proving Native Americans were humans or giving them sacramental access? There are at least two overlapping possibilities. First, the gift drew a parallel between Gregory the Great and Paul III as missionary popes. Gregory, during his papacy from 590 to 604, sent priests to convert pagans in the Germanies and England—a biographical detail directly mentioned in the records of the church congress (*junta eclesiástica*) held in Mexico City in April 1539 (Vera 1887:386).

That this particular scene involving Saint Gregory was chosen for feathery transformation is not surprising. An iconographic type incredibly popular from around 1400 to 1550, the saint's Mass was constantly reproduced in prints, altarpieces, and illuminated manuscripts. It was by far his most famous visualization. Recent scholarship has questioned what, exactly, the scene was meant to depict, but at the very least it engages with the mystery, literally, of the Eucharist: that bread and wine are transformed into the body and blood of Christ without changing their outward appearance (Bynum 2006). The scene relates to a legend involving Saint Gregory and a miraculous Mass. The following version was retold in 1604:

Another miracle was that Saint Gregory was saying Mass one day, and a woman arrived to take Communion (who had donated the bread which had been consecrated in the Mass), and at the moment which he [Gregory] said these words: "May the body of our Lord Jesus Christ protect your soul for the life eternal," he saw that the woman smiled, and putting the Form upon the altar, stopped his Mass: and right there, before the whole community, commanded that the woman should say why, at the moment she wanted to receive the body of the Lord, she had brazenly laughed. And the woman, after being silent for a while, finally said "because you said that the bread that I had made with my hands was the body of the Lord." Hearing this response, Saint Gregory, with the whole community, kneeled right there before the Altar to say a prayer to the Lord, and beg that he should open the eyes of the soul of that poor woman: and then the consecrated Form was converted into flesh, and in the presence of all those who were present, he showed it to the incredulous woman: and with this miracle she was reconciled, and the community remained confirmed in the Faith, and then a bit later the Host returned to take the appearance [*especie*] of bread which it had before.[29]

All of which suggests a second reason this image of Gregory was a fitting gift to send to the pope. Paul III's three decrees about Native Americans in 1537 were interventions into debates over ontological distinctions. And so it is entirely appropriate that, as a counter-gift, Huanitzin would remake in Mesoamerican featherwork a European image devoted to an ontological transformation central to Catholic faith. For early modern Catholics, the sacrament of Communion was not a symbolic act: the wafer and wine did not *symbolize* Christ's flesh and blood. In the moment of transubstantiation, they actually, literally became divine meat.

That the sixth-century pope Gregory was remembered in 1539 Mexico City as involved in the original conversion of the Germanies and England also pointed to more current events: those places were, in 1539, major sites for Protestant attacks against Catholicism. When Catholic inquisitors in 1539 Mexico City were seeking out for fiery destruction the sacred bundle of Huitzilopochtli, they were well aware that in many parts of Europe their own divine images were being sought out for fiery destruction by Reformed Christians.

And this brings us to yet another object from 1539: the second edition of *On the Origin of Errors*, Heinrich Bullinger's treatise against Catholic image worship (Figure 5.17). Printed in Protestant Zurich—which, like Mexico City, was part of the Holy Roman Empire of Charles V—the book has two parts. Part 1 attacks the use of images in Catholic worship. Part 2 attacks the Catholic Eucharist as yet another species of, literally, idolatry:

We now return to go over what logically followed upon the definition of transubstantiation. After they had persuaded themselves that no substance of either the bread or the wine remained in the sacrament of the Last Supper, but that the body and the blood of the Lord were actually contained therein, as a result they began to reason in the following manner: if it is the body, then the spirit and divine nature are also present in the body, since it is agreed that Christ's nature is indivisible or inseparable. They therefore began to supply canopies for the Sacrament, and cases, and little shrines, and to lie down before these objects with the feelings and disposition of a worshiper. Even in Mass they would prostrate themselves in adoration at the raising of the Eucharist.[30]

The true purpose of the Eucharist was unknown. The window of idolatry was flung open [*Aperiebatur idololatriae fenestra.*] The sacrament was carried in pomp, and was worshiped by the common people. Foolish superstition thrived inside houses and outside in rogation ceremonies. Women walked in the procession, decked out in meretricious finery; what of the fact that priests, adorned like lovers, ingratiated themselves more truly with boys than God with their soft chants?[31]

Communion, for Bullinger and many other Protestants, involved no ontological transformation. It was a symbolic act and nothing more (Baker 1980:101, 139).[32] At the very same time Huitzilopochtli's bundle was on the run, trying to escape the iconoclastic violence of Catholics, Catholic Communion wafers became targets for the iconoclastic violence of Protestants. This symmetry is appropriate: for their

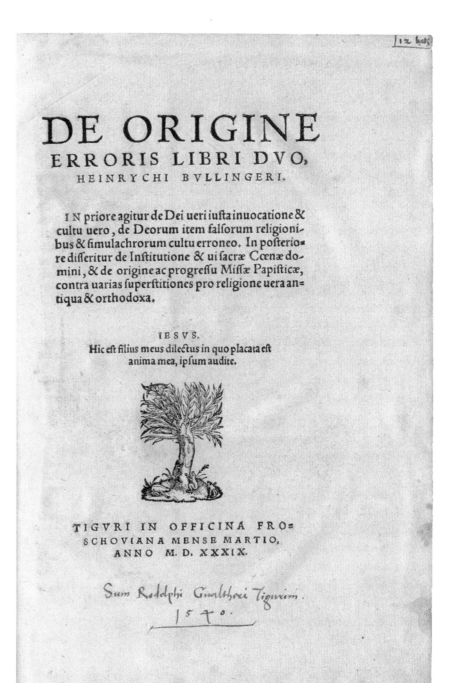

figure 5.17
The title page of *De origine erroris* (Bullinger 1539). Image courtesy of the Zentralbibliothek Zürich, Signaturangabe 5.501.

respective worshippers, both bundle and wafer were materialized divinities, sacred presences. And so on Sunday, August 8, 1535, the Cathedral of Geneva was attacked by a mob. The tabernacle in its main altar contained fifty consecrated Hosts. "If they really are gods," declared Protestant leader Mesgret, "they won't let themselves be eaten by a dog." The "white gods" were then presented to Mesgret's canine companion, who devoured them (Eire 1986:146).

Conclusion: Cartesian Animism

The interreligious fires of the 1530s were still burning a century later. In many ways, they reached their apotheosis in the three decades of Central European violence now known as the Thirty Years' War. Millions of people were slaughtered: soldiers and civilians, Catholics and Protestants. The fighting began in May 1618, when Ferdinand II (Holy Roman Emperor over an empire reduced to Bohemia, Hungary, and the Germanies) attempted to impose Catholicism on all of his subjects. The ensuing violence spread to France, Italy, and the Low Countries, and kings from throughout Europe (including Spain, Sweden, and Denmark) sent armies to participate. The conflicts ended in 1648 with the Peace of Westphalia, a settlement "agreed to by all the major powers of all the outstanding problems of western and central Europe" (Rabb 1975:74–82). Although the reigning pope, Innocent X, denounced this interreligious peace treaty, he was ignored by Protestants and Catholics alike. Violent conflicts between Christian sects were not banished from Europe in 1648, but their intensity had forever changed (Hamann 2016; Kaplan 2007).

The three decades of violence of the Thirty Years' War were the context in which René Descartes developed his philosophy and wrote his *Discourse on Method* (Figure 5.18). The *Discourse* directly references its blood-soaked political context. Descartes (who identified as Catholic all of his life) joined the army of the (Catholic) duke of Bavaria in 1619, and it was on November 10 of that year—in a town on the frontiers between rival Catholic and Protestant claimants for the crown of the Holy Roman Empire—that Descartes had the famous nocturnal visions inspiring his new theories of knowledge (Bird-David 1999:S79; Clarke 2006:58–59). As he writes in part 2 of the *Discourse*, "I was then in Germany, where the occasion of the wars which are not yet over there had called me; and as I was returning to the army from the coronation of the emperor" (Descartes [1637] 1998:6). Descartes was also well aware that the very writing of his *Discourse* was possible because (by the 1630s) he was living as an émigré in the relatively tolerant—and, above all, peaceful—United Provinces: "a country where the long duration of the war has led to the establishment of such well-ordered discipline

that the armies quartered here seem to serve only to make one enjoy the fruits of peace with even greater security" (Descartes [1637] 1998:17–18).

Before settling in the United Provinces, Descartes traveled extensively throughout Europe. And as a reader of Michel de Montaigne ([1580] 1958), he had armchair-traveled throughout the world. He was therefore well aware of the issue of multiculturalism—except that the culture concept had not yet been invented:

I had recognized in my travels that all those who have sentiments quite contrary to our own are not for that reason barbarians or savages, but that many of them use their reason as much as or more than we do. And I considered how one and the same man with the very same mind, were he brought up from infancy among the French or the Germans, would become different from what he would be had he always lived among the Chinese or the cannibals, and how, even down to the styles of our clothing, the same thing that pleased us ten years ago, and that perhaps will again please us ten years hence, now seems to us extravagant and ridiculous. Thus it is more custom and example that persuades us than any certain knowledge. (Descartes [1637] 1998:9)

Descartes knew that human propensities for ethnocentrism could easily be taken advantage of. ("Ethnocentrism," by the way, is the title of the chapter where Lévi-Strauss included the anecdote on inquisitions and the Antilles with which we began.) Over and over again in a letter from 1643, Descartes laments the power that the words of radical preachers had for inspiring their followers to religious violence: "A preacher excites his listeners to anger and hatred . . . against men of a different religion, which we already hate as the cause of all wars. . . . I would add that often public dissentions and wars have no other origin, and those most susceptible are those who, full of confidence in the wisdom of these dangerous doctors, have followed all their advice."[33]

The Thirty Years' War began with an attempt by a Catholic monarch to impose his religion by

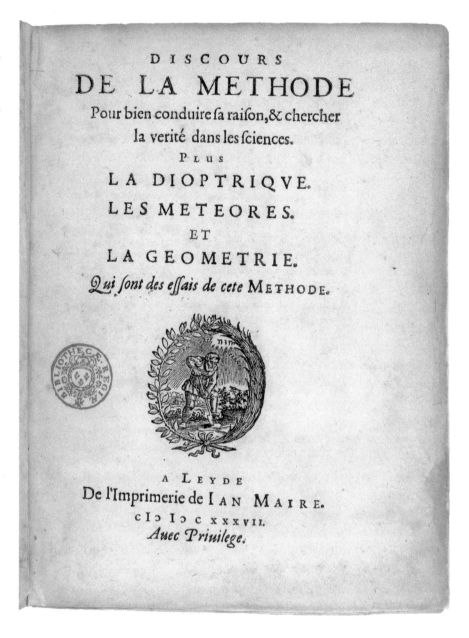

force. That this failed, and spectacularly, helps explain why Descartes uses strikingly self-effacing prose at the beginning of the *Discourse*. He does not want to force the reader to believe anything. Descartes's awareness of how ethnocentric violence often rests on unexamined assumptions, and of how easily humans can be deceived (by religious rhetoric, for example), also explains why he attempts to rebuild his personal philosophy from the ground up, interrogating all of his taken-for-granted ideas and mistrusting the influence of his fallible senses:

And if, my work having pleased me sufficiently, I here show you a model of it, it is not for the reason that I would wish to advise anyone to imitate it. Perhaps those with whom God has better shared his graces will have more lofty plans; but I fear that even this one here may already be too daring for many. The single resolution to rid oneself of all the opinions to which one has heretofore given credence is not an example that everyone ought to follow.

. . . For a long time I had noticed that in matters of morality one must sometimes follow opinions that one knows to be quite uncertain, just as if they were indubitable, as has been said above, but because I then desired to devote myself exclusively to the search for the truth, I thought it necessary that I do exactly the opposite, and that I reject as absolutely false everything in which I could imagine the least doubt, in order to see whether, after this process, something in my beliefs remained that was entirely indubitable. Thus, because our senses sometimes deceive us, I wanted to suppose that nothing was exactly as they led us to imagine. (Descartes [1637] 1998:9, 18)[34]

This "Cartesian objectivism" (Bird-David 1999:S87) was much stranger than its recent characterizations suggest. Patricia McAnany begins her chapter in this volume by discussing the complexity of ontological translation, and this is a key issue with Descartes. The introductory paragraph

to the *Discourse on Method* includes the claim that Descartes "proves the existence of God and of the human soul, which are the foundations for his metaphysics."[35] Although Descartes is often charged with inventing the mind/body dualism, the Cartesian word that English translations present as "mind" is, in the original French, *esprit*: soul or spirit.[36] Thought, for Descartes, takes place not in the brain, but in the soul.[37] He was not living in a secular, deanimated universe. "I think, therefore I am" was, for Descartes, proof that the *soul* existed.

Throughout the 1640s, Descartes wrote a number of letters explaining how the ontological mystery of transubstantiation could be explained—yet not secularized—by the particle physics of his new philosophy. But Catholic authorities were unconvinced, and Eucharistic implications are one reason why, in 1663, the Holy Office of the Inquisition placed the *Discourse* on its Index of Prohibited Books.[38]

NOTES

1 Adapted from Descartes 1637:3. That my chapter's wide-ranging but interconnected pensées (as one reviewer described them), each building on the next but with their own arguments and interpretations, echo the structure of Descartes's *Discours de la methode* (and the *Essais* by Montaigne that inspired him) is not incidental. Thanks to Art Joyce for making me see the Latourian implications of my reading of Descartes (Latour 1993). On historical constellations, see Hamann 2016.

2 On the concept of a "turn," see Latour 2014:13 and Boellstorff 2016; for critical evaluations of this "turn," see Turner 2009; Laidlaw 2012; Ramos 2012; Bessire and Bond 2014.

3 "Dans les Grandes Antilles, quelques années après la découverte de l'Amérique, pendant que les Espagnols envoyaient des commissions d'enquête pour rechercher si les indigènes possédaient ou non une âme, ces derniers s'employaient à immerger des blancs prisonniers afin de vérifier par une surveillance prolongée si leur cadavre était, ou non, sujet

à la putréfaction" (Lévi-Strauss 1952:12; reprinted in Lévi-Strauss 1973:384 and quoted and translated in Viveiros de Castro 1998:475). When retelling the anecdote in his *Tristes tropiques*, Lévi-Strauss (1955:80) alluded to its source: "Au même moment, d'ailleurs, et dans une île voisine (Porto-Rico, selon le témoignage d'Oviedo) les Indiens s'employaient à capturer des blancs et à les faire périr par immersion, puis montaient pendant des semaines la garde autour des noyés afin de savoir s'ils étaient ou non soumis à la putrefaction." The story was indeed recounted by Gonzalo Fernández de Oviedo y Valdés in the 1535 edition of his *La historia general de las Indias* (book 16, chap. 8:123v–124r). The tale was then retold by Girolamo Benzoni in his *La historia del mondo nvovo* (1565:9v–10r), a book subsequently reprinted (with added illustrations) as volume 4 of Theodor de Bry's *Americae* (1594).

4 The occidentalist essentialism (Carrier 1992:199) involved in generalizations about "Western-Cartesian thought" has not escaped criticism:

"[Pedersen] limits the alternative view he proposes by designating it 'non-Euro-American' (and 'non-Cartesian' as if these were the same thing), even though his own exposition of that alternative view draws heavily on a galaxy of indubitably 'Euro-American' thinkers" (Laidlaw 2012); "One major problem for Descola certainly relates to how what he calls 'naturalism' arose from whatever it is imagined it developed from (analogism, principally), for on his account it was nowhere to be found before it came to dominate thinking in seventeenth-century Europe" (Lloyd 2011:835). See also Turner 2009:18.

5 "Ie connû de là que i'estois vne substance dont toute l'essence ou la nature n'est que de penser, & qui pour estre n'a besoin d'aucun lieu ny ne depend d'aucune chose materielle, En sorte que ce Moy, c'est a dire, l'Ame par laquelle ie suis ce que ie suis, est entierement distincte du cors" (Descartes 1637:34; translated in Descartes [1637] 1998:19).

6 According to the *Oxford English Dictionary*, *anthropology* and its cognates appear in European languages during the sixteenth century. The *OED*'s earliest attestation in English is from 1593. For other discussions of Descartes's thought in relation to Europe's wars of religion, see Shenefelt and White 2013:16, 124–141.

7 See also López Luján et al. 2010. For sacred bundles in general, see Bassett 2015; Olivier 2006. On the dating of the *Boturini*, see Escalante Gonzalbo 2010:63–64, 101, 387; Tena 2009. See Kopytoff 1986 on the blurred boundaries of humans and objects, as well as for a "biographical" approach to material culture whose influence on these pages will be quite clear.

8 Thanks to Alanna S. Radlo-Dzur for her Nahuatl expertise throughout this essay. The first investigation (Archivo General de la Nación, Mexico [AGN], Inquisición, Volumen 37, Expediente 3, 20r–46v; González Obregón 1912:115–140) began on June 20 and 21, 1539, prompted by testimonies from Mateo and Juan, indigenous men resident in Mexico City's San Juan neighborhood. They described how their father had been asked by Moctezuma himself to carry the bundle of Huitzilopochtli out of besieged Mexico City and across the lake to safety in Azcapotzalco. They accused Pochtecatl Tlaylotla, a man baptized as Miguel, of storing the bundles in his Mexico City house when they were later returned from Azcapotzalco and then sent onward once again. Miguel had been arrested by mid-July and became the center of the investigation. Additional testimonies against him were gathered on October 14 (witnesses from Chiconauhtla and Tlatelolco—note that witnesses from Chiconauhtla were at the center of the July 1539 investigation of don Carlos Ometochtzin of Texcoco, a process that ended with his execution on November 30, 1539), October 24, and November 1 (witnesses from the Mexico City neighborhoods of Santa María and Santa Catalina). In the end, Miguel was sentenced to seclusion in Mexico City's Franciscan monastery. The second investigation (AGN, Inquisición, Volumen 42, Expediente 18, 147r–153v; González Obregón 1912:177–184; note that the published presentation of the documents somewhat obscures the incomplete nature of the surviving sheets of testimony in the original file) is much more fragmentary than the first; the only dated testimony is from December 2, 1539. The case is centered on the ruler of Culhuacan, don Baltasar, who is accused of helping to hide the sacred bundles of Tenochtitlan nearly two decades before. Three of the witnesses (including don Baltasar) are from Culhuacan; the fourth witness is Pochtecatl Tlaylotla, aka Miguel, who provides a direct connection between the two cases. Apparently, the investigation into don Baltasar attempts to pick up the trail of what happened to the bundles after they had returned to Mexico City from Azcapotzalco. Four of the five bundles named in the Pochtecatl Tlaylotla investigation are also named in the don Baltasar investigation: Huitzilopochtli, Cihuacoatl, Tlatlauhqui Tezcatlipoca, and Tepehua. In any case, the bundles were never found.

9 "Dixo: que lo que sabe es, que cuando los xpianos tomaron esta Cibdad de México, se acuerda este testigo que su padre, que se decía Tlatolatl, se huyó de esta Cibdad con un ídolo que decían que era el dios de los mexicanos muy antiquísimo, y fué á parar con el dicho ídolo á parar á Escapuzalco, y los señores de allí, que se decían Ocuicin é Tlilanci, le recibieron de muy buena voluntad y lo llevaron á una casa en que estuviese y guardase su ídolo, y le dieron cuatro ídolos otros á guardar, que se decían Tescatepocal y Ciguacuatl, y Telpuchtl y Tepegua, y le dixeron que los guardase todos; y que este testigo vía que su padre adoraba y ofrecía á los dichos

ídolos, y los ornaba con ornamentos como lo tenían por costumbre" (AGN, Inquisición, Volumen 37, Expediente 3, 22v; González Obregón 1912:118).

10 "Los indios llevaron dos envoltorios á Culhuacan, grandes y pesados, el uno era negro y el otro era azul, y que allí estuvieron cuatro ó cinco días, y que los guardaban mexicanos, y que ellos mismos los llevaron en una canoa; y que preguntando el dicho Don Baltasar por ellos, le dixieron unos que á Xilotepec los habían llevado, y otros que á Xaltoca, y otros que al Peñol, y á otras partes también le nombraron; y que los dichos envoltorios eran del gran ídolo de México Huizilopuchtly" (AGN, Inquisición, Volumen 42, Expediente 18, 149v; González Obregón 1912:181).

11 Parallel circulations of sacred bundles to sites involved in their primordial biographies were also taking place in Oaxaca (Hamann 2020:142–149).

12 "Dixo: que puede haber diez é siete años, poco más o menos, que llevaron de esta Cibdad al dicho pueblo de Culoacán el Ochilobos é otros muchos ídolos, y que los llevó Teuachichilayo, indio que es muerto, y los pusieron en una cueva que se dice Telacin, y allí estuvieron seis días" (AGN, Inquisición, Volumen 42, Expediente 18, 147r; González Obregón 1912:178).

13 "É que entonces, un viejo que se decía Nahueca, dixo á este testigo y á su hermano: i pobres de vosotros, ya sabéis cómo el cacique de Escapuzalco y Tlilanci é vuestro padre son todos muertos; porque el dicho Nahueca era principal viejo y que tenía cargo de las cosas de Tlilanci" (AGN, Inquisición, Volumen 37, Expediente 3, 21v–22r; González Obregón 1912:117).

14 AGN, Inquisición, Volumen 37, Expediente 3, 21r; González Obregón 1912:116.

15 "Muy privado de Montezuma y persona á quien el dicho Montezuma daba parte de sus secretos" (AGN, Inquisición, Volumen 37, Expediente 3, 21v; González Obregón 1912:116).

16 AGN, Inquisición, Volumen 42, Expediente 18, 149v; González Obregón 1912:179.

17 In addition to the work of Castañeda de la Paz, other key discussions of the *Boturini* include Boone 1991; Cummins 2015; Tena 2009.

18 It takes around ten to twelve years for a maguey cactus to reach maturity so that its sap can be harvested; thanks to Megan O'Neil for asking me about the numerics of maguey lives.

19 "Preguntado, si sabe dónde están ó quién tiene los ídolos de ochilobos, dixo: que este confesante era profeta y tenía la cuenta de los demonios y cargo de hacer las cosas que para ellos era menester, é que oyó decir á Tomólo, difunto, que era del mismo oficio que este confesante, que Palacatl, y Cuzcasuchatl, é Yzcuen, y Cocacal, indios vecinos de México, que andan con Don Diego, Señor de México, tienen é guardan á los dichos ídolos, porque sus padres de ellos los solían tener y guardar, y ellos, despues de la muerte de sus padres sucedieron en la guarda de los dichos ídolos y los traen é tienen junto á Tula, é que este que declara cree é tiene por cierto que ellos los tienen y saben de ellos, porque descienden de los que solían tener el mismo cargo; otro sí, dixo: que puede haber ocho ó diez años, poco más ó menos, que estando en el puebo de Escapuzalco este que declara y Don Diego, Señor que agora es de México, y Achacal, principal, y otros tres principales, platicando sobre que los padres habían prehendido á un principal sobre que diese el ochilobos, dixo el dicho Don Diego que le parecía que debían dar el ochilobos á los frailes: que qué les parecía; y el Achacatl, principal, dixo que no se debía dar, é que en ninguna manera no se les diese; y así determinaron que no se les debía dar ni diese é que así no se les dio" (AGN, Inquisición, Volumen 37, Expediente 3, 27r–27v; González Obregón 1912:123–124).

20 "It was created in 1539 to be sent to Pope Paul III in gratitude for his Papal Bull, issued in 1537, conceding that the Indian, as a being capable of reason, could receive the sacrament of baptism and communion" (Cummins 2002:116). "The inscribed date of 1539—the earliest for an existing featherwork—coincides with the year the news arrived in Mexico of the papal bull promulgated by Paul III proscribing the enslavement of Indians and defending their full rationality and consequent lawful access to the sacraments—including the Eucharist" (Estrada de Gerlero, Pierce, and Farago 2004:97). "As the surrounding Latin text explains, the image was created in Mexico City by Aztec feather workers in 1539 as gift for Pope Paul III, who two years before had issued a Papal Bull that recognized the capacity of Indians to receive the sacraments of baptism and communion" (Cummins 2009:81). See also Estrada de Gerlero 1994.

21 The Latin text and a Spanish translation of *Altitudo divini consilii* and *Sublimis deus* are published in Parish and Weidman 1992:306–312; the Latin text

and an English translation of *Sublimis deus* and *Veritas ipsa* are published in Panzer 1996:79–83.

22 Classic accounts of this "dispute" include Cañizares-Esguerra 2001; Church 1936; Gerbi 1973.

23 "OTRA BULA DE EL SEÑOR PAULO III. por la que declara capaces á los Indios de los Santos Sacramentos de la Iglesia, contra la opinion de los que los tenían por incapaces de ellos" (Lorenzana 1769:33). Lorenzana does not make this prejudice up; it is mentioned directly (and dismissed) in item 22 of the account of Mexico City's 1539 *junta eclesiástica* (Vera 1887:401). But although many other items in that account directly reference the recent bulls of Paul III (for example, see Vera 1887:286, 391–392, 402–403), no such reference occurs in connection with item 22—which surely would have been done had contemporaries seen some link between indigenous "capacity" and the papal decrees of 1537.

24 "You don't need to go to America to see savages," wrote Honoré de Balzac in 1844—they could be seen in the Burgundian countryside (quoted in Weber 1976:3). Views of the European peasantry as "savages and barbarians," even "a heathen population," would continue into the twentieth century (Hind 1984:20, 23; Levi 1963). For the deep history of wild internal others in the lands north of the Mediterranean, see Bartra 1994.

25 On the "discovery" of "Europe's internal savages" in the twelfth and thirteenth centuries, see Fernández-Armesto 1987:225.

26 "Quando yo le vi entrar en el Senado, imaginé que era algún animal en figura de hombre" (Guevara [1529] 1994:634; see also Abulafia 2008:21–23, 69; Martínez 2008:12).

27 "Vulgarmé[n]te solemos dezir animal, al hombre de poco discurso" (Covarrubias Orozco 1611:72r). Canary Islanders, too, were often compared to animals: see Fernández Armesto 1987:241.

28 Writing from New Spain in 1536, Friar Bernardino de Minaya described a theory that Indians were a "third species" of animal between monkeys and humans; this view was later critiqued by Francisco de Vitoria (Cruz y Moya 1944:2:46; Vitoria 1991:104).

29 "Otro milagro fue, q[ue] dizie[n]do vn dia Missa san Gregorio, y llega[n]dose à comulgar vna muger, que auia ofrecido el pan que el en la Missa auia consagrado, al tie[m]po que dixo aquellas palabras: *El cuerpo de nuestro Señor Iesu Christo guarde tu alma para la vida eterna*, vio que se sonreía la muger, y

poniendo la forma sobre el altar, acabò su Missa: y despues alli delante de todo el pueblo mandò à la muger que dixesse, porque en aquel punto que queria recebir el cuerpo del Señor, temerariamente se auia reydo. Y la muger, despues de auer callado vn rato, al fin dixo: Porque vos dixistes, que el pan que yo auia hecho con mis manos, era cuerpo del Señor. Oyendo ésta respuesta san Gregorio, con todo el pueblo se arrodillò alli delante del Altar à hacer oracio[n] al Señor, y suplicarle, que abriesse los ojos del alma à aquella pobre muger: y luego la forma consagrada se conuirtio en carne, y el en presencia de todos los que estauan presentes, se la mostrò à la muger incredula: y con éste milagro ella se reduxo, y el pueblo quedò confirmado en la Fê, y de alli à poco la Hostia boluio à tomar la especie de pa[n] que antes tenia" (Ribadneyra 1604:295).

30 "Redimus nunc, ac quid definitione[m] illa[m] Transsubstantionis sequutum sit perstringimus. Posteaquam ergo sibi persuaserant in sacramentis Coenae nihil superesse substantiae uel panis uel uini, sed uerum ibi contineri corpus & sanguinem domini, co[n]sequenter si ratiocionabantur. Si corpus est & anima igitur & diuinitas sunt una cum corpore, quando personam Christi constet esse indiuisibilem aut inseparabilem. Coeperunt ergo Sacramento parare tabernacula, & thecas, & aediculas, & coram his procumbere adorantis animo & affectu. In Missis quoq[ue] eleuationem eucharistiae prostrauerunt se ad adorandum" (Bullinger 1539:241r; translation by Erika Valdivieso).

31 "Ignorabatur uerus eucharistię usus. Aperiebatur idololatriae fenestra. Ferebatur enim in pompa sacramentu[m], et adorabatur a uulgo promiscuo. In domibus agrisq[ue] lustrandis mire stulta uigebat superstitio. Mulieres in pompa cultu ornatae meretricio incedebant: quid quod sacerdotes amasiorum more compti suaui cantu sese puellis ueris q[uam] deo insinuabant" (Bullinger 1539:242r; translation by Erika Valdivieso).

32 On Bullinger's "symbolic" views (which he shared with Huldrych Zwingli, his pastoral predecessor in Zurich), and the somewhat different understandings of John Calvin, see Rorem 1988. Luther, famously, was opposed to the doctrine of transubstantiation, but he did maintain that the presence of Christ in the wine and bread was actual and not merely symbolic (Dillenberger 1962:xxxii)—one of the debates within Reformed belief that helps

explain why Protestant-Protestant religious violence in early modern Europe could be as horrific as Protestant-Catholic conflicts.

33 "C'est pourquoi enfin, lorsqu'un prédicateur excite ses auditeurs à la colère et à la haine contre d'autres hommes, surtout contre des hommes riches et puissants, auxquels les dernières classes de la société ne sont que trop disposées à porter envie, ou contre des hommes d'une religion différente, que l'on hait déjà comme la cause de toutes les guerres. . . . Je pourrais ajouter que souvent les dissensions publiques et les guerres n'ont pas d'autre origine, et que ceux-là sont toujours les plus exposés, qui, pleins de confiance en la sagesse de ces dangereux docteurs, ont suivi tous leurs conseils" (Descartes [1643] 1988:354–355; see also 340, 353).

34 As with much of the *Discourse*, parallels to Latour's work are surprising and striking: "It is possible—and from a Western (from my Burgundian) point of view, desirable—that, in the distant future, we come to live within a common world defined as naturalism defines it. But to behave as if the settlement were already in place and as though it requires no negotiation to achieve it is a sure trigger to further warfare" (Latour 2004:458; see also note 24, above).

35 "En la 4, les raisons par lesquelles il prouue l'existence de Dieu, & de l'ame humaine, qui sont les fondemens de sa Metaphysique" (Descartes 1637:3; translated in Descartes [1637] 1998:1).

36 For seventeenth-century definitions of *esprit*, see Académie Françoise 1644:399.

37 For Descartes's ideas about thought, the soul, and the pineal gland, see Lokhorst 2013.

38 On the Index, transubstantiation, and Descartes's metaphysics, see Armogathe and Carraud 2005; Nadler 1988, 2013:168. Descartes was not alone in his attempts, in the seventeenth century, "to reconcile miracles with a mechanical universe"; see also Oakley 1984:67–92.

REFERENCES CITED

Abulafia, David
    2008   *The Discovery of Mankind: Atlantic Encounters in the Age of Columbus*. Yale University Press, New Haven.

Académie Françoise
    1644   *Le dictionnaire de l'Académie Françoise, dedié au Roy. Tome Premier. A-L*. Jean Baptiste Coignard, Paris.

Acosta, José de
    1954   *Obras del Padre José de Acosta*. Ediciones Atlas, Madrid.

Alberti, Benjamin, and Tamara L. Bray
    2009   Animating Archaeology: Of Subjects, Objects and Alternative Ontologies. *Cambridge Archaeological Journal* 19(3):337–343.

Allen, Catherine
    1998   When Utensils Revolt: Mind, Matter, and Modes of Being in the Pre-Columbian Andes. *RES: Anthropology and Aesthetics* 33:18–27.

Armogathe, Jean-Robert, and Vincent Carraud
    2005   The First Condemnation of Descartes's *Oeuvres*: Some Unpublished Documents from the Vatican Archives. *Oxford Studies in Early Modern Philosophy* 1:67–110.

Baker, J. Wayne
    1980   *Heinrich Bullinger and the Covenant: The Other Reformed Tradition*. University of Ohio Press, Athens.

Bartra, Roger
    1994   *Wild Men in the Looking Glass: The Mythic Origins of European Otherness*. University of Michigan Press, Ann Arbor.

Bassett, Molly
    2015   *The Fate of Earthly Things: Aztec Gods and God-Bodies*. University of Texas Press, Austin.

Benzoni, Girolamo
    1565   *La historia del mondo nvovo*. Francesco Rampazetto, Venice.

Bessire, Lucas, and David Bond

2014   Ontological Anthropology and the Deferral of Critique. *American Ethnologist* 41(3):440–456.

Bird-David, Nurit

1999   "Animism" Revisited: Personhood, Environment, and Relational Epistemology. *Current Anthropology* 40:S67–S91.

Boellstorff, Tom

2016   For Whom the Ontology Turns: Theorizing the Digital Real. *Current Anthropology* 57(4):387–487.

Boone, Elizabeth Hill

1989   Incarnations of the Aztec Supernatural: The Image of Huitzilopochtli in Mexico and Europe. *Transactions of the American Philosophical Society*, n.s., 79(2):i–iv, 1–107.

1991   Migration Histories as Ritual Performance. In *To Change Place: Aztec Ceremonial Landscapes*, edited by Davíd Carrasco, pp. 121–151. University Press of Colorado, Boulder.

2000   *Stories in Red and Black: Pictorial Histories of the Aztecs and Mixtecs.* University of Texas Press, Austin.

Bray, Tamara

2009   An Archaeological Perspective on the Andean Concept of *Camaquen*: Thinking through Late Pre-Columbian *Ofrendas* and *Huacas. Cambridge Archaeological Journal* 19(3):357–366.

Brilliant, Richard

1991   The Bayeux Tapestry: A Stripped Narrative for Their Eyes and Ears. *Word and Image* 7(2):98–126.

Brown, Bill

2006   Reification, Reanimation, and the American Uncanny. *Critical Inquiry* 23:175–207.

Brown, Linda A., and Kitty F. Emery

2008   Negotiations with the Animate Forest: Hunting Shrines in the Guatemalan Highlands. *Journal of Archaeological Method and Theory* 15:300–337.

Bry, Theodor de

1594   *Americae pars quarta.* Theodor de Bry, Frankfurt.

Bullinger, Heinrich

1539   *De origine erroris.* Officina Froschoviana, Zurich.

Bynum, Caroline Walker

2006   Seeing and Seeing Beyond: The Mass of Saint Gregory in the Fifteenth Century. In *The Mind's Eye: Art and Theological Argument in the Middle Ages*, edited by Jeffrey F. Hamburger and Anne-Marie Bouché, pp. 208–240. Princeton University Press, Princeton.

Camille, Michael

1989   *The Gothic Idol: Ideology and Image-Making in Medieval Art.* Cambridge University Press, Cambridge.

Cañizares-Esguerra, Jorge

2001   *How to Write the History of the New World: Historiographies, Epistemologies, and Identities in the Eighteenth-Century Atlantic World.* Stanford University Press, Stanford.

Carrier, James

1992   Occidentalism: The World Turned Upside-Down. *American Ethnologist* 19(2):195–212.

Castañeda de la Paz, María

2005   El Códice X o los anales del grupo de la *Tira de la Peregrinación*: Evolución pictográfica y problemas en su análisis interpretativo. *Journal de la Société des Americanistes* 91(1):7–40.

2007   *La Tira de la Peregrinación*: La ascendencia chichimeca de los tenochca. *Estudios de cultura náhuatl* 38:183–212.

2008   Codex Axcatitlan and the World of Torquemada: A Historiographic Puzzle in the Aztec-Mexica Sources. *Latin American Literatures Journal* 24(2):151–194.

Church, Henry Ward

1936   Corneille de Pauw, and the Controversy over His *Recherches philosophiques sur les américains. PMLA* 51(1):178–206.

Clarke, Desmond

2006   *Descartes, a Biography.* Cambridge University Press, Cambridge.

Covarrubias Orozco, Sebastián de

1611   *Tesoro de la lengva castellana o española.* Luis Sanchez, Madrid.

Cruz y Moya, Juan José de la

1944   *Historia de la santa y apostólica provincia de Santiago de predicadores de México en la Nueva España.* 2 vols. Porrua, Mexico City.

Cummins, Tom

2002   To Serve Man: Pre-Columbian Art, Western Discourses of Idolatry, and Cannibalism. *RES: Anthropology and Aesthetics* 42:109–130.

2009   The Golden Calf in America. In *The Idol in the Age of Art: Objects, Devotions and the Early Modern World*, edited by Michael W. Cole and Rebecca E. Zorach, pp. 77–104. Ashgate, Burlington, Vt.

2015   Here, There, and Now: Deictics and the Transposition of Orality to Image in Colonial Imagery. *Art in Translation* 7(1):64–94.

Dedieu, Jean Pierre

1991   "Christianization" in New Castile: Catechism, Communion, Mass, and Confirmation in the Toledo Archbishopric, 1540–1650. In *Culture and Control in Counter-Reformation Spain*, edited by Anne Cruz and Mary E. Perry, pp. 1–24. University of Minnesota Press, Minneapolis.

Descartes, René

1637   *Discours de la methode pour bien conduire sa raison, & chercher la verité dans les sciences, plus la dioptrique, les meteores et la geometrie qui sont des essais de cette methode.* Jan Maire, Leiden.

[1637] 1998   Discourse on Method. In *Discourse on Method and Meditations on First Philosophy*, translated by Donald A. Cress, pp. 1–44. Hackett, Indianapolis.

[1643] 1988   Lettre à Voet. In *La querelle d'Utrecht*, edited by Martin Schoock and translated by Theo Verbeek, pp. 321–400. Les impressions nouvelles, Paris.

Descola, Philippe

2005   *Par-delà nature et culture.* Gallimard, Paris.

Didi-Huberman, Georges

1995   *Fra Angelico: Dissemblance and Figuration.* Translated by Janet M. Todd. University of Chicago Press, Chicago.

Dillenberger, John (editor)

1962   *Martin Luther: Selections from His Writings.* Anchor Books, New York.

Durán, Diego

1964   *Book of the Gods and Rites and the Ancient Calendar.* Translated by Doris Heyden and Fernando Horcasitas. University of Oklahoma Press, Norman.

Eire, Carlos M.

1986   *War against the Idols: The Reformation of Worship from Erasmus to Calvin.* Cambridge University Press, Cambridge.

Escalante Gonzalbo, Pablo

2010   *Los códices mesoamericanos antes y después de la conquista española: Historia de un lenguaje pictográfico.* Fondo de Cultura Económica, Mexico City.

Estrada de Gerlero, Elena Isabel

1994   La plumaria expresión artística por excelencia. In *México en el mundo de las colecciones de arte, Nueva España I*, pp. 73–117. Azabache, Mexico City.

Estrada de Gerlero, Elena Isabel, Donna Pierce, and Claire Farago

2004   Mass of Saint Gregory. In *Painting a New World: Mexican Art and Life, 1521–1821*, edited by Donna Pierce, Rogelio Ruiz Gomar, and Clara Bargellini, pp. 94–102. Frederick and Jan Mayer Center for Pre-Columbian and Spanish Colonial Art at the Denver Art Museum, Denver, Colo.

Feria, Pedro de

1567   *Doctrina christiana en lengua castellana y çapoteca.* Pedro Ocharte, Mexico City.

Fernández-Armesto, Felipe

1987   *Before Columbus: Exploration and Colonization from the Mediterranean to the Atlantic.* University of Pennsylvania Press, Philadelphia.

Freedman, Paul

1999   *Images of the Medieval Peasant.* Stanford University Press, Stanford.

Gell, Alfred

1998   *Art and Agency: An Anthropological Theory.* Clarendon Press, Oxford.

Gerbi, Antonello

1973 *The Dispute of the New World: The History of a Polemic, 1750–1900.* Edited and translated by Jeremy Moyle. University of Pittsburgh Press, Pittsburgh.

González Obregón, Luis (director)

1912 *Publicaciones del Archivo General de la Nación III: Procesos de indios idolatras y hechiceros.* Tipografía Guerrero Hermanos, Mexico City.

Guevara, Antonio de

[1529] 1994 *Obras completas, II: Relox de príncipes.* Turner, Madrid.

Hallowell, Irving A.

1960 Ojibwa Ontology, Behavior, and World View. In *Culture in History: Essays in Honor of Paul Radin*, edited by Stanley Diamond, pp. 19–52. Columbia University Press, New York.

Hamann, Byron Ellsworth

2004 "In the Eyes of the Mixtecs / To View Several Pages Simultaneously": Seeing and the Mixtec Screenfolds. *Visible Language* 38(1):68–123.

2008 Chronological Pollution: Potsherds, Mosques, and Broken Gods before and after the Conquest of Mexico. *Current Anthropology* 59(5):803–836.

2013 Object, Image, Cleverness: The *Lienzo de Tlaxcala. Art History* 36(3):518–545.

2016 How to Chronologize with a Hammer, Or, The Myth of Homogeneous, Empty Time. *HAU: Journal of Ethnographic Theory* 6(1):69–101.

2018 The *Higa* and the *Tlachialoni*: Material Cultures of Seeing in the Mediterratlantic. *Art History* 41(4):624–649.

2020 *Bad Christians, New Spains: Muslims, Catholics, and Native Americans in a Mediterratlantic World.* Routledge, New York.

Heywood, Paolo

2012 Anthropology and What There Is: Reflections on "Ontology." *Cambridge Journal of Anthropology* 30(1):143–151.

Hind, Robert J.

1984 "We Have No Colonies": Similarities within the British Imperial Experience. *Comparative Studies in Society and History* 26(1):3–35.

Ingold, Timothy

2012 Toward an Ecology of Materials. *Annual Review of Anthropology* 41:427–442.

Kaplan, Benjamin

2007 *Divided by Faith: Religious Conflict and the Practice of Toleration in Early Modern Europe.* Belknap Press, Cambridge, Mass.

Kellogg, Susan

1980 Social Organization in Early Colonial Tenochtitlan-Tlatelolco: An Ethnohistorical Study. PhD dissertation, University of Rochester, Rochester, N.Y.

1995 *Law and the Transformation of Aztec Society.* University of Oklahoma Press, Norman.

Kohn, Eduardo

2015 Anthropology of Ontologies. *Annual Review of Anthropology* 44:311–327.

Kopytoff, Igor

1986 The Cultural Biography of Things: Commoditization as Process. In *The Social Life of Things*, edited by Arjun Appadurai, pp. 64–91. Cambridge University Press, Cambridge.

Laidlaw, James

2012 Ontologically Challenged. *Anthropology of This Century* 4. http://aotcpress.com/articles/ontologically-challenged/.

Latour, Bruno

1993 *We Have Never Been Modern.* Harvard University Press, Cambridge, Mass.

2004 Whose Cosmos, Which Cosmopolitics? Comments on the Peace Terms of Ulrich Beck. *Common Knowledge* 10(3):450–462.

2009 "Perspectivism": "Type" or "Bomb"? *Anthropology Today* 25(2):1–2.

2014 Anthropology at the Time of the Anthropocene: A Personal View of What Is to Be Studied. Distinguished Lecture, Annual Meeting of the American Anthropological Association, Washington, D.C.

Levi, Carlo

    1963   *Christ Stopped at Eboli.* Farrar, Straus, and Company, New York.

Lévi-Strauss, Claude

    1952   *Race et histoire.* UNESCO, Paris.

    1955   *Tristes tropiques.* Plon, Paris.

    1973   Race et histoire. In *Anthropologie structurale deux*, pp. 377–422. Plon, Paris.

Lloyd, G. E. R.

    2011   Humanity between Gods and Beasts? Ontologies in Question. *Journal of the Royal Anthropological Institute*, n.s., 17:829–845.

Lockhart, James

    1992   *The Nahuas after the Conquest.* Stanford University Press, Stanford.

Lokhorst, Gert-Jan

    2013   Descartes and the Pineal Gland. In *The Stanford Encyclopedia of Philosophy*, edited by Edward N. Zalta. https://plato.stanford.edu/archives/win2017/entries/pineal-gland/.

López de Palacios Rubios, Juan

    [1514] 1954   *De las islas del mar océano.* Translated by Agustín Millares Carlo. Fondo de Cultura Económica, Mexico City.

López Luján, Leonardo, Ximena Chávez Balderas, Norma Valentín, and Aurora Montúfar

    2010   Huitzilopochtli y el sacrificio de niños en el Templo Mayor de Tenochtitlan. In *El sacrificio en la tradición religiosa mesoamericana*, edited by Leonardo López Luján and Guilhem Olivier, pp. 367–394. Instituto Nacional de Anthropología e Historia and Universidad Nacional Autónoma de México, Mexico City.

Lorenzana, Francisco Antonio

    1769   *Concilios provinciales primero, y segundo, celebrados en la muy noble, y muy leal ciudad de México.* Imprenta de el Superior Gobierno, Mexico City.

Lynch, Michael

    2013   Ontography: Investigating the Production of Things, Deflating Ontology. *Social Studies of Science* 43(3):444–462.

Martínez, María Elena

    2008   *Genealogical Fictions: Limpieza de Sangre, Religion, and Gender in Colonial Mexico.* Stanford University Press, Stanford.

Martínez del Río de Redo, Maríta, and Elena Isabel Estrada de Gerlero

    1990   Mass of St. Gregory. In *Mexico: Splendors of Thirty Centuries*, edited by Kathleen Howard, pp. 258–260. Metropolitan Museum of Art, New York.

Montaigne, Michel de

    [1580] 1958   *The Complete Essays of Montaigne.* Translated by Donald M. Frame. Stanford University Press, Stanford.

Mundy, Barbara E.

    2015   *The Death of Aztec Tenochtitlan, the Life of Mexico City.* University of Texas Press, Austin.

Nadler, Steven M.

    1988   Arnauld, Descartes, and Transubstantiation: Reconciling Cartesian Metaphysics and Real Presence. *Journal of the History of Ideas* 49(2):229–246.

    2013   *The Philosopher, the Priest, and the Painter: A Portrait of Descartes.* Princeton University Press, Princeton.

Oakley, Francis

    1984   *Omnipotence, Covenant, and Order: An Excursion in the History of Ideas from Abelard to Leibniz.* Cornell University Press, Ithaca, N.Y.

Olivier, Guilhem

    2006   The Sacred Bundles and the Coronation of the Aztec King in Mexico-Tenochtitlan. In *Sacred Bundles: Ritual Acts of Wrapping and Binding in Mesoamerica*, edited by Julia Guernsey and F. Kent Reilly III, pp. 199–225. Boundary End Archaeological Research Center, Barnardsville, N.C.

Oviedo y Valdés, Gonzalo Fernández de

    1535   *La historia general de las Indias.* Juan Cromberger, Seville.

Panzer, Joel S.

    1996   *The Popes and Slavery.* Alba House, New York.

Parish, Helen-Rand, and Harold E. Weidman

1992   *Las Casas en México: Historia y obra
        desconocidas.* Fondo de Cultura
        Económica, Mexico City.

Park, Katherine

1998   Impressed Images: Reproducing
        Wonders. In *Picturing Science and
        Producing Art*, edited by Caroline A.
        Jones and Peter Galison, pp. 254–271.
        Routledge, New York.

Pauw, Cornelius de

1768–1769   *Recherches philosophiques sur les
             Américains, ou Mémoires intéres-
             sants pour servir à l'Histoire de l'Es-
             pèce humaine.* 2 vols. George Jacques
             Decker, Berlin.

Pérez de Perceval, José María

1992   Animalitos del señor: Aproximación a
        una teoría de las animalizaciones pro-
        pias y del otro, sea enemigo o siervo, en
        la España imperial (1550–1650). *Areas*
        14:173–184.

Prosperi, Adriano

1995   The Missionary. In *Baroque Personae*,
        edited by Rosario Villari and translated
        by Lydia G. Cochrane, pp. 160–194.
        University of Chicago Press, Chicago.

Rabb, Theodore K.

1975   *The Struggle for Stability in Early
        Modern Europe.* Oxford University
        Press, Oxford.

Ramos, Alcida Rita

2012   The Politics of Perspectivism. *Annual
        Review of Anthropology* 41:481–494.

Ribadneyra, Pedro de

1604   *Flos sanctorum, o Libro de las vidas de
        los santos.* Luis Sanchez, Madrid.

Rojas Rabiela, Teresa, Elsa Leticia Rea López, and
Constantino Medina Lima

1999   *Testamentos en náhuatl y castellano
        del siglo XVI.* Vol. 2 of *Vidas y bienes
        olvidados: Testamentos indígenas novo-
        hispanos.* Centro de Investigaciones y
        Estudios Superiores en Antropología
        Social, Mexico City.

Rojas Silva, Alejandra

2018   Gardens of Origin and the Golden Age
        in the Mexican *Libellus de medicinalibus
        indorum herbis* (1552). *Bulletin of Latin
        American Research* 37(S1):41–56.

Rorem, Paul

1988   Calvin and Bullinger on the Lord's
        Supper, Part I: The Impasse. *Lutheran
        Quarterly* 20:155–184.

Sahagún, Bernardino de

1950–1982   *Florentine Codex: General History of
             the Things of New Spain.* Edited and
             translated by Arthur J. O. Anderson and
             Charles E. Dibble. 12 vols. University of
             Utah Press, Salt Lake City, and School of
             American Research, Santa Fe, N.Mex.

Sahlins, Marshall

1981   *Historical Metaphors and Mythical
        Realities: Structure in the Early History
        of the Sandwich Islands Kingdom.*
        University of Michigan Press, Ann
        Arbor.

Seed, Patricia

1993   "Are These Not Also Men?": The Indians'
        Humanity and Capacity for Spanish
        Civilisation. *Journal of Latin American
        Studies* 25(3):629–652.

Shenefelt, Michael, and Heidi White

2013   *If A, Then B: How the World Discovered
        Logic.* Columbia University Press,
        New York.

Sillar, Bill

2009   The Social Agency of Things? Animism
        and Materiality in the Andes. *Cambridge
        Archaeological Journal* 19(3):367–377.

Taube, Karl A.

1993   The Bilimek Pulque Vessel: Starlore,
        Calendrics, and Cosmology of Late
        Postclassic Central Mexico. *Ancient
        Mesoamerica* 4:1–15.

Taylor, William B.

1979   *Drinking, Homicide, and Rebellion in
        Colonial Mexican Villages.* Stanford
        University Press, Stanford.

Tena, Rafael

2009   La cronología de la "Tira de la Peregri-
        nación." *Estudios de cultura náhuatl*
        40:121–129.

Turner, Terry S.

2009   The Crisis of Late Structuralism. Per-
        spectivism and Animism: Rethinking
        Culture, Nature, Spirit, and Bodiliness.
        *Tipití: Journal of the Society for the
        Anthropology of Lowland South America*
        7(1):3–40.

Vera, Fortino H.

    1887   *Colección de documentos eclesiásticos de México*. Vol. 2. Imprenta del Colegio Católico, Amecameca.

Vitoria, Francisco de

    1991   *Political Writings*. Edited by Anthony Pagden and Jeremy Lawrence. Cambridge University Press, Cambridge.

Viveiros de Castro, Eduardo

    1998   Cosmological Deixis and Amerindian Perspectivism. *Journal of the Royal Anthropological Institute*, n.s., 4:469–488.

    2004a   Exchanging Perspectives: The Transformation of Objects into Subjects in Amerindian Ontologies. *Common Knowledge* 10:463–485.

    2004b   Perspectival Anthropology and the Method of Controlled Equivocation. *Tipití* 2(1):3–22.

    2009   *Métaphysiques cannibales*. Presses Universitaires de France, Paris.

Weber, Eugen

    1976   *Peasants into Frenchmen: The Modernization of Rural France, 1870–1914*. Stanford University Press, Stanford.

Woolgar, Steve, and Javier Lezaun

    2013   The Wrong Bin Bag: A Turn to Ontology in Science and Technology Studies? *Social Studies of Science* 43(3):321–340.

Zedeño, María Nieves

    2009   Animating by Association: Index Objects and Relational Taxonomies. *Cambridge Archaeological Journal* 19(3):407–417.

6

"Metaphysical Subtleties and Theological Niceties"

Incarnation, Incantations, Animism, and the Powers of Pre-Columbian Visual Imagery

THOMAS B. F. CUMMINS

It is only through the habit of everyday life that we come to think it perfectly plain and common-place that a social relation of production should take on the form of a thing.

—KARL MARX,
Capital: A Critique of Political Economy

Corporate personhood is the legal notion that a corporation, separately from its associated human beings (like owners, managers, or employees), has some, but not all, of the legal rights and responsibilities enjoyed by natural persons (physical humans).

—WIKIPEDIA entry on "corporate personhood"

Right now if a human worker does, you know, $50,000 worth of work in a factory, that income is taxed. If a robot comes in to do the same thing, you'd think that we'd tax the robot at a similar level.

—WILLIAM GATES,
interview with Kevin Delaney, February 17, 2017

The Five men (Paria Caca who is composed of five men) ate the thorny oyster shell, making it crunch with a "cap cap" sound.

—ANONYMOUS,
The Huarochiri Manuscript

Introduction

OBJECT AND SUBJECT, ANIMATE AND INANI-mate, cultural and natural, rational and irrational are negotiated categories in all societies, no matter how the categories might be conceived, termed, or legislated. Within such distinctions are nonetheless universal ecologies that all peoples experience and internalize. Day and night, light and dark are, for example, universal and a leitmotif of this chapter, stitching local ecologies together. Each culture may deal with these universals in specific ways in which other objects, natural and human-made, are singled out as being endowed with special properties that often commingle the specifics of beauty, power, and the divine. As an art historian, I am interested in those elements that are singled out for representation in the first sense of the term as described by Bruce Mannheim (this volume), how they are formed, and in what materials. One might posit through asking such questions that the imaginary of power takes a material form that endows with authority the person or groups to whom they first pertain and embellish. I will, therefore, present various instances in which the particularities of cultural choices within the local ecologies are visualized.

Two propositions structure this chapter: one is to demonstrate by various different, some radically different, examples the cultural variation and historical contingency behind a seemingly universal notion of animation or transubstantiation. Thus, I will take the reader through various political, social, and cultural entities so as to focus primarily on the imperial objects and religious beliefs of sixteenth-century Spain, Mexico, and the Andes. However, beyond these imperial powers, there were many important chiefdoms in America that also collided with the Europeans in the sixteenth century and which are seldom discussed. They are nonetheless critical to my discussion, so this chapter ends with an analysis of some of the objects and spaces of the Muiscas of central Colombia and the Jama-Coaque of coastal Ecuador and the specificity of place and ecology in the construction of their objects and spaces.

The second and related proposition is to argue that we cannot simply reduce such variation to a dichotomy of "Western" and "indigenous"—there is both variation among the American examples, in terms of materials and meanings, and also commonality among American and European examples. Hence, one does best to look at these instances of "animacy," and how they supported or subverted authority, without imposing ontological distinctions, whether derived from anthropology or a kind of vulgar materialism of the New Archaeology.

Taking these rather straightforward premises into account, this chapter is indebted in many ways to John Berger's *Ways of Seeing* (1972) and, therefore, to Walter Benjamin's "Art in the Age of Mechanical Reproduction" ([1939] 1968). Both point to the modern conditions that have evacuated the aura that images, representations, and performances once seemingly possessed.[1] Whether or not this is wholly true is not at debate here, rather the notion of aura and its loss is, in terms of an analysis of Pre-Columbian images, important within the context of "Sacred Matter: Animism and Authority in Pre-Columbian America." Images and things had prodigious power to effect in America, participating fully in social and political power. They manifested the origins and continuous presence of divine authority. It is important to think about the loss of aura of such objects in the modern world because this loss extends to some archaeologists of the New Archaeology (now old) and their reductionist vision of society. Aura has no place as economy is the only true basis of power and is therefore solely of real intellectual interest. Society is reduced to an economic engine in which the concentration of power and authority in an elite is a logical and inevitable conclusion. The rest, the cultural trappings, is epiphenomenal (see also Weismantel, this volume). Art and ritual in this line of thinking are to be considered only so far as they are ideological projections or propaganda reflecting and expressing power relationships that jostle about within the one-dimensional category of political economy (see, for example, Covey 2006; D'Altroy 1992; Earle 1997; Marcus 1993).[2]

Art history has its counterpart in George Kubler, who wrote in *The Shape of Time* (1962b:27) that "iconology is a variety of cultural history" and, therefore, posited a Pre-Columbian art history that reinvigorated Focillon's ideas in *The Life of Forms* ([1934] 1942) with a more rational, scientific sense of stylistic creation and order (Kubler 1962a).[3] This fixation is a kind of rational imperative (material/formal) in which individuals solely act according to economic motives or artists create in a rational world of stylistic imperatives and form the basis of a descriptive analyses (e.g., the rise of chiefdoms) or a set of related works, disconnected from meaning. These approaches reduce cultural expressions to being essentially an undifferentiated tool for manipulation by the "elite" to establish and maintain their political power through expressing authority or for development of stylistic relationships. Kubler (1975:335) is very explicit about this when writing about Inka art, stating, "The intrinsic meaning of Inca art reinforces the general impression of an oppressive state. It is as if, with the military expansion of the empire, all expressive faculties, both individual and collective, had been depressed by utilitarian aims to lower and lower levels of achievement."

My critique does not mean that art and architecture were not concerned with or related to these issues. Rather, it is important to go beyond a rational functionalist/materialist paradigm to embrace a larger set of criteria that shape the nature of power and artistic production. It is to ask what more can be said about Pre-Columbian art, architecture, and performance within a broader sense of power and authority in which subject formation is a shared process with what might be considered the inanimate or nonhuman operating in a broader ontology than that imagined by materialists. Just as important, I will juxtapose and interweave descriptions of Western objects and practices not as a foil, but as something that can help put Eduardo Viveiros de Castro's (1998, 2004) ontological perspectivism into a wider analysis in which one can find correspondences between early modern European and Pre-Colombian and early colonial images and practices.[4] That is to say, this chapter moves between different categories of authority and representation that are constituted and exercised differently but that exist within the same historical time. Nonetheless, some areas in the cultural expression of political authority bring into relief forms of commensurability.

Art and Artifice

To begin, all objects and artisans under discussion operated within a fully sacral world that did not differentiate or even conceive of secular versus sacred spheres, and many Pre-Columbian objects and actions operated well outside of instrumental or utilitarian confines. Within this context,

I will move across and between differing levels of political and social complexity without making distinctions. Objects and images are common to all, and they constituted the materialization of accumulated knowledge transmitted from generation to generation and the talent, at times a very rare talent, to deploy that knowledge. The artists, their techniques, and the objects they produced could connect the past with the present through images, objects, making, singing, and dancing (Cummins 1994; Guss 1990). The special attention manifested in the creation and curation of things and spaces demands an accounting that recognizes not only what they may illustrate, but what they might have been able to do beyond the lifeless functionality of "political economy" or universalist structural analysis (Lévi-Strauss 1982).[5]

Societies understood and understand, and related and relate to, things and ideas through a variety of desires and needs,[6] some of which we may either be dimly or sharply aware, others that we will never know. The transformational relationship of the inanimate thing to animate personhood is nearly universal, and it is often a part of political power, perhaps best articulated for the archaeological world in the studies of ancient Mesopotamian art and architecture by Irene Winter (2010). And none of this should be so strange for those who live in the animated world of corporate capitalism and ecological conservation.

For some peoples of the modern West, there is a cultural world that is replete with distinct natural forces and resources. For others, these natural forces are a constituent part of their cultural world (Cummins 2003; Descola 1992; Guss 1990). There are also things that are animate to some and inanimate to others, and for a variety of reasons. For sixteenth-century Western culture, for example, various signs (alphabetic writing) speak across space and time to some (Europeans) but do not speak to others (non-Europeans; Acosta [1590] 2002; Anonymous [ca. 1607] 1991:1; Bry 1596:8–9; MacCormack 1988; Nebrija [1492] 2011). By this differentiation, the animate letters perform as a marker of Western cultural superiority (Cummins 2016b). Regardless, the concepts that stand behind

Descola's (1992; Kosiba, this volume) understanding of animism and Viveiros de Castro's (1998, 2004; Kosiba, this volume) ontological perspectivism in terms of the relationship of nature to culture, subject to object, allow us to look at Pre-Columbian images and objects and to ask how they might participate in the actualization of the world (cosmology) they inhabited. That is, while we cannot engage in the participant observation of Viveiros de Castro or Descola to record Pre-Columbian mythologies, rituals, and songs that would comprise the context or deixis that "speak of a state of being where self and other interpenetrate" (Viveiros de Castro 2004:464; see Severi 2007), we do have their residue in the form of the subject matter that was presented and special objects and special/sacred spaces and structures that were built, which offers a distinct but complementary perspective (Cummins 2008; Houston 2001).

The Inkas, the Aztecs, and the Spaniards

Transubstantiation, *kamay*, and *teixiptla* are three culturally specific, coeval phenomena of the sacred that act differently to transform or recognize the animate character of a substance, be it bread and wine, rock and wood, or body and dough. In each instance, smoke, song, and speech or breath brought into presence and present the longed for, desired, living sacred essence. These beliefs all came into political conflict through evangelization or reformation in sixteenth-century America and Europe. Despite their very real differences, words and objects joined together in these cultural arenas to make manifest the sacred in objects and bodies, often within politically charged and overlapping cultural spheres. Bernardino de Sahagún (1580:25v, 26r, 26v) offers an excellent example when he writes in Nahuatl and Latin about Aztec idolatry, and he singles out the wood-carver who made images for worship. The woodworker is not a random choice because the Latin text is from "The Book of Wisdom" (Edgar 2011:806). The Old Testament text describes the origin of idolatry and focuses on a woodworker who fells a tree, hews it into a log, and fashions it into an image. The Nahuatl text varies slightly and describes how the woodworker carefully carves the wood into a human figure, giving it a head, face, body, hands,[7] and then setting it up in his house. The woodworker makes offerings of food in the Latin text, but in the Nahuatl translation he also cuts his ears, bleeds himself, and weeps before the image. These are specifically Aztec forms of sacrifice and offering, and only someone who could read Nahuatl and knows Aztec rituals would be able to recognize this specificity.

Other passages concern the origin and making of idolatrous images in the appendix to the first book of Sahagún's *Historia general*. However, this is one of the very few that is illustrated. The image is divided into two sequential vertical panels of action (Figure 6.1). Viewed from the top, the first panel depicts two stages of production: the tree as it is cut and then as it is worked into a figure. In the second panel, we see a figure dressed in rich regalia standing before three supplicants offering baskets of tortillas. What is significant in the illustration (and something that does not appear in either the Latin or Nahua texts) is that the "idol" is not differentiated in appearance or being from the worshippers. In the text, it is the artifice of the woodwork that has made an "idol,"[8] but in the finished image, we see a living deity, performing within a Nahua understanding of the transformation of material to the sacred (*teixiptla*). Here, we see the contradiction or ontological distinction that exists between the Latin text and the Nahua image, as the one aims to describe the origins of idolatry while the other depicts, within this biblical framework, the Aztec transformational process. One might, therefore, think of the Aztec world as an amplification of Gell's (1998) notion of distributed personhood and see this as "distributed divinity," in which individuals and objects are transformed so as to participate in a social world in which there exists the copresence of personhood and divinehood.[9]

The woodworker performing in the Inka state of Tahuantinsuyu is called upon to do something similar but within a different ontological context. This person is termed a *kerokamayuq*, a title that combines the material wood *kero* with *kamayuq*, which in a pedestrian sense can be translated as

figure 6.1
Bernardino de Sahagún, *Historia general*, bk. 1, app. 1, fol. 26r, ca. 1580. Biblioteca Medicea-Laurenziana, Palat. 218–220, Florence.

"artisan" but whose root is *kamay*, which means to create in the sense of reshaping raw material to be something new so as to realize its latent animate force, most significantly in a vessel form that is itself called a *kero* (Allen 2015; Cummins 2002). At the same time, this creative act produces a set of objects that materially externalize or objectivize broad social and political Andean ideals, ideals and their objectification that were used within an Inka ideology of expansion and conquest. We certainly can say this about a charred *kero* found at Huanaco Pampa's plaza, a provincial space where the *kero* participated as a principal actor in what might be understood as a precapitalist Gramscian

"Metaphysical Subtleties and Theological Niceties" 173

figure 6.2
An Inka *kero* ritually buried at San Juan de Pariachi. Photograph courtesy of Luis Felipe Villacorta, Proyecto Arqueológico San Juan de Pariachi, Valle del Rimac.

hegemonic state ritual hosted by the Inkas and based upon an Andean norm of reciprocity (Cummins 2002:39–59, 99–118, fig. 1.3, 2015:175, fig. 10.15). Another example is a *kero* found ritually interred near the *usnu* (an Inka platform of various dimensions with a drain for libations) of San Juan de Pariachi (Villacorta 2003; Figure 6.2).[10] This *kero* may have been placed there in an act of "consecrating" this political structure just as, one might say, an altar is consecrated within a Catholic church.[11] These contexts of encounter with an Inka object should not be understood as distinct or belonging to different spheres of meaning. Rather, their occurrence and placement participate in a single cosmic world that is overtly politicized by state formation. From the *usnu* one might hear the

words of the semidivine Inka as a ritual toast would be offered to enact a sacred or political pact (Cummins 2002).

Metaphysical power is not just manifested by an object's or image's animated participation. It often first resides within the material itself before it takes a form. The transformation of material into subject/object realizes sacred potentials seen in Sahagún's illustration (see Figure 6.1). The coming into cultural being, the process, takes on a life force of its own as has been documented throughout America and the world (Lechtman 1996). For example, in Africa metalsmiths must create their own primary material, iron and bronze, before it can be cast, and even today they do so with many incantations and other rituals that include smelting furnaces formed in the shape of a woman's torso, as the "birth" of iron is equated to a human birth.[12]

The transformation of material is a fundamental cultural act, an act that is most often classified as being artistic or artisanal, which it is. But it is also most often tinged with religious and metaphysical significance, as Sahagún's passage and image demonstrate. As Hamann (this volume) points out, the deerskin pages of the Ñudzavui screenfolds were carefully prepared and the word for them was ñee ñuhu, "sacred skin." When sites of production are investigated archaeologically, they are often analyzed in rather cold terms of economic and material production. Perhaps that is all we can do, or perhaps we might also look for the unexpected or extraneous and not discount it as epiphenomenal.

Regardless of whatever can be said about sites of production as a part of a political economy, the Inka political expansion and expression were not merely a disingenuous manipulation of ritual, beliefs, spaces, and objects (Cummins 2002:99–105). Similarly, the incarnation of the sacred for the Aztecs took place within a highly charged politics of the sacred that was fully consistent with a broader understanding of the ontology of the world (Bassett 2015; Carrasco 2000). For example, the construction and renovation of the Templo Mayor was effected within two physical spaces and two intersecting time frames: one eschatological and the other sociopolitical. Time and space came together, creating and uniting the terror of the end-of-things and terror of the here and now, and the Templo Mayor gave material and spatial substance to those fears through sculpture, painting, architecture, and ritual. Of course, the political power of the Aztecs afforded the material expressions of these fears, but it could not affect their eventual cosmic outcome (Carrasco 2000).

This chapter progresses from such examples with ethnohistoric data to examine from the point of view of an art historian whether or not we can identify such instances in Pre-Columbian history for which we have often no texts and only have spaces and images. And if this is possible, then how? Might we suggestively and imaginatively interpret later textually recorded oral narratives that might

"reanimate" them for us?[13] To create this imaginative sphere is to suggest that we begin by thinking through what is most familiar, first within our own cultural parameters, and then those instances best known to us through the crisis of spiritual, political, and economic conquest of America. In doing so, we might be able to ask, for example, if a Wari *kero* made sometime around 700 CE was an animated object in some manner equal to the Inka pair found at Ollantaytambo for which ethnohistoric and contextual evidence exists (Cummins 2002:123–127). Were the Wari *keros* made in pairs, which was a fundamental ontological part of Inka cosmic, political, and cultural aesthetics (Cummins 2007:273–275)? And was the Wari example ever used in a state ritual of political alliance as were *keros* for Inka imperial formation or modern nineteenth-century state formation (Carrillo 1991:393; Cummins 2004:462–463)? Can the continuity of an object type such as a drinking vessel that has a mundane or utilitarian function, and also has simultaneous ritual, mystical, or political uses, be considered within Wittgenstein's proposition? He writes, "Every sign by itself seems dead. What gives it life?—In use it is alive. Is life breathed into it there?—Or is the use its life?" (Wittgenstein [1953] 2009:para. 432). This suggests that we can imaginatively proceed to think about archaeological objects in multiple, overlapping, competing, and even contradictory ways.

If we take the example of the well-known Moche theme "the revolt of the objects" depicted on the walls of buildings and ceramics (Quilter 1990), we are confronted with objects (vessels, weaponry, farming, and weaving utensils) that are subjects arising in some form of combat with humans and supernaturals. The seventeenth-century Quechua text of *The Huarochiri Manuscript* also mentions the voracious attack of animated mortars and pestles as they began to eat men and llamas began to herd men when the earth became dark for five days after the sun died (Anonymous [ca. 1607] 1991:53). Clearly, the Moche images and Quechua story express a similar and underlying theme that existed in the Andes for at least seven hundred years, as acknowledged by many scholars (Allen 2015:28; Quilter 1990:45–47).

But what has gone mostly unnoticed is that this darkened Andean world-upside-down is not dismissed by the Andean Christian author as merely a pagan myth, rather it is understood and interpreted within a cross-cultural typological relationship: "We think these stories tell of the darkness following the death of our Lord Jesus Christ. Maybe that is what it was" (Anonymous [ca. 1607] 1991:53). Here we read the capacity of one cosmology to be incorporated into another one; although in this case it is a Christian cosmology that incorporates an Andean one. This transposition of one reality into another is not uncommon, and it occurs, for example, among the Yekuana of modern Venezuela, who are capable of intertwining the reality of ongoing invasive and aggressive Western culture into their great origin poem referred to as Watunna (Guss 1990:12–14). This is a specific case of what Viveiros de Castro (1992:8) classifies as "ontological predation," a mythopoetic process of appropriation of the other through a struggle to replenish the self. Equally important, the Yekuana recount, just as the Huarochiri myth and Moche images seem to do, that once, a long time ago when chaos reigned, baskets (the sine qua non of Yekuana artistry that every male needs to master to become a complete

member) were animate, dangerous beings with deadly powers that had to be overcome in a cosmic struggle with man. The designs woven into the contemporary baskets are the malevolent elements that threatened the ancestors and are still an ongoing menace that must be restrained through song and weaving (Guss 1990:92–125). For the Yekuana, the relationship between subject and object, nature and culture, is a complex one that is not bound by the laws of political economy and is within the domain of artistry, as it is in so many cultures.

Conversely, what kind of sign is the cross scratched into the surface of a pair of keros long after their creation (Figure 6.3)? How does its presence alter whatever animated life originally had been engendered in them by the kerokamayuq? The crosses that were crudely scratched into each of the pair show the intersection of two animating forces: Andean and European. That each vessel had a cross etched into its surface asserts the power of the living cross to transform any idolatrous content that the keros might have possessed, performing almost as an apotropaic act against any future apostasy.[14] But because a cross has to be etched onto the surface of both vessels, the Christian act simultaneously recognizes the Andean vital force inherent

figure 6.3
A pair of transitional *keros* with a Christian cross etched into their surfaces, ca. 1550. Lambari Collection, Cuzco.

figure 6.4
"Last Supper," *Institución de la regla y hermandad de la Cofradía del Sanctissimo Sacramento*, fol. 6v, 1502. Houghton Library, MSTyp184, Harvard University.

in their being as a pair (see Kosiba, this volume). It was, therefore, not sufficient to mark just one.

These examples bring the discussion to some more familiar instances in which the Christian subject/object is innately animated. For example, Christ as god incarnate is inherently animated, possessing a divine force capable of producing the magic of miracles in human form. In other cases, the subject/object is transformed from one state of being to another (although all are one and the same, i.e., the trinity), and this is the "mystery" that must be accepted and not rationally understood. This is effected most often through ritual performance and incantations in the Catholic Mass. However,

for almost all Pre-Columbian objects, we can only dimly envisage the performances and rarely imagine hearing the words and music that brought them to life and death.

To demonstrate what is generally meant, it is important first to move to a very familiar act: the Christian animation of bread and wine and its transposition to sixteenth-century America. The mytho-historic founding act is depicted by a full-page miniature of the Last Supper from the 1502 *Institución de la regla y hermandad de la Cofradía del Sanctissimo Sacramento*, created in Toledo (Figure 6.4). We recognize the apostles and Christ seated at a table covered with loaves of bread and cups of wine. Christ's right hand is raised in the sign of benediction, and he holds in his left hand a chalice with a wafer that is embossed with the crucifixion, thus making the central image the Holy Sacrament. A blue border with a Latin text written in gold leaf frames the image. It reads, "for this is my body" (*hoc est corpus meum*) and then "for this is the Chalice of my Blood of the new and everlasting covenant" (*hic est enim Calix Sanguinis mei, novi et eterni te[stamenti]*). These are the most important mystical phrases spoken in the Catholic cosmos. They constitute the moment of consecration: the first is said over the host, and the second is said over the wine. The image of Christ holding both the host and the chalice, thus, conflates the historical moment of the Last Supper with the central mystery of the Catholic Mass, transubstantiation. That is, the accident, the bread and wine, maintain their outward appearance but what they are, their substance, is mystically transformed through Christ's original words now uttered by the priest. They, the bread and wine, represent in and of themselves what they have become, even though one cannot see Christ's human form, an issue to which we shall return.[15]

This illumination appears within a foundational manuscript that established the rules for the early modern confraternity dedicated to the Holy Sacrament by its founder, Teresa Enríquez, who earned the sobriquet "la loca del sacramento," which was bestowed by Pope Julius II in 1508 (Fernández Fernández 2001). The intensified veneration of the Holy Sacrament came to the New World with the establishment of similar confraternities.

This mystical act appears in the earliest extant Mexican Christian feather image that reached Europe: the representation of the sixth-century eucharistic miracle of the Mass of Saint Gregory (see Figure 5.16). The central element concerns the moment of transubstantiation, which was doubted by one of the parishioners. And so, Saint Gregory petitioned God so that the consecrated host and wine changed their appearance/accident into their substance, Christ's flesh and blood, seen in the guise of the Man of Sorrows rising from a sarcophagus and surrounded by the Arma Christi.[16] This

feather painting, made in Mexico City as a gift for the pope, demonstrates the animating force of the Christian Mass. Furthermore, the image argues that the host is, in and of itself, what it represents, even though its appearance does not change, except at this miraculous moment. It is the priest's incantation of Christ's words that animates the bread and wine. Christ's death, resurrection, and Second Coming form the central mystery of Christianity and must be accepted as ontologically true, just as an Aztec accepted *teixiptla* as the transformation of a man into a god incarnate, just as an Inka accepted the *ylla* and *huaca* and the presence of the divine (Salomon 1991, 2004).

Another illustration in the manuscript is also related to the struggle over signs of power and animation in the New World. It is the living cross, which the text says should be held in the right hand of the members of the confraternity in service and honor of God (Figure 6.5). In a pen-and-ink drawing done some eighty years later by Diego Muñoz Camargo ([1584–1585] 1981:fol. 239v) for the *Descripción de la provincia y ciudad de Tlaxcala*, we witness the apotropaic force residing within this powerful Christian object-sign (and also manifested by the two crosses on the pair of *keros*) as Western-style demonic figures fly around it like annoying mosquitos, wearing the recognizable empowering, transformative masks and headdresses. Such sacred Aztec paraphernalia, as well as the temples and plazas where they were utilized, operated within a unified cosmic field of the senses including sound, taste, and smell, such that for the Aztec the union of ornament and body transformed both and made the divine copresent. This supernatural power was not experienced by the Franciscans within an ontological perspective as articulated by Viveiros de Castro (see Kosiba, this volume); rather, all individuals participated in a universally animated cosmos in which there were opposing forces of benevolence and malevolence. This is also not an example of "double misunderstanding," as discussed by James Lockhart (1985, 1992) and others. It is rather to understand that for some (Spaniards) there were competing animated forces that could, on the one hand, disguise and

figure 6.5a

"Holy Cross," *Institución de la regla y hermandad de la Cofradía del Sanctissimo Sacramento*, fol. 7r, 1502. Houghton Library, MSTyp184, Harvard University.

figure 6.5b

Franciscans erect the first wooden cross in Tlaxcala, in Diego Muñoz Camargo, *Descripción de la provincia y ciudad de Tlaxcala*, fol. 239v, 1584–1585. Special Collections, University of Glasgow, Sp Coll MS Hunter 242 (U.3.15).

deceive and, on the other, enlighten and bestow grace (MacCormack 1991).

Christ is also imagined as the Sol Invictus through whom everlasting life is promised (Murry and Murry 1996:497).[17] Such belief has material repercussions, as any medieval archaeologist knows. Christ, within apocalyptic time, will appear in the east, arising just as the sun does, hence Christian churches should have an east–west axis with the apse in the east, the locus of Christ's presence. The priest performs with his back to the congregation, facing toward God, and Christ's body determines the spatial right and left as it appears in the east.[18] Hence, all imagery is in mirrored relationship to the worshipper facing the altar. The bodies of the politically powerful were sometimes interred in the nave, laid prone, hands folded, with the head to the west so that when they arose at the Second Coming they would face toward the altar and greet Christ's appearance in the east. The point is that any archaeological excavation of a tomb, sacred space, or in situ imagery must recognize that the objects and spaces are ordered and charged within a set of criteria that activates them in the sense that they actually do something whether, for example, it be to prepare for the Last Coming or something else (see Conklin, this volume).

For the Aztecs, humans and statues became gods incarnate by donning their ornaments; this is part of an Aztec concept called *ixiptla* (Clendinnen 1991:87–140, 236–263; Gruzinski 2001:50–52; Hvidtfeldt 1958; Townsend 1979:23–37). These manifestations of the Aztec sacred were demons for the Franciscans, but they were no less real, as I have discussed. They became recognized as the devil's deceit (*engaño*), just as were all other sacred manifestations in the Andes and elsewhere in the Americas (MacCormack 1991). The importance of the animating power of the regalia manifesting the sacred is demonstrated in Sahagún's depictions of the Aztec "pantheon." He equates the Aztec deities with Roman gods and heroes (Cummins 2016b). One may think of *ixiptla* as drawing down or into the form, be it body or statue, the vitalizing power of the sacred, which was something well understood as a concept in Renaissance Europe with the

reading of the third-century *Logos telios*, or the *Perfect Discourse*, in which Hermes describes how mankind was not divine and, thus, summoned the divinity of demons and angels and implanted it into images with sacred and divine rites. The powers of the supernatural are drawn into earthly images through the sacrifice of nature's herbs, stones, and spices, which have in themselves the power of divinity (Hermes Trismegistus [2nd–3rd centuries CE] 2007:94–95). Saint Augustine takes issue with these passages in terms of idolatry in his *City of God*, yet these Hermetic texts were widely read in Italy and Spain, and the *City of God* was a fundamental text in the New World. This is also a key element in Sahagún's deity images, as well as in his appendix to book 1 (see Figure 6.1).[19]

This digression demonstrates the familiarity that erudite friars had with some of the practices and concepts that were termed *ixiptla*. This understanding seems to be depicted in another drawing in the *Descripción de Tlaxcala*, in which Franciscan friars hold torches to the transforming ritual paraphernalia of the gods who control the twenty days of the *tonalamatl* (Muñoz Camargo [1584–1585] 1981:fol. 242r). The smaller figure to the viewer's right presumably holds codices that were also subject to destruction. But they are generically rendered, whereas the faces, the masks, that summoned the divine presence are individually rendered, such as Tlaloc with goggle eyes and Ehecatl with a birdlike beak.

The copresence of the divine, supernatural, spiritual, and mystical (or however one might term it) is either brought into the material or conjured out of it through ritualized labor, such that it is recognizably animate, incarnate, real.[20] A powerful aspect of this sacred essence was received through the sun's light and warmth, absorbed into the body, and known as *tonalli* (Hajovsky 2015:14–15, 68, 106–107). Locomotion, sound, and smell were afforded by the human body, and while the latter two are hardest to know and analyze, what moved through the streets was not, for the Aztecs, an actor or an impersonator. It was the divine or, as Hvidtfeldt (1958:98) wrote, the "'image' itself . . . which constitutes the 'god.'"

The regalia worn by warriors paralleled that of those who became deities (Olko 2005). Divine presence and military prowess intermingled within the sacred city of Tenochtitlan. The warrior's body was marked so as to instantiate through the individual the ideal of the warrior. For example, the hair of the most valiant was worn with a short twisted tuft at the front, where *tonalli* resided and was bound with a feathered adornment called a *quetzallalpiloni*, as depicted in the *Codex Mendoza* (Anonymous 1992, 3:fols. 64r–65r). The *quetzallalpiloni* were bestowed by Nahua rulers on the bravest warriors (Sahagún 1580). Degrees or ranks of valor were, in part, recognized by the number of captives taken in battle, as indicated by ritual paraphernalia. The pride in such dress was paralleled by the fact that some would become, through being captured themselves, sacrificed. Then they walked the streets of Tenochtitlan or Tlaxcala as deities for the fleeting moments remaining to them before their sacrificial deaths (Clendinnen 1991:236–263). Whether warrior or prisoner/deity, the brilliant reflection of the feathers worn through the bright streets of Tenochtitlan transformed visions of them from the stable to the ephemeral, fleeting, and precarious. It is a phenomenological experience that shifts any certainty of a fixed reality. Colors and images were transformed, according to how the wearer or viewer moved through a visual iteration of the precarious and momentary nature of Aztec reality.[21]

In America after evangelization began, mystical arenas shifted such that some Pre-Columbian objects and materials performed differently (Kosiba, this volume). The reframing of Inka weaving and Aztec featherwork for Christian purposes was perhaps the most spectacular (Phipps, Hecht, and Esteras Martín 2004; Russo, Fane, and Wolf 2015). One such arena was the atrium of the new Christian temple in the center of which a cross was erected. They were not merely apotropaic, as the image in the *Descripción de Tlaxcala* depicts, but were sites of devotion for Nahua Christian communities. The crown of thorns often represented metonymically the tortured head of Christ, while the instruments of his passion were distributed along the cross.

In some crosses, the void within the crown is filled with an Aztec sacred substance: obsidian, the smoking mirror of Tezcatlipoca. Are we to see, perhaps, the divine visage of Jesus Christ emerging from the dark interior of this magical material and highly valued substance?[22] One cannot know for certain; however, a framed piece of obsidian in the Dumbarton Oaks Collection is identified as a mirror. Possibly it is a portable altar, but at the very least, it is identified with the Franciscans in Mexico as the back of the frame carries the emblematic Franciscan shield with the five wounds of Christ. If it were a portable altar, it would have contained a consecrated host and the Franciscan friar would have placed the monstrance and chalice on it and peered into the dark surface as he conjured Christ's body into the wine and bread through magical Latin phrases. Did he see in his own visage the word incarnate within the reflective surface? We will never know.

These Christian signs, images, and objects have had a life in America from their first appearance until today, and they are invigorated and animated with both the forms and materials of the cultures that possessed and made them. As we contemplate these versions of the cross, we might again recognize Wittgenstein's ([1953] 2009):para. 432) proposition cited earlier: "Every sign by itself seems dead. What gives it life?—In use it is alive. Is life breathed into it there?—Or is the use its life?" Such a proposition moves away from Saussurean semiotics and its incorporation by Lévi-Strauss's structuralism and comes closer to the propositions of a pragmatics of language, meaning it is created as spoken as opposed to being exterior to speech. In other words, as José de Acosta ([1590] 2002:297) attempts to articulate for his reader what he heard about the transformation of Aztec sacrificial victims, they were dressed in brilliant regalia "so that the living likeness of the god would always be present."

Pacha, Huaca, Inti, and Beyond

The Andean world (Pacha) was also populated by divine personages moving among the living and the dead. Moche burials reveal that individuals were adorned with the attributes of supernaturals depicted in ceramics (Alva and Donnan 1994). The ruling Inka is said to have been the son of the sun (Inti). Pacha, in fact, encompasses more than just the earth. A sunlit sky is called *llipipin pacha*, *lippiyani* meaning "to have brilliance" (Holguín [1608] 1952:214). The material manifestation of this brilliance is not so much the feather or obsidian of the Aztecs but textiles (*cumbi*) and polished metal. The kinetic gold pieces created using multiple complex techniques throughout the Andes were the essence of "bling" (Lechtman 1996), and they moved, glistened, and sang as light hit their surfaces and bounced back into the eyes of the beholder. One normally experiences these incredible pieces in museums as static objects illuminated by a constant, unvaried source of artificial light. However, when they must be moved, as they were for the deinstallment of the Chimú pectoral (B-450) at Dumbarton Oaks, they reveal the magic of their being, springing into a set of surfaces, sounds, and sensations that cannot be captured by technical description or iconographic identification. One can only imagine how metal object and human body came together to transcend each other and become one with the light.

This phenomenon of light, movement, and sound has the same mesmerizing effect as the brilliant surfaces of Mexican featherworks. The world explodes in ways and forms we will never really experience. And as with the Aztecs, the great animating force is the sun, which for the Inkas was the paramount deity, who plays a critical role in the animation of the world. Adorning both bodies and walls, the politics of power was resplendent in its brilliance.

The mythical foundation of the Inka empire narrates this animating relationship, which is interpreted by the Spaniards as demonic deceit and political manipulation. An illustration from Martín de Murúa's *Historia general de Perú* (1616) shows the figure of Manco Capac standing above the mountain as he appears before his people, having emerged from Tambotocco, the cave of origin at Paccaritambo (Figure 6.6). A silver disk, a *purupuru*, is depicted on his chest and appears dull and tarnished. Murúa (1615:19r) tells how Manco

Capac emerged, brilliant in a gold dress, and that he caught the sun and by his reflection appeared divine, blinding those who looked at him—something akin to the notion of bling or the "sound" of light reflected from a precious surface. The intent of this and similar Spanish texts about Manco's appearance was not to attribute a miraculous or divine light to the founder of the Inka dynasty, as if he were a saint or Christ. Rather, the appearance of Manco was interpreted as a means of deceiving the simple Andeans who were easily awed by the dazzling effect produced by his golden ornaments, a sentiment echoed by the New Archeologists.

There is no doubt that the Sapa Inka (ruler) did have such garments, as recorded in the inventories of Atahualpa's ransom, the archaeological record, and dictionaries (Holguin [1608] 1952:214). However, Murúa's image and account miss the nature of the brilliance of Manco Capac's appearance, as the golden ornaments bedecking the Inka founder transformed the mortal body of the semidivine Inka, the son of Inti, to be joined with his father in emanating brilliant light.[23] Also, as Catherine Allen (2015:33) and Sabine MacCormack (1991:306) have recalled, the Inka monarch possessed a crystal as a prerequisite of sovereignty, an object whose refraction of sunlight linked the Inka with the sun's world-shaping power.

The divine sun also rises and sets. Its movement casts light and shadow across stone walls that were understood as sacred signs (Anonymous [ca. 1607] 1991:71–72; Cummins and Mannheim 2011:12–13). As Gerald Taylor (1976:235) and Frank Salomon (1991:16) note, the Andean world is much more animated than ours, activated through a force, *kamay*, that pulsates through the earth, water, and sky. Some manifestations of this energy are identified as *huacas*. The whole world possesses *kamay*. Outer appearance does not necessarily reveal *kamay*, what might be considered somewhat comparable to the notions imbued in the term *hypostasis*.

This Andean concept is manifested in a drawing by Guaman Poma de Ayala (Figure 6.7). He depicts a large stone that is being dragged from one site to the next. At a certain point, the stone becomes too tired, weeps blood, and eventually

figure 6.6
Manco Capac, founder of the
Inka dynasty, emerges from
Paccaritambo, color wash on
paper, in Martín de Murúa,
Historia general del Perú,
Ms. Ludwig XIII 16 (83. Mp.159),
fol. 19r, 1616. J. Paul Getty
Museum, Los Angeles.

comes to rest where it is. The stone has an irregular
outline, and within this natural form is sketched
an ashlar block, the form into which the material
would be shaped once it reached its destination.
In other words, the form of what it is to become
already exists within its natural state. What is visually expressed is, I believe, the Andean concept of
kamay, or the potentiality existent within any natural state to be realized as a metaphysical presence
of the sacred.[24] This animistic notion is further

intensified by the anthropomorphism of the stone
itself. Guaman Poma endows it with a pair of eyes
that look forward and in the direction it is moving
(Cummins and Mannheim 2011:11–12).

Endowing the stone with eyes is not an abstract
matter of anthropomorphizing the stone. Watching
and seeing (vision) are constituent parts of the
animated Andean world, including walls (Allen
2015:24–25). Whereas Western physical orientation
imagines turning the body to face the future with

figure 6.7
"Inca Urcun and the Tired Stone," painted by Guaman Poma de Ayala, in Martín de Murúa, *Historia del origen y genealogía real de los reyes del Piru, de sus hechos, costumbres, trajes, maneras de gobierno*, fol. 37v, begun ca. 1589, finished ca. 1613. Photograph by Thomas B. F. Cummins.

the back to the past, Quechua orientation faces the past with the back to the future. This notion of seeing the past is manifestly present in the added introduction of *The Huarochiri Manuscript*. Bemoaning the lack of writing in the Andes, the author writes: "If the ancestors of the people called Indians had known writing in earlier times the lives they lived

would not have faded from view until now. As the mighty past of the Spanish Viracocha is visible until now, so too would theirs be" (Anonymous [ca. 1607] 1991:41). The Quechua emphasis on seeing the past in relation to the technology of writing for recording is distinct from a European ontology that comes from Aristotle through Acosta and others, who

figure 6.8
Cave opening showing the *amaru* (large snake) and puma carved into the sides and emerging from the entrance/exit, Cuzco. Photograph by Thomas B. F. Cummins.

discuss the lack of phonetic writing in America. For Europeans, writing's capacity to transcribe sound allows those in the present to hear the past and speak to the future.[25] The Andean understanding of the significance of writing is that it allows one to see the past that has otherwise "faded from view," such that one can speak with personal, firsthand knowledge of ancient events if one is close to a ruin where that event took place (see Cummins 1998:141–143; Howard-Malverde 1990:73–83; Kosiba 2017).

Seeing and the different experiences of seeing are critical to Andean expressions of time and place, and the sun and moon, light and dark, interior and exterior are critical elements within Andean visions. It is not just the bedazzling semidivine who emerges from the interior who is animated. The point of emergence is itself charged. The moral force of the *ayllu*, the fundamental social and political structure of the Andes, and the Inkas

in particular, is dependent on the place of origin and the emergence of the apical ancestor. Hence, the Andean landscape is replete with natural and built places where the underworld breaks open into the light and air. One opening just to the north of Cuzco has a large snake, an *amaru*, and a jaguar *otorongo* emerging from the opening (Figure 6.8). The *amaru* and *otorongo* are, at least in the colonial period, emblematic of Inka royalty as depicted in a fictive Inka royal coat of arms by Martín de Murúa (1615:fol. 13r).

We do not know how this particular cave was used, but the figures are carved from the "living stone" and in relatively high relief such that they interact with the intense sunlight and shadow so as to give them higher relief than they actually have and make them appear to change as the sun moves across the sky. (The head of the feline has been destroyed, which, as with the crosses etched into the pair of *keros*, is an act that recognizes the power residing in the Inka image and object.) Similar figures are carved at the site today known as Puma Urqu, but which is almost certainly the Inka site of origin, Paccaritambo (Bauer 1992:120–123). A great urban grid-planned Inka center with the very best masonry, Maukullacta lies across from Puma Urqu on a hemispheric plain. The plan is open and oriented toward Puma Urqu. The Inka hallmark architectural features such as double- and triple-jamb niches and portals are extremely elaborate and emphasize the significance of the site. Again, we do not know what specific rituals would have been carried out in the large plaza, but the orientation of the site takes advantage of the natural terrain: the plan is an open U form, and the plaza opens toward Puma Urqu. This site is not merely epiphenomenal; it gives place and form to the origin of the Inkas, uniting them with a sacred living landscape (Kosiba 2015a, 2015b; Sherbondy 1982). Equally, the great plaza in Cuzco was the center that activated state ritual throughout Tahuantinsuyu, and it was endowed with aura and sacrality by being filled with pure sand brought from the shore of *mamacocha*, the ocean (Polo de Ondegardo y Zárate [1571] 1990:98).

Emergence into the Andean world, *pacha*, is a concept that integrates the physical, the temporal, and the moral as being experienced within a single complex relationship.[26] It preexists speech and action and allows them to occur in infinite variety within the notion and rules of *pacha* (Allen 2015:27; Salomon 1991:14–15). *Pacha* is also the moment and space that initiate the animated political rule of the Inkas based upon their apical ancestor. That is, the animation of anyone or anything necessitates an already animated space in which one can then physically join in celebratory, reciprocal Andean acts, feasting being paramount, that acknowledge past, present, and future relations. Only then can the politics of chiefdoms and empires proceed with the necessary moral authority to produce and build.[27]

Nature and Habitat: The Muisca and Jama-Coaque Peoples

For the Inkas and others, emergence from the earth's openings, or from bodies of water, such as Lake Titicaca, brings life and order to the world (Cummins 2002:60–68; Sherbondy 1982). But it is not just the emergence into the energizing light of the day, it also represents the entrance to the interior and darkness of the underworld. (For Christianity to begin, Christ first descended into and then reemerged from the cave as he rolled away the stone.) This is certainly true for the Inka, Maya (see McAnany, this volume), and Aztec peoples, for whom caves, natural and man-made, were foundational spaces of origin and return (Brady and Prufer 2005; Carrasco and Sessions 2010; Heyden 1981). Many religions, including Christianity, have built into their narratives and, therefore, their physical spaces the idea of descent into darkness and reemergence into light. For example, the return to the interior is a critical element in the religious beliefs of the Muiscas in the high plains of central Colombia, for whom we have reasonable ethnohistorical information (Francis 2007; Pérez de Barradas 1951). For the Muisca people, origin history, caves, and ritual preparation of leaders are intimately linked.

The Muisca origin myth tells that in the beginning was the darkness of the night where existed Chiminigagua, a spark of light. Chiminigagua was the creator deity whose first act was to create great black birds that Chiminigagua sent out to breathe air into the world so that "era lúcido y resplandeciente." Then the world became "claro e iluminado" as it is now (Simón [1629] 1981:367). The sun became the paramount deity, but there was also another important deity called Cuchavia, translated as "el aire resplandeciente" (Simón [1629] 1981:377). The emergence from dark nothingness to a beautiful, resplendent airy world is a common origin theme, be it in Christian, Inka, or Aztec origin histories. For the Muiscas, however, the preparation of a future ruler mimicked their creation myth in an extreme form. The author of *Epítome de la conquista del nuevo reino de Granada* (Anonymous [ca. 1539–1540] 2001) tells how when a boy or girl who would eventually become *zipa* or *psihipqua* (cacique) was selected, they were placed in a dark hut for several years, without ever leaving.[28] Aside from selected servants who would bring food and also occasionally give them a severe lashing, they would see or speak to no one. Upon emerging into the sunlight after this dark exile, they dressed in golden chest plates, earrings, nose rings, hats, and arm and leg bands (Anonymous [ca. 1539–1540] 2001:113–114). This transition from prolonged darkness and isolation to light and community creates a truly different resplendent person whose personal experience relives the Muisca origin myth. These adorned individuals would take up their place within the community as leaders and also intermediaries, go-betweens, with the divine, the sun and moon being the preeminent deities.[29] Carl Henrik Langebaek (2006:232) notes that the origin of the social order was based on the political order in which the cacique was the physical and metaphysical form of that order through inheritance from and incarnation of the sun. Langebaek goes on to say that some of the chroniclers detail a direct relationship between solar festivals and political leadership.

The relationship between origin/darkness and community/light within a sacred landscape is, therefore, fully incorporated into the Muisca cultural world, both past, present, and future, through representations, just as it was for the Aztec, Maya, Inka, and many other peoples. For example, Fray Pedro Simón ([1629] 1981:375; see also Vargas Murcia 2017:26–27) says of the petroglyphs that abound in this area that the Muiscas told him they had been made by the god who brought weaving to the world.[30] Called Nemterquetaba, as well as other names such as Bochica or Sue, which mean "sun" (Langebaek 2006:232),[31] this creator deity went from community to community teaching them how to weave. When he finished his teaching, he left "paintings" of the looms on the polished flat surface of a stone so that if the people forgot how to weave, they had the petroglyphs to remember.[32] The high planes are replete with these images on stones, many of which recall the painted designs on the few Muisca cotton tunics that have survived (Triana [1924] 1970).[33] In fact, cotton mantas were extremely valued among the Muiscas both before and after the Spanish arrival. However, unlike Quechua and Aymara traditions to the south, where the woven object was most important, the raw material of Muisca weaving, cotton,

was equally important and worshipped as an "idol" (Cortés Alonso 1960). Many of these sacred entities were kept with the ancestors, placed in the Muiscas' most sacred spaces, some of which were constructed within the earth and covered with paintings and painted textiles.[34] For example, a Dominican extirpator was led by a powerful and old priest named Siqasiosa to a cave where he "entered by going down a very dangerous and steep set of stairs . . . some twelve feet long, and it was covered with many mantas painted with figures of incredibly horrendous demons of different types . . . and the friar removed them all up as well as all the idols that twenty indios could carry" (Meléndez 1681:1:420).[35] Indeed, caves were important places for the living to communicate with their ancestors, as well as the divine. For example, we again hear from those who attempted to root out the devil's deception that "Fray Pedro Martir de Cardenas became aware of a cave where the Indios practiced their idolatries and he went there . . . entering within . . . found more than a hundred and fifty bodies seated in a circle according to the tradition of their ancestors, and in the middle was seated their lord . . . who was differentiated from the rest by his adornment of beads around his arms and neck and a headdress" (Meléndez 1681:1:422).[36]

In addition to the ancestors and effigies, space in the form of an architectural skeuomorph was also critical. Muisca subterranean spaces, either natural or man-made, were not only places of communion with the ancestors, but also spaces to perform religious rituals. If we think about the subterranean funeral chambers of Tierradentro (500–800 CE) in southern central Colombia, which were built by carving into the volcanic layer, then we can gain an idea of how these Muisca caves might have been understood to operate as spaces. The hollowed-out interiors of Tierradentro (Figure 6.9) took an architectural form that was probably not unlike structures built aboveground, which, until very recently, were still being built by the Páez.

The walls of the caves mimic a built interior but are carved into the living rock. A post-and-lintel system supports a central beam and the slanting rafters of a thatched roof. The interiors of these

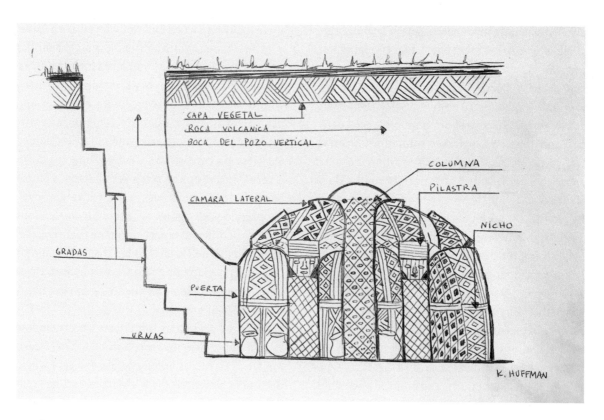

figure 6.9
A schematic drawing of a subterranean structure, Tierradentro, Colombia. Redrawn by Kyle Huffman.

carved tombs were also painted so as to make the stone appear even more like the interior of a built structure (Figure 6.10). Like the Muisca sanctuaries, the Tierradentro structures were visited and looted by Spaniards well into the eighteenth century (Santa Gertrudis Serra [1799] 1970:chap. 5). Furthermore, although the Muisca sanctuaries were most often found within natural caves rather than man-made ones, we might imagine that these cave interiors, as described by the sixteenth-century priests, were transformed into pseudo-realistic interior spaces complete with quasi-architectural features covered with textiles:

> They had dug and excavated a cavernous space in the form of a very large room, into which one entered by a very wide door. This was closed on the outside by very tightly packed earth, such that one could not distinguish it [the entrance] from the side of the cliff itself. Within the room they had a great bird made of wood and covered with feathers, much larger than life-size. The devil used this image as an instrument in order to speak with them, and to make speeches against the Holy Doctrine of the Gospels . . . [and] to foretell things that would happen to them . . . all simple minded people pay attention to such things, and they hold [the bird] in such great esteem, as it had been there for more than four hundred years in that place in which they venerated and obeyed it, sacrificing [to the image], among other many other offerings, innocent children, [and it] was attended in the room at night by many young maidens who were dedicated to its cult [and] who were changed from time to time. (Meléndez 1681:1:417)[37]

This sanctuary is described as an artificially made subterranean room, perhaps a bit like those in Tierradentro. It was used to convene the community in ritual activity that focused on a large wooden sculpture of a parrot, which served as a

figure 6.10
The interior of a Tierradentro sanctuary. Photograph courtesy of Santiago Giraldo.

kind of oracle.[38] The images of birds were animated by ventriloquism. This was also true for the sacrificed children (*mojos*) who, as Langebaek (1987:105) writes, "were taken from the eastern foothills [and] were kept in a structure known as the 'Casa del Sol.'" Equally important, Langebaek notes that the author of *El epítome* writes that the *mojos* communicated with the sun, speaking and receiving his answers. The "political" power of the cacique in relation to the *mojos* and the sun is explicitly described by Fernández de Oviedo ([1557] 1959:121), who writes that "the caciques or at least the highest ranking were never without these *mojos*."[39]

As already noted, tropical birds, especially parrots, were also sacrificed and treated like the *mojos* in part because they came from the same region as the sacrificed children and from where the sun arose (Zamora [1701] 1980:1:279). Alonso de Medrano ([1599] 2003:71, as cited in Langebaek 2006:233) mentions that the colored feathers of birds "were a great part of their idolatries and superstitions."

The sanctuaries, where the oracular intermediaries (*mojos* and parrots), the cacique, and the sun joined together to converse, are described as *plumerías* or *iglesias de plumerías* (Langebaek 2006:233–234). The sun was the Muisca people's principal deity, as it was for the Inkas and Aztecs. And the Muiscas understood a profound affinity between the sun and birds and the word *sue*, which, as noted previously, is one of the names for the sun deity and also means "bird."

These bird effigies became the site of verbal disputation between the Franciscan priests and the native priests (see also Rodríguez Freyle ([1636] 1986:84–86).[40] However, the ventriloquism was based on the capacity of the birds to mimic human speech (Rappaport and Cummins 2012). Zamora ([1701] 1980:1:279) writes that the Muiscas acquired hundreds of parrots from the lowlands and taught them to talk in their own language, and when the parrots spoke Muisca very well, they judged them ready to be sacrificed.[41]

figure 6.11
A Muisca cacique in a *cercado* (palisade), *tumbaga*, Cordillera Oriental, Muisca, 600–1600 CE. Colección Museo del Oro, Banco de la República, Acc. #032866. Photograph by Clark M. Rodríguez.

What these and other sources demonstrate is that these spaces (*iglesias de plumerías*) were activated by the voices of ancestors and talking birds. Here there was communion between various conditions of being (human/animal, alive/dead) that was palpable in an auditory way, in just the way that the sun is understood to be a natural force that enlightens and energizes through its palpable warmth and light. These are natural phenomena that manifest the power of the sacred that is communicated with and through the Muisca elite.

Muisca caves, however, were not the only sacred places where the integration of political power, ancestors, and the sacred spatially intersected. Circular palisades circumscribed the sacred, social, and political world of the Muiscas and constituted power within a cosmic sphere. The caciques were located in the centers of these enclosures (Langebaek 1987, 2006:228–230). Various accounts in the chronicles of wooden circular enclosures describe them as being in a labyrinthine form.[42] At the entrance,

large posts were erected where sacrifices were placed and shot with arrows (Simón [1629] 1981). A common motif in Muisca goldwork appears to reproduce in miniature this sacred space and the cacique within it (Uribe et al. 2013:30–36; Figure 6.11). The composition of these small golden pieces consists of a circular latticework enclosure in which a large standing or seated figure is placed. Two large posts mark the opening, and it is presumed that these are the posts described in the chronicles.

A ritual offering found in Pasca, Cundinamarca, and now in the Ethnological Museum of Berlin has a gold piece composed of four dividing walls within a circular fence at the back of which is an elaborately outfitted figure with two smaller attendants. This is interpreted as representing the labyrinthine structure of the *cercacdo* with the cacique in the center (Uribe et al. 2013:31). Other figures, such as those found at Cogua y Cota, Cundinamarca, are simply placed on a round platform with a causeway leading to them (Uribe et al.

figure 6.12a
A Jama-Coaque seated female in
an open fence (palisade), ceramic,
height 14.5 cm, maximum width
15.3 cm. Museo Antropológico,
Banco Central Guayaquil, Acc.
#GA-2-2293-82. Photograph by
Thomas B. F. Cummins.

figure 6.12b
A Jama-Coaque seated feline
with raised paws in an open fence
(palisade), ceramic, height 14.5 cm,
maximum width 15.3 cm. Museo
Antropológico, Banco Central
Guayaquil, Acc. #GA-2-2293-
82. Photograph by Thomas B. F.
Cummins.

figure 6.13
A Jama-Coaque standing parrot on a platform, ceramic, height 16.5 cm, maximum width 2.9 cm. Museo Antropológico, Banco Central Guayaquil, Acc. #GA-10-1670-80. Photograph by Thomas B. F. Cummins.

2013:61). In addition, large ceramic vessels represent the same concept, although the figure of the cacique dwarfs the *cercacdo* (Uribe et al. 2013:36). These ceramic vessels are containers for the gold pieces, which together constitute an offering. What is important here is that Muiscas found the structure of the *cercacdo* and the cacique within it to be so significant in their imaginary that it became a major subject of representation and subsequently a ritual offering.

The descriptions of Muisca sacred interior spaces, including the veneration of and communication with parrots and ancestors, suggest them to be part of a wider Andean practice of oracles and oracular sites such as Pachacamac and Chavín de Huantar (Curatola Petrocchi 2016, this volume; Curatola Petrocchi and Ziólkowski 2008), as well

as, perhaps, the Mayo Chinchipe–Marañón spiral temples at the very early sites of Santa Ana–La Florida and Monte Grande (ca. 3000 BCE). Also at Santa Ana–La Florida, several finely carved stone images of birds were recovered at the center of the spiral or labyrinth in a tomb (Valdez 2013). Clearly, birds were important agents, as indicated by a ritual burial of a macaw unearthed at the slightly later site of San Isidro in the same region (Olivera Núñez 2014:130–135). The *cercacdo* and the golden figurines of the enormous cacique seated within it refer to the cosmic space in which power is enacted and personified. The figurines, judging by the fact that they are found as ritual offerings (whatever that may mean), certainly create the imagined communicative space as something transportable from one realm of being to another.

figure 6.14

A Jama-Coaque standing parrot with human arms, ceramic, height 16.5 cm, maximum width 12.2 cm. Museo Antropológico, Banco Central Guayaquil, Acc. #GA-9-614-78. Photograph by Thomas B. F. Cummins.

These ethnohistorical and archaeological data for the Muiscas and southern Ecuador also relate to another early set of northern Andean coastal images for which we have little information other than the objects themselves. Through analogy with the aforementioned, it is possible to suggest interpretations of their animate world that is almost entirely lost to us: where the local ecology gives rise to different interests that intersect and diverge from the cultures both to the north and south.

Within the spectacular ceramic tradition of Jama-Coaque (500 BCE–1530 CE; Zeidler 2016), there is a corpus of small ceramic figurines of humans and animals that through size, form, iconography, and style are clearly related to each other and that seem to be similar in iconography and composition to the coeval Muisca ceramic and *tumbaga* sculptures of the *cercados*. These are different from the larger human figurines of women, men, warriors, musicians, and dancers who are often interpreted within a shamanistic context (Capua 1986; Gutiérrez Usillos 2011). This particular set of smaller figurines is composed of humans, animals, fantastic creatures, and plants that share the same sphere of being such that they can be substituted one for another, combined, and recombined in various ways. The figures are often placed on either an oval platform or within a circular latticework fence or *cercado*. Some of the figures are standing or seated men or seated women with babies on their laps and with parrots perched on a fence facing the main figure (Figure 6.12). The composition of these scenes is very much like those of the Muisca *cercados*. The round wooden

"Metaphysical Subtleties and Theological Niceties" 193

fences of the Jama-Coaque figurines probably do not represent chiefly structures as interpreted for the Muiscas, yet the formal and iconographic parallels of the two coeval traditions are striking and are probably not coincidental as they both mark an enclosed sacred or cosmic space.

Some figures are felines holding beads in the center of their upraised paws, a motif also found in the headdress of Moche ceramic figures. Others are parrots, endowed with human feet and bedecked with jewels (Figure 6.13). There is a clear visual syntagmatic chain in which one figurine alludes to the other absent ones. What cannot be determined is how this chain is linked other than visually.

Regardless, parrots are sculpted in an anthropomorphized form with human arms instead of wings (Figure 6.14). The arm gestures clearly index absent speech and intensify this anthropomorphism. Standing erect and gesticulating, they appear declamatory, as if we were seated or standing before Ovid, or perhaps Pliny the Parrot, whom the Muisca "las enseñan a hablar en su lengua."

In another example of this subset, we see a multifigure composition with a man and a parrot seated next to each other (Figure 6.15). From the front, they appear independent of each other, and the human male figure is larger than the parrot. However, they are attached in the back by a tube. As far as I can determine, this connection has no functional use. Rather, it seems to imply a direct connection between the two beings. Whatever the case, a seated human figure is linked to some important "natural" being such as figures seated on a throne in the form of yucca (Figure 6.16). Yucca is an important ritual crop on the coast of Ecuador that was cultivated very

figure 6.15
A Jama-Coaque seated male and parrot, ceramic, height 11.5 cm, maximum width 15.3 cm. Museo Antropológico, Banco Central Guayaquil, Acc. #GA-3-416-77. Photograph by Thomas B. F. Cummins.

figure 6.16
A Jama-Coaque seated male
on a manioc root, ceramic,
height 14.3 cm, maximum
width 19.3 cm. Museo
Antropológico, Banco
Central Guayaquil, Acc.
#GA-1-2729-84. Photograph
by Thomas B. F. Cummins.

figure 6.17
A Jama-Coaque male seated
on a fantastic mangrove
crab monster and a
mangrove crab monster
figure, ceramic, height
23.5 cm, maximum width
13.8 cm; height 2.9 cm,
length 16.5 cm. Museo
Antropológico, Banco
Central Guayaquil, Acc.
#GA-13-1064-78, Acc. #Ga-
4-2379-82. Photograph by
Thomas B. F. Cummins.

figure 6.18
A Jama-Coaque vessel with mangrove roots, ceramic, height 14.9 cm, maximum length 12.75 cm. Museo Antropológico, Banco Central Guayaquil, Acc. #GA-2-2729-84. Photograph by Thomas B. F. Cummins.

early (Chandler-Ezel, Pearsall, and Zeidler 2006) and from which chicha was being made when Europeans arrived.

The clear and intimate relationship between the seated figures and the tuber unites them in a common universe. This kind of composition occurs in other iterations and with other protagonists. For example, a similar human figure sits upon a kind of monstrous aquatic figure (Figure 6.17). Like the parrot, this being is linked in some kind of semiotic chain with the other figures, and whatever set of constructed relations that were expressed linguistically, through semantic schemes and narrative constructions, we can only intuit them through compositional patterns and iconography. However, if we move back into one of the elements of the

coastal environment, we can begin to suggest what is implied in this coastal cosmos, which is in part composed of mangrove.

The mangrove is a world apart, moved by the moon and tide, which when out reveals a thick, tangled, muddy, and difficult terrain. One moves about through land and water that has no clear division and is always changing. This local ecology is an important part of the Jama-Coaque cosmos and becomes a subject of their ceramics as tendrils and roots entangle their vessels (Figure 6.18). It is in the mangrove that different creatures swim and move about. And they too become subjects in the Jama-Coaque ceramic corpus. We see, for example, crab figures, important inhabitants of the mangrove forest;[43] however, one of the most

figure 6.19
A Jama-Coaque vessel
with mangrove roots and
a mangrove crab monster,
ceramic, height 14.9 cm,
maximum length 12.75 cm.
Museo Antropológico, Banco
Central Guayaquil, Acc.
#GA-2-2729-84. Photograph
by Thomas B. F. Cummins.

common figures is an amorphous shrimplike creature. There is no mistaking its relation to its habitat as it sometimes is depicted lurking among the exposed mangrove roots (Figure 6.19). Within the conventions of the ceramic composition of figures seated together are mangrove figures: a shrimplike creature and bivalves known as known as *pianguas* or mangrove clams, which are still collected today in Colombia and Ecuador. Sometimes they are also placed within this open fence (Figure 6.20). As the tide goes out, some clams attached to exposed roots begin to open and shut, producing an eerie cacophony. Here, just as with the mimicry of the human voice by the parrots, the mangrove comes alive with the clacking sound of bivalves, one of the most sacred materials in the Andean world, be it

spondylus, strombus, *pianguas*, or others. One also cannot but help think of the sound of the spiny oyster being eaten by the Andean god Pariacaca, "making it crunch with a 'cap cap' sound" (Anonymous [ca. 1607] 1991:116).

Within the corpus of Jama-Coaque ceramics, we see, among other things, a desire to represent an animate world that is particular to them, in which relations between entities fluidly move among humans, birds, felines, amorphous shrimplike beings, clams, and the mangrove. We can only glimpse their relationship through the artistry of Jama-Coaque ceramists, but we can be sure that the mangrove was fully a part of an animated world in which man, bird, and clams communicated in a social contract with the divine.

a

figure 6.20a
A Jama-Coaque mangrove clam with a shrimp- or dolphinlike figure on top and mangrove clams (*pianguas*), ceramic. Museo Antropológico, Banco Central Guayaquil, Acc. #GA-12-2229-864. Photograph by Thomas B. F. Cummins.

figure 6.20b
A Jama-Coaque mangrove clam with a shrimp- or dolphinlike figure on top within a fenced compound (*cercado*), ceramic, height 14.3 cm, maximum width 19.3 cm. Museo Antropológico, Banco Central Guayaquil, Acc. #GA-14-1063-78. Photograph by Thomas B. F. Cummins.

b

Conclusion

This chapter began with the familiar because of the tendency of some to romanticize ontological difference, especially between West and non-West, while criticizing a deadening materialism and formalism. This is not to say that there are not profound differences between the familiar and unfamiliar, but that there are also unacknowledged common grounds both historically and today. With Muisca and Jama-Coaque cultures we come to an entirely different environment, but one that is equally animated by creatures and their sounds, which become subjects of representation (in both senses of the term as determined by Mannheim, this volume), just as Eucharistic words spoken over bread and wine transform/animate them. Or, let us think about our own world that is animated by social and cultural imaginings such that corporations (United States), rivers (New Zealand), and forests

(Ecuador) are legislated as beings endowed with rights and privileges or that robots might be taxed for the tasks they perform in place of the human labor that they replace. These contemporary examples suggest that ontologies and animism are ever-changing categories and that just as those of one culture can be radically different from another, they can have unexpected common ground. How they play into political authority is not a teleological given. That is, they cannot be reduced to mere manipulative ideology. Marx ([1867] 1990:163), in his critique of political economy, understood the animated, transactional nature of the object and its transformation within capitalism: "A commodity appears at first sight an extremely obvious, trivial thing. But its analysis brings out that it is a very strange thing, abounding in metaphysical subtleties and theological niceties." Those subtleties and niceties both preexist commodities and extend into the future, beyond them.

NOTES

1 Benjamin's ([1939] 1968) and then Berger's (1972) discussion of the loss of aura in art refers to a specific Western phenomenon concerning the contradictory properties of uniqueness and reproducibility. Weber ([1905] 1930) understands this loss in a positive fashion or as the Enlightenment's gradual disenchantment with religion and the turn to a more rational world of Protestant Capitalism as articulated in his 1905 work *The Protestant Ethic and the Spirit of Capitalism*. The beginning of this process, however, is located in part in the Renaissance, as discussed by Belting (1994), when painting and sculpture began to be separated from religious veneration and became disassociated objects of aesthetic appreciation. This phenomenon historically intersects with the Western recognition of non-Western art in the late nineteenth and twentieth centuries as having social and aesthetic values that Western art (primarily painting and sculpture) had lost. Often called "Primitivism" with a decidedly negative connotation, it attributes to non-Western

objects an aesthetic value that also recognized their animism and social and cultural authenticity that the marketplace had, within a Marxist sense of the term, alienated from the object of Western artistic production (see also Kosiba, this volume).

2 To be fair, archaeology is a big tent and some research recognizes greater dynamics than mere political economy, especially in work done in the Maya area and central valley of Mexico, and in the Late Classic in particular. The Andes is, perhaps, less well developed in this area. Thankfully, Moche, Wari/Tiahuanaco, and Inka archaeological studies have demonstrated a much more expansive set of approaches in the past decades, some represented in this volume. Nearly forty years ago, I was informed by an archaeologist on my dissertation committee and one of his students that what I was studying was epiphenomenal and hence of no real importance. Most recently, in the introduction to a set of essays concerning *huacas* as sacred manifestations in the Andes, the editor also notes the problematic issue

of the "sacred" as being epiphenomenal and the normalizing division between secular and sacred once assumed in archaeology (Bray 2015:3, 8).

3 Again, to be fair, art history has certainly not always followed Kubler's stylistic approach, and iconography and attempts (sometimes a bit extreme) to attribute meaning to Pre-Columbian works have been a dominant part of its studies.

4 Viveiros de Castro's anthropological position, while based on field research, has, as is well known, its roots in Nietzsche's radical critique of reason, deriving ultimately from pre-Socratics such as Heraclites and rearticulated by Plato and his thesis that the mental formation and understanding of the world that one inhabits derive from particular perspectives.

5 Certain types of objects, including bodies of ancestors, show careful repair. Jama-Coaque ceramic molds are repaired so that they can be passed from generation to generation, thereby maintaining uniformity in style and iconography (Cummins 1994). Repairs sometimes demonstrate the aura that the object possesses. For example, people restored an early colonial *kero* (American Museum of Natural History, New York, AMNH B 1847) by taking a piece from another, presumably beyond repair, colonial *kero* and replacing a missing part of the older *kero*. It seems that this method of repair is not simply about replacement but maintenance of the integrity of the *kero* as an heirloom that was passed from generation to generation (Cummins 2002:1; see McAnany, this volume). Also, certain sites are repeatedly visited as sacred sites well past their apogee, including political centers of power such as Chavín de Huantar (Cummins 2008), Tiahuanaco, Tula, Teotihuacan, Rome, or Angkor Wat. Ancient places such Chavín de Huantar, Tiahuanaco, and Teotihuacan maintained their aura and were in a fashion curated as places where power was first produced.

6 For example, Bry (1626:1) writes, "God hath added herein a further grace, that as Men by the former [reason] exceed Beasts, hereby one man may excel another; and amongst Man, some are accounted Civil, and more both Sociable and Religious, by the use of letters and Writing, which others wanting are esteemed Brutish, Savage, Barbarous . . . by writing Man seems immortal, conserreth and consulteth with the Patriakes, Prophets, Apostles, Fathers, Philosophes, Historians and learners of the wisdom of the sages which have been in all times before him, yea by translations or learning Languages, in all places and Regions of the world; and lastly, by his owne writings, suruieth, himselfe, remains [literascriptament] through all ages a Teacher and Counseller to the last of men, yea hereby God holds conference with men, and in his sacred Scriptures; as at first in the Tablets of Stone, speakes to all." For other examples, see Cummins 2016b.

7 In the *Vulgate* (Edgar 2001:806–807), the woodworker takes wood that is either leftover, crooked, or full of knots and uses it to fashion an image of a man or "a beast."

8 *Artifice* first meant to make with skill. It came to denote in the sixteenth century not only the skill of an artist, but also the art of deception, which is probably due in part to Reformation fear and antipathy toward Catholic images. *Desengaño*, as it is termed in Spanish, or the devil's deceit through artifice and therefore idolatry, is the subject of Sahagún's *Appendix*. There is a bit of artifice in both senses of the English term as Sahagún uses Latin passages from the *Vulgate*'s "The Book of Wisdom," which universalizes Aztec idolatry by recounting the origin of idolatry through image making as recorded in the Old Testament (Edgar 2011:804–823). The image actually illustrates verses 11–14 of book 13, which appears on folio 25v and therefore is not just about the Aztec.

9 Bynum (2011:59) proposes that medieval images and material objects were perceived not only to memorialize the saint portrayed, but also to be actually inhabited by the saint. See also Carruthers 2008:275.

10 Cieza de León ([1554] 1984:136) writes that the Sapa Inka would give one *kero* to a local leader and keep the other as a sign of peace and agreement. Garcilaso de la Vega ([1609] 1943:54), El Inca, says that "estos vasos [queros y aquillas] porque el Çapa Inka los había tocado con la mano y con los labios, los tenían los curacas en grandíssima veneración, como a cosa sagrada; no bebían en ellos ni los tocaban, sino que los ponían como a ídolos donde los adoraban en memoria y reverencia de su Inka que les había tocado."

11 The Catholic altar must be activated by the act of consecration, which must include the placement of a relic or a consecrated host on the altar.

12 William Dewey, personal communication, 2016.

13 This line of thinking goes against Panofsky's (1944, 1960) argument of disjunction, a thesis employed by Kubler (1973, 1975) to argue against ethnographic and ethnohistoric analogy by which archaeologists and art historians might project specific iconographic identifications of images described at the time of conquest onto the interpretation of much earlier forms. I side here with a modified "direct historical approach" as developed by Strong and others, that allows us to identify at least certain general conventions that can be traced with great time depth and that clearly take on differing interpretations within specific cultures but nonetheless convey similar, shared concepts.

14 In some colonial *keros* depicting the Inka-Ri Colla-Ri theme, someone intentionally eradicated the anthropomorphized face of the sun by scratching out the *mopa-mopa* (the resin-based pigment applied to the vessel to form the figures). This iconoclastic act recognizes that the sun in these images could be interpreted and venerated as an Andean celestial divinity and, therefore, operates within a Western Christian ontology of images, which divides them into truthful or deceitful.

15 "Accident" (the outward appearance of a thing) and "substance" (what the thing is regardless of appearance) are fundamental (ontological) categories for understanding reality within Aristotelian philosophy and the neo-Aristotelian philosophy of Saint Thomas Aquinas.

16 Two of these miraculous Eucharistic hosts are now venerated as relics at Andechs Abbey in Upper Bavaria, Germany.

17 For the Nahuas, the power of the sun also energized and oriented the personhood of the Mexica through *tonalli* (Echeverría García 2014).

18 The Second Vatican Council (1962–1965) changed the position of the priest saying Mass so as to face the parishioners and allowed Mass to be said in the vernacular.

19 Too often modern scholars are a bit smug about their understandings of Pre-Columbian practices and suggest that early European observations were confused (cf. Bray 2015). However, closer and better readings of a variety of texts reveal a greater degree of understanding and even empathy than is acknowledged, such as that found in the work of Sahagún (1580), Betanzos ([1551] 1987), and the authors of the First and Second Councils of Lima.

20 Smell, dance, and sound are critical elements of that ritual, as one can see in Moche and Maya murals and ceramics (see Curatola Petrocchi, this volume). Here, the relationship between political authority, aesthetics, and animism is most clearly represented, such as at Bonampak, which Miller and Brittenham (2013) call "spectacle." However, the mixture of religion and ritual and their representation are more than what might be understood as spectacle. And whatever Maya ritual and religion are, they are not Benjamin's or Debord's ideas of spectacle and religion of the twentieth and twenty-first centuries. For example, Debord ([1967] 1977:thesis 20) writes, "The spectacle is the material reconstruction of the religious illusion," which is an elaboration of Karl Marx's ([1844] 1970:1) definition of religion as being "the sigh of the oppressed creature, the heart of a heartless world, and the soul of soulless conditions. It is the opium of the people. The abolition of religion as the illusory happiness of the people is the demand for their real happiness. To call on them to give up their illusions about their condition is to call on them to give up a condition that requires illusions. The criticism of religion is, therefore, in embryo, the criticism of that vale of tears of which religion is the halo." Music, a medium most difficult historically to access, is a shared artistic practice that has both magical and mystic capacities, as well as aesthetic ones that intermingle and produce effect across differing cultures and languages (see Certeau 1988:209–243; Tomlison 2009). Certeau (1988:213) notes that the European Jean de Léry ([1578] 1990:144) confesses he was ravished by music: "I received . . . such joy, hearing the measured harmonies of such a multitude, and especially in the cadence and refrain of the song, when at every verse all of them would let their voices trail, saying 'Heu, heuaure, heura, heuraure, heura, heura, oueh'—I stood there transported with delight. Whenever I remember it, my heart trembles, and it seems their voices are still in my ears." As Guss (1990) and Arnold and Dios Yapita (2001) have demonstrated, song is a medium that intersects with other artistic activities, combining them into a single synesthetic field of communication that also creates communion between object, animal, and human, past and present, present and future. We also have colonial evidence of the relationship between song, objects, and memory (Cummins 2002:135).

21 The ephemeral and the fragile are tropes in Nahua song-poems.

22 Again there is an overlap between the material and the sacred of medieval Christian art in Spain and Mexica (Aztec) art in the valley of Mexico. For example, the eyes of some of the witnessing apostles of the "Doubting Thomas" pier relief in the cloister at Silos (1088) were filled with a jet-black material to intensify the act of vision, just as Mexica sculptures often have eyes filled with obsidian to give emphasis to sacred vision.

23 Visions through brilliant lighting are also a common element of mystical revelation in the Old and New Testaments, as well as visions in medieval, early modern, and modern Christian Europe, especially Spain (Christian 1981a, 1981b). More important, perhaps, these brilliant visions continued well past the dawning of a rational Cartesian worldview and persisted into the twentieth century (Christian 1996:289–298).

24 Taylor (1976:235) discusses sixteenth- and seventeenth-century uses of the root *kama-*. As regards the verbal form, *kamay*, "nous le traduisons par 'animer' en donnant à ce terme la valeur multiple que lui accorde Garcilaso, c'est-à-dire: 'transmettre la force vitale et la soutenir, protéger la personne ou la chose qui en sont les bénéficiaires.' Le monde animé des Andes évoque un horizon beaucoup plus vaste que son équivalent occidental; toute chose qui possède une fonction ou une fin est animée afin que sa fonction ou sa fin puissent être réalisées: les champs, les montagnes, les pierres aussi bien que les hommes." As Cummins and Mannheim (2011) noted, the meanings of "animate" and "transmit a vital force" do not require the action *kamay* to have an agent. For this reason, the Third Council of Lima (1584:77v) chose to use the word *ruraque* (one who makes something) rather than *camaque* in the Quechua translation of the Nicene Creed. Were they to have used *camaque*, the translation would have been ambiguous, since *camaque* can also be understood as the agent of the vital force, an entity or person infused with a vital force, or as the prototype for a species or object. (They were not consistent in their usage, however; see Third Council of Lima 1584:5r.) The word *kamachisqa* is a nominalized (*-sqa*) causative (*-chi*) form of *kamay*. According to Taylor (1976:236), the causative suffix *-chi* indicates that the vital force is received

from elsewhere: "on fournit à l'autre la capacité ou l'autorisation d'agir."

25 "La causa de la invención de las letras primeramente fue para nuestra memoria, y despúes para que por ellas pudiésemos hablar con los ausentes y los que están por venir" (Nebrija [1492] 2011:chap. 3; see also Cummins 2016a).

26 *Pacha* has various glosses in early dictionaries including "ticci muyu pacha," which is translated as "toda la rondeza de la tierra, o el hemisfero que se vee." However, *ticci* means "origen principio fundamento cimiento caussa" (Holguín [1608] 1952:340).

27 Spaniards quickly learned of the source of moral authority when they prohibited feasting (Cummins 2002).

28 The authorship of the *Epítome de la conquista del nuevo reino de Granada* is debated. It is often attributed to the conquistador and founder of Bogotá, J(X)imenez de Quesada; however, Millán de Benavides (2001:1–97) argues that Alonso de Santa Cruz, royal cosmographer, compiled it through a variety of sources, among which were the papers of Ximenez de Quesada.

29 This kind of extreme deprivation is one way of creating the ecstatic condition common to most shamanic formations.

30 For a compendium of petroglyphs in the Muisca region, see the work of Triana ([1924] 1970), who drew them in 1924.

31 See Bohórquez Roa 2017 for a compendium of the different descriptions and names of this deity in the chronicles.

32 "Otros le llamaban a este hombre Nemterequetaba, otros le decían Xué. Este les enseñó hilar algodón y tejer mantas, porque antes de esto solo se cubrían los indios con unas planchas que hacían de algodón en rama, atadas con unas cordezuelas de fique unas con otras, todo mal aliñado y aun como a gente ruda. Cuando salía de un pueblo les dejaba los telares pintados en alguna piedra lisa brunida, como hoy se ven en algunas partes, por si se les olvidaba lo que les enseñaba" (Simón [1629] 1981:375).

33 See, for example, the superb surviving Muisca manta fragment (British Museum Acc# Am1842,1112.3) from an underground sanctuary in Gachancipá, Cundinamarca, found in 1842 or the colonial mural at Sutatausa depicting a *cacica* wearing a manta (Rappaport and Cummins 2012). The designs are similar to the Muisca rock paintings

and petroglyphs at Pandi and Soacha (Triana [1924] 1970:plates IV, VII, and XVIII).

34 Muisca also built religious sanctuaries aboveground, see Rodríguez Freyle (1636) 1986:81–83.

35 "Otros despues de apostara, y reducido por su predicaccion, le llebò tambien a una cueva, a la qual se bajaba por unas despeñaderos muy peligrosos, que tenia doze pies de largo, seis de ancho, y estaba entolada, con muchas mantas pintadas con figuras de demonios muy horrendas de diferentes hechuras, conforme el demonio se aparece a los sacerdotes, y el Padre sacò della tanto Ydolos, que pudo cagar dellos hasta viente Yndios, y entre ellos vino de la estaura de un Yndio, y este hizo, que el Sacredote le cargasse."

36 "Fray Pedro Martir de Cardenas... que tiendo noticia de una cueva donde los Yndios hazian sus idolatries, y enterrauan los cuerpos de uchos, que morian en su gentilidad.... Quitaron la losa de la puerta de la Cueva, y entrando dentro hallaron mas de ciento y cinquebnta cuerpos sentados en rueda al uso de sus antepasados, y en medio de todos estauá el Señor, o Cazique, que se diferenciaua de los demas en el adorno, de cuentas en los braços, y cuello, y una tocado, ò turbante en la cabeza, y junto a el cantidad de telas pequeñas, que los Yndios ofrecian."

37 "Estando el Padre Fray Diego Mancera sirviendo la doctrina del Pueblo del Quiqui jurisdiccion de la Ciudad de Tunxa, tuvo noticia, que los Indios del dicho pueblo, los demas comarcanos tenian un santuario general, donde todos, a ciertos tiempos, a haser sus ofrecimientos de oro, Esmeraldas, y otras cosas, con todas las ceremonias de su idolatria: Este santuario estaba en una peña, en que auian hecho, y abierto una cancavidad en forma de una sala muy grande, adonde se entrava por una puerta muy angosta, y esta cerrauan con una losa tan ajustada, que no se diferenciaba, por la parte de afuera, de la misma peña. Dentro de la sala tenian un pajaro de madera, todo cuerpo de pluma, de grandeza

de proporcionada. A este tomaba el demonio por instrumento para hablarles, y hacerles practicas contra la Doctrina santa del Evangelio, que los Religiosos les predicaban, pronosticandoles cosas por venir, con que à vueltas de una verdad les hazia creer muchas mentiras. Pero los simples a todo le dauan tanto credito, y hacian del tanta estima, que auia mas de quatrocientos años, que en aquel lugar le adoraban, y obedecian, sacrificandole, entre los demas ofrecimientos muchos, niños inocenetes, assitiendo en la sala de noche, cantidad de donzellas, que tenian dedicadas a su culto, que se mudaban a cierto tiempo."

38 Fray Esteban de Asensio ([1585] 1921:43) writes that caciques and other leaders were buried with their wives in a tomb. Their prepared bodies were placed next to a gold papagayo. I thank Carl Langebaek for this citation and his generosity in providing other sixteenth-century citations.

39 "Los caciques, o a lo menos los más principales, nunca están sin esos mojas."

40 In a *visita* to extirpate idolatry in the area of Boyaca in 1577, a number of Guacamayos were seized as idols in religious sanctuaries (Cortés Alonso 1960:228, 231, 237, 245).

41 "Las enseñan a hablar en su lengua y cuando hablaban muy bien las juzgaban dignos de sacrificio."

42 "Las maneras de sus casas y edificios, aunque son de madera y cubiertas de un heno largo que allá hay, son de la más extraña hechura y labor que se ha visto, especialmente las de los caciques y hombres principales, porque son a manera de alcázares, con muchas cercas alrededor, de manera que acá suelen pintar el laberinto de Troya. Tienen grandes patios, las casas de muy grandes molduras y de bulto, y también pinturas por todas ellas" (Anonymous [1539–1545] 2001).

43 Crabs are also represented in the preceding Chorrera culture from which the Jama-Coaque ceramic tradition derives.

Acosta, José de

[1590] 2002   *Natural and Moral History of the Indies.*
Edited by Jane E. Mangan. Translated
by Frances López-Morillas. Duke
University Press, Durham, N.C.

Allen, Catherine

2015   The Whole World Is Watching: New
Perspectives on Andean Animism.
In *The Archaeology of Wak'as:
Explorations of the Sacred in the Pre-
Columbian Andes*, edited by Tamara L.
Bray, pp. 23–46. University Press of
Colorado, Boulder.

Alva, Walter, and Christopher Donnan

1994   *The Royal Tombs of Sipan.* Fowler
Museum of Cultural History, University
of California, Los Angeles.

Anonymous

[1541–1542]   *The Codex Mendoza.* 4 vols. Edited by
1992   Frances Berdan and Patricia Anawalt.
University of California Press, Berkeley.

Anonymous

[ca. 1607] 1991   *The Huarochiri Manuscript: A Testament
of Ancient and Colonial Andean Religion.*
Translated by Frank Salomon and
George L. Urioste. University of Texas
Press, Austin.

Anonymous

[ca. 1539–1540]   Epítome de la conquista del nuevo
2001   reino de Granada. In *Epítome de la conquista del nuevo reino de Granada: La
cosmografía española del siglo XVI y el
conocimiento por cuestionario*, edited by
Carmen Millán de Benavides, pp. 123–129.
Pontificia Universidad Javeriana, Bogotá.

Arnold, Denise Y., and Juan de Dios Yapita

2001   *River of Fleece, River of Song: Singing
to the Animals, an Andean Poetics of
Creation.* Saurwein, Markt Schwaben.

Asensio, Esteban de

[1585] 1921   *Historia memorial.* Edited by Atanasio
López, O.F.M. *Archivo Ibero-Americano*
15:67–94, 129–151.

Bassett, Molly

2015   *The Fate of Earthly Things: Aztec Gods
and God-Bodies.* University of Texas
Press, Austin.

Bauer, Brian

1992   *The Development of the Inca State.*
University of Texas Press, Austin.

Belting, Hans

1994   *Likeness and Presence: A History of the
Image before the Era of Art.* Translated
by E. Jephott. University of Chicago
Press, Chicago.

Benjamin, Walter

[1939] 1968   The Work of Art in the Age of Mechanical Reproduction. In *Illuminations:
Essays and Reflections*, edited by Hannah
Arendt, translated by H. Zohn, pp.
214–218. Schocken Books, New York.

Berger, John

1972   *Ways of Seeing.* Penguin,
Harmondsworth.

Betanzos, Juan de

[1551] 1987   *Suma y narración de los Incas Capa-
cruna que fueron señores de la ciudad
de Cuzco y de todo lo a ella subjetado.*
Atlas, Madrid.

Bohórquez Roa, Andrés Camilo

2017   *Bochica en las crónicas de Indias.*
Independently published, Bogotá.

Brady, James E., and Keith Prufer (editors)

2005   *In the Maw of the Earth Monster:
Mesoamerican Ritual Cave Use.*
University of Texas Press, Austin.

Bray, Tamara L.

2015   Introduction. In *The Archaeology of
Wak'as: Explorations of the Sacred in
the Pre-Columbian Andes*, edited by
Tamara L. Bray, pp. 1–22. University
Press of Colorado, Boulder.

Bry, Theodor de

1596   *Alphabeten vnd aller art characteren.*
Theodor and Johann Theodor de Bry,
Frankfurt-am-Main.

Bry, Theodor de, and Johann Theodor de Bry

1626   *Caracters and diversitie of letters vsed by
divers nations in the world: The antiquity, manifold vse and varietie thereof:
With exemplary descriptions of very
many strang alphabets curiously cutt in*

brasse by Iohn Theod: De Bry deceased.
Frankfurt.

Bynum, C. W.

2011   *Christian Materiality: An Essay on
Religion in Late Medieval Europe.* Zone
Books, Cambridge, Mass.

Capua, Constanza di

1986   El shamán y el jaguar: Iconografía de
la ceramica prehistórica de la costa
ecuatoriana. *Miscelánea antropológica
ecuatoriana: Boletín de los Museos del
Banco Central del Ecuador* 6:157–170.

Carrasco, Davíd

2000   *City of Sacrifice: The Aztec Empire and
the Role of Violence in Civilization.*
Beacon Press, Boston.

Carrasco, Davíd, and Scott Sessions (editors)

2010   *Cave, City, and Eagle's Nest: An Inter-
pretive Journey through the Mapa de
Cuauhtinchan No. 2.* University of
New Mexico Press, Albuquerque.

Carrillo, Leonardo Altuve

1991   *Choquehuanca y su arenga a Bolivar.*
Planeta, Buenos Aires.

Carruthers, M. J.

2008   *The Book of Memory: A Study of Memory
in Medieval Culture.* 2nd ed. Cambridge
University Press, Cambridge.

Certeau, Michelle de

1988   *The Writing of History.* Translated by
T. Conley. Columbia University Press,
New York.

Chandler-Ezell, Karol, Deborah M. Pearsall, and
James A. Zeidler

2006   Root and Tuber Phytoliths and Starch
Grains Document Manioc (*Manihot
esculenta*), Arrowroot (*Maranta arun-
dinacea*), and Lleren (*Calathea* sp.) at
the Real Alto Site, Ecuador. *Economic
Botany* 60(2):213–220.

Christian, William

1981a   *Apparitions in Late Medieval and Renaissance Spain.* Princeton University Press,
Princeton.

1981b   *Local Religion in Sixteenth-Century
Spain.* Princeton University Press,
Princeton.

1996   *Visionaries: The Spanish Republic
and the Reign of Christ.* University of
California Press, Berkeley.

Cieza de León, Pedro de

[1554] 1984   *El señorío de los Incas.* Historia 16,
Madrid.

Clendinnen, Inga

1991   *Aztecs: An Interpretation.* Cambridge
University Press, Cambridge.

Cortés Alonso, Vicenta

1960   Visita a los santuarios indígenas de
Boyacá en 1577. *Revista Colombiana de
Antropología* 9:199–274.

Covey, Alan

2006   *How the Incas Built Their Heartland:
State Formation and the Innovation of
Imperial Strategies in the Sacred Valley,
Peru.* University of Michigan Press,
Ann Arbor.

Cummins, Tom

1994   La tradición de figurinas de la costa ecuatoriana: Estilo tecnológico y el uso de
moldes. In *Technología y organización
de la céramica prehispánica en los Andes,*
vol. 1, edited by Izumi Shimada, pp. 157–
172. Pontificia Universidad Católica del
Perú Fondo Editorial, Lima.

1998   "Let Me See! Reading Is for Them":
Colonial Andean Images and Objects
"como es costumbre tener los caciques
señores." In *Native Traditions in the
Postconquest World,* edited by Elizabeth
Boone and Tom Cummins, pp. 91–148.
Dumbarton Oaks, Washington, D.C.

2002   *Toasts with the Inca: Andean Abstraction
and Colonial Images on Kero Vessels.*
University of Michigan Press, Ann Arbor.

2003   Nature as Culture's Representative:
A Change of Focus in Late Formative
Iconography. In *Archaeology of Formative
Ecuador,* edited by J. Scott Raymond and
Richard Burger, pp. 423–464. Dumbarton
Oaks, Washington, D.C.

2004   *Brindis con el Inca: La abstracción
andina y las imágenes coloniales de los
queros.* Universidad Nacional Mayor de
San Marcos, Lima.

2007   Queros, Aquillas, Uncus, and Chulpas:
        The Composition of Inka Artistic
        Expression and Power. In *Variations in
        the Expression of Inka Power*, edited by
        Richard L. Burger, Craig Morris, and
        Ramiro Matos Mendieta, pp. 266–309.
        Dumbarton Oaks, Washington, D.C.

2008   The Felicitous Legacy of the Lanzón. In
        Chavín: Art, Architecture, and Culture,
        edited by William Conklin and Jeffrey
        Quilter, pp. 277–302. Monograph
        61. Cotsen Institute of Archaeology,
        University of California, Los Angeles.

2015   Inka Art. In *The Inka Empire: A Multi-
        disciplinary Approach*, edited by Izumi
        Shimada, pp. 165–196. University of
        Texas Press, Austin.

2016a   From Many into One: The Transfor-
        mation of Pre-Columbian Signs into
        European Letters in the Sixteenth
        Century. In *Sign and Design: Script as
        Image in a Cross-Cultural Perspective
        (300–1600 CE)*, edited by Jeffrey
        Hamburger, pp. 83–105. Dumbarton
        Oaks Research Library and Collection,
        Washington, D.C.

2016b   Towards a New World's Laocoön:
        Thoughts on Seeing Aztec Sculpture
        through Spanish Eyes. In *Altera roma*,
        edited by John Pohl and Claire Lyons,
        pp. 195–235. Cotsen Institute, University
        of California, Los Angeles.

Cummins, Tom, and Bruce Mannheim
2011   "Boiling Bloody Stones": The Kinetics
        of the Body and Soul amongst the
        Inca. *RES: Anthropology and Aesthetics*
        50:5–21.

Curatola Petrocchi, Marco
2016   La voz de la huaca: Acerca de la natura-
        leza oracular y el transfondo aural de la
        religión andina Antigua. In *El Inca y la
        huaca: La religión del poder y el poder de
        la religión en el mundo andino antiguo*,
        pp. 259–316. PUCP, Lima.

Curatola Petrocchi, Marco, and Mariusz Ziólkowski
(editors)
2008   *La función de los oráculos en el mundo
        andino antiguo*. PUCP-IFEA, Lima.

D'Altroy, Terrance
1992   *Provincial Power in the Inka Empire*.
        Smithsonian Institution Press,
        Washington, D.C.

Debord, Guy
[1967] 1977 *The Society of the Spectacle*. Translated
        by F. Perlman and J. Supak. Black and
        Red, Detroit.

Descola, Philippe
1992   Societies of Nature and the Nature of
        Society. In *Conceptualizing Society*,
        edited by Adam Kuper, pp. 107–126.
        Routledge, London.

Earle, Timothy
1997   *How Chiefs Come to Power: The Political
        Economy in Prehistory*. Stanford Univer-
        sity Press, Stanford.

Echeverría García, Jaime
2014   Tonalli, naturaleza fría y personalidad
        temerosa: El susto entre los nahuas del
        siglo XVI. *Estudios de cultura náhuatl*
        48:177–212.

Edgar, Swift (editor), with Angela Kinney
2011   *The Poetical Books*. Vol. 3 of *The Vulgate
        Bible*. Harvard University Press, Cam-
        bridge, Mass.

Fernández de Oviedo, Gonzalo
[1557] 1959 *Historia general y natural de las Indias*.
        Vol. 3. Biblioteca de Autores Españoles,
        Ediciones Atlas, Madrid.

Fernández Fernández, Amaya
2001   *Teresa Enríquez: La loca del sacra-
        mento*. Biblioteca de Autores Cristianos,
        Madrid.

Focillon, Henri
[1934] 1942 *The Life of Forms in Art*. Yale University
        Press, New Haven.

Francis, J. Michael
2007   *Invading Colombia: Spanish Accounts
        of the Gonzalo Jiménez de Quesada
        Expedition of Conquest*. Pennsylvania
        State University Press, University Park.

Garcilaso de la Vega, El Inca
[1609] 1943 *Comentarios reales de los Incas*. Emecé
        Ediciones SA, Buenos Aires.

Gell, Alfred

1998 *Art and Agency: An Anthropological Theory.* Oxford University Press, Oxford.

Gruzinski, Serge

2001 *Images at War: Mexico from Columbus to Blade Runner (1492–2019).* Duke University Press, Durham, N.C.

Guss, David

1990 *To Weave and Sing: Art, Symbol, and Narrative in the South American Rainforest.* University of California Press, Berkeley.

Gutiérrez Usillos, A.

2011 *El eje del universo: Chamanes, sacerdotes y religiosidad en la cultura Jama Coaque del Ecuador prehispánico.* Museo de América, Ministerio de la Cultura, Madrid.

Hajovsky, Patrick Thomas

2015 *On the Lips of Others: Moteuczoma's Fame in Aztec Monuments and Rituals.* University of Texas Press, Austin.

Hermes Trismegistus

[2nd–3rd century CE] 2007 *Asclepius: The Perfect Discourse of Hermes Trismegistus.* Edited and translated by Clement Salaman. Duckworth, London.

Heyden, Doris

1981 *Caves, Gods, and Myths: World-View and Planning in Teotihuacan.* Edited by Elizabeth P. Benson. Dumbarton Oaks Research Library and Collection, Washington, D.C.

Holguín, Diego González

[1608] 1952 *Vocabulario de la lengua general de todo el Peru: Llamada lengua quichua o del Inca.* La Universidad Nacional de San Marcos, Lima.

Houston, Stephen D.

2001 Peopling the Classic Maya Court. In *Theory, Comparison, and Synthesis.* Vol. 1 of *Royal Courts of the Maya,* edited by Takeshi Inomata and Stephen D. Houston, pp. 54–83. Westview Press, Boulder, Colo.

Howard-Malverde, Rosaleen

1990 *The Speaking of History: "Willapaakushayki" or Quechua Ways of Telling the Past.* Institute of Latin American Studies, London.

Hvidtfeldt, Arild

1958 *Teotl and Ixiptlatli: Some Central Conceptions in Ancient Mexican Religion.* Munksgaard, Copenhagen.

Kosiba, Steve

2015a Of Blood and Soil: Tombs, Wak'as, and the Naturalization of Social Difference in the Inka Heartland. In *The Archaeology of Wak'as: Explorations of the Sacred in the Pre-Columbian Andes,* edited by Tamara L. Bray, pp. 167–212. University Press of Colorado, Boulder.

2015b Tracing the Inca Past: Ritual Movement and Social Memory in the Inca Imperial Capital. In *Perspectives on the Inca,* edited by Monica Barnes, Inés de Castro, Javier Flores Espinoza, Doris Kurella, and Karoline Noack, pp. 178–205. Linden Museum, Sonderband/Tribus, Stuttgart.

2017 Ancient Artifice: The Production of Antiquity and the Social Roles of Ruins in the Heartland of the Inca Empire. In *Antiquarianisms: Contact, Conflict, Comparison,* edited by Benjamin Anderson and Felipe Rojas, pp. 72–108. Oxbow Books, Oxford.

Kubler, George

1962a *The Art and Architecture of Ancient America: The Mexican, Mayan and Andean Peoples.* Penguin, Baltimore.

1962b *The Shape of Time: Remarks on the History of Things.* Yale University Press, New Haven.

1973 Science and Humanism among Americanists. In *The Iconography of Middle American Sculpture,* pp. 163–167. Metropolitan Museum of Art, New York.

1975 History—or Anthropology—of Art? *Critical Inquiry* 1(1):757–767. Reprinted 1985 in *Studies in Ancient American and European Art: The Collected Essays of George Kubler,* edited by Thomas F. Reese, pp. 406–412. Yale University Press, New Haven.

Langebaek, Carl Henrik

1987   *Mercados, poblamiento e integración étnica entre los muiscas, siglo XVI.* Colección Bibliográfica, Banco de la República, Bogotá.

2006   De las palabras, las cosas y los recuerdos: El infiernito, la arqueología, los documentos y la etnología en el estudio de la sociedad muisca. In *Contra la tiranía tipológica en arqueología: Una visión desde suramérica*, edited by C. Langebaek and C. Gnecco, pp. 215–257. Universidad de los Andes, Bogotá.

Lechtman, Heather

1996   Cloth and Metal: The Culture of Technology. In *Andean Art at Dumbarton Oaks*, vol. 1, edited by Elizabeth Boone. Dumbarton Oaks, Washington D.C.

Léry, Jean de

[1578] 1990   *History of a Voyage to the Land of Brazil, Otherwise Called America.* Translated by J. Whatley. University of California Press, Berkeley.

Lévi-Strauss, Claude

1982   *The Way of the Masks.* University of Washington Press, Seattle.

Lockhart, James

1985   Some Nahua Concepts in Postconquest Guise. *History of European Ideas* 6(4):465–482.

1992   *The Nahuas after the Conquest: A Social and Cultural History of the Indians of Central Mexico, Sixteenth through Eighteenth Centuries.* Stanford University Press, Stanford.

MacCormack, Sabine

1988   Atahualpa y el libro. *Revista de Indias* 48(184):693–714.

1991   *Religion in the Andes: Vision and Imagination in Early Colonial Peru.* Princeton University Press, Princeton.

Marcus, Joyce

1993   *Mesoamerican Writing Systems: Propaganda, Myth, and History in Four Ancient Civilizations.* Princeton University Press, Princeton.

Marx, Karl

[1844] 1970   *Critique of Hegel's Philosophy of Right.* Cambridge University Press, Cambridge.

[1867] 1990   *Capital: A Critique of Political Economy.* Vol. 1. Translated by Ben Fowkes. Penguin, New York.

Medrano, Alonso de

[1599] 2003   Descripción del Nuevo de Granada [1598]. Introduction and transcription by M. Francis. *Anuario colombiano de historia social y de la cultura* 30:341–360.

Meléndez, Juan

1681   *Tesoros verdaderos de las Yndias.* Vols. 1–2. En la Imprenta de Nicolas Angel Tinassio, Rome.

Millán de Benavides, Carmen

2001   *Epítome de la conquista del nuevo reino de Granada: La cosmografía española del siglo XVI y el conocimiento por cuestionario.* Pontificia Universidad Javeriana, Bogotá.

Miller, Mary, and Claudia Brittenham

2013   *The Spectacle of the Late Maya Court: Reflections on the Murals of Bonampak.* University of Texas Press, Austin.

Muñoz Camargo, Diego

[1584–1585] 1981   *Descripción de la ciudad y provincia de Tlaxcala de las Indias y del mar océano para el buen gobierno y ennoblecimiento dellas.* Universidad Nacional Autónoma de México, Mexico City.

Murry, Peter, and Linda Murray

1996   *The Oxford Companion to Christian Art and Architecture.* Oxford University Press, Oxford.

Murúa, Martín de

1615   *Historia general del Piru.* Ms. Ludwig XIII 16. J. Paul Getty Museum, Los Angeles.

Nebrija, Antonio de

[1492] 2011   *Gramática sobre la lengua castellana.* Barcelona.

Olivera Núñez, Quirino

2014   *Arqueología alto amazónica: Los orígenes de la civilización en el Perú.* Apus Graph Ediciones, Lima.

Olko, Justyna

2005   *Turquoise Diadems and Staffs of Office: Elite Costume and Insignia of Power in Aztec and Early Colonial Mexico.* Polish Society for Latin American Studies and the Centre for Studies on the Classical Tradition, University of Warsaw, Warsaw.

Panofsky, Erwin

1944   Renaissance and Renascences. *Kenyon Review* 6(2):201–236.

1960   *Renaissance and Renascences in Western Art.* Almqvist and Wiksell, Stockholm.

Peréz de Barradas, José

1951   *Los Muiscas antes de la conquista.* Vol. 2. Consejo Superior de Investigaciones Cientificas, Madrid.

Phipps, Elena, Johanna Hecht, and Cristina Esteras Martín

2004   *Colonial Andes: Tapestries and Silverwork, 1530–1830.* Metropolitan Museum of Art, New York.

Polo de Ondegardo y Zárate

[1571] 1990   *El mundo de los Inca.* Edited by G. González and A. Alonso. Historia 16, Madrid.

Quilter, Jeffrey

1990   The Moche Revolt of the Objects. *Latin American Antiquity* 1(1):42–65.

Rodríguez Freyle, Juan

[1636] 1986   *Conquista y descubrimiento del nuevo reino de Granada.* Historia 16, Madrid.

Russo, Alessandra, Diana Fane, and Gerhard Wolf (editors)

2015   *Images Take Flight: Feather Art in Mexico and Europe, 1300–1700.* Hirmer, Munich.

Sahagún, Fray Bernardino de

1580   *Historia general de las cosas de Nueva España.* Electronic document, https://www.wdl.org/en/item/10096/view/1/87/.

Salomon, Frank

1991   Introductory Essay. In *The Huarochiri Manuscript: A Testament of Ancient and Colonial Andean Religion,* by Anonymous [ca. 1607], translated by Frank Salomon and George L. Urioste. University of Texas Press, Austin.

2004   Andean Opulence: Indigenous Ideas about Wealth in Colonial Peru. In *Colonial Andes: Tapestries and Silverwork, 1530–1830,* by Elena Phipps, Johanna Hecht, and Cristina Estera Martín, pp. 114–124. Metropolitan Museum of Art, New York.

Serra, Juan de Santa Gertrudis

[1799] 1970   *Maravillas de la naturaleza.* Biblioteca Banco Popular, Bogotá.

Severi, Carlo

2007   *Le principe de la chimère: Une anthropologie de la mémoire.* Ed. Rue d'Ulm- Musée du Quai Branly, Paris.

Sherbondy, Jeanette

1982   El regadío, los lagos y los mitos de origen. *Allpanchis* 17(20):3–53.

Simón, Fray Pedro

[1629] 1981   *Noticias historiales de las conquistas de tierra firme en las Indias Occidentales.* Biblioteca Banco Popular, Bogotá.

Taylor, Gerald

1976   Camay, camae et camasca dans le manuscrit quechua de Huarochirí. *Journal de la Société des Américanistes* 63:231–244.

Third Council of Lima

1583–1585   *Doctrina christiana y catecismo para instrvccion de los Indios, y de las de mas personas, que han de ser enseñadas en nuestra Sancta fé. Con un confessionario, y otras cosas necessarias para los que doctrinan, que se contienen en la pagina siguiente.* Antonio Ricardo, Lima.

Tomlison, Gary

2009   *The Singing of the New World: Indigenous Voice in the Era of European Contact.* University of Cambridge Press, Cambridge.

Townsend, Richard

1979   *State and Cosmos in the Art of Tenochtitlan.* Dumbarton Oaks, Washington, D.C.

Triana, Miguel

[1924] 1970   *El jeroglífico chibcha.* Biblioteca Banco Popular, Bogotá.

Uribe, María Alicia, Eduardo Londoño, Juan Pablo Quintero, and Marcos Martinón-Torres

2013   *Historias de ofrendas muiscas: Catálogo virtual de la exposición temporal en el Museo del Oro, Bogotá D.C.* Electronic document, http://www.banrepcultural.org/museo-del-oro/exposiciones-temporales/historias-de-ofrendas-muiscas.

Valdez, Francisco

2013   *Primeras sociedades de la alta Amazonía: La cultura mayo chinchipe-marañón.* Institut de Recherche pour le Développement, Quito.

Vargas Murcia, Laura Liliana

2017   De nencatacoa a San Lucas: Mantas muiscas de algodón como soporte pictórico en el nuevo reino de Granada. *UCOARTE: Revista de la historia del arte de la Universidad de Córdoba,* 25–43.

Villacorta, Luis Felipe

2003   Palacios y ushnus: Curacas del Rímac y gobierno inca en la costa central. *Boletín de Arqueología PUCP* 7:151–187.

Viveiros de Castro, Eduardo

1992   *From the Enemy's Point of View: Humanity and Divinity in an Amazonian Society.* Translated by C. Howard. University of Chicago Press, Chicago.

1998   Cosmological Deixis and Amerindian Perspectivism. *Journal of the Royal Anthropological Institute,* n.s., 4(3):469–488.

2004   Exchanging Perspectives: The Transformation of Objects into Subjects in Amerindian Cosmologies. *Common Knowledge* 10(3):463–484.

Weber, Max

[1905] 1930   *The Protestant Ethic and the Spirit of Capitalism.* Translated by T. Parsons. Scribner, New York.

Winter, Irene

2010   *On Art in the Ancient Near East.* 2 vols. Brill Academic, Boston.

Wittgenstein, Ludwig

[1953] 2009   *Philosophical Investigations.* 4th ed. Edited and translated by P. M. S. Hacker and Joachim Schulte. Wiley-Blackwell, Oxford.

Zamora, Fray Alonso de

[1701] 1980   *Historia de la provincia de San Antonino del Nuevo Reyno de Granada.* 4 vols. Instituto Colombiano de Cultura Hispánica, Bogotá.

Zeidler, James

2016   Modeling Cultural Responses to Volcanic Disaster in the Ancient Jama-Coaque Tradition, Coastal Ecuador: A Case Study in Cultural Collapse and Social Resilience. *Quaternary International* 394:79–97.

7

The Lanzón's Tale

MARY WEISMANTEL

The study of religion is or ought to be the study of what human beings do to, for, and against the gods really present—using "gods" as a synecdoche for all the special suprahuman beings with whom humans have been in relationship in different times and places—and what the gods really present do with, to, for, and against humans.

—Robert Orsi, *History and Presence*

"THE GODS REALLY PRESENT"—HOW better to describe the powerful beings whose living presence was so much a part of life in the Pre-Columbian Americas? In this chapter, I consider the long relationship between humans and their "gods really present" at one of the most famous and enigmatic archaeological sites of the Andes, the Peruvian site of Chavín de Huantar,[1] and I do so from the perspective of one of the most famous and enigmatic of Chavín's stone monoliths, the carved granite shaft known as the Lanzón.[2]

Chavín is an ideal site from which to contemplate the themes of this volume: animacy and

authority. In the introduction, Steve Kosiba asks us to consider animist practice and political authority as these were enacted within reciprocal, triangular relationships between humans, objects, and places. In this chapter, I focus on one example of these relationships: what John Janusek (2015:339) calls the "mutual subjectivity of stone and flesh" between a stone monolith of enduring power and its human interlocutors.[3]

Each section of the chapter considers this lithic–human relationship from a different angle, like a viewer who walks around a three-dimensional sculpture so as to see it in its entirety. The first section is an illustrated narrative, "The Lanzón's Tale," that takes a lithic-centered perspective. This narrative is intentionally provocative in several ways. One is simply in the fact that it is a somewhat novel form of presentation—completely different from a graph, a table, or a photograph.[4] If stories and drawings are strange companions to archaeological writing,[5] however, they are not at all strange to Chavín, or to indigenous knowledge production and transmission, where narrative is strongly valorized. Over its long history, a penumbra of stories and legends must have grown up around this place and its secret stone, and since people traveled to the site for brief, intense experiences, its impact could never be measured solely by quantifiable facts. This was a mythic place—one that was most significant in the form of tales told and retold after the fact.

The second provocation is to our conventional anthropocentrism as archaeologists studying ancient American animist societies: could momentarily abandoning this position allow us to better appreciate the history of a site like Chavín and the motivations and actions of the indigenous South Americans who built, inhabited, cared for, visited, and worshipped there?

In the sections that follow, I return to a more conventional authorial voice, from the lithic to the fleshly side of the equation. What was it that drew so many humans, most of whom already worshipped other stones and respected other authorities elsewhere, to place themselves in the Lanzón's presence?[6] I begin by considering human authority in a place where the greatest power resided in nonhuman actors and then ask about specific qualities of the stone that made humans perceive it as so compelling. These include its multispecies animality and its complicated relationship to temporality. As a stone, it has existed far longer than any human, but as a being surrounded by stone in a volcanic landscape, it also embodies the constant threat to survival posed by active geological processes in the Andes. I end the chapter by considering how in all of these aspects—as a deity, a fearsome beast, a creature of immeasurable antiquity, and an avatar of the unstable earth—the Lanzón evoked human emotions that we often call "fear," but which also encompass "awe" and "reverence."

The Site

Chavín is an ideal site from which to contemplate the themes of this volume. It is undoubtedly a good place to think about animacy: nonhuman beings and places have been "humming with conscious life" throughout the ancient Americas, but few places have hummed with the intensity and duration of this site.[7] The "humming" sacrality of this particular place has captured human attention for several millennia. Its known history as a focus of indigenous worship and pilgrimage may have begun far before 1500 BCE and encompassed parts of the Initial period, an apogee in the Early Horizon, and a resurgence in the early colonial period. It has a modern history as well: it was well known as an archaeological site in the nineteenth and twentieth centuries; is currently thriving as a national icon of Peru and an international World Heritage site; and it appears poised to enjoy continued fame and attention in the near and distant future.

This site is an equally good place to think about questions of authority. Chavín is a locus classicus in South American archaeology for interrogating the relationship between art, religion, and politics. The evidence that Chavín had an expansive influence far beyond its narrow highland valley during the first millennium BCE in western South America is generally considered to be overwhelming. It includes objects inscribed with Chavín's distinctive iconographic style found at far-flung regional centers and objects from those distant centers found in the ritual complex at Chavín de Huantar itself. As with the Olmec in Mesoamerica, mid-twentieth-century archaeologists spoke of a "Chavín horizon" and engaged in sometimes heated debates over whether stylistic influence necessarily indicated political authority: was Chavín the capital of a polity, the center of a religious cult, neither, or both? Dumbarton Oaks, the publisher of this volume, has a special relationship to these debates.[8]

This chapter explores the relationship between these two facets of the site: its significance as a sacred and intensely animate place and the authority it exercised over the humans who came to or lived there. My goals in doing so are twofold. Narrowly, the unusual aspects of Chavín make it a good place to think our way toward more nuanced and site-specific models that might replace the sometimes mechanistic evolutionary models that have been so influential in the Andes. As Steve Kosiba ably summarizes in the introduction to this volume, archaeological thinking about the relationship between political and religious power is currently in flux, with many researchers now critical of models that have been, up until recently, widely accepted.

Unquestionably, long-term change in the Andes involved the growing concentration of power in the hands of a few. But this broad generalization may not capture the anomalous characteristics of Chavín, which differs markedly from many coeval sites in western South America. Although the site had a larger resident population than was once thought, its massive ceremonial complex was never intended merely to preside over its own narrow valley; instead, it was oriented toward the heterogenous and cosmopolitan travelers who came from far beyond its own region and whose primary political and religious identities were claimed elsewhere (Contreras 2015:214–215; Kembel 2008; Sayre 2010). For this reason, models that explain how a political center controls its surrounding populations may be relevant to many Pre-Columbian sites, but they cannot capture the power that made Chavín.

I also have a broader question in mind: whether, in studying the animist societies of the ancient Americas, we might need to open up our conceptualization of "authority" to encompass nonhuman actors, and if so, how that might change our research and writing practices. I do so somewhat playfully, but the question is a serious one. Social scientists have traditionally envisioned "authority" as an exclusively human phenomenon exercised by human leaders over their human followers (Kosiba, this volume). This conceptualization of authority is an awkward fit with animacy, which may be best defined as a life lived in relationship with other persons, only some of whom are human (Harvey 2005:xi; Sillar 2006). It may seem self-evident that people built Chavín—but to put humans at the center of the story may be to miss how the political ecology of the site worked. The people who erected stone monoliths invested them with both animacy and authority, especially in the indigenous Andes, where stone was and is considered to be alive and potentially powerful (Bray 2015; Dean 2010).

The Monolith

The protagonist of "The Lanzón's Tale" is a monolithic carved granite shaft that played (and plays) a central role in the complex and shifting assemblages of built environments, objects, and persons that constitute Chavín. As at Tiwanaku (Janusek, this volume), the fame of Chavín is inextricably bound to its carved stones, many of which are iconic, not only for Pre-Columbian archaeologists, but for the Peruvian public as well (Cummins 2008). However, not all its monoliths are the same. Stones like the Obelisk Tello and the Stela Raimundi are known for their elaborate carvings of intertwined hybrid creatures; it is from these stones that we learned to appreciate the distinctive Chavín style, as deciphered by John Rowe and Donald Lathrap in classic articles on iconography.[9] Oddly, however, the carving on the site's most famous monolith, christened the Lanzón, or Giant Lance, by Julio C. Tello, is relatively crude, lacking the complexity for which the Chavín style is famous. Nevertheless, as Rowe ([1967] 1977) recognized, this stone holds a special place in the history of the site, of Peru, and of the ancient Americas.

The Lanzón captures the imagination above all for its dramatic location, hidden in a chamber at the heart of the network of stone passageways known as the *galerías* (Figures 7.1–7.3). Its antiquity also makes it distinctive: the monumental complex at Chavín is ancient, but the Lanzón is even older—a fact that remains undisputed in the midst of otherwise acrimonious disagreements over other aspects of the site's chronology. According to a widely accepted reconstruction of events, this granite prism is the earliest and most significant of all Chavín's monoliths. It may have begun life as a naturally occurring stone, worshipped long before the rest of the site was built; the entire temple complex may then have been gradually constructed around this originary "god really present" (although in its distant past, it may have been brought to the site from elsewhere). Over the centuries, as Chavín—and the Lanzón—grew in importance, successive generations built on an ever more monumental scale and completely entombed the stone and its network of

figure 7.1
The Lanzón
stela. www.
CyArk.com.

figure 7.2
Replica of the
Lanzón stela in
the Museo de la
Nación, Lima.
Wikimedia
Commons.

figure 7.3
Detail of the Lanzón
stela, depicting the
principal deity of
Chavín, Building B.
www.CyArk.com.

surrounding galleries, turning the monolith into an underground deity (Rick 2004) (Figure 7.4). The site plan of the temple complex, with its series of larger and smaller plazas, pathways and staircases, and, finally, network of galleries that lead to the Lanzón, all reinforce the view that this most hidden object, nested in the innermost sanctum, is also the most central and most holy.

The previous description presents the Lanzón as seen by archaeologists and therefore, we might argue, is the best available approximation of how it would have been seen by the Pre-Columbian people who built the site and worshipped the stone. In the story that follows, I retell the tale differently, making the Lanzón the site's originary and central pivot, the center of the action. The challenges are obvious, given the gaps in the archaeological record. Nevertheless, with these limitations in mind, I give you the history of Chavín from the point of view of its oldest continuous inhabitant.

I call this somewhat mischievous approach a "strategic decentering of the human," along the lines of Spivak's (1988) well-known "strategic essentialism." The choice to be deliberately playful—a kind of interaction that is inherently multimodal and interactive—strikes me as in keeping with the

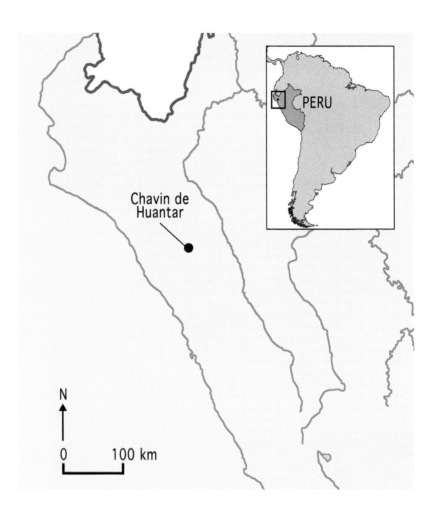

figure 7.4
Map of Chavín
de Huantar,
Peru, and its
surrounding
regions.

Chavin de
Huantar

PERU

N

0   100 km

overall theoretical and methodological project of this volume. Rather than a somber, ideologically driven representation of a singular "truth" about the ancient Andes, a playful narrative that claims only a partial perspective might get us closer to the messy, generative processes of everyday political and ritual life in all their ontological and affective multiplicity.

The most playful aspect of this experiment is the illustrations, which are the result of a collaboration with a young artist, Sam Molina-Wong (Figures 7.5–7.12). As soon as I envisioned this narrative exercise, I wanted to make pictures as well as words, but I realized that it would be impossible to accurately illustrate the earliest phases of the site, since the archaeological evidence remains buried under the massive stones of later phases. Even for later phases, any reconstruction must be largely speculative. To assist me in solving this problem, I enlisted Sam. I did not, however, employ him as

a scientific illustrator whose depictions would be judged by their exactitude. Instead, I wrote a storyboard for him, gave him access to a pile of illustrated publications, and encouraged him to express the tale creatively. I had no idea if the experiment would be successful. The resulting drawings surprised me very much, and this surprise, to my mind, made the experiment a success, since it brought me to consider questions about the life of the Lanzón that we have come to take for granted, some of which I will discuss.

This kind of experiment is only one tool in the archaeologist's toolkit—and one that should be used sparingly. As researchers, we are bound to high standards of accuracy: the drawings that illustrate this chapter could never replace conventional archaeological illustrations, nor can narratives like "The Lanzón's Tale" be more than an adjunct to factual presentations of the evidence. Nevertheless,

figure 7.5
The young Lanzón receives offerings. Original watercolor and ink drawing by Sam Molina-Wong, 2016.

figure 7.6
The Lanzón requests a body. Original watercolor and ink drawing by Sam Molina-Wong, 2016.

figure 7.7
Sculpting the Lanzón. Original watercolor and ink drawing by Sam Molina-Wong, 2016.

figure 7.8
The Lanzón's new body.
Original watercolor
and ink drawing by
Sam Molina-Wong, 2016.

figure 7.9
The Lanzón in the temple.
Original watercolor
and ink drawing by
Sam Molina-Wong, 2016.

figure 7.10
The aging Lanzón inside the
temple complex. Original
watercolor and ink drawing by
Sam Molina-Wong, 2016.

figure 7.11
Viewing the Lanzón in historic times.
Original watercolor and ink drawing by
Sam Molina-Wong, 2016.

figure 7.12
The Lanzón as a United Nations World Heritage
Site. Original watercolor and ink drawing by
Sam Molina-Wong, 2016.

this kind of "serious play" has its uses (Van Dyke
and Bernbeck 2015:4 and passim; Weismantel 2011).
It makes us think more clearly about our narrative
choices and their conceptual, political, and historical underpinnings: who speaks here, and why?

Here, then, is "The Lanzón's Tale."

The Lanzón's Tale

From the Lanzón's point of view, we begin the story
some time before 1500 BCE—perhaps long before—
somewhere in the north-central highlands of Peru.
This part of the story is mostly lost to us, but we can
imagine that as a young, striking-looking stone,
it began to attract local followers who visited it to
pray, bring offerings, and conduct rituals. As its
reputation grew, it eventually felt the need to be
enclosed in a temple. And so it motivated its people
to build one for it: a small, rather humble temple
in the highland style, probably circular and semi-
subterranean. But this was only the beginning.
As worshippers came from farther away and from
other altitudes and ecosystems, the Lanzón needed
a place of greater chthonic and spatial significance,
one that could better express its more cosmopolitan identity. Its humans, then, were further motivated to take it to the place where it could assume
the role of an axis mundi: the valley of Chavín. In
this location—high in the mountains, but warm
with air from lower altitudes, isolated and possessed of dramatic natural entrances from several
different directions—its followers built its new temple, enclosing it again in stone. This was not a safe
choice, given the volatility of the local geology, but
safety was not something that the Lanzón or its followers sought.

At some time during its early life, the stone felt
a desire to let its humans see it in a form that they
could better understand, and so it allowed them
to shape it, making visible its eyes, its nostrils, its
hands. This was a relational act: like an alien in
a science-fiction film, this lithic being took on a
more animal form, with orifices and features that
facilitated its relations with humans. It also better
enabled offerings of fluids by having a cruciform

channel carved into its head. At this point in its history, then, its stony surfaces were modified to increase its capacity to interact with other kinds of substances and bodies, whether liquid or mammalian.

We can take a cue from biographies of human leaders and characterize this young period as in some ways the happiest. The Lanzón felt intensely alive: its temple home was humming with water and life, and its connections to its followers were frequent and direct, feeding its growth. The next centuries were good as well, as the Lanzón and Chavín both continued to grow, at times exponentially, attracting fame as well as wealth in the form of offerings. According to some interpretations of the site, the travelers who came were exclusively individuals who were beautiful and powerful themselves: elegantly dressed elites who came with their retinues, carrying the most beautiful and valuable of gifts. The air was alive: with sounds, not only of rushing water, but of voices and trumpets raised in song or prayer; with color and movement, and the flashes of light reflected from polished hematite mirrors; and, from farther away, with the smells of food cooking, of pack llamas resting in their corrals.

This was the period when the site became truly monumental, as the humans who belonged to the Lanzón continued to encase it in more and more layers of living stone. They dug underground tunnels that linked the temple to the river and transported enormous stones to line them. They built a kind of artificial mountain around the original temple, laced with a network of chambers, galleries, and channels. The temple complex that they built was alive: it respirated like a biological creature, filled with circulating fluid and air, light and darkness, sounds and silences. Like the Lanzón, this mountainous building was made of stone, but it felt like a mammalian body as well, with its seemingly organic galleries and breathy sounds. When it rained, it was transformed again: the sounds of the water coursing through its body pounding and echoing like a giant drum. And everything about it served the Lanzón's ends: its sacred body was protected from view, and yet the entire building, the built environment around it, and the valley itself

were shaped to funnel people toward it—even if not everyone was allowed to enter its inner sanctum.

During this period, new carvings were being made, but these served the Lanzón, too. They were shiny and flat and displayed so as to draw people from the outside of the site gradually inward. The entrance to its stony home was reconfigured into an enclosed pathway that led through a circular plaza, and this too was carved with human and jaguar figures who moved in procession toward the ancient prism, bringing offerings and playing trumpets in its honor. New monoliths were erected in public places and covered in incised designs, but these were secondary to the Lanzón, which remained the central, secret axis that gave the entire complex its meaning and shape. These new stones were beautiful, but they were different: rather than giving them expressive features that could allow them to communicate, their carvings wrapped them in shallow designs like a body wrapped in woven fabric. And in turn, the new stelae and constructions enclosed and wrapped the Lanzón itself, enhancing rather than competing with its power.

From there, the story follows a familiar political arc, also known to us from books and movies about the lives of famous men. Like many a great leader, the Lanzón allowed itself to become increasingly isolated as its fame, importance, and power grew. As the new larger temples and plazas were built to accommodate the increased volume of travelers, fewer and fewer of them were allowed access to the Lanzón itself. Although it was still surrounded by an aura of fame, that fame was a thing of mystery and whispers; in contrast, the exterior stones had designs that could not only be seen, but also copied, taken away, and repeated elsewhere. The Lanzón reveled in its exalted status, but it also felt old and alone. Priests served it, but they also kept it in isolation; it had many servants, but there were fewer and fewer whom it knew well.

And so we can begin to speak of its long decline. Rarely seeing outsiders, no longer fed by the bodily interactions with human worshippers, the stone felt its power dimming; around it, the very walls of its temples began to buckle under their own weight. Eventually, it was almost completely abandoned.

Those who knew and understood it were somehow no longer there; ignorant newcomers built houses on what had been sacred space, and the Lanzón settled into a few centuries of elderly gloom.

But this was far from the last chapter. Chavín's longevity, the durability and monumentality of the temple complex, and the enduring pull of the sacred space itself eventually brought people back. First came its sixteenth-century florescence, when colonial documents attest to its legendary status as a holy place visited by pilgrims from across Peru. Now, five hundred years later, the flow of visitors is more modest, but its reputation as a United Nations World Heritage site reaches global dimensions. The local population is still there, serving and tending to the stones and feeding its guests. The priests are archaeologists now, and the pilgrims are tourists. As three-thousand-year-old stories go, this is a pretty good one.

Encounters

In this half of the chapter, I return to a more balanced perspective but not to an entirely anthropocentric point of view. The first section considers some of the various kinds of interactions—or intra-actions (Barad 2012)[10]—through which authority was produced; the following two sections focus on two aspects of the encounters between pilgrims and the big stones that were vibrantly and dangerously alive. The first of these, "Encountering Animal Others," considers the stones as multispecies animals and the encounters in light of ethnographic accounts of Amazonian animism. The next section, "Encountering a Geomorph," turns to various forms of lithic vitality: the Lanzón's stony substance, its incredible antiquity, and its position as axis mundi.

Recent archaeological investigations suggest that the entire site of Chavín de Huantar may have been deliberately constructed as an instantiation of the destructive, life-giving geophysical forces that shape the Andes (Contreras 2015); in this light, we can see the Lanzón as a still more concentrated instantiation of these forces. The final section, "On

Fear," uses this idea to revisit the affective experience of coming to Chavín. Rather than mere terrified dupes, worshippers may have come to the site with full knowledge of the implications of their actions. Seeking a transformative experience with a chthonic being from which they might emerge either newly empowered or utterly destroyed, they may have faced this momentous occasion with heightened emotions that included not only deathly fear, but also life-affirming desire. As a religious practice, this conscious embrace of an ambivalent lithic force seems appropriate for the indigenous residents of western South America, who thrived for millennia in an environment that was both fertile and lethally volatile.

Authority, Human and Nonhuman

All forms of power at the site were relational, including that of the stones (Watts 2013). In "The Lanzón's Tale," we saw that its power depended on drawing human actors into its orbit; as Janusek (2015:238) says, the animacy of sacred monoliths "required human engagement." From the perspective of human actors, the stones themselves may have motivated people to travel to the site, quarry and transport other stones, construct buildings, perform rituals, and create art—and obey human leaders whose directives were understood to be in service of the "gods really present."

My thinking about those human leaders is quite different from explanations of indigenous American politics in which beliefs in speaking stones or jaguar shamans solely reflect an "ideology meant to mask the brute and all-too-human machinations of power" (as Kosiba critiques in this volume). Researchers who adopt this approach have tended to represent Chavín as a place of theocratic totalitarianism where rulers deliberately manipulated a credible "lay public" through deceptive spectacles (e.g., Rick 2004:80). While we can agree that human authority figures exerted control over what happened at the site, and used their connection to the stones to influence other humans, we can nonetheless stop short of the further assumption that these leaders were cynically duplicitous in their religious practices. I am especially wary of this assumption because of its deep and pernicious roots in colonial campaigns to discredit indigenous religion and religious authorities; we should be mindful of the fact that some ethnohistoric sources are not neutral descriptions but carefully crafted documents designed to justify campaigns of extirpation.

Comparative, cross-cultural, and historical evidence suggests a more likely scenario: that like religious leaders elsewhere, the human leaders of Chavín believed implicitly in their own faith. This could have been true even though their relationship with the "gods really present" was different—more intimate, more knowing—than that of ordinary people and even though they likely crafted performances of religiosity designed to create particular effects for particular audiences. Like most forms of authority, human authority at the site was a balance of subordination and superordination: if the most powerful humans were *leaders* of other humans, they were also *servants* or *caretakers* of beings more powerful than themselves (Fausto, this volume).

Another antidote to generic political models is to think more deeply about the experience of travelers to Chavín. A model of fearful, blind obedience to local leaders seems especially misplaced at a pilgrimage site, to which travelers come voluntarily in search of personally rewarding encounters with famous nonhuman presences. Both comparative and archaeological forms of evidence suggest alternative scenarios. Modern and historical accounts of religious pilgrimages describe experiences that are embodied and interactive; focused on nonhuman sacred persons or objects such as icons, tombs, or images rather than on human priests; and heavily weighted toward personal transformation and the crafting or acquisition of narratives and material evidence to bring back home. Resident religious figures may be actively sought out for their esoteric wisdom, their close relationship to the sacred, and their ability to conduct rituals and provide access to restricted areas, but the respect in which these figures are held only indirectly translates into forms of coercive political power, and these may only operate in very limited contexts.

As I have argued elsewhere, the phenomenological evidence of the stones themselves, such as the features of scale and design that imposed slow, unpredictable interactions with human eyes and bodies, suggests that interactions between stone and flesh created sensory, cognitive, and emotional experiences that were specific to each encounter, rather than delivering an overdetermined experience that drove home a single political or ideological message (Weismantel 2013a, 2015a). When groups with a shared identity traveled to and experienced the site together, their encounters with the sacred may have involved interpretive processes that were dialogic and collaborative (Weismantel 2015b). This is not to say that ritual activity at Chavín was entirely participatory, let alone egalitarian. Rather, as Daniel Contreras (2015:226) argues, it "seems to have simultaneously involved both inclusionary/participatory/communitarian and exclusionary/hierarchical components." And in that hierarchy, no human stood above the stones themselves.

There does, however, seem to be a hierarchy among the *stones*, one that places nonhumans above humans. In this regard, Chavín offers an interesting comparison to Tiwanaku, where Janusek (this volume) finds that the monoliths fall into different classes, ranked in importance. His hierarchy places two classes of anthropomorphic figures at the top and the feline *chachapumas* at the bottom. At Chavín, in contrast, depictions of the human figure—and the human political hierarchies and forms of subjectification it represents—pale in significance when compared to nonhuman bodies. Spatial evidence reinforces these inverted hierarchies: at Tiwanaku, the *chachapumas* serve as entry figures to inner sanctums dominated by anthropomorphic figures, whereas at Chavín, small human figures lead toward the entrance to the galleries that hold the nonhuman Lanzón.

This contrast points to a possible difference in the purpose and outcomes of encounters between humans and stones. For Janusek (this volume), Tiwanaku's monoliths were deployed in order to produce "firmly beholden geopolitical subjects" subjected to localized human political authority. Similarly, the site as a whole was dedicated to achieving centrality as a place that dominated local places and populations geography, socially, ideologically, and politically, as was true of many Pre-Columbian monumental sites.

Chavín—and the Lanzón—were playing a very different game. The difference can be seen in Chavín's location and site design.[11] Although the scale of the architecture, the sheer quantity of monumental stone, and the vast ambitions of its builders are stunning, Chavín does not overwhelm from a distance. Instead, the overall experience is of a place that is rather secretive. Access to the site begins with arduous travel (Cummins 2008), followed by a series of dramatic discoveries, and then a departure (Weismantel 2013a, 2013b). Movement toward and through the site seems designed as a journey rather than a destination, as though meant for people whose geopolitical home was elsewhere.[12] This built environment lays claim to a more profound but more diffuse kind of significance, one that transcended its locality or any human genealogies or polities. (Although individuals undoubtedly enhanced their power in their home polities through claims of having been to Chavín, as when prosperous Muslims gain stature by making the pilgrimage to Mecca.)

To make this transcendent claim, the important stones at Chavín signify not as human personages, ethnic groups, lineages, or ancestors, but in a more universal idiom of nonhuman biota and stony geomorphs. However, different stones deploy and emphasize these two aspects differently—differences that shaped travelers' experiences at the site and what they took home with them when they left.

Upon entering the more accessible areas of the site, Pre-Columbian visitors saw a lot of carved stones: the ashlars mounted on temple exteriors, the twin pillars variously known as "Black and White" or "Falcon," and possibly stelae such as the Raimundi or Tello, which may have been erected in exterior places like plazas. These sculptures are smooth and highly polished, with planar surfaces and shallow inscriptions (Weismantel 2014). There is no obvious relationship between medium and image, between the lithic surface and the biotic imagery. The riotous intertwining of mammals, reptiles, birds, and plants in the designs is seemingly indifferent to the stone beneath and resembles designs found on other media such as clay, metal, or painted cloth. This is the kind of imagery that traveled, becoming the distinctive Chavín or "Chavinoid" style found elsewhere, and indeed, the images seem almost packaged to go. Wrapped around the surface like cloth, the designs invite visitors to mentally unwrap them and carry them home in order to wrap them around new objects of stone, clay, metal, or cloth.

In contrast, the Lanzón retains aspects of its original, somewhat irregular shape. Its surfaces are rougher, the carving simpler, larger, and deeper; the lines appear to give the stone biotic features—hands, a spine, a face—that bring out its original form, rather than existing separately from it. Alone among the major monoliths at the site, the Lanzón appears to be a stone come to life. Nevertheless, while animality may have been more present on the public stones than on this more secretive stone, the Lanzón may sometimes have taken visible and aural form as a powerful animal—one that was larger than the stone itself.

Encountering Animal Others

Although images of animal-human hybrids are characteristic of Pre-Columbian and indigenous art across the Americas, the emphatic animality at Chavín is striking. In some art styles, such hybrid figures are predominantly human, their animal features subordinate parts of an anthropomorphic whole. Elsewhere, animal (or vegetable) features may even appear as a costume covering a human body, for example in Paracas textiles or at Khonkho Wakane, where Janusek (2015:350) describes the monoliths as "anthropomorphic personage[s] *decorated with* zoomorphic imagery" (my emphasis). At Chavín, the balance is reversed: whereas human features are present, animality predominates. On one of the most iconic of Chavín statues, the Obelisk Tello, the dominant figures are caimans or *amarus* (Urton 2008).

As has often been noted, this more-than-human imagery of caimans, jaguars, raptors, and hallucinogenic plants also evokes a distant ecology, in keeping with the site's hybrid, expansive, cosmopolitan relationship to geography. The architecture at Chavín de Huantar is eclectic, expressing elements of both coastal and highland style (Burger 1992). Both these regions, at various moments in their long histories, experienced explosive growth, political centralization and expansion, and accumulated wealth, and attracting visitors from these regions was important to Chavín. But the ecological imagery on the monoliths does not evoke either of them. Instead, it recalls Amazonia—a place that later state societies such as the Inka (as well as contemporary residents of the Andes) would associate with deep shamanic knowledge and power and with mystical connections between human and nonhuman species (Lathrap 1973).

Ethnographic accounts of shamanic encounters from Amazonia, then, are a possible source for interpreting the iconography at Chavín. But unlike the relatively simple human-jaguar encounter that Eduardo Viveiros de Castro (1998, 2012) proposes as the prototypical Amazonian interspecies encounter, the carvings on the Chavín monoliths include many bodies and many species (Weismantel 2013a, 2013b). This multiplicity evokes ethnographic descriptions of the most powerful shamans, who have acquired multiple bodies and souls from others, and befits such a famous holy place: the stones do not embody an ordinary encounter with an ordinary being; instead, they bring viewers into contact with superhuman beings who have incorporated, ingested, or become not just one but many others over their long lives.

This animality may extend not only to the stelae, but also to the enormous stone armature that surrounds the Lanzón. While other newer buildings on the site feature theatrical or performative facades with staircases and doorways that would allow costumed figures to appear before audiences gathered in the open spaces below, this network of "underground" *galerías* is enclosed and inward facing. This has led scholars to speculate that, at least in later centuries, few or even no worshippers may have been allowed into the presence of this most secluded figure. However, comparative data from Pachacamac suggest a provocative possibility: the creature inside may have manifested itself sensorially to those who could not enter. Curatola Petrocchi (this volume) cites ethnohistoric accounts of Pachacamac in which the entity who lived inside the temple made itself visible in the form of a fearsome "serpent or feline," wrapping itself around the building and shrieking and roaring in a terrifying manner. At Chavín, Curatola Petrocchi argues that the well-known "phantasmagoric acoustic effects" produced by water coursing through the *galerías* were the sounds of an enormous creature both alive and distinctly animal. If we put together Janusek's astute observation in this volume about the shared identity of monoliths and their monumental enclosures with Curatola Petrocchi's reference to Moche ceramic portrayals of temples as serpents, or as wrapped in serpents, we can think of the temple housing the Lanzón as a larger manifestation of the animal-stone itself, as its carapace or outer living shell. One might further speculate that the famous tenon heads that once adorned the external walls of the site, which were visible before one entered into the complex, might have evinced the multiple captured souls that live within a powerful shaman's body—like the multiple, smaller animal-persons that make up the big figures in Chavín art: the snake hair, the open-mouth joints.

Apparently, the concept of temple as animal body is something that I communicated to Molina-Wong before I was fully aware of it myself. When he first showed me his drawings, I was taken aback by his decision to represent the building that encases the Lanzón as a kind of crouching reptilian, but he was surprised by my surprise. To him, this was a logical response to several things that had impressed him about the site. One was the ubiquity of reptilian and nonmammalian imagery—snakes, caimans, even the scaly feet of birds—in Chavín art. Another was my description of being inside the *galerías* as like being inside the entrails of an enormous stony creature. He, too, had interpreted the acoustical effects of the *galerías* as evidence that the building possessed an animal vitality. His drawing and Curatola Petrocchi's chapter make me wonder if in thinking about buildings as embodied we might consider whether those bodies are (nonhuman) animal bodies.

Encountering a Geomorph

The Amazonian analogy can only take us so far. The power of these monoliths vastly exceeded that of the wild animals encountered by jungle shamans and not only because their iconography incorporates so many species. The Lanzón is more powerful than any animal because it is not only an animal. It is also a carved and living stone, which adds still more dimensions to its multiplicious being. I turn now to two of those dimensions: the Lanzón as a historical personage whose great antiquity embodies the *slow time* of stone and the Lanzón as a geomorph that embodies the *fast time* of volcanic activity.

—————

To be at Chavín is to be surrounded by the overwhelming presence of massive stones—not only the carved monoliths, but also the huge shaped boulders that comprise much of the built environment. The Lanzón, too, embodies the stoniness of stone. Embedded in earth, encased in a claustrophobically small chamber, it projects an inescapable sense of immobility. Unlike the other monoliths, it has no copies; its carvings cannot be unwrapped from its oddly shaped stone body (Cummins 2008) and so do not travel. While other works of Chavín art have spread their imagery widely across the Andes, the Lanzón gained fame while remaining rooted in place, like an heirloom that accrues value by its refusal to circulate. This significance is embedded in the site design of nested enclosed spaces, which positions the Lanzón in the last, most intimate, ultimate place. It is the site's heart, its conatus, and is thus inseparable from it.

SLOW TIME

A monolith takes its meaning from its rocky substance, but also from its status as an artifact: an object quarried, transported, and carved by human hands (although over time, the makers may no longer have been conceptualized as human). Traces of these labors are part of the stones, making them at once living animals, living stones, and living artifacts. In an animistic world, the act of making is not generally conceptualized as creating something entirely new; as vital matter, the substances used to

craft an artifact are lively and active participants (Joyce and Gillespie 2015; Roddick 2015) that shape the process and the outcome (Conneller 2012). If this is true of ordinary stone or clay, how much more so would it be true of an energetically powerful place such as Chavín? It is noteworthy that as the centuries went on, many human acts of making at the site took the form of enclosing and rearranging sacred objects and places rather than making something new. In these later phases, and perhaps throughout its life, the construction of the site was a relational act—a response to a primordial place whose agency was greater than that of any living human carver or builder.

One source of this power is age: these objects, and this site, are very, very old. Curiously, this antiquity is itself ancient. The site's origins are impossible to ascertain since its earliest levels are blocked by later phases of massive stone construction. However, it was certainly a very old place in the colonial period, when Spanish writers commented on the indigenous pilgrims flocking to Chavín from great distances and in great numbers. These seventeenth-century travelers were returning to a sacred ruin: a place that had been abandoned for some centuries and then came back to life as a place of worship. Even at the site's apogee a thousand years before, antiquity inhered in the place and its stones; its builders are likely to have seen themselves as enclosing and celebrating an ancient place rather than constructing a new one.

Antiquity, then, encases the Lanzón like the patina that encrusts New Orleans (Dawdy 2016) and adds to the sense of the site as possessed of a secret, hidden power. Awareness of Chavín's great age would have been conveyed through dense, overlapping layers of history, rumor, and myth that emanated far beyond the site, reaching distant human communities, embedding themselves in social memory, and drawing generations of pilgrims toward their source. Over time, these encounters slowly added another layer of meaning as they were repeated endlessly on a temporal scale vastly greater than a human life. An animistic sensibility might perceive this accumulated history as embedded in the site and its stones, like the shiny patinas or pitted surfaces that differentiate old things from new ones.

Fast Time

This time span, extending so far beyond biotic mortality, makes the site a space that bridges human and geological temporalities. However, geologic time is not always slow: in the volatile environment of the Andes, it can manifest itself with catastrophic suddenness. Recent work at Chavín by Contreras (2015) suggests that this significance of stone as volatile rather than stable may be embodied in the site as a whole.

Contreras's (2015) research has established that the boundary between built environment and surrounding ecosystem is less fixed and more expansive than may be apparent. The site's builders did more than construct monumental architecture; they also engaged in an enormous engineering project that reconfigured the entire platform upon which that architecture rests, as well as the flow of rivers around it. Contreras (2015:519) underlines the volatility of this setting, a place where "seismic hazards are magnified by a steep and landslide-prone landscape capable of producing catastrophic debris flows of astonishing speed and power." The residents of Chavín would have witnessed and endured earthflow movement, landslide activity, and river channel avulsion. Nevertheless, they chose to build a sacred and precious site here. Contreras (2015:523) offers two especially provocative suggestions: first, they may have purposefully located the sacred core of the ceremonial center in the most vulnerable area of the valley; and second, their engineering activities may actually have exacerbated the risk rather than mitigating it, as they repeatedly moved earth and water in ways designed to provoke its cataclysmic potential.

It may be, then, that deliberate exposure to encounters with potentially deadly nonhuman powers is integral to the very construction of the site. As Contreras (2015:522) notes, this gives a new meaning and urgency to the notion of the Andean landscape as animate. I would suggest that it also offers another perspective on the evolutionary paradigms discussed previously, which postulated that indigenous leaders manipulated false fears through false gods—an assumption based on two interrelated premises, one about the nature of power over nonhumans and one about power over humans. The first premise is that humans can and do control the nonhuman world but not through religion. They achieve control through technologies based on a "realistic" knowledge that nonhuman things are inert and passively await human manipulation. Thus, any recognition of the power of the nonhuman world is either a foolish error or—the second premise—a deliberate lie designed to achieve domination not over "nature," but over other humans.

However, the impending environmental catastrophes of the twenty-first century are forcibly introducing new forms of "realism": what seems real now is not the powerlessness of inert matter, but the limitations of human technologies and the dangers of underestimating the vital forces of the nonhuman world. In turn, this leads to a reassessment of what counts as collective wisdom and what is misguided fallacy: as we contemplate survival in an increasingly volatile global environment, we may find growing relevance in the millennium-old attitude of indigenous South Americans who never underestimated the destructive forces of the nonhuman world and who survived and thrived as a result. Nowhere is this attitude more apparent than at Chavín, a place designed for worshipful intimacy with the earth's most fearsome powers.

On Fear

It is almost a cliché about Chavín to say that its art and architecture inspired fear in its visitors. This statement is supported by the fearsome imagery at the site itself, which bristles with claws and fangs, and by ethnohistoric descriptions of the comparable site of Pachacamac, which offer a compelling picture of terrified worshippers and frightening sensory experiences (Curatola, this volume). But what does it mean to feel "fear," and does it preclude other emotions? There is a curious ambiguity in descriptions of the Lanzón: its mouth has been described as "snarling" because of its predatory dentition, but also as "smiling" because of its upturned shape. Molina-Wong's drawings capture the peculiar ambivalence of this awkward monster, whose toes turn inward and whose hand is raised in what looks like a tentative greeting. This expression, simultaneously welcoming and menacing, may express an affective quality characteristic of Chavín, which could be described as "fearful joy" or "joyful fear."

The Pleasures of Fear

Fear takes multiple forms, from deep trauma in the face of real violence to the pleasurable goose bumps induced by scary stories and haunted houses (to which Chavín, with its many acoustical and visual "special effects," has often been compared). Consider, for example, the Hebrew word that biblical scholars translate as "fear" or "awe" of God. Religious scholar Andy Tix rejects modern exegetical attempts to separate positive and negative aspects of this emotion; it is, he says, uncategorizable except in its intensity. He focuses instead on its two observable effects: the physiological response of trembling and the relational response of complete submission to the deity.[13]

Similarly, recent scholarship on affect does not discuss it as an interior state of mind, but as a bodily experience that is culturally produced; it preexists individuals, entering from outside and changing subjectivities (Williams 2010). This conceptualization captures something of the affective aura of Pachacamac and Chavín, which could not be dissociated from the place itself and intensified as people ventured further inside.

Affect theorists also argue against thinking of emotions as occurring singly. Expressions like "black humor" or "I laughed till I cried" hint at the ambiguity of our affective responses, and accounts of pilgrimages, as, for example, to the Virgin of Guadalupe, describe them as emotionally multivocalic: solemn and sacred but also festive and celebratory. Travelers to Chavín may have experienced pleasurable anticipation and desire, as well as fear. Philosopher Caroline Williams describes Spinoza's concept of affect as encompassing "a full medley of passions" that all living things seek out as necessary

to their flourishing and experience as bodily states. She differentiates between them, not as positive or negative, but according to their intensity and effect: "That which increases the body's power of action is called by Spinoza an affect of joy (*laetitia*), in contrast to those that hinder and restrain the body's power, which he labels 'sadness'" (William 2010:254). This conceptualization of living things seeking out intense experiences in order to increase their "power of action"—and finding the very intensity of that seeking "joyful"—is a powerful model to bring to Chavín. It fleshes out the word *transformation*, frequently used to describe Pre-Columbian encounters with the "gods really present"—a thought that brings us back to the animality of Chavín's stones and our exploration of Amazonian analogies.

Transformative Fear

Twentieth- and twenty-first-century Amazonians seek knowledge and power through encounters with jaguars and anacondas, whether in life, in dreams, or in myth. Simultaneously benign and threatening, the Lanzón resembles the ambivalently friendly and lethal jaguars of the Bororo myth "Fire of the Jaguar," analyzed by Terence Turner (2017). Its body language and facial expression may represent all of the following: I like meeting you; I may nourish and help you; I may devour you.

The Bororo myth is the narrative form of a life-crisis ritual and depicts the transformation of a boy into a man. This is something else I would like to bring to Chavín: the model of transformative ritual as practiced by indigenous South Americans. When a group of ancient travelers left their community and undertook the journey to Chavín, they were motivated by a desire not simply to *see* works of art or religious icons, but to *meet* the living animal stones in embodied encounters that they expected to be transformative (Weismantel 2014, 2015a). They approached the space generated by a sacred monolith knowing that it could be a space of learning, of transformation, or of death. What happened there depended on the capacity of the stone's human interlocutors to face, absorb, and survive what they found.

Faced with transformative experiences from which they might emerge either newly empowered or utterly destroyed, those who ventured to Chavín could have experienced an intoxicating mix of life-affirming desire and deathly fear. This affective valence is precisely the "intensity" that Spinoza says all living beings seek and that he called "joy."

Living with Fear

The pilgrimage to Chavín has a mythic quality to it, reminiscent not only of Amazonian myth but of other journeys that culminate in a transformative encounter, such as North American indigenous vision quests or European tales like those of Theseus and the Minotaur. Similarly, Molina-Wong was partially inspired by the Japanese animated television series *One Punch Man* in which a puny human hero defeats enormous cannibalistic monsters. These twenty-first-century monsters are surprisingly similar to those at Chavín in that they are often manifestations of geophysical forces such as the ocean. European monsters and dragons, too, are chthonic, earthbound, and mineral. The difference is not in how humans imagine monsters but in the kind of encounters we wish to have with them. For Saint George or One Punch Man, these hybrid creatures, who combine animal, human, and geophysical qualities, are frightening and abhorrent, an ontological threat that must be destroyed so that humans can flourish.

At Chavín, on the other hand, such hybridity was godlike, and ancient Native Americans sought out monsters' chthonic powers, not to destroy them, but to enter into their presence with as much intimacy as they dared. Within this indigenous paradigm, growth and transformation did not come from destroying a nonhuman enemy, but from allowing oneself to be changed through submission to a more powerful other—an image of transformation more like the Judeo-Christian "fear and trembling before God." And if we return to the perspective of the long-lived Lanzón rather than the many short-lived humans, what mattered to Chavín itself was not any single individual's transformation (or death), but the collective thriving of human and nonhuman alike.

What, then, of all the violent imagery? Janusek (this volume) offers one possible explanation when

he observes that the death symbolized by transformational figures such as the Tiwanaku *chachapumas* need not be literal. Violent imagery abounds during rites of passage because during such rites, the "raw" person must be sacrificed so that a new, more vital person can be born. The death that people feared as they entered ritual spaces may not have been a literal, immediate, and physical death.

But that insight is not exactly apt for Chavín, where Contreras demonstrates that the threat of death was not merely symbolic but real and present, not merely individual but collective, embodied in the volatile geological dynamics of the region. This suggests a final, geomorphological level of meaning for those entering the close spaces where the Lanzón resides. This experience—risky, volatile, and deadly but also beautiful, pleasurable, and enriching—may have been a microcosm, spatially and temporally, of the valley of Chavín de Huantar itself.

This chapter has considered the relationship between animacy and authority at a place where humans went to confront powers that were greater than themselves. In looking at this encounter with a god who was "really present," to borrow Orsi's phrase, I have paid more attention to what humans perceived those powers might "do with, to, for, and against" them than I have to what humans might do in making and worshiping their gods. What I discovered in the process is that in the Lanzón, ancient South Americans encountered a being who embodied both the fast and slow temporalities of the Andean earth itself. In its incredible antiquity, it made lithic time "really present" within a human-made space; in its destructive manifestations, it evinced the predatory animal's lightning-fast pounce and the mountain's capacity to erupt into flame, flood, and liquid rock. And yet if it created around itself a halo of fear and dread, it also gave rise to an unforgettable ceremonial center, a great architectural and artistic achievement nestled in a fertile and welcoming valley that has supported a human community for thousands of years.

In building in a volatile place and then daring and provoking it, the builders of Chavín engaged in risky endeavors that both mimicked the individual traveler's visit to the ceremonial center and reenacted what it means to live in western South America more generally. On the one hand, seismic unpredictability and coastal flooding make this a notoriously unstable and difficult environment; extremes of altitude and tropical climates are also often hypothesized to be more challenging than life in the temperate zones. But the archaeological record tells a different story: one of productive agricultural regimes, expansive states and empires, and a generally animate world where humans and all of their creative and political enterprises flourished for millennia. The people who built and came to places like Chavín were well aware of this dynamic opposition between thriving and dying; as we struggle to understand our own relationship to an increasingly volatile global environment, we may find some relevance in the attitude of indigenous South Americans more than a millennium ago, who appear to have embraced uncertainty at every scale.

NOTES

1. In lieu of a site map, I suggest viewing the short video tour of Chavín available at the UNESCO website. The audio script is not informative or completely accurate, but the video provides three-dimensional visual access to the major aspects of the site discussed in this chapter. See http://whc.unesco.org/en/list/330/video.

2. Because of its prominence in the history of Andean archaeology, Chavín has long been a touchstone for archaeological theory in the Americas. Stellar figures in Andean studies, including Julio C. Tello (1943), John Rowe ([1967] 1977), Donald Lathrap (1973), R. Tom Zuidema (1992), and Gary Urton (2008), among others, have worked there or written important essays about its distinctive material record, especially its iconic carvings of multispecies hybrid creatures (jaguar/raptor/reptile/human).

3. I have also discussed this topic in previous articles, see Weismantel 2013a, 2013b, 2014, 2015a, 2015b.

4. On the genres of archaeological writing, see Joyce 2008.

5. On the use of storytelling in archaeology, see Brown, Clarke, and Frederick 2016; Spector 2016.

6. Equally compelling is the question of what motivated other actors, especially those who built the site and carved the stones, but that is beyond the scope of this chapter.

7. Like Catherine Allen (this volume), I am using a capacious definition of the term *animacy*, embracing both what Philippe Descola defines as "animism" and that which he calls "analogism" (Descola 2013); like her, I will borrow from him (and her) the felicitous phrase "humming with conscious life" to describe an animate nonhuman world—an especially appropriate phrase given Curatola Petrocchi's lovely chapter on sound and the sacred in the Andes in this volume.

8. They were first aired and recorded during memorable conferences on the Pre-Columbian past held at Dumbarton Oaks, and these questions were revisited in 2018, when a conference once more explored the nature of Chavín's influence over people who lived at great distances from the site and inhabited a wide variety of ecological zones. See https://www.doaks.org/research/pre-columbian/scholarly-activities/reconsidering-the-chavin-phenomenon-in-the-21st-century.

9. See also later studies by Cummins (2008), Urton (2008), and others.

10. For feminist philosopher Karen Barad, objects and persons do not precede their interaction; rather, they emerge into being through their interactions, or "intra-actions," with one another. This philosophy is well suited to the Pre-Columbian Andes, where people and things similarly were seen to come into being relationally, through their intra-actions with one another—and with places, sacred and mundane.

11. For detailed analyses of highland and coastal site designs and their impact on viewers, see Moore 1996, 2005.

12 Although as Contreras (2009) notes, the visual rela-
    tionship to the local population was also important.
13 See https://thequestforagoodlife.wordpress.com/
    2017/03/06/what-is-awe/.

REFERENCES CITED

Barad, Karen

2012   Nature's Queer Performativity. *Kvinder,
        køn og forskning* 1–2:25–53.

Bray, Tamara L. (editor)

2015   *The Archaeology of Wak'as: Explorations
        of the Sacred in the Pre-Columbian Andes.*
        University Press of Colorado, Boulder.

Brown, Steve, Anne Clarke, and Ursula Frederick
(editors)

2016   *Object Stories: Artifacts and Archaeolo-
        gists.* Routledge, New York.

Burger, Richard

1992   *Chavin and the Origins of Andean
        Civilization.* Thames and Hudson,
        London.

Conneller, Chantal

2012   *An Archaeology of Materials: Substantial
        Transformations in Early Prehistoric
        Europe.* Routledge, London.

Contreras, Daniel A.

2009   Reconstructing Landscape at Chavín de
        Huantar, Peru: A GIS-Based Approach.
        Journal of Archaeological Science
        36(4):1006–1017.

2015   Landscape Setting as Medium of Com-
        munication at Chavín de Huántar,
        Peru. *Cambridge Archaeological Journal*
        25(2):513–530.

Cummins, Tom

2008   Felicitous Legacy of the Lanzón. In
        Chavín: Art, Architecture, and Culture,
        edited by William J. Conklin and Jeffrey
        Quilter, pp. 279–304. Cotsen Institute of
        Archaeology, University of California,
        Los Angeles.

Dawdy, Shannon Lee

2016   *Patina: A Profane Archaeology.* Univer-
        sity of Chicago Press, Chicago.

Dean, Carolyn

2010   *A Culture of Stone: Inka Perspectives
        on Rock.* Duke University Press,
        Durham, N.C.

Descola, Philippe

2013   *Beyond Nature and Culture.* University
        of Chicago Press, Chicago.

Harvey, Graham

2005   *Animism: Respecting the Living World.*
        Wakefield Press, Cambridge.

Janusek, John

2015   Of Monoliths and Men: Human-
        Lithic Encounters and the Production
        of an Animistic Ecology at Khonkho
        Wankane. In *The Archaeology of
        Wak'as: Explorations of the Sacred in
        the Pre-Columbian Andes,* edited by
        Tamara L. Bray. University Press of
        Colorado, Boulder.

Joyce, Rosemary A.

2008   *The Languages of Archaeology: Dialogue,
        Narrative, and Writing.* John Wiley and
        Sons, Malden, Mass.

Joyce, Rosemary A., and Susan D. Gillespie (editors)

2015   *Things in Motion: Object Itineraries
        in Anthropological Practice.* School of
        American Research Press, Santa Fe.

Kembel, Silvia R.

2008   The Architecture at the Monumental
        Center of Chavín de Huantar: Sequence,
        Transformations, and Chronology. In
        Chavín: Art, Architecture, and Culture,
        edited by William J. Conklin and Jeffrey

Quilter, pp. 35–84. Cotsen Institute of
Archaeology, University of California,
Los Angeles.

Lathrap, Donald W.

1973   Gifts of the Cayman: Some Thoughts
        on the Subsistence Basis of Chavin.
        In *Variation in Anthropology: Essays
        in Honor of John C. McGregor*, edited
        by Donald W. Lathrap and J. Douglas,
        pp. 91–105. Illinois Archaeological
        Survey, Urbana.

Moore, Jerry D.

1996   *Architecture and Power in the Ancient
        Andes: The Archaeology of Public
        Buildings.* Cambridge University Press,
        Cambridge.

2005   *Cultural Landscapes in the Ancient Andes:
        Archaeologies of Place.* University Press of
        Florida, Gainesville.

Rick, John

2004   The Evolution of Authority and Power at
        Chavín de Huántar, Peru. *Archaeological
        Papers of the American Anthropological
        Association* 14:71–89.

Roddick, Andrew

2015   Geologies in Motion: Itineraries of Stone,
        Clay, and Pots in the Lake Titicaca Basin.
        In *Things in Motion: Object Itineraries
        in Anthropological Practice*, edited
        by Rosemary A. Joyce and Susan D.
        Gillespie. School of American Research
        Press, Santa Fe.

Rowe, John

[1967] 1977   Form and Meaning in Chavín Art. In
              Peruvian Archaeology: Selected Readings,
              edited by John Rowe and Dorothy
              Menzel, pp. 72–103. Peek, Palo Alto, Calif.

Sayre, Matthew P.

2010   Life across the River: Agricultural,
        Ritual, and Production Practices at
        Chavin de Huantar, Peru. PhD disserta-
        tion, University of California, Berkeley.

Sillar, Bill

2009   The Social Agency of Things? Animism
        and Materiality in the Andes. *Cambridge
        Archaeological Journal* 19(3):367–377.

Spector, Janet

2016   What This Awl Means. In *Object Stories*,
        pp. 29–34. Routledge, New York.

Spivak, Gayatri Chakravorty

1988   Can the Subaltern Speak? In *Can the
        Subaltern Speak? Reflections on the
        History of an Idea*, edited by Rosalind C.
        Morris, pp. 21–78. Columbia University
        Press, New York.

Tello, Julio

1943   Discovery of the Chavín Culture in
        Peru. *American Antiquity* 9(1):135–160.

Turner, Terence S.

2017   *The Fire of the Jaguar.* University of
        Chicago Press, Chicago.

Urton, Gary

2008   The Body of Meaning in Chavín Art. In
        Chavín: Art, Architecture, and Culture,
        edited by William J. Conklin and Jeffrey
        Quilter, pp. 217–238. Cotsen Institute of
        Archaeology, University of California,
        Los Angeles.

Van Dyke, Ruth M., and Richard Bernbeck (editors)

2015   *Subjects and Narratives in Archaeology.*
        University Press of Colorado, Boulder.

Viveiros de Castro, Eduardo

1998   Cosmological Deixis and Amerindian
        Perspectivism. *Journal of the Royal
        Anthropological Institute* 4(3):469–488.

2012   Cosmological Perspectivism in
        Amazonia and Elsewhere. *HAU:
        Masterclass Series* 1:45–168.

Watts, Christopher

2013   Relational Archaeologies: Roots and
        Routes. In *Relational Archaeologies:
        Humans, Animals, Things*, edited by
        Christopher Watts, pp. 1–20. Routledge,
        London.

Weismantel, Mary

2011   Obstinate Things. In *The Archaeology
        of Colonialism, Gender, and Sexuality*,
        edited by Barbara Voss and Eleanor
        Casella, pp. 303–323. Cambridge
        University Press, Cambridge.

2013a   Coming to Our Senses at Chavín de
        Huantar. In *Making Senses of the Past:
        Toward a Sensory Archaeology*, edited
        by Jo Day, pp. 113–136. Publications
        of the Center for Archaeological
        Investigations, Southern Illinois
        University, Carbondale.

2013b   Inhuman Eyes: Looking at Chavín de Huantar. In *Relational Archaeologies: Humans, Animals, Things*, edited by Christopher Watts, pp. 21–41. Routledge, New York.

2014   Slippery and Slow: Chavín's Great Stones and Kinaesthetic Perception. In *Sensational Religion: Sense and Contention in Material Practice*, edited by Sarah Promey, pp. 605–624. Yale University Press, New Haven.

2015a   Encounters with Dragons: The Stones of Chavín. *RES: Anthropology and Aesthetics* 65–66:37–53.

2015b   Looking Like an Archaeologist: Viveiros de Castro at Chavín de Huantar. *Journal of Social Archaeology* 15(3):139–159.

Williams, Caroline
2010   Affective Processes without a Subject: Rethinking the Relation between Subjectivity and Affect with Spinoza. *Subjectivity* 3(3):245–262.

Zuidema, R. Tom
1992   An Andean Model for the Study of Chavín Iconography. *Journal of the Steward Anthropological Society* 20(1–2):37–54.

Cosmopolitical Bodies

Living Monoliths, Vital Tectonics, and the Production of Tiwanaku

JOHN WAYNE JANUSEK

ONE CAN NARRATE THE HISTORY OF RELIgious institutions as so many projects of monumental assembly, transformation, and destruction. The ongoing construction of temples for any major Western religion—Holy Roman Catholicism, Byzantine Orthodoxy, Medieval Islam—comprised a peculiar cartography. Each constituted a hierarchical regime focused on a central temple—respectively, Saint Peter's Basilica, the Hagia Sophia, and the Great Mosque of Córdoba—supported by a vast geography of satellite temples, productive landscapes, and subject communities. Each regime valorized particular practices as the appropriate gestures and actions of devout subjects. Yet these expansive institutions were at any given moment comprised of multiple, vital communities. They were ambitious, globalizing projects that demanded "universal" engagements with the world by subverting local practices and places in order to create a coherent cosmopolitical order grounded in a particular set of practices and ontological dispositions.

Tiwanaku was a comparable geopolitical project. It emerged after 500 CE as an urban ceremonial center in the southern Lake Titicaca basin of the South American Andes. By 700 CE, Tiwanaku was a bustling city centered on sprawling monumental campuses that drew pilgrims, diplomats, and others from across the Andes for recurring ritual events (Janusek 2004, 2008, 2015b; Kolata 1993, 2003; Posnansky 1945; Vranich 2006, 2009). While Tiwanaku can be interpreted as a "religious" phenomenon, I focus attention on its emergent *fame*—its expansive spatiotemporal prestige and power (sensu Munn 1986)—and its ongoing production as an influential *ecoregime*. By this, I mean a field of articulations that assembled mountains, celestial movements, water flows, humans, and nonhuman lithic persons as a coherent, if shifting, master geopolitical cartography. I adapt Arturo Escobar's (1999) notion of "nature regime" as a particular engagement with and *appropriation of* the nonhuman to a Pre-Columbian situation in which "nature" as a master category for all things

233

nonhuman had no purchase on human engagements with the biophysical world they inhabited (Descola 2013; Sahlins 2008).

Tiwanaku incorporated monumental campuses intent on directing human attention to specific features, materials, and flows in the center's surrounding landscape. Its temples incorporated powerful classes of stone, including sandstone quarried from sacred peaks in the local Corocoṛo range and volcanic andesite and basalt from more distant peaks across the lake (Janusek and Williams 2016). Temples afforded visual relations with such peaks, often meshing them with alignments that featured recurring celestial movements on the horizon (Benitez 2009, 2013). Such alignments coordinated the diverse productive and ritual rhythms of the communities that Tiwanaku sought to incorporate to create a coherent, hegemonic calendar. Furthermore, Tiwanaku incorporated an elaborate water network centered on a ring of channels that surrounded the monumental core (Janusek and Bowen 2018). Several temples afforded vistas to key places in the network, including springs at the foot of Mount Kimsachata, due south of the center. Tiwanaku constituted a vast, shifting assembly of elements and materials that facilitated dramatic ritualized engagements with its biophysical surroundings.

The anthropomorphic sculptures, or monoliths, that occupied key locations in this assembled landscape formed the crux of this project (Janusek and Guengerich 2015). I argue that carved anthropomorphic sculptures secured Tiwanaku's coalescence as a centralizing regime in a Late Formative (100 BCE–500 CE) geopolitical field of competing ritual-political centers and their interdigitated political communities (Janusek 2015a, 2015b; Stanish 2003). Monoliths are arguably Tiwanaku's most celebrated archaeological objects. Since the early nineteenth century, explorers and scientists have marveled at their size and intricate carved iconography. This is somewhat ironic. First, monoliths have never figured centrally in interpretations of Tiwanaku's geopolitical consolidation. Most studies of monoliths focus on their carved iconography (Berenguer 1998; Makowski 2002) rather than

squarely addressing their contextual importance or lithic materiality. An enduring emphasis on iconography has effectively reduced monoliths to inert, if visually evocative, "art objects" (see Dean 2006). Second, many monoliths were found above ground, and hewing to an archaeological orthodoxy fixed on stratigraphy, most archaeologists have summarily ignored them.

I explore the idea that monoliths were powerful animate personages who punctuated Tiwanaku's urban landscape and propelled its fame and geopolitical expansion. Political vitality resided in their material origins and the monumental temples they inhabited, as well as in their recurring engagements with humans and other monolithic beings. Monoliths were quarried near dramatic peaks and placed in strategic locations. Some stood in satellite centers of Tiwanaku's immediate hinterland. The material composition and spatial context of any monolith were critical for its ritual and geopolitical import. Furthermore, by 700 CE, many monoliths collectively comprised a regimen of three ranked classes. Together, they formed dynamic, interrelated assemblages (sensu Bennett 2009; DeLanda 2006) in relation to the specific temples they populated and the particular biophysical features and flows they indexed. I argue that Tiwanaku geopolitical consolidation coincided with the expanding fame of its animate monolithic beings.

Monumental Spaces and Monolithic Inhabitants

Tiwanaku was a vibrant city and a center for cyclical, periodic ritual gathering in 500–800 CE (Figure 8.1). Located near the southern edge of Lake Titicaca in the south-central Andes, its population pulsated dramatically according to the rhythm of recurring ceremonial events. In this regard, it breaks the mold for understanding urbanism according to traditional models beholden to the conceptual imperative of "permanent occupation." Cyclical mobility and calendrical festivals were central to Tiwanaku's prestige. Unlike Pre-Columbian cities such as Cuzco and Huari, Tiwanaku was a

figure 8.1
Tiwanaku and related sites and locations in the southern Lake Titicaca basin. Image by John Janusek.

centripetal center, designed to bring people in. It was built to draw pilgrims and others into its two core monumental campuses: one to the northeast, focused on the Akapana and Kalasasaya platforms, another to the southwest, focused on Pumapunku (Figure 8.2). The two campuses formed a dual urban axis (Kolata and Ponce Sanginés 2003). Each major structure was a temple incorporating a large axial staircase that presented an ideal that all could scale the terraced platforms during ritual events and enter the raised, intimate sunken courts they enclosed. However exclusive these sunken courts were in practice, or became over time (Janusek 2004), they housed several of Tiwanaku's most imposing, and likely most important, monolithic personages.

Movement into Tiwanaku and through its monumental campuses was profoundly ritualized. Some people traveled long distances—coming from the eastern and western Andean valleys

and the northern Lake Titicaca basin—to participate in recurring ceremonies (Blom 2005; Janusek and Blom 2006). Travel toward Tiwanaku likely was enacted as pilgrimage. Numerous small Tiwanaku monumental complexes in the altiplano maintained no permanent habitation and yet mark key routes of travel across ecological zones (e.g., Kachwirkala [Portugal 1998:82–87] and Simillake [Browman 1981:416]). This is reminiscent of contemporary pilgrimage to Bolivia's Virgin of Copacabana, during which families traveling to the shrine, located on the south shore of Lake Titicaca, stop at a sequence of small ritual locales situated in mountain passes and other locations to pour libations and pray. Movement in Tiwanaku itself, toward and through its monumental campuses, funneled pilgrims through elaborate staircases and carved lithic portals that punctuated gradations of increasingly intimate spaces. Visitors ascended

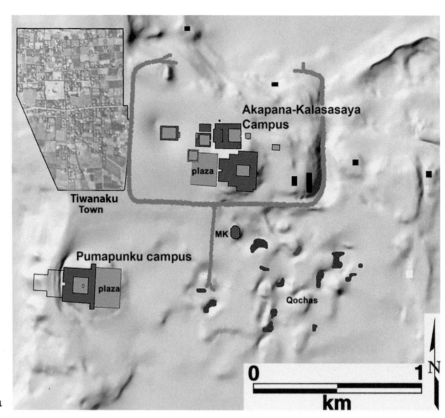

figure 8.2
Tiwanaku's two monumental campuses: a) the northeast (Akapana-Kalasasaya) campus surrounded by a perimeter canal; and b) the found locations of several monoliths in the northeast campus (view facing south). Image by John Janusek.

figure 8.3
The view east from atop Pumapunku highlighting the view of Mount Illimani (a); and the view west from the balcony platform of Kalasasaya highlighting the view of Mount Ccapia (b). Photographs by John Janusek.

eastward into the Pumapunku and Akapana platforms and westward through the Kalasasaya toward the Putuni platform (Vranich 2009). Ascending Pumapunku and Akapana facilitated dramatic visual encounters with the peak of Mount Illimani, to the east, while movement through Kalasasaya facilitated a dramatic view of Mount Ccapia, to the west, Tiwanaku's primary source of volcanic stone (Janusek and Williams 2016) (Figure 8.3).

Sunken courts and other enclosed spaces within or near these terraced platforms housed one or more monoliths. They included the early Sunken Temple

a   b   c

figure 8.4
Three of Tiwanaku's five known presentation monoliths, shown to relative scale: a) Fraile; b) Bennett; and c) Ponce.
Fraile consists of sandstone and stands 2.8 m high (including its buried plinth); Bennett consists of sandstone and
stands 7.3 m high; and Ponce consists of andesite and stands 3.2 m high. Photographs by John Janusek (a and c);
photograph courtesy of Clare Sammells (b).

and the central sunken courts of the Akapana, Pumapunku, Kalasasaya, and Putuni platforms. In several cases, monoliths were found in situ or at least near where they presumably stood in Pre-Columbian times. Archaeologists found the enormous Bennett Monolith next to the Bearded Monolith and two smaller monoliths in the Sunken Temple (Bennett 1934:428–444); a farmer located the Fraile Monolith on Kalasasaya's west platform (Schaedel 1952:250); and Carlos Ponce's team located the eponymous Ponce Monolith under its sunken court (Ponce Sanginés 1995:230). The Pumapunku Monolith, found on the eponymous campus's west platform (Posnansky 1945, 2:183), originally stood there or in its central sunken court. Several *chachapumas*, or stone human-feline composite beings, were found near monumental entrances (Kolata 1993; Posnansky 1945:vol. 2). Yet many stone sculptures have been found in places that are likely ex situ. Despite orthodox archaeological strictures regarding stratigraphy, we can nevertheless study patterned relations among classes and scales of monoliths in Tiwanaku's core region to approach some understanding of their past contexts and geopolitical gravity.

Movement into and through Tiwanaku brought pilgrims and others in contact with its imposing monolithic personages. At the telluric heart of Tiwanaku's project were presentation monoliths, their arms positioned symmetrically over their front torsos. Presentation monoliths were Tiwanaku's primary lithic beings and possibly the primary focus of human–lithic transactions. These monoliths are known only from Tiwanaku itself. Directly associated with some presentation monoliths, and situated in local monumental complexes or satellite sites, extended-arm monoliths were guardians or attendants for presentation monoliths. *Chachapumas* manifested part human, part nonhuman guardians of megalithic portals and monumental entrances. The latter most directly surveilled the ongoing production of appropriately gestured, clothed, and ritualized subjects as they entered Tiwanaku's temples. Relations among these lithic beings, fortified by their respective emplacements, sought to produce generations of gesturally correct, fully ritualized "Tiwanaku" human subjects.

Tiwanaku's Monolithic Assemblages

This section introduces Tiwanaku's cast of monolithic characters, organized according to their principal classes and scales: presentation, extended-arm, and *chachapuma* beings.

Presentation Monoliths

Presentation monoliths comprise Tiwanaku's most celebrated class of monolithic being. They also were Tiwanaku's most imposing lithic personages. Five are known, four of sandstone and one of andesite, and they vary dramatically in height, style, and execution. Each is a standing personage wearing elaborate clothing and showing clearly defined arms and legs (Figure 8.4). Each clutches to its chest a stylized drinking chalice, or *kero*, in its left hand and another object in its right. On three presentation monoliths, the personage clearly holds in its right hand a tablet for ingesting snuff (Torres 2002). On two others, the images are highly eroded but their remnant iconography is similar; we can surmise that all held snuff tablets. Thus, presentation monoliths clutched two paired, complementary objects to their chests: *keros* and snuff tablets. Their frontal gestures identify them as "presentation" figures (Bandy 2013), lithic beings who offer those objects or their contents to their human interlocutors.

Keros facilitated consumption of fermented chicha, native corn- or quinoa-fermented beer, while snuff tablets facilitated consumption of the dried resins of hallucinogenic plants and herbs (Figure 8.5). *Keros* are ubiquitous at Tiwanaku sites, and wooden snuff tablets are common in tombs on the dry coast. Presentation monoliths clutched artifacts iconic of Tiwanaku and indexical of the "transformed" substances (fermented chicha, processed psychotropic snuff) that facilitated transformations in consciousness that were perhaps deemed requisite for apprehending Tiwanaku's monolithic personages. Considering hallucinogens alone, Tiwanaku iconography frequently presents *Anadenanthera* pods (Knobloch 2000), which grow on trees in the nearby upper eastern Andean valleys. The substances and their iconic vehicles may have facilitated an appropriate ritual attitude for

a

b

figure 8.5
a) A snuff tablet (Wassén 1972); and b) a *kero* depicting Tiwanaku iconography. Photograph by John Janusek (b).

entering Tiwanaku's innermost sancta and transacting with these ancient personages.

Presentation monoliths stood in Tiwanaku's principal monumental courts and enclosures. The two stylistically earliest, Fraile and Pumapunku, were found in association with two of Tiwanaku's earliest platforms: Kalasasaya and Pumapunku, respectively. Both are relatively small (<3 m tall),[1] consist of Corocoro sandstone, and present minimal bodily decor, collectively indicating their

early production. Found on Kalasasaya's west platform, Fraile may have originally inhabited its sunken court but was removed once that court was reconstructed and the later andesite Ponce Monolith erected therein. Early explorers found the Pumapunku Monolith lying on Pumapunku's west esplanade (Posnansky 1945:2:183). It likely either stood in Pumapunku's sunken court or on this platform, greeting pilgrims and diplomats as they scaled its west stairway.

Bennett and Ponce are Tiwanaku's most studied presentation monoliths (see Figure 8.4). Bennett stood in Tiwanaku's early Sunken Temple and Ponce in Kalasasaya's refurbished sunken court. They may have stood such that they could "view" one another through a "window" formed by Kalasasaya's primary east entrance (Kolata 2003:198). Standing an imposing 7.3 m tall, Bennett is the largest known Tiwanaku monolith and, like Fraile and Pumapunku, consists of Corocoro sandstone. Bennett stood in a Late Formative temple that had been refabricated after 500 CE to adapt to changing ritual practices and monumental technologies. The temple's reconstruction maintained its Late Formative style, perhaps as a material testament of a reformulated Tiwanaku past (Janusek 2008:130). Furthermore, Bennett stood alongside the decidedly earlier Late Formative–period Bearded Monolith (Figure 8.6). It is significant that the Sunken Temple faced due south, toward Kimsachata, a prominent local peak in the Corocoro range that provided both sandstone for Bennett and the aquifer that fed Tiwanaku (Janusek and Bowen 2018). Its orientation also created a visual path with the south celestial pole that rotates directly over Kimsachata's peak (Benitez 2009; Vranich 2009).

The Ponce Monolith stood in Kalasasaya's sunken court and consisted of Ccapia andesite (Janusek et al. 2013). While Bennett's temple home faced Kimsachata, Ponce's faced west toward Ccapia, its own place of origin. The setting sun in 800 CE passed over the northernmost pilaster of the west balcony wall, also quarried from Ccapia, and shed a ray of light through Kalasasaya to illuminate the Ponce Monolith. Ponce stands just over 3 m high and presents intricate scenes carved in low relief (Figure 8.7). Incising hard volcanic stone demanded new technical specialties (Protzen and Nair 2013) and, thus, new specialized communities of practice (Janusek and Williams 2016; sensu Lave and Wenger 1991; Roddick 2016).

The torsos of Bennett and Ponce feature ritual processions that originate from a central scene on their backs. On Bennett, the scene is a solar figure raising two objects in its outstretched hands; on Ponce, it is a ritual act consisting of two specialists

figure 8.6
The Sunken Temple's Bearded Monolith, Late Formative in style and carved of deep red sandstone. Photograph by John Janusek.

facing a kind of "offering table" over which stands a similar solar figure. Variably masked and bedecked profile figures move out in procession from these central back scenes toward the frontal gesture of the monolithic being who holds a *kero* and a snuff tablet (Janusek 2008:138). Incised monolithic processions

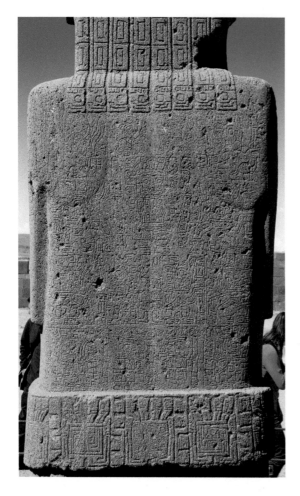

figure 8.7
The intricately carved backside of the andesite
Ponce Monolith, highlighting subtle bodily details
(scapulae, vertebral column). Photograph by
John Janusek.

likely index the recurring ritual processions that
led priests, pilgrims, diplomats, and others toward
these monolithic personages in their temples.

Presentation monoliths were the primary
monolithic personages humans confronted once
they entered Tiwanaku and journeyed into one of
its major platform temples. They were the primary
animate, ancestral lithic beings who welcomed
interlocutors to Tiwanaku's festivities. Yet if presentation monoliths inspired reciprocal engagement, it
was not precisely equal (Figure 8.8). Each monolith
clutches a *kero* with its left arm and left hand and
a snuff tablet with its right arm in an impossibly
depicted left hand. As Cummins (2002:64) puts it,

"What makes this gesture impossible anatomically
is that the fingers and thumbs all face in the wrong
direction." The iconographic acrobatics required to
depict this unnatural gesture demand explanation.
It was clearly important that presentation monoliths present the two objects and their contents with
two left hands, but why? Institutionalized Inka
practices of offering chicha may help us understand
this gesture. The chronicler Inca Garcilaso de la
Vega ([1609] 1943, bk. 6, chap. 21:48–49) noted that
the Inka ruler offered a vessel of chicha to someone
of inferior status with his left hand and to someone of equal or superior status with his right. For
example, during the Inti Raymi festival, held at the
austral winter solstice, the Inka ruler (Sapa Inka)
stood in Cuzco's main plaza facing the rising sun,
holding two gold vessels (Cummins 2002:108–109).
He raised the vessel in his right hand as an offering to the sun, Inti, the primary Inka deity and the
ruler's "father." He then poured the contents into a
basin that fed into Coricancha, the temple dedicated
to Inti. Next, the Inka drank from the *kero* in his left
hand and offered the rest to his constituent subjects
in the plaza.

Presentation monoliths may have precipitated
similar reciprocal obligations. As Marcel Mauss
(1967) noted decades ago, gifting is the essence of
political practice. Tiwanaku monoliths invited
transactions with humans, but those transactions
transpired according to very specific terms. If Inka
analogy is pertinent to understanding Tiwanaku
monoliths, their hands had no other choice but to
be the left hands that offer iconic vessels and their
fermented, intoxicating liquids to supplicants
and devotees. Coming to Tiwanaku, entering its
monumental campuses, addressing its principal
monoliths, and engaging monolithic gestures of
weighted hospitality were critical for becoming a
dedicated Tiwanaku subject. It is also worth turning the Inka analogy on its head. As Cummins
(2002:64–65) notes, early Inka sculptors, who
studied Tiwanaku's monuments and whose leaders
were interested in creating their own hegemony,
may have adopted their own gestural aesthetics
from Tiwanaku monolithic sculptures. Might the
body politics of Inka chicha offerings derive from

figure 8.8
The front-center gesture of the Ponce personage, emphasizing the presentation of a *kero* and snuff tablet with "two left hands." Photograph by John Janusek.

their astute observations of Tiwanaku's monolithic personages?

Extended-Arm Attendants

Extended-arm monoliths complemented presentation personages, yet they have drawn very little attention. Extended-arm monoliths constitute beings with arms and hands stretched down tightly along the sides of their bodies. They differ from presentation monoliths in two other key respects. First, they differ in their spatial contexts. While presentation monoliths are known only from Tiwanaku, extended-arm monoliths have been found at Tiwanaku and at least four nearby centers. Second, they differ in relative scale. Presentation monoliths range from 2.8 to 7.3 m in height. Extended-arm monoliths appear in three different size ranges. Large (>2 m tall) monoliths in this class appear to

have accompanied taller presentation monoliths, while medium-size monoliths (0.8–1.7 m) occupied local courtyards and strategic regional centers such as Lukurmata and Lakaya. Smaller statuettes (0.25–0.60 m) are known from a local residential courtyard (e.g., Akapana West) (Mattox 2013:60–61) and two local Tiwanaku centers (Portugal 1998:248–249, 259–261).

Extended-arm monoliths embodied male guardians or attendants. Many large and medium-size extended-arm monoliths emphasize muscular physiques. The andesite Suñawa Monolith is a prime case (Figure 8.9). Found near Tiahuanaco's town plaza (Schaedel 1948), it stands 3.1 m tall and shows a male with broad shoulders, prominent pectorals, and large hands. A pair of solar faces with radiating headdresses covers the breasts. The personage takes a disciplined stance with muscled

figure 8.9
The andesite Suñawa
Monolith, which
stands approximately
3.1 m high. Photograph
by John Janusek.

arms and oversized hands. An incised weapon decorates each of his front shoulders: an axe on the left, a spear-thrower on the right (Figure 8.10). Decorating his scapulae are striking Tiwanaku images of sacrifice. Suñawa's scapulae present the only profile human decapitators known to Tiwanaku stone sculpture. Yet Suñawa's back torso presents a flowering segmented plant, a clear image of emergent life. Meanwhile, forward-flying profile figures decorate Suñawa's upper shoulders. Scapular decapitators, shoulder flyers, and frontal weapons may comprise a narrative of sacrifice and generation that complements the back-to-front ritual processions of presentation monoliths.

The andesite Pachakama Monolith complements Suñawa (Figure 8.11). At 3.1 m, it stands the same height. Like Suñawa, Pachakama celebrates a solar being, in this case depicted as a single face with a radiating headdress on its front torso. Though the two monoliths were found in different places of Tiwanaku, it is possible they constituted a pair. They manifest key differences that were likely construed as complementary. While Suñawa wears a squared, feathered cap, Pachakama wears a bulbous turban. This is significant because most inhabitants of Tiwanaku demonstrated one of two broad styles of cranial modification (Blom 2005; Janusek and Blom 2006). Some affiliated

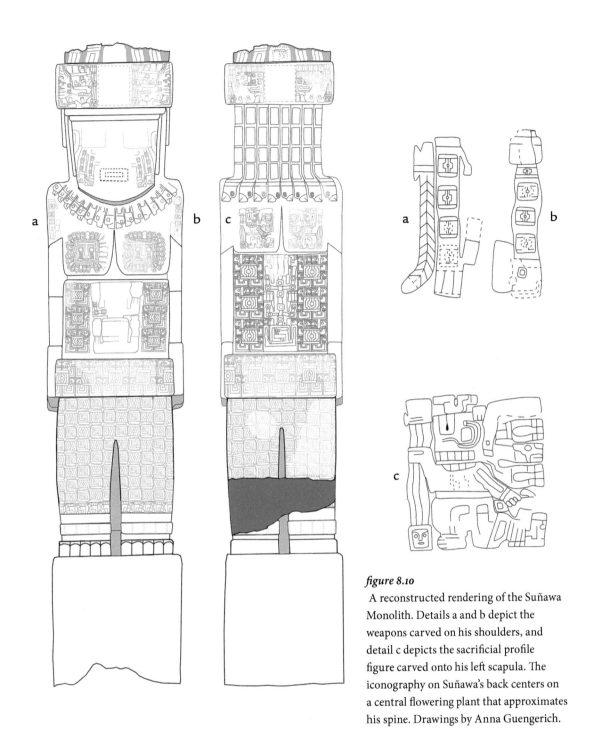

figure 8.10

A reconstructed rendering of the Suñawa Monolith. Details a and b depict the weapons carved on his shoulders, and detail c depicts the sacrificial profile figure carved onto his left scapula. The iconography on Suñawa's back centers on a central flowering plant that approximates his spine. Drawings by Anna Guengerich.

communities practiced techniques of flattened cranial modification, conducted by tying a contraption of boards to a child's soft head, while others practiced techniques that produced annular modification, conducted by tying a contraption of ropes or woven turban-like garments around a child's head (Blom 2005). Woven-hat styles—some squared or "four cornered," others long, bulbous, and conical—emphasized differences in head shapes.

The Kochamama triad lends support to this monolithic pairing (Figure 8.12). It comprises a trio of large sandstone sculptures first documented by Max Uhle (1895). It consists of two paired extended-arm monoliths, both 2.5 m tall, standing on either

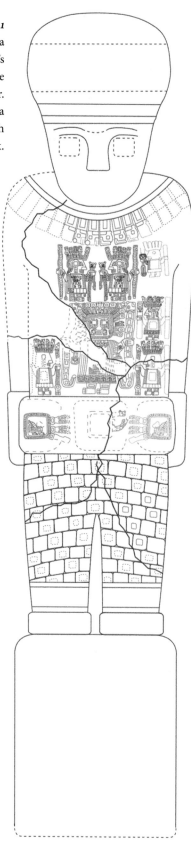

figure 8.11
The andesite Pachakama
Monolith, Suñawa's
likely complement. Note
the distinctive headgear.
Drawing by Anna
Guengerich, photograph
by John Janusek.

a

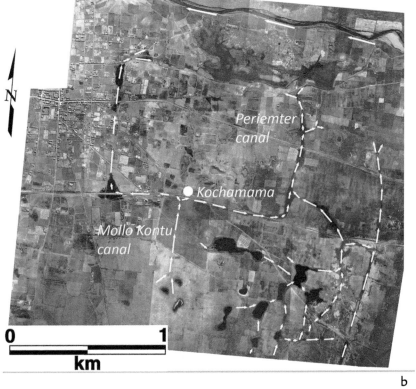

b

figure 8.12
The Kochamama triad, centered on the Kochamama Monolith: a) anonymous photo, taken at the turn of the twentieth century; and b) the found location of the triad near the intersection of Tiwanaku's Mollo Kontu and Perimeter Canals. Image by John Janusek.

side of a much taller, gaunt presentation monolith known as Kochamama (4.35 m; Posnansky 1945:2:185–204). Like the aforementioned andesite monoliths, they are paired but not identical; they differ in form and iconographic details. This trio, by all accounts found in situ, indicates that at least some extended-arm monoliths accompanied a single larger presentation monolith as paired attendants. It suggests that Suñawa and Pachakama, which also stood the same height, may have accompanied a single presentation monolith. The material composition of the andesite attendants indicates a likely central personage. Monoliths of the Kochamama triad all consist of red sandstone quarried from the Corocoro range south of Tiwanaku. Suñawa and Pachakama both consist of gray Ccapia andesite, and the only Ccapia andesite presentation monolith is the Ponce. I suggest that the two monoliths formed a pair of attendants for the Ponce, whether or not they both originally stood in Kalasasaya.

Extended-arm monoliths formed a class of attendants. In one case, paired sandstone monoliths flanked a sandstone presentation monolith, and in another, two andesite monoliths may have been associated with the Ponce Monolith. While presentation monoliths present androgynous features covered with elaborate garments, large extended-arm monoliths emphasize male physiques; at least one depicts sacrificial figures and weaponry. As a class they embody attendants or guardians, and perhaps for certain situations monolithic warriors.

Chachapumas

Chachapumas comprised a third class of Tiwanaku stone sculpture (Figure 8.13) that Posnansky (1945:2:204) considered "humanized animals." They differ markedly from presentation and extended-arm monoliths. Each embodies the corporeal, transformative consubstantiation of human (*chacha*, "man" in Aymara) and nonhuman animal form. Arthur Posnansky and others since consider their consubstantial counterparts to be feline (*puma*, "predatory feline" in Aymara) beings. Yet ear positions suggest that some were human-camelids. *Chachapumas* were not directly associated with other monoliths. In situ finds indicate

a   b

figure 8.13
The front and right axe-bearing sides of paired *chachapumas*, 1 (a) and 2 (b), found in Pumapunku and standing 95 and 94 cm high, respectively. Image by John Janusek.

that *chachapumas* were associated with the stone portals and staircases that drew people into monumental ritual enclosures (Posnansky 1945:2:206). Among large *chachapumas* (0.6–1.0 m high), most consist of nearly identical pairs, and in some documented cases, a pair of *chachapumas* framed an entrance into one of Tiwanaku's key temples, such as Pumapunku.

Large *chachapumas* depict snarling human-nonhuman beings in a kneeling or crouched position. All consist of volcanic stone, some of them durable, dark basalt. Posnansky (1945:2:205) noted that they "express ferocity." They embodied aggression, human sacrifice, and interpersonal violence. Stylistically early sculptures hold an axe in the right hand and a decapitated human head in the left. Later sculptures, which included the Akapana and at least one unfinished *chachapuma*, hold a decapitated head in both hands in front of their torsos (Figure 8.14). The violence embodied in these transformational beings contrasts with the far more subtle, latent, protective violence of extended-arm monoliths and specifically Suñawa. For that reason, some archaeologists have concluded that they indicate Tiwanaku's inherently violent, militarily expansive character (Ponce Sanginés 1981). I disagree with this conclusion. Archaeologists have found remarkably little bioarchaeological or artifactual evidence for military violence (e.g., raids, battles) at Tiwanaku sites (Janusek 2008). Most evidence for human violence consists of a dozen or so human remains that show sacrificial traumas on or near the foot of the Akapana temple (Blom and Janusek 2004; Manzanilla and Woodard 1990; Verano 2013). While *chachapumas* may have indexed violence, and specifically the human sacrifices that took place around Akapana, their associations with temple entrances suggest a more profound and intimate role in Tiwanaku. Those entrances constituted portals between relatively mundane spaces and the inner sanctums that housed Tiwanaku's most powerful monoliths and facilitated charged human–monolithic engagements. *Chachapumas* guarded those portals.

Chachapumas were intimately involved in the production of appropriate human subjects. I argue

this based on their found contexts within Tiwanaku and in relation to other sculptural classes, drawing on Bloch's (1992) study of violent acts and imagery during rites of passage globally. He concludes that rites of passage most fundamentally transform "raw" humans (in some cases, children) into newly constituted and more fully empowered members of a community—a Maussian social persona, a Foucauldian political subject. They involve the sacrifice of "homegrown native vitality" to a new vitality gained relationally with other beings, whether, according to Bloch, jaguars, eagles, bears, or deer. This frequently requires the violent conquest of a raw person as depicted in violent imagery (e.g., axes, decapitation). A person's newly acquired vitality reflects the transcendental vitality of an entire community, but it comes with a price. Newly "animated" humans are empowered via their conscription to the communal institutions that transcend and encompass them interpersonally and that will, henceforth, dramatically condition their bodily practices and lives as fully vitalized subjects.

Chachapumas effected similar transformations in an encompassing network of animate monolithic personages. Standing in pairs before monumental entrances and portals, they guarded passage into Tiwanaku's most ritually potent and intimate inner sancta. Passing through these portals constituted transformative rites of passage. In the inner sancta their entry afforded, humans approached Tiwanaku's presentation personages, some flanked by extended-arm attendants, seeking to consummate the act of becoming a legitimate, empowered, fully vitalized ritual person. This new status was produced relationally via engagements with *chachapumas*, presentation monoliths, and their extended-arm attendants. *Chachapumas* were transformative beings that not-so-subtly welcomed various grades of "raw" humans to their new roles as Tiwanaku ritual-political subjects. Once constituted as legitimate persons who successfully performed Tiwanaku ritual attitudes—as manifested in a presentation monolith's central gesture of engagement, for example—they now embodied the monolithic transcendental as newly vitalized, and yet firmly beholden, geopolitical subjects.

figure 8.14
The basalt Akapana *chachapuma* was found lying near the base of the west entrance of the eponymous structure during excavations (Kolata 1993:126–129) in the late 1980s. Photograph by John Janusek.

Scaled Monolithic Embodiments

Each of Tiwanaku's three monolithic classes appears in specific places and in various size ranges. Presentation monoliths were restricted to Tiwanaku's monumental campuses and were relatively large. Small presentation monoliths were stylistically earliest and likely were later eclipsed or even decommissioned with the inauguration of the massive Kochamama, Bennett, and Ponce Monoliths. Extended-arm monoliths and *chachapumas* appear in three scaled size ranges that correlate with specific contexts of

engagement. In relation to the exclusive centrality of presentation monoliths, the sizes and contexts of these two classes map an intriguing cartography of scalar geopolitics in Tiwanaku's ritual-political heartland.

Extended-arm monoliths appear in three size ranges, the aforementioned Suñawa, Pachakama, and Kochamama pair constituting their known large embodiments. They also appear in a medium size range, either as slim, elegant figures in dark basalt or shorter, squatter personages in andesite. All emphasize the male physique and appear to embody guardian attendants. Two squat andesite sculptures from Tiwanaku may have formed a pair (Figure 8.15). The Angrand, first described in 1844, was located ex situ (Prümers 1993). The Putuni was found near the center of the courtyard of the Putuni complex (Ponce Sanginés 1995:236), located on the west side of Kalasasaya, and attached to an elite residential complex known as the "multicolored palace" (Couture and Sampeck 2003). The courtyard likely was a proprietary ceremonial space for one of Tiwanaku's most prominent high-status lineages, and the Putuni Monolith its primary patron monolithic personage. Intriguingly, Angrand and Putuni are similar in style and dimensions, and both were decapitated in an act of ritual destruction.

Medium-sized extended-arm monoliths are the largest monoliths found outside of Tiwanaku itself (Figure 8.16). They are known only from two particularly strategic sites north of Tiwanaku.[2] Lukurmata served as a key port on Lake Titicaca and both Lukurmata and Lakaya served as centers for organizing agricultural production in the extensive adjacent floodplain of the Katari River (Janusek and Kolata 2003; Kolata 1991). Located at the north edge of a montane valley that links it to Tiwanaku across the Taraco range, Lakaya was a center for the ongoing movement of farmers and produce. Lukurmata incorporated two medium-sized extended-arm monoliths similar in height and squat proportions to those at Tiwanaku, and they may have constituted an asymmetrical pair. Uhle (1895) located the fragments of two similarly asymmetrical monoliths at nearby Lakaya. They

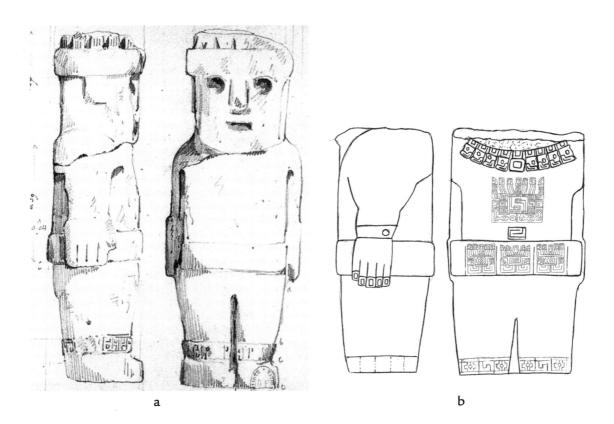

figure 8.15

a) The Angrand Monolith; and b) the decapitated and "deplinthed" Putuni Monolith. The Angrand was first noted by the French diplomat Léonce Angrand in 1848 (Prümers 1993:figs. 71–73), and the Putuni was excavated by Carlos Ponce Sanginés (1981:fig. 99, 1995:236, fig. 157) under the center of the Putuni courtyard in the mid-1970s (Portugal 1998:196–197). Angrand stands 1.3 m high and the remnant Putuni 0.82 m high.

consist of the head and torso of one and the decapitated head of a larger personage.

Extended-arm beings also appear as small statuettes. Only three have been found in situ and all consist of andesite. One was found at Sullkatata near the port of Guaqui, several kilometers southwest of Tiwanaku (Portugal 1957, 1998:259–261), and the head of another was found on the Island of Koati on Lake Titicaca (Portugal 1998:248–249). Archaeologists found the third at the edge of a small pool just west of a stone-paved courtyard southwest of Akapana (Figure 8.17) (Mattox 2013:60–61). The base of the pool consisted of micro-laminated soils deposited via recurring water action and was fixed with a plugged drain. The statuette may have stood in the pool. Below deposits of thin lamina was a small feature of hard clay that, Mattox suggests,

cemented the statuette in place. In any case, it is clear that miniature extended-arm personages inhabited local Tiwanaku courtyards and surrounding sites.

Chachapumas formed a parallel gradient of scaled personages, and all known instances consist of volcanic stone. The largest guarded Tiwanaku's monumental campuses. *Chachapumas* appear in three other size ranges; medium-sized sculptures (60–80 cm), statuettes (25–50 cm), and figurines (<10 cm). A few medium-sized *chachapumas* are housed in European museum collections. A *chachapuma* at the musée du quai Branly, Paris, may have once formed a portal pair with another recently restored and originally acquired by the twentieth-century collector Frederico Diez de Medina (Querejazu Lewis 1983). One with an unusual harness is housed at the Náprstek

a   b

figure 8.16

The two squat extended-arm monoliths from Lukurmata standing (a) 1.25 m and (b) 1.5 m high (Bennett 1936:493–494). Photographs by Max Uhle, 1895, courtesy of the Penn Museum at the University of Pennsylvania.

Museum, Prague (Figure 8.18) (Nestler 1913:fig. 2).[3] Uhle collected a fourth at the lower end of the medium-size gradient from Copacabana, Bolivia, for the Ethnologisches Museum of Berlin (Eisleb and Strelow 1980:87). Several other fragments are known from Tiwanaku, including a *chachapuma* head found in the Putuni courtyard in 2009 (Luis Viviani, personal communication, 2010).

Chachapuma statuettes also were paired and may have guarded entrances to local temples and houses. Like medium-sized and statuette extended-arm personages, statuette *chachapumas* are known from Tiwanaku peripheral areas and key local centers. The Soria family unearthed a pair of unfinished *chachapuma* statuettes near the plaza of the town of Tiahuanaco, some 500 m

northwest of Tiwanaku's northeast monumental campus (Figure 8.19). Others were found at the center of Iruhito on the Desaguadero River, a key route for boat and llama caravan travel. Excavations of a small Tiwanaku platform at the site recovered two pairs of *chachapuma* statuettes (Pérez Arias 2014:29–31).

It is likely significant that, of all monolithic genera, only *chachapumas* were carved as figurines (<5 cm tall). Some were perforated to be worn as bodily adornments, perhaps not unlike the way a devout Christian wears a diminutive cross on her neck (Figure 8.20). It is intriguing that the most visually violent and profoundly transformative of Tiwanaku's monolithic genera were worn as personal icons. These were the beings that

figure 8.17
The extended-arm Mattox
Monolith, found near a
pool southwest of Akapana
and standing 30 cm high.
Photograph courtesy of
Wesley Mattox.

figure 8.18
The *chachapuma*
personage currently
housed at the
Náprstek Museum,
Prague, standing
45 cm high.
Photograph courtesy
of the Náprstek
Museum, Prague.

figure 8.19
The Soria *chachapumas* of Tiwanaku, each standing 31 cm high. Photograph by John Janusek.

figure 8.20
A *chachapuma* figurine standing 3.72 cm high. Photograph by John Janusek, courtesy of the Museo de Metales Preciosos, La Paz.

converted nonsocialized persons into newly vitalized, empowered Tiwanaku subjects. Kept close to the body, miniature incarnations of Tiwanaku's transformers were powerful avatars for an appropriately gestured and bedecked Tiwanaku ritual-political subject.

Crafting Subjects, Gathering Fame

Temples and Their Living Lithic Inhabitants

Monumental campuses routinely corner discussion of Tiwanaku's ritual-political centrality. The carved monoliths associated with these ensembles have been sidelined in interpretations of Tiwanaku's ritual practices and political expansion. I argue they were living lithic beings at the fulcrum of Tiwanaku geopolitics. I suggest we invert the traditional perspective of Tiwanaku: monoliths did not just stand within particular monumental enclosures; those enclosures were built to provide an appropriate home for specific ancestral monolithic personages. Monoliths were the focus of Tiwanaku's expanding fame and geopolitical gravity. This accords with Estete's (1918) description of the wooden Pachacamac idol that the Spanish encountered and burned in 1535. He precociously perceived that the idol was not a representation within a Catholic church. Rather, the wooden idol *was* Pachacamac, however "filthy" and "poorly carved" (Kosiba, this volume), and its temple *was* its home. Likewise, and as Mary Weismantel persuasively argues for the Lanzón personage at Chavín de Huantar (2013, this volume), Tiwanaku celebrated monolithic personages as *the* focal beings of ritual engagement and the temples they inhabited as their homes.

Tiwanaku geopolitical expansion followed the expanding fame of these beings. By "fame," I mean celebrity and specifically Nancy Munn's (1986:114–118) notion of the spatiotemporal expansion of a person's name and influence. For Munn, expansive and yet ultimately intimate transactions frequently generate fame. In Gawa, the hard-won circulation of a well-known kula object trumpets the names of donor and recipient alike across the South Pacific, recalibrating their standing in a transregional

geography of islands. Just so, successfully creating and commodifying a pop song may render an artist a "household name," a mega-kula feat that may be conscripted down the road in a "cover" recorded by a recipient artist, thereby expanding her own fame. In both situations, the "things" exchanged or created (kula object or "hit") accrue life histories and powers of their own, affecting the actions and desires of people distant in space, social relation, or generation. Tiwanaku monoliths garnered fame via their transactions with humans during cyclically orchestrated, recurring events that brought humans and monoliths into contact. People came in pilgrimage to engage them, many from distant Andean regions and different ecological zones. Stopping at auspicious places en route to pay tribute to local landscape beings, pilgrims enacted a "kinesthetic mapping of space" (Sallnow 1987:184). Carefully choreographed processions directed pilgrims toward Tiwanaku, through its labyrinthine corridors, and into the monumental temples that were the monoliths' intimate homes. This is not to suggest that everyone was allowed into their innermost sanctums or was brave enough to enter; as at Pachacamac, most visitors likely were content to visit Tiwanaku for ritual events and simply *approach* the monumental homes.

Monolithic personages ordered space by gathering and condensing Tiwanaku's biophysical landscapes. They indexed specific montane—sandstone or volcanic—places of origin in their expressive materiality, as well as in the orientations and material construction of their temples, not via abstract representation or nostalgia. Like miniature animate stone objects "birthed" of mountains in the contemporary Andes (Allen 2016; de la Cadena 2015:107), Tiwanaku monoliths were quarried fragments of those mountains. Their materiality and iconography embodied the teeming, generative telluric essence of those imposing features. Their temple homes afforded privileged views of those mountains, perceptually appropriating their vital power to Tiwanaku's urban landscape. More than just fragments of those landforms, monoliths embodied their totalities in condensed form, shaped into particular beings that instantiated the mythical personhoods of their ancestral mountains of origin. Monolithic beings were the focal components of an emergent, seductive ecoregime.

Monolithic personages and their temples also maintained a rigorous temporal rhythm. We do not know the exact cycles that brought humans and monoliths into transactional engagements in Tiwanaku. Yet Tiwanaku's temple orientations offer clues. Earlier Late Formative sunken temples directed attention southward toward the heliacal rise and set of nighttime celestial events (Benitez 2009, 2013). These included the nightly rotation of the Milky Way and the seasonal rise of the Yacana dark cloud constellation (Urton 1988). All later temples, beginning with Kalasasaya, emphasized solar setting and rising points. By Tiwanaku 1 (500–800 CE), regular equinox and solstice events likely organized Tiwanaku's social and ritual calendar. These events scheduled major political events and drew thousands of pilgrims, relatives, specialists, and others to Tiwanaku. A key reason for coming to Tiwanaku was to approach, apprehend, supplicate, and make offerings to its monolithic personages. In its attention to celestial movements and temporal rhythms, Tiwanaku's seductive ecoregime was not just geopolitical but profoundly cosmopolitical.

Monoliths were powerful animate beings who sought the production of appropriately ritualized Tiwanaku persons. Whatever expansionist ambitions Tiwanaku leaders nurtured were firmly rooted in the city's fundamentally calendrical, centripetal foundation. During ceremonial events, temples facilitated transformative human–lithic engagements. Those engagements came with an obligatory price; they transformed anxious pilgrims into newly vitalized, yet beholden and obligated Tiwanaku subjects. Tiwanaku's five hundred years of enduring fame indicate that subsuming a primal, raw, pre-enlightened identity to an enlightened, vitalized, cosmopolitan Tiwanaku identity was considered a redemptive bargain.

Cosmopolitical Bodies

Cyclically recurring ceremonies rendered monolithic sculptures vital beings who collectively embodied emergent geopolitical relations. In the preceding Late Formative period (200 BCE–500 CE), stone sculptures were common across the Lake Titicaca basin. Each region promoted a range of sculptural styles. While centers in Escoma, in the east-central basin, emphasized architectural panels, centers in the southern basin, including Khonkho Wankane and Tiwanaku, celebrated anthropomorphic sculptures (Janusek 2015a; Roddick and Janusek 2018). Tiwanaku's emergence as the primary center in the basin corresponded with an apparent monopoly on stone sculptural production and display (Janusek 2006). From this point forward, after 500 CE and continuing until Tiwanaku's decisive disintegration after 1000 CE, major anthropomorphic stone sculptures were limited to Tiwanaku alone.

Sculptors designed a threefold plan for monoliths. The largest and most centrally placed were presentation personages, which became the focus of Tiwanaku's expanding geopolitical fame. Flanking them, physically or conceptually, were beefed-up, decidedly masculine, and in some cases weaponed extended-arm monoliths. At least one extended-arm monolith, Suñawa, combined sacrificial and generative imagery. Paired *chachapumas* guarded the portals that directed ritual participants into Tiwanaku's temple homes and inner sanctums. These sacrificers ensured that all who passed through Tiwanaku's most sanctified portals were intent on becoming beholden subjects. Tiwanaku's threefold monolithic program sought to interpellate fleshly humans as appropriately gestured ritual-political subjects (sensu Althusser 1972), yet the swath of activities that occurred at Tiwanaku during major ceremonial events—exchanges, deals, offerings, feasts, "brushes with celebrities"—empowered those subjects with cosmopolitan relations and expansive identities (sensu Bell 1992; Ortner 2005).

Tiwanaku's monolithic program condensed messy geopolitical relations. Presentation monoliths were the most important stone sculptures that humans apprehended in their pilgrimage to Tiwanaku. Their central placement in temples and their focal gestures, in which each clutches a *kero* with the left arm and a snuff tablet with the right arm, designate them as hosts that welcomed pilgrims and others. *Keros* indexed fermented chicha and snuff tablets psychotropic resins, both consciousness-transforming substances that were likely deemed critical for inducing a proper ritual attitude. Yet presentation beings offer those objects with two left hands, a physically impossible feat that rendered recipients as supplicant subjects. Presentation monoliths affected a generous gesture mitigated by their manner of presentation. They were not in the business of offering a free (beer) lunch. They were in the business of circulating reciprocal obligations, articulating hierarchical geopolitical relations, and, most fundamentally, producing beholden human subjects in the Lake Titicaca basin and beyond.

Chachapumas did the dirty work of ensuring that those who entered Tiwanaku were worthy. Consubstantial beings-in-transformation themselves, *chachapumas* sought to transform "raw" humans into appropriately gestured, minded, and bedecked persons. Passing through Tiwanaku's portals and into the intimate homes of presentation monoliths and their extended-arm attendants was a dramatic ritual passage. *Chachapumas* reminded pilgrims that this passage required sacrifice. It required the ritual rebirth of an unenlightened person as an enlightened, vitalized, and attitudinally appropriate Tiwanaku "citizen." Perhaps because of their fundamentally personal, violent roles, many *chachapumas* were targeted for ritual mutilation at the time of Tiwanaku's geopolitical disintegration (Janusek 2008:295).

Scaled relations among monoliths embodied hierarchical cosmopolitical relations in Tiwanaku's immediate hinterland. Presentation monoliths inhabited Tiwanaku's primary temples, at least some of them attended by large (>2 m) extended-arm monoliths. Medium-sized extended-arm monoliths inhabited the courts of Tiwanaku residential complexes and strategic regional centers such as Lukurmata and Lakaya. Extended-arm statuettes occupied at least one local residential complex and two regional centers. Large paired *chachapumas* (>1 m) guarded the entrances to Tiwanaku's core temples, while smaller paired *chachapumas* guarded local temples and residences at Tiwanaku and key regional sites (e.g., Iruhito).

Chachapuma figurines likely served as avatars of personal transformation. The three classes of monoliths and their scaled relations produced hierarchically positioned fleshly subjects.

Networks of animate things assembled in ritual to condense geopolitical relations appear elsewhere in the Pre-Columbian Andes. The Cuzco hinterland during Inka expansion consisted of at least 328 powerful *wak'as*: outcrops, springs, boulders, river junctions, and so forth—material things that "manifested the superhuman" (Salomon 1991:17). The Inka devised a system of paths that radiated from their principal temple, Coricancha, and linked these *wak'as* together as a master assembly that ordered space, time, and society for Cuzco and its hinterland (Bauer 1998; Zuidema 1964, 1990). In other regions, diverse polities were linked together in mythic narratives and ritual practices that centered on imposing, animate ancestral peaks (*apus*) or springs venerated by ethnically disparate communities. The Huarochirí Manuscript narrates turbulent, often tawdry relations among major *wak'as* near the Peruvian coast (Salomon 1991). It centers on the relation between the mighty highland *apu* Pariacaca and his lowland female sibling and water shrine Chaupi Ñamca, each the focus of pilgrimage and worship for diverse political communities. The *wak'as* embodied their multiplex communities, and the narrative presents an ideal complementarity—simultaneously social, ritual, political, and ecological—that subsumed tortured histories of conflict and migration. The manuscript narrates an ecoregime centered on powerful places that afforded cosmopolitical order to an otherwise messy, fraught geopolitical history.

Ontological Frontiers of Tiwanaku's Ecoregime

Becoming a Tiwanaku subject carried weight in the Middle Horizon Titicaca basin. It afforded redemptive ontological dispositions toward the world, health, and the afterlife. Pilgrims, traders, diplomats, and others came to Tiwanaku for these reasons, as well as political and economic opportunities. Many left as transformed persons who, as Victor Turner (1974:166–230) suggests, returned to a different home. Tiwanaku's monoliths and their temple homes constituted structured assemblages that, during astronomically scheduled ceremonial events, facilitated the relational coproduction of animate ancestral monoliths and newly vitalized and empowered persons. The monoliths that inhabited its core temples were central to Tiwanaku's expansive prestige and emergent ritual-political power.

Yet Tiwanaku's monolithic project did not have total purchase over the experiences and ontologies of the diverse communities that affiliated with the center. Ontology as a "radical alterity" of being has come to sound a lot like familiar essentialized concepts such as "cosmology" and "culture" (Kosiba, this volume; also Graeber 2015). Despite the successful historical production of predominant unimodal ontologies—Holy Roman theology, Western science—people may shift moment to moment, situationally, among ontological dispositions, understood here as "different practical understandings of the nature of material reality" (Harris and Robb 2010:670). For example, communities whose lives and rituals proceed according to a particular juncture of ontological dispositions are at some point or another, if not regularly, in intensive contact with other communities and their distinctive, deeply conditioned engagements with the material world. All told, a Cuban diviner's *ache* powder "is power," and not just *like* power, only for a specific set of ritual contexts (Holbraad 2007), just as a particular monolith momentarily constituted the material essence of a politicized Bolivian Aymara community in a politically charged June solstice ritual in 2002 (see Janusek 2015a:335–336). In the lived world, ontologies are not fixed. They are dynamic, situational dispositions.

Even as it strove to encompass the diverse identities and divergent political interests of its ritual adherents, Tiwanaku's monolithic program never fully encapsulated the multiplex dispositions of its affiliated communities. Changing spatial orientations emphasize shifting priorities and political relations. The Kalasasaya platform differed dramatically in orientation and landscape relations from the Late Formative Sunken Temple, and the Pumapunku differed in form and axial orientation from both Kalasasaya and Akapana. The transition from Late Formative to Tiwanaku urbanism

marks a dramatic transformation in Tiwanaku's ecoregime and its attendant ritual practices and ontological dispositions. Monoliths shifted from embodying barely dressed ancestral personages without legs, emplaced as if rising from the earth, to humanlike beings standing firmly on the ground, bedecked in elaborate attire (Janusek 2006). Furthermore, monolithic production shifted dramatically from having proliferated across the Lake Titicaca basin to being restricted to Tiwanaku and a few specific, strategically located nearby centers. Temples shifted from primarily north–south orientations fixed on the cycles of nighttime lunar and stellar movements to east–west orientations that integrated these cycles with annual solar cycles, fixing in place, via monolithic temple homes, a more systematic, encompassing, hegemonic calendar.

Tiwanaku's temples sought to incorporate the social diversity so prominent in its residential compounds and human bodily modifications (Blom 2005; Janusek 2004; Janusek and Blom 2006). Each was a ritual place that gathered a particular network of communities. Each differed from others in construction, composition, and celestial-terrestrial alignments. Each also housed a presentation monolith and, in some cases, its extended-arm attendants. Although presentation monoliths shared a common facial visage, gesture, and stance, they varied significantly in size, dress, iconography, and bodily form. I suggest that a presentation monolith and its temple gathered a unique ritual-political community, many of whose members likely came from distant locales in the south-central Andes and whose perceptual engagements with the biophysical world differed substantially. Tiwanaku's ecoregime, attuned to carefully constructed assemblages of monoliths and their temple homes, sought to anchor these differences to a common set of ontological dispositions and ritual practices.

Monolithic assemblages afford insight into sociopolitical and ontological tensions inherent in the ecoregime they worked hard to create. Tiwanaku was a cosmopolitan city that gathered communities from multiple ecological locales in the south-central Andes (Janusek 2002, 2004, 2008). A systematic program for creating ancestral monoliths and their temples went some way toward rendering Tiwanaku a common home. Yet a full consideration of monolithic assemblages reveals faults in this program. First, many sculptures not treated here fall outside of the categories I have summarized (see Portugal 1998). Second, there exist several "unfinished" extended-arm and *chachapuma* monoliths. One extended-arm sculpture, the basalt Workers' Monolith, presents roughly incised lines marking places where deep carving never materialized. The prevalence of unfinished monoliths points to the gravity that ongoing production had in Tiwanaku. What we interpret as "incomplete" monoliths may have been significant as vital stone personages in process. Their prevalence suggests the possibility that not simply monoliths as fully figured "beings" but also monoliths "coming into being" were valued and empowered.

Third, two extended-arm monoliths, Suñawa and Pachakama, were sculpted in an attempt to unite diverse communities into a common Tiwanaku fold, reminiscent, in lithic form, of the geopolitical embodiment narrated in the Huarochirí manuscript. The two extended-arm monoliths, both of Ccapia andesite, manifest distinct personages, as expressed most visibly in their different headdresses. Their headgear presented the two complementary styles worn by many of the diverse communities affiliated with Tiwanaku (Frame 1991). Blom and I (2006) posit that these styles corresponded to two broad techniques of infant cranial modification that remained lifelong embodiments of community identification. Multiple techniques produced a diverse range of artfully crafted skulls. Suñawa and Pachakama may have embodied Tiwanaku's different political communities, condensing them in lithic form as dual attendants subject to the Ponce Monolith, one of Tiwanaku's largest presentation personages.

Tiwanaku's ecoregime and political community began to disintegrate before 1000 CE. This corresponded with shifts in regional climatic conditions that included decreased annual rainfall and lowering lake levels, resulting in a retreating lake edge (Binford et al. 1997). Insofar as monolithic personages and temple homes had been central to

urban centrality and expansive ritual-political fame since the Late Formative period, this was a major transformation. The Late Intermediate period communities that coalesced in the process of Tiwanaku disintegration rejected these centralizing manifestations of a geopolitical phenomenon that had run its course (Janusek 2008; Janusek and Kolata 2003). A dramatic turn from monoliths and monuments and toward more mobile, pastoral livelihoods manifested a resurgence of productive practices and ontological dispositions that had been vital, if subdominant, among the communities who earlier identified as "Tiwanaku." These practices and understandings now constituted key anchors for inhabiting Titicaca's biophysical world in the face of challenging new environmental conditions and shifting productive and political imperatives.

Monolithic destruction accompanied this dramatic geopolitical shift (Janusek 2008:295). Curiously, all known presentation monoliths are intact. Some medium-sized extended-arm monoliths and many *chachapumas*, on the other hand, are strategically mutilated. One *chachapuma*, a basalt sculpture presumably found in situ in front of Akapana's primary entrance, was ritually defaced. This pattern may provide clues for Tiwanaku's disintegration. It indicates that the transformative sculptural beings most directly and intimately associated with the sacrificial production of Tiwanaku subjects received the brunt of the fury that accompanied the rejection of Tiwanaku's once seductive, empowering ecoregime.

Conclusions

Monoliths shaped Tiwanaku's emergent geopolitical network. Culminating a millennial formative tradition, Tiwanaku sculptors developed an intricate, articulated program of monolithic classes and scalar relations. Presentation monoliths were primary ancestral personages and Tiwanaku's storied monumental campuses their temple homes. The largest extended-arm personages were their attendants and smaller versions or statuettes lithic ancestral personages for local centers and residential complexes. *Chachapumas* guarded the portals that afforded entrance into Tiwanaku's temples and assured that those who entered adopted an appropriate ritual attitude. If the things that presentation personages held provide insight into this attitude, it included a consciousness enhanced by drinking fermented chicha and ingesting psychotropic resins. This was clearly vital for an anxious or impassioned person seeking to enter one of Tiwanaku's temples and to transact with—in voice, gesture, offering, or some other manner—its resident ancestral personages.

Still, monolithic animacy was uneasy, contingent, and contested, as it inevitably was when Tiwanaku's intricate ecoregime, expansive fame, and ritual-political power were rejected after 1000 CE. Monoliths were rendered animate and accrued fame not through some essential ontology or theoretical attribution; rather, they accrued power through witnessed actions and engagements that occurred in cyclically recurring rituals enhanced by mind-altering substances and flickering braziers. Driving Tiwanaku's emergent fame, monoliths—in particular, presentation monoliths—were the stars of this show. Very possibly, Tiwanaku human leadership and political hierarchy were secondary to and hinged on transactive encounters with Tiwanaku's intricate and classed assemblages of potent monolithic beings.

Recent engagements with Tiwanaku monoliths involve ontological contradictions, ambiguities, and, ultimately, new understandings that emerge from unexpected, immediate, and transformative engagements with monoliths. The intersection of politically jostling communities in Tiwanaku today is reminiscent of the landscapes held in tension among capitalists, biodiversity scientists, and local communities in Latin America described by Escobar (1999). There are, for example, Bolivian authorities for whom the Bennett Monolith and the site of Tiwanaku embody the civilized primordial origins of a quasi-socialist "plurinational state." Carted to the capital of La Paz in the 1930s, Bennett stood in a central exhaust-choked roundabout plaza for nearly seventy years as a material embodiment of Bolivia's past. There are the nineteenth-century industrialists who, in the course of building a railway through Tiwanaku, dynamited monoliths to create its rubble roadbed. There are also the hundreds of tourists who visit Tiwanaku daily. Broadly holding the site and its monoliths in reverence, most are awed with Tiwanaku's monoliths and excited to take a selfie with one.

There is also the Aymara-identifying community of Tiwanaku itself, whose relations to the site's monoliths are uneasy and complex. Many are ambivalent when discussing the theoretical proposition that "monoliths live" but light up to tell a story about having come into contact with one (apostrophizing Hallowell's [1960] precocious point that the animacy of a stone or any other presumably living thing is empirical, *witnessed* while awake or in a dream). Older community members unanimously note that Tiwanaku's monoliths live lives parallel to those of humans. For one thing, when they become animate, they do so at night. Stories of their animation frequently begin with a flash of blinding light.

Tiwanaku monoliths remain potent today, if again via multiplex experiences of the biophysical world and a new conjunction of geopolitical networks. Every year, on the June solstice, thousands of tourists descend on the ruins to witness the sun rise over the temples that enclosed Bennett and Ponce, choreographed by a now world-famous *amauta*, or ritual master, and a host of attendants. The initial inauguration of President Evo Morales, in January 2006, strategically took place at the site, featuring those same temples and the Ponce Monolith. For the Aymara who inhabit the town of Tiahuanaco, Bennett, Suñawa, and other monoliths are "alive" in a much more engaged manner than they are for the curious tourist or nationalist.

Yet Tiwanaku's emergent fame in a new world of globalizing capital accumulation and national pride may well come at the price of the animate power of its monoliths for the community. Local narratives are rapidly disappearing as an older generation of Tiahuanaco community members pass on. Younger generations throng to the city of El Alto at an explosive rate and generally demonstrate little interest in monoliths or their parallel lives. An older friend mentioned to me that people do not witness monoliths at night like they once did. When I casually asked why that might be, she paused and suggested, "Well, stones live by night, and since light [electricity] came to Tiahuanaco [in the 1980s], now it is never dark."

Acknowledgments

The research presented in this chapter is part of a broader initiative that I am conducting in coordination with Anna Guengerich of Vanderbilt

University. I am indebted to many persons and places including, in Tiahuanaco, Julio Condori, Mario Pachaguaya, Irene Delavaris, Cesar Calisaya, Clemente Quispe, and Gloria and Anna Ramirez. In La Paz, Jose Luis Paz consistently produced national permits and Wolfgang Schüler and Julia Durango graciously provided a home. Funding was secured via Vanderbilt Unrestricted Retention funds and Vanderbilt's Robert Penn Warren Center for the Humanities.

NOTES

1 Both monoliths stood on pedestals. Fraile's is buried under the Kalasasaya west platform, and Pumapumku's was broken from the monolith shortly after it was first recorded. Early photographs and renderings indicate both pedestals stood approximately 80 cm high.

2 I recorded a medium-sized extended arm monolith from the site of Cerro Churo, near the Middle Horizon center of Wari, Peru (600–1000 CE) in June 2018 (see Pérez Calderón 2013).

3 The quai Branly *chachapuma* (inventory #71.1938.6.1) was collected by Alcide d'Orbigny in 1833; the Náprstek *chachapuma* was collected by Julius Nestler in 1909–1912 (inventory #50724).

REFERENCES CITED

Allen, Catherine J.
2016   The Living Ones: Miniatures and Animation in the Andes. *Journal of Anthropological Research* 72(4):416–441.

Althusser, Louis
1972   Ideology and Ideological State Apparatuses. In *Lenin and Philosophy and Other Essays*, pp. 121–176. Translated by Ben Brewster. Monthly Review Press, Ann Arbor, Mich.

Bandy, Matthew
2013   Tiwanaku Origins and Early Development: The Political and Moral Economy of a Hospitality State. In *Visions of Tiwanaku*, edited by Alexei Vranich and Charles Stanish, pp. 135–150. Cotsen Institute of Archaeology, University of California, Los Angeles.

Bauer, Brian
1998   *The Sacred Landscape of the Inca: The Cuzco Ceque System*. University of Texas Press, Austin.

Bell, Catherine
1992   *Ritual Theory, Ritual Practice*. Oxford University Press, Oxford.

Benitez, Leonardo
2009   Descendants of the Sun: Calendars, Myths, and the Tiwanaku State. In *Tiwanaku: Papers from the 2005 Mayer Center Symposium at the Denver Art Museum*, edited by Margaret Young-Sánchez, pp. 49–82. Denver Art Museum, Denver.

2013　What Could Celebrants See? Sky, Landscape, and Settlement Planning in the Late Formative Southern Titicaca Basin. In *Advances in Titicaca Archaeology 2*, edited by Alexei Vranich and Abigail R. Levine, pp. 89–104. Cotsen Institute of Archaeology, University of California, Los Angeles.

Bennett, Jane

2009　*Vibrant Matter: A Political Ecology of Things.* Duke University Press, Durham, N.C.

Bennett, Wendell C.

1934　Excavations at Tiahuanaco. *Anthropological Papers of the American Museum of Natural History* 34(3):359–494.

1936　Excavations in Bolivia. *Anthropological Papers of the American Museum of Natural History* 35(4):329–530.

Berenguer R., Jose

1998　La iconografía del poder en Tiwanaku y su rol en la integración de zonas de frontera. *Boletín del Museo Chileno de Arte Precolombino* 7:19–37.

Binford, Michael W., Alan L. Kolata, Mark Brenner, John Wayne Janusek, Matthew T. Seddon, Mark Abbott, and Jason H. Curtis

1997　Climate Variation and the Rise and Fall of an Andean Civilization. *Quaternary Research* 47:235–248.

Bloch, Maurice

1992　*Prey into Hunter: The Politics of Religious Experience.* Cambridge University Press, Cambridge.

Blom, Deborah E.

2005　Human Body Modification and Diversity in Tiwanaku Society. *Journal of Anthropological Archaeology* 24:1–34.

Blom, Deborah E., and John Wayne Janusek

2004　Making Place: Humans as Dedications in Tiwanaku. *World Archaeology* 36(1):123–141.

Browman, David

1981　New Light on Andean Tiwanaku. *American Scientist* 69(4):408–419.

Couture, Nicole C., and Kathryn Sampeck

2003　Putuni: A History of Palace Architecture in Tiwanaku. In *Tiwanaku and Its Hinterland: Archaeology and Paleoecology of an Andean Civilization*, vol. 2, edited by Alan L. Kolata, pp. 226–263. Smithsonian Institution Press, Washington, D.C.

Cummins, Thomas B. F.

2002　*Toasts with the Inca: Andean Abstraction and Colonial Images on Quero Vessels.* University of Michigan Press, Ann Arbor.

Dean, Carolyn

2006　The Trouble with (the Term) Art. *Art Journal* 65(2):24–32.

de la Cadena, Marisol

2015　*Earth Beings: Ecologies of Practice across Andean Worlds.* Duke University Press, Durham, N.C.

DeLanda, Manuel

2006　*A New Philosophy of Society: Assemblage Theory and Social Complexity.* Continuum, London.

Descola, Philippe

2013　*Beyond Nature and Culture.* University of Chicago Press, Chicago.

Eisleb, Dieter, and Ranate Strelow

1980　*Altperuanische Kulturen Tiahuanaco III.* Museum für Völkerkunde, Berlin.

Escobar, Arturo

1999　After Nature: Steps toward an Antiessentialist Political Ecology. *Current Anthropology* 40(1):1–20.

Estete, Miguel de

[1535] 1918　Noticia del Perú. *Boletín de la Sociedad Ecuatoriana de Estudios Históricos Americanos* 1(3):312–335.

Garcilaso de la Vega, Inca

[1609] 1943　*Comentarios reales de los Incas.* Emecé Editores SA, Buenos Aires.

Graeber, David

2015　Radical Alterity Is Just Another Way of Saying "Reality": A Reply to Eduardo Viveiros de Castro. *Journal of Ethnographic Theory* 5(2):1–41.

Hallowell, A. Irving

1960　Ojibwa Ontology, Culture, and World View. In *Culture in History: Essays in Honor of Paul Radin*, edited by Stanley Diamond, pp. 19–52. Columbia University Press, New York.

Harris, Oliver J. T., and John Robb

2010   Multiple Ontologies and the Problem of the Body in History. *American Anthropologist* 114(4):668–679.

Holbraad, Martin

2007   The Power of Powder: Multiplicity and Motion in the Divinatory Cosmology of Cuban Ifá (or Mana, Again). In *Thinking through Things: Theorising Artefacts Ethnographically*, edited by Amira Henare, Martin Holbraad, and Sari Wastell, pp. 189–225. Routledge, London.

Janusek, John Wayne

2002   Out of Many, One: Style and Social Boundaries in Tiwanaku. *Latin American Antiquity* 13(1):35–61.

2004   *Identity and Power in the Ancient Andes: Tiwanaku Cities through Time.* Routledge, London.

2006   The Changing "Nature" of Tiwanaku Religion and the Rise of an Andean State. *World Archaeology* 38(3):469–492.

2008   *Ancient Tiwanaku.* Cambridge University Press, Cambridge.

2015a   Of Monoliths and Men: Human-Lithic Encounters and the Production of an Animistic Ecology at Khonkho Wankane. In *The Archaeology of Wak'as: Explorations of the Sacred in the Pre-Columbian Andes*, edited by Tamara L. Bray, pp. 335–365. University Press of Colorado, Boulder.

2015b   Tiwanaku Urban Origins: Distributed Centers and Animate Landscapes. In *Early Cities in Comparative Perspective, 4000 BCE–1200 CE*, edited by Norman Yoffee, pp. 223–252. Cambridge University Press, Cambridge.

Janusek, John Wayne, and Deborah E. Blom

2006   Identifying Tiwanaku Urban Populations: Style, Identity, and Ceremony in Andean Cities. In *Urbanization in the Preindustrial World: Cross-Cultural Perspectives*, edited by Glenn Storey, pp. 233–251. University of Alabama Press, Tuscaloosa.

Janusek, John Wayne, and Corey Bowen

2018   Tiwanaku as Telluric Waterscape: Water and Stone in a Highland Andean City. In *Powerful Places in the Ancient Andes*, edited by Justin Jennings and Edward Swenson, pp. 209–246. University of New Mexico, Albuquerque.

Janusek, John Wayne, and Anna K. Guengerich

2015   Demanding Hosts: Extended Arm Monoliths and Tiwanaku Geopolitics. Paper presented at the 56th Annual Meeting of the Institute of Andean Studies, Berkeley.

Janusek, John Wayne, and Alan L. Kolata

2003   Prehispanic Rural History in the Katari Valley. In *Tiwanaku and Its Hinterland: Archaeology and Paleoecology of an Andean Civilization*, vol. 2, edited by Alan L. Kolata, pp. 129–172. Smithsonian Institution Press, Washington, D.C.

Janusek, John Wayne, and Patrick Ryan Williams

2016   Telluric Techné and the Lithic Production of Tiwanaku. In *Making Value, Making Meaning: Techné in the Precolumbian World*, edited by Cathy L. Costin, pp. 95–128. Dumbarton Oaks, Washington, D.C.

Janusek, John Wayne, Patrick Ryan Williams, Mark Golitko, and Carlos Lémuz Aguirre

2013   Building Taypikala: Telluric Transformations in the Lithic Production of Tiwanaku. In *Mining and Quarrying in the Ancient Andes: Sociopolitical, Economic, and Symbolic Dimensions*, edited by Nicholas Tripcevich and Kevin J. Vaughn, pp. 65–98. Springer, New York.

Knobloch, Patricia J.

2000   Wari Ritual Power at Conchopata: An Interpretation of *Anadenanthera colubrina* Iconography. *Latin American Antiquity* 11(4):387–402.

Kolata, Alan L.

1991   The Technology and Organization of Agricultural Production in the Tiwanaku State. *Latin American Antiquity* 2(2):99–125.

1993   *Tiwanaku: Portrait of an Andean Civilization.* Blackwell, Cambridge.

2003   Tiwanaku Ceremonial Architecture and Urban Organization. In *Tiwanaku and Its Hinterland: Archaeology and Paleoecology of an Andean Civilization*, vol. 2, edited by Alan L. Kolata, pp. 175–201. Smithsonian Institution Press, Washington, D.C.

Kolata, Alan L., and Carlos Ponce Sanginés

2003   Two Hundred Years of Archaeological Research at Tiwanaku: A Selective History. In *Tiwanaku and Its Hinterland: Archaeology and Paleoecology of an Andean Civilization*, vol. 2, edited by Alan L. Kolata, pp. 18–29. Smithsonian Institution Press, Washington, D.C.

Lave, Jean, and Etienne Wenger

1991   *Situated Learning: Legitimate Peripheral Participation.* Cambridge University Press, Cambridge.

Makowski, Krysztof

2002   Los personajes frontales de báculos en la iconografía tiahuanaco y huari: Tema o convención? *Boletín de la Arqueología PUCP* 5:337–374.

Manzanilla, Linda, and Eric Kenneth Woodard

1990   Restos humanos asociados a la pirámide de Akapana (Tiwanaku, Bolivia). *Latin American Antiquity* 1(2):133–149.

Mattox, Christopher Wesley

2013   Materializing Value: A Comparative Analysis of Status and Distinction in Urban Tiwanaku, Bolivia. MA thesis, McGill University, Montreal.

Mauss, Marcel

1967   *The Gift: Forms and Functions of Exchange in Archaic Societies.* W. W. Norton, New York.

Munn, Nancy

1986   *The Fame of Gawa: A Symbolic Study of Value Transformation in a Massim (Papua New Guinea) Society.* Duke University Press, Durham, N.C.

Nestler, Julius

1913   Beiträge zur Kenntnis der Ruinstätte von Tiahuanaco. *Mitteilungen der K. K. Geographischen Gesellschaft in Wien* 56(4):226–236.

Ortner, Sherry B.

2005   Subjectivity and Cultural Critique. *Anthropological Theory* 5(1):31–52.

Pérez Arias, Adolfo Enrique

2014   *Arqueología en el Río Desaguadero: Excavaciones en Iruhito.* Junior, La Paz.

Pérez Calderón, Ismael

2013   Arqueología en Ayacucho. *Boletín de Lima* 35(172):19–34.

Ponce Sanginés, Carlos

1981   *Tiwanaku: Espacio, tiempo, y cultura.* Los Amigos del Libro, La Paz.

1995   *Tiwanaku: 200 años de investigaciones arqueológicas.* Producciones CIMA, La Paz.

Portugal Ortiz, Max

1957   Sullkatata. In *Arqueología boliviana, Primera Mesa Redonda*, edited by Carlos Ponce Sanginés, pp. 226–234. Biblioteca Paceña, La Paz.

1998   *Escultura prehispanic boliviana.* Universidad Mayor de San Andrés, La Paz.

Posnansky, Arthur

1945   *Tihuanacu: The Cradle of American Man.* Vols. 1–2. J. J. Augustin, New York.

Protzen, Jean-Pierre, and Stella Nair

2013   *The Stone of Tiahuanaco: A Study of Architecture and Construction.* Cotsen Institute of Archaeology, University of California, Los Angeles.

Prümers, Heiko

1993   Die Ruinen von Tiahuanaco im Jahre 1848: Zeichnungen und Notizen con Léonce Angrand. *Beiträge Zur Allgemeinen und Vergleichended Archäologie* 13. Philipp Von Zabern, Mainz.

Querejazu Lewis, Roy

1983   *El mundo arqueológico del Cnl. Federico Diez de Medina.* Los Amigos del Libro, La Paz.

Roddick, Andrew

2016   Scalar Relations: A Juxtaposition of Craft Learning in the Lake Titicaca Basin. In *Knowledge in Motion: Constellations of Learning across Time and Place*, edited by Andrew Roddick and Ann Stahl, pp. 126–154. University of Arizona Press, Tucson.

Roddick, Andrew, and John Wayne Janusek

2018   Moving between Homes: Landscape, Mobility, and Political Action in the Titicaca Basin. In *Powerful Places in the Ancient Andes*, edited by Justin Jennings and Edward Swenson, pp. 287–322. University of New Mexico Press, Albuquerque.

Sahlins, Marshall

2008 *The Western Illusion of Human Nature.* Prickly Paradigm Press, Chicago.

Sallnow, Michael J.

1987 *Pilgrims of the Andes: Regional Cults in Cuzco.* Smithsonian Institution Press, Washington, D.C.

Salomon, Frank

1991 Introductory Essay: The Huarochiri Manuscript. In *The Huarochiri Manuscript: A Testament of Ancient and Colonial Andean Religion*, pp. 1–38. Translated by Frank Salomon and George Urioste. University of Texas Press, Austin.

Schaedel, Richard P.

1948 Monolithic Sculpture of the Southern Andes. *Archaeology* 1(2):66–73.

1952 An Analysis of Central Andean Stone Sculpture. PhD dissertation, Yale University, New Haven.

Stanish, Chales

2003 *Ancient Titicaca: The Evolution of Complex Society in Southern Peru and Northern Bolivia.* University of California Press, Berkeley.

Torres, Constantino

2002 Iconografía tiwanaku en la parafenalia inhalatoria de los Andes centro-sur. *Boletín de la Arqueología PUCP* 5:427–454.

Turner, Victor

1974 *Dramas, Fields, and Metaphors.* Cornell University Press, Ithaca.

Uhle, Max

1895 Official Notes of Research in Bolivia Submitted to the Department of Archaeology and Paleontology of the University of Pennsylvania. University of Pennsylvania Museum of Archaeology and Anthropology, Philadelphia.

Urton, Gary

1988 *At the Crossroads of the Earth and Sky: An Andean Cosmology.* University of Texas Press, Austin.

Verano, John W.

2013 Excavations and Analysis of Human Skeletal Remains from a New Dedicatory Offering at Tiwanaku. In *Advances in Titicaca Basin Archaeology 2*, edited by Alexei Vranich and Abigail R. Levine, pp. 167–180. Cotsen Institute of Archaeology, University of California, Los Angeles.

Vranich, Alexei

2006 The Construction and Reconstruction of Ritual Space at Tiwanaku (A.D. 500–1000), Bolivia. *Journal of Field Archaeology* 31(2):121–136.

2009 The Development of the Ritual Core of Tiwanaku. In *Tiwanaku: Papers from the 2005 Mayer Center Symposium at the Denver Art Museum*, edited by Margaret Young-Sanchez, pp. 11–34. Denver Art Museum, Denver.

Wassén, S. Henry

1972 A Medicine-Man's Implements and Plants in a Tiahuanacoid Tomb in Highland Bolivia. *Etnologiska Studier* 32. Erlanders Boktryckeri Aktiebolag, Göteborg.

Weismantel, Mary

2013 Inhuman Eyes: Looking at Chavín de Huantar. In *Relational Archaeologies: Humans, Animals, Things*, edited by Christopher Watts, pp. 21–41. Routledge, New York.

Zuidema, R. Tom

1964 *The Ceque System of Cuzco: The Social Organization of the Capital of the Inca.* E. J. Brill, Leiden.

1990 *Inca Civilization in Cuzco.* Translated by J.-J. Decoster. University of Texas Press, Austin.

On the Threshold of the *Huaca*

Sanctuaries of Sound in the Ancient Andean World

MARCO CURATOLA PETROCCHI

THE EXTRAORDINARY RELEVANCE OF THE sonic-aural dimension in the ancient Andean system of religious beliefs and practices has only recently begun to be discerned. Perhaps the first to grasp its real significance was Constance Classen, who in one of the essays gathered in *Worlds of Sense* (1993:106) posited, though in very general terms, that the ancient people of the Andes had to live "in a world set into motion by sound." Later, Claudette Columbus, in a seminal essay titled "Soundscapes in Andean Context" (2004), drew attention to the profound semiotic implications of sound in pre-Hispanic ritual practices and how the latter could condense and encode a vast and coherent system of meanings, beliefs, and collective representations. Likewise, Jeremy Moore (2005:149), examining the dynamics of pre-Hispanic processions and also on the basis of ethnographic analogies, proposed that the "audial domain" could represent an essential component of them. For her part, Mónica Gudemos (2008:116–118, 133–134), in studying the choreographic-musical sequences of the rituals of the major annual Inka festivals, not only recognized that sound fulfilled a preponderant ritual role in those ceremonial occasions but also noticed that one of the most common and striking characteristics of ancient Andean ceremonial spaces was their location on sites with some natural sound source or particular architectural or structural features that were meant to give out or amplify sound, such as canals through which water runs loudly. Along this same line, in my essay "La voz de la huaca" (2016), I settled that the Andean religion at the time of the Inkas was indeed a system of beliefs and ritual practices of a strongly aural nature, focused on sensing and interpreting certain sounds, regarded as extra-human voices, of the universe surrounding humanity. Actually, I highlighted that in the ancient Andean world the attribute that distinguished things and places infused with life-force (*camac*), and therefore considered living sacred entities (*huacas* [*wak'a*]), was essentially sound and that the Andean places of cult were thought of primarily as spaces where one could hear the voices of

267

the gods. Established in strategic sites and carefully conditioned to elevate the perception of sounds of nature or others produced through different systems and devices, and to offer intense auditive experiences, these shrines represent the most perfect and generalized case of aural spaces and structures created by an ancient society (Curatola Petrocchi 2016:303–304, also 2015:115). In this chapter, I mean to show how the configuration of some Inka sites of worship concorded with particular stories and traditions in which deities manifested themselves and spoke to humans, or perhaps vice versa, as certain Inka stories expressed specific oracular practices that took place in sanctuaries specially prepared to hear the god's "voice."

The Sanctuary of the Four Talking Fountains

In his two chronicles, the *Historia del origen y genealogía real de los reyes ingas del Piru* (Galvin Manuscript, ca. 1590) and the *Historia general del Perú* (1613), the Mercedarian friar Martín de Murúa twice recounted, with slight variations, the forbidden and tragic love story of Chuquillanto, a young and beautiful girl, "*ñusta* daughter of the Sun"[1]—an Inka noble devoted to the service of the Sun God and belonging to an important category of state servants named *acllacuna*, the "chosen women"[2]—and a shepherd called Acuytapia, who tended a flock of white llamas reserved for the sun cult (Murúa [1613] 1987:329–337, chaps. 91–92, [1590] 2004a:244–250, [1590] 2004b:fols. 144–147v). The story tells how the two lovers were petrified and turned into two large pillars of rock on top of Pitusiray Mountain, close to Calca, in the Yucay Valley.[3] In his illustrated chronicle, Felipe Guaman Poma de Ayala ([1615] 1980:1:93 [113], 160 [183 (185)], 243 [268 (270)], 248 [275 (277)]) pointed out this mountain—illustrating it and its two tapered peaks with accuracy—as a major oracular *huaca* in Antisuyu. Likewise, Guaman Poma probably also made the five watercolor illustrations that accompany the text of the story of Chuquillanto and Acuytapia in the Galvin Manuscript of Murúa's ([1590] 2004b:fols. 145v, 146,

146v, 147, 147v) chronicle, despite suggestions that two of them could have been the work of another hand (Trever 2011:52). Whoever the author may be, the two drawings illustrate the central episode in which Chuquillanto—conscientiously following the instructions given to her in dreams by a nightingale (*ch'eqollo*)[4]—sings, in the middle of the night, lying at the center of four fountains of "crystal-clear fresh water" in the sun sanctuary where she lives (Figure 9.1). Chuquillanto softly sings the words "micuc usutu cuyuc utussi cusin" (the plowman who eats the moving *utussi* [totora reed?] is happy), and the four fountains rapidly reply in turn, repeating the same lyrics. As suggested by the nightingale, the young girl interprets the quick reply of the fountains as a good omen and an encouragement to continue her relationship with Acuytapia. The story tells how the water of each of the fountain-baths, in which the *aclla* of the sanctuary performed their ablutions, ran in the direction of one of the four *suyus*, that is, the four macro-regions that formed the Inka empire. Even the name of each fountain is specified: *silla puquio* (fountain of pebbles)[5] was the Chinchaysuyu fountain; *llullucha puquio* (fountain of the confervae)[6] that of Collasuyu; *oqhoruru puquio* (fountain of the watercress)[7] of Contisuyu; and *chiclla puquio* (fountain of the frogs)[8] of Antisuyu. In the first of Murúa's chronicles—that of 1590 (2004a:249, fol. 145)—it is specified that every *aclla* at the site bathed only in the fountain corresponding to the *suyu* of which she was a native. As for the sacred fountains, it is said that when the shepherd Acuytapia, who was in the field tending to the Sun God's flock, first saw Chuquillanto coming toward him with another *aclla* and addressing him, he at first believed that those two beautiful creatures were the embodiment of "some of the four crystal-clear fountains celebrated throughout the highlands" (Murúa [1590] 2004a:247–248, fol. 144).

The belief that water can speak is an ancient and widespread one in the Andean tradition. I should recall in this regard the testimony given by the *yatiri* (Aymara healer) from Toconce, a small village in Antofagasta, Chile, who told anthropologist Victoria Castro (1988:117) that the ancestors

figure 9.1
Martín de Murúa,
*Historia del origen, y
genealogía real de los reyes
ingas del Piru*, fol. 145v, 1590.

"spoke with water; they spoke with the earth, with water, with the air," as well as the more categorical and revealing statement made by a peasant from Huarochirí, in the highland of Lima, when questioned by Frank Salomon about the nature and essence of Pariacaca, the paramount local deity, who was identified with a high snow-covered peak and whom historical sources from the sixteenth and seventeenth centuries describe as a powerful oracle in Inka times. The Huarochirian peasant replied to Salomon's question with these precise words: "Pariacaca is the sound water makes in the stream

in winter. By listening to it, you can tell whether it will be a good year for crops" (Salomon and Niño-Murcia 2011:232). The belief that Andean deities can manifest themselves and "speak" through water is fully consistent with the Andean notion of *sami*, which Catherine Allen studied in the small community of Soncco, about 60 km northeast of Cuzco, and which clearly has the same connotations as the ancient notion of *camac*, the "animating force" that Gerald Taylor (1974–1976) and Frank Salomon (1991:16) unraveled thanks to their philological analysis of the Quechua Huarochirí manuscript (1609), as well as the colonial Quechua dictionaries. Allen (2002:33, 36), in fact, not only explains *sami* as an "animating essence" but also recalls how, in the Sonquinos' system of beliefs and representations, "rivers and streams provide a tangible manifestation of the *sami's* flow." In addition, the term *sami* corresponds to what the Aymara shepherds of the Macha area, in the province of Chayanta, northern Potosi, call *animu*. Ethnomusicologist Henry Stobart (2006:27), who spent extended periods with them, posits that the Machas use the term to refer to "the animating quality or essence of living things," which in their conception is consubstantial not only to the beings of the animal kingdom but also to phenomena of nature like the mountains and certain rocks. In addition, Stobart (2006:27–30, 2007) points out that the word *animu* is also used to indicate all forms of sound. This establishes a clear semantic connection between "sound" and "animating energy" and indicates that for Andeans sound traditionally constitutes the primary manifestation of every being endowed with life. The notion of *animu* has also been thoroughly analyzed by Xavier Ricard Lanata (2007:77–90), based on his observations among the Quechua-speaking shepherds of the Ausangate massif, in the Cuzco region. According to this people, the animating force—or "essence in act" (*esencia en acto*), as Ricard (2007:82–83) prefers to define the term *animu*—would be distributed, as a kind of emanation, by the *apus* (lords, sacred mountains) that manifest themselves and make their voices heard to shamans only through the sound of the wind. Similarly, Carolyn Dean (2011:30) emphasizes, in a seminal study of the aesthetics and symbolic dimension of Inka fountains, how the sound of water, along with the movement and the reflection of light on the water itself, gave an impression of animateness—an effect that was intentionally sought by those who built these hydraulic works. Likewise, Mónica Gudemos (2008:133–134) notes how many ancient Andean ceremonial spaces are characterized precisely by their locations that are endowed with some natural source of sound or by having works such as canals or ducts meant to give out sound when water flows or drafts go through.

In fact, as Jeanette Sherbondy (1982:74, 1992:60) and other scholars have pointed out, many *huacas* (deity-shrines) in the Cuzco *ceque* system are represented precisely by springs, fountains, baths, and canals, or by rocks and structures that were close to watercourses or hydraulic works (Bauer 1998:23; Bray 2013:166).

It, thus, comes as no surprise that in one of the idolatry trials held in 1662 by the extirpator Bernardo de Noboa, one of the most sacred sites of the people of San Pedro de Mangas in the colonial province of Cajatambo (central-northern highlands of Peru) was a spring called Rimay Puquio (Spring that Speaks), located not too far from the village. The community's Indian priests headed there in procession on certain ceremonial occasions, accompanied by young women—in the document described as "virgin or single women"—playing drums (*tinyas*) and carrying pitchers full of *chicha*. In the spring, the priests made sacrifices, burned offerings, and called upon the deity of the place as "the owner of the *puquio*" and "the mother who raises water." This extra-human entity appeared and spoke with them under the guise of a woman "of such great height"—we read in the deposition given by one of the Indian women summoned to confess in the trial—"that she competed with the big mountain adjacent to the said town of Mangas" (Duviols 2003:600, 612, 619).[9]

As for the "single" or "virgin" women who took part in the oracular rituals of the Mangas community, they clearly correspond, *mutatis mutandis*, to the "daughters of the Sun," that is, the *acllacuna* of the Inka empire mentioned in the tale of Chuquillanto related by Murúa. In light of the historical and ethnographic information provided, the story told by Murúa, with its four fountains that spoke to an *aclla*, turns out to be fully consistent with the system of Andean collective representations and ritual practices. But this is not all. The fact is that when in both his texts and in a drawing of the Galvin manuscript Murúa ([1613] 1987:331–332, [1590] 2004a:249, fols. 144v–145, [1590] 2004b:fol. 145v) indicates the existence of a shrine "with large and sumptuous palaces of the Sun, many rooms superbly built" and above all with four fountains,

figure 9.2
A satellite view of Chachabamba. Courtesy of Google Earth.

each one located on each of the four cardinal directions, this was not a mere legend or a figment of the chronicler's fantasy, but instead a precise reference to specific sacred Inka sites, as is proven by the sanctuary of Chachabamba. This site lies on the left bank of the Vilcanota River, 5 km away as the crow flies from the Inka citadel of Machu Picchu and about 40 km away from the section of this same river that is known as the Yucay Valley. Chachabamba was first located and studied in 1940 by the Wenner Gren Scientific Expedition to Hispanic America led by Paul Fejos (1944:37–41).[10] The site is at present being jointly studied and excavated by Peru's Ministry of Culture and the Centre for Andean Studies of the University of Warsaw in Cuzco, headed by Mariusz Ziólkowski.[11]

Chachabamba lies at a crossroad and close to where a brook, known as Chachabamba or Santa Rita, running down the mountain from south to west of the site, flows into the Vilcanota River (Figure 9.2). Therefore, the sanctuary of Chachabamba lies on what in the Andes is known as a *tinku*—a Quechua term that indicates "the union of two things" (Holguín [1608] 1952:342)[12]—just like the Coricancha, the great Inka oracular temple in Cuzco dedicated to the Sun God, or the

ancient sanctuary of Chavín de Huántar (first millennium BCE), which, according to archaeological evidence and documentary sources,[13] was also a major oracle. That Chachabamba was a place of worship is clearly indicated by the small temple of the *huaca*-boulder that was the main structure at the site (Figures 9.3 and 9.4). Built atop a large boulder that dominates the Vilcanota riverbank and with the very same rock, polished and carved, protruding inside and taking up almost all of its inner area, this structure is conceptually similar to other major sacred Inka buildings that enclose outcrops, like the Temple of the Sun (the so-called Torreón) of Machu Picchu, the Intiwatana in Pisac, or the House of the Rock at Caquia Xaquixaguana (now known as Huchuy Qosqo). However, it should be noted that unlike the latter, the southern side of the small temple at Chachabamba is completely open, facing a plaza with restricted access that is delimited on its three other sides by as many buildings. On its frontal side, facing the plaza, the sacred boulder has a large seat and a small four-step stairway exquisitely carved, following a formal pattern that is fully analogous to that of the "ceremonial stone" found near the so-called Watchman's Hut at Machu Picchu (Figure 9.5) and the "carved stone

figure 9.3
The front (south side) of the *huaca*-boulder temple at Chachabamba. Photograph by Marco Curatola Petrocchi.

figure 9.4
The back (north and west sides) of the *huaca*-boulder temple at Chachabamba. Photograph by Marco Curatola Petrocchi.

with steps" at Saywite (Dean 2010:pl. 6). Another large seat is carved on the opposite (north) side of the stone facing the Vilcanota River. This is a key part of the site. The strong, ceaseless sound of the river roaring thunderously a few meters below the boulder is heard throughout all of the shrine, thus giving rise to a highly emotional aural experience. For those in the plaza, it is as if the sound were coming from within the sacred rock itself. Yet the most striking characteristic of the archaeological site of

figure 9.5
The ceremonial stone
near the Watchman's
Hut at Machu Picchu.
Photograph courtesy of
Donato Amado.

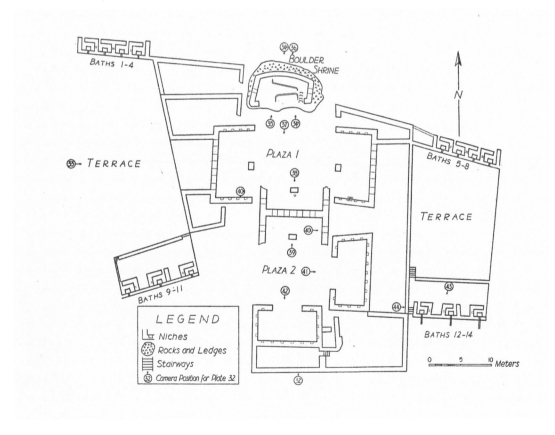

figure 9.6
A plan of Chachabamba. Reprinted from Fejos 1944:38, by permission of the Wenner-Gren Foundation
for Anthropological Research, Inc., New York.

figure 9.7
Drone photography
of Chachabamba.
Courtesy of the Dirección
Desconcentrada de Cultura
de Cusco, Ministerio de
Cultura, Peru.

Chachabamba, which somehow connects it with the tale of Chuquillanto, is that it has four sets of baths on its corners: two rows of four bath-fountains on its northeastern and northwestern corners, and two rows of three bath-fountains on its southeastern and southwestern corners, according to a fully symmetrical pattern (Figures 9.6–9.8). The supply of water in these baths was ensured by a complex, branching hydraulic system that was fed by a stone canal that derived the water from the brook south of the site. Chachabamba shows that shrines like the one described in the tale of Chuquillanto and

figure 9.8
Bath-fountains on Chachabamba's southwestern corner. Photograph by Marco Curatola Petrocchi.

Acuytapia, with the four "talking" fountains, actually existed in the Inka world. This, therefore, suggests that in the ancient Andes the ontological and epistemological dualism separating the world of the senses from the world of ideas, which was so deeply ingrained in the Western tradition from Plato to Descartes, did not exist.

The Sanctuary of the Speaking Sun Fountain

Perhaps the most famed "talking" fountain of the Inka world was that of Susurpuquio, where, according to the Inka traditions surrounding the rise of their empire, the Sun God appeared to the prince Inca Yupanqui, who would shortly thereafter become ruler under the name of Pachacuti. At Susurpuquio, the Sun announced the future power

and glory that awaited Inca Yupanqui and urged the prince to render the cult that was due to him. This event marked the beginning of Inka expansion and, historiographically speaking, can be considered the watershed that separates the legendary history of the first eight Cuzco rulers from that of the final members of the dynasty, emperors of Tahuantinsuyu and "children of the Sun," whose life and feats were recorded in song, *quipus* (knotted-string record devices), painted boards, and other data-recording media. The apparition of the Sun at Susurpuquio is related by the chroniclers Pedro Sarmiento de Gamboa ([1572] 2001:87, chap. 27) and Cristóbal de Molina ([ca. 1574] 2008:21–22), as well as by the Jesuit priest Bernabé Cobo ([1653] 1964:2:78–79, bk. 12, chap. 12). However, all the latter did was repeat what had already been said by Molina, who achieved a deep knowledge of the history and religion of the Inkas, as well as their language, during the many years he was the parish priest of the Hospital de Naturales in Cuzco. The *Fábulas y ritos de los Incas*, which Molina wrote around 1574, is, in fact, the more detailed account of the myth of the Sun's apparition at Susurpuquio. Molina ([ca. 1574] 2011:17) says the Sun called Pachacuti "from within the spring," saying, "Come here, son, do not be frightened: because I am the Sun, your father, and I know that you will conquer many nations. Take very great care to worship me and remember me in your sacrifices." Once again, we see that the deity, in this case the Sun God himself, appears and speaks to humans through a spring or a fountain.

Susurpuquio apparently simply means "a flowing spring" (Calvo Pérez 2008:21). In a well-known paper on "the image of the Sun and the Susurpuquio *huaca*," Tom Zuidema (1974–1976:204, 213–214) posited that this *huaca* must have been located in Callachaca, a royal estate appanage of Prince Amaru Tupa, the son of Pachacuti and brother to Tupa Yupanqui. Callachaca is located on a hill on the left side of the Huatanay Valley, less than 4 km as the crow flies east of Huacaypata, the main plaza of Cuzco (Niles 1987:15–21). Zuidema came to this conclusion on the basis of a laconic and obscure reference made by Joan de Santa Cruz Pachacuti Yamqui, an Indian nobleman from the province of Canas and Canchis and author of a history of the Inka kings written around 1613 in a quite convoluted Andean Spanish. Pachacuti relates that on the eve of the decisive battle against the Chanca people about to attack Cuzco, the future Inca Pachacuti, who had apparently been headed toward Yuncaypampa (possibly the modern-day village of Yuncaypata), decided instead to turn back to Cuzco "even before arriving at Callachaca." On a hillock close to Lucri, he "had a vision of a young man, who announced his victory over the invaders" (Pachacuti Yamqui Salcamaygua [ca. 1613] 1993:217, fol. 18). Lucri (Lucrepata) is a place close to the city, less than 1 km east of Huacaypata, and therefore relatively distant from Callachaca. Despite that, both Zuidema (1974–1976:213) and Brian Bauer (1998:86–87) believe that Susurpuquio may have been the spring in Callachaca known as Susumarca, due also to a slight assonance of their names. Susumarca

is mentioned as the eighth *huaca* on the fifth Antisuyu *ceque* (line) in the *Relación de los adoratorios huacas del Cuzco*, a very detailed account of the sacred places around the capital of the Inkas that was written around 1559, quite probably by the *corregidor* Polo de Ondegardo,[14] and inserted in full by Father Bernabé Cobo in his mid-seventeenth-century chronicle *Historia del Nuevo Mundo* ([1653] 1964:2:177, bk. 13, chap. 14).

Unlike Callachaca, the site of Lucri, mentioned by Pachacuti, is in the vicinity of the center of the ancient city of Cuzco. Father Molina states that Inca Yupanqui had a vision while he was going to visit his father, Inca Viracocha, at Caquia Xaquixaguana, a major Inka settlement some 18 km as the crow flies north of Cuzco above Calca. It should be pointed out, however, that Molina does not make the slightest reference to the Chanca war. He presents the story as the foundational myth of the empire and of the Sun cult. In other words, if we abide by Molina's account, the spring of Susurpuquio must have been somewhere along the road that led from Cuzco to Caquia Xaquixaguana, the initial stretch of which corresponds to the first Antisuyu *ceque*. As reported by the *Relación de los adoratorios huacas del Cuzco*, this *ceque* began at Coricancha. It first went across Rimac Pampa ("the plain, the flat space that speaks") and then passed through the ravine of Patallacta, where there was a sacred fountain called Pacha "in which the Inca washed himself on a given time," as well as another one called Corcorchaca, to which ground shells were offered. Next, the road passed near Amaru Marcahuasi, which was the house of Amaru Tupa, the brother of Tupa Yupanqui. According to the 1559 account, the following *huaca* on the first Antisuyu *ceque* was Tipucpuquio, a warm-water fountain Bauer identified as a spring close to the community of Huaylla Cocha, and next came another sacred fountain called Quinuapuquio, which had two "springs-water dispensers" and in all likelihood is the monumental fountain nowadays known as Tambomachay. As a matter of fact, Tambomachay was originally the name of another sacred place close by, where Inca Pachacuti used to stay whenever he went hunting and which probably is the

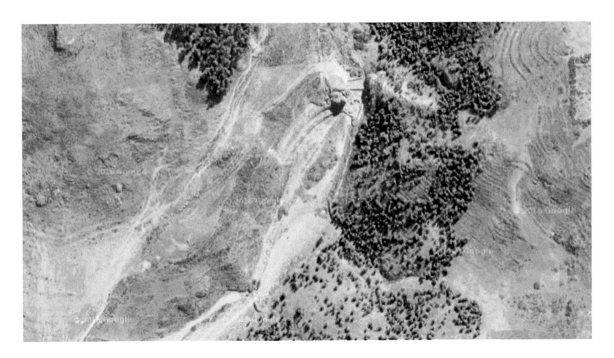

figure 9.9
A satellite view of the archaeological site at Chuspiyoq. Courtesy of Google Earth.

site currently called Pucapucara (Bauer 1998:76–77; Cobo [1653] 1964:2:175, bk. 13, chap. 14). It is, thus, clear that there were many "*huaca*-fountains" along the Antisuyu road, but not one called Susurpuquio, the extraordinary importance this one had in Inka history and religious ideology notwithstanding.

Still, between the *huacas* of Amaru Marcahuasi and Tambomachay (Pucapucara) is an archaeological site not yet studied, which has certain features that suggest it may well have been the celebrated place where the Sun God appeared before Pachacuti, foretelling the rise of the empire and establishing his cult among the Inka. It is an Inka architectural complex of a clearly ceremonial nature located in the ravine of Chuspiyoq (Place of the Flies), less than 3 km to the northeast of Coricancha (Figure 9.9).[15] The site is distinguished by a huge and quite special rock formation with a high protuberance on its frontal-upper part (Figure 9.10) and a large, meticulously carved, rectangular-shaped concavity on its frontal-lower part (Figure 9.11), quite similar to that of many other sacred stones (*huacas*), like that of Incallacta, located in a deep ravine of restricted access northwest of the site and associated with a

waterfall (Figure 9.12). The concavity evokes the shelter of Titicala, the sacred rock in the sanctuary of the island of Titicaca, or of the Sun, from which, according to Inka belief, the Sun first emerged (Figure 9.13; Ramos Gavilán [1621] 1988:116, 124, chaps. 17 and 19; cf. Bauer and Stanish 2001:196–202). Titicala had an oracular character, as was noted by the first Spaniards, Diego de Agüero and Pedro Martín de Moguer, who explored the Inka province of Collao. Pedro Sancho ([1534] 1606:344), the secretary of conquistador Francisco Pizarro who recorded their testimony, wrote in his 1534 *Relación para Su Magestad* that the inhabitants of the Lake Titicaca plateau "went to make their offerings and sacrifices to a large stone called Thichicasa that is on an island, *where or because the devil hides there and speaks to them.*"[16]

The rock at Chuspiyoq is related to, and fully integrated with, a sophisticated hydraulic system with canals, fountains, and even a pond that was created by a big stone dam that was built some 210 m down the ravine. The rock is on the northernmost end of this small artificial lake that—if the site really had a symbolic or formal correspondence

figure 9.10
The sacred rock at Chuspiyoq. Photograph courtesy of Donato Amado.

figure 9.11
The rectangular-shaped concavity of the sacred rock at Chuspiyoq. Photograph by Marco Curatola Petrocchi.

figure 9.12
The sacred stone at Incallacta, Bolivia. Photograph by Marco Curatola Petrocchi.

figure 9.13
Titicala, the sacred rock on the island of the Sun. Photograph by Marco Curatola Petrocchi.

figure 9.14
The stone dam of the artificial lake at Chuspiyoq. Photograph by Marco Curatola Petrocchi.

figure 9.15
The ceremonial platform, the western canal, and the crevice of the sacred rock at Chuspiyoq. Photograph by Marco Curatola Petrocchi.

with the oracular shrine of Titicaca—may have been a representation of Lake Titicaca itself (Figure 9.14). The sacredness of the Chuspiyoq rock is highlighted by the fact of its being situated at the *tinku* (meeting) of two stone canals. One of these canals runs from east to southeast and passes its last section at the foot of the aforementioned "rectangular-shaped concavity." The other canal, which had its water flow controlled by means of a kind of fountain-bath-sluice on well-carved stone blocks, goes along the upper west part of the rock formation, alongside the base of a platform that seems to have been a true *ushnu* (Inka sacred platform for ritual performance; Figure 9.15). Then the canal comes down from west to southwest of the rock, significantly increasing its gradient. In this latest section, its bed is fully stepped and is flanked on its right side by a stone staircase (Figure 9.16). The

figure 9.16
The stepped canal and the staircase of the sacred rock at Chuspiyoq. Photograph by Marco Curatola Petrocchi.

canal ends in a fountain that empties its waters into the pond close to the southernmost part of the rock, on the same spot where the east–southeast canal also drains away. A monumental fountain lies just a few meters away, at the center of the pond's northern shore. It is formed by a large stone-slab backdrop and an unusually wide basin on finely worked stone blocks and empties directly into the pond (Figure 9.17). Behind the fountain and in front of the "rectangular-shaped concavity" on the sacred rock is a courtyard with restricted access. A big rectangular, prismatic, altarlike stone overlooks the courtyard; it leans toward the enclosure's northern side and is aligned with the fountain (Figure 9.18). East of the altar, the courtyard is delimited on its northern and eastern sides by niched structures like those found in major Inka religious centers consecrated to the Sun, like

Pacarictambo (Maukallaqta) and Pachacamac. They are also similar to Pachacuti's mausoleum at Patallacta (modern-day Kenko) and above all to the shrines of Aqchapay (modern-day Quillarumiyoq, in the Ancahuasi district in Anta, Cuzco; Bauer and Barrionuevo Orosco 1998:77) and Tipón (in the Oropesa district in Quispicanchi, Cuzco), which have many structural and functional similarities with Chuspiyoq. Immediately behind the east niched wall, in the shelter of the slope of the ravine, is another canal that flows into the pond, precisely in front of the point where the two canals on the sacred rock pour their water in the same basin. It should also be noted that the sacred rock at Chuspiyoq has a long, deep, and narrow transverse fracture that partially separates it from the slope to which it belongs and on which the aforementioned ceremonial platform rests (see Figure

figure 9.17
The monumental fountain and the ceremonial courtyard with niched walls at Chuspiyoq. Photograph by Marco Curatola Petrocchi.

figure 9.18
The prismatic stone altar at Chuspiyoq. Photograph by Marco Curatola Petrocchi.

figure 9.19
The crevice of the sacred rock at Chuspiyoq. Photograph by Marco Curatola Petrocchi.

9.15). The crevice is so narrow that only one person at a time can pass through it (Figure 9.19). It is, in fact, almost invisible unless one passes in front of its entrance, which is at the upper end of the stone staircase flanking the canal to the west of the rock. This does not seem to be a mere coincidence and suggests that the staircase was especially made for someone who had to climb it and "disappear" into the rocks; or vice versa, for someone who had to come out of the crack and walk down to the pond, someone who had to make his appearance as if out of nowhere in some highly dramatic ritual performance. On the opposite side—the boulder's eastern side—the crack ends just in front of the prismatic stone altar (Figure 9.20).

Finally, it is worth pointing out what may actually be no more than a simple curiosity or coincidence: when seen from the altar stone—that is, from the east—the upper part of the big sacred rock appears to be an impressive human head in profile that points northward and is looking upward (Figure 9.20). Depictions of stones that end in a human head and which were major *huacas* can be found in three of Guaman Poma's drawings: one in the Galvin manuscript (Murúa [1590] 2004b:fol. 96v) and two in the *Nueva corónica y buen gobierno* (Guaman Poma de Ayala [1615] 1980:1:235 [261 (263)], 242 [268 (270)]; Figure 9.21). One of these drawings, showing the "idols and *huacas* of Antisuyo," includes two stone pillars with human heads atop Pitusiray, which is

figure 9.20
The east side of the sacred rock at Chuspiyoq. Photograph by Marco Curatola Petrocchi.

precisely the mountain connected with the tale of Acuytapia and Chuquillanto. Lisa Trever posits that the depiction of stone idols with certain anthropomorphic traits in Guaman Poma is probably due to late medieval Christian imagery. However, this does not seem to be true in the case of these three drawings, whose iconography has no correspondence to the European tradition, or in the case of another illustration of the Galvin manuscript that represents a talking stone with human eyes very similar to the prismatic stone altar at Chuspiyoq (Murúa [1590] 2004b:fol. 37v). We should also bear in mind that in the Andes there is an ancient and widespread belief that rocks can be a metamorphic state of both humans and animals (Dean 2015:224; Duviols 1978), whose original traits an attentive observer can distinguish in the stone. And as Trever (2011:42) herself points out, "seeing figures in stone *huacas* was, and remains, part of a process of visual imagination and active engagement between object and viewer."

Clearly, the sacred stone of Chuspiyoq demanded a strong aural and visual commitment of those who approached it; this enabled it to provide an extraordinary sensorial, emotional, mnemonic, and imaginative experience in which the physical and the ontological were indissolubly fused.

Some significant aspects of the sanctuary at Chuspiyoq—a shrine located along the path where the rise of Tahuantinsuyu was foretold to Pachacuti and that was symbolically related to the place where the Sun first came out; a site with architectural elements and features typical of the most sacred religious centers in the empire, like Pacarictambo, the origin place of the Inkas that according to Bauer (1992:122) could be an oracle, or Pachacamac, the pan-Andean sanctuary whose oracular god was believed to be the forefather of all *huacas* (Curatola Petrocchi 2011, 2016:278–281); a large rock in an unusual and intriguing shape, in full accordance with all the formal characteristics of many primary

figure 9.21
Felipe Guaman Poma de Ayala, *El primer nueva corónica y buen gobierno*, 261 [263], 1615. Courtesy of the Royal Danish Library (GKS 2232 4º).

Inka *huacas*; an aural holy place, provided with a monumental fountain, a canal with a stepped bed and regulated water flow, and a whole complex hydraulic system capable of giving out different sounds; a ceremonial space where ritual performances entailing the sudden disappearance or apparition of some personage took place—suggest that the Chuspiyoq sanctuary may well have been Susurpuquio, the famed spring where the Sun spoke to Inca Pachacuti and foretold the rise of the empire. If that was the case, the Inkas should congregate there to evoke and relive in a dramatic way that extraordinary founding event of their glorious history as masters of the Andes and of their identity

as chosen people of the Sun God. And if it was not so, it must still have been an important *huaca* the Inkas approached in order to listen to, and possibly even see, some powerful extra-human being.

Sanctuaries of Sound

As I mentioned at the beginning of this chapter, shrines of a strong aural nature—such as those of Chachabamba and Chuspiyoq—were quite common in the Andes and represent a long-standing religious tradition. In most of them, the sound of rushing water was a primary component, being regarded as the voice of the deity itself, which the local priests had the capability to understand. Thus, the oracle of Catequil in Huamachuco (northern Peruvian highlands) and various sites related to it in modern-day Ecuador, where its cult was widespread by Inca Huayna Capac (ca. 1493–1527), are all characterized by the presence of springs and fountains where water flows "with an exceptional force"—in the words of John Topic, Theresa Topic, and Alfredo Melly (2002:326)—and, therefore, in a very loud way. For their part, Helaine Silverman and Donald Proulx (2002:212), based on precise ethnographic observations they made in Usaca, a community in the lower Nazca Valley (southern coast of Peru) that has numerous underground watercourses, concluded that the deities of the ancient Nazca (third–sixth centuries CE) must have constantly demonstrated their presence and omnipotence through the sound that the rushing subterranean waters give out, which in many places is perceived as a "roar" that comes out of the earth.

In regard to sanctuaries characterized specifically by sound architectural structures, many northern Peru highland ceremonial centers of the Early Horizon (first millennium BCE) have inside their buildings elaborate stone conduits for ritual manipulations of water flow, like the stepped canal in the interior of one of the platforms at the site of Huacaloma, in the Cajamarca Valley, in which the descending water must have produced a resounding gurgling (Moseley 1985:49, 1992:143; Silva Santisteban 2001:38; Terada and Onuki 1985:209). However, the case better studied and more emblematic is that of Chavín de Huantar, the great oracular U-shaped sanctuary situated at the confluence of two streams in the upper Conchucos Valley. Its templar structures contain underground drains, as well as different sets of corridors, small chambers, and air ducts, that constitute true boxes of resonance for any sound produced inside the complex, including the gurgle of rushing water in the drainage system (see Lumbreras, Gonzáles, and Lietaer 1976). Archaeoacoustic studies carried out in the galleries and ducts of the Old Temple—that is, the sanctum sanctorum, where the monumental image of a god with feline features known as El Lanzón,

or the Great Image (Weismantel, this volume), is located—indicate that the whole building was rigorously planned to create, both inside and in the sunken circular plaza immediately outside, phantasmagoric acoustic effects directly related to the oracular activity (Kolar 2012, 2013).

The Akapana, the imposing stepped pyramid that dominates the grand ceremonial center of Tiwanaku (first millennium BCE), near the southern shores of Lake Titicaca, seems to have had analogous characteristics. Like Chavín, Tiwanaku was a holy place and a major long-distance pilgrimage destination. In addition, the iconographic evidence, such as the representation of the Staff God, seems to indicate that there could have been some cultic correspondence between the two sacred centers (Rowe 1962:21). Alan Kolata has suggested that the complex hydraulic system of the Akapana, the most sacred building at Tiwanaku, must have produced significant sound effects. His excavations of the structure revealed the presence of a "sophisticated and monumental system of interconnected surface and subterranean drainage ducts" of finely crafted stones (Kolata 1993:111–116, 2003:184). This hydraulic system drained the large amount of water that fell during the rainy season, from December to March, and accumulated in the enormous sunken patio on the summit of Akapana, from where it was discharged from terrace to terrace in the form of cascades through canals that were both open and underground. Kolata (1993:109, 2003:187) considers Akapana to have represented a sacred mountain with its springs and torrents running down its sides and claims the water must have given out an intense and vibrating roar that made the entire structure shake as it flowed down and along the canals inside the pyramid. This is fully consistent with William Isbell (2013) and Alexei Vranich's interpretation of the nature of Tiwanaku (Isbell and Vranich 2004:172–175, 181). According to these scholars, Tiwanaku was above all an oracular center, intentionally endowed with an extraordinary spectacularity. Its siting, spatial organization, and monumental facilities permanently being refurbished and renovated, along with its landscape, dominated by the snow-capped peaks of Illimani, the sacred mountain par excellence of the local Aymara populations (Reinhard 1987:43–45), essentially sought to instill an intensely emotive and mystical experience in the many pilgrims who visited the place. And what more astounding and shattering experience could these pilgrims have had than hearing at the climax of their approach to the oracular deity of the site its roaring voice rising from the very entrails of Akapana.

The Sanctuaries of the Whistling Serpent

Moving from the macro to the micro, the production of sound related to templar structures can also be observed in the Moche whistling ceramic vessels depicting architecture. Whistling vessels were produced by different ancient cultures of the North Coast of Peru, like the Vicús (second century BCE–sixth century CE), the Virú-Gallinazo (second century BCE–seventh century CE), and the Moche (third–eighth centuries CE). These vessels, which have a resonating chamber and one or two whistles, can produce sound—depending on their shape—when blown into from the outside, that is, when an individual is puffing directly into them, or from the inside by oscillation of the liquid inside. In the latter case, pouring water or some other liquid into the vessels, which often have a double chamber, creates a pocket of air that is then compressed by liquid displaced when the vessel is tilted. In this way, the air is pushed out through the whistle, which emits a high-pitched and lengthy sound. It has been verified that this whistling can have intense psycho-acoustic effects. In fact, as stated by Daniel Statnekov (1987:27–63) and Don Wright (1992), the sounds made by whistling vessels, which are characterized by low-frequency differential tones, bring about a remarkable increase in auditive sensibility and may cause visual or auditory hallucinations in the form of human and animal voices (Pérez de Arce 2004:29). It is possible that the *cántaros* (pitcher) *huacas* referred to in mid-seventeenth-century records of idolatries for the colonial province of Cajatambo (central-northern highlands of Peru), which "spoke" when

a spurt of water from a fountain flowed into them, belonged to this same class of objects (Curatola Petrocchi 2016:289). As stated previously, many whistling vessels represent architectural structures. Juliet Wiersema (2010:74, 2015:137) suggests that because they emit sound, or "speak," the Moche must have considered them to be "animated." Moreover, this scholar believes that these vessels were mimetic representations of real architectural structures, which due to their sound effects were thought of as the abodes of powerful extra-human entities.

The pottery studied and published by Wiersema (2010:275, fig. 2.37, 2015:135, figs. 5.26–5.27) includes a modeled ochre-and-cream-painted Moche IV vessel (MNAAAHP C-54615) with an elegant architectural structure atop its body (Figures 9.22 and 9.23). This structure consists of a single-chamber quadrangular building with a gabled roof adorned with a double step-shaped comb. Wiersema (2011:176, 182, 186, 188, 2015:106–118) describes it as "of the enclosed gabled type" and identifies it as a small-scale representation of the restricted-access chapel of primary ritual importance that arose on top of Moche pyramid complexes (*huacas*) and in which blood offerings and sacrifices were carried out. In the case of this Moche IV vessel, the chapel represents the sanctum sanctorum of a step pyramid. In fact, as Wiersema (2011:168, 188, 2015:106–108) has pointed out by means of a comparative analysis of analogous architectural ceramic models, the ochre and cream line-bands that run around the lower section of the vessel's body are an artistic convention for representing terraces, while the fourteen-stepped motives that are repeated around the upper half of the body represent the stairs leading to the most sacred part of the Moche *huacas*; in this specific case, they evince the absolute sacredness of the space they delimit. Therefore, the Moche vessel represents a step pyramid with a small temple on its summit that has a single frontal access point and walls decorated with three wide reddish parallel bands. The whistling mechanism of the vessel is hidden inside this scale model temple, which, acting as a resonance chamber, makes it seem as if the sound is coming from its interior.

figure 9.22
Moche IV architectural whistling vessel. Museo Nacional de Arqueología, Antropología e Historia del Perú C-54615. Photograph by Marco Curatola Petrocchi.

figure 9.23
Detail of the Moche IV architectural whistling vessel of Figure 9.22. Museo Nacional de Arqueología, Antropología e Historia del Perú C-54615. Photograph by Marco Curatola Petrocchi.

figure 9.24
The tropical rattlesnake *Crotalus durissus*. Photograph courtesy of Boris Klusmeyer.

A giant feline-headed serpent modeled in high relief lies on the floor around the temple. The creature, which slithers around the entire structure, has an enormous body covered with colored spots and a terrifying feline head with raised and open lips, apparently growling and grinding its teeth. Its snout lies on the threshold of the small temple's doorway, as if the monstrous serpent were about to slither inside. The very specific form of the rhomboid-shaped spots of its body and the way its tail is depicted—darker, thinner, and sharply bent in relation to the rest of the body—suggest that it is *Crotalus durissus*, a venomous pit viper more commonly known as a South American or tropical rattlesnake (Figure 9.24). This is a serpent of mostly nocturnal habits whose dark tail has a series of horny rings, the "rattles," that collide with each other and give out a sound vaguely similar to castanets when the animal slithers.

The association of the feline-headed serpent with the stepped-crest temple atop a stepped pyramid on the Moche whistling vessel is not fortuitous, since an analogous scene is found on other Moche architectural vessels that show the animal dwelling inside, as if the temple was its abode. In some cases, the serpentlike monster peeps out of the door of the small temple (Wiersema 2011:180–181, fig. 184 [Museo Amano 469], fig. 185 [Museo Larco, ML002901]), while in others it is shown slithering over the roof (Wiersema 2011:186–187, fig. 191

[Museo Larco, ML002904], fig. 192 [Museo Larco, ML002903]).

The scene of a sacred place to which access is restricted and in which bloody sacrifices take place, where a threatening and terrifying serpent appears at night and inside which a whistle is heard, as is shown and even "modulated" by the Moche whistling bottle I have described, has a striking resemblance to the ritual of consultation with the oracle of Pachacamac, as it was reported by sixteenth- and seventeenth-century chroniclers. One of them is don Pedro de la Gasca, the president of the Lima Audiencia (high court), who visited Pachacamac in the late 1540s, when the sanctuary still retained some of its past magnificence. In a short account written to Emperor Charles V and his court, Gasca ([1551–1553] 1998:30–31) relates how the Indians claimed that when they consulted Pachacamac the god usually appeared as a terrible and savage animal, like a serpent or a feline, often looking very angry and requiring offerings and human and animal sacrifices in order to placate his wrath.[17] Further details on the oracular rite that took place at Pachacamac are provided by the Jesuit José de Acosta in his *Historia natural y moral de las Indias*, published in 1590. Acosta is a particularly reliable chronicler. His data on Andean religion derive both from diligent field observations and from oral and written reports by great experts in Inka history and Andean society, like the aforementioned Polo de Ondegardo and Cristóbal de

Molina. In regard to the Pachacamac shrine, Acosta ([1590] 2008:168, bk. 5, chap. 12) states that he knew from a trustworthy source that in ancient times "the demon used to speak" and "to give answers" there, and on some occasions he appeared in the shape of "a colorful serpent."[18] The chronicler also describes, albeit briefly, the rite of consultation of the deity. He claims this usually took place at night. The priests would enter the sanctum sanctorum walking backward and then ask their questions with their backs turned toward the Pachacamac idol and with their bodies and heads leaning toward the ground. Then they waited for a response from the god, who finally manifested himself with a hair-raising and hideous "whistle" or "shriek."[19] Analogous information regarding the way the oracular rites unfolded, specifically referring to Cuzco, is found in the *Historia del célebre santuario de Nuestra Señora de Copacabana*, published in 1621 by Friar Alonso Ramos Gavilán. Ramos Gavilán acquired an extensive knowledge of Andean religion during the many years he spent carrying out pastoral duties in different places in the southern Peruvian highlands and in the high Titicaca plateau. He uses almost the same words as Acosta does regarding Pachacamac to say that in Cuzco the Andean priests consulted the *huacas* in the early hours of the night, bowed and with their backs facing the sacred oracular images, which usually answered by giving out some sort of terrifying whistle. And when speaking specifically of Coricancha, where this kind of ritual took place regularly, Ramos Gavilán explains that the deities who dwelled there, that is, Punchao (Young Sun) and Pachayachachic (Viracocha-Pachacamac), sometimes appeared in the shape of a multicolor serpent, just like Acosta claims Pachacamac often did.[20] Friar Antonio de la Calancha later emphasized the same topic in the first volume of his monumental *Corónica moralizada del Orden de San Agustín en el Perú*, which was published in 1638. Although Calancha was a relatively late chronicler, who followed Acosta and Ramos on this point, his chronicle provides the most detailed account of all regarding the oracle of Pachacamac. As a matter of fact, it includes all of the information gathered by the Augustinian order, which was in charge of

figure 9.25
The idol of Pachacamac with figures of felines and feline-headed serpents. Museo de sitio de Pachacamac. Ministerio de Cultura, Peru. Photograph courtesy of Daniele Giannoni.

the Pachacamac parish during the second half of sixteenth century. Calancha says that the priests of Pachacamac, the Sun, Viracocha, and the other major Andean deities all used to consult their gods when night fell and that the latter answered them with a "whistle."[21]

Finally, it is worth pointing out that the figures of the feline-headed serpents and the felines carved in bas-relief on the famous wooden idol (Figure 9.25) that was found in 1938 by Alberto Giesecke in the upper terrace of the so-called Painted Temple—that is, the temple of Pachacamac (Paredes Botoni 1985:79–80)—could easily have been representations of the snake and feline mentioned in Pedro de la Gasca's account or of the "colorful serpent" referred to by José de Acosta, in which guise Pachacamac showed himself to his priests. In effect, if the idol is an image of the Pachacamac god, as the historical sources[22] and its very own location indicate, it is very likely that the theriomorphic figures found lengthwise on the wooden stick are representations of the shape in which the deity manifested himself in his temple. Iconologically, both in its appearance and context, the feline-headed serpent of the Pachacamac whistling oracle is the same monstrous serpentlike being that dwelled in the whistling temple of the Moche IV architectural vessels.

Concluding Remarks

The similarity between the ritual of consulting the Pachacamac god described by the chroniclers and the scene represented on the Moche whistling architectural vessel is both surprising and cogent, and it indicates the existence of a long Andean oracular tradition of the central and northern Peruvian coast, at least from the Early Intermediate Period to the Late Horizon, according to which the deities used to reveal themselves and express their will in the most hidden part of their shrines through particular high-pitched sounds. Similarly, the Inka sanctuaries in which the voices of the gods materialized through the sound of rushing water seem to be the last link in an equally or more ancient

highlands oracular tradition, with antecedents in Tiwanaku, Nazca, and possibly Chavín. What is evident is that the sacred places of the ancient Andean world must emit some kind of sound, conceived as the voice of the divinity living there: a "voice" that all people approaching the threshold of the sanctuary could hear but whose "language" only the high priests of the deity could understand and translate into words comprehensible to the faithful. It was that "voice," that sound loaded with esoteric meanings and cultural significance, that defined the animateness and, therefore, the sacredness of a rock or any other object or place and differentiated it from simple inanimate matter.

In the essay "Vita" of the Einaudi *Enciclopedia*, the biologist Antoine Danchin (1982:1146) points out how in the collective imagination of Western society any entity's "living" status has been traditionally recognized by two characteristics: the capacity for movement and reproduction. Since ancient Greece, according to Danchin, "movement" would have been the indicator par excellence for fixing the difference between inanimate matter and living beings, that is, those endowed with a motor-element that gives them life. The data and evidence gathered in the present study confirm what I posed in "La voz de la huaca" (Curatola Petrocchi 2016) and demonstrate that, unlike Western tradition, in the pre-Hispanic Andes the attribute that characterized entities endowed with life force (*camac*) was fundamentally sound.

Certainly, the Inka, the last and most highly developed sociopolitical formation in the ancient Andean world, were the ones who created the greatest number of sanctuaries of a markedly aural nature. Chuspiyoq and Chachabamba are just two of the many shrines that the lords of Cuzco built in the imperial heartland, to which they devoted vast resources, and where they used all of their craftsmanship in stonework and in managing water, as well as their inimitable architectural landscaping skill. These sacred sites, wherein the sonic-aural elements vivified, strengthened, and charged the visual elements with meaning, gave their visitors an intense and direct sensorial experience of the empire's majesty, its mythical past, and its historical memory that was both emotive and cognitive. It was through these shrines that the Inka transformed their capital city, its environs, and the whole nuclear area of Tahuantinsuyu into a type of mega–Holy Land, one where the Sun God and the *huacas* continuously manifested their presence and expressed their will by making their voices heard—voices that had normative, performative, and authority-legitimizing roles on a scale that was probably even greater than that of the sacred texts of many ancient Mediterranean and Near Eastern societies (cf. Curatola Petrocchi 2008).

NOTES

1 "*Ñusta*. Princesa, o señora de sangre yllustre" (González Holguín 1952:264).

2 "*Acllacuna*. Las mujeres religiosas que estauan en recogimiento escogidas para el seruicio de su Dios el Sol" (González Holguín 1952:15).

3 For analytical studies on the tale of Chuquillanto and Acoytapia, see Alberti 1985 and Dedenbach-Salazar 1990.

4 "*Chheccollo* Ruiseñor. *Checcolloy runa*. El veloz apresurado en hablar" (González Holguín 1952:106).

5 In the 1590 chronicle of Murúa it is written "*Siclla puquio* que significa fuente de guijos" (Murúa 2004b:249, f. 145r). Probably the correct word is *silla*, since in the vocabulary of Domingo de Santo Tomás (1951:350) it is found "*sillarumi*, cascajo" and in the one of González Holguín the same term is translated as "China piedrecillas menudas" (1952:326), while *siklla* has another meaning, being a "planta campestre de muy hermosa flor azul" (Lira and Mejía 2008:448). In the 1613 text of Murúa the same fountain is called "*Sulla puquio*," glossed as "fuente de guijas" (1987:332, chap. XCI). Sabine Dedenbach-Salazar (1990), based on the entry "*Sulla sulla*. Rocio" of the vocabulary of González Holguín (1952:331) has proposed as translation "fuente del rocío," but it is probable that the word *sulla* was a mere error of the scribe and the original word was *silla*.

6 "*Lulluchha*. Ouas de los charcos" (González Holguín 1952:218).

7 In the Murúa text of 1590 it is written *Ocoruru puquio* (2004b:249), while in that of 1613 *Ocorura puquio* (1987:332, chap. XCI). "*Oqhorúru*, y más comúnmente *oqorúru*, m. *Bot*. Berro, género de plantas crucíferas que se desarrollan en lugares muy húmedos" (Lira and Mejía 2008:297).

8 In the Murúa chronicle of 1590 it is written *Chuclla puquio* (2004b:249), while in that of 1613 *Siclla puquio* (1987:332, chap. XCI). "Rana, animal terrestre: *checlla* [*Chiqlla*], o *hampato* [*hampatu*]" (Domingo de Santo Thomas 1951:196; 2013:2:655).

9 Causa de ydolatría contra los yndios ydolatras echiseros del pueblo de señor San Francisco de Mangas, 9 de agosto-21 de octubre de 1662 (Archivo Arzobispal de Lima, legajo V, expediente 2, ff. 30v, 52, 58v–59). Duviols 2003:577–656. See in particular pp. 597–598, 612–613, 619, 645–646, and 654.

10 The site of Chachabamba is mentioned also by Rowe (1946:222, 228), Angles Vargas (1988:3:220–229) and Hyslop (1990:124–125).

11 I am deeply grateful to Dominika Sieczkowska, codirector of the excavations at Chachabamba, for having pointed out the existence of this site to me, during the Interdisciplinary Seminar Pisac 2016 (Centro Académico Valentín Paniagua, Pisac, July 5–9).

12 "*Tincuc mayu*, junta de dos rios" (Anonymous 1951:84); "*Tinku*: Unión, encuentro, junta, juntura de dos cosas" (Lira and Mejía 2008:495).

13 Two early seventeenth-century sources describe—on the basis of local oral traditions—the sanctuary of Chavín as an oracular centre. One is the *Compendio y descripción de la Indias Occidentales* (1628), of the Carmelite Vázquez de Espinosa (1969:332–333, second part, bk. IV, chap. 54, n° 1732), and the other is the account of the mission that the Jesuits Pablo Joseph de Arriaga, Luis de Teruel, and Ignacio López made to the provinces of Ocros and Lampas, in the *corregimiento* of Cajatambo, in 1618 (*Letras annuas de la Provincia del Perú*) (Duviols 2003:725).

14 Magistrate representing the Spanish crown.

15 I am very grateful to the historian Donato Amado Gonzáles, from the Dirección Desconcentrada de Cultura de Cusco, Ministerio de Cultura del Perú, for showing me the Chuspiyoq sanctuary in July 2014.

16 "In mezzo desto [lago] sono due isolette picciole, nell'una delle quali è una moschea, & casa del Sole, la quale è tenuta in gran venerazione, & in essa vanno a fare le loro offerte, & sacrificij in una grande piedra, che è nell'isola, che la chiamano Thichicasa, doue, ò perche il Diavolo vi si nasconde, & gli parla, ò per costume antico, come gli è, ò per altro, che non si è mai chiarito, la tengono tutti quelli della prouincia in grande stima, & gli offeriscono oro, & argento, & altre cose. Vi sono meglio di seicento Indiani al servitio di questo luogo, & più di mille done, che fanno Chicca per gettare sopra quella piedra Thichicasa" (Sancho 1606 [1534]:344). The original text, in Spanish, of the Sancho chronicle has been lost. Fortunately, there remains the Italian translation published in 1606, in the third volume of the monumental collection of travel accounts compiled by the Veneto native geographer and humanist Giovanni Battista Ramusio (1485–1557).

17 "Pachacama parecía en diversas figuras de animales y ordinariamente en los más feos y bravos, como son serpientes y tigres, y respondía a los que les preguntaban mostrando muchas veces estar enojado y que se había de desenojar con sacrificios y, así, le sacrificaban sangre humana y otros animales" (Gasca 1998:31 [n. 33]).

18 "En este templo hay relación cierta que hablaba visiblemente el demonio, y daba respuestas desde su oráculo, y que a tiempo vían una culebra muy pintada" (Acosta 2008:168, bk. V, chap. 12).

19 "Ordinariamente era de noche, y [los ministros hechiceros] entraban las espaldas vueltas al ídolo—andando hacia atrás: y doblando el cuerpo e inclinando la cabeza poníanse en una postura fea, y así consultaban. La respuesta de ordinario era una manera de silvo temeroso, o con un chillido que les

ponía horror" (Acosta 2008:168, Bk. V, Chap. 12). The Inca Garcilaso de la Vega, possibly based on Acosta, repeats that "los sacerdotes y el rey entraban en su [of Pachacamac] templo a adorarle, las espaldas al ídolo (y también al salir) para quitar la ocasión de alzar los ojos a él" (Garcilaso 1991:1:394, bk. VI, chap. XXXI).

20 "Pagávales el demonio a estos bárbaros del Pirú sus sacrificios, sólo con hablarles, que en el templo que avía en el Cuzco dava respuestas, y les hablaba visiblemente, y a tiempos le vían en forma de una culebra muy pintada. El modo que tenía de consultar a las guacas los Indios era, que a primera noche entravan las espaldas vueltas al Idolo, agobiando el cuerpo hazía tras, inclinando la cabeça y aassí le consultavan la respuesta que el demonio les dava, era de ordinario una manwera de silvo temeroso [. . .] En esta casa del Sol en el Cuzco, tenía un Idolo llamado Punchao, en forma de un Sol [. . .] Este era el Dios principal de los Incas, en cuyo servicio se esmeraban, y en el del Idolo llamado Pachayachachic (que es como si dixéramos el hazedor del cielo)" (Ramos Gavilán 1988:166–167, bk. I, chap. XXVII).

21 "El modo de consultar dudas, o pedir respuestas los Sacerdotes en casos futuros o mercedes presentes, era entrar a prima noche vueltas las espaldas al ídolo, agobiando el cuerpo. Respondía con un silvo temeroso, i decía razones confusas, todas encaminadas a muertes o estragos de los Indios, vaticinio cruel i señorío infame" (Calancha 1974–1982:3:839, bk. II, chap. XI).

22 "Y así entramos con ella en una cueva muy pequeña, tosca, sin niguna labor; y en medio estaba un madero hincado en la tierra con una figura de hombre hecha en la cabeza de él" (Estete [?] 1968:383).

"Por todas las calles deste pueblo y a las puertas principales dél, y a la redonda desta casa, hay muchos ídolos de palo, y los adoran a imitación de su diablo" (Estete 1985:137).

Acosta, José de

[1590] 2008 *Historia natural y moral de las Indias.* Edited by Fermín del Pino-Díaz. Consejo Superior de Investigaciones Científicas, Madrid.

Alberti Manzanares, Pilar

1985 Los amores de Chuquillanto y Acoitapia: Análisis de los dos manuscritos atribuidos a Murúa. *Revista española de antropología americana* 15:183–207.

Allen, Catherine J.

2002 *The Hold Life Has: Coca and Cultural Identity in an Andean Community.* Smithsonian Institution, Washington, D.C.

Angles Vargas, Víctor

1988 *Historia del Cusco incaico.* 3 vols. Cusco.

Anonymous

[1586] 1951 *Vocabulario y phrasis en la lengua general de los indios del Perú, llamada quichua.* Edited by Guillermo Escobar Risco. Universidad Nacional Mayor de San Marcos, Lima.

Bauer, Brian S.

1992 *The Development of the Inca State.* University of Texas Press, Austin.

1998 *The Sacred Landscape of the Inca: The Cuzco Ceque System.* University of Texas Press, Austin.

Bauer, Brian S., and Wilton Barrionuevo Orosco

1998 Reconstructing Andean Shrine Systems: A Test Case from the Xaquixaguana (Anta) Region of Cusco, Peru. *Andean Past* 5:73–87.

Bauer, Brian S., and Charles Stanish

2001 *Ritual and Pilgrimage in the Ancient Andes: The Island of the Sun and the Moon.* University of Texas Press, Austin.

Bray, Tamara L.

2013 Water, Ritual, and Power in the Inca Empire. *Latin American Antiquity* 24(2):164–190.

Calancha, Antonio de la

[1638]
1974–1982 *Corónica moralizada del Orden de San Agustín en el Perú.* Edited by Ignacio Prado Pastor. 6 vols. Lima.

Calvo Pérez, Julio

2008 Léxico quechua. In *Relación de las fábulas y ritos de los Incas*, by Cristóbal de Molina, pp. 203–272. Fondo Editorial, Universidad San Martín de Porres, Lima.

Castro, Victoria

1988 Entrevista a un yatiri de la localidad de Teconce, II Región, Chile (agosto, 1979). In *Plantas medicinales de uso común en Chile*, vol. 3, edited by Cristina Farga, Jorge Lastra, and Adriana J. Hoffmann, pp. 117–119. Ediciones Paesmi, Santiago.

Classen, Constance

1993 *Worlds of Sense: Exploring the Senses in History and Across Cultures.* Routledge, London.

Cobo, Bernabé

[1653] 1964 Historia del Nuevo Mundo. In *Obras del P. Bernabé Cobo*, edited by Francisco Mateos, vols. 1–2, pp. 1–275. Biblioteca de Autores Españoles 91–92. Atlas, Madrid.

Columbus, Claudette Kemper

2004 Soundscapes in Andean Context. *History of Religions* 44(2):153–168.

Curatola Petrocchi, Marco

2008 La función de los oráculos en el imperio inca. In *Adivinación y oráculos en el mundo andino antiguo*, edited by Marco Curatola Petrocchi and Mariusz Ziólkowski, pp. 15–69. Fondo Editorial de la Pontificia Universidad Católica del Perú and Instituto Francés de Estudios Andinos, Lima.

2011 ¿Fueron Pachacamac y los otros grandes santuarios del mundo andino antiguo verdaderos oráculos? *Diálogo andino* 38:5–19. Universidad de Tarapacá, Chile.

2015 Deities. In *Encyclopedia of the Incas*, edited by Gary Urton and Adriana von Hagen, pp. 112–116. Rowman and Littlefield, Lanham, Md.

2016 La voz de la huaca: Acerca de la naturaleza oracular y el transfondo aural de la religión andina antigua. In *El Inca y la huaca: La religión del poder y el poder de la religión en el mundo andino antiguo*, edited by Marco Curatola Petrocchi and Jan Szemiński, pp. 259–316. Fondo Editorial de la Pontificia Universidad Católica del Perú and the Hebrew University of Jerusalem, Lima.

Danchin, Antoine

1982   Vita. In *Enciclopedia*, edited by Ruggiero Romano, vol. 14, pp. 1146–1205. Giulio Einaudi editore, Torino.

Dean, Carolyn

2010   *A Culture of Stone: Inka Perspectives on Rock*. Duke University Press, Durham, N.C.

2011   Inka Water Management and the Symbolic Dimensions of Display Fountains. *RES: Anthropology and Aesthetics* 59–60:22–38.

2015   Men Who Would Be Rocks: The Inka Wak'a. In *The Archaeology of Wak'as: Explorations of the Sacred in the Pre-Columbian Andes*, edited by Tamara L. Bray, pp. 213–238. University Press of Colorado, Boulder.

Dedenbach-Salazar Saénz, Sabine

1990   El tema del pastor en la literatura andina: El pastor Acoytapia y Chuquillanto, hija del Sol; Una ficción de la crónica de Murúa [ca. 1600]. In *Trabajos presentados al simposio "RUR" 6. El pastoreo altoandino: Origen, desarrollo y situación actual*, edited by Jorge A. Flores Ochoa, pp. 3–13. CEAC, Cuzco.

Domingo de Santo Tomás, fray

[1560] 1951   *Lexicon, o vocabulario de la lengua general del Peru*. Edited by Raúl Porras Barrenechea. Instituto de Historia, Universidad Nacional Mayor de San Marcos, Lima.

Duviols, Pierre

1978   Un symbolisme andin du double: La lithomorphose de l'ancêtre. In *Actes du XLIIe Congrès International des Américanistes, Congrès du Centenaire. Paris, 2–9 Septembre 1976*, vol. 4, pp. 359–364. Société des Américanistes, Paris.

2003   *Procesos y visitas de idolatrías: Cajatambo, siglo XVII*. Fondo Editorial de la Pontificia Universidad Católica del Perú and Instituto Francés de Estudios Andinos, Lima.

Estete, Miguel de

[1534] 1985   La relación del viaje que hizo el señor capitán Hernando Pizarro por mandado del señor gobernador, su hermano, desde el pueblo de Caxamalca a Parcama y de allí a Jauja. In *Verdadera relación de la conquista del Perú*, by Francisco de Xerez, edited by Concepción Bravo, pp. 130–148. Historia 16, Madrid.

Estete, Miguel de (?)

[1536] 1968   Noticia del Perú. In *Biblioteca peruana*, vol. 1, pp. 345–402. Editores Técnicos Asociados S.A., Lima.

Fejos, Paul

1944   *Archaeological Explorations in the Cordillera Vilcabamba, Southeastern Peru*. Viking Fund Publications in Anthropology 3, New York.

Garcilaso de la Vega, Inca

[1609] 1991   *Comentarios reales de los Incas*. Edited by Carlos Araníbar. 2 vols. Fondo de Cultura Económica, Lima.

Gasca, Pedro de la

[1551–1553] 1998   *Descripción del Perú*. Edited by Josep M. Barnadas. Centro de Estudios Regionales Andinos Bartolomé de las Casas, Cuzco.

González Holguín, Diego

[1608] 1952   *Vocabulario de la lengua general de todo el Perú: Llamada lengua qquichua o del Inca*. Edited by Raúl Porras Barrenechea. Universidad Nacional Mayor de San Marcos, Lima.

Guaman Poma de Ayala, Felipe

[1615] 1980   *El primer nueva corónica y buen gobierno*. Edited by John V. Murra and Rolena Adorno. 3 vols. Siglo Veintiuno, Mexico City.

Gudemos, Mónica

2008   Taqui Qosqo Sayhua: Espacio, sonido y ritmo astronómico en la concepción simbólica del Cusco incaico. *Revista española de antropología americana* 38(1):115–138.

Hyslop, John

1990   *Inca Settlement Planning*. University of Texas Press, Austin.

Isbell, William H.

2013   Nature of an Andean City: Tiwanaku and the Production of Spectacle. In *Visions of Tiwanaku*, edited by Alexei Vranich and Charles Stanish, pp. 167–196. Cotsen Institute of Archaeology Press, University of California, Los Angeles.

Isbell, William H., and Alexei Vranich

2004   Experiencing the Cities of Wari and Tiwanaku. In *Andean Archaeology*, edited by Helaine Silverman, pp. 167–182. Blackwell, Malden, Mass.

Kolar, Miriam

2013   Tuned to the Senses: An Archaeo-acoustic Perspective on Ancient Chavín. *The Appendix* 1(3). http://theappendix. net/issues/2013/7/tuned-to-the-senses-an-archaeoacoustic-perspective-on-ancient-chavin.

Kolar, Miriam, with John W. Rick, Perry R. Cook, and Jonathan S. Abel

2012   Ancient *Pututus* Contextualized: Integrative Archaeoacoustics at Chavín de Huántar, Peru. In *Music Archaeology of the Americas.* Vol. 1 of *Flower World*, edited by Matthias Stöckli and Arnd Adje Both, pp. 23–53. Ekho Verlag, Berlin.

Kolata, Alan L.

1993   *The Tiwanaku: Portrait of an Andean Civilization.* Blackwell, Cambridge, Mass.

2003   Tiwanaku Ceremonial Architecture and Urban Organization. In *Urban and Rural Archaeology.* Vol. 2 of *Tiwanaku and Its Hinterland: Archaeology and Paleoecology of an Andean Civilization*, edited by Alan L. Kolata, pp. 175–201. Smithsonian Institution Press, Washington, D.C.

Lira, Jorge A., and Mario Mejía Huamán

[1944] 2008   *Diccionario quechua-castellano/ castellano-quechua.* Editorial Universitaria, Universidad Ricardo Palma, Lima.

Lumbreras, Luis, Chacho Gonzáles, and Bernard Lietaer

1976   *Acerca de la función del sistema hidráulico de Chavín.* Investigaciones de Campo 2. Museo Nacional de Antropología y Arqueología, Lima.

Molina, Cristóbal de

[ca. 1574] 2008   *Relación de las fábulas y ritos de los Incas.* Edited by Julio Calvo Pérez and Henrique Urbano. Fondo Editorial, Universidad San Martín de Porres, Lima.

[ca. 1574] 2011   *Account of the Fables and Rites of the Incas.* Edited by Brian Bauer, Vania Smith-Oka, and Gabriel E. Cantarutti. University of Texas Press, Austin.

Moore, Jerry D.

2005   *Cultural Landscapes in the Ancient Andes: Archaeologies of Place.* University Press of Florida, Gainsville.

Moseley, Michael E.

1985   The Exploration and Explanation of Early Monumental Architecture in the Andes. In *Early Ceremonial Architecture in the Andes*, edited by Christopher B. Donnan, pp. 29–57. Dumbarton Oaks Research Library and Collection, Washington, D.C.

1992   *The Incas and Their Ancestors: The Archaeology of Peru.* Thames and Hudson, London.

Murúa, Martín de

[1590] 2004a   *Codice Murúa. Manuscrito Galvin: Historia y genealogía de los reyes incas del Perú.* Edited by Juan Ossio. Testimonio, Madrid.

[1590] 2004b   *Historia de origen y genealogía real de los reyes ingas del Piru.* Facsimile ed. Testimonio, Madrid.

[1613] 1987   *Historia general del Perú.* Historia 16, Madrid.

Niles, Susan

1987   *Callachaca: Style and Status in an Inca Community.* University of Iowa Press, Iowa City.

Pachacuti Yamqui Salcamaygua, Joan de Santa Cruz

[ca. 1613] 1993   *Relación de antigüedades deste reyno del Pirú.* Edited by Pierre Duviols and César Itier. Institut Français d'Études Andines, Lima, and Centro de Estudios Regionales Andinos Bartolomé de las Casas, Cuzco.

Paredes Botoni, Ponciano

1985   La huaca pintada o el templo de Pachacamac. *Boletín de Lima* 41:70–84.

Pérez de Arce, José

2004   Análisis de las cualidades sonoras de las botellas silbadoras prehispánicas de los Andes. *Boletín del Museo Chileno de Arte Precolombino* 9:9–33.

Ramos Gavilán, Alonso

[1621] 1988   *Historia del Santuario de Nuestra Señora de Copacabana*. Edited by Ignacio Prado Pastor. Ignacio Prado P., Lima.

Reinhard, Johan

1987   Chavín y Tiahuanaco: Una nueva perspectiva de dos centros ceremoniales andinos. *Boletín de Lima* 51:35–52.

Ricard Lanata, X.

2007   *Ladrones de sombra: El universo religioso de los pastores del Ausangate (Andes surperuanos)*. Instituto Francés de Estudios Andinos y Centro Bartolomé de las Casas, Cuzco.

Rowe, John H.

1946   Inca Culture at the Time of the Spanish Conquest. In *The Andean Civilizations*. Vol. 2 of *Handbook of South American Indians*, edited by Julian H. Steward, pp. 183–330. Bureau of American Ethnology Bulletin 143. Smithsonian Institution, Washington, D.C.

1962   *Chavín Art: An Inquiry into Its Form and Meaning*. The Museum of Primitive Art, New York.

Salomon, Frank

1991   Introductory Essay: The Huarochirí Manuscript. In *The Huarochirí Manuscript: A Testament of Ancient and Colonial Andean Religion*, edited by Frank Salomon and George L. Urioste, pp. 1–38. University of Texas Press, Austin.

Salomon, Frank, and Mercedes Niño-Murcia

2011   *The Lettered Mountain: A Peruvian Village's Way with Writing*. Duke University Press, Durham, N.C.

Sancho, Pedro (Pero Sanco)

[1534] 1606   Relatione per sua Maestà di quel che nel conquisto & pacificatione di queste prouincie della nuoua Castiglia, & successo, & della qualità del paese dopo che il Capitano Fernando Pizarro si partì, & ritornò a sua Maestà: Il rapporto del conquistamento di Caxamalca, & la prigione del Cacique Atabalipa. In *Delle navigationi et viaggi raccolte da M. Gio. Battista Ramusio: Volume terzo*, pp. 333–346. I Giunti, Venice.

Sarmiento de Gamboa, Pedro

[1572] 2001   *Historia de los Incas*. Miraguano Ediciones and Ediciones Polifemo, Madrid.

Sherbondy, Jeanette E.

1982   The Canal System of Hanan Cuzco. PhD dissertation, University of Illinois, Urbana-Champaign.

1992   Water Ideology in Inca Ethnogenesis. In *Andean Cosmologies through Time: Persistence and Emergence*, edited by Robert V. H. Dover, Katharine E. Seibold, and John H. McDowell, pp. 46–66. Indiana University Press, Bloomington.

Silva Santisteban, Fernando

2001   *Cajamarca: History and Landscape*. Minera Yanacocha, Lima.

Silverman, Helaine, and Donald A. Proulx

2002   *The Nasca*. Blackwell, Malden, Mass.

Statnekov, Daniel K.

1987   *Animated Earth*. North Atlantic Books, Berkeley, Calif.

Stobart, Henry

2006   *Music and the Poetics of Production in the Bolivian Andes*. Ashgate, Burlington, Vt.

2007   Ringing Rocks and Roosters: Communicating with the Landscape in the Bolivian Andes. Proceedings of the conference "Sound and Anthropology: Body, Environment and Human Sound Making," University of St Andrews, St Andrews. https://www.st-andrews.ac.uk/soundanth/work/stobart/.

Taylor, Gerald

1974–1976   *Camac, camay* et *camasca* dans le manuscrit quechua de Huarochirí. *Journal de la Société des Américanistes* 63:231–244.

Terada, Kazuo, and Yoshio Onuki

1985   *The Formative Period in the Cajamarca Basin, Peru: Excavations at Huacaloma and Layzon, 1982*. Report 3 of the Japanese Scientific Expedition to Nuclear America. University of Tokyo Press, Tokyo.

Topic, John R., Theresa Lange Topic, and Alfredo Melly

2002 Catequil: The Archaeology, Ethnohistory and Ethnography of a Major Provincial Huaca. In *Andean Archaeology I: Variations in Sociopolitical Organization*, edited by William H. Isbell and Helaine Silverman, pp. 303–336. Kluwer Academic and Plenum Press, New York.

Trever, Lisa

2011 Idols, Mountains, and Metaphysics in Guaman Poma's Pictures of Huacas. *RES: Anthropology and Aesthetics* 59–60:39–59.

Vázquez de Espinosa, Antonio

[1628] 1969 *Compendio y descripción de las Indias Occidentales*. Edited by Balbino Velasco Bayón. Biblioteca de Autores Españoles 231. Ediciones Atlas, Madrid.

Wiersema, Juliet B.

2010 The Architectural Vessels of the Moche of Peru (C.E. 200–850): Talismans for the Afterlife. PhD dissertation, University of Maryland, College Park.

2011 La relación simbólica entre las representaciones arquitectónicas en las vasijas mochica y su función ritual. In *Modelando el mundo: Imágenes de la arquitectura precolombina*, edited by Cecilia Pardo, pp. 164–191. Mali, Lima.

2015 *Architectural Vessels of the Moche: Ceramic Diagrams of Sacred Space in Ancient Peru*. University of Texas Press, Austin.

Wright, Don

1992 Peruvian Whistling Vessels: Pre-Columbian Instruments that Alter Consciousness through Sound. In *Music and Miracles*, edited by Don J. Campbell, pp. 156–162. Quest Books, Wheaton, Ill.

Zuidema, R. Tom

1974–1976 La imagen del Sol y la huaca de Susurpuquio en el sistema astronómico de los Incas en el Cuzco. *Journal de la Societé des Américanistes* 63:199–230.

10

Buried Alive

Buildings, Authority, and Gradients of Being in Northern Yucatan, Mexico

SCOTT HUTSON, JACOB WELCH, SHANNON PLANK, AND BARRY KIDDER

APPROXIMATELY TWO THOUSAND YEARS ago, people in what is now the Mexican state of Yucatan built an 18 km long stone causeway that connected four towns: Ucí, Kancab, Ucanha, and Cansahcab (figure 10.1) (Kurjack and Andrews 1976; Maldonado 1995). Mapping and excavations by the Ucí-Cansahcab Regional Integration Project (UCRIP) show that when this happened, Ucí was three times larger than the other three towns in terms of population size and monumental architecture (Hutson and Welch 2014). The towns that likely came under the authority of Ucí when linked to the causeway had their own leaders, and each had buildings at their cores that manifest access to and organization of local labor and resources. In particular, Ucanha had a building—Structure 92c-SubIV—that refers symbolically to leadership. Regional authority along the causeway underwent several transformations in Pre-Columbian times, and Structure 92c-SubIV played an active role in the maintenance of authority. Studies of other Maya architecture, both ancient and contemporary,

suggest that a building like Structure 92c-SubIV could have been alive (Stuart 1998; Vogt 1998).

The notion that a building can be alive brings us to the fraught anthropological discourse on "animism" (Kosiba, this volume). Not long ago, Graham Harvey (2006:xi) defined animists as "people who recognize that the world is full of persons, only some of whom are human, and that life is always lived in relationship with others." It is not always certain, however, what criteria differentiate persons from nonpersons or, more basically, what should be considered alive. Do nonhumans exist as persons merely because humans attribute personhood to them? Similarly, do inert objects live only because humans project life onto them? Alternatively, do nonhuman persons exist independently of human attribution? Or, taking a middle ground, does personhood or life grow from events and interactions in the process of everyday experience?

Some anthropologists (Henare, Holbraad, and Wastell 2007) have argued that what we refer to as animism differs from our own world so radically

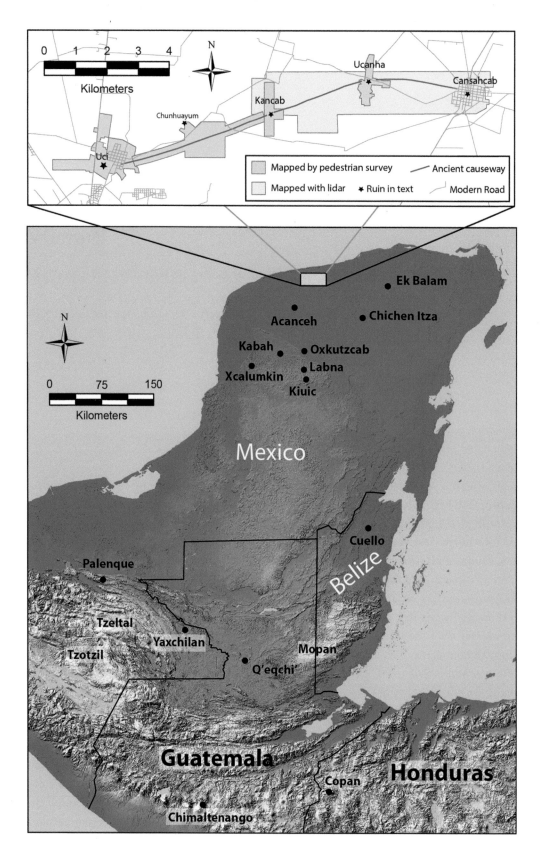

figure 10.1

A map of the Maya region, showing sites and areas mentioned in the text. Map by Scott Hutson.

that we may not be able to answer such questions. Indeed, Maya reality, in which stones live (Stuart 1996), plants get angry (Laughlin 2000:106), and tortilla griddles speak (Tedlock 1985:85), troubles our own interpretive categories (Harrison-Buck 2012; Hendon 2012). To get at the role that nonhuman persons play in the constitution of authority, however, we must be able to make some sense of who these persons are. In other words, before we begin the analysis, we must argue that "animists" are not so ontologically different that they completely elude interpretation. We, therefore, begin this chapter by challenging the idea that different ontologies are incommensurable. If this were the case, Maya ontologies would forever evade our understanding of them. We then use ancient Maya texts and iconography, as well as Maya ethnohistory and ethnography, to develop local answers to the questions about animacy, life, and personhood that we and others have posed. Grounded in these answers, we explore the life of Structure 92c-SubIV at Ucanha and make the case that this building was understood by the ancient Maya as a person and that its personhood derived from the protective role it played. This role was critical to the establishment and reestablishment of authority at Ucanha.

Animism, Modernism, and Radical Alterity

In 1941, Sol Tax wrote of the highland Maya of Guatemala that "like classical 'primitives,' their minds are clouded with animism: sun and earth, river and hill, are anthropomorphized; animals talk; plants have emotions; it is possible for a hoe to work alone; such things as fire and maize are capable of direct punitive action" (1941:38). Though Tax did not refer to Edward Tylor, his use of the word *primitive* in the same breath as *animism* clearly recalls Tylor's 1871 book *Primitive Cultures*. In that book, Tylor embraced a modernist standpoint in which the human self is separate from and looks out upon an objective world of nature (Bird-David 1999; Descola 2013; Latour 1993). When Tylor sifted through secondhand accounts of indigenous people who attribute human characteristics to all manner of

animals, vegetables, and minerals, he saw this as a misreading of "nature" (Kosiba, this volume). In the evolutionary approach to which Tylor was a major contributor, animism preceded the supposedly more developed views of the Western world. Animists have not yet learned to keep nature and culture apart; they continue to intermingle them, treating bears, for example, as if they were people. Tylor noted that in the West, animism survives only in children, who know no better, and séance-hosting spiritualists, such as those in London whom Tylor investigated firsthand (Stocking 1971).

Whereas Tylor appears to dismiss animism as an incorrect way of knowing the world, a stage from which most humans have long since advanced, later analysts such as Émile Durkheim and Claude Lévi-Strauss saw ways in which indigenous knowledge of "nature" did indeed have a foundation in reality (Bird-David 1999:70). Though it has become fashionable to say that none of these figures "took animism seriously" (e.g., Alberti and Marshall 2009:351; Haber 2009:418; Holbraad 2009:433), Severin Fowles (2013) makes the case that Tylor, Durkheim, and others were quite invested in animism. They, along with Protestant reformers and several other Western intellectuals, saw early modern religion as corrupt and felt that a return to "primitive religion" would put society on a more democratic course. According to Tylor, "a return to older starting points may enable [the anthropologist] to find new paths, where the modern track seems stopped by impassable barriers" (quoted in Fowles 2013:17).

Nevertheless, the question of how to take animism seriously has not been resolved. Several writers (Descola 2013; Holbraad 2009; Viveiros de Castro 2004) argue that recent attempts to understand animism retain a modernist separation of nature and culture that inhibits our capacity to understand animism on its own terms. These writers claim that keeping a separation between nature and culture restricts us to unproductive discussions of epistemology, causing us to miss the more radical challenges that animism poses in the realm of ontology. We often read that animists imbue material objects with nonmaterial characteristics: spirit, personhood, animacy, and more (Holbraad

2009). This attribution of life to the nonliving immediately gives rise to a contradiction. How can an inert thing be considered animate? The contradiction only holds if we insist, following a Western scientific, objective perspective, that a material object is just a material object. The premise in this perspective is that there is only one nature, namely an objective, "real" reality, independent of human experience (Ingold 2000:95). Following this premise, there is only one world, but there are many ways of knowing it and accounting for it. In other words, there is only one ontology (the ontology of the natural sciences, in which objects are just objects) but many epistemologies. From this perspective, animism would be a "more or less exotic way of accounting for the state of a world that our own system of conceptualization has established" (Descola 2013:33). From the perspective of Western ontology, Maya reality, in which rocks jump, griddles speak, and plants get angry, violates the objective rules of nature and, therefore, appears not as a valid reality but as a confused, exotic account of a universal, scientific reality (Kosiba, this volume). Yet reducing other realities to mere accounts of a single underlying reality prioritizes one particular ontology over all others and, as Martin Holbraad (2009:433) maintains, asserts the intellectual superiority of the West.

Eduardo Viveiros de Castro and others advocate that an approach to animism should instead begin from the premise that there are multiple ontologies. In other words, rather than anthropologist and animist inhabiting the same world but seeing it from different perspectives, anthropologists and animists occupy radically different worlds (Kosiba, this volume). To say that others inhabit a world that is radically different from our own, however, makes interpretation difficult. If interpretation involves "expanding familiar categories to illuminate unfamiliar instances" (Henare, Holbraad, and Wastell 2007:6), then we cannot interpret someone else's world because anything expressed with the help of our own familiar categories merely recapitulates our own cosmology. In other words, to take a different ontology seriously means that we can never understand other worlds. If this were the case, anthropology would lose relevance. Unable to understand other ways of life, anthropologists would not be able to use outsiders' ideas to critique our own (Graeber 2015:7; cf. Marcus and Fisher 1988). In lieu of interpretation, Amira Henare, Martin Holbraad, and Sari Wastell (2007:6) state that the goal should be to provide a "satisfactory description." But can we really achieve such a description? To the extent that description uses familiar terms to render an unfamiliar thing intelligible, it is not clear how description differs from what they define as interpretation. In fact, when those who embrace the position of radical alterity produce accounts of alien ontologies, some of these accounts, such as Alejandro Haber's (2009) case study of ancient "meat caches" in northwest Argentina, do indeed make sense of foreign practices through interpretation.

The ability to build a compelling understanding of someone else's world rests on the principle that worlds/ontologies are not always radically different. Furthermore, this possibility for commensurability and mutual understanding comes in part from the notion that "worlds" are not airtight. They are not eternally sealed off from the kinds of historical interactions (trade, migration, colonization) that require building common ground with outsiders (Clifford 1997; Weismantel 2015). Finally, even insiders often disagree with each other about the parameters of the "world" they occupy. The debate between David Graeber (2015) and Eduardo Viveiros de Castro (2015) over charms in Madagascar helps illustrate these points. Viveiros de Castro takes exception to Graeber's claim that a certain charm cannot prevent hail from falling on crops. Yet debating or doubting the efficacy of charms is common enough to be considered a pastime in the Malagasy communities where Graeber worked. Furthermore, *fanafody*, the form of medicine that encompasses charms, has been in continuous dialogue with non-Malagasy forms of medicine over the last several centuries and has "continuously incorporated foreign techniques, objects, and ideas" (Graeber 2015:10). *Fanafody*'s long and continued articulation with non-Malagasy ideas suggests that the world in which *fanafody* primarily operates is not so radically different as to be incommensurate with outside perspectives. Likewise, millennia of interaction between different Maya groups and between Maya speakers and non-Maya speakers, not to mention over a hundred years of anthropological investigation, boost our confidence that concepts like that of a living building are not beyond translation.

Maya Life and Personhood

We learn about Maya concepts of animacy and life from ethnographic, historic, and ancient sources. Of course, ethnographic sources come from a very different era than when Ucí flourished. Yet massive transformations (the fall of the Classic period, Spanish conquest and colonialism) did not greatly alter certain ontological aspects of indigenous heritage (Astor Aguilera 2010:81; Farriss 1984:8; Stross 1998:31). Just as neighboring regions in ancient Oaxaca each had different ways of animating buildings, suggesting potential differences in ontologies (Joyce, this volume), concepts of life certainly varied among Maya people in different places facing different circumstances. Nevertheless, "Maya communities participate in a shared frame of reference about living things. They endorse the claim that things might talk, entreat, assail, dissent, hunger, thirst, and assist" (Houston 2014:75, 80–81). In this section, we give shape to this frame of reference by looking closely at Maya understandings of life and personhood with particular attention to what these mean for stone buildings, such as Ucanha 92c-SubIV. We will draw several conclusions: (1) life is a matter of degree, a gradient as opposed to an alive/not alive dichotomy; (2) persons among the Maya are lively beings who often have souls and important roles in society; and (3) life and personhood normally depend on relations with other persons and are therefore fleeting.

Ethnographies from the Maya area reveal a bewildering array of things that exhibit some kind of life: houses, hammocks, altars, shrines, temples, time, brooms, bridges, crosses, crystals, caves, cookware, stones, stalactites, saints, salt, ceramic censers,

sewing machines, maize, masks, mountains, musical instruments, grinding basins, fires, ancestors, and more (Astor Aguilera 2010; Boremanse 2000; Brady et al. 2005; Stross 1998; Stuart 1996; Tedlock 1985:84; Vogt 1976:18–19). Yet not all things live (Astor Aguilera 2010:114). In particular, the ancient Maya do not show hides, leather, clay, straw, thatch, and leaves as animate (Houston 2014:98).

To get at what it means to be alive, we start with human life. In many contemporary Maya societies, something similar to the Tzotzil Maya concept of *ch'ulel* animates human life. Evon Vogt (1976:18) translates *ch'ulel* as "soul." Words like *vitality* and *energy* also capture the essence of the concept and work well as a translation for an ancient Maya word for life, *kux* (Houston 2014:78). Nonhumans may also have *ch'ulel*. Other Maya languages have cognate words attached to similar concepts, and many of these descend from the ancient Maya glyph *k'uh* (read as "god" but also referring to royal blood) and *k'uhul* ("sacred," "divine") (Houston 2014:81; Houston and Stuart 1996:291–292; McAnany, this volume; Ringle 1988). For contemporary Maya, *ch'ulel* circulates in the blood and is centered in the heart. For Maya past and present, strength and vitality equate with heat, and the heat of fires can give life to new houses (Gossen 1974; Houston 2014:98; Stuart 1998:417; Taube 1998; Watanabe 1992:87). One's animacy is also one's breath or wind (Hanks 1990:86), known in Classic-period texts as *ik'* (Houston and Taube 2000:267). Blowing into an entity can animate and give strength (Duncan and Hofling 2011:204; Stross 1998:32). Likewise, vital energy can leave its host in times of sickness and fright and when the host no longer acts in ways that are intelligible to others (Vogt 1976:18–21; Watanabe 1992:87–88).

Rather than an entity either being alive or not, there are gradations of energy. For example, stone stelae that depict Maya kings buzz with life. Some have names (Stuart 1996:151), others were carefully housed, fed, and memorialized over centuries (O'Neil 2009), and in a few cases a stela's text states that it is an embodiment or extension of a king or god and that mutilation could extinguish its life (Houston 1998; Houston and Stuart 1996; Stuart 1996:159–160). David Stuart (1996:157) has noted that both kings and stone carvings merited wrapping and bundling with cloth—*k'altun*—to protect their divine essence. To the extent that carvings such as Stela F at Copan also commemorate the completion of *k'atuns* (periods of seventy-two hundred days), these stones materialize time and motion (Reilly 2006:15). Other stones—obsidian blades, flint knives—have much lower energies (Houston 2014; Hruby 2007). At the least lively end of the spectrum, most common rocks would appear to be completely dormant, though their vitality might be awakened with tedious polishing (Houston 2014:93–97; Stuart 2010). So different stones express different capacities for life. Thus, interrogating the ontological status of an entire category of things (see Brown and Emery 2008:311–314) overlooks the notion that animacy falls on a gradient, colored by shades of gray, not black or white.

At the lively end of the spectrum, many entities could be considered persons. For many Maya groups, being a person means having a place in society. "Having a place" refers to several different conditions, not the least of which is having a destiny. Destiny, involving prognostication about one's character and one's profession, is determined in part through the qualities of the particular day (in the 260-day calendar, the 365-day calendar, the lunar cycle, etc.) on which one was born (Monaghan 1998). Having one's proper place in the calendar (deriving from one's day of birth or naming day) means being part of a totality. At the core of ancient Maya calendars, one finds units of twenty (months with 20 days, *k'atuns* that bundle together twenty periods of 360 days, etc.). The number twenty is, therefore, associated with totality and completion, no surprise given that the Maya used a vigesimal counting system. Monaghan notes that the word for person (*vinik* or *winik*) is also the word for twenty in many Maya languages. The calendar system could also endow a person with a name, derived from the day of birth. For many Mesoamerican groups, the name refers to the soul (Stross 1998:32; Stuart 1998:395–396). Among ancient and modern Maya, the souls to which names refer are not new, unique entities pertaining exclusively to a single biological being. Rather, souls are regenerated or

recycled; ruling lineages reused the same names, skipping generations (see McAnany, this volume; also Carlsen and Prechtel 1991; Gillespie 2000b). One's name acknowledges one's ancestors. Souls leave the human body at death, as breath expires. Ancient and modern Maya worked hard to usher it quickly and safely on its journey away from the realm of the living so that it could eventually return to inhabit a new being (Scherer 2016; Vogt 1976:22–24). In many ways, then, being a person is about being part of a broader system, about occupying a role in a collectivity.

If being a person and having a soul mean having a name and having a place among one's forebears and the totality of time, they also mean being an intelligible member of society. Working in Chimaltenango, the central town of Mam speakers in highland Guatemala, John Watanabe finds that soul loss occurs when one loses his or her social sensibility (see also McAnany, this volume). "Chimalteco souls derive not from some innate essence but from relative participation in an inclusive nexus of social interaction" (Watanabe 1992:90). Having a soul means being able to relate to others properly: "an existential eloquence of continual engagement with other individuals predicated on established cultural precedents" (Watanabe 1992:91). Here, having a soul means more than being alive. It means having a self in the sense of being able to act intelligibly in the context of a socially shared orientation to the world (Hallowell 1955; Monaghan 1998). Following this line of thought, beings among the Maya, even human beings, are not born as persons. They become persons through socialization. Their souls slowly gain strength and stability as they learn to relate properly to others.

To what extent can nonhumans be persons? The highland Maya make a sharp distinction: only humans have animal companions, a phenomenon that dates at least back to the Classic period (Gossen 1994; Houston and Stuart 1989; Vogt 1976:18; Watanabe 1992:87). Nevertheless, it is clear that humans are not the only beings with souls and, therefore, not the only persons. Paul Kockelman's fieldwork among the Q'eqchi' of Guatemala suggests that personhood, like life, can be assessed on a gradient. Kockelman argues that personhood derives from inalienable possessions such as body parts, names, kin, clothing, and place. "Some nonhuman entities (for example, animals, mountains, houses, and gods) possess some of these objects, and some human entities (for example, the dead, destitute, immature, and ill) do not possess all of them . . . the number of such objects individuals possess correlates with their degree of personhood" (Kockelman 2007:351). Santiago, the patron saint of Chimaltenango, provides an example of a nonhuman with a robust personhood and perhaps even a degree of sentience (Watanabe 1992:72–78). Santiago is made of wood and dresses as a Chimalteco. The Chimaltecos who pray to him in the Mam language consider him a Chimalteco, though Santiago was not born one. He rejected Chimaltenango the first three times he was brought there before finally resigning himself to a life in Chimaltenango's church after Chimaltecos whipped him hard enough to leave scars on his back. He is not a perfect Chimalteco, and he cannot respond to every request made of him, but he performs customary rites at the local shrines as often as people will take him. Not quite saintly, Santiago is a regular Chimalteco whose personhood is not guaranteed. As Watanabe (1992:78) explains, "he must constantly demonstrate his personhood through proper behavior, or risk losing it."

Since our archaeological case study focuses on architecture, we address where buildings fall on this gradient of personhood. Many researchers note that the ancient Maya equated buildings with humans and other animals. They made some doors look like mouths (Andrews 1995; Proskouriakoff 1963:52; Schele and Freidel 1990:71–72) and used body-part terms to refer to parts of buildings (mouth = door, hair = thatch roof, etc.) (Laughlin 1975; Stuart 1998:395). Some ancient buildings were bundled as if being clothed (Plank 2004:180; Wagner 2006). Michael Carrasco and Kerry Hull (2000) argue that ancient buildings were seen as turtles. Hieroglyphic texts show that some buildings received names (Houston and Stuart 1994), quite important given that possessing a name implies possession of a soul. Certain buildings

act like humans: texts at Yaxchilan suggest that a building can impersonate another place (McAnany and Plank 2001:107), while texts at Chichen Itza imply that a lintel can be the lord of the door it covers (Plank 2004:165). David Stuart (1998:396) argues that the red paint often found on buildings represents blood, the vital stuff of Maya life. Circular shrines in Belize likely made sounds in the wind and contained items (speleothems) considered to be alive (Harrison-Buck 2012).

One of the most illuminating sources of information regarding the potential personhood of buildings comes from house dedication ceremonies. Such ceremonies among the Tzotzil and Tzeltal Maya of the Mexican Highlands serve to ensoul the house (Stross 1998; Vogt 1998; see McAnany, this volume). Based on his work among the Tzotzil, Vogt (1998:26) stated that ensoulment "transforms a physical structure into one with a soul: with a place in and significance for society." Since having an intelligible and significant place in society meets the criteria for personhood discussed previously, ensoulment of a structure equates to actualization as a person. The house's place in Tzotzil society is to protect its occupants. Of the many different steps in house dedication rites, Vogt (1998:26) notes that the erection of a cross outside of the house "symbolizes" ensoulment. Linda Brown and Kitty Emery (2008) take this passage to mean that other steps in the dedication rite, such as offerings placed in the floor, are not part of the process of ensoulment. Our approach differs: to the extent that ensoulment enables the house to take its place in society as a protector, other steps in the dedication ceremony that prepare the house to fulfill its role as a guardian should also be considered part of the process of ensoulment. Among the Tzotzil, one of these steps includes a ritual circuit around the house, which "delineates the area safe from the demons and the Earth lord" (Vogt 1998:26). At each corner and in the center of each of the four walls, the shaman offers candles, chicken broth, and cane liquor to the ancestral gods and the earth lords. Another step includes offerings of the blood, feathers, and heads of hens and roosters placed in a hole dug into the center of the dirt floor. This step compensates the

Earth Lord (Vogt 1998:25) in return for the extraction of building materials (mud, vines, tree products) from his domain. Without such offerings, the Earth Lord will enslave the house's occupants or, at the very least, shake the house. Similar offerings to the four corners and the center during new house ceremonies have been documented among the Yucatec and Mopan Maya (Redfield and Villa Rojas 1934:146; Thompson 1930:69). In addition to demarcating boundaries and making offerings, ensoulment of nonhuman entities can include giving that entity a name, clothing it, purifying it, and feeding it (Stross 1998).

Making explicit reference to these ceremonies, archaeologists often identify subfloor offerings found through excavation as part of dedication rites that ensoul buildings (Freidel and Schele 1989; Mock 1998; Stuart 1998). We agree with this identification while also agreeing with Stuart (1998:374) that these buildings may already contain life before people ensoul them. In other words, there is a distinction between being alive and being a person. The materials incorporated into houses are considered animate, particularly quarried stone (Houston 2014:91) and wood from trees, which have blood-like sap and play a central role in Maya concepts of power, descent, centrality, and life (Astor Aguilera 2010; Carlsen and Prechtel 1991; Schele and Freidel 1990). Construction materials are "part of an animated forestscape whose agency does not wane once they reside in nonforested domains" (Brown and Emery 2008:330). Since these forest products can threaten the residents of the house, the offerings in the center of the floor should also be seen as compensation to them. The offerings to the forest products incorporated in the house suggest that a house is already alive. Thus, ensoulment is not the creation of life. It is the creation of personhood. Of course, the example of Santiago of Chimaltenango shows that personhood for the Maya cannot merely be created, it must be maintained. We will address this point in the context of ancient Maya buildings once we present the building at the core of our case study, Structure 92c-SubIV. We now turn to this structure, whose details suggest it was the seat of authority at Ucanha over many centuries.

Built and Bundled: Structure 92c-SubIV and Late Preclassic Politics

The Ucí-Cansahcab Regional Integration Project (UCRIP) seeks to understand transformations that brought about and resulted from the construction of the 18 km long causeway that linked four sites with monumental architecture and numerous rural households. As of 2018, UCRIP excavations consist of roughly one thousand shovel tests, over three hundred test pits at one hundred different platforms, and broad excavations of portions of over a dozen buildings. Excavations have uncovered offerings of full pots, likely containing food, in platforms of all sizes, from the smallest rural house platforms to the central plaza platform at Kancab (Hutson, Lamb, and Medina 2017; Joyce, this volume, also considers how social status affects participation in offerings to buildings). In most cases, these offerings were part of the original construction events, though in two cases (Structure N148 of the Chunhuayum site and Structure 44 at Kancab) they were placed when an earlier platform underwent modification. We interpret these as offerings to other-than-human beings. These offerings attempted to ensure the safety of the inhabitants but also brought "renewed life and continue[d] the cycle of being" (Becker 1993:67–68; Taube 1994; Vogt 1998:25). If this interpretation is correct, these offerings suggest that the buildings in which they are found were considered persons. These offerings may also reflect the possibility that materials in the building were considered alive and that offerings were needed so that these materials would not endanger the occupants (Brown and Emery 2008:329–330; see also Kosiba, this volume). In this context, we now turn to Ucanha Structure 92, a being whose long life was consequential to local authorities.

Pre-Columbian architecture at Ucanha covers approximately 2.2 km², of which 95 percent has been mapped with total station, LiDAR, or tape, compass, and GPS. We have chronological data on 8 percent of the approximately four hundred domestic compounds at the site. The earliest period of occupation is the Middle Preclassic period (800–300 BCE), during which an estimated 18 percent

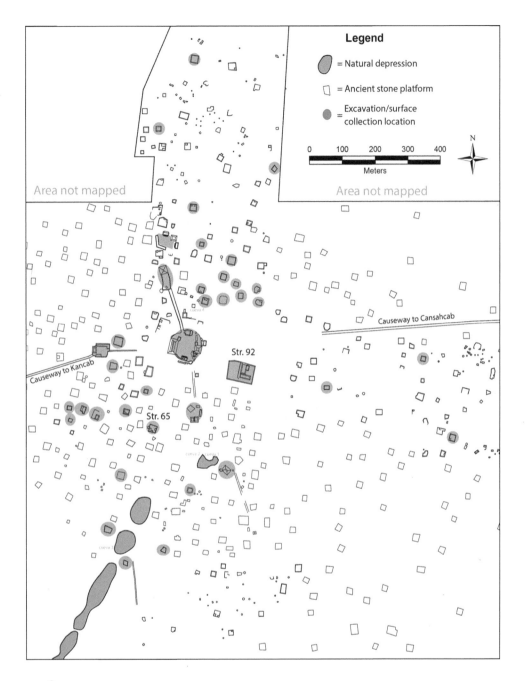

figure 10.2
A map of Ucanha, showing the locations of Structure 92 and Structure 65. Map by Scott Hutson.

of the domestic compounds were occupied. The ensuing Late Preclassic saw a major expansion, as we estimate, based on test pitting, that 84 percent of the site's domestic compounds were occupied. Population dropped in the Early Classic but then peaked in the Late Classic, during which 91 percent of the domestic compounds were occupied.

Located 80 m east of Ucanha's main group (Figure 10.2), Structure 92 is an 80 m × 55 m × 2 m platform supporting two superstructures that today reach a height of 5 m above the natural ground surface (Figure 10.3). It is Ucanha's largest platform by surface area and mound volume, nearly double the size of the site's largest pyramid.

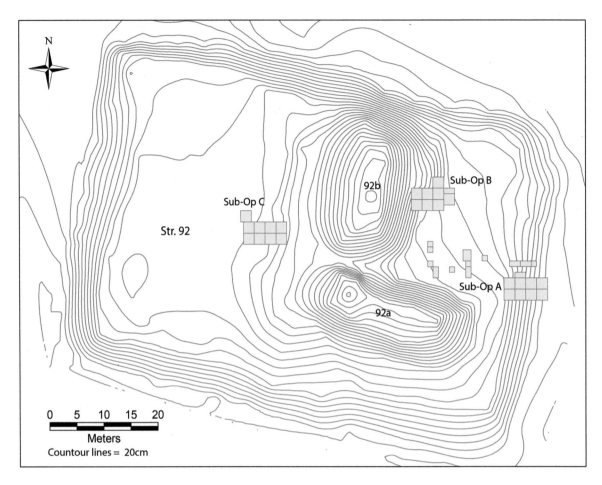

figure 10.3

A map of Structure 92, Ucanha, showing the location of excavations in 2014. Map by Scott Hutson and Jacob Welch.

Excavations in 2014 (122 m²) and 2017 (436.25 m²) revealed numerous construction stages. The final construction stages, which comprise the majority of the platform by volume, were completed in the Late Classic period.

Near the center of the platform, a 36 m² exposure (Sub-Op C) in 2014 revealed a well-preserved portion of Structure 92c-SubIV's west wall, buried by Late Classic–period fill. Additional excavations in 2017 uncovered more of 92c-SubIV's floor plan. Though the excavations showed that the Maya destroyed the south part of 92c-SubIV to make space for another Late Preclassic construction phase, the remains of the north part of the structure indicate that 92c-SubIV's floor consisted of a single room with a door to the west. The room's walls were plastered and measure

50 cm wide at their bases and consist of superimposed courses of stone, each course one stone wide (Figure 10.4). At most, four courses of the wall were preserved, reaching a maximum height of 90 cm above 92c-SubIV's plaster floor. The west wall features a rounded door jamb. At a distance of 2.5 m south of the door jamb, the wall of a new building (92-SubV) cut through the southern portion of 92-SubIV, leaving no traces of 92c-SubIV further south. The walls of 92c-SubIV were built on a plastered substructural platform 84 cm high. A step on the west side of the platform leads up to the doorway. The width of the building, from the west wall to the east wall, is 3.5 m. The full length is not known, but the length from the doorjamb to the exterior of the northern wall is 3.15 m. Pottery recovered from the sealed context below the floor

figure 10.4
Structure 92c-SubIV, looking east. The excavation unit bounded by pink string measures 2 m × 2 m. Photograph by Jacob Welch.

consists entirely of Late Preclassic material, indicating a Late Preclassic construction date.

At the base of the exterior face of the superstructure's west wall, a red-painted motif depicting a woven mat extends horizontally along the full length of the portion of the west wall (Figure 10.5). Typically, this mat motif is referred to as POP (or POHP), meaning "mat" in contact-period Yucatec (and other Maya languages). The glyph for the first month of the 365-day calendar carries a woven mat icon. Bishop Diego de Landa's sixteenth-century Yucatec Maya informants referred to this month as *pop* (Tozzer 1941). Maya scholarship often emphasizes the association between mats and governance (Bey and May Ciau 2014; Fash et al. 1992; Schele and Mathews 1998:137). The *Popol Vuh* refers to Quiche

lords as "keepers of the mat" (Tedlock 1985:203). The reed mat was used as an index for royalty in Maya art (Stone and Zender 2011:81). When adorning buildings, the mat motif often is said to mark a structure as a *popol nah*. In colonial dictionaries, as well as the Chronicle of Calkini, *popol nah* (translated literally in Yucatec as "mat house") carries the meaning "council house" (Ringle and Bey 2001:276). Yucatec dictionaries also name another type of council house (i.e., the *nikteil naah*) connected with flower and textile motifs (Schele 1998). Structures with mat, textile, and flower motifs are found across the Maya area and interpreted as council houses at sites such as Palenque (Schele 1998), Acanceh (Miller 1991), Copan (Cheek 2003; Fash et al. 1992), Chichen Itza, Ek Balam (Ringle

figure 10.5

The mat motif at the base of the west wall's exterior, Structure 92c-SubIV, Ucanha. The mat motif measures approximately 20 cm from top to bottom. Photograph by Jacob Welch.

and Bey 2001), Kabah, Labna, and Kiuic (Bey and May Ciau 2014). These structures date to the Late Classic period. Examples of Late Preclassic mat structures come only from Uaxactun (Valdés 1987) and Ucanha. While excavations demonstrate that 92-SubIV was not a deep room, the remaining portions could represent the northern end of a range structure—one form suggested for the *popol nah*.

The idea that buildings with mat motifs were council houses has come under scrutiny (Foias 2013; Plank 2004:141; Stone and Zender 2011). Andrea Stone and Marc Zender note that the mat sign more often reads JAL, as opposed to POP. The JAL sign does not exclusively signify mats; it also represents other woven material, including cloth, plaited hair, or twists of rope (Stone and Zender 2011:81). Therefore, Stone and Zender (2011:81) posit that the motif likely highlights the "economic value of woven cloth and the residents of palatial compounds,"

rather than marking a structure as a council house. Weaving was a major part of royal and noble identity among the Classic Maya (Hendon 1991; McAnany 2010:185; Miller and Martin 2004:94). Jeff Kowalski and Virginia Miller (2006) argue that textile patterns incorporated into the facades of various buildings in northern Yucatan attest to the economic importance of weaving and may refer to creation, given that creation is described in the *Popol Vuh* as an act of crafting. Though we have uncovered no direct evidence (e.g., spindle whorls, bone awls, etc.) of weaving at Structure 92, reading the mat sign as JAL does not require that weaving took place at the building.

We argue that Structure 92 indexes the emergence of formal authority at Ucanha in the Late Preclassic period, even if we cannot be certain that the mat motif signified governance by council. Excavations across Ucanha show that the site

figure 10.6
Red-painted vertical bands on the substructure of 92c-SubIV. Photograph by Jacob Welch.

grew to be many times larger than in the preceding period, and its house platforms were located unusually close to each other (see Hutson and Welch 2014:table 1). Centralized decision-making may have mitigated site-wide conflicts and tensions arising from such growth and crowding. Furthermore, settlement data published elsewhere (Hutson et al. 2016) suggest that Ucanha's authority at the end of the Late Preclassic extended beyond the site, thus creating a need for coordinated leadership. Rather than seeing the causeway as linking four previously independent sites, the causeway could instead be viewed as linking two settlement clusters—one consisting of Ucí and Kancab, the other consisting of Ucanha and Cansahcab—comprising two political units (eastern and western) separated by a buffer of very lightly populated space (Hutson et al. 2016). Since Ucanha had a higher population and larger monuments than Cansahcab, we envision Ucanha as the

capital of the eastern polity. Ucí unquestionably led the western polity, and its eventual growth to approximately three times the size of Ucanha suggests it subordinated or incorporated the eastern polity once the causeway was complete.

Excavations of 92c-SubIV show that the Maya treated 92c-SubIV differently than other buildings and indicate that this building was a person. One line of evidence consists of vertical swaths of red paint on the north and west faces of the substructure (Figure 10.6). Stuart (1998:396) has suggested that red paint on monuments "represents blood, where the soul is believed to reside, thus lending them a certain animate and precious quality." The painted mat design stands as a second line of evidence. Shannon Plank (2004:180) has offered epigraphic evidence showing that buildings adorned with textile patterns (such as the mat on 92c-SubIV) were "hung with textiles and were probably conceived as being 'dressed' for various

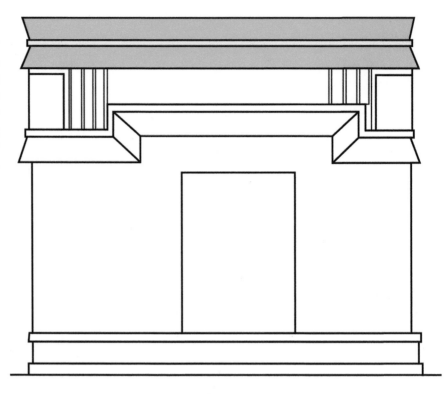

figure 10.7
A schematic drawing of a
Puuc structure highlighting
a common roof element that
makes the building appear
bound and cinched. Drawing
by Scott Hutson, after
Andrews 1995:158.

occasions." Among the Tzeltal Maya, living things are clothed in order to establish a boundary that will protect and ensoul them (Stross 1998:32). We might also say that the mat motif of 92c-SubIV bundles the structure. The ancient Maya bundled ancestors (Saturno et al. 2005), stelae (Stuart 1996), insignia of office such as headbands worn by kings (Stross 1988), and tools for blood sacrifice (Wagner 2006). All of these are powerful objects, some (stelae in particular) unquestionably alive. A broad range of Native American groups spoke with, sang to, made offerings to, and danced in the presence of bundled, bound, wrapped, or clothed entities (Astor Aguilera 2010:64, 102; Guernsey and Reilly 2006). Bundling may also preserve heat and vitality (Wagner 2006:64). Bundling of buildings may indicate that they, too, were persons. When Maya builders erected a new structure on top of an old one, they sometimes covered the old building—which might be left entirely intact, as in the case of the fabulously adorned Rosalila temple at Copan (Agurcia Fasquelle 2004), or destroyed, as in the case of Structure 5E-52 at Yaxuna (Freidel, Suhler, and Cobos Palma 1998)—with a layer of white stucco or marl. Elisabeth Wagner (2006) argues that the white wrapping protects and purifies the bundled entity. Stuart (1996:157) noted earlier that both kings and stone stelae underwent bundling ceremonies—*k'altun*—in order to protect and contain the divine essence. Such wrapping is equivalent to a human burial and likewise may function to ensure regeneration (Carlsen and Prechtel 1991) and to ensure that the soul passes to a later building (Freidel 1995; Wagner 2006:68). Architectural dedicatory texts at Yaxchilan, Xcalumkin, and Chichen Itza state that the buildings and doorways being dedicated are bound (*k'al*), which serves to protect these spaces (Plank 2004:46; see also Duncan and Hofling 2011). Decorative elements on Puuc structures create the impression that these buildings are bound and cinched (Figure 10.7).

Zender (2018) recently offered an alternative translation for *k'al* as "to raise up." Rather than referring to the tying of headbands on rulers in coronations scenes on stelae, Zender argued that the verb references the holding of a headband over the acceding king's head. This shifts focus to the critical moment in a coronation ceremony when a priestly attendant holds a headband over a ruler as an audience bears witness. Similarly, the use of the verb on lintels highlights their lifting over doorways. Stephen Houston and colleagues (2017) point out that the text of Laxtunich's Lintel 1 references its lifting. The lintel depicts mythic subjects lifting a lintel into place, highlighting the event as an important moment in Laxtunich's history and transforming the ritual event into a mythic act of creation that crystalized the power of Laxtunich's authority and the nature of the site's human hierarchy (Houston et al. 2017). Under this framework, the use of the mat could symbolize the ritual act of the building's creation, as opposed to the bundling of the building. Regardless of the exact translation of the verb *k'al*, the evidence of bundling occurs abundantly in ancient Maya iconography. Additional lines of evidence for the personhood of Structure 92c-SubIV derive from how it was treated during and after the remodeling of Structure 92, as we discuss in the following section.

Buried and Unburied: Structure 92c-SubIV and Late Classic Revitalization

The Late Classic period witnessed a political transformation. At the end of the Late Preclassic, Ucí reached its peak. Excavations in 2016 revealed that 94 percent of Ucí's architectural compounds were occupied, making Ucí three times the size of the second largest settlement on the causeway, Ucanha. Ucí consolidated its authority over the other three large sites in the area—Ucanha, Kancab, and Cansahcab—by chaining them to Ucí with the causeway. In the Late Classic period, however, Ucí shrank: only 61 percent of its compounds were occupied. In contrast, Ucanha grew slightly: 91 percent of its architectural compounds were occupied, as compared to 84 percent in the Late Preclassic period. In addition to Structure 92, we have conducted broad excavations in three other contexts at Ucanha: two domestic compounds (Structures 65 and 239) and the north structure (Structure 149) of the main group. All three excavations

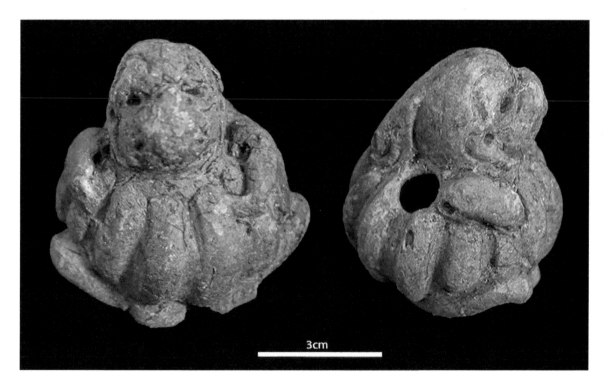

figure 10.8
An ink pot from Structure 65, Ucanha, showing front and side views. Photograph by Barry Kidder.

figure 10.9
A map of the Ucí site core, showing Structure E1N1-14. Map by Scott Hutson.

show significant labor inputs or greater economic diversity in the Late Classic period. Excavations at Structure 65 revealed the accouterments of a scribe—a bark beater and a simian ceramic inkpot (Figure 10.8)—as well as several architectural construction episodes, such as expansion of the basal platform with new retaining walls. At Structures 239 and 92, we also found two more bark beaters, which indicates that the production of paper for books or clothing was a component of Late Classic life at Ucanha. Excavations at Structure 149, on the north side of Ucanha's main plaza, show remodeling in the Late Classic period. Though we have not excavated the structures on the east, south, and west sides of the main plaza, they were probably also modified in the Late Classic period (and perhaps rebuilt, like Structure 149). Recent test pitting in the central plaza also uncovered a Late Classic burial. Finally, in the Late Classic period, Structure 92 became the 80 m × 55 m platform we see today, undergoing an enlargement that gave it the majority of its volume. Ucí has a similarly large platform, Structure E1N1-14 (Figure 10.9). Though damaged by bulldozers in the 1950s, Structure E1N1-14 once measured approximately 75 m × 60 m × 4 m, twice the volume of Structure 92 at Ucanha.

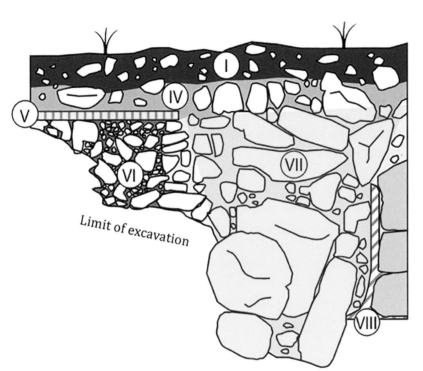

Limit of excavation

figure 10.10
A west to east profile of a portion of Op 92c, showing Structure 92c-SubIV (VIII), the redeposited fill in front and to the west of it (VII), and the floor destroyed in the process of ancient excavation (V). Drawing by Jacob Welch.

Recent excavations of 84 m² at E1N1-14, however, suggest that a large portion of it was built in the Late Preclassic period. People at Ucanha would have been aware of massive E1N1-14, a possible Late Preclassic palace at Ucí, and appear to have imitated it when expanding Structure 92. In sum, while Ucí lost population, Ucanha thrived in the Late Classic and its leaders did things—such as rebuilding the main group and expanding Structure 92 to ape Ucí's E1N1-14—that required major control of labor and that seemed to reassert a position of independent authority in the region.

As part of the enlargement of Structure 92, the builders removed the upper reaches of the 92c-SubIV superstructure but carefully buried the rest in fill, preserving the wall and its plaster coating to a height of 90 cm. While builders destroyed the southern extent of 92c-SubIV to make room for 92c-SubV, they took special care to preserve this portion of the building. The ancient Maya specifically chose this fragment of the building to incorporate into the new construction, a building practice observed across Mesoamerica (e.g., Temple of the Warriors at Chichen Itza). The act of dismantling a part of the building does not indicate the dismantling of its significance. Rather, its significance was preserved in the structure's northern side, which served as the core for a Late Preclassic building (92c-SubV) and later a Late Classic open-air platform (92c-SubI). The plaster floor capping this platform is 25 cm above the top of what currently remains of the 92c-SubIV wall (Figure 10.10). A final construction phase added approximately 30 cm to the height of the platform. If the platform in its final iteration had a plaster floor, it is not preserved, as is the case in most other constructions not subsequently buried. After the construction of 92c-SubI, people broke through 92c-SubI and V's plaster floors and dug a pit that exposed what was preserved of the western face of the 92c-SubIV wall. The pit was then carefully filled with large stones, leaving the wall intact once again. This fill contrasts starkly with the top 60 cm of the original fill under the 92c-SubI floor, which consists of smaller stones (Figure 10.10).

Interestingly, we have no evidence for the ancient excavations of 92C-SubV, which stood as a large, more elaborate Late Preclassic structure. Instead, the ancient Maya specifically targeted 92c-SubIV. Despite being an earlier phase of construction, this particular phase of building was remembered by the ancient Maya, who chose not to excavate 92c-SubV.

The burial, disinterment, and reburial of Structure 92c-SubIV recalls La Venta Offering 4, a tableau of sixteen human figurines and six celts (Drucker, Heizer, and Squier 1959). Long after the offering was buried, people dug a pit through several floors and exposed the heads of the figurines and then reburied them. Philip Drucker, Robert Heizer, and Robert Squier (1959:154) note that "the point of especial interest in this is the very accurate manner in which this inspection hole was located directly over the elliptical area occupied by the offering." As with those who dug up Offering 4, the diggers who exposed and then reburied the wall of Structure 92c-SubIV must have known what they were looking for and where to find it. Knowledge of the location of this feature may have become social memory passed from one generation to the next. To the extent that the building was a kind of person, knowledge of its location would have been like knowledge of the burial of an ancestor, underscoring the intertwining of social and physical houses (Gillespie 2000a). This intertwining was visible among the twentieth-century Chorti, who referred to ancestral lines as houses (otot) (Wisdom 1940:248–250; see also Vogt 1969:140–144). That Ucanha's Late Classic leaders remembered the location of a previously buried feature is not unique for the Maya area (Chase and Chase 1996; Coe 1990; Escobedo 2004). At Cuello, people remembered the original buried center-point of an earlier patio for hundreds of years, even after subsequent architectural modifications created a new center-point to the patio (Hammond 2010). We propose that the diggers at Ucanha exposed the mat motif as a way to show onlookers that Ucanha was once powerful enough to have had a mat house. Such a demonstration may have been part of an attempt to convince those present that there was indeed precedent and justification for Ucanha to become a seat of authority in the Late Classic, just as it was in the Late Preclassic, before succumbing to Ucí. Knowledge of this buried building and interactions with it may have helped differentiate nobles from others, as Arthur Joyce (this volume) notes for the Valley of Oaxaca.

We see the careful burial, excavation, and reburial of Structure 9c-SubIV as an additional line of evidence that the structure was perceived and treated as a person. We mentioned in a previous section that personhood cannot simply be created, it must maintain itself. As persons, players of a socially significant role, buildings interact with other people. Rather than being mere containers unchanged by those who reside within them, Maya buildings have biographies built from the kinlike relations in which they are entangled. Houses mesh with humans. A new Tzotzil Maya house is likened to a newborn child, and in its infancy, after construction is complete, the people who will live in the house place strands of their hair in the cracks of the walls, signifying that the house and its occupants belong to one another (Vogt 1976:55). A new house needs the same care as a newborn child; souls are not yet tightly tethered to either of them (see Loren's chapter for discussions of health and personhood). Insofar as the Maya equate houses with humans, the life of a house does not necessarily thrive on its own. Houses have to be fed (Nash 1970:16–17; see also Brown and Emery 2008:330). The Tzotzil also believe that a piece of a human's soul gets attached to those spaces where humans work and sleep. When a person dies, relatives must undo this intermingling, loosening the soul from the house (Vogt 1998:28; see also Scherer 2016). In Chimaltenango and other highland communities, afterbirth is buried in the floor of sweatbaths and, in order to avoid or mitigate crises, adults return to the sweatbaths that contain their afterbirth to make offerings (Houston 1996:139; Wagley 1949:23). One of Wagley's Mam informants stated that receiving the placenta of additional newborns makes the sweatbath happy. At Ucanha, the continuing interactions involving the building—the care it was given during its burial, disinterment, and reburial—suggest that 92c-SubIV, like any proper social person, was embedded in long-term relations with other actors.

Discussion

Thus far, we have argued that Structure 92c-SubIV served as a mat house, the spatial locus of leadership at Ucanha, and we placed it in the context of a regional political history in which Ucanha's authority expanded beyond the site in the Late Preclassic period, contracted as it fell under the dominion of Ucí, and expanded again in the Late Classic period. We have also argued that 92c-SubIV was a living, bleeding, clothed person with a long biography of interaction with others. In this section, we link these two themes—politics and personhood—in an attempt to contribute to the book's broader goal of critically reconsidering authority in light of the roles played by nonhuman persons.

If the generalized notion of Maya personhood consists of playing a role in a collectivity, of occupying an intelligible and interactive place in a social whole, what role did 92c-SubIV play, and how did it relate to authority? In short, the building's role was to support and protect authority. In the most literal sense, a mat house supports authority: the mat is the seat on which the leaders sit. Of course, ruling institutions must also be supported figuratively. Authority must be perceived and materialized (DeMarrais, Castillo, and Earle 1996; Latour 2005). Painting the mat motif on the facade of Structure 92c-SubIV durably instantiates the structure as the fount of authority. But the mat motif does not just communicate the building's status as the physical and symbolic core of the site's leadership. The building also protects Ucanha's leaders. Authority depends, in part, on ensuring that the ruling institution is in good health (Golden and Scherer 2013:399). Good health, be it for humans, animals, or buildings, means having a vital soul, and, as Patricia McAnany's chapter (this volume) demonstrates, management of souls was a central concern at many ancient Maya settlements. In the same way that walls serve as physical boundaries, ritual circuits along the four corners, four sides, and center of a new house erect social boundaries that give the house a role as a protector. The ensouled house guards the occupying family from demons attempting to enter the house, causing soul loss and sickness. In Structure 92c-SubIV, protection came from being bound. Whereas architectural dedication texts at sites such as Yaxchilan, Xcalumkin, and Chichen Itza state that the buildings were bound (Plank 2004:46), 92c-SubIV was symbolically bound by the textile/mat motif painted along its base. Among Yucatec speakers of Oxkutzcab, binding an altar (by fixing spirits to their appropriate places), which William Hanks (1990:337) compares to binding a house (by tying beams together with vines), offers protection and boundaries, defending the shaman against attacks from marauding spirits. From beyond the Maya world, several structures at Mitla, Oaxaca, were also bound in woven textile and matlike motifs (Guernsey 2006:31). We suggest that the binding of ancient structures also offered protection (Stuart 1996), perhaps in a way not completely unrelated to the amulets/*higas* discussed by Diana DiPaolo Loren (this volume). The textile painted on Structure 92c-SubIV can also be said to clothe the structure, a process that, like binding and ritual circuits, establishes boundaries and mediates interactions with the external world (Stross 1998:32).

The mat motif projects an image of good health: it communicates that Ucanha's leaders were protected from spiritual attack. Yet taking the Maya seriously means acknowledging that the mat motif is more than an image. It actively fends off malicious nonhuman beings. Humans within and beyond Ucanha might contest the power of its leaders, but contestation can also come from nonhumans. This perspective accepts the Mesoamerican notion that these other beings, glossed as spirits and demons in the ethnographies, are not precisely "supernatural" but inhabit the same realms as humans and form reciprocal, interdependent relations with humans (Monaghan 2000; Tedlock 1985). Thus, a critical take on authority grounded in a Pre-Columbian perspective would make the case that authority, the recognition of the legitimacy of a leader's acts, claims, and decisions, is not established solely through interactions between human leaders and human followers. It is also established through interactions between humans and nonhumans, as well as interactions among nonhuman persons, such as those between a spirit and a building.

The discussion of the personhood of Structure 92c-SubIV enables comments not just on authority, but also animacy. Here, we return to the question, posed in the introduction, of whether nonhuman persons are animate in themselves or animated by humans or something in between. In a previous section, we stated that personhood among the Maya is fleeting: it comes and goes, depending in part on the state of relations with others. Personhood, in other words, is not an essence, but a process of acts and entanglements. This appears to be at the crux of the famous interchange between Irving Hallowell (1960:24) and his much-quoted informant from the Berens River band of Ojibwe in Manitoba, Canada. When Hallowell asked whether all stones are alive, the old man replied "No! But some are." On the Yucatan Peninsula, as along the Berens River, being alive often depends on object biographies and social relations. Life accrues not solely from an essence within but from the frequency and richness of interactions. Sitting in a tent during a storm, an Ojibwe husband can hear what a thunderclap says, while his wife cannot, because the husband has a special relationship with the thunderbird, which appeared to the husband in a dream during his puberty fast (Hallowell 1960:34; Ingold 2000:102–106). Different things are located in different relational webs, such that a being that is alive for one person may not be for another.

Reflecting on his ethnographic work in Quintana Roo, Mexico, Miguel Astor Aguilera (2010:114) writes, "My j'meen [shaman] consultants only perceive a stone, a wooden cross, a crystal and so forth as having volition if they know, through direct relationship and communication with the object, that it has agency." Potentially anything can come into a relationship with a person. Therefore, whether or not a human treats a particular thing as a social being, an interlocutor, or some other force to be reckoned with depends on chance encounters, personal experiences, and the rest of the contingencies that we often call "context." We have seen this in ethnographic accounts of Maya houses, whose lives literally and figuratively intertwine with the lives of human occupants, and in the extended social life of 92c-SubIV. These examples suggest that for

the Maya, life unfolds in the course of "those very relations that are set up by virtue of a being's positioning in the world, reaching out into the environment—and connecting with other selves" (Ingold 2000:104, 2011:69–73). This kind of approach, in which life is not given automatically or independently of relations, can be called relational and has been explored among the ancient Maya (Hendon 2010; Hendon, Joyce, and Lopiparo 2014; Hutson 2010). McAnany (this volume) applies a relational approach with regard to personal destiny and the rejuvenation of souls.

The relational approach presented here and applied to Maya buildings such as Structure 92c-SubIV could be construed to mean that life depends on relations with humans. But must humans always be involved? Tim Ingold (2007, 2011), Manuel de Landa (1997), and Jane Bennett (2010), drawing inspiration from Gilles Deleuze and Felix Guattari (1987), stress that materials are "alive" because the substances of which they are composed are continuously in flux: rotting, eroding, cracking, wetting, drying. Durable objects seem stable only because their rate of change is too slow for human discernment. As noted previously, Maya materials, particularly those quarried or felled, have their own energy (Houston 2014), but it does not necessarily arise from the mechanical instability of the physical substances that compose them. In fact, humans can amplify the life in stones by polishing them. Yet in some instances, animacy may not be contingent at all on humans. The Q'eqchi' Maya consulted by Brady and colleagues (2005) see speleothems as alive because they grow and sweat on their own (see also Stone 2005). Indeed, in spite of the importance of reciprocity to certain forms of life, a few other-than-human persons, particularly malevolent ones, such as the *witz* of the Mam Maya or the night spirits of the Q'eqchi', do not need human acknowledgment. Though humans can strike deals with them in pursuit of certain outcomes (Boremanse 2000; Watanabe 1992:74–76), *witz* and night spirits can live without reciprocal engagement with humans. As to be expected, Maya understandings of the life and matter overlap only partially with the new materialisms (see also McAnany, this volume).

Conclusion

In this chapter, we have explored the ways a building—Structure 92c-SubIV at Ucanha—could be a person. We have also placed this building in a context of dynamic regional politics in order to see how its life was intertwined with the changing fortunes of leaders at Ucanha and their evolving relationship with leaders at Ucí. Discussing the personhood of nonhumans necessarily engages scholarship on animism. Though some have argued that "animist ontologies" are singular and inscrutable (Henare, Holbraad, and Wastell 2007), we concur with David Graeber (2015) and Mary Weismantel (2015) that people with such ontologies have long and complex histories of interaction with other groups and other ontologies, not to mention critical interpretive stances on their own worlds in the contexts of other worlds. These reflections and interactions establish the conditions for the possibility of understanding something of Maya ontologies, past and present.

Our take on buildings as persons highlights the broader question of what animates entities that Western ontologies often consider inanimate (see also Kosiba, this volume). Is a building alive and animate because of its relation with humans, or, as suggested in new materialisms literature (Bennett 2010; Deleuze and Guattari 1987), does it live because it contains an essential energy independent of humans? Maya ethnographic sources do provide examples of life independent of humans, but, taking into account a broader sweep of material (iconographic, archaeological, and ethnohistoric), the balance of these beings form social relations with humans and either depend on these relations or can at least be influenced by humans (Houston 2014:79). We, therefore, see a relational approach as most appropriate to our case study.

Relational aspects of Maya personhood include possessing a name (which links the entity to ancestors and to the calendar), a place (in terms of time, destiny, space, and social role), and the social intelligibility that enables long-term entanglements with other persons. Personhood among the Maya was not a strictly dichotomous, all-or-nothing essence but a matter of degree. Structure 92c-SubIV had life because it bled and was made from materials that live. But more than being alive, this structure played a social role. It was bundled and clothed like other persons and powerful beings. This allowed it to protect the leaders of Ucanha and to contribute to their authority in the Late Preclassic period. By playing this role, the structure acquired a place in society and a degree of personhood. The strong relations it formed with other people may account for the building's longevity. It was carefully preserved and remembered, even when buried and out of sight. It was open to and affected by ongoing relations as times and fortunes changed. At the least, it was vital enough, centuries after painters bound it with a mat motif, for leaders to exhume it and reuse it as part of new strategies for an ascendant populace.

REFERENCES CITED

Agurcia Fasquelle, Ricardo

2004   Rosalila, Temple of the Sun-King. In *Understanding Early Classic Copan*, edited by Ellen E. Bell, Marcello A. Canuto, and Robert J. Sharer, pp. 101–111. University of Pennsylvania Museum of Archaeology and Anthropology, Philadelphia.

Alberti, Benjamin, and Yvonne Marshall

2009   Animating Archaeology: Local Theories and Conceptually Open-Ended Methodologies. *Cambridge Archaeological Journal* 19(3):345–357.

Andrews, George F.

1995   *Architecture of the Puuc Region and the Northern Plains Areas.* Vol. 1 of *Pyramids and Palaces, Monsters and Masks: The Golden Age of Maya Architecture.* Labyrinthos, Lancaster, Calif.

Astor Aguilera, Miguel

2010   *The Maya World of Communicating Objects: Quadripartite Crosses, Trees, and Stones.* University of New Mexico Press, Albuquerque.

Becker, Marshall

1993   Earth Offering among the Classic Period Lowland Maya: Burials and Caches as Ritual Deposits. In *Perspectivas antropológicas en el mundo maya*, edited by Ma. Josefa Iglesias Ponce de León and Franciso de Asís Ligorred Perramón, pp. 45–74. Sociedad Espanola de Estudios Mayas, Madrid.

Bennett, Jane

2010   *Vibrant Matter.* Duke University Press, Durham, N.C.

Bey, George J., and Rossana May Ciau

2014   The Role and Realities of Popol Nahs in Northern Maya Archaeology. In *The Maya and Their Central American Neighbors: Settlement Patterns, Architecture, Hieroglyphic Texts, and Ceramics*, edited by George E. Braswell, pp. 335–355. Routledge, New York.

Bird-David, Nurit

1999   "Animism" Revisited: Personhood, Environment, and Relational Epistemology. *Current Anthropology* 40:S67–S91.

Boremanse, Didier

2000   Sewing Machines and Q'echi World View. *Anthropology Today* 16(1):11–18.

Brady, James E., Allan B. Cobb, Sergio Garza, Cesar Espinosa, and Robert Burnett

2005   An Analysis of Ancient Maya Stalactite Breakage at Balam Na Cave, Guatemala. In *Stone Houses and Earth Lords: Maya Religion in the Cave Context*, edited by Keith M. Prufer and James E. Brady, pp. 213–224. University Press of Colorado, Boulder.

Brown, Linda A., and Kitty F. Emery

2008   Negotiations with the Animate Forest: Hunting Shrines in the Guatemalan Highlands. *Journal of Archaeological Method and Theory* 15(4):300–337.

Carlsen, Robert S., and Martin Prechtel

1991   The Flowering of the Dead: An Interpretation of Highland Maya Culture. *Man* 26(1):23–42.

Carrasco, Michael D., and Kerry Hull

2002   The Cosmogonic Symbolism of the Corbeled Vault in Maya Architecture. *Mexicon* 24(2):26–32.

Chase, Arlen F., and Diane Z. Chase

1996   Maya Multiples: Individuals, Entries and Tombs in Structure A34 of Caracol, Belize. *Latin American Antiquity* 7:61–79.

Cheek, Charles D.

2003   Maya Community Buildings: Two Late Classic Popol Nahs at Copan Honduras. *Ancient Mesoamerica* 14(1):131–138.

Clifford, James

1997   *Routes: Travel and Translation in the Late Twentieth Century.* Harvard University Press, Cambridge, Mass.

Coe, William R.

1990   *Excavations in the Great Plaza, North Terrace, and North Acropolis of Tikal.* Tikal Reports. University Museum, University of Pennsylvania, Philadelphia.

Deleuze, Gilles, and Felix Guattari

1987   *A Thousand Plateaus: Capitalism and Schizophrenia.* University of Minnesota Press, Minneapolis.

DeMarrais, Elizabeth, Luis Jaime Castillo, and Timothy Earle

1996   Ideology, Materialization, and Power Strategies. *Current Anthropology* 37(1):15–32.

Descola, Philippe

2013   *The Ecology of Others.* Translated by J. Lloyd. Prickly Paradigm Press, Chicago.

Drucker, Philip, Robert F. Heizer, and Robert Squier

1959   *Excavations at La Venta, Tabasco, 1955.* Smithsonian Institution Bureau of American Ethnology Bulletin 170.

U.S. Government Printing Office, Washington, D.C.

Duncan, William N., and Charles Andrew Hofling

2011   Why the Head? Cranial Modification as Protection and Ensoulment among the Maya. *Ancient Mesoamerica* 22:199–210.

Escobedo, Hector

2004   Tales from the Crypt: The Burial Place of Ruler 4, Piedras Negras. In *Courtly Art of the Ancient Maya*, edited by Mary Ellen Miller and Simon Martin, pp. 277–279. Fine Arts Museum of San Francisco, San Francisco.

Farriss, Nancy M.

1984   *Maya Society under Colonial Rule: The Collective Enterprise of Survival.* Princeton University Press, Princeton.

Fash, Barbara W., William L. Fash, Sheree Lane, Rudy Larios, Linda Schele, Jeffrey Stomper, and David S. Stuart

1992   Investigations at a Classic Maya Council House at Copan, Honduras. *Journal of Field Archaeology* 19:419–442.

Foias, Antonia E.

2013   *Ancient Maya Political Dynamics.* University Press of Florida, Gainesville.

Fowles, Severin M.

2013   *An Archaeology of Doings: Secularism and the Study of Pueblo Religion.* SAR Press, Santa Fe, N.Mex.

Freidel, David A.

1995   Preparing the Way. In *The Olmec World: Ritual and Rulership*, edited by Michael Coe, pp. 1–9. Princeton University Press, Princeton.

Freidel, David A., and Linda Schele

1989   Dead Kings and Living Mountains: Dedication and Termination Rituals of the Lowland Maya. In *Word and Image in Mayan Culture: Explorations in Language, Writing, and Representation*, edited by William F. Hanks and Don S. Rice, pp. 233–243. University of Utah Press, Salt Lake City.

Freidel, David A., Charles K. Suhler, and Rafael Cobos Palma

1998   Termination Ritual Deposits at Yaxuna: Detecting the Historical in Archaeological Contexts. In *The Sowing and the Dawning: Termination, Dedication and Transformation in the Archaeological and Ethnographic Record of Mesoamerica*, edited by Shirley Boteler Mock, pp. 135–144. University of New Mexico Press, Albuquerque.

Gillespie, Susan D.

2000a   Maya "Nested Houses": The Ritual Construction of Place. In *Beyond Kinship: Social and Material Reproduction in House Societies*, edited by Rosemary A. Joyce and Susan D. Gillespie, pp. 135–160. University of Pennsylvania Press, Philadelphia

2000b   Rethinking Ancient Maya Social Organization: Replacing "Lineage" with "House." *American Anthropologist* 102(3):467–484.

Golden, Charles, and Andrew Scherer

2013   Territory, Trust, Growth, and Collapse in Classic Period Maya Kingdoms. *Current Anthropology* 54(4):397–435.

Gossen, Gary

1974   *Chamulas in the World of the Sun.* Harvard University Press, Cambridge, Mass.

1994   From Olmecs to Zapatistas: A Once and Future History of Souls. *American Anthropologist* 96(3):553–570.

Graeber, David

2015   Radical Alterity Is Just Another Way of Saying "Reality": A Reply to Eduardo Viveiros de Castro. *HAU: Journal of Ethnographic Theory* 5(2):1–41.

Guernsey, Julia

2006   Late Formative Period Antecedents for Ritually Bound Monuments. In *Sacred Bundles: Ritual Acts of Wrapping and Binding in Mesoamerica*, edited by Julia Guernsey and F. Kent Reilly III, pp. 22–39. Boundary End Archaeology Research Center, Barnardsville, N.C.

Guernsey, Julia, and F. Kent Reilly III

2006   Introduction. In *Sacred Bundles: Ritual Acts of Wrapping and Binding in Mesoamerica*, edited by Julia Guernsey and F. Kent Reilly III, pp. v–xiv. Boundary End Archaeology Research Center, Barnardsville, N.C.

Haber, Alejandro F.

2009 Animism, Relatedness, Life: Post-Western Perspectives. *Cambridge Archaeological Journal* 19(3):418–430.

Hallowell, Irving A.

1955 *Culture and Experience.* University of Pennsylvania Press, Philadelphia.

1960 Ojibwa Ontology, Behavior, and World View. In *Culture in History: Essays in Honor of Paul Radin*, edited by Stanley Diamond. Columbia University Press, New York.

Hammond, Norman

2010 La persistencia de la memoria: Quince siglos de acción ritual en Cuello, Belice. In *El ritual en el mundo maya: De lo privado a lo público*, edited by Andrés Ciudad Ruiz, Ma. Josefa Iglesias Ponce de León, and Miguel Sorroche Cuerva, pp. 69–82. Sociedad Española de Estudios Mayas, Madrid.

Hanks, William

1990 *Referential Practice: Language and Lived Space among the Maya.* University of Chicago Press, Chicago.

Harrison-Buck, Eleanor

2012 Architecture as Animate Landscape: Circular Shrines in the Ancient Maya Lowlands. *American Anthropologist* 114(1):64–80.

Harvey, Graham

2006 *Animism: Respecting the Living World.* Columbia University Press, New York.

Henare, Amira, Martin Holbraad, and Sari Wastell

2007 Introduction: Thinking through Things. In *Thinking through Things: Theorizing Artefacts Ethnographically*, edited by Amira Henare, Martin Holbraad, and Sari Wastell, pp. 1–31. Routledge, London.

Hendon, Julia A.

1991 Status and Power in Classic Maya Society: An Archaeological Study. *American Anthropologist* 93:894–918.

2010 *Houses in a Landscape: Memory and Everyday Life in Mesoamerica.* Duke University Press, Durham, N.C.

2012 Objects as Persons: Integrating Maya Beliefs and Anthropological Theory. In *Power and Identity in Archaeological Theory and Practice: Case Studies from Ancient Mesoamerica*, edited by E. Harrison-Buck, pp. 82–89. University of Utah Press, Salt Lake City.

Hendon, Julia A., Rosemary A. Joyce, and Jeanne Lopiparo

2014 *Material Relations: The Marriage Figurines of Prehispanic Honduras.* University Press of Colorado, Boulder.

Holbraad, M.

2009 Ontology, Ethnography, Archaeology: An Afterword on the Ontography of Things. *Cambridge Archaeological Journal* 19(3):431–441.

Houston, Stephen D.

1996 Symbolic Sweatbaths of the Maya: Architectural Meaning in the Cross Group at Palenque, Mexico. *Latin American Antiquity* 7:132–151.

1998 Finding Function and Meaning in Classic Maya Architecture. In *Function and Meaning in Classic Maya Architecture*, edited by Stephen D. Houston, pp. 519–538. Dumbarton Oaks, Washington, D.C.

2014 *The Life Within: Classic Maya and the Matter of Permanence.* Yale University Press, New Haven.

Houston, Stephen D., James Doyle, David Stuart, and Karl Taube

2017 A Universe in a Maya Lintel IV: Seasonal Gods and Cosmic Kings. https://decipherment.wordpress.com/2017/09/04/.

Houston, Stephen D., and David Stuart

1989 *The Way Glyph: Evidence of "Co-essences" among the Classic Maya.* Research Reports on Ancient Maya Writing 30. Center for Maya Research, Washington D.C.

1994 *Classic Maya Place Names.* Studies in Pre-Columbian Art and Archaeology 33. Dumbarton Oaks, Washington, D.C.

1996 Of Gods, Glyphs, and Kings: Divinity and Rulership among the Classic Maya. *Antiquity* 70:289–312.

Houston, Stephen D., and Karl Taube

2000 An Archaeology of the Senses: Perception and Cultural Expression in Ancient Mesoamerica. *Cambridge Archaeological Journal* 10:261–294.

Hruby, Zachary X.

2007   Ritualized Lithic Production at Piedras Negras, Guatemala. In *Rethinking Craft Specialization in Complex Societies: Archaeological Analyses of the Social Meaning of Production*, edited by R. Flad and Zachary X. Hruby, pp. 68–87. Archeological Papers of the American Anthropological Association 17. American Anthropological Association, Washington, D.C.

Hutson, Scott R.

2010   *Dwelling, Identity and the Maya: Relational Archaeology at Chunchucmil*. Altamira, Lanham, Md.

Hutson, Scott R., Barry Kidder, Céline Lamb, Daniel Vallejo-Cáliz, and Jacob Welch

2016   Small Buildings and Small Budgets: Making LiDAR Work in Northern Yucatan, Mexico. *Advances in Archaeological Practice* 4(3):268–283.

Hutson, Scott R., Céline Lamb, and David Medina

2017   Political Engagement in Household Ritual among the Maya of Yucatan. In *Beyond Integration: Religion and Politics in the Precolumbian Americas*, edited by Stacy Barber and Arthur Joyce, pp. 165–188. Routledge, London.

Hutson, Scott R., and Jacob Welch

2014   Sacred Landscapes and Building Practices at Ucí and Kancab Yucatan, Mexico. *Ancient Mesoamerica* 25(2):421–439.

Ingold, Tim

2000   *The Perception of the Environment: Essays on Livelihood, Dwelling, and Skill*. Routledge, London.

2007   Materials against Materiality. *Archaeological Dialogues* 14(1):1–16.

2011   *Being Alive: Essays on Movement, Knowledge and Description*. Routledge, London.

Kockelman, Paul

2007   Inalienable Possession and Personhood in a Q'eqchi'-Mayan Community. *Language in Society* 36(3):343–369.

Kowalski, Jeff Karl, and Virginia E. Miller

2006   Textile Designs in the Sculptured Facades of Northern Maya Architecture: Women's Production, Cloth, Tribute, and Political Power. In *Sacred Bundles: Ritual Acts of Wrapping and Binding in Mesoamerica*, edited by Julia Guernsey and F. Kent Reilly III, pp. 145–174. Boundary End Archaeology Research Center, Barnardsville, N.C.

Kurjack, Edward B., and E. Wyllis Andrews V

1976   Early Boundary Maintenance in Northwest Yucatan, Mexico. *American Antiquity* 41(3):318–325.

Landa, Manuel de

1997   *A Thousand Years of Nonlinear History*. Zone Books, Cambridge, Mass.

Latour, Bruno

1993   *We Have Never Been Modern*. Harvester-Wheatsheaf, New York.

2005   *Re-Assembling the Social*. Oxford University Press, Oxford.

Laughlin, Robert

1975   *The Great Tzotzil Dictionary of San Lorenzo Zinacantan*. Smithsonian Contributions to Anthropology 19. Smithsonian Institution Press, Washington, D.C.

2000   Poetic License. In *The Flowering of Man: A Tzotzil Botany of Zinancatán*, edited by Dennis Eugene Breedlove and Robert M. Laughlin, pp. 101–108. Smithsonian Institution, Washington, D.C.

Maldonado C., Rubén

1995   Los sistemas de caminos del norte de Yucatan. In *Seis ensayos sobre antiguos patrones de asentamiento en el area maya*, edited by E. Vargas Pacheco, pp. 68–92. Universidad Nacional Autónoma de México, Instituto de Investigaciones Antropológicas, Mexico City.

Marcus, George E., and Michael M. J. Fisher

1988   *Anthropology as Cultural Critique: An Experimental Moment in the Human Sciences*. University of Chicago Press, Chicago.

McAnany, Patricia A.

2010   *Ancestral Maya Economies in Archaeological Perspective*. Cambridge University Press, Cambridge.

McAnany, Patricia A., and Shannon Plank

2001   Perspectives on Actors, Gender Roles, and Architecture at Classic Maya Courts and Households. In *Theory, Comparison and Synthesis*. Vol. 1 of *Royal Courts of the Ancient Maya*, edited by Takeshi Inomata and Stephen D. Houston, pp. 84–129. Westview Press, Boulder, Colo.

Miller, Mary E., and Simon Martin

2004   *Courtly Art of the Ancient Maya.* Fine Arts Museums of San Francisco, San Francisco.

Miller, Virginia E.

1991   *The Frieze of the Palace of the Stuccoes, Acanceh, Yucatan, Mexico.* Dumbarton Oaks Research Library and Collection, Washington, D.C.

Mock, Shirley Boteler (editor)

1998   *The Sowing and the Dawning: Termination, Dedication and Transformation in the Archaeological and Ethnographic Record of Mesoamerica.* University of New Mexico Press, Albuquerque.

Monaghan, John

1998   The Person, Destiny, and the Construction of Difference in Mesoamerica. *RES: Anthropology and Aesthetics* 33:137–146.

2000   Theology and History in the Study of Mesoamerican Religions. In *Ethnology*. Vol. 6 of *Supplement to the Handbook of Middle American Indians*, edited by John Monaghan, pp. 24–49. University of Texas Press, Austin.

Nash, June

1970   *In the Eyes of the Ancestors: Belief and Behavior in a Maya Community.* Yale University Press, New Haven.

O'Neil, Megan

2009   Ancient Maya Sculptures of Tikal, Seen and Unseen. *RES: Anthropology and Aesthetics* 55–56:119–134.

Plank, Shannon E.

2004   *Maya Dwellings in Hieroglyphs and Archaeology: An Integrative Approach to Ancient Architecture and Spatial Cognition.* BAR International Series 1324. British Archaeological Reports, Oxford.

Proskouriakoff, Tatiana

1963   *An Album of Maya Architecture.* University of Oklahoma Press, Norman.

Redfield, Robert, and Alfonso Villa Rojas

1934   *Chan Kom: A Maya Village.* Carnegie Institute of Washington Publication 448. Carnegie Institute of Washington, Washington, D.C.

Reilly, F. Kent, III

2006   Middle Formative Origins of the Mesoamerican Ritual Act of Bundling. In *Sacred Bundles: Ritual Acts of Wrapping and Binding in Mesoamerica*, edited by Julia Guernsey and F. Kent Reilly III, pp. 1–21. Boundary End Archaeology Research Center, Barnardsville, N.C.

Ringle, William M.

1988   *Of Mice and Monkeys: The Value and Meaning of T1016c, the God C Hieroglyph.* In Research Reports on Ancient Maya Writing 18. Center for Maya Research, Washington, D.C.

Ringle, William M., and George J. Bey III

2001   Post-Classic and Terminal Classic Courts of the Northern Maya Lowlands. In *Data and Case Studies*. Vol. 2 of *Royal Courts of the Ancient Maya*, edited by Takeshi Inomata and Stephen D. Houston, pp. 266–307. Westview Press, Boulder, Colo.

Saturno, William, David Stuart, Karl Taube, and Heather Hurst

2005   *The Murals of San Bartolo, El Peten, Guatemala. Part 1: the North Wall.* Ancient America 7. Center for Ancient American Studies, Barnardsville, N.C.

Schele, Linda

1998   The Iconography of Maya Architectural Façades during the Late Classic Period. In *Function and Meaning in Classic Maya Architecture*, edited by Stephen D. Houston, pp. 479–518. Dumbarton Oaks Research Library and Collection, Washington, D.C.

Schele, Linda, and David A. Freidel

1990   *A Forest of Kings: The Untold Story of the Ancient Maya.* William Morrow, New York.

Schele, Linda, and Peter Mathews

1998 *The Code of Kings: The Language of Seven Sacred Maya Temples and Tombs.* Scribner, New York.

Scherer, Andrew K.

2016 *Mortuary Landscapes of the Classic Maya.* University of Texas Press, Austin.

Stocking, George W.

1971 Animism in Theory and Practice: E. B. Tylor's Unpublished "Notes on Spiritualism." *Man* 6:88–104.

Stone, Andrea

2005 Divine Stalagmites: Speleothems in Maya Caves and Aesthetic Variation in Maya Art. In *Aesthetics and Rock Art*, edited by T. Heyd and J. Clegg, pp. 215–233. Ashgate, Aldershot.

Stone, Andrea, and Marc Zender

2011 *Reading Maya Art: A Hieroglyphic Guide to Ancient Maya Painting and Sculpture.* Thames and Hudson, New York.

Stross, Brian

1988 The Burden of Office: A Reading. *Mexicon* 10(6):118–121.

1998 Seven Ingredients in Mesoamerican Ensoulment: Dedication and Termination in Tenejapa. In *The Sowing and the Dawning: Termination, Dedication, and Transformation in the Archaeological and Ethnographic Record of Mesoamerica*, edited by Shirley Boteler Mock, pp. 31–39. University of New Mexico Press, Albuquerque.

Stuart, David

1996 Kings of Stone: A Consideration of Stela in Ancient Maya Ritual and Representations. *RES: Anthropology and Aesthetics* 29–30:148–171.

1998 "The Fire Enters His House": Architecture and Ritual in Classic Maya Texts. In *Function and Meaning in Classic Maya Architecture*, edited by Stephen D. Houston, pp. 373–425. Dumbarton Oaks, Washington, D.C.

2010 Shining Stones: Observations on the Ritual Meaning of Early Maya Stelae. In *The Place of Stone Monuments: Context, Use, and Meaning in Mesoamerica's Preclassic Transition*, edited by Julia Guernsey, John E. Clark, and Barbara

Arroyo, pp. 283–296. Dumbarton Oaks Research Library and Collection, Washington, D.C.

Taube, Karl

1994 The Birth Vase: Natal Imagery in Ancient Maya Myth and Ritual. In *The Maya Vase Book*, vol. 4, edited by Barbara Kerr and Justin Kerr, pp. 652–685. Kerr Associates, New York.

1998 The Jade Hearth: Centrality, Rulership, and the Classic Maya Temple. In *Function and Meaning in Classic Maya Architecture*, edited by Stephen D. Houston, pp. 427–478. Dumbarton Oaks Research Library and Collection, Washington, D.C.

Tax, Sol

1941 World View and Social Relations in Guatemala. *American Anthropologist* 43:27–42.

Tedlock, Dennis

1985 *Popol Vuh: The Definitive Edition of the Mayan Book of the Dawn of Life and the Glories of God and Kings.* Simon and Schuster, New York.

Thompson, J. Eric S.

1930 *Ethnology of the Mayas of Southern and Central British Honduras.* Field Musuem of Natural History Publication 274. Field Museum of Natural History, Chicago.

Tozzer, Alfred M.

1941 *Landa's* Relación de las Cosas de Yucatan: *A Translation.* Papers of the Peabody Museum of American Archaeology and Ethnology 17. Peabody Museum of American Archaeology and Ethnology, Cambridge, Mass.

Tylor, E. B

[1871] 1958 *Religion in Primitive Culture.* Vol. 1 *of Primitive Culture.* Harper and Row, New York.

Valdés, Juan Antonio

1987 Uaxactun: Recientes investigaciones. *Mexicon* 8(6):125–128.

Viveiros de Castro, Eduardo

2004 Exchanging Perspectives: The Transformation of Objects into Subjects in Amerindian Ontologies. *Common Knowledge* 10:463–485.

2015 Who's Afraid of the Ontological Wolf: Some Comments on an Ongoing Anthropological Debate. *Cambridge Anthropology* 33(1):2–17.

Vogt, Evon Z.

1976 *Tortillas for the Gods.* Harvard University Press, Cambridge, Mass.

1998 Zinacanteco Dedication and Termination Rituals. In *The Sowing and the Dawning: Termination, Dedication, and Transformation in the Archaeological and Ethnographic Record of Mesoamerica*, edited by Shirley Boteler Mock, pp. 21–30. University of New Mexico Press, Albuquerque.

Wagley, Charles

1949 *The Social and Religious Life of a Guatemalan Village.* Memoirs of the American Anthropological Association 71. American Anthropological Association, Menasha, Wis.

Wagner, Elisabeth

2006 White Earth Bundles: The Symbolic Sealing and Burial of Buildings among the Ancient Maya. In *Jaws of the Underworld: Life, Death, and Rebirth among the Ancient Maya*, edited by P. R. Colas, G. L. Fort, and B. L. Persson, pp. 55–69. Verlag Anton Saurwein, Markt Schwaben.

Watanabe, John

1992 *Maya Saints and Souls in a Changing World.* University of Texas Press, Austin.

Weismantel, Mary

2015 Seeing Like an Archaeologist: Viveiros de Castro at Chavin de Huantar. *Journal of Social Archaeology* 15(2):139–159.

Wisdom, Charles

1940 *The Chorti Indians of Guatemala.* University of Chicago Press, Chicago.

Zender, Marc

2018 "The Crown Was Held above Him": Rethinking Classic Maya Accession. Paper presented at the Eighth Annual Maya at the Lago Conference, Davidson, N.C.

11

Animating Public Buildings in Formative-Period Oaxaca

Political and Ontological Implications

ARTHUR A. JOYCE

ARCHAEOLOGISTS, ETHNOGRAPHERS, AND ethnohistorians are increasingly recognizing the prevalence of practices in both ancient and modern Mesoamerica through which vital, life-giving forces were manifest and exchanged among animate entities including earth, rain, maize, mountains, ancestors, humans, deities, and buildings (e.g., Barber and Olvera Sánchez 2012; Harrison-Buck 2012, 2015; Joyce and Barber 2015; López Austin 1988, 1989; Monaghan 1995, 2000; Stross 1998; Vogt 1976). Relations among these entities could be simultaneously sacred, practical, and inseparable from everyday life (Hutson and Stanton 2007). Drawing on ethnographic and ethnohistoric research as sources of analogy to explore the Pre-Columbian past, archaeologists have begun to investigate what Eleanor Harrison-Buck (2015) calls the "animic cosmos." Yet archaeologists have generally focused on a generic understanding of such practices and their ontological implications, which has been dominated by research on Aztec and Maya religion. This is undoubtedly in

part the result of the paucity of comparative work by Mesoamerican ethnographers and ethnohistorians. As John Monaghan (2000:26) argues, "comparative work on Mesoamerican religion is so thin that at this point it is more productive to concentrate on what is generally true about Mesoamerican theology than to focus on the variables which may account for differences." Likewise, these practices are often seen as instantiating a broad overarching ontology, which risks falling into a new structuralism with a stable and enduring ontological base, constraining the ways in which people reproduced and transformed social life. As argued by Edward Swenson (2015), however, ontologies are products of social negotiation and are not necessarily determinative of materialities, ideologies, practices, or political formations. Archaeologists are beginning to consider how ontologies are multimodal and activated situationally within different social-material contexts (Harris and Robb 2012; Harrison-Buck 2012; Joyce and Barber 2015; Loren, this volume). Ontologies can also at times

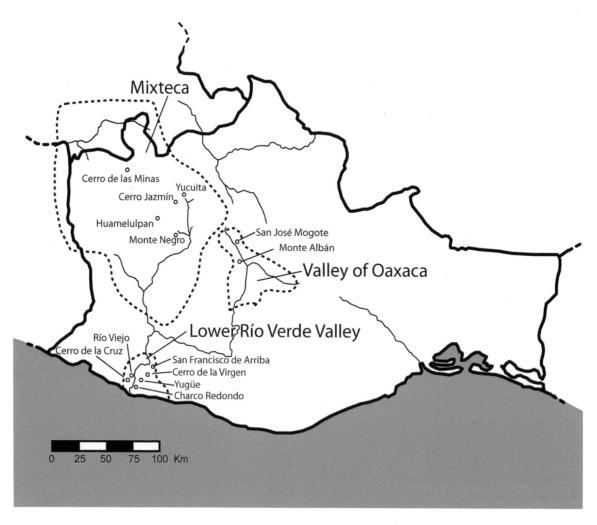

figure 11.1

Map of Oaxaca, showing regions and archaeological sites mentioned in the text. Map by Arthur Joyce.

be authorized and regulated by social authorities, leading to pressures for uniformity (Harris and Robb 2012).

In this chapter, I explore variability in later Formative-period (700 BCE–300 CE) animating practices in Oaxaca with a focus on the animation, feeding, and de-animation of public buildings. By public buildings, I refer to nonresidential architectural settings, often monumental in scale, that were loci of ceremonial practices with participants ranging from large groups to more limited and exclusive engagements. Although public gatherings also occurred at residences, I omit considerations of domestic settings in order to narrow the focus of the chapter. Drawing on ethnographic and ethnohistoric analogies, I compare evidence for these practices in three regions of Oaxaca: the Valley of Oaxaca, the lower Río Verde Valley, and the Mixteca (Figure 11.1). The analysis examines the Formative period because in all three regions this period has been a major focus of research and because data are more accessible and systematically reported. The findings show that animating practices associated with public buildings varied greatly among these regions. I consider how this variability was entangled with political life and if these differences reflect alternative understandings of personhood relating to either humans, buildings, or both. I begin with a discussion of some of the complexities of understanding indigenous

Mesoamerican concepts and practices of animation, drawing largely on ethnographic and ethnohistoric evidence.

Animating Practices in Mesoamerica

In Mesoamerica, social life was enmeshed with a wide variety of living entities animated by vital, life-giving forces (Furst 1995; López Austin 1988, 1989; Monaghan 1995, 2000; Stross 1998). Because vital forces could be transferred, transformed, and concentrated among beings, social life was constituted not simply through the interactions of people but also through ongoing relations among people and other-than-human animate beings. Based on ethnohistoric documents, it is clear that there was no unitary animating force similar to the soul. The Aztec identified three vital forces: *tonalli*, *teyolia*, and *ihiyotl* (Furst 1995; López Austin 1988). Likewise, *ch'ulel* among the Maya is multifaceted and divisible (Freidel, Schele, and Parker 1993; Harrison-Buck 2015:117–118; Hutson et al., this volume; McAnany, this volume), and some of its aspects share properties with Aztec vital forces (Furst 1995:153–154; López Austin 1988:219–230). Similar beliefs in multiple animating forces and their distributed nature are found in other indigenous groups in Mesoamerica, including the Mixe and Chatino of Oaxaca (Greenberg 1981:91–92; Lipp 1991:43–46).

Being imbued with vital forces did not mean that all animate entities were equivalent or human-like. As noted by ethnographers, ethnohistorians, and archaeologists, different beings manifest different kinds and degrees of these forces (Freidel, Schele, and Parker 1993:181–185; López Austin 1988, 1989; Monaghan 1995:197–198). Certain beings, especially deities and rulers, concentrated vital forces beyond those of others, which gave them greater power and ability to affect the world (see Hutson et al., this volume). The properties and capacities of animate beings to transfer, transform, link, and concentrate vital forces were not necessarily inherent to particular objects or actions, but were created through relations among diverse entities and the acts that assembled them, requiring

that people and other animate beings engage with the various animate aspects of their world in myriad ways. Scott Hutson and colleagues (this volume) make this point in their discussion of personhood among the Maya. Maya persons, whether human or other-than-human, are constituted through ongoing relations with people, ancestors, deities, and other animate entities, including acts of animation involving the transfer of vitality (Stross 1998; cf. Loren, this volume). Personhood, like life more generally, can, therefore, be assessed along a gradient (Hutson et al., this volume).

Power infused relations among animate entities, including humans (Brown and Emery 2008; López Austin 1988, 1989; McAnany 1995; Monaghan 2000, 2009). The most powerful entities included what María Nieves Zedeño (2009) terms "index objects," which had the ability to transfer vitality to other beings, and entities that could communicate and mediate between animate beings, what Timothy Pauketat (2013) terms "witnesses." In Mesoamerica, index objects included dripping water, blood, spit, breath, marine shells, wind, jade, obsidian, and speleothems (Brown and Emery 2008; Harrison-Buck 2012; Mock 1998), while entities such as mirrors, flutes, human hearts, and images of deities had the ability to connect different realms of existence, allowing gods and ancestors to view and interact with the living and vice versa (Barber and Olvera Sánchez 2012; López Austin 1989:123–124; Olivier 2003:240–265). Buildings were often considered to be powerful animate beings that assembled varied entities such as people, divinities, ancestors, celestial bodies, life, death, and time, thereby constituting broader communities (Joyce and Barber 2015; Stross 1998). People, including rulers and religious specialists, were also powerful mediators, assembling and concentrating animate entities (Freidel, Schele, and Parker 1993; Schele and Miller 1986). Ancestors, as well as the "living," were seen as animate beings with abilities to impact the world, and this relationship continues for many Native Americans today (McAnany 1995).

Relations among people and other beings were often negotiated and transformed through ritualized practices (sensu Bell 1992). These practices included a wide range of acts through which vital forces were transferred, transformed, and concentrated among animate entities (Brown and Emery 2008; Joyce and Barber 2015; Monaghan 1990, 2009; Stross 1998). I term these acts "animating practices." For example, the vitality of humans and other beings, including deities, could be merged and dispersed, as with Aztec "man-gods" and nagualism (López Austin 1988; see also Kosiba, this volume). Upon death, the vital essence of the Aztec "man-god" was dispersed to different destinations, including returning to the deity from whom it originated. As social personae, many other-than-human beings went through a life cycle that included birth and death and was often marked by ritualized acts through which vital forces were transferred (Stross 1998). Another practice sometimes associated with animate other-than-human beings like buildings was the act of "feeding" or giving sustenance to maintain the animateness of things, just as humans must eat to live (McAnany, this volume; Stross 1998:33). Monaghan (1995) argues that eating and feeding are fundamental practices that materialize and reiterate social relationships within the household and the community.

Sacrifice in Mesoamerica can also be considered a form of animating practice involving transactions of vitality between humans and divinities, typically where it is released from one animate being to sustain, feed, or animate another (Freidel, Schele, and Parker 1993:202–207; López Luján 2005:35–37). In Aztec ethnohistory, for example, deities hungered for vital forces and, if these were not received through sacrifice, might languish to the point of no longer maintaining the cosmic order (López Austin 1988). The blood of sacrificial victims was, at times, smeared on wooden and stone figures to feed the deities within (Freidel, Schele, and Parker 1993:202). In addition to blood sacrifices, a wide variety of offerings also transferred vitality to deities (Freidel, Schele, and Parker 1993:204; López Luján 2005:35–37). Copal incense, maize dough, jade, and other objects were burned to release their force. Offerings were emplaced in public buildings to animate and sustain them as living beings (Mock 1998). Temples were often associated with particular deities and

acted as portals through which divinities were contacted (Freidel, Schele, and Parker 1993:204; Matos Moctezuma 1988). At least some tribute payments made to rulers were referred to as "sacrifices" (Monaghan 2009). Like deities, rulers could also be revitalized through sacrificial blood (López Austin 1988:251–252). Of course, the fact that rulers could take on the guise of deities, incorporate aspects of the essence of the deity, and become what Alfredo López Austin (1989) terms a "man-god" shows that the distinction between rulers and deities could be decidedly fuzzy.

Transactions of the vital force in sacrifice activated and recapitulated a sacred covenant between humans and deities that was established as a fundamental aspect of the cosmic creation. In both ancient and modern Mesoamerican creation stories, the current world was the result of a sacred covenant whereby people petitioned deities for agricultural fertility and prosperity in return for sacrificial offerings (Freidel, Schele, and Parker 1993:65–66; Monaghan 1990; Tedlock 1996). Since humans literally consumed the gods as maize, earth, and rain, both sides of the exchange can be seen as forms of sacrifice through which vital forces were transferred. As argued by Monaghan (1990, 2009), death itself was a sacrificial act through which people fed the gods. López Austin (1988:321) argues that the act of depositing the dead in the earth "was a direct delivery of the body to the lords of vegetation and of rain. It was like sowing a seed that would germinate beneath the ground and grow inside of the hollow, sacred mount, from which surged the water that fed all the rivers and all the clouds." Because sacrifice was a debt owed to the gods for the creation of the current world, humans were in a decidedly inferior position in these transactions. The sacred covenant, therefore, establishes sacrifice as a fundamental condition of human existence involving relations of debt and merit between humans and the gods (Monaghan 1990, 1995).

Animating practices are probably best documented archaeologically for buildings, including public buildings and residences (Freidel, Schele, and Parker 1993; Joyce and Barber 2015; Mock 1998). Birth rites, usually conceptualized as rituals of animation, dedication, or ensoulment, and death rites, termed rituals of closure or termination, continue to be carried out in houses by many indigenous Mesoamerican groups (Greenberg 1981; Mock 1998). It is not surprising, therefore, that public buildings were loci of animating practices often involving the emplacement of objects such as ceramic vessels, jade, and the remains of humans and animals whose vital forces were transferred to the structure (Mock 1998). Like that of humans, the vitality of buildings and associated objects at death could also be released through burning and breakage (Stross 1998; Stanton, Brown, and Pagliaro 2008).

Animating practices were often elements of more complex ritual sequences involving other kinds of ceremonial acts unrelated to the transferal of vitality. An example of the complex ritual sequences associated with the animation of buildings can be seen among the Tzotzil Maya. Linda Brown and Kitty Emery (2008) point out that the different components of houses (posts, thatch, daub) come from the animate earth and forest and so are alive even before any human involvement. Drawing on Evon Vogt (1976), Brown and Emery argue that ritualized practices associated with house construction include offerings made to repay the earth for the use of these materials, as well as practices designed to "ensoul" the building so as to incorporate it into a social order. The offerings made to the Earth Lord involve the sacrifice of chickens by the builders, who bury the remains in a hole beneath the center of the house floor and pour chicken broth and sugarcane liquor on the roof, which is followed by a ritual meal. These are seen as acts of feeding, which continue through the life of the house, and if not properly carried out, the house may pursue vengeance against the occupants. The ensouling of the building requires a ritual specialist and the raising of a house cross, additional sacrifices to the Earth Lords, travel to sacred mountains where offerings are made to ancestral gods, and another ritual meal. These acts provide the house with an "inner soul" through the transferral of the vital force, ch'ulel, and so can be described as an animating practice involving both humans and divinities (see Kosiba, this volume; McAnany, this

volume). This example illustrates the complexity of actors and actions associated with the raising of a house. Humans were clearly involved in the actions designed to feed and ensoul the house, although in this case the primary agents in the act of animation were deities.

In Oaxaca, animating practices associated with buildings are best documented ethnographically for the Chatino, and these resemble the patterns discussed for the Maya (Greenberg 1981:85–98). During house-raising ceremonies, several offerings, including food, fine china, and a sacrificed chicken, are placed into pits dug into the floor. The initial offering in the center of the house feeds its "heart," where the life force burns. Later subfloor offerings are given to the house altar and to the Fire God, who embodies the ancestors whom one feeds and from whom one is fed. Elsewhere in Mesoamerica, ethnographic data demonstrate variation in the means through which buildings are animated (e.g., La Fuente [1977] 1949; Lipp 1991; Mock 1998).

Based on ethnohistoric and ethnographic examples, the animating practices that are the most archaeologically visible will be those that involve the emplacement of offerings beneath the floors of public buildings in order to animate the structure. Making somewhat simplistic assumptions and acknowledging that animating practices are far more diverse than those associated with buildings, I propose three means of differentiating among offerings involved in the animation, feeding, and termination of public buildings. Offerings emplaced during the initial construction or sequential rebuilding or remodeling of public buildings are likely to have been the result of acts of initial animation. These acts include those that bring to life the inanimate, as well as those that assemble (sensu DeLanda 2016) already animate entities into emergent relational fields involving personhood, community, and urbanity, among others (Hutson et al., this volume; Joyce n.d.; Joyce and Barber 2015). Offerings sequentially emplaced through time, independent of episodes of building and remodeling, are more consistent with acts of feeding and nurturing buildings and associated divinities. Evidence of practices that closed public buildings and released their vital forces should occur around the time of abandonment. In archaeological and ethnographic contexts in Mesoamerica, termination ceremonies often include some combination of the covering of buildings with sediment and the destruction of structures and associated objects (Becker 1993; Hutson et al., this volume; Mock 1998; Stanton, Brown, and Pagliaro 2008). Using these analogical tools in the following sections, I use archaeological data from later Formative-period Oaxaca to describe variability in the assembled entities and acts through which public buildings were animated, sustained, and closed.

Animating Public Buildings in the Valley of Oaxaca

The Valley of Oaxaca is the largest highland valley in southern Mexico and has been inhabited by Zapotecs probably since at least the Formative period. Evidence for later Formative-period animating practices associated with public buildings in the Valley of Oaxaca comes primarily from San José Mogote and Monte Albán.

The earliest evidence of animating practices in the Oaxaca Valley comes from San José Mogote and is associated with Mound 1 (Figure 11.2), which was a platform built over a natural hill at the beginning of the Middle Formative–period Rosario Phase (700–500 BCE) (Marcus and Flannery 1996). Mound 1 faced a large open plaza and significantly exceeded the scale and prominence of earlier buildings. The plaza allowed for the involvement of greater numbers of people in public ceremonies, although the platform's summit would have been restricted. The scale and organization required to build Mound 1 suggest that the leaders of the community wielded greater power, although at the time of its construction clear evidence for hereditary status distinctions is lacking (Blanton et al. 1999:36–42; Joyce 2010:111–117).

Shortly before the construction of the initial version of the platform on Mound 1 (Structure 19B), at least five pits were dug into the surface of the hill and filled with secondary human interments covered with red pigment (Flannery and Marcus 2015). Accompanying the burials were ceramic vessels, a figurine, two bowls made from marine shells, jadeite beads, and a fish otolith (Figure 11.3). Kent Flannery and Joyce Marcus (2015:104) suggest that these were higher-status youths who were honored by being interred prior to the construction of an important temple. I suggest that these are also the first clear examples of offerings associated with animating rituals in buildings viewed as living, other-than-human divine beings. They are consistent with patterns seen throughout Mesoamerica in which offerings are emplaced prior to or at the onset of building construction (Joyce and Barber 2015; Mock 1998). The pits in Mound 1 also contain items that have been identified as index objects with animating properties identified in archaeological, ethnohistoric, and ethnographic cases, including red pigment, marine shell, greenstone, and human bodies (Freidel, Schele, and Parker 1993; Harrison-Buck 2012; Mock 1998).

Following the construction of Structure 19B, a temple (Structure 28) was built on top of the platform (Flannery and Marcus 2015:141–147). Ceramic vessels found in the fill of Structure 19B, as well as the contents of another pit, are likely candidates for offerings involved with the animation of either Structure 19B or Structure 28. The pit contained three ceramic vessels, a bowl carved from a limpet shell, and a possible gourd vessel. In each of the corners of the recessed floor of the temple, people placed an offering of a single ceramic vessel.

At circa 500 BCE, people from San José Mogote and surrounding communities founded the mountaintop city of Monte Albán, which rapidly grew into the region's largest community (Marcus and Flannery 1996). One of the earliest activities at Monte Albán was the construction of the site's ceremonial center, located in the Main Plaza precinct, which far exceeded in scale Mound 1 at San José Mogote (Figure 11.4). Public buildings were built around the Main Plaza, and many were the foci of animating practices, as well as other kinds of ritualized acts.

Later Formative-period offerings at Monte Albán show continuities and differences in animating practices relative to Rosario Phase San José

figure 11.2

Mound 1 at San José Mogote. Photograph by Arthur Joyce (Joyce and Barber 2015:fig. 6 © The Wenner-Gren Foundation for Anthropological Research).

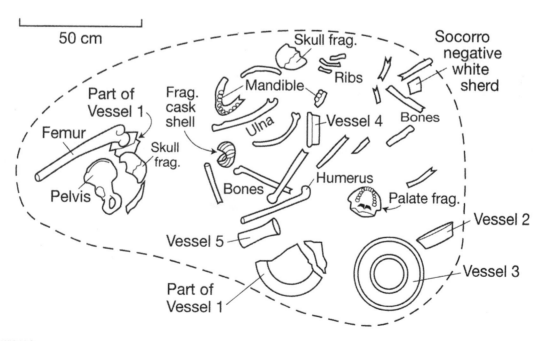

figure 11.3

Plan view of Burial 66, a secondary burial intrusive into Stratigraphic Zone F of Mound 1 at San José Mogote (Flannery and Marcus 2015:fig. 6.6).

figure 11.4
The Main Plaza of Monte Albán. Photograph by Arthur Joyce (Joyce 2010:fig. 5.3).

Mogote. Animating practices associated with public buildings at Monte Albán ranged from ritualized acts involving the emplacement of modest offerings of a few ceramic vessels or human burials (Caso [1935] 2003:268, [1939] 2002:177–178; Caso and Bernal 1952:58, 151) to incredibly elaborate offerings featuring exotic and highly valued objects, both locally made and imported. For example, an offering beneath the temple on Building VG on the North Platform included six ceramic vessels, two necklaces of greenstone and shell, a mother-of-pearl mosaic, and the skeletons of two women who may have been sacrificial victims (Marcus and Flannery 1996:183). An offering associated with a probable public building on the southeastern end of the North Platform consisted of ceramic bowls, two bird effigy vessels, an anthropomorphic vessel, twenty-three stone balls, and two whale ribs (Figure 11.5) that had been notched so as to make them into musical instruments (Caso, Bernal, and Acosta 1967:103–105). In another temple on the North Platform, an offering box contained a

ceramic bowl, a shell, two jade ear ornaments in the form of flowers, and the remains of two mosaic masks, one of jade and turquoise and the other of pyrite and shell (Caso, Bernal, and Acosta 1967:138).

A series of offerings was placed in two stone-lined pits that penetrated into the Nisa Phase (100 BCE–200 CE) version of the South Platform (Figure 11.6) (Gámez Goytia 2002). One of the pits had an offering consisting of eighty-one unfired cylindrical vessels coated with cinnabar, twenty-six with lids, and a greenstone bead. The other pit had at least three periods of use, beginning with the placement of five unfired hollow clay cylinders and four lids. A second offering placed above the first consisted of fourteen bowls and a shell pendant. Above these vessels were two unfired clay objects; one contained a greenstone bead covered in hematite and cinnabar, while the other was covered in hematite. The repeated placement of offerings in the pits suggests that they were used in the ongoing feeding of the South Platform as an animate being. It is possible that the vessels held food or drink or some other

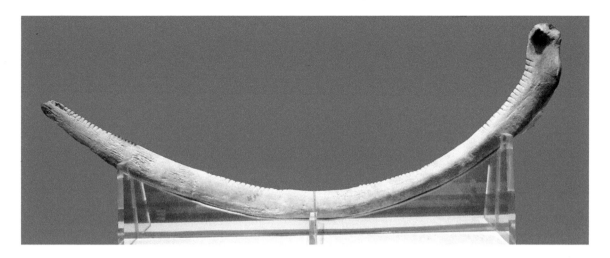

figure 11.5
A whale rib from an offering in the North Platform at Monte Albán. Photograph by Arthur Joyce.

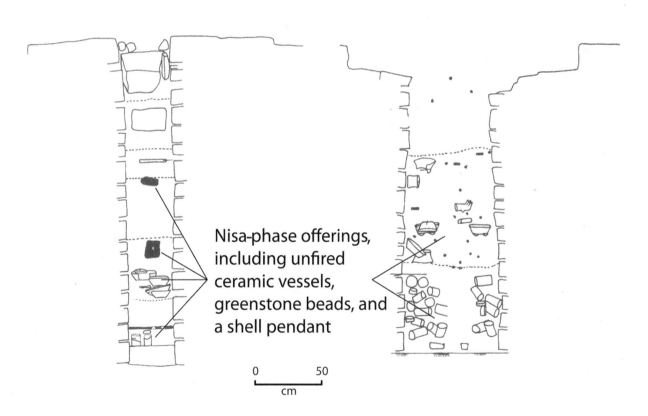

Nisa-phase offerings, including unfired ceramic vessels, greenstone beads, and a shell pendant

0   50
cm

figure 11.6
Stone-lined pits with offerings in the South Platform (Gámez Goytia 2002:figs. 7 and 8).

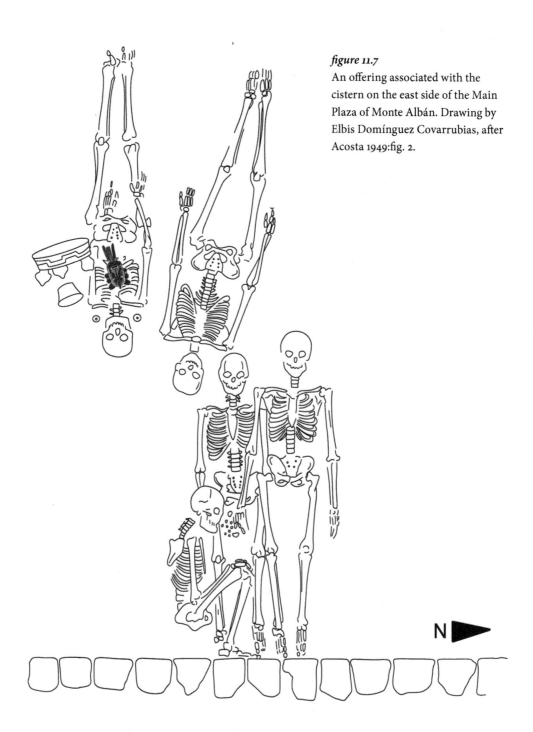

figure 11.7
An offering associated with the cistern on the east side of the Main Plaza of Monte Albán. Drawing by Elbis Domínguez Covarrubias, after Acosta 1949:fig. 2.

N ▶

substance that nourished the building. It is also possible that the cinnabar and hematite were iconic references to sacrificial blood, as they were in the Maya region (Freidel, Schele, and Parker 1993:244).

The most elaborate later Formative-period offering was Burial XIV-10, found on a stone pavement on the eastern side of the Main Plaza (Acosta 1949). It contained two adult males, two adult females, and a subadult accompanied by ceramic vessels and ornaments of jade, marine shell, and pearl (Figure 11.7). The males were interred wearing stone mosaic pectorals, including an elaborate jade bat mask with eyes and teeth of marine shell (Figure 11.8a). Interments like this one are unusual at Monte Albán since it is rare to find burials in public settings, leading several scholars to suggest that

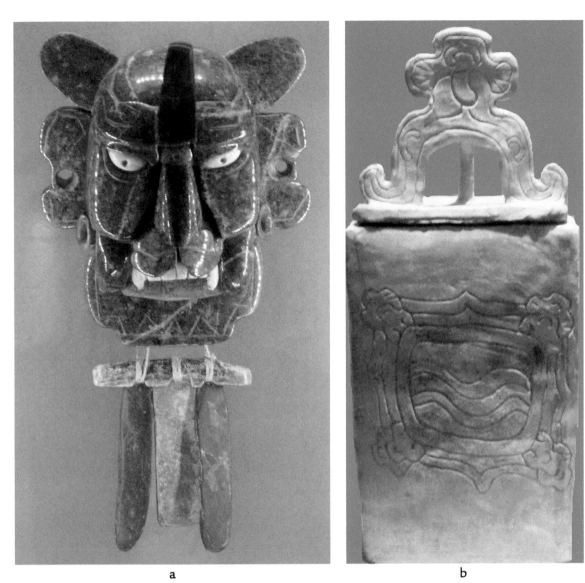

| a | b |

figure 11.8
Objects included in the offering associated with the cistern on the east side of the Main Plaza of Monte Albán (not to scale): a) jade bat mask; and b) ceramic box incised with the glyph for "water" and images of maize sprouts. Photographs by Arthur Joyce.

the interments may have been sacrificial victims (Flannery 1983:104; Joyce 2010:156). The offering was emplaced at the time of the closure and burial of an elaborate stone cistern and may have been associated with termination rituals. Excavations in the vicinity of the burial yielded five ceramic boxes with lids that may also have been deposited during the termination ritual (Urcid 2011). The boxes were incised with the glyph for "water" and images of maize sprouts (Figure 11.8b). Found near the cistern

was evidence for ritual feasting, including ovens that contained hundreds of small bowls and extensive evidence of burning (Marcus Winter, personal communication, 2017).

During the Nisa Phase at San José Mogote, a series of two-room temples was built on Mound 1, and although some were poorly preserved, others included offerings frequently placed in stone boxes (Flannery and Marcus 2015). Several offerings associated with the temples included possible sacrificial

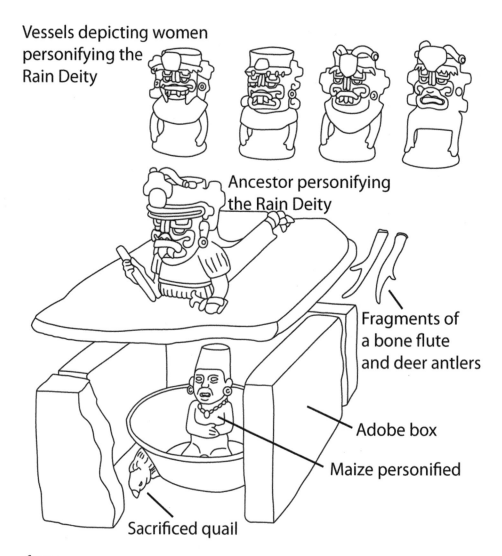

Vessels depicting women personifying the Rain Deity

Ancestor personifying the Rain Deity

Fragments of a bone flute and deer antlers

Adobe box

Maize personified

Sacrificed quail

figure 11.9
An offering of an adobe box and effigy vessels from Structure 35 at San José Mogote. Drawing by Elbis Domínguez Covarrubias, after Urcid 2009:fig. 2.

victims or ancestors. For example, interred beneath Structure 36 were the partial remains of a child who may have been cooked and eaten (Flannery and Marcus 2015:233), along with an adult secondary burial. A ceramic vase and a skull with its atlas vertebra still attached were discovered in the fill of Structure 13. Subfloor offerings in Structure 19 included a stone masonry box containing an incense brazier depicting the Old God or God of Ancestors and four turtle shells. Nearby was the burial of a woman and child stuffed into a small pit and accompanied by ceramic vessels, mother-of-pearl buttons, and stone beads.

The most elaborate offerings on Mound 1 were associated with Structure 35 (Flannery and Marcus 2015:246–273). A stone box beneath the inner room of the temple contained two jadeite statues; the largest was nearly half a meter tall and depicted a naked male who, Flannery and Marcus (2015:264) argue, may have represented a sacrificial victim. Beneath an area of Structure 35's floor showing evidence of intense burning, presumably of incense, was an adobe box, as well as a tableau of anthropomorphic ceramic effigy vessels and other objects (Figure 11.9). Javier Urcid (2009) argues that the central vessel embodied an ancestor manifesting the Rain God and holding a lightning bolt in one hand. The vessel lay on top of the adobe box. The ancestor was assisted by four anthropomorphic vessels depicting women who also personified the Rain God. Sitting in a bowl within the box was a vessel depicting the personification of maize. Adjacent to the bowl were the remains of a quail, possibly sacrificed to petition the Rain Deity for fertility. Just outside the box were fragments of a bone flute and a pair of deer antlers. Urcid (2009) interprets this tableau as depicting an element of the Zapotec creation narrative related to the Rain God, who is assisted by lesser attendants from the four quarters of the world, freeing maize from the mountain of sustenance to feed humanity.

The later Formative-period evidence from the Valley of Oaxaca is consistent with practices designed to animate, terminate, and possibly feed public buildings. Of the three types of animating practices, acts that animated public buildings during their initial construction were most strongly supported by the evidence, although it was not always possible to determine the exact context of offerings, especially at Monte Albán. Data from the cistern on the east side of the Main Plaza suggest termination ceremonies. The only features that seem consistent with acts of feeding are the South Platform offerings sequentially deposited in pits.

Although the details and scale of the offerings vary, the objects within the offerings reference a relatively restricted set of themes. Common materials had semiotic associations with humans merging with deities (deity masks and vessels depicting the personification of the Rain Deity), sacrifice/ancestors (human and animal remains, red pigment), water/rain (shell, greenstone, whalebone), maize and fertility (greenstone, vessels depicting maize personified, flower ornaments), and perhaps food and drink (ceramic vessels and possibly their contents). Taken together, these materials invoke the sacred covenant whereby humans offer sacrifices to deities in return for rain, maize, and ultimately sustenance. In many cases, the offerings assembled objects that referenced sacrifice with others that referenced fertility, such as greenstone and shell accompanying human bodies or ceramic

vessels covered with red pigment. I interpret the offerings as means through which vital forces were transferred through sacrifice, whether to animate buildings, deities, or both. The ability of the objects bundled within the offerings to transfer vital forces was enhanced by the presence of both index objects and witnesses. Some of the more elaborate offerings likely activated the covenant as offering and simultaneously cited liturgical narratives related to the covenant. In particular, the offering associated with Structure 35 at San José Mogote depicts the story of the Rain God providing maize to people in return for sacrificial offerings.

Most of the public buildings where offerings were found were in highly restricted locations that would have limited the number of participants, although others may have been able to observe from a distance. Such a spatial separation contributed to social distinctions likely related to status, as well as access to the divine. This applies particularly to the summit of Mound 1 at San José Mogote and the North Platform at Monte Albán (Figure 11.10). The use of exotic and valuable materials in many of the offerings—often imported from distant regions and including jade, marine shell and pearl ornaments, whale ribs, elaborate anthropomorphic vessels, deity masks, cinnabar, important ancestors, and sacrificial victims—also suggests that participants were restricted to the nobility. The presence of offerings in the public buildings suggests that they were living, divine beings and community members. The close proximity of elite residences to public buildings at both San José Mogote and Monte Albán (Flannery and Marcus 2015; Joyce 2010) implies that nobles were caretakers of these animate buildings and had primary access to them. This new centrality of the ruler in the entanglements through which divinities were contacted would have been a source of great political and spiritual power. Other offerings were more modest. One or two ceramic vessels emplaced in fill during the construction of a public building could represent the more informal actions of workers or ceremonies carried out by small groups of commoners.

A few of the offerings were made in places that would have allowed for large audiences to

figure 11.10
The North Platform at Monte Albán. Photograph by Arthur Joyce.

participate without obvious spatial barriers, especially ceremonies involving the cistern at Monte Albán and to a lesser extent the South Platform offerings. The evidence suggests that the cistern offering was dramatic and impressive in scale, involving a complex set of ritualized practices such as the interment of prominent people and perhaps human sacrifice, as well as ritual feasting.

Overall, the evidence from the Formative-period Valley of Oaxaca indicates that animating practices associated with public buildings were largely a prerogative of the nobility and carried out in restricted settings. As I discuss in the next section, animating practices in the lower Río Verde Valley differed from the patterns seen in the Valley of Oaxaca.

Animating Public Buildings in the Lower Río Verde Valley

The lower Río Verde Valley, located on the Pacific Coast of Oaxaca, was likely inhabited by Chatino speakers until the arrival of highland Mixtecs

around 1100 CE (Joyce 2010). The earliest evidence for animating practices associated with public buildings dates to the Late Formative Minizundo Phase (400–150 BCE). During the Terminal Formative period (150 BCE–250 CE), an urban center developed at Río Viejo on the west bank of the river, which grew to 225 ha. Practices involving initial animation, feeding, and closure occurred in public buildings at multiple sites in the region (Joyce and Barber 2015). Public buildings also typically have evidence for large-scale ritual feasts, which may have been carried out in conjunction with animating acts.

Evidence of animating practices carried out during the initial construction or sequential remodeling of public buildings was found at San Francisco de Arriba and Cerro de la Virgen. At San Francisco de Arriba, people left ritual caches in the fill of different construction phases of a restricted public building on the site's acropolis (Workinger 2002:185–214). Most of the offerings consisted of several ceramic vessels. The largest offering, however, consisted of 356 greenstone beads, twenty-seven rock-crystal beads, 109 beads of an unidentified stone, two greenstone bird-head pendants, two rock-crystal pendants,

fragments of iron ore, nine locally produced miniature gray ware jars, and disarticulated animal bones. At the hilltop site of Cerro de la Virgen, a series of animating offerings was also discovered in a small and spatially restricted public building (Structure 1) reached by a stairway east of the site's large public plaza (Brzezinski, Joyce, and Barber 2017). An elite family, perhaps the community's rulers, lived in a residence only 30 m south of Structure 1 (Barber 2013). The earliest of the offerings was placed beneath the center of the initial version of Structure 1 and consisted of a small stone figure, two miniature stone thrones, a broken but nearly complete stone Rain Deity mask, fragments of a second mask, and several ceramic vessels (Figure 11.11). The stone figure exhibits a "mantle" that covers the back of the human figure and resembles the silk and husk of a maize cob, suggesting an image of personified maize (Figure 11.12). All of the stone objects with the exception of the figurine were intentionally broken during or prior to emplacement. Given that vital forces are divisible (Furst 1995), it is possible that the breaking of the objects was an act of sacrifice designed to transfer their life force to the building (Stross 1998).

Subsequent versions of this building were animated primarily through the emplacement of ceramic vessels in platform fill.

The most impressive offerings in terms of scale involved the ongoing feeding and sustenance of public buildings as animate beings, often carried out in accessible spaces. At the site of Yugüe, Sarah Barber (2013) excavated a public building that contained a series of offerings emplaced through time. One offering included twenty ceramic vessels and another consisted of fifty low-fired, coarse brown ware cylinders (Figure 11.13). A third offering consisted of two cooking jars buried beneath an occupational surface. The presence of shellfish in one of the jars suggests that human food was used as a form of sustenance provided to the divine and raises the possibility that vessels appearing empty when excavated once contained perishable food items.

The most impressive offering related to the feeding of a public building comes from a patio associated with a public complex (Complex A) adjacent to the large ceremonial plaza at Cerro de la Virgen (Brzezinski 2015). The offering covered 62 m² and included 260 ceramic vessels in

a

figure 11.11
Terminal Formative–period animating offering beneath Structure 1 at Cerro de la Virgen: (a) stone objects (Brzezinski et al. 2017:fig. 5); (b) offering in situ (Joyce and Barber 2015:fig. A.18). Photographs by Jeff Brzezinski.

b

figure 11.12
A stone figure depicting the personification of maize. Photographs by Jeff Brzezinski.

granite-slab compartments that were emplaced over an extended period of time (Figure 11.14). Additional offerings consisting largely of ceramic vessels and granite slabs have been found in other public buildings on and near the plaza, including one that yielded eighty-two whole vessels in an excavated area of only 4 m² (Brzezinski 2019). The granite-slab compartments occur only at Cerro de la Virgen and illustrate how practices associated with the emplacement of offerings varied somewhat from community to community in the lower Río Verde Valley (Joyce and Barber 2015). It is possible that the granite-slab compartments, like the stone boxes in the Oaxaca Valley, facilitated the revisiting of particular offerings after their initial emplacement (also see Hutson et al., this volume).

Cemeteries and isolated burials found in public buildings may have also involved the transference of vital forces to sustain and animate buildings (Figure 11.15). Communal cemeteries have been discovered in public buildings at Cerro de la Cruz, Yugüe, and Charco Redondo (Barber et al. 2013; Joyce 1994), often in close association with evidence of ritual feasting and offerings (Joyce and Barber

2015). If death itself was a sacrificial act through which people fed the gods (López Austin 1988:321; Monaghan 1990, 2009), then human interments in cemeteries could have been animating offerings as well. Although cemeteries are rare in other parts of Mesoamerica, bodies were, at times, interred in public buildings, including victims of human sacrifice (Schele and Freidel 1990; Sugiyama 1989). Bodies buried in cemeteries in the lower Río Verde Valley were frequently disturbed by later interments, much like sequential offerings of ceramic vessels. Indeed, caching and burial share a number of characteristics that have led archaeologists to see parallels between the two practices (Becker 1993; Hendon 2000). For example, Marshall Becker (1993) has argued for treating burials and caches as "earth offerings" of analogous, if not identical, meanings. Considered in the context of animate buildings, the interment of the dead in public spaces may represent a sharing or transference of vital forces between different kinds of community members: the living, the dead, other-than-human animate spaces, and deities.

Like the human bodies themselves, offerings that accompanied burials in cemeteries may have

a

b

figure 11.14
Sections of the Cerro de la Virgen offering. Photograph by Jeff Brzezinski (Joyce and Barber 2015:fig. 3b).

nourished the buildings. Although most interments were unaccompanied by offerings, a few notable ones were present. A young man in the cemetery at Yugüe, who was probably a high-status ritual specialist, was interred wearing a pyrite mirror and holding an elaborately incised bone flute (Barber and Olivera Sánchez 2012). The complex iconography represents a personified image of the flute as an animate entity whose breath or voice makes manifest an ancestor impersonating the rain deity for purposes of agricultural fertility, as suggested by references to maize, rain, and wind (Figure 11.16). Like the flute, the pyrite mirror, as well as inlays of pyrite in the teeth of another interred individual, may have also been a witness that allowed deities or ancestors to communicate with the living and vice versa (Olivier 2003:240–265).

Surprisingly, and in contrast to the public buildings at outlying sites like Cerro de la Virgen and Yugüe, the acropolis at the urban center of Río Viejo lacks evidence for practices that would have animated and fed the building (Joyce and Barber 2015). The acropolis was by far the largest structure in the region (Figure 11.17), and its construction likely required the mobilization of labor from nearby communities, as well as from Río Viejo (Joyce, Levine, and Barber 2013). Despite large-scale excavations over the course of four field seasons, however, offerings meant to animate or sustain the building are virtually unknown. It is possible that offerings involving the initial animation of the acropolis lie deeply buried in its earliest construction levels. Sequential offerings designed to feed and sustain buildings at other sites, however, are always located in accessible places near the surface of public buildings and should have been easily exposed by the excavations. The only ceremonial practices that are visible on the acropolis are those related to ritual feasting and termination ceremonies.

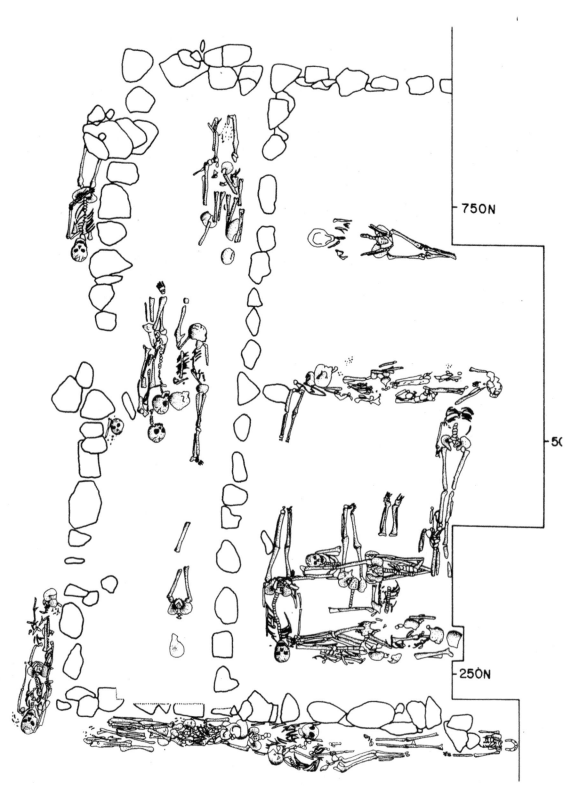

750N

250N

figure 11.15
The cemetery at Cerro de la Cruz (Joyce 1994:fig. 9).

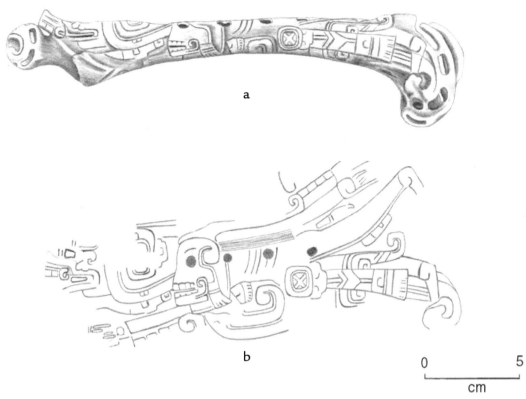

figure 11.16
An offering of an incised bone flute from the burial of a ritual specialist at Yugüe: a) a drawing of the flute (Barber and Olvera Sánchez 2012:fig. 6a); and b) a rollout of the imagery (Barber, Sánchez, and Olvera 2009:fig. 4).

Termination rituals were carried out during the later Formative period in the lower Río Verde Valley probably as a means of releasing vital forces from buildings and associated objects. In most cases, these included relatively modest rituals in restricted public settings involving the destruction of the building by fire and the emplacement of modest offerings in pits (Barber 2013; Brzezinski 2015). On Río Viejo's acropolis, termination practices were much larger in scale and were carried out over a significant period of time, perhaps several decades (Figure 11.18). The acropolis was terminated and abandoned at the very end of the Terminal Formative period, as Río Viejo declined in size and political prominence (Joyce 2010). Termination ceremonies involved the burning of public buildings, followed by the capping of the acropolis by thin fill layers, some containing high densities of broken ceramics. In several areas, pits were then dug into these fill layers in which sherds and whole or partial vessels were placed.

These practices resemble evidence of termination ceremonies found in other parts of Mesoamerica (e.g., Hutson et al., this volume; Mock 1998; Stanton, Brown, and Pagliaro 2008).

Overall, the evidence from the lower Río Verde Valley shows that animating practices were carried out in public buildings throughout the region and included both the interment of objects and perhaps human bodies (Joyce et al. 2016). The scale of some offerings, particularly involving the sustenance of public buildings, far exceeded the Formative-period offerings in the Valley of Oaxaca. In fact, at Yugüe, San Francisco de Arriba, and especially Cerro de la Virgen—sites where public buildings have been extensively investigated—most areas of Formative-period public space that were excavated yielded impressive subfloor offerings. The scale of both human bodies and offerings emplaced in public buildings is distinctive relative to practices elsewhere in Mesoamerica. Curiously, the one

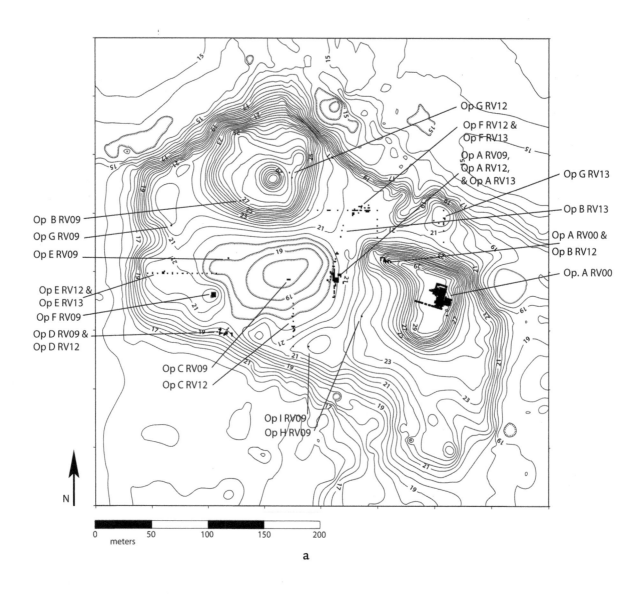

Op G RV12

Op F RV12 &
Op F RV13

Op A RV09,
Op A RV12,
& Op A RV13

Op G RV13

Op B RV13

Op A RV00 &
Op B RV12

Op. A RV00

Op B RV09

Op G RV09

Op E RV09

Op E RV12 &
Op E RV13

Op F RV09

Op D RV09 &
Op D RV12

Op C RV09

Op C RV12

Op I RV09

Op H RV09

N

0   50   100   150   200
meters

a

b

figure 11.17
The acropolis at Río Viejo: a) a topographic map showing the locations of excavations; and b) a photograph of the acropolis. Drafted and photographed by Arthur Joyce.

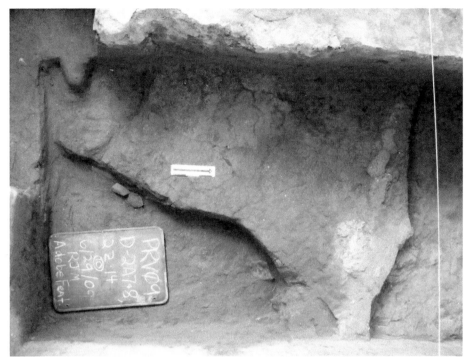

figure 11.18
Termination rituals at
the Río Viejo acropolis:
a) the remnants of
a burned building;
and b) a pit filled
with broken ceramic
vessels. Photographs by
Robert Markens and
Jeff Brzezinski.

a

b

exception to this pattern in the lower Río Verde Valley region was the acropolis at Río Viejo.

Our data suggest that public buildings viewed as living, divine beings were central to the constitution of community in the lower Río Verde Valley (Joyce and Barber 2015). Animating practices instantiated communities as people, ancestors, deities, witnesses, and index objects came together in ceremonies that transferred vital forces to public buildings or released those forces at closure. The interment of human bodies in public buildings linked these structures to the households and families from which the deceased originated, while ornaments linked offerings to living bodies. The interment of locally made pottery tied public buildings to the varied producers and production loci of the vessels. Feasts, perhaps associated with animating ceremonies, instantiated community in commensalism, creating bonds and obligations much like modern indigenous fiestas do in Mesoamerica (Greenberg 1981; Monaghan 1995). In feasting, people shared in the sustenance provided by deities in return for acts of sacrifice as defined by the sacred covenant.

At the same time, animating practices in more restricted public settings, such as on the acropolis at San Francisco de Arriba or Structure 1 at Cerro de la Virgen, likely instantiated social distinctions related to status and access to the divine. The evidence suggests that these ceremonies were carried out by nobility with most of the community excluded. Structure 1 at Cerro de la Virgen was located in close spatial proximity to an elite residence, implying that the residents may have been primarily responsible for the care of the animate building. Offerings included exotic imported goods (greenstone, stone masks) and works that required specialized skill to manufacture (stone artifacts in Structure 1 at Cerro de la Virgen), which were typically restricted to the elite. Although none of the offerings seem to communicate liturgies to the same extent as the Structure 35 offering at San José Mogote, they certainly contain references to the sacred covenant in the form of iconography and substances referencing the Rain Deity, sacrifice, and possibly personified maize (Brzezinski, Joyce, and Barber 2017).

Animating Public Buildings in the Mixtec Highlands

The highland Mixteca region is located to the west of the Valley of Oaxaca and was inhabited by Mixtec-speaking peoples in the Pre-Columbian era, as it is today. During the later Formative period, perhaps a dozen urban hilltop centers emerged in the Mixteca, and public architecture has been excavated at Yucuita, Monte Negro, Cerro Jazmín, Huamelulpan, and Cerro de las Minas (Acosta and Romero 1992; Gaxiola 1984; Pérez Rodríguez et al. 2017; Winter 1982, 2007).

Unlike in the Valley of Oaxaca and the lower Río Verde Valley, evidence from the Mixteca indicates that animating practices may not have been associated with public buildings at this time, since offerings have not been reported (Acosta and Romero 1992; Gaxiola 1984; Pérez Rodríguez et al. 2017; Winter 1982, 2007). At Monte Negro and Cerro Jazmín, the burning of some public buildings at the time of their abandonment, as well as instances of whole vessels left on the floors of temples, raises the possibility of termination rituals (Acosta and Romero 1992:75–87; Pérez Rodríguez et al. 2017), although this pattern is not common at other sites and could have resulted from other kinds of abandonment processes. Possible animating offerings in the Mixteca are limited to human interments found in a few public buildings (Acosta and Romero 1992; Jeffrey Blomster, personal communication, 2017; Pérez Rodríguez et al. 2017), and four skulls with holes drilled in the forehead for suspension accompanied by an elaborate offering associated with an altar at Huamelulpan (Gaxiola 1984:47–55). More excavations are needed in public buildings before we can be definitive about the lack of animating practices, however.

Conclusions

The results of this comparative study show major variation in Formative-period animating practices in public buildings in Oaxaca. In the Valley of Oaxaca, animating practices were largely restricted to the elite and involved exotic and highly valued objects. In the lower Río Verde Valley, practices involving the initial animation of public buildings, especially if they were spatially restricted, were likely limited to elites and involved special offerings, while those associated with the ongoing sustenance of buildings appear to have been accessible to the larger community. In the Mixteca, clear evidence for animating practices has not been found. Needless to say, the data from the three regions show that animating practices varied greatly.

One question raised by this review is whether the variability in animating acts simply reflects different means through which vital forces were transferred to buildings based on similar understandings of the nature of being, or did this variation instantiate significantly different ontologies (cf. Kosiba, this volume; Swenson 2015)? Taking into consideration all of the animating entities bundled in offerings within public buildings in the Valley of Oaxaca and the lower Río Verde Valley, I see a considerable degree of overlap (e.g., ceramics, greenstone, human and animal remains, bodily ornaments, deity masks, objects depicting personified maize, etc.). One element with significant variation, however, is the human agents contributing to animating practices. In the Valley of Oaxaca, such acts appear to have been carried out primarily by elites, while in the lower Río Verde Valley the broader community and elites were entangled in the materialities through which public buildings were animated. This raises the possibility that what distinguished the nature of nobles and non-nobles, especially in regard to how they related to other animate entities, differed in the Valley of Oaxaca relative to the lower Río Verde Valley. Specifically, nobles in the Valley of Oaxaca had abilities that allowed them to contribute to animating agency, while commoners did not. It is also possible that the ontological aspects of the animating abilities of elites were to some extent authorized by political authorities. This does not appear to have been the case in the lower Río Verde Valley, where elites and commoners alike contributed to and engaged with animating agencies.

The data from the Mixteca seem even more puzzling, although Monaghan (1998:50) anticipated the results of this study based on his ethnographic research. He found that among the contemporary Mixtecs of Nuyoo, all things were viewed as alive, with the exception of burned rocks (Monaghan 1995:98). Why then would buildings or other things need to be animated (Monaghan 1998:50)? He anticipates at most a simple offering to the Earth Lords at the onset of construction, rather than specifically animating practices. Although I am not arguing for continuity between one small section of the Mixteca today and a much larger area two thousand years ago, the parallel is intriguing. Does

the lack of evidence for animating practices in the Mixteca also suggest a distinct ontology, such that life was the initial state of being for nearly all entities or that humans lacked the agency to transfer vital forces to buildings? If so, then public buildings in the Mixteca also seemingly lack evidence for the kinds of relationships that constitute personhood among the Maya (Hutson et al., this volume). In contrast, some of these relationships, involving the care and nourishment of public buildings, can be seen in the Formative-period Valley of Oaxaca and in the lower Río Verde Valley region.

Ontological questions aside, the evidence strongly indicates that animating practices had political implications, at least in the Valley of Oaxaca and the lower Río Verde Valley (Joyce and Barber 2015). In both regions, animating practices were among a suite of religious innovations that developed during the later Formative period, including the massive scaling up of public architecture and ceremony, human sacrifice, and the earliest manifestations of divinities like the Rain God. Regardless of why buildings began to be subjects of animating practices, the people and other-than-human beings that came together to animate these buildings increasingly differentiated nobles and commoners and contributed to unequal wealth and political power.

Public buildings themselves were likely important sources of political power, particularly for elites in the Valley of Oaxaca who engaged with animate buildings in ceremonial performances and acted as their caretakers. As instantiations of the animating forces that were transferred to and concentrated within public buildings, these structures were powerful beings and likely conduits between humans and the divine. The spatially restricted settings, exotic materials, and specialized knowledge and abilities that were fundamental components of animating acts in the Valley of Oaxaca made nobles central to the practices through which public buildings were animated. These features were evident even in some of the earliest animating practices at San José Mogote and only became more prominent with the founding of Monte Albán as assemblages involving nobles and public buildings increasingly mediated between people and divinities. The centrality of nobles in animating practices was established, whether it was a result of their inherent being or simply because elites had the knowledge, influence, connections, and economic resources to sponsor the construction of public buildings and acquire the exotic materials necessary for their animation. The presence of modest offerings in construction fill at Monte Albán leaves open the possibility that commoners made animating offerings, if only informally.

In the lower Río Verde Valley, special staging, restricted participation, exotic objects, and special knowledge and abilities are also evident in practices involving the initial animation of buildings such as at Structure 1 at Cerro de la Virgen (Brzezinski, Joyce, and Barber 2017). As in the highlands, these practices contributed to the increasing differentiation of coastal elites from commoners. The materiality of animating practices on the coast, however, was more constraining in this regard relative to conditions in the highlands. As argued by myself and Barber (2015), public buildings were central to the assemblages that constituted local communities like Cerro de la Cruz, Yugüe, and Cerro de la Virgen. Although local leaders were prominent in the initial animation of these buildings, the larger community was involved in their ongoing feeding and sustenance through the emplacement of the bodies of ancestors, as well as ceramic vessels and their contents. The persistence and durability of the bones of ancestors and ceremonial offerings emplaced within public facilities at outlying sites tightly bound community members—local elites and commoners alike—to these animate buildings who, as social beings, were community members as well. The construction of the acropolis at Río Viejo engaged people from multiple communities in a large-scale collective works project and created the capacity for reorganizing and expanding the scale of assemblages that could have stabilized a politically centralized polity and driven greater inequalities in wealth, status, and access to the divine, as it did in the Valley of Oaxaca. At the same time, people were pulled away from their obligations to local community members, including public buildings, creating sites of tension and potential conflict between local and regional collectivities and authorities. These tensions are seen in the lack of offerings in the acropolis, which would have directly competed with the feeding of public buildings in local communities. The result was that the multi-community links and centralized political authority that could have come to define a polity were fleeting and unstable, and Río Viejo collapsed shortly after its emergence as a political center.

Overall, the results of this study indicate that animating practices in Mesoamerica could be highly variable in both their expression and political implications. While animating practices associated with public buildings facilitated political inequality and centralization in the Valley of Oaxaca, the materiality of animate buildings constrained the scaling up of political authority in the lower Río Verde Valley.

Acknowledgments

I would like to thank the Instituto Nacional de Antropología e Historia for permission to carry out field research in the lower Río Verde Valley. I thank Steve Kosiba, John Janusek, and Tom Cummins for inviting me to participate in the Dumbarton Oaks symposium and in the resulting volume, as well as for their input on this chapter, and I thank Stacy Barber, Jeff Blomster, Jeff Brzezinski, Scott Hutson, Steve Kosiba, John Monaghan, Verónica Pérez Rodríguez, Javier Urcid, and two anonymous reviewers for providing helpful suggestions.

Acosta, Jorge R.

1949   El pectoral de jade de Monte Albán. *Anales del Instituto Nacional de Antropología e Historia* 3:17–25.

Acosta, Jorge R., and Javier Romero

1992   *Exploraciones en Monte Negro, Oaxaca: 1937–1938, 1938–1939, y 1939–1940.* Instituto Nacional de Antropología e Historia, Mexico City.

Barber, Sarah B.

2013   Defining Community and Status at Outlying Sites during the Terminal Formative Period. In *Polity and Ecology in Formative Period Coastal Oaxaca*, edited by Arthur A. Joyce, pp. 165–192. University Press of Colorado, Boulder.

Barber, Sarah B., Arthur A. Joyce, Arion T. Mayes, José Aguilar, and Michelle Butler

2013   Formative Period Burial Practices and Cemeteries. In *Polity and Ecology in Formative Period Coastal Oaxaca*, edited by Arthur A. Joyce, pp. 97–134. University Press of Colorado, Boulder.

Barber, Sarah B., and Mireya Olvera Sánchez

2012   A Divine Wind: The Arts of Death and Music in Terminal Formative Oaxaca. *Ancient Mesoamerica* 23(1):9–24.

Barber, Sarah B., Gonzalo A. Sánchez, and Mireya Olvera Sánchez

2009   Sounds of Death and Life in Meso-america: The Bone Flutes of Ancient Oaxaca. *Yearbook of Traditional Music* 41:40–56.

Becker, Marshall J.

1993   Earth Offering among the Classic Period Lowland Maya: Burials and Caches as Ritual Deposits. In *Perspectivas antropológicas en el mundo maya*, vol. 2, edited by María Josefa Iglesias Ponce de León and Francisco de Asís Ligorred Perramón, pp. 45–74. Publicaciones de la S.E.E.M., Barcelona.

Bell, Catherine

1992   *Ritual Theory, Ritual Practice.* Oxford University Press, New York.

Blanton, Richard E., Gary M. Feinman, Stephen A. Kowalewski, and Linda M. Nicholas

1999   *Ancient Oaxaca.* Cambridge University Press, Cambridge.

Brown, Linda A., and Kitty F. Emery

2008   Negotiations with the Animate Forest: Hunting Shrines in the Guatemalan Highlands. *Journal of Archaeological Method and Theory* 15(4):300–337.

Brzezinski, Jeffrey S.

2015   Excavaciones en Cerro de la Virgen. In *El proyecto Río Verde, informe técnico de la temporada de 2013*, edited by Arthur A. Joyce and Sarah B. Barber, pp. 288–509. Final report submitted to the Consejo Nacional de Arqueología, Instituto Nacional de Antropología e Historia, Mexico City.

2019   Terminal Formative Religion and Political Organization on the Pacific Coast of Oaxaca, Mexico: The Perspective from Cerro de la Virgen. PhD dissertation, University of Colorado, Boulder.

Brzezinski, Jeffrey S., Arthur A. Joyce, and Sarah B. Barber

2017   Constituting Animacy and Community in a Terminal Formative Bundled Offering from the Coast of Oaxaca, Mexico. *Cambridge Archaeological Journal* 27(3):511–531.

Caso, Alfonso

[1935] 2003   Las exploraciones en Monte Albán, temporada 1934–35. In *Obras de Alfonso Caso 2: El México antiguo (Mixtecas y Zapotecas)*, by Alfonso Caso, pp. 259–348. El Colegio Nacional, Mexico City.

[1939] 2002   Resumen del informe de las exploraciones en Oaxaca durante la 7a y la 8a temporadas, 1937–1938 y 1938–1939. In *Obras de Alfonso Caso 1: El México antiguo (Mixtecas y Zapotecas)*, by Alfonso Caso, pp. 153–185. El Colegio Nacional, Mexico City.

Caso, Alfonso, and Ignacio Bernal

1952 *Urnas de Oaxaca.* Memorias del Instituto de Antropología e Historia 2. Instituto Nacional de Antropología e Historia, Mexico City.

Caso, Alfonso, Ignacio Bernal, and Jorge R. Acosta

1967 *La cerámica de Monte Albán.* Memorias 13. Instituto Nacional de Antropología e Historia, Mexico City.

DeLanda, Manuel

2016 *Assemblage Theory.* Edinburgh University Press, Edinburgh.

Flannery, Kent V.

1983 The Development of Monte Albán's Main Plaza in Period II. In *The Cloud People: Divergent Evolution of the Zapotec and Mixtec Civilizations,* edited by Kent V. Flannery and Joyce Marcus, pp. 102–104. Academic Press, New York.

Flannery, Kent V., and Joyce Marcus

2015 *Excavations at San José Mogote 2: The Cognitive Archaeology.* Prehistory and Human Ecology of the Valley of Oaxaca 16. Memoirs of the Museum of Anthropology, University of Michigan, 58. Museum of Anthropology, University of Michigan, Ann Arbor.

Freidel, David A., Linda Schele, and Joy Parker

1993 *Maya Cosmos: Three Thousand Years on the Shaman's Path.* William Morrow, New York.

Furst, Jill L.

1995 *The Natural History of the Soul in Ancient Mexico.* Yale University Press, New Haven.

Gámez Goytia, Gustavo

2002 El eje sagrado en Monte Albán: Elemento central de la arquitectura religiosa zapoteca. In *La religión de Los Binnigula'sa',* edited by Victor de la Cruz and Marcus Winter, pp. 197–217. Fondo Editorial, IEEPO, Oaxaca.

Gaxiola, Margarita

1984 *Huamelulpan: Un centro urbano de la Mixteca Alta.* Colección Científica, Instituto Nacional de Antropología e Historia, Mexico City.

Greenberg, James B.

1981 *Santiago's Sword: Chatino Peasant Religion and Economics.* University of California Press, Berkeley.

Harris, Oliver J. T., and John Robb

2012 Multiple Ontologies and the Problem of the Body in History. *American Anthropologist* 114(4):668–679.

Harrison-Buck, Eleanor

2012 Architecture as Animate Landscape: Circular Shrines in the Ancient Maya Lowlands. *American Anthropologist* 114(1):64–80.

2015 Maya Religion and Gods: Relevance and Relatedness in the Animic Cosmos. In *Tracing the Relational: The Archaeology of Worlds, Spirits, and Temporalities,* edited by Meghan E. Buchanan and B. Jacob Skousen, pp. 115–129. University of Utah Press, Salt Lake City.

Hendon, Julia A.

2000 Having and Holding: Storage, Memory, Knowledge, and Social Relations. *American Anthropologist* 102(1):42–53.

Hutson, Scott R., and Travis W. Stanton

2007 Cultural Logic and Practical Reason: The Structure of Discard in Ancient Maya Houselots. *Cambridge Archaeological Journal* 17(2):123–144.

Joyce, Arthur A.

1994 Late Formative Community Organization and Social Complexity on the Oaxaca Coast. *Journal of Field Archaeology* 21(2):147–168.

2010 *Mixtecs, Zapotecs, and Chatinos: Ancient Peoples of Southern Mexico.* Wiley-Blackwell, Malden, Mass.

n.d. Assembling the City: Monte Albán as a Mountain of Creation and Sustenance. In *New Materialisms Ancient Urbanisms,* edited by Timothy R. Pauketat and Susan M. Alt. Routledge, London, in press.

Joyce, Arthur A., and Sarah B. Barber

2015 Ensoulment, Entrapment, and Political Centralization: A Comparative Study of Religion and Politics in Later Formative Oaxaca. *Current Anthropology* 56(6):819–847.

Joyce, Arthur A., Sarah B. Barber, Jeffrey S. Brzezinski, Carlo J. Lucido, and Victor Salazar Chavez

2016   Negotiating Political Authority and Community in Terminal Formative Coastal Oaxaca. In *Political Strategies in Pre-Columbian Mesoamerica*, edited by Sarah Kurnick and Joanne Baron, pp. 61–96. University Press of Colorado, Boulder.

Joyce, Arthur A., Marc N. Levine, and Sarah B. Barber

2013   Place-Making and Power in the Terminal Formative: Excavations on Río Viejo's Acropolis. In *Polity and Ecology in Formative Period Coastal Oaxaca*, edited by Arthur A. Joyce, pp. 135–164. University Press of Colorado, Boulder.

La Fuente, Julio de

[1949] 1977   *Yalálag: Una villa zapoteca serrana.* Instituto Nacional Indigenista, Mexico City.

Lipp, Frank J.

1991   *The Mixe of Oaxaca: Religion, Ritual, and Healing.* University of Texas Press, Austin.

López Austin, Alfredo

1988   *Human Body and Ideology: Concepts of the Ancient Nahuas.* Vol. 1. University of Utah Press, Salt Lake City.

1989   *Hombre-Dios: Religión y política en el mundo náhuatl.* 2nd ed. Universidad Nacional Autónoma de México, Mexico City.

López Luján, Leonardo

2005   *The Offerings of the Templo Mayor of Tenochtitlan.* Rev. ed. Translated by Bernard R. Ortiz de Montellano and Thelma Ortiz de Montellano. University of New Mexico Press, Albuquerque.

Marcus, Joyce, and Kent V. Flannery

1996   *Zapotec Civilization: How Urban Society Evolved in Mexico's Oaxaca Valley.* Thames and Hudson, London.

Matos Moctezuma, Eduardo

1988   *The Great Temple of the Aztecs: Treasures of Tenochtitlan.* Thames and Hudson, London.

McAnany, Patricia A.

1995   *Living with the Ancestors.* University of Texas Press, Austin.

Mock, Shirley Boteler (editor)

1998   *The Sowing and the Dawning: Termination, Dedication, and Transformation in the Archaeological and Ethnographic Record of Mesoamerica.* University of New Mexico Press, Albuquerque.

Monaghan, John

1990   Sacrifice, Death, and the Origins of Agriculture in the Codex Vienna. *American Antiquity* 55:559–569.

1995   *The Covenants with Earth and Rain.* University of Oklahoma Press, Norman.

1998   Dedication: Ritual or Production? In *The Sowing and the Dawning: Termination, Dedication, and Transformation in the Archaeological and Ethnographic Record of Mesoamerica*, edited by Shirley Boteler Mock, pp. 47–56. University of New Mexico Press, Albuquerque.

2000   Theology and History in the Study of Mesoamerican Religions. In *Ethnology.* Vol. 6 of *Supplement to the Handbook of Middle American Indians*, edited by John Monaghan, pp. 24–49. University of Texas Press, Austin.

2009   Sacrificio y poder en Mesoamérica. In *Bases de la complejidad social en Oaxaca, memoria de la cuarta mesa redonda de Monte Albán*, edited by Nelly M. Robles García, pp. 181–197. INAH, Mexico City.

Olivier, Guilhem

2003   *Mockeries and Metamorphoses of an Aztec God: Tezcatlipoca, the "Lord of the Smoking Mirror."* University Press of Colorado, Boulder.

Pauketat, Timothy R.

2013   *An Archaeology of the Cosmos: Rethinking Agency and Religion in Ancient America.* Routledge, New York.

Pérez Rodríguez, Verónica, Antonio Martínez Tuñón, Laura R. Stiver Walsh, Gilberto Pérez Roldán, and Fabiola Torres Estévez

2017   Feasting and Building an Urban Society in Cerro Jazmin, Oaxaca, Mexico. *Journal of Field Archaeology* 42(2):115–128.

Schele, Linda, and David A. Freidel

  1990   *A Forest of Kings: The Untold Story of the Ancient Maya.* William Morrow, New York.

Schele, Linda, and Mary Ellen Miller

  1986   *The Blood of Kings: Dynasty and Ritual in Maya Art.* Kimbell Art Museum, Fort Worth, Tex.

Stanton, Travis W., M. Kathryn Brown, and Jonathan B. Pagliaro

  2008   Garbage of the Gods? Squatters, Refuse Disposal, and Termination Rituals among the Ancient Maya. *Latin American Antiquity* 19(3):227–247.

Stross, Brian

  1998   Seven Ingredients in Mesoamerican Ensoulment. In *The Sowing and the Dawning: Termination, Dedication, and Transformation in the Archaeological and Ethnographic Record of Mesoamerica,* edited by Shirley Boteler Mock, pp. 31–39. University of New Mexico Press, Albuquerque.

Sugiyama, Saburo

  1989   Burials Dedicated to the Old Temple of Quetzalcoatl at Teotihuacan, Mexico. *American Antiquity* 54(1):85–106.

Swenson, Edward R.

  2015   The Materialities of Place-Making in the Ancient Andes: A Critical Appraisal of the Ontological Turn in Archaeological Interpretation. *Journal of Archaeological Method and Theory* 22(3):677–712.

Tedlock, Dennis

  1996   *Popol Vuh.* 2nd ed. Simon and Schuster, New York.

Urcid, Javier

  2009   Personajes enmascarados: El rayo, el trueno y la lluvia en Oaxaca. *Arqueología mexicana* 16(96):30–34.

  2011   Sobre la antigüedad de cofres para augurar y propiciar la lluvia. *Arqueología mexicana* 19(110):16–21.

Vogt, Evon Z.

  1976   *Tortillas for the Gods: A Symbolic Analysis of Zinacanteco Rituals.* Harvard University Press, Cambridge, Mass.

Winter, Marcus

  1982   *Guía zona arqueológica de Yucuita.* Centro INAH Oaxaca, Oaxaca.

  2007   *Cerro de las Minas: Arqueología de la Mixteca Baja.* 2nd ed. Centro INAH Oaxaca, Oaxaca.

Workinger, Andrew

  2002   Coastal/Highland Interaction in Prehispanic Oaxaca, Mexico: The Perspective from San Francisco de Arriba. PhD dissertation, Vanderbilt University, Nashville.

Zedeño, María Nieves

  2009   Animating by Association: Index Objects and Relational Taxonomies. *Cambridge Archaeological Journal* 19:407–417.

12

The Material Ambivalence of Health and Spirituality in Colonial Northeastern New Spain

DIANA DIPAOLO LOREN

FRANCISCAN FATHER GASPAR JOSÉ DE SOLÍS'S 1767–1768 diary of his yearlong mission-inspection tour provides the reader with some tantalizing details on the aspects of daily life for Native Americans and Spaniards living in northeastern New Spain (present-day western Louisiana and eastern Texas). His diary documented mission communities, with notations on small details—what houses looked like, what foods were available, what people wore—as well as the struggles of daily life, such as lack of adequate supplies from Mexico City, hostilities between Spaniards and Native Americans, the threat of starvation, and also constant waves of disease and sickness. Threading through the document is a discussion of how successful Franciscan fathers were in converting the indigenous population to Catholicism. Yet, as the diary makes clear, the priests were less than popular. Many Native Americans actively scorned the Franciscans, only coming to them in the hour of death to receive "Holy Baptism, although it is suspected that many ask for it as

a natural remedy for obtaining bodily health" (Kress, Solís, and Hatcher 1931:65).

It is not surprising that Native Americans and Spaniards came to Franciscan priests for healing, as they were known to be healers. During the eighteenth century, theories of disease and illness were intertwined with Catholic doctrines regarding spiritual well-being. Spanish settlers in frontier locations such as northeastern New Spain often sought medical treatment from priests, who were schooled to tend to the religious and medical needs of their communities (Foster 1953; Loren 2014). Father Solís even documented medicinal plants along his journey to share that knowledge with other Franciscans: "The 28th we passed through a very beautiful plain, surrounded by thick woods called La Escaramuza: from here begins the Virgin Viperine, herb of many virtues, very medicinal" (Kress, Solís, and Hatcher 1931:33).

Solís's diary also included documentation of other healers in the region, namely Native American shamans and dances (*mitotes*) performed to encourage individual and community well-being (Kress, Solís, and Hatcher 1931:41–68). Franciscans scorned not only Native American healing practices but also the work of *curandero/as*, male or female practitioners of folk medicine who treated a variety of medical and spirituals concerns, including childbirth, fever, and the evil eye (*mal de ojo*) (Guerra 1976). Reading through archival accounts reveals that the inhabitants of northeastern New Spain were somewhat ambivalent regarding who they visited to receive relief from ailments. Just as Native Americans sought treatment from Father Solís, Spanish and mestizo settlers also visited *curandero/as* and priests (Goldberg 2017). This suggests that we reconsider the presumed boundary between Native American and Catholic bodily and healing ontologies as these boundaries were more fluid in everyday lived experience, suggesting some convergence of practice when bodies were ailing. What I suggest is that on this colonial frontier, while ontological understandings of illness differed, the enactment of healing, and animacy of material culture in treatment, at times came from a place of ambivalence. This case study provides an opportunity to see beyond the kinds of ontological essentialisms and dichotomies that often lie within current literature.

This ambivalence found at the intersection of magic, medicine, and religion has left a residue in the archaeological record. Small objects, such as crucifixes, amulets, and even eggshells, were used in practices of bodily and spiritual healing. These inanimate objects took on meaning and significance in the hands of the healer or the afflicted where they were charged with metaphysical power. Lost, discarded, or purposefully buried, they have become artifacts that require attention to reanimate them in our historical memory. In this chapter, I consider how material culture found in the archaeological record of two sites—Mission Dolores and Presidio Los Adaes—in northeastern New Spain was used to heal and protect bodies through practices of faith, spirituality, and medicine. Amulets and religious items are the focus in this discussion, as they were objects used on or near corporeal bodies that were used by Native American, Spanish, and mestizo people in the practices of faith and medicine in lived experience.

Eighteenth-Century Northeastern New Spain

In the early eighteenth century, the northeastern border of New Spain abutted the western border of French Louisiana along the Red River. Nuestra Señora de Los Dolores de Los Ais and San Miguel de Linares de Los Adaes were two of six missions established in 1716–1717 on the northeastern frontier of New Spain so that Franciscans could begin converting local Ais and Adai Caddo communities to Christianity (Weber 1992). Mission Dolores was short-lived, abandoned in 1719. Skirmishes on the Spanish-French border related to the War of Quadruple Alliance (1717–1720) led to efforts to further secure the border against the French, resulting in the construction of several presidios in the region and the reestablishment of Mission Dolores close to its initial location in the early 1720s. In 1721, the presidio of Nuestra Señora del Pilar de Los Adaes was built adjacent to Mission San Miguel, about 60 miles away from Mission Dolores (Figure 12.1) (Corbin et al. 1990; Gregory 1984; Gregory et al. 2004).

The communities at Los Adaes (both the presidio and the mission) and Mission Dolores differed slightly in regard to their populations. Los Adaes and Mission Dolores together had a total population of four hundred individuals. At Los Adaes, this included Franciscans, Spanish and mestizo military personnel, and civilian families and Caddo Adai people (Avery 1995, 1996; Gregory 1984; Gregory et al. 2004; Perttula 1992). At Mission Dolores, the population was Franciscan priests and lay brothers, as well as Spanish and mestizo military personnel and families, surrounded by the Ais (Avery 2008; Carlson and Quinn 1996; Corbin et al. 1990).

The mission and presidio communities in northeastern New Spain were expected to be self-sufficient and pious. Regulations for soldiers and settlers stipulated that they should not blaspheme or swear, they must attend Mass, they must be industrious in growing grains and raising livestock for daily consumption, and they must limit

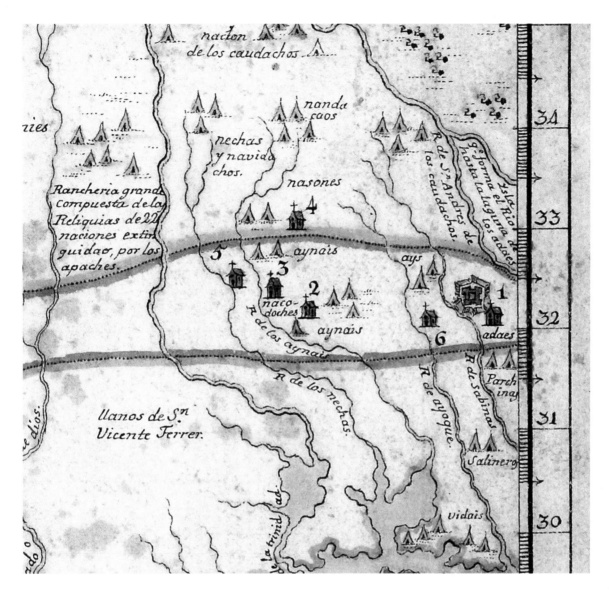

figure 12.1
Detail of *Plano corographico e hydrographico de las provincias . . . de la Nueba España*, 1728, by Francisco Álvarez Barreiro, depicting both the Mission Dolores and Los Adaes communities © British Library Board, Cartographic Items Additional MS. 17,650.b.

their interactions with Native Americans to the encouragement of Catholic conversion (Naylor and Polzer 1988:259–279). Unsurprisingly, life in these remote communities rarely mirrored this imperial vision of segregated indigenous and European worlds. Supplies of goods were infrequent from San Antonio and Mexico City, resulting in numerous shortages of daily necessities such as soap and clothing (Jackson 1995). The Spanish population suffered from malnutrition and illness. Numerous

waves of illness were recorded in 1754 alone, with relief coming from priests and members of the presidio community who compounded medicines (Bexar Archives 1754). With cessation of hostilities between Spain and France in 1763, the Marqués de Rubí and Father Gaspar José de Solís were sent out to inspect the missions and presidios along the eastern frontier. As a result of these inspections, Mission Dolores, Mission San Miguel, and Los Adaes were closed; they were deemed unnecessary to frontier border maintenance, and their inhabitants migrated to Louisiana and other communities in Spanish Texas.

Archaeological excavations at Los Adaes presidio were conducted in the late twentieth century by Pete Gregory (1973, 1980, 1982, 1984, 1985), who located the governor's house inside the presidio walls and three structures outside the presidio (Avery 1996). Kathleen Gilmore, Jim Corbin (1977; Corbin, Alex, and Kalina 1980; Corbin et al. 1990), Shawn Carlson (Carlson and Quinn 1996), and George Avery (2008) all conducted different excavations at Mission Dolores beginning in the 1970s and made progress toward determining the scope of the deposits and identifying architectural remnants not disturbed by highway construction. Cumulatively, these excavations revealed trash pits, the remains of numerous structures, and perimeter walls related to the mission, while also indicating that the majority of the mission building was destroyed by highway construction earlier in the twentieth century.

Materiality, Animacy, and the Colonial Body

Archaeologists continue to redefine their understanding of the relationship between people and things. Those who employ the broadly defined "New Materialism" suggest that we reconceptualize human interactions with things and disavow the passive nature of objects, as found in actor network theory (e.g., Latour 2005), materialist approaches (e.g., Miller 2005), entanglement theory (e.g., Hodder 2012), and symmetrical approaches (e.g., Olsen 2010). The focus shifts toward how people and things together construct material worlds and environments, moving away from agency placed solely in the realm of the human subject (Ingold 2007; Joyce, this volume; Robb 2010). How people understand things is framed by context and their ontological beliefs, but in some contexts, new environments impact current ontologies. In the case of northeastern New Spain, missions and presidios brought new people (and their ontologies) together in unfamiliar ways. Ontological presuppositions

were challenged and relationships to things shifted so that they became significant or meaningful in new ways (see Kosiba, this volume). In periods of substantive change, then, we need to consider a more situated context, as familiar networks and assemblages were changed by new relationships between bodies and things.

The need to transcend the dualisms (human and nonhuman, colonist and colonizer, nature and culture) that have continued to haunt archaeological interpretations emerges in ontological discussions. This is challenging work, as some theory "simply recreates the dualities it seeks to eradicate" (Harris and Cipolla 2017:93). Others find the answer in greater attention to ontological questions about the reality of "worlds" as people understand them and the pluralizing of ontologies (e.g., Alberti 2016; Harris and Robb 2012; Hutson et al., this volume; Strathern 1988, 1992; Viveiros de Castro 1998). Eduardo Viveiros de Castro (1998), for example, presents perspectivism as another way destabilize Western assumptions. Yet while he asks us to imagine a world where a shaman can turn into a jaguar, we are still left with the problem of dueling ontologies: that of the indigenous American and that of the Westerner (see Kosiba, this volume). There are still more ontologies to consider, particularly with regard to the body, healing, and illness.

Oliver Harris and John Robb (2012) place the body at the center of their discussion of ontologies, folding in relevance of the material world to explore how all groups have more than one way of engaging with their bodies. They argue that blurred boundaries between ontologies more accurately described lived experience for non-Western and Western peoples and that, in practical action, "people alternated between different understandings more or less seamlessly" (Harris and Robb 2012:670). Contradictions are inherent, and people move through multiple ontologies simultaneously as there is no one exclusive way of knowing one's body. This assertion holds as we consider the body in sickness and health.

Anthropologist Annemarie Mol (2002:6) argues along a similar vein for "the body multiple," stating that "no object, no body, no disease is singular." Rather, the body and its diseases reflect the multiplicity of reality in practice. Ontologies are not fixed; rather, they are "brought into being, sustained, or allowed to wither away in common, day-to-day, sociomaterial practices" (Mol 2002:6). Illness and healing practice are not about a shared, coherent ontology. What is illness? What does it mean to heal and how is comfort achieved? As Mol (2002) demonstrates, there are different metaphysical and material strategies for achieving what is perceived as "health." The ways in which diseases are embodied and how materials are animate in healing can entail different, and often multiple, ontologies.

My concern here is on bodily objects found in the archaeological record: the small animate items that attend to bodily concerns (Loren 2019). The world of bodily objects, while rare numerically in the archaeological record, is quite robust in terms of scope. Bodily objects include "small finds": closures for clothing such as buttons and buckles, jewelry and personal adornments, and needlework tools such as thimbles and needles (Beaudry 2006; Deagan 2002; Galke 2009; Joyce 2005; Loren 2010, 2014, 2019; Loren and Beaudry 2005; White 2005; White and Beaudry 2009). Bodily objects are those that materialize the needs and desires of the physical and spiritual body; they are embodied in different practices of presenting and performing one's body, healthy or otherwise (Chaplin 2003; Joyce 2005; Loren 2019).

When used in healing, items of material culture—crucifixes, amulets—were animate in relation to multiple bodily ontologies, even in colonial contexts when certain ontologies were forced on indigenous populations. Joyce (this volume) emphasizes the animacy of the built environment as it manifests power and authority. This much is true, as can be seen in his discussion of Pre-Columbian Oaxaca architecture, but power and authority can also be found in animating practices associated with small things. The small finds that I discuss were recovered from a colonial location: Spanish presidios and missions meant to convert and control Native American communities. Power imbalances were inherent in those landscapes, and small finds provide insight into the reaches of colonial power and the ambivalence to it in action.

The population of New Spain was to be Catholic. Indigenous peoples were to be converted, and efforts were put in place to maintain the religion of most Catholics. Imperial anxieties regarding the physical and spiritual state of the colony and those relations that disrupted ordered colonial hierarchies and threatened imperial loyalties were palpable, marked and recorded in historical accounts, documented by sumptuary laws, and preserved in colonial archives (Lindman and Tarter 2001; Loren 2007; Stoler 2009). In this archive, health and appearance emerge as important facets of imperial control over individual bodies and the body politic. Unhealthy bodies were seen as a threat to colonization, which was successful when colonized and colonizer espoused cleanliness, hard work, and morality (Goldberg 2017:3). As Mark Goldberg (2017:41) notes, this work fell to priests as "conversion involved multiple areas of instruction: Catholic prayer, colonial politics and law, husbandry, and diet and household living; Spanish marital traditions and gender, sexual, and familial norms; and the right way to dress." Linen was distributed for the production of clothing; men were to wear linen shirts, pants, hats, and a rosary, while women were to wear blouses, skirts, linen underskirts, camisoles, and petticoats, as well as shoes, earrings and necklaces, and rosaries (Goldberg 2017:47). Yet the lived reality of colonialism rarely matched these ideals, as both colonizers and colonized peoples often constituted and reconstituted identities to stabilize uncertain environments and curb anxieties around the flesh, disease, and sin.

Eighteenth-century European medicine was built on the belief that the body was composed of four humors: black bile, yellow bile, phlegm, and blood (Foster 1953). The causes of illnesses—such as pneumonia, influenza, smallpox, tumors—were tied to mechanical imbalances of these four humors. The classification of these imbalances differed in Europe. Some argued that "anima" (the soul) was at the heart of everything and that disease was the soul's attempt to reestablish bodily order, whereas other physicians took the view that the body was a machine and disease was the body's way of expelling foreign matter (Shyrock 1960).

Body and soul were implicated in these ontologies as imbalance could also be caused by sin or witchcraft. Balance could then be restored to the body through diet, prayer, bloodletting, purging, vomiting, and ingestion or the application of certain compounds (Foster 1953; Shyrock 1960).

Spanish accounts indicated that religious and healing practices in many indigenous communities were tied to competing forces of good and evil (Swanton 1942:219–226). Practices of healing, including the application and ingestion of herbs as well as the performance of songs and ceremonies, were longstanding in Native American communities in northeastern New Spain (Swanton 1942:224–226). Rituals intended to aid individuals, such as those carried out to cure illness and commemorate death, also took place under the supervision of shamans. Although viewed with suspicion, Spanish priests also took careful note of Native American uses of local plants and herbs to use in their own healing practices (Goldberg 2017:17). These represented broad ontological assumptions about how the Native Americans and Spanish viewed their bodies, complicated in colonial politics. How these ontologies were re-created or disregarded in practical action, however, is another matter.

In New Spain, surgeons and pharmacies were rare outside of Mexico City. A number of different diseases and maladies impacted the population of northern New Spain during the eighteenth century, including dysentery, smallpox, and influenza (Foster 1953; Nava 1795). Infectious diseases were endemic in the Spanish mission and presidio communities. For example, a 1754 account notes waves of influenza and other ailments that plagued the communities in northeastern New Spain (Bexar Archives 1754). In addition to prayer, Franciscan priests utilized herbal remedies brought from Europe and some that were popular with Native Americans. A few soldiers became renowned as lay surgeons, and some presidios acquired trained surgeons.

Physical health and spiritual salvation were closely connected in the eighteenth century. Caring for the sick was part of the Seven Corporal Works of Mercy (charitable acts of mercy for bodily needs) and carried out by priests (Guerra 1969). Tending to medical needs, as well as spiritual needs, fell into the hands of priests as a part of their daily routine. This practice was spiritual and pragmatic: to save souls, the body must be healed. Members of the Jesuit and Augustinian religious orders ministered to people in remote regions of New Spain where access to doctors and surgeons was rare or nonexistent. Priests and religious missionaries wrote many of the first medical books in New Spain. For example, Jesuit brother Juan de Esteyneffer's *Florilegio medicinal*, published in Mexico in 1712, combined European medical knowledge with knowledge of indigenous herbs found in New Spain (Kay 1977). Produced for missionaries, the *Florilegio* was a sourcebook for the diagnosis and treatment of diseases, surgical methods, and the composition of common medicines. The *Florilegio* and other medical books included prayers, as well as *novenas*, for preventing and curing disease (Guerra 1969, 1976).

Eighteenth-century folk medicine performed by someone formally schooled in the "physick," or more formal medicine, drew from knowledge about the world as it was then understood (Foster 1953; Goldberg 2017; Graham 1976). While folk medicine was used for physical care (illness, childbirth, pregnancy), it was also used for curing *mal de ojo* (evil eye) and other disorders considered to be causes of illness, such as shame, fear, anger, envy, and longing (Foster 1953). Practitioners of *curandería* could be male or female. Within New Spain, they were distinguished from priests by their magical curative powers, which the *curandero/a* attributed to God (Graham 1976; Quezada 1991). *Curandería* was a hybridized healing practice, containing elements derived from both indigenous and Spanish cultures, in which a male or female healer prayed for spiritual cleansing and protection against evil spirits or the acts of a *brujo* (witch) who had the power to cast the *mal de ojo* and imbalance humors (Foster 1953). The *curandero/a*'s rituals consistently used such Catholic symbols as crucifixes, rosaries, and holy pictures.

Archival accounts suggest that the populations of Los Adaes and Mission Dolores were ambivalent in their preference for Catholic or folk healing. For example, Solís noted in 1768 the important role of priests in attending to the physical and spiritual wellness of the community:

> This mission of Señor San Miguel de Cuellar de los Adays [sic] is situated in a dense forest of thick trees, pines, post oaks, pin oaks.... The ministers (who only occupy themselves in ministering to all the white people of the royal presidio and ranches, of which there are some) suffer many needs, and even lack the necessary things. By the time that aid reaches them, which is given to them by the piety of the King, Our Lord (may God guard him), they have already suffered and had these experience.... The people live on the corn and do not have any sown fields. The flesh of the bulls that is furnished them is very bad. All seed, such as corn, frijoles etc. is scarce. There is only an abundance of whiskey, with which they are provided by the French of Nachitos [sic] who are seven leagues from here. In regard to the organization of the mission, there is no Indian congregation, because although they are numerous they do not wish to congregate, and go to the presidio rather than to the mission. What has been and is a consolation, as I have been assured by the old men, since many of the first who came in to settle in this country are still living, is that all of the Indians, both men and women, old and young, send for the Father in the hour of death, wherever they may be in order that he may "*echar el Horco Santo*," that is administer the Holy Baptism, although it is suspected that many ask for it as a natural remedy for obtaining bodily health. (Kress, Solís, and Hatcher 1931:64–65)

In comparison, in 1778 Franciscan father Juan Agustín Morfí described the actions of local Caddo *curandero/as*: "The multitude of medicine men (*curanderos*) with which this nation is flooded, contribute powerfully to the maintenance of faith . . . to deceive a superstitious people, who, instructed in advance in their favor, believe without examination, whatever these imposters propose to them" (quoted in Swanton 1942:223, emphasis in original).

Religious officials were often highly suspicious of the curative powers of the *curandero/as*, and in some Spanish colonial contexts these healers were persecuted and punished for idolatry and witchcraft (Quezada 1991). Knowledge of the body and humors, as well as the kinds of performances involved with acts of curing, differed between the two groups of healers: priests and *curandero/as*. Franciscan healers dispensed medicine and spiritual advice and quietly prayed over the bodies of the ill, while *curandero/as* (both Native American and non–Native American), who also dispensed medicine and spiritual advice, prayed, danced, and performed in more elaborate healing ceremonies (Foster 1953; Goldberg 2017). In this context, caring for the body was embedded in social practices that recognized various ways and means of healing spirit and flesh.

Bodily Objects of Health and Spirituality

Throughout his travels, Father Solís would remark on the places he stopped to say Mass: "On the 24th, feast day of the Patron Señor San Joseph, we said mass, and planted a large cross as the Ritual commands" (Kress, Solís, and Hatcher 1931:57). The importance of material culture in Catholic Mass needs almost no elaboration. Yet in the archaeological record, the residue of worship is admittedly faint. What remains from religious and other spiritual and healing practices are small items, such as crucifixes, amulets, and pharmaceutical vials. Even with this small signature, these artifacts provide insight into spiritual and healing practices and how material culture was used to soothe body and soul.

Two categories of bodily objects recovered from archaeological excavations at Los Adaes and Mission Dolores are highlighted here. The first includes religious items, such as crucifixes and medals, that were worn on the body or placed on the body during sacraments, including last rites. The second category includes amulets or nondevotional items that were worn on the body and used in folk practice (Deagan 2002; Loren 2014). Religious items and amulets are objects of adornment—worn on the body and clothing to communicate, symbolize, accessorize, and embody aspects of one's social life (Deagan 2002; Loren 2007, 2010, 2014; Loren and Beaudry 2006; White 2005). While rare in many archaeological contexts, these artifacts are significant small finds linked to lived experience. Bodily objects could create meaning, indicate membership, bring about dissonance, and underscore beauty in different contexts when worn by different users. For example, the archaeological work on glass beads recovered from the Spanish colonial communities of Saint Augustine and Pensacola has suggested that beads were used not only as jewelry but also for rosaries and particularly (in certain contexts) as amulets and magical protection for women (Deagan 2002). While my own work on health and illness focuses on small finds, bodily objects can be more monumental in scale. Scott Hutson and colleagues (this volume) discuss Pre-Columbian Yucatan structures as animate, made from materials that lived: "the ensouled house" guards the body from illness and protects the occupants from spiritual attacks, especially in the context of political dynamics, when the body was at risk.

Religious Adornments:
Devotional Medals and Crucifixes

Crucifixes and other religious items are objects of adornment that contain the residues of religious proselytization in the New World. In New World contexts, they often symbolized the reassurance that Christianity was accepted and maintained by colonial peoples in place of other religions (Deagan 2002; Loren 2010, 2014). Crucifixes and religious medals held certain meanings for baptized individuals, but rosary beads and other Christian symbols took on different meanings when combined with other items to purposefully and publicly embody faith in the context of religious conversion.

No religious artifacts have been recovered from Mission Dolores. Religious objects recovered from Los Adaes excavations include a copper alloy crucifix, a medallion depicting the Holy Family with a drilled hole under a broken loop attachment, and a Saint John of Matha medal. The crucifix and medals were recovered from domestic contexts with other diverse items of clothing and adornment,

including a gilt paste shoe buckle, tinkler cones, glass beads, and plain copper alloy buttons, which suggest that these religious symbols were incorporated into the creative fashions worn by Los Adaes residents (Loren 2014).

Given that many of the individuals living at Mission Dolores and Los Adaes were Catholic, the low number of religious artifacts seems to be, at first glance, somewhat surprising. Would not the Franciscan father, lay brothers, or Catholic soldiers have forgotten or lost more items? Franciscans were also distributing religious items among the newly converted. Were these discarded or lost? Maybe not, particularly as these symbols may have been so important, and perhaps powerful, in their lives that they carefully guarded them and kept them safe. Crucifixes from a rosary or holy medals were kept close to the body, to both signify faith and to do the work of healing and protecting the body. Rosaries employed during last rites would have stayed with the priest, worn over his cassock and communicating his role in that society.

Equally important to consider, however, is the ambivalence with which these items may have been considered. In a context in which illness was common and comfort was hard to achieve, the power embodied by religious items differed according to who owned or used them and when and how they were used. While religious items were tangible objects of faith, they may have been worn or employed in other ways: to mimic the faithful, especially when worn with other bodily objects such as amulets and charms.

Amulets: Higas

Kathleen Deagan (2002:87–105) provides a lengthy list of amulets recovered from Spanish colonial sites, all of which were intended to protect the wearer from illness or to help the individual withstand or bring about certain bodily processes: teething, nosebleeds, hemorrhage, or conception. These practices of using protective adornments often derived from European homelands. Amulets are used to protect the body, and were often worn on the body itself, but they differ from religious medals or crucifixes in that they are not "used as intermediaries between their owner and a higher power" (Deagan 2002:87). Rather, these items are invested with meanings and beliefs that imbue them with power, sometimes magical in nature but always meant to protect the physical and spiritual body.

One common amulet in the Spanish colonial world was the *higa*. *Higas* are fist-shaped charms that had roots in Moorish traditions and were commonly used throughout early modern Spain and the Spanish New World as protective charms (Deagan 2002:95–99). Worn on or near the body, they were employed by some to ward off *mal de ojo* and other maladies, to protect children, and to maintain good health (Hildburgh 1955). Made from coral, bone, silver, and other metals, *higas* would have been worn as jewelry: as earrings, on a necklace, or pinned to clothing (Foster 1953). Some *higas* were also attached to horse bridles. Bridle jinglers (*coscojos*) were a common component of Spanish colonial horse gear and made a tinkling sound when the horse and rider were in motion. One common type of *coscojos* was the *higa*, worn to protect the rider from bullets and illness (Deagan 2002:95; Gregory 1973:48–49, 177). As with religious ornaments, it is important to consider that *higas* may have been used for their material, rather than spiritual, properties. The sound, particularly the tinkling of metal against metal, may have been more important than the protection afforded by shape.

At Los Adaes, twenty-four *higas* have been recovered from various locations in the presidial community, including the area of the barracks and inside the south wall of the presidio (Gregory 1973, 1980, 1982, 1984, 1985). The majority of copper alloy *higas* are simple or abstract in shape and would have been used as *coscojos*. Other *higas* recovered at Los Adaes were made from silver and had holes for suspension, suggesting that they may have also been worn as jewelry or attached to clothing (Figure 12.2). Several *higas* were also recovered from Mission Dolores, including abstract copper alloy *higas* that hung from horse gear and jet *higas* that would have been worn close to the body (Figure 12.3) (Corbin 1977; Corbin et al. 1990:77).

At Los Adaes, *higas* outnumber religious medals, and at Mission Dolores, *higas* are the only evidence of bodily objects that attended to health and spiritual well-being. While it could be argued that *higas* were more easily lost—perhaps broken from a bridle or lost from a cord around the neck—this reasoning alone does not explain the prevalence of these items in Catholic contexts in northeastern New Spain. The evidence suggests that amulet use may have been as important, or perhaps more important, than the use of religious items in these communities. Another interpretation, however, is that amulets and religious items were both needed in communities that sought relief from various ailments. One example can be found in the excavations at Los Adaes.

Curandería at Los Adaes

Hiram Gregory and colleagues (2009) postulate, based on a specific set of artifacts recovered from a domestic cooking pit at Los Adaes, that one of the house's occupants was a practitioner of *curandería*. In a cooking pit feature, a brass wick trimmer, eggshell fragments, and tubular blue and red glass beads were found in association with a Saint John of Matha medal at the bottom of the pit. Gregory and colleagues (2009) argue that this unusual cluster was the intentional result of folk medicine rituals. George Foster (1953:208–209) notes that in the *curandería* of New Spain the most common form of divining and curing the evil eye involved the use of a chicken egg, as the egg draws out the "eye" from the patient. Other items used by a *curandero/a* include candles, pictures of saints, animal bones, herbs, and holy water—all items that closely resemble those recovered from the cooking pit (Gregory et al. 2009). The feature excavated and interpreted by Gregory and his colleagues adds a particularly nuanced perspective of bodily care in colonial New Spain, revealing how community members cared for one another through faith and healing (Loren 2014). While it is unlikely that Franciscan priests were responsible for this activity, these practices were part of a repertoire of spiritual and bodily healing principles employed by community members in search of relief by any means necessary.

figure 12.2
Silver *higas*. Photograph by Don Sepulvado.

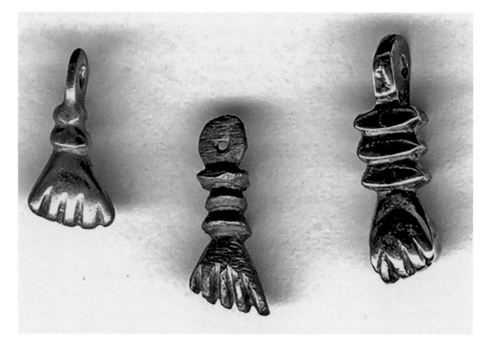

figure 12.3
Jet *higas* from
Mission Dolores.
Photograph by
George Avery.

What becomes clear in this discussion is that colonial peoples in northeastern New Spain sought both bodily and spiritual healing from a variety of different individuals: licensed physicians, priests, and *curandero/as* and other healers. Prayer helped some, while others turned to science. While some of these practices went against what was approved by colonial officials, the goals may not have been a reaction to colonization, but rather the result of ambivalence to receive healing in an expedient manner. The material culture used in these practices carried hope to those seeking comfort or protecting themselves along the frontier. Religious medals, crucifixes, and *higas*, as well as practices of *curandería*, were all necessary to daily life, to sustain and to protect body and soul.

Concluding Thoughts

Religious items and amulets found at Los Adaes and Mission Dolores indicate how bodily objects were necessary in northeastern New Spain, integral to safeguarding spiritual and bodily well-being on the frontier. Such items were vibrant; they carried power when passed over the body or from hand to hand. Native Americans and Europeans had different ontologies regarding their bodies and how to treat them. Franciscan priests viewed *curandero/as* as transgressors of morality (Quezada 1991), but their knowledge and practices offered relief from many ailments. Historical narratives, such as those offered by Solís, suggest that colonial peoples sought healing through priests, as well as *curandero/as*, indicating that relief was sought from anyone who could provide it and with any objects that carried the power to do so.

The use of both amulets and devotional medals for their prophylactic and curative powers does not suggest that *curandero/as* were preferred over Franciscans, but rather that the use of different adornments represented embodied knowledge of practical action. Through practice, ontologies were called into question and, in some cases, fictionalized. The assemblage suggests intentional action meant to care for and protect one's body by including a *higa* or a devotional medal over or under clothing. These bodily objects recovered from the archaeological record are the tangible remains of the corporeal predicament of colonialism. They focus our attention on the relationship between people and things in a context where bodies needed healing. They highlight intentional but ambivalent practical actions meant to care for and protect one's body by any means necessary on a remote frontier.

Acknowledgments

I would like to thank Pete Gregory and George Avery for their support of my research on Los Adaes materials. It was Gregory's interpretation of *curandería* at the presidio that inspired my work on health and the body at Los Adaes and Mission Dolores. My larger study of colonial clothing and adornment, health, sin, and the body has benefited from discussions with Mary Beaudry, Trish Capone, Joyce Chaplin, Charlie Cobb, Tom Cummins, Steve Kosiba, and Christina Hodge.

Alberti, Benjamin
2016   Archaeologies of Ontology. *Annual Review of Anthropology* 45:163–179.

Avery, George
1995   More Friend than Foe: Eighteenth-Century Spanish, French, and Caddoan Interaction at Los Adaes, a Capital of Texas Located in Northwestern Louisiana. *Louisiana Archaeology* 22:163–193.

1996   Annual Report for the Los Adaes Station Archaeology Program, Department of Social Sciences, Northwestern State University, Natchitoches, La.

2008   *Mission Dolores Replication Project: Geophysical Survey and Shovel Testing, May 2008.* Technical Report, Center for Regional Heritage Research, Department of Social and Cultural Analysis, Stephen F. Austin State University, Nacogdoches, Tex.

Beaudry, Mary C.
2006   *Findings: The Material Culture of Needle-work and Sewing.* Yale University Press, New Haven.

Bexar Archives
1754   Translation of Citizens of San Fernando v. Jacinto de Barrios y Jáuregui Demanding the Repeal of Measures Enacted by the Governor on September 13, 1754. Dolph Briscoe Center for American History, University of Texas, Austin. Electronic document, http://www.cah.utexas.edu/projects/bexar/gallery_doc.php?doc=e_bx_002029, accessed November 16, 2017.

Carlson, Shawn Bonath, and Kendra L. Quinn
1996   *Archaeological Investigations at Mission Dolores de Los Ais (41SA25), 1995–96, San Augustine County, Texas.* Technical Report 1. Historic Sites Research, College Station, Tex.

Chaplin, Joyce E.
2003   *Subject Matter: Technology, the Body, and Science on the Anglo-American Frontier, 1500–1676.* Harvard University Press, Cambridge, Mass.

Corbin, James E.
1977   *Archeological Research at 41SA25, Mission Dolores de Los Ais 1977: A Preliminary Report Submitted to the Texas Historical Commission.* Stephen F. Austin State University, Nacogdoches, Tex.

Corbin, James E., Thomas C. Alex, and Arlan Kalina
1980   *Mission Dolores de Los Ais.* Papers in Anthropology 2. Stephen F. Austin State University, Nacogdoches, Tex.

Corbin, James E., Heather A. Brown, Mary G. Canavan, and Sharon Toups
1990   *Mission Dolores de Los Ais (41SA25), San Augustine County, Texas.* Papers in Anthropology 5. Texas State Department of Highways and Public Transportation, Highway Design Division, Stephen F. Austin State University, Nacogdoches.

Deagan, Kathleen A.
2002   *Personal Portable Possessions.* Vol. 2 of *Artifacts of the Spanish Colonies of Florida and the Caribbean, 1500–1800.* Smithsonian Institution Press, Washington, D.C.

Foster, George M.
1953   Relationships between Spanish and Spanish-American Folk Medicine. *Journal of American Folklore* 66(261):201–217.

Galke, Laura J.
2009   The Mother of the Father of Our Country: Mary Ball Washington's Genteel Domestic Habits. *Northeast Historical Archaeology* 38(1):29–48.

Goldberg, Mark Allan
2017   *Conquering Sickness: Race, Health, and Colonization in the Texas Borderlands.* University of Nebraska Press, Lincoln.

Graham, Joe S.
1976   The Role of the *Curandero* in the Mexican American Folk Medicine System in West Texas. In *American Folk Medicine: A Symposium*, edited by Wayland Debs Hand, pp. 175–189. University of California Press, Berkeley.

Gregory, Hiram F.
1973   Eighteenth-Century Caddoan Archaeology: A Study in Models

and Interpretations. PhD dissertation, Southern Methodist University, Dallas, Tex.

1980 *Excavations: 1979, Presidio Nuestra Señora del Pilar de Los Adaes*. Office of State Parks, Louisiana Department of Culture, Recreation, and Tourism, Baton Rouge.

1982 *Excavations: 1982, Presidio Nuestra Señora del Pilar de Los Adaes*. Office of State Parks, Louisiana Department of Culture, Recreation, and Tourism, Baton Rouge.

1984 *Excavations: 1981–82, Presidio de Nuestra Señora del Pilar de Los Adaes*. Williamson Museum, Northwestern State University, Natchitoches, La.

1985 *Excavations: 1984, Unit 227, Presidio Nuestra Señora del Pilar de Los Adaes*. Office of State Parks, Louisiana Department of Culture, Recreation, and Tourism, Baton Rouge.

Gregory, Hiram F., George Avery, Francis X. Galán, Steve Black, Mariah Wade, Jay C. Blaine, and Aubra L. Lee

2009 Los Adaes: 18th-Century Capital of Spanish Texas. Electronic document, http://www.texasbeyondhistory .net/adaes/index.html, accessed November 15, 2013.

Gregory, Hiram F., George Avery, Aubra L. Lee, and Jay C. Blaine

2004 Presidio Los Adaes: Spanish, French, and Caddoan Interaction on the Northern Frontier. *Historical Archaeology* 38(3):65–77.

Guerra, Francisco

1969 The Role of Religion in Spanish American *Medicine*. In *Medicine and Culture*, edited by F. N. L. Poynter, pp. 179–188. Wellcome Institute of the History of Medicine, London.

1976 Medical Folklore in Spanish America. In *American Folk Medicine: A Symposium*, edited by Wayland Debs Hand, pp. 169–174. University of California Press, Berkeley.

Harris, Oliver J. T., and Craig N. Cipolla

2017 *Archaeological Theory in the New Millennium: Introducing Current Perspectives*. Routledge, New York.

Harris, Oliver J. T., and John Robb

2012 Multiple Ontologies and the Problem of the Body in History. *American Anthropologist* 114(4):668–679.

Hildburgh, W. L.

1955 Images of the Human Hand as Amulets in Spain. *Journal of the Warburg and Courtauld Institutes* 18(1/2):67–89.

Hodder, Ian

2012 *Entangled: An Archaeology of the Relationships between Humans and Things*. Wiley-Blackwell, Oxford.

Ingold, Tim

2007 Materials against Materiality. *Archaeological Dialogues* 14(1):1–16.

Jackson, Jack

1995 *Imaginary Kingdom: Texas as Seen by the Rivera and Rubí Military Expeditions, 1727 and 1767*. Edited and translated by Jack Jackson. Texas State Historical Association, Austin.

Joyce, Rosemary

2005 Archaeology of the Body. *Annual Review of Anthropology* 34:139–158.

Kay, Margarita Artschwager

1977 The *Florilegio Medicinal*: Source of Southwest Ethnomedicine. *Ethnohistory* 24(3):251–259.

Kress, Margaret Kenney, Fray Gaspar José de Solís, and Mattie Austin Hatcher

1931 Diary of a Visit of Inspection of the Texas Missions Made by Fray Gaspar José de Solís in the Year 1767–68. *Southwestern Historical Quarterly* 35:28–76.

Latour, Bruno

2005 *Reassembling the Social: An Introduction to Actor-Network-Theory*. Clarendon, Oxford.

Lindman, Janet Moore, and Michele Lise Tarter (editors)

2001 *A Center of Wonders: The Body in Early America*. Cornell University Press, Ithaca.

Loren, Diana DiPaolo

2007 Corporeal Concerns: Eighteenth-Century Casta Paintings and Colonial Bodies in Spanish Texas. *Historical Archaeology* 41(1):23–36.

2010   *The Archaeology of Clothing and Bodily Adornment in Colonial America.* University Press of Florida, Gainesville.

2014   Dress, Faith, and Medicine: Caring for the Body in Eighteenth-Century Spanish Texas. In *Archaeology of Culture Contact and Colonialism in Spanish and Portuguese America*, edited by Pedro Paulo A. Funari and Maria Ximena Senatore, pp. 143–154. Springer, Cham.

2019   Intimacies of Glass in Early 18th-Century Louisiana. In *The Historical Archaeology of Shadow and Intimate Economies*, edited by James A. Nyman, Kevin R. Fogle, and Mary C. Beaudry. University Press of Florida, Gainesville.

Loren, Diana DiPaolo, and Mary C. Beaudry

2005   Becoming American: Small Things Remembered. In *Historical Archaeology*, edited by Martin Hall and Stephen Silliman, pp. 251–271. Blackwell, Oxford.

Miller, Daniel (editor)

2005   *Materiality.* Duke University Press, Durham, N.C.

Mol, Annemarie

2002   *The Body Multiple: Ontology in Medical Practice.* Duke University Press, Durham, N.C.

Nava, Pedro de

1795   Letter to the Governor of Texas Concerning the Discovery of Cure for "Sickness of Seven Days." Bexar Archives 2S68, Roll 24. Dolph Briscoe Center for American History, University of Texas, Austin.

Naylor, Thomas H., and Charles W. Polzer (editors)

1988   *Pedro de Rivera and the Military Regulations for Northern New Spain, 1724–1729.* University of Arizona Press, Tucson.

Olsen, B.

2010   *In Defense of Things: Archaeology and the Ontology of Objects.* AltaMira Press, Lanham, Md.

Perttula, Timothy K.

1992   *The Caddo Nation: Archaeological and Ethnohistoric Perspectives.* University of Texas Press, Austin.

Quezada, Noemi

1991   The Inquisition's Repression of *Curanderos.* In *Cultural Encounters: The Impact of the Inquisition in Spain and the New World*, edited by Mary Elizabeth Perry and Anne J. Cruz, pp. 37–57. University of California Press, Berkeley.

Robb, John

2010   Beyond Agency. *World Archaeology* 42(4):493–520.

Shyrock, Richard Harrison

1960   *Medicine and Society in America, 1660–1860.* Cornell University Press, Ithaca.

Stoler, Ann Laura

2009   *Along the Archival Grain: Epistemic Anxieties and Colonial Common Sense.* Princeton University Press, Princeton.

Strathern, Marilyn

1988   *Gender of the Gift: Problems with Women and Problems with Society in Melanesia.* University of California Press, Berkeley.

1992   *Reproducing the Future: Anthropology, Kinship, and the New Reproductive Technologies.* Manchester University Press, Manchester.

Swanton, John Reed

1942   *Source Material on the History and Ethnology of the Caddo Indians.* University of Oklahoma Press, Norman.

Viveiros de Castro, Eduardo

1998   Cosmological Deixis and Amerindian Perspectivism. *Journal of the Royal Anthropological Institute* 4:469–488.

Weber, David J.

1992   *The Spanish Frontier in North America.* Yale University Press, New Haven.

White, Carolyn L.

2005   *American Artefacts of Personal Adornment, 1680–1820: A Guide to Identification and Interpretation.* AltaMira Press, Lanham, Md.

White, Carolyn L., and Mary C. Beaudry

2009   Artifacts and Personal Identity. In *The International Handbook of Historical Archaeology*, edited by T. Majewski and D. Gaimster, pp. 209–225. Springer, New York.

Southern Quechua Ontology

BRUCE MANNHEIM

In memory of three mentors, recently departed:
Paul Friedrich, Dennis Tedlock, and Tom Zuidema

THIS CHAPTER SETS OUT A RESEARCH agenda for comparative studies of ontology both social and material, one that contextualizes some of the work represented among the South American chapters in this volume.[1] I center it in an integrated set of studies of southern Quechuas, including ethnography, history, prehistory, grammar, and cognition, with an emphasis on animacy, agency, and spatial orientation. I locate the project squarely within what has been called "the ontological turn" in anthropology, a cluster of analytical approaches that share only the most abstract of precepts: a rejection of the social as bounded by the activities of humans; an opening to the agency of other-than-humans (a position that was already well established by philosophers studying causality); and an ethnographic view of language and culture as actively engaged in making the world we take for granted, rather than representing it. *Representation* is a contested term, used differently in different research traditions. Here, I want to acknowledge two radically different uses,

one that is grounded in folk ideas of language and cultural forms "standing for" things (I'll call this "representation$_1$") and another that means roughly "essential properties" of an expression (I'll call this use "representation$_2$"). Representation$_1$ is commonplace in interpretative anthropology, archaeology, art history, and literary studies. Representation$_2$ is commonplace in mathematics, linguistics, and cognitive science. When I call for "an ethnographic view of language and culture as actively engaged in making the world we take for granted, rather than representing it," I am rejecting representation$_1$ in favor of representation$_2$ (see Cummins, this volume).[2]

Scholars working in one or another of the varieties of "the ontological turn" range in their approaches, from aprioristic-and-philosophical to ethnographic-and-empirical. Though I place myself on the empirical edge of the range, my goal is nomological: to identify interdependencies among social practices, regardless of whether they are social (e.g., a particular kind of kinship

371

system), material (e.g., settlement patterns), linguistic (e.g., the structure of grammatical person), or cognitive (e.g., spatial orientation). The compatibilities and incompatibilities among practices permit researchers to establish *relational typologies* that can be tested comparatively. In his recent book *Par delà nature et culture* (2005, translated as *Beyond Nature and Culture*, 2013), Philippe Descola sketches a typological framework to account systematically for differences in the social ontologies among distinct societies in native South American and beyond. Particularly important in this regard is his typology of forms of agency, differentiated along two parameters: inherence—or shared inner substance—and physical appearance. Together these two parameters define four social regimes: naturalism (dominant in Europe since the eighteenth century), animism, totemism, and analogism, all of which configure relationships between human and other-than-human entities. For example, a social ontology in which humans and some species of animals are treated as having the same *inherence*—conscious awareness—and different physical *appearance* (some are jaguars, some humans) would be characterized as "animist." Each of these larger categories itself encompasses a range of social configurations that similarly lend themselves to typology. The purpose here is not to pigeonhole societies into social ontologies like "naturalist" or "animist" or even "animic-analogical," but to establish relational grids that allow us to compare social configurations and to provide insights into how ethnographic phenomena are configured—to establish relationships of compatibility, incompatibility, and determination among them. The research strategy outlined here is classically structuralist, pioneered by the Russian linguist Nikolai Trubetzkoy (1939) in his study of sound systems *Grundzüge der Phonologie* (*Principles of Phonology*) and ported to social anthropology by Claude Lévi-Strauss in his *Les structures élémentaires de la parenté* (*Elementary Structures of Kinship*). Neither pigeonholes nor inert structures, relational dependencies are fallible empirically and allow researchers to identify constraints on social configurations.

Finally, until very recently, anthropologists treated the world as "good to think" (to steal a phrase), as an always already constituted set of affordances for representation.[3] There have been notable exceptions, such as Edward Sapir (1929) and Irving Hallowell (1960, 1991; see Strong 2017), but even relativists such as Benjamin Lee Whorf tended to see culture and language as variables against a constant, uniform world. The so-called ontological turn strikes a novel path in suggesting that the material interactions of people and their physical and social worlds can vary from society to society and over time (see Alberti 2016; Kohn 2016; Swenson 2015:678; Viveiros de Castro 2004). Under traditional representational approaches, the differences between a set of practices in one culture and another were treated as matters of distinct knowledge and belief; ethnographers treated other cultures as densely symbolic, with people speaking in figures; archaeologists interpreted the serpent carved into rock as *standing for* water. Under ontological approaches, the nature of the world, of the interactions between humans and the world, and of social relations vary from society to society.[4] Social authority and political power manifest not only in relationships among humans and their institutions but also are imbricated in the world. Where I differ from other researchers working within this program is that I regard ontological variability as limited, constrained by cognitive processes (not representations$_1$; see Mannheim 2015a),[5] restricted by the compatibility or incompatibility of social forms and institutions with each other (cf. Descola 2005:119, 137), and constrained historically.

Though my goal is ultimately comparative, in this chapter I draw on material mainly from the southern Andean highlands, from the Inka period up to the present—from agriculturalists and pastoralists who spoke and speak Southern Peruvian Quechua. As a research strategy, gathering systematic evidence from a single cultural and linguistic tradition enables us to uncover the mechanisms intrinsic to relationships of compatibility and incompatibility and to formulate comparative hypotheses. Detailed evidence is provided in a dozen recent consilient studies drawing on the disciplinary perspectives of linguistic anthropology, cultural anthropology, history, linguistics, and the history of art, including collaborations with colleagues at the University of Michigan and elsewhere.[6] I focus on four interrelated fields. Within each field is a range of practices, also interrelated, that makes it fruitful to consider them together, and there are also interrelationships among the sets.[7]

1. Properties of the world. Kinds of objects vary in the properties attributed to them and in the relationships that they have to other kinds.
2. Frame of reference. Languages and cultures vary in the ways in which they articulate the relationship between people and the world. A primary distinction comparatively is between "allocentric" and "egocentric" frames of reference (Danziger 2010; Levinson 2003), with subtypes for both. In "allocentric" systems (like Quechua), social interaction (in all activities, important and mundane) is anchored primarily in the physical space surrounding the interaction rather than in the participants; in contrast, in "egocentric" systems (like English), the frame of reference is projected from the vantage point of the speaker.
3. Agency. Quechua grammar and social practices presuppose and implicate forms of social agency that attribute agentive powers to places and to other objects, things we would consider inanimate.
4. Causal structures. Concepts emerge from more general and broad knowledge that people have about the world; in other words, concepts are embedded in overarching theories. These tacit theories establish ontologies (in the first sense), causal relationships, and unobservable entities specific to cognitive domains such as "living kinds" and "artifacts." Critical in the domain of causal structures is that Quechua adults are *naturalists* with respect to living kinds and U.S. English-speaking adults *artifactualists*, the cross-cultural variability in domain membership notwithstanding.

Properties of the World

"Properties of the world" conveys the usual sense of *ontology*, particularly outside of anthropology. In Quechua, these can include such commonplaces as the fact that *maki* refers to hand and arm without distinguishing between them; a pencil has an *uma*, "head," and a *siki*, "ass and loins"; rocks and mountains have insides in which beings live; named places are individuals (much as people are) and have particular personalities; a lake and the ocean are the same kind of object; the same verb, *hisp'ay*, is used for a liquid leaving the body, regardless of whether it is urine, blood from a wound, menstrual blood, or feces. It also includes more complex properties of the world, such as the fact that artifacts are frequently named with verbs for the activity one does with them regardless of form, so that *tiyana* is a place to be, a seat and a place to be seated, whether it is a chair, a stool, a bench, or a rock; textiles have mouths; and mountains have portals. Properties attributed to everyday objects also vary culturally: one does not herd animals, one guides (*pusay*) or follows them (*qhatikuy*) as they move under their own agency. Similarly, an irrigation canal does not carry water; just as herd animals can be guided, the canal guides (*pusay*) the water. The objects "in the world" for Quechua speakers[8]—and "in the world" for their Inka ancestors[9]—are not the same objects as for Spanish speakers or English speakers, and the activities of irrigation water, animal herds, and named places are not the same as apparently similar objects in English. This is not a matter of "symbolic richness" or of "figurative language"—these truly form the world in which Quechua speakers and English speakers live, and they are different worlds, as Sapir (1929:207) proposed.

The relationships among different kinds of things—objects and actions—vary culturally. In Southern Quechua, conceptually related objects and events are taken up in semantic couplets, pervasive not only in *waynus* (huaynos; and so heard in many everyday settings; Mannheim 1998b) but also in ritual song (Arnold and Yapita 1998; Mannheim 2015d, drawing on Felipe Guaman Poma de Ayala's [(1615) 1987] description of a rite in

figure 13.1
Guaman Poma de Ayala, *Primer nueva corónica y buen gobierno*, ca. 1615, pp. 318/320.

Inka Cuzco; Figure 13.1). For example, in a *waynu* from the 1960s, Urpischallay, the singer, asks,

> Maytaq chay munakusqayki
> Maytaq chay wayllukusqayki
> But where is your desire (*munakusqa*)?
> But where is your affection (*wayllukusqa*)?

And then asserts,

> Mayullawaqchá aparachiwanki
> Qaqallawaqchá ñit'irachiwanki

Perhaps you've had river (*mayu*) carry me off
Perhaps you've had rock (*qaqa*) crush me

In the first couplet, the verb *munay*, "to want," is paired with the verb *waylluy*, "to care for, with shows of affection." These are a semantic minimal pair in Quechua—they are as closely related to each other semantically as two words can be, with no third value coming between them (so no verb for "slightly affectionate," for example). But what do we make of the second couplet, in which *river*

figure 13.2
The western slope of Machu Picchu, with terraces and worked boulders, dating to ca. 1500. Photograph courtesy of Thomas B. F. Cummins.

(*mayu*) pairs with *rock* (*qaqa*)? These two are also a conceptual minimal pair, and the stem *qaqa* (rock as a substance) is, in turn, paired with *rumi*, "individuated stone." The river/rock couplet is common in Quechua song, and its patterning is no different from that of more transparent couplets such as *munay*, "want" / *waylluy*, "to care for with shows of affection." These couplets entail specific ontic relationships among the objects that they refer to and so project them into the Quechua world.

Thus, famously, in Machu Picchu living stone is carved into tapered fissures, crossing agricultural terraces, so as to flow across the mountainside as a rushing river would, flowing toward the Urubamba River below (Cummins and Mannheim 2011:8–12; Figure 13.2). Similarly, stepped fret designs around portals carved into living stone, which can be activated either by water flowing through them or by liquid being poured on them—a motif found at

multiple Inka sites—are not figurations of water but are indexes (actually meta-indexes) that signal the ontic bind between *mayu* and *qaqa* as substances (Figure 13.3; Cummins and Mannheim 2011; also see Dean 2010). The lexical relations diagrammed by semantic couplets—and in the case of *mayu* and *qaqa*, extended into the built environment[10]—are indexes of the relative complexity of closely related concepts. In the song passage quoted previously, *waylluy*, "to desire affectionately" (the marked, more complex member of the relationship, +), is related to *munay*, "to want" (the less complex, unmarked member of the relationship, Ø), as *pusay*, "to guide" (+), is related to *apay*, "to carry" (Ø), by a formal realignment of the argument structure and a kind of conceptual presupposition, whereas *wasi*, "house" (+), is related to *llaqta*, "settlement" (Ø), by existential presupposition. What these pairs have in common—besides a tighter conceptual connection

figure 13.3
Stepped fret indexes on a boulder in the Saphi River above Cuzco, dating to ca. 1500. Photograph courtesy of
Thomas B. F. Cummins.

with each other than with other associated words—
is the hierarchy between the members of each pair,
a hierarchy whose basis is relative to conceptual
domain. Implicit in each semantic couplet is a structural alignment between the members of a lexical
pair, inducing a cognitive focus on commonalities
and specific differences and enhancing their storage
in long-term memory (Gentner and Lasaga Medina
1998; Markman and Gentner 1997). Semantic couplets, and indeed the physical arrangement of the
built environment, are the external stimuli through
which conceptual relationships are sustained and
transmitted (Mannheim 1998b).

Similarly, social ontology—what there is in
the social world and the relationships that persons of distinct kinds have to each other—is
grounded in song and narrative, below the threshold of awareness (Mannheim 2015c). Three mechanisms—semantic presupposition (Chierchia and

McConnell-Ginet 1990:280; Karttunen 1974),[11]
implicature (Grice 1975; Sperber and Wilson 1986),
and interactional lamination (Goffman 1979:24;
Irvine 1996; Mannheim 2015c)[12]—are built into
practices in such a way that to interpret an utterance, even nonconsciously, requires one to acqui-
esce to the ontic commitments entailed by the
utterance, including (or perhaps especially including) social commitments. Listening to a song about
a thrush that has been imprisoned by the government might entail acquiescing to the arbitrary
power of the state (Mannheim 2015c:47–48); listening to a narrative in which a rock is the trace of a
narrative protagonist entails both the physical existence of the protagonist and the truth of the narrative (Allen 1994:91ff). To understand any talk at all
requires the listener to draw on these mechanisms;
hence, the acquiescences are inescapable, and—
like other social processes that unfold in the small

spaces of everyday life—habitual (Canessa 2012). In these cases, public material practices—singing to a camelid, singing about love lost, or carving live rock to resemble water flowing down a hillside—entail specific ontic commitments on the part of their users.

Frame of Reference

In *At the Crossroads of the Earth and Sky*, Gary Urton (1981:61–62 and elsewhere) describes a curious fact about the stellar observations of the Quechua-speaking agriculturalists of Maras, Cuzco: rather than anchor their observations directly in the observer, as we do, they anchor them sometimes in the mountains on the horizon and most often from the position of the celestial river, the Milky Way, which systematically shifts the observations to its position in the night sky. (The lyric from Disney's *Peter Pan*, "The second star to the right," would be utterly incomprehensible to them, anchored as it is in the position of the observer.) Another way to describe this would be to say that the agriculturalists are identifying celestial bodies *allocentrically*, by establishing a relationship between two objects outside of the speech situation; in contrast, we (and Peter Pan) do so *egocentrically*.[13] And so Urton (1981:38) learned that "one cannot understand the sky without first understanding the earth," without understanding that celestial observations are anchored by the named mountains on the horizon. In contrast, we establish a direct relationship between the object that we are observing and ourselves (who are within the speech situation, as shown by the use of the word *right*). We and the agriculturalists from Maras have different observational points and, more broadly, different systems of *frame of reference*.

Frame of reference is a cognitive/linguistic system that partitions space and locates people within space by a single set of principles that coordinates cognition, language, and physical movement. Substantial comparative research (e.g., Danziger 2010; Haviland 1998; Levinson 2003; Levinson and Wilkins 2006; Majid et al. 2004)—largely

experimental—shows variability among languages, constrained within a set of narrow typological parameters. The frame of reference system constrains gestures, the relationship of behaviors to the immediate topography, movement through the landscape, the semantics of grammar, and such large-scale matters as engineering (allocentric engineering is constructed relationally, rather than on a grid—see Brezine 2011) and settlement pattern. Inasmuch as the *frame of reference* is habitual, structured, and nonconscious, the physical relationships within a specific *frame of reference* appear to individuals to be features of the world rather than features of the culture.

Frame of reference systems identify an *object* as a figure against a *ground*, the linkage established by an *anchor* (Danziger 2010; Levinson 2003).[14] Here is the point at which it becomes linguistic. If the anchor is a participant in the speech situation, such as the speaker or the addressee, the frame of reference is *egocentric*. If the anchor is not part of the speech situation, say it is a place or a llama or a cardinal direction, then the frame of reference is *allocentric*. Egocentric frame of reference is anchored in the "I's" and "you's";[15] allocentric frame of reference is anchored elsewhere, for example, in a feature of the landscape or in the relationship between two objects. Within these two types, the anchor can be identified with the ground or not. If an egocentric anchor is part of the ground, the frame of reference is *direct egocentric* (essentially the case in English or in Spanish); if it is not part of the ground, it is *relative* or *relational deixis* (a common—but not the only—system in Mesoamerica). Similarly, if an allocentric anchor is part of the ground it is *intrinsic* or object centered. If it is not part of the ground, it is *absolute*. In living populations, each of these distinctions can be identified through experiments using nonlinguistic stimuli. Comparative research has identified additional frame of reference schemes that build on these, such as a geocentric frame that is based on unique identifications of landmarks and has identified circumstances that afford a shift from one frame of reference to another (e.g., whether the participants are in an enclosed space), but for the purposes of our discussion the basic typology will suffice.[16]

Though frame of reference is technically established by means of experiment and defined by means of language, the dominant frame of reference spills out into all fields of endeavor, including interactions with the natural and built environments. Though the gold standard for identifying frame of reference is experimental, which means that it can be done only with living populations, the material signatures of an allocentric absolute system are clear enough that it should be possible to read the frame of reference back from settlement pattern and other aspects of material culture for archaeologically attested peoples. No population has a single frame of reference. Rather, each seems to have a basic frame of reference that undergirds a range of social practices—from grammar to settlement pattern—with additional strategies available for specialized situations.

Up to now, little work on frames of reference has been carried out among native South Americans. Sérgio Meira (2006:350) identifies Tiriyó (Carib) as primarily absolute and object centered, that is, allocentric; Konrad Rybka (2016) identifies two allocentric frames of reference as primary in Lokono, an Arawakan language of Guiana, and suggests that "relative" (egocentric) frame of reference has few grammatical affordances; and Joshua Shapero (2014, 2017a, 2017b), working with Ancash Quechua agriculturalists and pastoralists in Huaraz (which is a good experimental proxy for the Southern Quechua/Inka pattern) observes a basic allocentric-absolute pattern. According to Shapero (2017a), pastoralists show a stronger allocentric-absolute bias than agriculturalists, regardless of exposure to Spanish (which is primarily egocentric). In Ancash Quechua, the allocentric-absolute frame of reference means that spatial orientation is established with reference to external physical objects (which can be mobile, such as a cow, or fixed, such as a particular mountain). In addition, the primary frames of reference are overlain with a geocentric frame, one in which people move through the landscape by means of named, and singular, places.

Shapero's point about the distribution of frame of reference within the community is also critical and, in part, responds to Allen's query (this volume). It is perfectly feasible for individuals with distinct frames of reference to interact with each other, but they will systematically misunderstand each other's spatial orientation. Sometimes this has interactional consequences, sometimes not, but the case of an ethnographer who orients egocentrically asking directions of a local who orients allocentrically will be familiar to many. The ethnographer gets lost.

Frame of reference is a critical linchpin of Andean ontology, one that has implications across multiple fields of practice, including personhood (Mannheim, Davis, and Velasco 2018), local-level social organization, landscape and movement through landscape (Kosiba 2015b), settlement pattern, political organization, exchange and redistribution, and mortuary practices. For example, a lineage structure—and by extension, a system of ancestor veneration—is built up by projecting an apical ancestor from an ego and requires an egocentric frame of reference. That Quechua speakers use an allocentric frame of reference would predict that there are no lineages as such but that inheritance is established through much shallower social configurations, and consequently would also predict the absence of systems of ancestor veneration.[17] Indeed, though scholars have suggested that both existed in the Inka state, arguably there is no clear archaeological evidence of either one. The earliest historical evidence is similar. A striking feature of early colonial documents claiming royal descent (pre-1580 or so)[18] is that they conform to a residentially based house model—rather than a lineage—with no identified ancestor further than a three-generation remove from the claimant. The Inka "royal dynasty" is a single marked exception, but the historiography of the royal dynasty is far more complex than a simple king list would suggest (Covey 2006; Ramírez 2006; Yaya McKenzie 2011; Zuidema 1964). The order of royal names in pre-1580 Spanish sources may have been signaling social hierarchy rather than chronology (Yaya McKenzie 2011:49ff; indeed, in the case of the chronicler Diez de Betanzos [(1551) 2015], within a single elite house, Qhapaq ayllu).

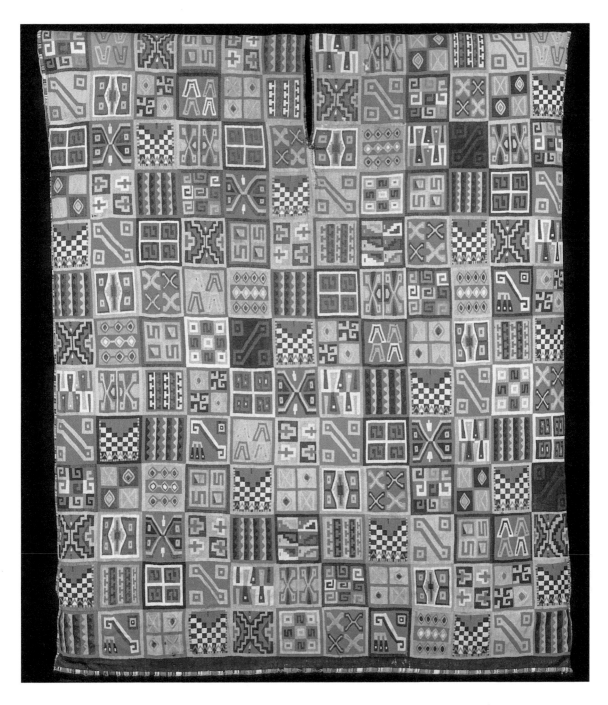

figure 13.4
The Dumbarton Oaks tunic. Note the miniature *unku* tunics woven into the design of the tunic. Pre-Columbian Collection PC.B.518, Dumbarton Oaks Research Library and Collection, Washington, D.C.

Sources from the earliest period after Spanish colonization of Peru generally show the shallow inheritance structure that is characteristic of residence-based kinship systems (a specific kind of "house society" or *société à maison*; Yaya McKenzie 2011:33–34)[19] and consistent with an allocentric frame of reference, as the social unit is constituted externally to an ego and identified with a physical place. Individuals are recruited to the "house," potentially by multiple mechanisms ("house" in

figure 13.5
The Radicati Khipu Collection, MALI, Lima, Peru. Photograph courtesy of Gary Urton.

this case referring to an actual house structure or to a patio group). People move through the social unit—self-identified with the place—and are buried in the place (in the Late Intermediate Period and in the Inka Horizon, often in house burials but also in localized aboveground tombs [Kosiba 2015a] and in mortuary structures built into the side of a tutelary mountain [Velasco 2018; Wernke 2013:140–143]). In the case of Inka Cuzco, the ruler himself was the embodiment of his place of residence. His title—and perhaps name—*was* Cuzco (Ramírez 2005:chap. 2).[20] In short, I would suggest that consistent with an allocentric frame of reference, the Inkas were a *société a maison*, as indeed are their contemporary descendants.

Frame of reference also plays a critical (external) role in Inka and contemporary Quechua *principles of semiotic interpretation*. The visual and literary art of the early colonial period (sixteenth and seventeenth centuries) is divided between forms that functioned by means of allocentric principles, forms that functioned by means of egocentric principles, and composites that could be interpreted through both systems, each one accounting for many, but not all, of the properties of an object (Mannheim 1998a, 2019:chap. 9). Spaniards introduced visual forms that required an egocentric frame of reference to be interpretable using a mix of perspective and other compositional techniques, such as color and spatial hierarchy, to construct a two-dimensional system of representational art that contested the primarily (though not exclusively) geometric forms used by native Andeans.

In contrast, native Andean visual and literary forms used several strategies to build the interpretation into the object itself. For example, the "Warikza arawi" song text in Guaman Poma has a synecdoche of the whole within the song text itself in the form of two interspersed couplets in Quechua (Mannheim 2015d:224); the Dumbarton Oaks tunic

has multiple representations of a tunic, perhaps of the tunic itself, woven into it (Figure 13.4); Inka *khipus* have summary strings that interpret the data coded into them (Figure 13.5) (Urton 2010:65), similarly building the interpretation into the object itself. Other objects repeat structural relationships in nested hierarchies, a common strategy followed in Southern Quechua textiles, a strategy of *involution* in which a single relationship or figure is replicated at several levels of scale (see Figure 13.6, a woman's shawl from the Lares Valley of Cuzco). A similar strategy of structural involution (and fractal embedding) is followed in the internal structure of the radial *ziqi* lines that connect named sacred places to the landscape surrounding Inka Cuzco, in which a tripartite system of ranks organizes

segments of the system, with five levels of embedding going from the smallest structures (the places themselves) to the largest (the four sections that made up the Inka capital as a microcosm of the entire state; Zuidema 1964) (Figures 13.7 and 13.8). A third strategy was to use a smaller-scale object to signal the presence or the proximity of an object organized by the same principles, as for example the Sayhuite stone (Figure 13.9), in which the parts of a settlement, including houses organized around patios and irrigation canals, are carved into the stone. These strategies constructed a world of objects and forms that were self-interpreting—an *introversive* semiosis (Allen 1997, 1998; Mannheim 2019:chap. 9; Molinié 2012; Smith 2010, 2016). The effect on the viewer—the social subject—was to be

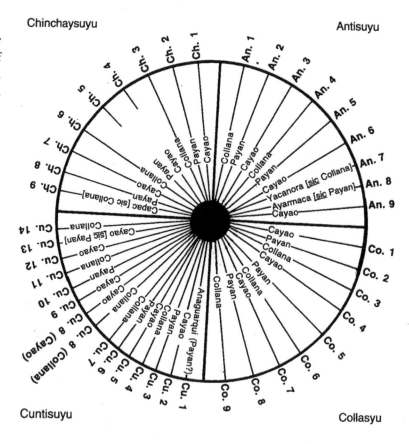

figure 13.7
A conceptual organization of
nested *ziqi* lines, Inka Cuzco.
Courtesy of Brian Bauer.

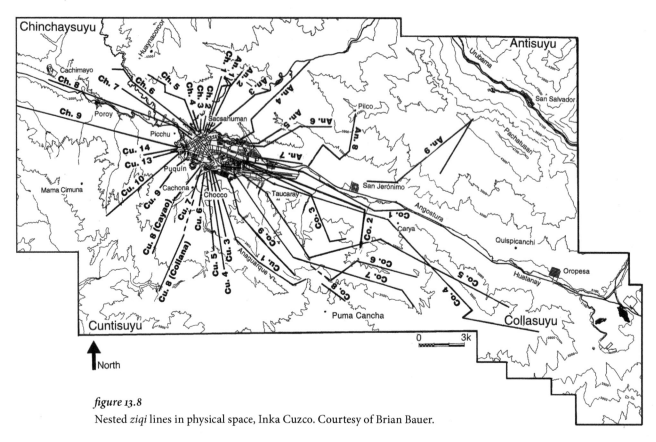

figure 13.8
Nested *ziqi* lines in physical space, Inka Cuzco. Courtesy of Brian Bauer.

figure 13.9
The Sayhuite miniature settlement template.

pushed away from the object, which could live an interpretative life of its own perfectly well without a viewing subject. The key distinction here is that *extroversive* semiosis establishes a direct relationship with the interpreter as an embodied social subject, precisely in the way that egocentric frames of reference do (Benveniste 1971:chap. 21). In contrast, Inka *introversive* semiosis achieved semiotic closure object to object, just as allocentric frames of reference do. Though the Inkas did indeed use representational forms, they typically did so in portable objects such as drinking vessels and miniatures (see Allen 1997, 1998, 2016; Cummins 2002).

Quechua allocentrism ties every interaction into a tacit relationship between the participants and the surrounding landscape. It is not surprising, then, that Inka settlements were

planned—to varying extents—to create "a synthesis between environment and settlement, not only by accommodation to natural features, but also by modifying the landscape" (Hyslop 1990:300), an observation supported by subsequent Inka scholars (Bauer 1998; Hastorf 1993:54–56; Van de Guchte 1990:330–348, 1999). The Inkas took advantage of natural features—rivers, rock outcroppings, mountains, valleys—embellishing them with terraces and fill and sometimes extending them to accommodate the settlement, but never ignoring them. From smallest to largest, state installations were wedded to particular places, and these places were not just objects of veneration but the ground of the smallest acts of everyday linguistic reference. It is not surprising, then, that the political order was literally inscribed in the landscape, meaning that the political order was treated as a feature of the world rather than a contrivance. The expansion of the state, even in the Inka heartland itself, involved the erasure of specific parts of a prior settlement and its reconfiguration within an Inka order (Kosiba 2012).

The *ziqi* system provides an especially dramatic example of the inscription of a political order on the landscape (see Figure 13.7). A three-rank relational hierarchy repeated itself, from the smallest places, including natural formations and built places, to a template for the organization of the state as a whole. Each node in the system was associated with a specific social segment, ranked according to its position in the whole. *Ziqi* sight lines defined a set of irrigation districts, determining each group's rights to specific sources of water (and hence to specific agricultural lands). Social segments were associated with sacred places ranked along the same sight lines and were responsible for tending them on specific ritual occasions, sequenced by position on the system of sight lines (Bauer 1998; Sherbondy 1985; Zuidema 1964). In the expansion of the state into the Colca Valley (modern-day Arequipa), the Inkas reproduced the hierarchies of Cuzco, inscribed in the local landscape (Wernke 2013:11–38).

Six mountains in the vicinity of Cuzco formed a relational matrix around the Inka capital. As the Inkas expanded, they established secondary centers such as Vilcashuamán and Huánuco Pampa, "other Cuzcos," *ranti* or stand-ins for the Inka capital itself (Christie 2007; Coben 2006; Santillana 2012:117–121; Stanish 2012; Van de Guchte 1990:53; on *ranti*, see Mannheim 2015a:210). Along with the establishment of secondary centers, the Inkas replicated key architectural features of Cuzco itself and renamed the principal mountains around the secondary centers to match their counterparts in Cuzco: Wanak'auri, Pitusiray, Sawasiray, and so forth. One could, in effect, make an offering to Wanak'auri through its *ranti*. The Inkas replicated both their relational position among the named mountains and the secondary *ranti* status of the other Cuzcos. In an allocentric world, the space of social action is delineated by objects and places. It would be easy to think of speakers who establish frames of reference using allocentric strategies as "animists" but for the fact that frame-of-reference theory precisely delimits the mechanisms and scope of an allocentric frame of reference in a way that a theory of animism does not. In addition, while animism is normally attributed to people on an ad hoc, case-by-case basis, a specific frame of reference (or a skein of related frames of reference) can be identified in living communities through formal experimental methods. A strategy for extending frame of reference to prehistory is to identify the social and material entailments of a specific frame of reference (such as settlement pattern, or lineage-oriented mortuary practices) in specific material assemblages.

Agency

Much of the anthropological discussion of ontological relativity centers around the topic of agency: What kinds of entities can be agentive and how? Do mountains and other places have causal powers (in the sense of Harré and Madden 1975)? Do they communicate with people, and if so, under what conditions? Do domestic or other animals have agency apart from that attributed to them by humans? Do they communicate with us, and do they understand us? *Agency* is a deeply contested term across the social sciences; every scholar who makes reference to it engages it differently and takes positions—overtly or tacitly—on a variety of issues that are key to the social sciences: individual/collective/institutional; conscious/nonconscious; sentient/nonsentient beings; inherent in social beings/inherent in social positions (often hybrids of sentient beings and objects). These are not simply a checklist that can be filled out in advance of an analysis. Each parameter enables or restricts causal explanations of social phenomena, by archaeologists, social anthropologists, linguistic anthropologists, philosophers, and sociologists.

Agency is constituted institutionally, socially, and grammatically and is not simply an aleatory power, a wrench thrown into the machinery of norms that can be associated with biological individuals and potentially others. Seen as "causal powers," agency inheres in any object (a causal power of the page that you are reading right now is the light it reflects, which, given the appropriate social and linguistic conventions, affords your reading it; a combined causal power of altitude, oxygenation, and light affords the possibility of growing maize in a particular field; and so forth). Seen as socially, institutionally, and grammatically constituted, agency inheres in entities and events other than individual humans: the devil made me do it; the government lies; the cat wants to leave; my car decided not to start; a volcano shoots out lava because "it wants to give out the energy to go back to its equilibrium" (the last a statement from an English-speaking adult in Ann Arbor, part of a study by Sánchez et al. [2016]; example from unpublished transcripts); the capture and killing of Osama bin Laden was "a miracle performed from the grave by Pope John Paul II " (*La República*, Lima, May 2, 2011). In an ethnographic context, a statement like the one about the volcano might lead an ethnographer to conclude that the people she is working with are animists. So, too, would the attribution of the capture and killing of bin Laden to a miracle from beyond, wrought by the late pope, although it was in fact made by the then-president of Peru, who only weeks earlier denounced many of his countrymen as "animists."[21] The moral of the story is that accounts of animism—and agency more generally—must be constructed systematically (see Kockelman 2017), not anecdotally, and are dependent on the stance of the observer. A distinction that has informed and bedeviled discussions of animism since Tylor (1871:452–453) has been between causal structures of the world that are features of nature and attributions of agency to features of the world that have causal powers by virtue of social attribution (my uncle Fernando, the admissions committee of my university department, Mount Wanak'auri [see Kosiba, this volume]). According to this view, an animist would be someone who identifies the second kind of causal relationship as an instance of the first, without recognizing that they only have agency because some people believe them to

have agency. But the distinction quickly crumbles under its own weight because it is, itself, relative to how particular observers—ethnographers or archaeologists—drew the line between these two domains to begin with (Bird-David 1999:68). (An early critique of Tylorian anthropology by Evans-Pritchard [1933:284] raises this point explicitly.[22])

Quechua grammar and social practices presuppose and implicate forms of social agency that attribute agentive powers to places (Allen 2015b; Bray 2015; de la Cadena 2010, 2015; Salas Carreño 2012; Sillar 2009) and to other objects, such as emotions and beer (Mannheim and Salas Carreño 2015). Agency—and more generally sociality and animacy—are first of all posited by grammar and installed in multiple grammatical subsystems, where they are both inculcated in individuals and maintained below the speakers' thresholds of awareness. The systems that are particularly important include person, relative pronouns, nominal classification systems (Senft 2000), and syntactic agreement.[23] For example, Quechua has three syntactic agreement systems: a dominant nominative-accusative system, in which (for many verbs) agency is attributed to the subject of the sentence, much as in English; an ergative system that only appears in subordinate clauses, in which the agent of the action has to be formally marked as such; and a semantic alignment system, in which the agent can be either subject or the object of a transitive verb. Each of these systems subclassifies nouns with respect to prospective agents. The entire system is not accessible to the conscious awareness of the speakers, so that the entire system replicates itself, as it were, in the background of everyday life. The effects can be subtle. Consider, for example, some of the ways a Quechua speaker can indicate that they desire beer (from Mannheim and Salas Carreño 2015):

(a) Cervezata munani.
   "I (agent) want (or like) beer."
(b) Cervezata munashani.
   "I (agent) am wanting beer."
(c) Cervezata uhyanayashani.
   "I (agent) am about to drink beer."

(d) Cerveza uhyanayawashan.
   "I (recipient) want to drink beer (agent)"
   (literally, "The beer wants
   to be drunk by me").
(e) Cerveza uhyanayakuwashan.
   "I (recipient) want to drink beer (agent)"
   (i.e., single-mindedly—
   you would not want to interrupt someone who
   says this).
(f) Cervezanayawashan.
   "I (recipient) want to drink-beer (verb)."

In the first three examples (a–c), the agent of desire is the speaker. In the next three (d–f), the agent is the beer, and though it is the beer that is desired, the speaker is the recipient of the desire, not its agent. In the last example, *beer* is even used as a verb. In each successive sentence, the desire is increasingly urgent and uncompromising. The stylistically neutral and most common way of expressing desire to drink beer is (d), in which the beer is the agent of desire and the speaker the recipient of externally generated desire. Compare English, in which desire is uncompromisingly agentive, at least in the grammatical sense. The Quechua grammatical pattern does shape (and is shaped by) a Quechua etiology or causal structure of desire, much in the same way that a covert grammatical pattern in the English pronoun system affords a distinction between social beings and nonsocial beings (Hill and Mannheim 1991), social beings consisting essentially of those beings that English speakers speak to—including humans, cats, their computers, and ships. The Quechua etiology of desire looks animistic from the perspective of the English one. Neither a Quechua nor an English speaker normally relies on facts of the natural world to defend their etiology of desire.

Just as obligatory as grammatical categories is the pragmatic structure of interaction—who can speak to whom directly, who can be referred to in their presence as a nonparticipant in interaction, and so forth. Verbs can trigger unconscious presuppositions as to the agency of the entity on which they are predicated. Camelid herders in southern Peru speak to individual animals in their herds and

interpret—understand—their well-being through the sounds they make (Arnold and Yapita 1998; Caine 2019). This is effectively cross-species conversation, in which some but not all of the requisites of human conversational interaction are present. Relevant here, too, is the attribution of agency to herds in the verbs used for taking them to pasture. Quechua speakers follow their herds—*qhatiy*—they do not lead them. The herds have agency in their movement from corral to pasture; the herder constrains their movement by guiding them from one place to another. Overall, anthropologists have paid little attention to the structure of social interaction in Andean societies, even among humans, much less, for example, the structures of verbal mediation that take place when a herder speaks to one of her alpacas (Caine 2019) or when a mountain speaks to a smallholder through the mediation of an *altumisayuq* (keeper of the high table) or during a divination with the assistance of a place (but see Platt 1997). All require verbal mediation but with different kinds of participants serving as mediational bridges.

What of places, both local (such as the underside of a staircase) and regional (such as the landmark mountain Apu Ausangate)? Guillermo Salas and I proposed that places have agency not as a first principle (e.g., because they are deemed to have agency in an abstract cosmology) but because they are socially attributed agency in food-sharing practices (also see Salas Carreño 2016). The key point here is that agency—and the forces and things that are agentive (or "animistic") in Quechua culture (and were agentive for the Inkas)—must be approached *grammatically* (agency is, among other things, a grammatical notion that is built up in distinctively different ways in different languages, sometimes for formal reasons), *historically* (sensitive to changes in the kinds of forces and objects that are attributed agency, but also to the reasons, political and religious, for which Westerners have construed certain practices as "animistic"), and *ethnographically* (in showing how the attribution of agency to particular forces and objects is part of an assemblage of material practices that, in turn, entail specific ontic commitments on the part of the practitioners).

Causal Structures

Cognitive psychologists have adduced evidence that concepts emerge from more general and broad knowledge that people have about the world.[24] Moreover they are not atomistic "building blocks" of thought (Keane 2006); rather, from the very beginning they are embedded in overarching theories (e.g., Gelman and Coley 1991; Gelman and Williams 1998; Gopnik and Wellman 1994; Keil 1991; Murphy and Medin 1985; Simons and Keil 1995; Wellman and Gelman 1998). These tacit theories, or *domains*, establish ontologies (in the first sense of this chapter, that is, "what there is" in the world), causal relationships, and unobservable entities specific to the domains. From this point of view, the early acquisition of concepts is not strictly perceptual in origin but is related to broader ontological configurations (e.g., a distinction between animate and inanimate entities) and to expectations regarding the causal laws of which the concepts are part (e.g., a dog is initially classified as a living being, an agent capable of autonomous movement). The tacit theories that scaffold concept formation are specific to domains (psychology, biology, physics, and so forth) and have domain-specific object-ontologies built into them, and these are, in turn, attributed to the kinds subsumed by them. (Kinds are routinely subsumed under multiple domains.) Central to this account are two observations: that there is a disjunction between appearances and underlying realities, the underlying realities bound to an ontological configuration (the "domain"), so that the construal of an underlying reality is domain specific; and that kinds have underlying psychological essences (Gelman 2003).

While the same domains are found across cultures, there is cross-linguistic and cross-cultural variability in the recruitment of concepts to domains. For example, in Quechua, both mountains and rocks are living kinds, whereas in English neither is (see the earlier section "Properties of the World"). Linguistic and social factors, such as syntactic generics (Mannheim et al. 2011) and other grammatical affordances (syntactic agreement, in "Agency," previously), identify concepts as kinds and assign them to domains.

Distinct domains may have distinct causal structures assigned to them. An English-speaking adult might explain a zebra's stripes as allowing it "to get away from predators" (Sánchez et al. 2016:appendix S4), assigning a teleological causal structure to the concept in which the zebra's stripes benefit the animal itself. Conversely, for both Quechua- and English-speaking adults, properties of artifacts are normally explained in terms of a human-directed teleology of design: clocks are for telling time, a *tiyana* is for sitting. These findings generalize to the domains of "living kinds" and "artifacts," respectively.

For living kinds, however, Quechua adults commonly explain their properties by appealing to an inevitable natural order of the animal world (frogs catch flies because "that's the way they are"), whereas U.S. adults have more of a "design" perspective on biological features, constructing explanations of animal features in an artifactualist mode (Gelman et al. 2015; Sánchez et al. 2016:754). Within Descola's fourfold typology of ontological regimes—naturalism, animism, totemism, and analogism—Quechua adults tend toward naturalism with respect to living kinds, and U.S. adults tend toward something that falls outside of this scheme, artifactualism, the cross-cultural variability in domain membership notwithstanding. Languages and societies differ in the causal structures that they assign to conceptual domains, differences that can be detected both developmentally and comparatively. What implications do these differences have for interactions between humans and living kinds in the two societies? What are the externalities, linguistic and cultural, that give shape to these differences? These questions can be answered only through a combination of experimental research with immersive ethnography.

Conclusion

This chapter introduces an analytical framework for approaching ontological differences among societies in a systematic way, along with their social and material consequences. It is constructed around two axes: At a foundational level, ontologies are constituted at arm's length by and for the people who use them—*worlding* (Descola 2014), constrained by *core cognition* (Carey 2009), *concepts-and-theories* (Murphy and Medin 1985; Wellman and Gelman 1998), and historically constituted indexical assemblages (Parmentier 2016:34; Silverstein 1976, 2003; all discussed in Mannheim 2015a). In turn, ontological structures are parts of comprehensive fields, whose interrelationships overflow the traditional distinctions among disciplines. The interrelationships are of interest here, for example, that frame of reference entails specific features of the social landscape or the visual culture and that reciprocally these afford the transmission of frame of reference to succeeding generations. The task of the anthropologist is on the one hand to identify these relationships in their full concreteness and on the other to identify relations of compatibility and entailment that can be investigated comparatively. Interrogating a

single feature of the social landscape, such as social agency or animism, is not especially useful in itself and, indeed, more often than not leads us back to one of the traditional culs-de-sac of social anthropology and archaeology: an anecdotal comparison of ourselves and others. More fruitful is to show the implications of each structure or practice across multiple domains, interactionally and interdiscursively; to show how they are integrated with each other when they are compatible and to show why they exclude each other when they are not.

In this chapter, I sketched the outlines of a theory of constrained ontological relativity and showed how it can be implemented in systematic accounts of Inka and contemporary Quechua language, culture, and society. Though I have only scratched the surface, I hope that the reader will have seen the fruitfulness of a strategy in which we can make empirical claims about the possible relationships among specific social practices, claims that are fallible and hence worthy of our consideration.

NOTES

1 An earlier version of this chapter was presented at the Workshop on Translating worlds, at the Social Science Matrix, University of California, Berkeley, January 2016, organized by William Hanks and Carlo Severi, to whom I am grateful for their challenging discussion points. I am also grateful to Catherine J. Allen, Anne Marie Creighton, Katherine Dimmery, Georgia Ennis, Susan A. Gelman, Margarita Huayhua, Webb Keane, Michael Lempert, Joyce Marcus, and Frank L. Salomon for their critiques of prior drafts.

2 For a related discussion of the use of "representation" in the history of art in the Andes, see Dean 2014. A related set of issues emerges around the notion of "belief." Uncritical use of "belief" as an analytical term tends to treat all societies as crypto-calvanists. But even more restricted views do not distinguish clearly among "belief" as a descriptive device used by ethnographers; as an operative category of self-representation by ritual specialists within a culture, as in the examples from Kogi and Arhuaco, discussed by Giraldo (this volume); and as an enregistered overlay designed to reformulate local cultural practices in the service of non-local interests (as in Mannheim's [2018] discussion of the linguistic overlay in Southern Quechua and Galinier and Molinié's [2006] study of New Age "Neo-Indians.") In addition, there are technical semantic and pragmatic issues around belief ascription both ethnographic (for example, whether mental states of others can only be attributed through quotation as in Quechua, or even attributed at all, as in many Melanesian societies; Robbins and Rumsey 2008) and technical (belief ascriptions have very specific semantic and pragmatic properties; Heny [ed.] 1980; Linsky 1983).

3 Keane (2016:29ff), discussing the notion itself of "affordance," observes that affordances work "with other sources of information such as cultural routines," "not as a matter of contemplation but in the course of practical activity," and are social. Affordances are at once fully social and fully cognitive characteristics of all material and social activities and structures with causal powers. My use of "afford" and "affordance" here is largely consistent with his.

4 For a succinct discussion of the ways in which an ontological approach differs from more traditional representationalist (symbolic) approaches, see Pedersen 2011:180–181 and Salomon 2018:184–204.

5 I follow W. V. O Quine (1961) in assuming an a priori, precultural ontological austerity, the ontology populated culturally and linguistically, constrained by universal cognitive processes. As Quine (1961:1) so pithily wrote: "Entification begins at arm's length." See Mannheim 2015b for an explicit account of how this works.

6 These include Cummins and Mannheim 2011; Gelman et al. 2015; Mannheim 1998a, 1999, 2015a, 2015b, 2015c, and 2019; Mannheim and Gelman 2015; Mannheim et al. 2011; Mannheim and Salas 2015; Salas 2016, 2019; Sánchez Tapia et al. 2016; and Shapero 2017a, 2017b.

7 The purpose of these fields is to organize the evidence in this chapter. In Mannheim, Davis, and Velasco (2018), we work with a different but overlapping set of fields, with an eye toward future comparisons among native South American societies.

8 When I use the expression "Quechua speaker," I refer to speakers of the monolingual or the Quechua-dominant bilingual registers of Quechua, not to speakers of the Spanish-regimented "overlay." For an explanation of these differences see Mannheim and Huayhua (2016) and Mannheim (2018). Experimental research by Margarita Huayhua (2018), drawing on Pérez Silva et al. (2009), shows that the difference between the monolingual and Quechua-dominant bilingual registers of Quechua on the one hand and the Spanish-regimented overlay on the other is observable to speakers of both, below their thresholds of awareness, and is a focus of social discrimination.

9 They are subject, of course, to standard processes of linguistic change, including the linguistic changes discussed in Mannheim (1991) and the register effects discussed in Mannheim and Salas (2015) and Mannheim (2015b).

10 I use the expression "built environment" with some trepidation, as instances like the carved living stone in Machu Picchu suggest that the Inkas did not distinguish "natural" from "built" environments (Dean 2007).

11 Levinson (1983:181–184) and Karttunen (2016), among others, have suggested that presupposition is not a linguistically uniform mechanism. That does not affect the proposal here.

12 Presupposition and implicature are two forms of tacit inference that are primarily propositional, although in aggregate they can have far-reaching ontic effects. In real-time interaction, both these forms of inference operate at the same time, interlocking with each other and with tacit inferences promoted by the structure of the social interaction itself. Social interaction is layered or *laminated,* and the structure of lamination promotes tacit inferences in ways that are similar to presupposition and implicature, and so reproduces the ontic landscape in which the interaction takes place.

13 The distinction between "egocentric" and "allocentric" is well established in neuroscience, cognitive psychology, art history, and linguistic anthropology, with senses that overlap. Neither makes the moral claims that might be suggested by lay uses of "egocentric."

14 Quechua visual forms often play with figure-ground reversals; in this account, the anchor would shift accordingly.

15 Technically, this should use the participation roles identified by the sociologist Erving Goffman (1979): principal (the person whose point of view is being expressed), addressee, and other ratified participant.

16 Levinson and his collaborators (Levinson and Wilkins 2007) and Shapero (2017b) use a closely related three-category typology with similar formal properties. Since both typologies include a primary split between allocentric and egocentric frames of reference, the differences between Levinson's typology and Danziger's does not materially affect the argument here.

17 Indeed, in contemporary Southern Quechua communities it is critical to maintain a distance between the living and the dead. While the recent noninfant dead are buried in individual graves and fed ritually on All Saints Day, their bones are eventually disinterred and added to an ossuary heap, in which they lack any distinguishable social identity (Allen 1988, 2015a; Robin 2008; Salas 2019).

18 Mannheim (2015c) identifies a "generic fade" in colonial sources on the Inka, in which references to particular events and practices are replaced with generic statements about classes of events and practices. This can be traced by comparing the specific language used in two or more descriptions of "the same" events.

19 "*Société à maison*" is a framework for kinship analysis, developed since the late 1970s; see Lévi-Strauss 1974, 1979; Feeley-Harnik 1980; Carsten and Hugh-Jones 1995; Gillespie 2000; Hamberger 2012. Sendón (2016) develops a comparable model based on colonial and republican parish records from Marcapata (Cuzco).

20 Inka king lists, products of the colonial encounter, which evolved over the course of the sixteenth century (Covey 2006) consist of a mix of a house name (Qhapaq), titles, and a smattering of individual names. That the Inka personified Cuzco, and so spoke *as Cuzco* and was referred to *as Cuzco* reflected a broader pattern—maintained even today—in which people share an essence with their place of origin (see de la Cadena 2015:102; Mannheim 1991:50; Oxa Diaz 2005:236–237).

21 A similar point is made by Sahlins (2014:288–289), who puts the matter pithily: "We are one of the others."

22 See Searle 2010 and Gouvea 2016 for similar distinctions that have the same kind of problem once they are operationalized cross-culturally.

23 On syntactic agreement as a determinant of language and culture-specific properties of agency, see Silverstein 1976; Duranti 1994, 2004; Ahearn 2001; Vapnarsky 2013; Kockelman 2014 and 2017; and Enfield 2015. On the role of person systems, see Hill and Mannheim 1991 and Klaiman 1992.

24 Anthropologists and sociologists have traditionally used the word "structure" in a scalar sense, giving it scope over social practices and interactions, even when they have prioritized the latter. In contrast, my use of the word "structure" here and elsewhere is nonscalar, to refer to pattern or organization of any kind.

Ahearn, Laura M.

2001 Language and Agency. *Annual Review of Anthropology* 30:109–137.

Alberti, Benjamin

2016 Archaeology of Ontologies. *Annual Review of Anthropology* 45:163–179.

Allen, Catherine J.

1988 *The Hold Life Has: Coca and Cultural Identity in an Andean Community.* Smithsonian Institution Press, Washington, D.C.

1994 Time, Place, and Narrative in an Andean Community. *Schweizerische Amerikanisten-Gesellschaft* 57–58:89–95.

1997 When Pebbles Move Mountains. In *Iconicity and Symbolism in Quechua Ritual*, edited by Rosaleen Howard-Malverde, pp. 73–84. Oxford University Press, New York.

1998 When Utensils Revolt: Mind, Matter, and Modes of Being in the Pre-Columbian Andes. *RES: Anthropology and Aesthetics* 33:18–27.

2015a The Sadness of Jars: Separation and Rectification in Andean Understandings of Death. In *Living with the Dead in the Andes*, edited by Izumi Shimada and James L. Fitzsimmons, pp. 304–328. University of Arizona Press, Tucson.

2015b The Whole World Is Watching: New Perspectives on Andean Animism. In *The Archaeology of Wak'as: Explorations of the Sacred in the Pre-Columbian Andes*, edited by Tamara Bray, pp. 23–45. University of Colorado Press, Boulder.

2016 The Living Ones: Miniatures and Animation in the Andes. *Journal of Anthropological Research* 72(4):416–441.

Arnold, Denise Y., and Juan de Dios Yapita

1998 *Río de vellón, río de canto: Cantar a los animales, una poética aymara de creación.* HISBOL, La Paz.

Bauer, Brian S.

1998 *The Sacred Landscape of the Inca: The Cusco Ceque System.* University of Texas Press, Austin.

Benveniste, Émile

1971 *Problems in General Linguistics.* University of Miami Press, Miami.

Bird-David, Nurit

1999 Animism Revisited: Personhood, Environment, and Relational Epistemology. *Current Anthropology* 40 (suppl.):67–91.

Bray, Tamara (editor)

2015 *The Archaeology of Wak'as: Explorations of the Sacred in the Pre-Columbian Andes.* University of Colorado Press, Boulder.

Brezine, Carrie

2011 The Tactile Abstract. Unpublished manuscript, University of Michigan, Ann Arbor.

Caine, Allison

2019 Restless Ecologies in the Andean Highlands. PhD dissertation, University of Michigan, Ann Arbor.

Canessa, Andrew

2012 *Intimate Indigeneities: Race, Sex, and History in the Small Spaces of Andean Life.* Duke University Press, Durham, N.C.

Carey, Susan D.

2009 *The Origin of Concepts.* Oxford University Press, New York.

Carsten, Janet, and Stephen Hugh-Jones (editors)

1995 *About the House: Lévi-Strauss and Beyond.* Cambridge University Press, Cambridge.

Chierchia, Gennaro, and Sally McConnell-Ginet

1990 *Meaning and Grammar: An Introduction to Semantics.* MIT Press, Cambridge, Mass.

Christie, Jessica Joyce

2007 Did the Inca Copy Cuzco? *Journal of Latin American and Caribbean Anthropology* 12:164–199.

Coben, Lawrence S.

2006 Other Cuzcos: Replicated Theaters of Inka Power. In *Archaeology of Performance*, edited by Takeshi Inomata and Lawrence S. Coben, pp. 223–259. Altamira Press, Lanham, Md.

Covey, R. Alan

2006   Chronology, Succession, and Sovereignty: The Politics of Inka Historiography and Its Modern Interpretation. *Comparative Studies in Society and History* 48(1):166–199.

Cummins, Thomas B. F.

2002   *Toasts with the Inca.* University of Michigan Press, Ann Arbor.

Cummins, Thomas B. F., and Bruce Mannheim

2011   The River around Us, the Stream within Us: The Traces of the Sun and Inka Kinetics. *RES: Anthropology and Aesthetics* 59–60:5–21.

Danziger, Eve

2010   Deixis, Gesture, and Cognition in Spatial Frame of Reference Typology. *Studies in Language* 34(1):167–185.

Davidson, Donald

1984   On the Very Idea of a Conceptual Scheme. In *Inquiries into Truth and Interpretation*, pp. 183–198. Oxford University Press, Oxford.

Dean, Carolyn

2007   The Inka Married the Earth: Integrated Outcrops and the Making of Place. *Art Bulletin* 89:502–518.

2010   *A Culture of Stone: Inka Perspectives on Rock.* Duke University Press, Durham, N.C.

2014   Reviewing Representation: The Subject-Object in Pre-Hispanic and Colonial Inka Visual Culture. *Colonial Latin American Review* 23:298–319.

de la Cadena, Marisol

2010   Indigenous Cosmopolitics in the Andes. *Cultural Anthropology* 25(2):334–370.

2015   *Earth Beings.* Duke University Press, Durham, N.C.

Descola, Philippe

2005   *Par-delà nature et culture.* Gallimard, Paris.

2013   *Beyond Nature and Culture.* University of Chicago Press, Chicago.

2014   Modes of Being and Forms of Predication. *Hau* 4:271–280.

Diez de Betanzos, Juan

[1551] 2015   *Suma y narración de los Incas, que los Indios llamaron Capaccuna, que fueron señores de la ciudad del Cuzco, y de todo lo à ella subjeto.* Edition consulted, *Juan de Betanzos y el Tahuantinsuyo: Nueva edición de la Suma y narración de los Incas*, edited by Francisco Hernández Astete and Rodolfo Cerrón-Palomino. Fondo Editorial de la Pontificia Universidad Católica del Perú, Lima.

Duranti, Alessandro

1994   *From Grammar to Politics: Linguistic Anthropology in a Western Samoan Village.* University of California Press, Berkeley.

2004   Agency in Language. In *A Companion to Linguistic Anthropology*, edited by Alessandro Duranti, pp. 451–473. Blackwell, Malden, Mass.

Enfield, N. J.

2015   Linguistic Relativity from Reference to Agency. *Annual Review of Anthropology* 44:207–224.

Evans-Pritchard, Edward E.

1933   The Intellectualist (English) Interpretation of Magic. *Bulletin of the Faculty of Arts, University of Cairo,* 1:282–311.

Feeley-Harnik, Gillian

1980   The Sakalava House (Madagascar). *Anthropos* 75:559–585.

Galinier, Jacques, and Antoinette Molinié

2006   *Les néo-Indiens, une religion du IIIe millénaire.* Odile Jacob, Paris.

Gelman, Rochel, and Earl Williams

1998   Enabling Constraints for Cognitive Development and Learning: Domain Specificity and Epigenesis. In *Cognition, Perception and Language.* Vol. 2 of *Handbook of Child Psychology*, edited by D. Kuhn and R. S. Siegler, pp. 575–630. 5th ed. Wiley, New York.

Gelman, Susan A.

2003   *The Essential Child.* Oxford University Press, New York.

Gelman, Susan A., and John D. Coley

1991   Language and Categorization: The Acquisition of Natural Kind Terms. In *Perspectives on Language and Cognition:*

Interrelations in Development, edited by Susan A. Gelman and James P. Byrnes, pp. 146–196. Cambridge University Press, Cambridge.

Gelman, Susan A., Bruce Mannheim, Carmen Escalante, and Ingrid Sánchez Tapia

2015 Teleological Talk in Parent-Child Conversations in Quechua. *First Language* 35:359–376.

Gentner, Dedre, and José Lasaga Medina

1998 Similarity and the Development of Rules. *Cognition* 65(2–3):263–297.

Gillespie, Susan D.

2000 Lévi-Strauss: Maison and société à maisons. In *Beyond Kinship: Social and Material Reproduction in House Societies*, edited by Rosemary A. Joyce and Susan D. Gillespie, pp. 22–52. University of Pennsylvania Press, Philadelphia.

Goffman, Erving

1979 Footing. *Semiotica* 25:1–29.

Gopnik, Alison, and Henry M. Wellman

1994 The Theory Theory. In *Mapping the Mind: Domain Specificity in Cognition and Culture*, edited by Lawrence A. Hirschfeld and Susan A. Gelman, pp. 257–293. Cambridge University Press, Cambridge.

Gouvea, Rodrigo A. dos S.

2016 On the Intentionality-Relative Features of the World. *Filosofia unisinos* 17(2):149–154.

Grice, H. Paul

1975 Logic and Conversation. In *Syntax and Semantics 3: Speech Acts*, edited by Peter Cole and Jerry L. Morgan, pp. 41–58. Academic Press, New York.

Guaman Poma de Ayala, Felipe

[1615] 1987 *El primer nueva corónica y buen gobierno.* Edited by John V. Murra and Rolena Adorno. 3 vols. Historia 16, Madrid.

Hallowell, A. Irving

1960 Ojibwa Ontology, Behavior, and World View. In *Culture in History: Essays in Honor of Paul Radin*, edited by Stanley Diamond, pp. 19–52. Columbia University Press, New York.

1991 *The Ojibwa of Berens River, Manitoba: Ethnography into History.* Harcourt Brace Jovanovich, Fort Worth, Tex.

Hamberger, Klaus

2012 La maison en perspective: Un modèle spatial de l'alliance. *L'Homme* 194:7–40.

Harré, Rom, and E. H. Madden

1975 *Causal Powers: A Theory of Natural Necessity.* Basil Blackwell, Oxford.

Hastorf, Christine A.

1993 *Agriculture and the Onset of Political Inequality before the Inka.* Cambridge University Press, Cambridge.

Haviland, John B.

1998 Guugu Yimithirr Cardinal Directions. *Ethos* 26:25–47.

Heny, Frank (editor)

1980 *Ambiguities in Intensional Contexts.* Kluwer, Dordrecht.

Hill, Jane H., and Bruce Mannheim

1991 Language and World View. *Annual Review of Anthropology* 21:382–406.

Huayhua, Margarita

2018 Strangers in Our Own Land: Social Oppression in the Southern Andes. Unpublished book manuscript, University of Massachusetts, Dartmouth.

Hyslop, John

1990 *Inka Settlement Planning.* University of Texas Press, Austin.

Irvine, Judith T.

1996 Shadow Conversations. In *Natural Histories of Discourse*, edited by Michael Silverstein and Greg Urban, pp. 131–159. University of Chicago Press, Chicago.

Karttunen, Lauri

1974 Presupposition and Linguistic Context. *Theoretical Linguistics* 1(1):181–194.

2016 Presupposition: What Went Wrong? *Proceedings of SALT (Semantics and Linguistic Theory)* 26:705–731.

Keane, Webb

2006 Signs Are Not the Garb of Meaning: On the Social Analysis of Material Things. In *Materiality*, edited by Daniel Miller, pp. 182–205. Duke University Press, Durham, N.C.

2016   *Ethical Life: Its Natural and Social Histories.* Princeton University Press, Princeton.

Keil, Frank C.

1991   Theories, Concepts, and the Acquisition of Word Meaning. In *Perspectives on Language and Cognition: Interrelations in Development,* edited by Susan A. Gelman and J. P. Byrnes, pp. 197–221. Cambridge University Press, Cambridge.

Klaiman, M. H.

1992   Inverse Languages. *Lingua* 88:227–261.

Kockelman, Paul

2014   *Agent, Person, Subject, Self.* Oxford University Press, Oxford.

2017   Semiotic Agency. In *Distributed Agency,* edited by N. J. Enfield and Paul Kockelman, pp. 25–38. Oxford University Press, Oxford.

Kohn, Eduardo

2016   Anthropology of Ontologies. *Annual Review of Anthropology* 44:311–327.

Kosiba, Steven

2012   Emplacing Value. In *The Construction of Value in the Ancient World,* edited by John K. Papadopoulos and Gary Urton, pp. 97–126. Cotsen Institute, University of California, Los Angeles.

2015a   Of Blood and Soil: Tombs, Wak'as, and the Naturalization of Social Difference in the Inka Heartland. In *The Archaeology of Wak'as: Explorations of the Sacred in the Pre-Columbian Andes,* edited by Tamara Bray, pp. 167–212. University of Colorado Press, Boulder.

2015b   Tracing the Inca Past: Ritual Movement and Social Memory in the Inka Imperial Capital. In *Perspectives on the Inca,* edited by Monica Barnes, Inés de Castro, Javier Flores Espinoza, Doris Kurella, and Karoline Noack, pp. 178–205. Linden-Museum, Sonderband/Tribus, Stuttgart.

Levinson, Stephen C.

1983   *Pragmatics.* Cambridge University Press, Cambridge.

2003   *Space in Language and Cognition.* Cambridge University Press, Cambridge.

Levinson, Stephen C., and David Wilkins (editors)

2006   *Grammars of Space: Explorations of Cognitive Diversity.* Cambridge University Press, Cambridge.

Lévi-Strauss, Claude

1949   *Les structures élémentaires de la parenté.* PUF, Paris.

[1976] 1984   La notion de "maison." In *Paroles données,* pp. 189–191. Plon, Paris.

[1979] 1982   Nobles sauvages. In *Culture, science et développement: Mélanges en l'honneur de Charles Moraze,* pp. 41–55. Privat, Toulouse. Translated as "The Social Organization of the Kwakiutl." In *The Way of the Masks,* translated by Sylvia Modelski, pp. 163–187. University of Washington Press, Seattle.

Linsky, Leonard

1983   *Oblique Contexts.* Unversity of Chicago Press, Chicago.

Majid, Asifa, Melissa Bowerman, Sotaro Kita, Daniel B. M. Haun, and Stephen C. Levinson

2004   Can Language Restructure Cognition? The Case for Space. *Trends in Cognitive Sciences* 8(3):108–114.

Mannheim, Bruce

1991   *The Language of the Inka since the European Invasion.* University of Texas Press, Austin.

1998a   A Nation Surrounded. In *Native Traditions in the Post-Conquest World,* edited by Elizabeth Boone and Tom Cummins, pp. 381–418. Dumbarton Oaks, Washington, D.C.

1998b   "Time, not the syllables, must be counted": Quechua Parallelism, Word Meaning, and Cultural Analysis. *Michigan Discussions in Anthropology* 13:245–287.

1999   Iconicity. *Journal of Linguistic Anthropology* 9:107–110.

2015a   All Translation Is Radical Translation. In *Translating Worlds: The Epistemological Space of Translation,* edited by Carlo Severi and William F. Hanks, pp. 199–219. University of Chicago Press, Chicago.

2015b   La historicidad de imágenes oníricos quechuas sudperuanos. *Letras* 123:5–48. Lima.

2015c The Social Imaginary, Unspoken in Verbal Art. In *The Routledge Handbook in Linguistic Anthropology*, edited by Nancy Bonvillain, pp. 44–61. Routledge, New York.

2015d What Kind of Text Was Guaman Poma's Warikza arawi? In *Unlocking the Doors to the Worlds of Guaman Poma and His Nueva corónica*, edited by Rolena Adorno and Ivan Boserup, pp. 161–182. Museum Tusculanum Press, Copenhagen.

2018 Xavier Albó's "The Future of the Oppressed Languages of the Andes" in Retrospect. In *Indigenous Languages, Politics, and Authority in Latin America: Historical and Ethnographic Perspectives*, edited by Alan Durston and Bruce Mannheim, pp. 207–230. University of Notre Dame Press, South Bend, Ind.

2019 The Horn of Time. Manuscript, Department of Anthropology, University of Michigan, Ann Arbor.

Mannheim, Bruce, Allison R. Davis, and Matthew C. Velasco

2018 Cranial Modification in the Central Andes: Person, Language, Political Economy. In *Social Skins of the Head: Bodies, Beliefs, and Ritual in Ancient Mesoamerica and the Andes*, edited by Maria Cecilia Lozada and Vera Tiesler, pp. 223–233. University of New Mexico Press, Albuquerque.

Mannheim, Bruce, and Susan A. Gelman

2013 El aprendizaje de los conceptos genéricos entre niños quechua hablantes monolingües. *Bulletin de l'Institut Français d'Études Andines* 42(3):353–368.

Mannheim, Bruce, Susan A. Gelman, Carmen Escalante, Margarita Huayhua, and Rosalía Puma

2011 A Developmental Analysis of Quechua Generics. *Language Learning and Development* 7:1–23.

Mannheim, Bruce, and Margarita Huayhua

2016 El quechua es un idioma multi-registral. In *Dilemas de la gobernabilidad en el Sur Andino al 2021*, edited by Anael Pilares, pp. 152–156. Centro de Estudios Regionales Andinos "Bartolomé de las Casas," Cuzco.

Mannheim, Bruce, and Guillermo Salas Carreño

2015 Wak'a: Entifications of the Andean Sacred. In *The Archaeology of Wak'as: Explorations of the Sacred in the Pre-Columbian Andes*, edited by Tamara Bray, pp. 46–72. University of Colorado Press, Boulder.

Markman, Arthur B., and Dedre Gentner

1997 The Effects of Alignability on Memory. *Psychological Science* 8(5):363–367.

Meira, Sérgio

2006 Approaching Space in Tiriyó Grammar. In *Grammars of Space: Explorations of Cognitive Diversity*, edited by Stephen C. Levinson and David Wilkins, pp. 311–358. Cambridge University Press, Cambridge.

Molinié, Antoinette

2012 La monnaie sauvage: Une énigme andine de la monnaie. In *Monnaie antique, monnaie moderne, monnaies d'ailleurs . . . : Métissages et hybridations*, edited by P. Pion and B. Fornoso, pp. 175–187. Colloques de la Maison René-Ginouvès 8. De Boccard, Paris.

Murphy, Gregory L., and Douglas L. Medin

1985 The Role of Theories in Conceptual Coherence. *Psychological Review* 92:289–316.

Oxa Diaz, Justo

2005 Vigencia e la cultura andina en la escuela. In *Arguedas y el Perú de hoy*, edited by Carmen María Pinilla, Gonzalo Portocarrero Maisch, Cecilia Rivera, and Carla Sagástegui, pp. 235–242. SUR, Casa de Estudios del Socialismo, Lima.

Parmentier, Richard

2016 *Signs and Society*. Indiana University Press, Bloomington.

Pedersen, Morten Axel

2011 *Not Quite Shamans: Spirit Worlds and Political Lives in Northern Mongolia*. Cornell University Press, Ithaca.

Pérez Silva, Jorge Ivan, Jorge Acurio Palma, and Raúl Bendezú Araujo

2009 *Contra el prejuicio lingüístico de la motosidad: Un estudio de las vocales del castellano andino desde la fonética acústica*. Instituto Riva Agüero, Pontificia Universidad Católica del Perú, Lima.

Platt, Tristan

    1997   The Sound of Light: Emergent Communication through Quechua Shamanic Dialogue. In *Creating Context in Andean Cultures*, edited by Rosaleen Howard, pp. 196–226. Oxford University Press, New York.

Quine, Willard van Orman

    1961   *Word and Object*. MIT Press, Cambridge, Mass.

    1968   Ontological Relativity. *Journal of Philosophy* 45:185–212.

Ramírez, Susan E.

    2005   *To Feed and Be Fed: Cosmological Bases of Inca Authority*. Stanford University Press, Stanford.

    2006   Historia y memoria: La construcción de las tradiciones dinásticas andinas. *Revista de indias* 66:13–56.

Robbins, Joel, and Alan Rumsey

    2008   Introduction: Cultural and Linguistic Anthropology and the Opacity of Other Minds. *Anthropological Quarterly* 81:407–420.

Robin Azevedo, Valérie

    2008   *Miroirs de l'autre vie: Pratiques rituelles et discours sur les morts dans les Andes de Cuzco (Pérou)*. Société d'Ethnologie, Nanterre.

Rybka, Konrad Arkadiusz

    2016   *The Linguistic Encoding of Landscape in Lokono*. LOT, Utrecht.

Sahlins, Marshall D.

    2014   On the Ontological Scheme of *Beyond Nature and Culture*. Hau 4(1):281–290.

Salas Carreño, Guillermo

    2012   Religious Change and Ideologies of Social Hierarchy in the Southern Peruvian Andes. PhD dissertation, University of Michigan, Ann Arbor.

    2016   Places Are Kin. *Anthropological Quarterly* 89:813–838.

    2019   *Lugares parientes: Comida y cohabitación en la emergencia de mundos andinos*. Fondo Editorial de la Pontificia Universidad Católica del Perú, Lima.

Salomon, Frank L.

    2018   *At the Mountain's Altar: Anthropology of Religion in an Andean Community*. Routledge, New York.

Sánchez Tapia, Ingrid, Susan A. Gelman, Michelle A. Hollander, Erika M. Manczak, Bruce Mannheim, and Carmen Escalante

    2016   Development of Teleological Explanations in U.S. English-Speaking and Peruvian Quechua-Speaking Preschoolers and Adults. *Child Development* 87(3):747–758

Sapir, Edward

    1929   The Status of Linguistics as a Science. *Language* 5:207–214.

Searle, John R.

    2010   *Making the Social World*. Oxford University Press, New York.

Sendón, Pablo F.

    2016   *Ayllu, parentesco y organización social en los Andes del sur peruano*. Fondo Editorial de la Pontificia Universidad Católica del Perú, Lima.

Senft, Gunter (editor)

    2000   *Systems of Nominal Classification*. Cambridge University Press, Cambridge.

Shapero, Josh

    2014   Gestures in Native South America: Ancash Quechua. In *Body, Language, Communication*, edited by Cornelia Müller, Alan Cienki, Ellen Fricke, Silva Ladewig, David McNeill, and Sedinha Teßendor, pp. 1193–1206. De Gruyter, Berlin.

    2017a   Does Environmental Experience Shape Spatial Cognition? *Cognitive Science* 41:1274–1298.

    2017b   Speaking Places: Quechua Language, Cognition and Pastoral Life in the Ancash Highlands. PhD dissertation, University of Michigan, Ann Arbor.

Sherbondy, Jeanette E.

    1985   Organización hidráulica y poder en el Cuzco de los Incas. *Revista española de antropología americana* 17:117–153.

Sillar, Bill

2009 The Social Agency of Things: Animism and Materiality in the Andes. *Cambridge Archaeological Journal* 19(3)367–377.

Silverstein, Michael

1976 Shifters, Linguistic Categories, and Cultural Description. In *Meaning in Anthropology*, edited by Keith Basso and Henry Selby, pp. 11–55. University of New Mexico Press, Albuquerque.

2003 Indexical Order and the Dialectics of Sociolinguistic Life. *Language and Communication* 23:193–229.

Simons, D., and Frank C. Keil

1995 An Abstract to Concrete Shift in the Development of Biological Thought: The *Insides* Story. *Cognition* 56:129–163.

Smith, Benjamin

2010 Of Marbles and (Little) Men: Bad Luck and Masculine Identification in Aymara Boyhood. *Journal of Linguistic Anthropology* 20:225–239.

2016 Turning Language Socialization Ontological: Material Things and the Semiotics of Scaling Time in Peruvian Aymara Boyhood. *Language and Communication* 46:42–50.

Sperber, Dan, and Dierdre Wilson

1986 *Relevance*. Blackwell, London.

Stanish, Charles

2012 The Revaluation of Landscapes in the Inca Empire as Peircean Replication. In *The Construction of Value in the Ancient World*, edited by John K. Papadopoulos and Gary Urton, pp. 80–88. The Cotsen Institute, University of California, Los Angeles.

Strong, Pauline T.

2017 A. Irving Hallowell and the Ontological Turn. *Hau* 7:468–472.

Swenson, Edward

2015 The Materialities of Place Making in the Ancient Andes: A Critical Appraisal of the Ontological Turn in Archaeological Interpretation. *Journal of Archaeological Method and Theory* 22(3):677–712.

Trubetzkoy, Nicolai S.

1939 *Grundzüge der phonologie*. Cercle Linguistique de Prague, Prague.

Tylor, Edward B.

1871 *Primitive Culture, Researches into the Development of Mythology, Philosophy, Religion, Art, and Custom*. Vol. 1. John Murray, London.

Urton, Gary

1981 *At the Crossroads of the Earth and the Sky*. University of Texas Press, Austin.

2010 Recording Measure(ment)s in the Inka Khipu. In *The Archaeology of Measurement*, edited by Iain Morley and Colin Renfrew, pp. 54–68. Cambridge University Press, New York.

van de Guchte, Maarten

1990 Carving the World: Monumental Sculpture and Landscape. PhD dissertation, University of Illinois, Urbana-Champaign.

1999 The Inca Cognition of Landscape: Archaeology, Ethnohistory, and the Aesthetic of Alterity. In *Archaeologies of Landscape*, edited by Wendy Ashmore and A. Bernard Knapp, pp. 149–168. Blackwell, Malden, Mass.

Vapnarsky, Valentina

2013 Le passif peut-il éclairer les esprits? Agentivités, interactions et esprits-maîtres chez les Mayas. *Ateliers d'Anthropologie*. Electronic document, https://journals.openedition.org/ateliers/9449?lang=fr, accessed March 1, 2019.

Velasco, Matthew

2018 Ethnogenesis and Social Difference in the Andean Late Intermediate Period (AD 1100–1450). *Current Anthropology* 59:98–106.

Viveiros de Castro, Eduardo

2004 Perspectival Anthropology and the Method of Controlled Equivocation. *Tipti* 2:3–22.

Wellman, Henry M., and Susan A. Gelman

1998   Knowledge Acquisition in Foundational Domains. In *Cognition, Perception and Language*. Vol. 2 of *Handbook of Child Psychology*, edited by D. Kuhn and R. S. Siegler, pp. 523–573. 5th ed. Wiley, New York.

Wernke, Steven A.

2013   *Negotiated Settlements: Andean Communities and Landscapes under Inka and Spanish Colonialism.* University Press of Florida, Gainesville.

Yaya McKenzie, Isabel

2011   *The Two Faces of Inca History: Dualism in the Narratives and Cosmology of Ancient Cuzco.* Brill, Leiden.

Zuidema, R. Tom

1964   *The Ceque System of Cuzco.* Brill, Leiden.

14

Purpose, Belief, and Political Action in the Sierra Nevada de Santa Marta

SANTIAGO GIRALDO

A VERY RECENT EXCHANGE IN AUGUST OF 2016 on the Facebook page of *Aluna* regarding my archaeological and ethnographic work highlights, in a rather funny way, some of the more obvious reasons why a number of scholars—such as Lucas Bessire (2014), Lucas Bessire and David Bond (2014), Michael Cepek (2016), David Graeber (2015), Paolo Heywood (2012), and James Laidlaw (2012)—seriously question the call by authors like Martin Holbraad (2007, 2012) to accept narratives and ideas regarding "multi-natural reality" and animistic beliefs in a literal sense, in both ethnographic and archaeological settings. *Aluna* is the second documentary by filmmaker Alan Ereira wherein he conveys to the world the dire warning emitted by the *mamas*,[1] the Kogi priests, regarding the ecological catastrophe that will befall us all if we continue to disregard the "Law of the Mother."[2] The following is an excerpt of the exchange on Facebook between the participants, who were discussing a feature article printed in the local daily about a conference at Universidad del Norte,

a private university in the city of Barranquilla, located on Colombia's northern coast, where I presented on August 4, 2016.[3] Names are as they appear on this public page, though at least one of them seems to be fake as far as I have been able to determine.[4]

Joshua Babbish: It must be included in this article that the Kogi do not want people in their ancestral lands. To have people screwing with their offerings and architecture is extremely offensive.

Burns Stewart: The article does mention that noninvasive archaeological techniques were used, but doesn't say if the Mamos' permission was given. I'd like to think permission was granted, as the article states that part of the study included codesigned projects with indigenous communities.

Joshua Babbish: Well then, for this article to be well written, "permission was given by the

figure 14.1

The Ashanti shrine (Abosomfie) at Besease, now a neighborhood of Kumasi in Ghana, where we were kicked out by the shrine guardian after *mama* Crispín tried to hide a *marumsama* bag filled with objects of power in a doorframe. Photograph by Santiago Giraldo.

Mamos," must be included. As far as I see this article teeters on disrespecting everything the Kogi warned the younger brother of in "Aluna" and "From the Heart of the World." i feel it speaks of the younger brothers mismanaged investments into technological crap and invasive behavior too lightly. That is just my impression of the article, and that pisses me off (you aren't Burns Stewart). I feel someone could read this and get it in their head that they might be able to visit and check out how cool it is, it's architectural mastery, or whatever. the Mamos repeat Timelessly how terrible this kind of behavior is. They repeat explicitly that they do not want people in "the (intentionally) lost city," That fact should at least

be mentioned out of respect for the love and true concern they express to help us younger brother.

Joshua Babbish: Alan Ereira where do the Mamos stand on this? I find the integrity of this article unacceptable.

Burns Stewart: hi again, found an academic paper produced in 2009 by the lead archeologist, Santiago Gilardo, which confirms authorisation to conduct studies of La Ciudad Perdida by Kogi civic and spiritual authorities. Link to the article.

Burns Stewart: hi again. i emailed the Organización Gonawindua Tayrona to ask if permission for the archeological study was granted. https://gonawindwa.org/

Joshua Babbish: Excellent work, mate!

Fiona Laveau: Permission can be a slippery slope. Always keep respect in your hearts

Since the 1950s, when Gerardo Reichel-Dolmatoff and his wife, Alicia Dussán, first published their monograph on the Kogi (1985), a mighty entanglement between the indigenous groups currently living in the Sierra Nevada de Santa Marta, the Tairona polities that disappeared at the beginning of the seventeenth century, and archaeological sites and artifacts has ensued.[5] Time and time again, I have been asked to "take what the indigenous peoples say" about the Tairona, about places such as Teyuna-Ciudad Perdida Archaeological Park, and about Tairona artifacts and objects in a literal way. Not merely as historically and socially contingent perceptions, opinions, propositions, intellectual and critical discourses, and discussions, and least of all as political and pragmatic statements imbued with power or as defined courses of action aimed at fulfilling political agendas. In almost every presentation I have given, be it in Colombia or abroad, in public or in academic settings, someone in the audience has asked a question that goes something like this: Well, this is all very interesting. But have you asked the Kogi or the Arhuaco or the Wiwa about what these things are? They are the direct descendants of the Tairona, aren't they? They should be able to give you some straight answers.[6]

Maria del Rosario Ferro, a colleague who has also worked in the Sierra Nevada de Santa Marta for many years and conducted ethnographic research among the Kogi and Arhuaco for her dissertation, has over the past twenty years or so asked me similar questions: Why don't I use what the *mamas* say about these objects? Why don't I believe in what they say about them? How indeed can we reconcile these positions, and where are they incommensurable? At least within the archaeology of the Tairona, Alberti and Bray's (2009) calls to incorporate "animism" into analysis are actually old hat. Warwick Bray (2003), Anne Legast (1998), Matthew Looper (2003), Augusto Oyuela-Caycedo (1998, 2002, 2005), and Clemencia Plazas (2014) have pulled in ethnographic examples to explain Tairona objects,

their symbolism, and their use in ritual practices, both ancient and contemporary. As in Holbraad's (2012) approach of taking subject propositions literally, many of the documentaries, movies, and ethnographic and popular literature available on the Kogi and the Arhuaco hinge precisely on a romanticized, literal view—of taking everything they say about the state of the world, environmental conservation, archaeological remains, and the other-than-human beings they believe in as "truth." As the Facebook exchange shows, these propositions and the Kogi themselves are considered predominantly from a romanticized Western, Euro-American perspective rather than as a group of people deploying particular and strategic "ontological claims" to further their own political interests. This is possible because in translating their beliefs related to other-than-human entities to a wider audience, Kogi leaders have been able to further indigenous territorial expansion and politico-religious demands within Colombia in unprecedented ways. Indigenous peoples in the Sierra Nevada de Santa Marta harness, quote, and deploy these supernatural beings constantly as efficacious political tools in their day-to-day dealings with the Colombian government, NGOs, universities, media, and corporations working within their area of influence, and they have won important legal battles at various levels on this basis alone. To be clear, this does not imply a criticism of claims and arguments by either side. Rather, what surfaces from these emerging and evolving claims and counterclaims is a fascinating, dynamic, and constantly changing political arena that should not be reduced to "alternative and incommensurable ontologies." Not only is this latter view overly simplistic, it completely misses the point made time and time again by the indigenous priests and authorities that it is their worldview and "original" law that applies to everyone's reality.

This chapter, like most of my archaeological and ethnographic work, seeks to disentangle this relationship, as well as to produce open-ended, historicized accounts as to what the various intellectually creative processes initiated by Kogi and Arhuaco *mamas* and civil authorities seek to do, be they related to ancient objects, sacred spaces in the sierra, or even foreign peoples and places. I am not alone in this of course. In the past twenty years or so, a number of anthropologists working among the Kogi and Arhuaco have tried to distance themselves from this romanticizing position, as have archaeologists beginning to work on the Tairona (Rodríguez 2014). We remain, as David Graeber (2015:35) has recently put it, on the side of the skeptics who wish to consider these ontologies as socially and historically situated claims rather than incommensurable realities and alternate and parallel worlds.

Political Animation among the Kogi and Arhuaco

In the following paragraphs, I provide a brief and abbreviated account of how, according to the indigenous peoples of the Sierra Nevada de Santa Marta in Colombia, the known universe came to be.[7] This is especially important because it is these myths that are cited by indigenous authorities as sources of various "original laws" applicable to all creatures living in this and other planes of existence. They also allow us to understand what types of beings populate the world and its different levels, how they relate to one another, and what must be done by humans to make the world a livable place. Political authority among the indigenous groups of the Sierra Nevada de Santa Marta is usually shared between the village headman, known as the *comisario* (*maku* in Koguian and Ijku), and the priest, known as a *mama*.[8] The village headman handles the day-to-day affairs of the community, coordinates labor and meetings, and enforces any punishments meted out by way of his *cabos* (corporals). But it is the *mama* who must deal on a daily basis with all other-than-human entities, communicate with them to understand what they want, and guide the behavior of the community accordingly so that they may "live well" and avoid disasters, disease, and tragedy.

At the zero moment of history, the great mother Haba Gaulchovang, a creature of *aluna* (i.e., the plane of nothingness where everything exists in pure spirit-thought form), created nine levels or "places-like-shelves" as they are usually called by

Kogi and Arhuaco priests. The Sierra Nevada de Santa Marta, the massive pyramid-shaped mountain they inhabit, is the place where the mother chose to begin her creation, as her spirit-thought unwound itself as thread from an endless spindle driven from the peaks of the mountain to the other side of the world. The mountain is metonym and body for the Great Mother, thus the constant mention of it being "the heart of the world," given that it is where creation took place and where her presence is strongest. After nine months, the great mother gave birth to nine sons,[9] who became the original fathers (*hate*). At this time there were no women at all, so the sons were married to things (pots, looms, metates, and other such artifacts) and masturbated endlessly. One of the sons proceeded to trick the Great Mother, using his *poporo* stick to place a bead, one of her nails, and one of her hairs on her belly button and then push them inside her.[10] After nine months, the Great Mother gave birth to nine daughters, who then became the original mothers (*haba*). From these original mothers and fathers, daughters and sons of the Great Mother came and continue to come. This is to say that the Great Mother birthed and continues to birth every human and nonhuman being and entity in the world (gold, quartz, pottery, water, forests, crops, helicopters, whisky, cell phones, marriage, car brands, disease, etc.). As such, in Kogi and Arhuaco cosmopolitics, every single thing and being that exists originally existed in spirit-thought and is "owned" or controlled either by the Great Mother or by an original mother or father. The fathers and mothers who own everything are immortal and cannot be killed or destroyed by human actions, and they are considered to be rather fickle entities who are constantly imposing their demands on human beings. Yet because they own everything, and because humans in their daily lives are constantly taking, touching, using, doing, or thinking about things, these mothers and fathers must be paid through *sewa* (koguian) or *aburu* (ikun), offerings that stand for food. Via these offerings, human beings must constantly feed the Great Mother and the mothers and fathers in *aluna* or risk their disfavor and wrath.

figure 14.2
Crispín making an exit or closing offering to the guardian of Tiwanaku after visiting the site, which he declared to be "devoid of owners and power, only the guardian remains." He later joined members of the "Concejo de Amautas" in a closing ceremony as well. Photograph by Santiago Giraldo.

The Great Mother and the original fathers and mothers who are her sons and daughters manifest themselves through certain places in the landscape, some of which are considered to be "original," "of the Mother," or existing since the Great Mother created the world. These are called *eyzuama* (*koguian*) or *ka'dukwu* (*ijkun*) and are usually guarded by a priest who lives nearby with his family and apprentices and conducts all rituals and offerings related to the Great Mother and the mothers and fathers, who manifest themselves in that particular location. As I will explain further along, these types of places, original or otherwise, can be found in potentially unlimited numbers anywhere in the world, and offerings to specific mothers and fathers

can or should be made at these locations. More conveniently for political action, they can be "found" or "located" via divination, such that other-than-human entities can potentially manifest themselves anywhere in the world and even in sacred places of other peoples, cultures, and religions, rendering those places "sacred" and part of Kogi or Arhuaco tradition and cosmopolitics. In addition and according to the *mamas* I have spoken with, they are considered to exist in relational resonance to one another, something that requires offerings to be made following certain patterns: first in one place, then in another, and so forth depending on the issue that needs to be solved. Indeed, one of the tasks constantly undertaken by *mamas* involves restoring,

figure 14.3
Crispín making an offering of coca leaves and corn husks to the fathers and mothers of the great Mekong. Photograph by Santiago Giraldo.

healing, or creating communication between these places so that they can "work together."

The four indigenous groups who currently live in the Sierra Nevada consider themselves to be the firstborn of these original fathers and mothers, thus making them "elder brothers" to all other human beings.[11] Some stories also mention the birth in that ancient time of the *mamas*, the religious specialists who deal on a daily basis with the mothers and fathers. All other human beings and nonhuman entities and animals were born later from these same fathers and mothers, making us, according to them, the not-so-bright younger brothers who came after and were sent to faraway lands by the Great Mother due to our greediness and lawlessness. What this means is that all human beings,

other-than-human entities, animals, and things are part of an extended kinship system that goes all the way to the Great Mother. In this sense, as opposed to what Eduardo Viveiros de Castro (2015) argues rather generally for Amazonian societies and, by extension, other indigenous societies of the Americas, the Kogi and Arhuaco do not live in a different "nature" or "ontology." Rather, it is an all-encompassing mode of being in which there seem to be no radically different others, only kin who are more or less close to one another. Multi-naturalism and perspectivism appear to be completely meaningless in these societies. Rather, for them, the Law of Sé (Law of the Mother) applies to all of us and has applied to all humans and nonhuman entities since the world was created. We are, in effect, inescapably within her creation. This, as we shall see, is interpreted by *mamas* as a fact granting them authority over us, the nonindigenous younger brothers, something they have actually begun to pursue via legal decrees within Colombia that mandate protection of these sacred places where communication with all other-than-human entities is possible.[12]

Apart from the Great Mother and her sons and daughters, other other-than-human entities, quasi-human beings, and metapersons must also be dealt with. One of the most important ones is *heisei*, or death and disease, considered to be evil, the opposite of life, fertility, fecundity, and the Great Mother. All ancestors who are not mothers or fathers are *heisei*, and offerings must also be made to them. Some of these ancestors end up as stones (*jatankana in koguian atinkunu in ijkun*), outcroppings, or particular places in our world and should not be disturbed or made angry, as some are thought to be quite evil. Much like the mothers and fathers, *heisei*, in all its permutations, must be fed via offerings to keep it at bay. At least up to around thirty or forty years ago, all Tairona archaeological sites were also *heisei*, and it was forbidden to live in them or even near them.[13] Touching artifacts taken from Tairona sites was thought to bring death and disease, and recovered artifacts had to be brought to a *mama* immediately. More recently, this perception has changed, and ancient Tairona towns and structures are now argued to be "sacred places" where offerings must be made or that must even be inhabited permanently, though many are still perceived to be quite dangerous and out of bounds. Levels of danger or safety for habitation related to these places vary widely throughout the sierra depending on when the places were first settled and by whom. Due to the potency and power (both positive and negative) of ancient places and objects and their associated other-than-human entities, spiritual work aimed at securing permission to live in these places is continuous and unending. I will explain how *mamas* transform spaces of *heisei* into habitable spaces where life can prosper and how these practices are linked to a particularly powerful political agenda of territorial appropriation and expansion.

A particularly interesting set of beings are *jauja*, who, according to some *mamas*, are tiny men with long hair, big feet, and no eyes and who are supposedly Teiruna. One of my Kogi friends indicated, much to the contrary, that they were *not* tiny but rather "normal" sized and that what made them somewhat dangerous were their incredibly beautiful women who would lead lone men astray after meeting them in the forest. *Jauja* cannot speak, they say, because they spend their time "in thought" or moving back and forth between *aluna* and our plane of existence. For this reason, they like to reside in archaeological sites, which are liminal spaces between both planes. *Jauja* appear to be neither good nor evil, and what they want is mostly unknown. Yet their very existence is also somewhat uncertain. Some of my indigenous friends say they have seen them while others say that they have never heard of such a creature. In any case, their presence is usually signaled by knee-high, round houses identical to those built by the Kogi and meant to give them shelter.

As opposed to many Amazonian examples, like those mentioned in Carlos Fausto's chapter, there appears to be no positive association between headmen or priests and felines such as jaguar and puma. Rather, the felinization of humans should be avoided and is thought to be extremely dangerous. In the myth of Kashindukue (Fischer 1989:93; Reichel-Dolmatoff 1985:vol. 2), for example, one of the original fathers slowly becomes a lawless man-eating puma (*nebbi*) who must eventually be caught and killed by a *mama*. Authority is predicated on the *mama*'s ability to "talk to" the *nebbi* and convince him to leave human beings alone and, if need be, hunt down the jaguar or puma that is killing people or livestock. In this sense, animals, plants, trees, insects, minerals, metals, and meteorological phenomena are not considered to be persons, even though they might have been people originally or even an original father or mother; they seem to be considered other-than-human entities with thought, agency, and varying degrees of consciousness. A good strong *mama* with authority should be able to communicate with these entities, which in the case of certain birds, bats, or insects are considered to be messengers between humans and the mothers and fathers. Rumaldo and Jose María Lozano, two of the *mamas* I work with, insist that a good *mama* must be "heavy with knowledge" (*pesado*) about these entities; hard, transparent, and bright as a quartz crystal; and able to dazzle his audience and constituency (much like the sun) with his stories and counsel. Indeed, their power and authority rest upon demonstrating that they *can* communicate, enter into, and establish relations with the spirit-thought plane that is *aluna*, in which all these other-than-human entities exist, and use that knowledge to guide human action in this plane.

A final kind of other-than-human entity is constituted by animated objects meant to fulfill certain duties, such as archaeological artifacts and structures still buried within their contexts and other things and "contraptions" animated by a *mama*. Opinions regarding what various types of archaeological artifacts are and what they do vary somewhat. For example, when *mamas* have visited the Gold Museum in Bogotá or other museums throughout the world housing Tairona objects, some have said that the gold objects, especially the anthropomorphic figurines, are ancient people or original fathers or mothers or, in the case of more generic objects, that they belong to *hate nyui*, the sun. Despite the varying interpretations as to exactly who they are, they are indeed considered to be animate or at least conscious entities that are locked away behind glass, far away from their original locations and in dire need of nourishment. Ferro (2015:chap. 3) notes that *mamas* visiting the museum have constantly indicated to the archaeologists and curators that the objects need to be fed *yui*, sexual fluids placed on cotton fluff, food for the ancestors. Stone beads are *sewa* and according to the type of stone and color constitute offerings to different fathers and mothers. Perhaps more importantly for our purposes, what *mamas* point out is that the museum exhibits have "messed up" the original relationship between the "artifact" and different other-than-human entities, given that the artifacts would have been placed and oriented in certain manners and organized according to gender and purpose so as to communicate more effectively with the fathers and mothers. In this sense, both *sewa* and archaeological artifacts and structures "do work" as long as they physically exist in their original votive context, operating as spiritual food for an other-than-human entity. As such, each offering or object enfolds within it and in relation to other offerings a relational and political indexicality set in motion by the *mamas*, whoever makes an offering, or ancient known or unknown entities that manifest themselves at archaeological sites.

It is for this reason that archaeological work within the indigenous territories of the Sierra Nevada de Santa Marta is fraught with tension. To some *mamas*, excavating ancient objects and taking them out of the Sierra Nevada destroys the relational qualities between these entities, impeding them from communicating properly with the various fathers and mothers who own the rain, thunder, crops, fertility, disease, and a host of other phenomena. Others believe that we are disturbing *heisei* places, and because we make no offerings whatsoever will bring upon the community various misfortunes. In mid-August 2016, during my last conversation with *mama* Rumaldo regarding excavations we had made in the central terraces during June, he came to the conclusion that what we do as archaeologists was a form of "honoring the ancestors" (as long as we do not excavate tombs) because we were trying to understand them in a sort of "backward-looking divination." Yet, he insisted, he was going to *divinar* (divine) what the appropriate *sewa* might be that should be used as offerings.

Given that any thing and any social or natural phenomenon can potentially be considered an other-than-human entity that is either fully or partly conscious and that is owned by a mother or a father, one of the main problems for indigenous peoples in the Sierra Nevada is determining when, how, where, and in which contexts one must "feed" these entities with offerings. A crucial aspect is the unknowability, for those who are not *mamas* or diviners, of what is going on in *aluna* and what exactly it is that these other-than-human entities want and demand. As Graeber (2015:28) notes for

figure 14.4

Crispín placing a rock brought from the Sierra Nevada de Santa Marta behind a Buddha effigy statue at Pha That Luang in Laos. Some of the effigy statues he declared to be *atinkunui*, that is, "alive" with some other-than-human entity. Here at the Golden Stupa, he bought brass figurines of a tiger, an elephant, and a cobra to make offerings to their fathers and mothers in his *kankurúa* (temple and surrounding areas) in the Sierra Nevada de Santa Marta. Photograph by Santiago Giraldo.

figure 14.5

One of the various decree-protected places located within Pueblito Archaeological site at Tayrona National Park. The sign indicates the name of the place (Haba Terugama, "Mother of Steps/Connections"), that visitor entry is forbidden, and the specific legal decrees protecting it. The place itself is a crevasse located between two granite boulders a couple of meters away from the main paved stone path used by visitors. Photograph by Santiago Giraldo.

his Malagasy interlocutors, I hear in my own conversations with *mamas* and common people about the mothers, fathers, and other-than-human entities that affect daily life a lot about what "I don't know," followed by "We have to divine" (Teniendo que divinar). Thus, the epistemological solution to this daily quandary is divination by the *mamas* or an experienced diviner and *alunashiguaishi*, also known as *confesación* (confession).[14] It is precisely through these practices that a *mama* knows what someone in the community has done, has thought, has considered doing, or is about to do; whether rains or drought will come; if a baby in utero will be a *mama*; and which mothers and fathers must be fed, the exact type of offering or *pagamento* that must be made, in which *eyzuama* or sacred place, and when. It is, thus, through these practices,

decisions, and courses of action that power and authority become condensed in the *mama*.

Divinatory Authority

Divination among the Kogi and Arhuaco is an extremely powerful and flexible tool that allows *mamas* and renowned diviners to consult the Great Mother's opinion on any conceivable question and to communicate with other-than-human entities. In relation to day-to-day questions posed by members of the community—"Will my baby be fine?" or "My beans have a fungus, what sort of offering should I make to the father/owner of beans?" or "May my son marry such-and-such woman?"—and to determinations of the source of a sickness or disaster that has recently befallen the community, the term *alunashiguaishi*, usually translated as "confession" (*confesación*), is used in conjunction with divination. In *alunashiguaishi*, the person is interrogated, sometimes for days, by the *mama* on everything they have done, thought, or thought about doing since the last time they did *alunashiguaishi*, such that a long conversation ensues. *Confesación* (note the Catholic overtones here) can be public or private, but the *mama*, as he pays close attention to what the person is saying, will also be divining. In the case of social transgressions, *alunashiguaishi* permits the *mama* to accurately determine what action or thought has caused trouble with one or several fathers and mothers and to subsequently suggest what must be done to fix this problem. Its ex post facto nature allows the *mama* to tailor his answer most appropriately.

Mamas commonly use four main kinds of divination, but the most powerful of all is the *zhatukua*, which involves dropping (preferably ancient) stone beads into a gourd filled with water and reading the bubbles as they emerge to the surface. *Mamas* perceive the bubbles as the voice of the Great Mother or the mothers and fathers and hold conversations with them on the topics being addressed. Though a *mama* can divine anywhere, very important questions or issues require that divination take place in *eyzuamas*, the places where the voice of the Great Mother is thought to be strongest. And depending on the level of complexity of the question, a *mama* will usually need multiple divinations to come up with a proper answer, especially if the first one is wildly unpopular with people. For example, I have seen two cases in which different *mamas* have divined differently on whether male children can or cannot play football. In one case, it was divined that the fathers and mothers did not like it, especially because the ball could hit an ancient stone or something owned by them, thus causing some evil thing to befall the community. Ergo, no football, at least in public and within the indigenous town, but the kids told me that "they were playing where they would not be seen by those sour old men" (*viejos amargados*) because they did not believe that playing could upset any *hate* or *haba*. In the other town,

the *mama* divined that it was all well and good that the kids played football.

Thus, divination is a historically and politically contingent practice that is flexible and powerful enough to provide the answers that a *mama* and the accompanying authorities need to sort out any type of situation. For example, I have witnessed cases in which a major development project is first divined as "bad" because it will physically alter a sacred site and thus the mother or father that resides in that place will be irritated or affected. Yet months or even years later, it is then divined to be "good" when proper compensation is agreed upon, be it in the form of land acquisitions or money. Western objects and technologies bought or acquired by indigenous peoples in the Sierra Nevada are also incorporated into daily life via divination simply by finding the appropriate father or mother to whom offerings must be made for using cell phones, radios, video or still cameras; drinking whisky; riding on a helicopter or airplane; or using solar panels and lamps.[15] At least in theory there are no absolutely incommensurable objects or practices because everything can be traced, in one way or another, to the Great Mother or an original father or mother. It is precisely this flexibility that makes divination so powerful, because as I mentioned previously, both the *mama* and the community understand that whatever is divined can be negotiated if it makes little sense, is not clearly understood, or is received with grumbling and dissatisfaction. This is reminiscent of an example used by Reichel-Dolmatoff (1985:129) wherein divination indicated that the Great Mother wanted an entire town to be moved elsewhere but the villagers did not agree with this interpretation and refused to move the town. As with the kids who refused to stop playing football, divination should not be taken in a literal way. Rather, whatever propositions are made are assumed to be open to negotiation, renegotiation, and change depending on a shifting sociopolitical context.

If we put this in different, more "ontologically minded" terms, other-than-human entities are also entitled to change their opinion on the various issues faced by human beings and the state of the world as we know it. I will highlight two examples that illustrate this flexibility, which in turn creates political opportunities. Daniel Rodríguez (2014, n.d.) has recently studied a case between the Don Diego and Palomino Rivers, where Arhuaco populations from the south side of the sierra were granted access to land belonging to a Kogi population. These lands were made available as the road connecting Santa Marta and Riohacha was finally built in the late 1960s, allowing mestizo homesteaders fleeing violence in other parts of the country to settle broad swaths of unoccupied lands in different parts of the Sierra Nevada de Santa Marta along the coastline. Because areas such as these are usually colonized first by mestizo homesteaders, the Kogi were quite worried that they would lose a foothold in the area, but they did not have sufficient population to create new towns, plus the area was perceived as sacred, dangerous, and off limits due to the large number of abandoned Tairona towns and structures on the landscape. In this situation, several Kogi *mamas* agreed with an Arhuaco *mama* who wanted to bring in young couples of the latter ethnic group to settle in the area and serve as a buffer against the homesteaders. Young families' access to agricultural land is an increasingly complicated issue among the indigenous groups because older, more prestigious men usually own the best lands, so young families tend to be forced out of their hometowns when land for cultivation becomes scarce.

In this case, the Arhuaco *mama* recognized that he faced a complicated problem on two fronts: the land was Kogi and thus the other-than-human entities populating the landscape were outside of his control. To compound this, as farms and small villages were established people found a great many Tairona archaeological sites with terraces and paths and other sorts of infrastructure, meaning that these were spaces of *heisei* and the ancients, which could cause serious misfortune to the population under the *mama*'s care. As Rodríguez (n.d.:33) puts it, what followed was a concerted effort by both *mamas* to secure permission from the other-than-human entities that "owned" the land, the ancient structures, and all the resources needed to establish viable farms and villages. In this way, an area

previously thought to be out of bounds was "domesticated" by constant divination and work in *aluna* by sets of *mamas* intent on gaining permission from the Great Mother, the fathers and mothers, *heisei*, and the ancients. In the ensuing time, and as relations between Arhuaco and Kogi have soured, the Arhuaco *mamas* charged with these populations have continued making offerings, working in "spiritual" terms with the other-than-human entities they have come to know, and enabling them to secure their legitimacy in this newly colonized territory that continues to be dangerous. This, of course, was only possible because human action is thought to be effective in convincing these entities to change their position from "no human beings allowed" to "human beings allowed as long as they make the appropriate offerings."

The second example comes from my own ethnographic work on how *mamas* are able to incorporate sacred places and objects belonging to other, radically different, societies into their worldviews and to enter into relationships with the other-than-human entities that reside in them. To understand this, I have been working with *mama* Crispín Izquierdo, an Arhuaco priest who was told by his father that his mission was to create links between sacred places located in different countries and the sacred places located in the Sierra Nevada de Santa Marta. I was able to understand how he did this because in 2013 the Colombian equivalent of the State Department (*cancillería*) financed four trips to five different countries as part of a photographic exhibit called *The Black Line*. The exhibit, shot by my friend Jorge Gamboa, shows Crispín, other *mamas*, and their apprentices as they make their offerings to the Great Mother and the fathers and mothers in some of the fifty-four sacred places that surround the Sierra Nevada de Santa Marta.

As part of a soft diplomacy effort by the Colombian government as it tried to open new embassies in Southeast Asia and Africa, the exhibit was designed to represent a "deep Colombia," beyond the usual images of narcos and violence commonly shown in the media the world over. For Crispín, the trips were the perfect opportunity to create "spiritual links" between the Sierra Nevada de Santa Marta and

figure 14.6

The "contraption" placed by *mama* Rumaldo Lozano on an archaeological terrace at Teyuna-Ciudad Perdida Archaeological Park. I named it a "super *nuizhi*" because Rumaldo indicated that "of course the device is alive, can't you see it moves?" and that he had "chanted it with life" just like the *nuizhi* (wicker woven representations of bats) placed on the crossbars of a *nuhue* (men's house and ritual space) that are meant to take prayers, speeches, and offerings to the *habas* and *hates* in *aluna*. This particular device was meant to take the thoughts and offerings of visitors to the fathers and mothers. Notice the addition of Tibetan prayer flags. Photographs by Santiago Giraldo.

figure 14.7

Offering contexts and assemblages of various types were placed within terrace fills at Pueblito and Teyuna-Ciudad Perdida Archaeological sites during the building process of each structure. Objects placed in the fill layers may include ceramic drinking cups and cooking pots, like those recovered in trench 12 at Pueblito (Giraldo 2010); polished stone ax-heads and objects; beads of different materials; and gold artifacts. For the current indigenous populations of the Sierra Nevada de Santa Marta, offering contexts are meant to "do work" on behalf of their offerer/owner for as long as they remain undisturbed and undamaged. For this reason, removing contemporary or ancient objects or disturbing any sort of offering context, be it through excavation, looting, or vandalism, is perceived by *mamas to* disturb the "work" that is being done and cause the ire of the other-than-human entity for whom the offering was made (i.e., its owner). Photograph by Santiago Giraldo.

other distant and different places and peoples that surely had fathers and mothers who needed to be in contact with the fathers and mothers present in the Sierra Nevada de Santa Marta. So this motley crew of Arhuaco priest, photographer, and anthropologist traveled together to Cambodia, Laos, Ghana, Peru, and Bolivia. Now Crispín has traveled quite widely, and he shuffles back and forth between Bogotá, where he works as an alternative medicine healer, and his *kankurúa* (temple) and domains in the sierra. He is, of all the Kogi and Arhuaco *mamas* I know, one of the worldliest and most generous with his knowledge. But imagine if you will an almost perfect setting for exploring how one supposedly rigid, traditional, and unchanging "Amerindian ontology" deals with places and peoples quite beyond the Kogi and Arhuaco imagination.

On every trip, Crispín's luggage was full of *aburu*, the Arhuaco equivalent of *sewa*, the offerings needed to feed the mothers and fathers and ancestors of the places and peoples we were visiting. Seashells, stones, coca leaves, cotton fluff and thread, corn husks, and ancient beads traveled with us and were used to make offerings in whatever sacred place was available in the cities we visited. As the anthropologist, I was usually called in to provide the information needed to determine what was considered sacred and "original" from each place. In Phnom Penh and Vientiane, Crispín made offerings of *aburu* to the fathers and mothers of the Mekong, rice, Asian elephants, tigers, and cobras, putting them "in connection" and resonance with the mothers and fathers of corn and all other crops imported from the Americas. In the great Buddhist wats, he placed stones brought from the Sierra Nevada, hiding them behind bronze or stone Buddhas and effigies that through divination with *bunkueika* he determined to be other-than-human entities. In Ghana, he made offerings at Volta Lake and in sacred groves, exchanged powerful objects with Fante elders, and, very dangerously, placed a *marunsama*, a cloth bag filled with objects of power meant to communicate with the fathers and mothers, on the threshold of an Ashanti shrine. This last act got us kicked out by the shrine's guardian, who immediately perceived that the *mama* was somehow trespassing and doing something sacrilegious.

While in Bolivia, Crispín made offerings to the guardian of the ancient Andean city of Tiwanaku and in Tiwanaku itself with members of the *consejo de amautas*. In later conversations, he mentioned that he had found Tiwanaku to be "empty," devoid of power, its fathers and mothers long gone, and that only the guardian remained strong. In Peru, offerings were made at the site of Pachacamac, south of Lima, within the Temple of the Sun.

In all these places, Crispín collected stones or soil or took pieces of vegetation. He bought figurines of tigers, snakes, and elephants at a wat in Laos and in Ghana was gifted with kente cloth and a warrior shirt sewn with charms and wards. In explaining the process through which links between these other-than-human entities are created, he made it quite clear that an exchange of objects was necessary for them to be able to communicate with one another. He took the objects, soil, cloth, and vegetation samples to his *kankurúa* in the Sierra Nevada de Santa Marta, where through divination he would be able to find the appropriate place to make offerings to the fathers and mothers who owned these people, places, and things. Through the offerings, he could then "heal" the damages to these places and "pay back" what was owed to those mothers and fathers, using the samples he collected to communicate effectively with them. For his own purposes and standing within the Arhuaco community and before his fellow *mamas*, being able to set up relationships in "spirit" with these mothers and fathers granted him added prestige and power, as well as more followers.

What I wish to highlight with these examples is that divination for the Kogi and Arhuaco is an extremely powerful and creative tool that, at least in theory, allows them to effectively communicate with practically any other-than-human entity anywhere in the world, assuring the commensurability of other indigenous and nonindigenous peoples, places, objects, and practices with their own ontological scheme of things. As such, it provides endless opportunities to rethink, reformulate, and discuss what exactly other-than-human entities

figure 14.8

Different *mamas* will have differing, and often times contradictory, opinions on the specific function and identity of figurines, but in general they agree on their status as other-than-human entities meant to do some type of spiritual work. The fact that they are displayed within a showcase far from the original context of the offering means that they can no longer do their work, are "hungry" for spiritual sustenance (and should be fed), and cannot interact with other, other-than-human entities in proper fashion. This, of course, presents curators with a complicated and mostly insurmountable dilemma regarding how to treat these artifacts.

require of human beings and, of course, how this translates into praxis. Ably negotiating and dealing with these entities on a daily basis is a crucial element of political authority for a *mama* and is considered to be a never-ending task. The art of politics among Kogi and Arhuaco populations involves a careful balancing act of putting into agreement spiritual and human social worlds that are constantly shifting and changing.

Literal Animism, or, How to Extend Your Power and Authority the Ontological Way

I began this chapter with an exchange aimed at showing how effectively the Kogi had been able to translate their beliefs to an audience throughout the world that takes their view on animism and the Great Mother in literal and unquestioning ways. This is also broadly applicable to the Arhuaco, though their prestige and credentials among environmentalists and New Agey folk are somewhat less than that of the Kogi. As Juan Orrantia (2002a, 2002b) and Astrid Ulloa (2005) have noted, indigenous beliefs in the Sierra Nevada de Santa Marta fit in perfectly with romantic environmentalist discourses and have allowed for the creation of alliances between indigenous organizations, global NGOs, and government institutions that seek a sort of indigenous esoteric truth to believe in unquestioningly.[16] This has been incredibly productive for these indigenous groups, resulting in land acquisitions, funding for all sorts of development projects, and the protection, by law, of sacred places and in general what they consider to be the sacred landscape of the Sierra Nevada de Santa Marta. Part of the success of this project has resulted from their efforts at making the nonindigenous "younger brothers" understand the Law of the Mother and accept, at least partly, their reality in an unproblematic fashion.[17] As I pointed out at the beginning of this chapter, they have made great efforts through their own publications, documentaries, websites, speeches, activism, and spokespersons to educate us and convince us of the truth value of their propositions.[18] Or to put it

bluntly, they have actively sought to extend their "ontological authority" over the nonindigenous "younger brother" as a political course of action aimed at granting them de facto higher levels of territorial autonomy and sovereignty, even though the Colombian constitution only provides for a limited form of indigenous autonomy.

The sacred landscape of the Sierra Nevada de Santa Marta and the spirit world are mobilized as the most powerful negotiating instruments precisely because *mamas* and indigenous authorities have seen that the Colombian government, NGOs, private corporations, and lawyers take propositions regarding the Great Mother, sacred places, and all the other-than-human entities in a very simplistic and literal way. Since 1973, the Colombian government has accepted requests by the indigenous authorities to provide ever more strict legal protection to sacred places in the Sierra Nevada de Santa Marta, be they inside or outside their legally assigned territory.[19] As a result, land claims by the indigenous groups have systematically targeted plots of land said to contain these sacred places because their very "sacredness" goes unquestioned by NGOs, government institutions, and their funders.[20] Put differently, claims and requests to the Colombian government, the Colombian constitutional court, or NGOs for protecting and acquiring nonsacred plots of land (i.e., those devoid of other-than-human entities) are taken much less seriously or have very little priority, as are requests made by indigenous villages and towns for health and educational services. Taking animistic beliefs and practices among the indigenous groups of the Sierra Nevada de Santa Marta in a literal sense has continued the tradition of exoticizing and romanticizing those indigenous peoples.

In contrast, what this chapter has tried to illustrate is that among these indigenous peoples the relationship between human authority and all other-than-human entities that populate the world is far more complex and nuanced and is ultimately based on open-ended and never-ceasing negotiations that are situated forms of political practice. It is clear that not everyone strictly follows or believes in what the *mamas* say and that what the other-than-human

figure 14.9

A mighty spread of *aburu*, offerings to be made as spiritual food to the various fathers and mothers, on behalf of a number of Arhuaco (Ijku or Wintukwa) couples soon to be married. Seashells, coral, sea urchins, ancient beads, semiprecious stones and stones of various types, corn husks and seeds, and several other types of offerings have been arranged from front to back according to their provenance: things from the sea, the lowlands, midlevel altitude, and high altitude, as well as ancient objects. This ensures that all other-than-human entities that manifest themselves throughout the landscape may be properly appeased. This case is especially complicated because the couples are being married due to various faults they have committed (including premarital intercourse) and have, of course, irritated many of these other-than-human entities. Photograph by Daniel Rodríguez, town of Katansama, Sierra Nevada de Santa Marta, 2013.

entities say should or has to be done and that, in turn, these entities oftentimes change their opinions on what human beings should do. But the knowledge acquired through divination about what these entities supposedly want does appear to grant power. On one hand, the ability to communicate with these entities creates conditions wherein power may emerge to be deployed. On the other hand, authority follows when belief in what the *mama* says about what the other-than-human entities have prescribed happens to have the desired effect, despite what the skeptics might say.

1 Throughout this chapter, I refer to them as *mamas*, but the term *mamo* or even *mamu* is also commonly used in the general literature on the area. All of these terms refer to the same specialists.

2 A short clip of the film and the explanation behind its making is available at http://www.alunathe movie.com/

3 http://www.elheraldo.co/tendencias/los-secretos -arqueologicos-que-revela-ciudad-perdida-276953

4 I was eventually contacted by someone calling himself Stewart Burns from Glasgow via email regarding whether I did or did not have authorization by the *mamos* to conduct research at Teyuna-Ciudad Perdida Archaeological Park. The exchange can be read at https://www.facebook.com/AlunaMovie/, as a post placed on August 27, 2016.

5 Though I have to add that doña Alicia told me in 2010 that their "writings were taken too literally and used in rather opportunistic fashion" most of the time.

6 The question was actually posed at the end of my presentation for the Dumbarton Oaks symposium that was the foundation for this volume.

7 Accounts of Kogi cosmopolitical narratives can be found in Konrad Preuss's (1993 [1926]) and Gerardo Reichel-Dolmatoff's ethnographies (1985), as well as a compilation by Manuela Fischer (1989). There are, as usual, several competing versions on how the universe came to be, and internal discussions between *mamas* (priests or religious specialists) and their followers regarding which is the "truer and more accurate" version are ongoing and quite intense (as are discussions regarding the nature and intentions of the original *hates and habas,* and recently deceased kin).

8 Since the early 1980s and the constitution of the indigenous *resguardos* in the Sierra Nevada de Santa Marta, relationships with the government are usually handled by an indigenous organization led by a governor known as the *cabildo*. Though originally this governor was under the authority of the *mamas,* of late he, along with his counselors, has acquired more power and authority, creating an indigenous professional bureaucracy that handles all government fund transfers, NGO donations, and relationships with corporations for prior consultation discussions taking place under ILO Convention

169. The indigenous governor works closely with his allied *mamas* and sometimes with a wider council of *mamas* when negotiating with the government, NGOs, or corporations. Though certainly powerful in his own right, the governor holds very little authority in indigenous towns (excepting his own) and cannot really deal with other-than-human entities, the mother, or the original *hates* and *habas.*

9 After masturbating with her wooden staff, goes one story.

10 The *poporo* is the gourd used to store the powdered lime made from shells used to chew coca. When young men are considered to reach adulthood, they are given a *poporo* by the *mama*, which is thought to represent the uterus of the great mother. The stick used to reach the lime is considered to be a phallus, and thus the act of *poporear* is akin to sex and intimately related to male virility, sexuality, and fertility.

11 Kogi, Arhuaco, Wiwa, and Kankuamo.

12 This objective is also pursued via indigenous media productions, such as those of Amado Villafañe, an Arhuaco photographer and videographer who sees his job as "extending by visual means the messages sent by *mamas* and our way of conceptualizing our sacred territory and defending our rights." In several conversations I have had with Amado on this topic, he conceives these indigenous documentaries as "unmediated" information to be used in furthering their political objectives. He explains in some detail his work in this video interview (in Spanish): https:// www.youtube.com/watch?v=eM-vziWD3oA

13 Oral histories collected by Reichel-Dolmatoff (1985) in the 1940s in various Kogi towns mention that they considered the Teiruna (Tairona) to be "another tribe" who had much knowledge, but that their relationship had been created when a couple of Kogi lineages had married Teiruna daughters.

14 All *mamas* that I know of constantly engage in divination in its various forms. From what I have been told, some common people and women can also engage in the simpler forms of divination such as *kashivita* (finger divination) or *kuina* (itch divination), and there appear to be some relatively renowned women diviners that use the *zhatukua* (gourd, water, and archaeological bead divination), but it is unclear how they "learned to divine." Arhuaco *mamas* prefer to divine using *bunkueika,*

a miniature cloth bag with beads and stones that is shaken and the arrangement of the beads and stones is then interpreted.

15 Diana Bocarejo (2002) was one of the first ethnographers to notice that *mamas* were making offerings in certain places for objects that were distinctly Western and saying that X father or mother was the father of helicopters, or whisky, or motorcycles, or the mother of machine-woven cotton cloth. Upon being questioned about this, the *mamas* indicated that all these apparently foreign objects had indeed been made "originally" and in *aluna* by the Great Mother or were owned by a father or a mother already. Some had been sent away until the "younger brother" brought them back, or the Great Mother created the "British" (*los ingleses*) younger brothers to make steel objects (like machetes, hoes, needles, picks, and shovels) and send them back to the Elder Brothers via trade. For the past four years, I have sold and traded solar lamps with the Kogui and Wiwa population of the Buritaca river basin. When I asked which entity owned them, they pointed out that it was very probably *hate mulkuakui* (father sun).

16 My own skepticism is usually met with perplexity by *mamas* accustomed to having all sorts of people accept their esoteric powers over other than human entities as a given. New-Agey folk consider my disbelief to be disrespectful.

17 In any exchange between indigenous authorities of the Sierra Nevada de Santa Marta and non-indigenous peoples, one of the most frequent phrases that is heard, in a tone of evident frustration, is "the younger brother does not understand anything."

18 The websites of Kogi and Arhuaco indigenous organizations make it abundantly clear that the Law of the Mother is not a myth, but something that applies to all human beings and must be respected to avoid catastrophes.

19 In 1973, the Colombian Government emitted Resolution 002 (Ministerio de Gobierno Resolución 002) that declared the territory contained within the Black Line a Theological Zone where an undetermined number of places fundamental to their concept of universal equilibrium were located. This protection was later extended by Resolution 0837 of 1995 that explicitly named all fifty-four sacred sites, and Bills T-849 of 2014 and T-005 of 2016 (see Ministerio del Interior 1995 and Corte Constitucional de Colombia 2014, 2016). Since 2012, the Colombian Ministry of Culture has been tasked with creating a "Master List" of all indigenous sacred sites in the Sierra Nevada de Santa Marta and producing a legal resolution protecting them. As I have tried to show, given the potentially infinite number of sacred places, the endeavor seems to be doomed to failure.

20 As one example among many, Amazon Conservation Team has only funded the acquisition of plots of land for the Kogi that contain sacred places; see http://www.amazonteam.org/water-wildlife-and -hope-rejuvenating-kogi-sacred-site.

REFERENCES CITED

Alberti, Benjamin, and Tamara L. Bray
    2009   Introduction. *Cambridge Archaeological Journal* 19:337–343.

Bessire, Lucas
    2014   *Behold the Black Caiman: A Chronicle of Ayoreo Life*. University of Chicago Press, Chicago.

Bessire, Lucas, and David Bond
    2014   Ontological Anthropology and the Deferral of Critique. *American Ethnologist* 41(3):440–456.

Bocarejo, Diana
    2002   Indigenizando "Lo Blanco": Conversaciones con arhuacos y kogis de La Sierra Nevada de Santa Marta. *Revista de antropología y arqueología* 13:3–44.

Bray, Warwick

2003   Gold, Stone, and Ideology: Symbols of Power in the Tairona Tradition. In *Gold and Power in Ancient Costa Rica, Panama, and Colombia,* edited by Jeffrey Quilter and John W. Hoopes, pp. 301–344. Dumbarton Oaks, Washington, D.C.

Cepek, Michael

2016   There Might Be Blood: Oil, Humility, and the Cosmopolitics of a Cofán Petro-Being. *American Ethnologist* 43(4):623–635.

Corte Constitucional de Colombia

2014   Electronic document, http://www.corte constitucional.gov.co/relatoria/2014 /t-849-14.htm, accessed October 25, 2016.

2016   Electronic document, http://www.corte constitucional.gov.co/relatoria/2016/ t-005-16.htm, accessed October 25, 2016.

Ferro, Maria del Rosario

2015   Between the Magic of Magic and the Magic of Money: The Changing Nature of Experience in the Sierra Nevada de Santa Marta. PhD dissertation, Columbia University, New York.

Fischer, Manuela, and Konrad Theodor Preuss

1989   *Mitos kogi.* Colección 500 Años 20. Ediciones Abya-Yala, Quito.

Giraldo, Santiago

2010   Lords of the Snowy Ranges: Politics, Place, and Landscape Transformation in Two Tairona Towns in the Sierra Nevada de Santa Marta, Colombia. PhD dissertation, University of Chicago, Chicago.

Graeber, David

2015   Radical Alterity Is Just Another Way of Saying "Reality": A Reply to Eduardo Viveiros de Castro. *HAU: Journal of Ethnographic Theory* 5(2):1–41.

Heywood, Paolo

2012   Anthropology and What There Is: Reflections on "Ontology." *Cambridge Anthropology* 30(1):143–151.

Holbraad, Martin

2007   The Power of Powder: Multiplicity and Motion in the Divinatory Cosmology of Cuban Ifá (or Mana, Again). In *Thinking through Things: Theorising*

Artifacts Ethnographically, edited by Amiria Henare, Martin Holbraad, and Sari Wastell, pp. 189–225. Routledge, New York.

2012   *Truth in Motion: The Recursive Anthropology of Cuban Divination.* University of Chicago Press, Chicago.

Laidlaw, James

2012   Ontologically Challenged: A Review of Morgan Axel Pedersen's *Not Quite Shamans: Spirit Worlds and Political Lives in Northern Mongolia. Anthropology of This Century* 4. Electronic document, http://aotcpress. com/articles/ontologically–challenged, accessed November 11, 2016.

Legast, Anne

1998   La fauna muisca y sus símbolos. *Boletín de arqueología* 13(3):5–105. Bogotá.

Looper, Matthew

2003   From Inscribed Bodies to Distributed Persons: Contextualizing Tairona Figural Images in Performance. *Cambridge Archaeological Journal* 13:25–40.

Orrantia, Juan Carlos

2002a   Esencialismo desde el corazón del mundo: Información como legitimación del riesgo. *Revista de antropología y arqueología* 13:45–77.

2002b   Matices Kogi: Representaciones y negociación en la marginalidad. *Revista colombiana de antropología* 38:45–76.

Oyuela-Caycedo, Augusto

1998   Ideology, Temples, and Priests: Change and Continuity in House Societies in the Sierra Nevada de Santa Marta. In *Recent Advances in the Archaeology of the Northern Andes: In Memory of Gerardo Reichel Dolmatoff,* edited by Augusto Oyuela-Caycedo and J. Scott Raymond, pp. 39–53. Institute of Archaeology, University of California, Los Angeles.

2002   El surgimiento de la rutinización religiosa: La conformación de la elite sacerdotal tairona-kogi. *Revista de arqueología del Área Intermedia* 4:12–45.

2005   El surgimiento de la rutinización religiosa: Los orígenes de los tairona-kogis. In *Chamanismo y sacrificio: Perspectivas arqueológicas y etnológicas en sociedades indígenas de America del Sur*, edited by Jean Pierre Chaumeil, Roberto Pineda, and Jean-François Bouchard, pp. 141–163. Fundación de Investigaciones Arqueológicas Nacionales, Banco de la República, Bogotá, and Instituto Francés de Estudios Andinos, Lima.

Plazas, Clemencia

2014   El humano-murciélago en el área intermedia norte: Distribución, formas y simbolismo. PhD dissertation, Centro de Investigación y Docencia en Humanidades del Estado de Morelos, Mexico City.

Preuss, Konrad Theodor

1926–1927   *Forschungsreise zu den Kagaba. Beobachtungen, Textaufnahmen und sprachliche Studien bei einem Indianerstamme in Kolumbien, Südamerika*. 2 vols. Anthropos, St-Gabriel-Mödling.

Reichel-Dolmatoff, Gerardo

1985   *Los Kogi: Una tribu de la Sierra Nevada de Santa Marta*. 2 vols. 2nd ed. Procultura, Nueva Biblioteca Colombiana de Cultura, Bogotá.

Rodríguez, Daniel

2014   La materialidad prehispánica: Lo hegemónico y lo disidente; Campesinos, indígenas y científicos; Estudio de caso en La Lengüeta, Sierra Nevada de Santa Marta. MA thesis, Universidad de los Andes, Bogotá.

n.d.   Desenmarañando la madeja: Una exploración de la historia reciente del Sector de la Lengüeta—Sierra Nevada de Santa Marta. Unpublished manuscript, Bogotá.

Ulloa, Astrid

2005   *The Ecological Native: Indigenous Peoples' Movements and Eco-Governmentality in Colombia*. Routledge, New York.

Viveiros de Castro, Eduardo

2015   *The Relative Native Essays on Indigenous Conceptual Worlds*. HAU Books, Chicago.

15

Shifts in the Light

A Journey through Varied Perspectives on Animacy and Authority in the Americas

CATHERINE J. ALLEN

TRAVELERS IN THE HIGH ANDES DISCOVER that every turn in the road, the crest of every hill, confronts them with a new panorama. These are places where Andean travelers will stop and greet landscape features that have just come into view—mountain peaks, valleys, lakes, rivers, cultivated fields. They blow upon their coca, sending the leaves' aroma to these living places, activating relationships with the terrain through which they intend to pass. Groups of pilgrims journeying to particularly powerful places supplement these greetings with music, libations of alcohol, and, sometimes, elaborate invocations. Such changes in one's perceptual field are called *alqa* in Quechua, a word that applies at a more intimate level to any marked change in slope or shift from light to shadow. These shifts mark boundaries and provide definition; color shifts in weaving can be characterized by the same term.

Reading this book reminded me of just such a mountainous journey with new panoramas revealing familiar landmarks from new angles. As I read the foregoing chapters, familiar themes appeared and reappeared in new and sometimes surprising guises. As it happens, the *journey* is one of these themes. This book touches upon many journeys, some long past and some in the present day, all revealing complex articulations of people, places, and objects: Huitzilopochtli (in bundle form) journeys from Aztlan to Tenochtitlan via a series of resting places, and after the fall of Tenochtitlan noblemen entrusted with hiding the bundle retrace its journey in reverse. A Kogi priest travels the world, creating spiritual links between distant places and those in his native Sierra Nevada de Santa Marta. Andean pilgrims journey from afar to powerful places like Chavín, Tiwanaku, and the shrines around Cuzco. Late Preclassic Yucatec Maya travel from town to town along a magnificent causeway. Upper Xinguano people travel from village to village along a "galaxy" of straight, radiating roads. And in a kind of walking meditation, Wari' mourners visit places, gardens, and trees associated in memory with deceased loved ones. These journeys differ in distance, duration, and motivation, yet in one way or another they are all transformative experiences, often with overt political and social ramifications.

Archaeologists take us on journeys through time as well. We have seen the Yucatec settlement of Uci grow in size and influence through the Preclassic period, developing a chain of satellite settlements attached to its causeway, only to dwindle during the Classic period while Ucanha experienced a revitalizing florescence. As a stratigraphic sequence, the Preclassic/Classic site of K'axob in northern Belize takes us on a journey through phases of domestic life, human burial, and soul revitalization. Buildings themselves undergo similar temporal journeys as they are successively brought to life, deactivated, and later revitalized. Chavín's Lanzón, while stationary in space, leads us on a trajectory through time as Chavín grows in influence and grandeur, recedes into obscurity, and then rises to new prominence as a World Heritage Site.

The journeys discussed in this book have much in common with journeys elsewhere in the world. Xinguano roads and Maya causeways should hardly surprise contemporary Americans or Europeans who are always "on the go" over a vast network of highways. The wandering Mexica bring to mind the Israelites in the wilderness. Pilgrimage sites like Tiwanaku and Chavín bring to mind Lourdes and Mecca. Yet within the overarching commonality of the human condition, every journey and every journeying tradition has its peculiarities.

Think of this chapter as a metaphorical journey through themes and questions raised by the other chapters in this book. Like Huitzilopochtli's bundle, I will wander a bit between leaving one home base and arriving at another. As in a mountainous journey, I will pause to take in new vistas when the view shifts. I represent my discussion as a journey because a sequential review of themes shares structural characteristics with physical journeying. My (rather mixed) metaphor also incorporates aspects of "memory lane," for the "vistas" bring to mind

familiar situations I have known close-up during my years of research in the Andes.[1] A bit farther away are ethnographic regions of Mesoamerica and Amazonia, which I know only secondhand, along with some approaches and ideas that I am still incorporating into my mental landscape. I see them stretching into the distance like far-off mountain ranges.

Steve Kosiba defines our quest in his introductory chapter, asking how authority is "claimed and constituted in societies where things and places are persons who can explicitly play social roles, have voices, influence decisions, demand recognition, and instill order." This volume's authors address animacy in Mesoamerica and South America ontologically, as a way of being-in-the-world that determines the character of relations of authority and deference; these, in turn, inform social action. Within this perspective, the human person is decentered, giving way to interdependencies and interactions inhering within assemblages of things and people. As Scott Hutson and colleagues (citing Ingold 2000, 2011) comment, "Life is not [viewed as] given automatically or independent of relations."

Native North American writer Scott Momaday (1976:80) refers to this kind of interdependency as "reciprocal appropriation" (also see Allen 2016a:424; Basso 1996:64). In a similar vein, Marisol de la Cadena proposes the term *intra-action*, alluding to the concept introduced by theoretical physicist Karen Barad (2007) to describe situations in which entities bring each other about *within* a relation (as opposed to *interaction*, in which the entities preexist their relation). "Rather than being instilled in the individual subject," writes de la Cadena (2015:102), "the substance of the *runakuna* [humans] and the other-than-humans that make an *ayllu* [community] is the coemergence of each with the others" (see also Kosiba, this volume). Human life is not a matter of interacting with other humans while acting on objects, but of intra-acting with the whole range of animate beings in the universe. This constant flux of intrarelationship is central to ontological understanding of all bodies, human and nonhuman.

Setting Out

We cross the threshold, close the door behind us, and set out on the journey. Before moving on we must pause and acknowledge our point of departure.

The *house* begins our metaphorical journey. In the indigenous American contexts that are explored in this book, buildings are experienced as entities with which humans have living, interactive relationships. We have seen the Kuikuro chief's house as a locus of authority, pride, fear, deference, and communal expectation, while the Wari' house is unbearably imbued with affect, so much so that after an occupant's death it must be dismantled and burned. Our own point of departure is the Dumbarton Oaks Research Library, in whose Pre-Columbian collection archaeology, history, ethnography, and aesthetics mingle happily and speak to each other. It is a perfect starting point for an exploration of the constitution of authority in the indigenous Americas, a world in which society extends beyond the human to include things like houses and mountains.

In foregoing chapters, archaeological understanding of ancient Mesoamerican buildings is informed by ethnographic accounts of houses among Tzotzil-speaking Maya and other Mexican and Central American peoples. These houses are "ensouled." Family and house belong to each other. Just as family members share nourishment with each other, they must nurture the house. Like a newborn baby, a new house is actualized as a person with initiatory offerings and fed throughout its life with specific substances. For their part, houses act as protective guardians and moral custodians of their occupants' welfare.

Similarly, in Sonqo, the Andean community where I did fieldwork,[2] the house (*wasitira*) is a self-contained microcosm. My friend Luis likened the house to "a mother hen who keeps us warm under her wings." She is a small, dark, cozy structure made of adobes and thatch. As in Mexico and Central America, family and house share a reciprocal commitment. "*Wasitira* must be treated well, for a disrespected house turns cold and unwelcoming. She is, moreover, a witness to whatever occurs within her walls, and she stands at the end of a chain of chthonic authority extending to the snow-capped mountain lords" (Allen 2015:24). Within her walls, there is no escaping her watchful authoritative presence. As a self-contained microcosm, moreover, she enjoys a unique spatial orientation. Within the house, east is defined by the door, "the sun's entering place" (*intiq haykuna*), even if, from an outsider's perspective, the door faces, for example, south.

Completion of a new house is marked by a ritual called, in Southern Peruvian Quechua, *wasichayay*, a term that indicates that the completed structure is being realized, or brought into existence, as a house. Living earth, water, tree limbs, and grass have been assembled and coaxed—as adobes, roof beams, and thatch—into a new set of relationships. *Wasichayay* acknowledges and celebrates an identity inhering in these relationships. Strictly speaking, the ceremony does not so much ensoul or animate the *wasitira* as wake her up with dance, drink, food, and cooking fires, thus ushering her into family life. Hutson and colleagues (this volume) interpret Mesoamerican houses similarly: "There is a distinction between being alive and being a person. The materials incorporated into houses are considered animate. . . . Thus, ensoulment is not the creation of life. It is the creation of personhood." This is literal, not metaphoric, personhood: houses are other-than-human persons. Ritual ensouls the relationship, not the material.

And so we have crossed the threshold and closed the door. If we were abandoning the building we might need to perform some ceremony of closure or termination—even burial. But as we leave our house intact and inhabited—no demolition, smashed pots, or (as far as I know) bodies buried in the living room—we say, "Good-bye for now," and go on our way.

Our Path:
The Scree-Filled Slope of Equivocation

As I step through the door, blink, and reorient myself, I see that I have embarked on a slippery vertiginous path. It seems as though an abyss yawns on one side and a rock wall looms on the other. *The rock wall denies comparison: every society, every practice, every object is unique, pristine, silent. The abyss denies difference: in its depths everything washes together into sameness. The rock wall says, "Animistic worlds of Native American societies—past and present—are so essentially different from ours (and probably from each other) as to defy understanding. Why bother to try?" The abyss says, "There really aren't any essential differences, so what's the big deal?" Our path makes its way between these two extremes. There are ontological differences, and these differences matter.*

I am wary of the term *ontology*, which properly refers to a theoretical discourse (*logos*) about the nature of existence. Because I doubt that any society can be characterized as "having" a self-contained, internally consistent theory of being, I prefer to think in terms of ontological orientations or dispositions. Members of a society may share certain orientations to existence; that is, they share deeply ingrained, usually tacit assumptions about what the world is and how it works. These assumptions inform social action. Kosiba addresses this issue in his introduction, observing that contemporary anthropologists use the term *ontology* to refer to "tacitly understood, but not always consciously acknowledged, *dispositions toward reality* or, put simply, those 'things that go without saying.'" Used in this sense, *ontology* refers to a mode of intra-relationship.

Bruce Mannheim's chapter argues that differences in ontological orientation reflect divergences in cognitive frames of reference that can be studied linguistically. The *egocentric* system of English and Spanish speakers, for example, projects its frame of reference from the vantage point of the speaker, whereas the *allocentric* system of Quechua is "anchored primarily in the physical space surrounding the interaction rather than in the participants." With differences originating at such a basic level, we have to wonder how mutual comprehension is even possible. Yet people can and do manage to communicate across ontological divides. To some extent, we even shift our ontological stances as necessity dictates. As John Janusek comments, citing Harris and Robb (2010:670), "People may shift moment to

moment, situationally, among ontological dispositions, understood here as 'different practical understandings of the nature of material reality.'" How is this possible if cognitive frames of reference are formed so early in life and at such a basic level?

In their introduction to *The Dialogical Emergence of Culture*, Bruce Mannheim and Dennis Tedlock address this problem in the context of ethnographic practice. For an ethnographer attempting to communicate with interlocutors across different frames of reference, what emerges is "a peculiar kind of dialogue and a peculiar zone of emergence, at once constitutive of and constituted by radical cultural difference" (Mannheim and Tedlock 1995:15). Eduardo Viveiros de Castro (2004:7) takes an analogous approach, describing ethnography as translation: "To translate is to situate oneself in the space of the equivocation and to dwell there. . . . It is to communicate by differences." He goes on to characterize "controlled equivocation" as "a properly transcendental category of anthropology" (2004:10).[3]

The notion that we progress through equivocation—that is, by recognizing and exploring our misunderstandings—has relevance for the issues Santiago Giraldo raises in his chapter on belief and political action in the Sierra Nevada de Santa Marta. Giraldo critiques the "ontological turn" in the social sciences as promoting essentialized visions of culturally distinct peoples living isolated from one another in incommensurable realities. His purpose is to refute this kind of essentialism by demonstrating how the Kogi/Arhuaco deploy "particular and strategic 'ontological claims' to further their own political interests": "Indigenous peoples in the Sierra Nevada de Santa Marta harness, quote, and deploy these supernatural beings constantly as efficacious political tools . . . and they have won important legal battles at various levels on this basis alone. . . . [This] constantly changing political arena . . . should not be reduced to 'alternative and incommensurable ontologies.'" Giraldo ranges himself "on the side of the skeptics," preferring to consider ontologies as contingent and socially situated rather than incommensurable and parallel worlds.

The Kogis/Arhuacos' remarkable deployment of a global totalizing vision succeeds because it intersects with (indeed, manipulates) a different ontological orientation characteristic of liberal democracies that espouse Enlightenment-derived principles of pluralism and tolerance (tinged with existential angst). The Kogi *mamas* operate masterfully within this space of equivocation; what emerges is "a fascinating, dynamic, and constantly changing political arena."

Ontologies exist not in an ideational neverland, but in social practice; they play out through relationships among social actors who translate each other's actions and words in ways they can (partially) understand. Inevitably, they will be incommensurable in some respects but not in others. Translation across radical difference is inherently approximate and may fail completely, as in Mannheim's example of the egocentrically oriented North American ethnographer trying to follow directions given by an allocentrically oriented Quechua speaker: "It is perfectly feasible for individuals with distinct frames of reference to interact with each other, but they will systematically misunderstand others' spatial orientations." This partiality of connections is simply part of the human condition (Strathern 2004)—like approaching a limit we can never actually reach.

The "space of equivocation" may emerge slowly and to some extent below the threshold of awareness. For example, I could converse comfortably with Andean interlocutors once I had learned some Quechua, and for the most part we understood each other well enough. Huddled beside the fire on a frigid night, Basilia and I recognized, for example, that the building in which we sat was a house (*wasi*) and that the night was cold outside. Apparently transparent to each other, we discussed the house's construction, contents, and history. When I mentioned the cold weather and my appreciation of her cozy hearth, Basilia tsk-tsked over my thin gringo clothing and wrapped me up in a heavy wool blanket. It took time and many conversations to notice that my Andean friends' experience of the house—their intra-relationship with it—was qualitatively different from mine. The realization struck home, for example, when I was chided for my clumsy, heavy-handed potato peeling—not because I was wasting time and food but because I was causing the potatoes pain, which would offend both *wasitira* and *q'uncha* (fireplace/stove). Similarly, one day I arrived at Basilia's house to find her talking to her *q'uncha*. She had just finished reshaping the cooking surface of this small adobe stove and was preparing to offer it a libation of cane alcohol. "Little Mother," she said, "please cook well for me." With the libation and words she invoked a relationship with the stove in which the two—woman and stove—were connected in a bond of mutual responsibility. A few months later, I joined don Erasmo as he expressed a similar mutuality with his new battery-operated radio, greeting it with a libation and the words, "Kuska wiñasun. Ama malograpunki!" (Let's grow together. Please don't break down!) (Allen 1998:20).

Through such conversations, the realization emerged that we had different ways of experiencing materiality—and that for my acquaintances matter itself could be a seat of moral authority. Marisol de la Cadena (2015) describes a similar process of realization in her conversations with Mariano Turpo, an important peasant leader who attributed much of his movement's success to the support and participation of Mount Ausangate. She finally had to accept the ambiguity inherent in her situation: "I learned to identify radical difference . . . as that which I 'did not get' because it exceeded the terms of my understanding. . . . For example: I could acknowledge [earth beings' existence] through Mariano and Nazario, but I could not know them the way I know mountains are rocks" (de la Cadena 2015:63).

One way to make sense of ambiguous concepts that one "does not get" is to make partial connections with something closer to one's familiar experience. Although we run the risk of slipping downslope and mistaking partial connection for equation, noting similarities is useful insofar as it helps us explore the differences. We can relate the *wasichayay* ceremony, for example, to a "housewarming party" or to the Christian custom of "blessing" a new house. Sprinkling a house with holy water bears similarities to the Andean awakening of a house with libations of alcohol. Yet the differences are equally profound, as a Christian website is quick to point out, warning its readers, "As a tradition, a house blessing is something we are free to choose or not choose to do. To avoid trusting in superstition, we should remember that it is God who blesses, not a picture in a frame or water from a shaker" (https://www.gotquestions.org/house-lessing.html). For my Andean acquaintances, this would exactly miss the point. Libations feed the awakening house *literally, not metaphorically*.[4]

In comparing how materiality was conceived in the Old and New Worlds during the contact period, both Tom Cummins and Byron Hamann find partial connections in the theme of transubstantiation. In his chapter, Cummins avers, "The transformational relationship of the inanimate thing to animate personhood is nearly universal, and it is often a part of political power." He points to *transubstantiation*, *kamay*, and *teixiptla* as "culturally specific, coeval phenomena of the sacred that act to transform or recognize the animate character of a substance, be it bread and wine, rock and wood, or body and dough."

It is worth amplifying the contrast inherent in the comparison: in *transubstantiation*, the wafer undergoes a transformation of substance from inanimate to animate while its outer appearance remains the same. *Kamay*, on the other hand, is a creative process grounded in the recognition of matter's inherent potential animation. Communion wafers are not alive in the same way—or more precisely, Catholic communicants do not relate to them as such, that is, as responsive to and effective on human life—prior to their transubstantiation into the real (not symbolic) body of Christ. Andean rocks do live, intrinsically. Their modes of life may change due to human agency; they may be more or less active and, if bereft of relationships, even go dormant over long periods of time, but they are never not alive (cf. Dean 2010).

A Play of Contrasts

By this time my tunnel vision has opened up, and I realize that our path is not really so narrow, nor bounded by such steep extremes on either side. Looking upslope

and down, I notice other paths that we have chosen not to follow. Upslope, a dead-end approach dismisses "animism" as just another mystifying ideology obscuring "the brute and all-too-human machinations of power" (Kosiba, this volume). Downslope, the typological approach forged by Philippe Descola ([2005] 2013) wends its way through the weeds. Is that the path I should be following? I have been referring to Andean cultures as "animistic," but according to Descola's system, they are properly termed "analogical."

Descola's system makes a crucial distinction between interiority and exteriority.[5] The former refers to subjective experience, that is, the way we are encapsulated within our individual bodies; the latter refers to how we experience the physical world beyond our bodies. Cultures differ in how they identify with internal and external experience and how they relate the two to each other. Descola proposes four basic "schema for integrating experience." One of these is animism: "the attribution by humans to nonhumans of an interiority identical to their own" (Descola [2005] 2013:129). Animists, in his terminology, assume that existent beings (human and nonhuman) share the same kind of subjectivity but have different kinds of bodies. Analogism, another of his schema, operates on the assumption that beings differ from each other in both dimensions, subjective and physical: "[Analogism is] a mode of identification that divides up the whole collection of existing beings into a multiplicity of essences, forms and substances separated by small distinctions . . . so that it becomes possible to recompose the system of initial contrasts into a dense network of analogies" (Descola [2005] 2013:201).

According to this scheme, most (probably all) Andean and Mesoamerican cultures are analogistic. Indeed, anyone familiar with the play of relationships in their respective ethnographic and ethnohistoric records will recognize the accuracy of this designation. Nevertheless, I agree with Marshall Sahlins (2014:281) that analogism can be understood simply as animism with a hierarchical emphasis. Descola recognizes that the analogical world may be "humming with conscious life" but argues that this analogical life is different in kind from that of animistic cultures. In an analogical regime, he says, "every existing being is different from every other one on account of the plurality of its components and the diverse modes of their combination . . . humans and [nonhumans] do not share the same culture, the same ethics, and the same institutions (Descola [2005] 2013:213).

But often, in the Andes, they do share the same culture, ethics, and institutions. *Tirakuna* (earth beings) are often described as having a hierarchically organized society parallel to that of humans; condors, too, are described in these terms. *Condenados* (souls of the undead) have their villages. In Apurimac, Peter Gose (1994) learned that on their way to the afterlife souls must pass through a sequence of villages occupied, respectively, by dogs, guinea pigs, and cooking pots. The "revolt of the utensils" is a theme that crops up in Andean iconography and narrative. And while my Andean acquaintances clearly distinguish their subjectivities from those of their houses, the two classes of beings can and do communicate.

Whatever terminology we use (Stensrud [2010:42] opts for the term *animic-analogical*), what interests me is the way the physical world, as expressed in the behavior and discourse of many indigenous Americans, is "buzzing with conscious life." Insofar as this animation emerges through a play of relationships, Descola's "analogism" points us in the right direction.

The play of relationships—especially synecdochal relationships in which part and whole contain each other—is basic to the constitution of the Andean world, which is called *pacha* in Quechua and Aymara. *Pacha* is sometimes translated into English as "space-time" because the word denotes both a moment in time and a location in space (e.g., Manga Qespi 1994). While space-time is a fairly familiar concept, other aspects of *pacha* are more elusive to "Western" thinking. For one thing, *pacha* can exist at any scale (cf. Salomon 1991:14). Depending on the context, *pacha* is the whole cosmos or an instantaneous located event. Every place, every microcosm, is *pacha*, contained by and containing other microcosms; every moment is nested within other moments. Thus, one's perspective can expand and contract indefinitely. Another aspect of the *pacha*

concept is even more elusive: while objectively material, *pacha* is a *collective state of consciousness*, an intersubjective convergence of the sensible entities, human and nonhuman, that compose it. The world (at whatever scale) is a confluence of matter, activity, and *intra-relationship*—a material, lived-in moment.

A Shift in the Light

As I move along the trail, a snowcapped mountain pokes its head into my line of sight. It reminds me of Mount Ausangate, the great apu *(mountain lord) of the Cuzco region. He is the top* kamachikuq *(authority, one who makes things happen). Ausangate, in turn, takes my thoughts back to Basilia's tiny house in the community of Sonqo. This is no non sequitur: house and mountain are intrinsically connected.*

The house witnesses everything that passes within her walls. I was told that if family members misbehave or a thief enters while they are away, the house knows about it. She does not, however, give up this information easily. Her inhabitants have to call on the services of a *paqu* (ritual specialist) who is skilled at communicating with powerful places. The *paqu* invokes the authority of Mount Ausangate, who proceeds to activate a chain of authority beginning with other high peaks, moving on down through a descending hierarchy, and finally reaching the round bald pate of Antaqaqa Hill, Sonqo's local *kamachikuq*. Antaqaqa commands *wasitira* to give up her secrets to the ritual specialist, who then interprets her response through configurations of coca leaves. Thus, even when we have left our house behind, we feel her resonance in connections of authoritative substance running through the landscape. Similar relationships between houses and powerful places pertain in Mesoamerica as well; for example, in highland Chiapas, where the "ensouling" of a new building requires that a ritual specialist carry offerings to sacred mountains with ancestral connections (Vogt [1976] cited by Joyce, this volume).

Thus, my ethnographic experience of the humble adobe house is germane to understanding how agency emerges through the articulation of human and nonhuman beings. *Wasitira* is a node of articulation between humans and powerful places (*tirakuna*, earth beings) in the landscape. On one hand, as an earth being herself, the house is intrinsically related to other earth beings, including the most powerful regional mountain lords. On the other hand, she owes her existence to human agency. Alfred Gell's (1998) concept of "distributed personhood" is useful for thinking about these connections.[6] *Wasitira* participates in her family's distributed personhood, as well as in the distributed personhood of mountain peaks and other powerful places. Indigenous American regimes like Tiahuanaco and Cuzco systematized and centralized many such relationships, integrating them on a grand scale. Human authority derived in part from a demonstrated ability to maneuver effectively within these relationships. De la Cadena's study of Mariano Turpo's political leadership explores this kind of authority in a contemporary context. Although embedded with a modern nation-state, Turpo's community chose him as their leader "because of his ability to negotiate both with the *hacendado* (landowner) and with earth-beings" (de la Cadena 2015:46). Turpo himself experienced his political successes in terms of his relationship with Mount Ausangate. In the precontact Andes as well, authority entailed the ability to intervene in chains of communication among powerful places.

Similarly, "one of the tasks constantly undertaken by [Kogi and Arhuaco] *mamas* involves restoring, healing, or creating communication between these places so that they can 'work together'" (Giraldo, this volume). They consider their pyramid-shaped mountain home to be the body of the Great Mother and "the heart of the world." Utterly confident of their place at the center of the world, they consider even distant sites elsewhere in the world to be manifestations of the Great Mother. Because all sacred places, local and global, exist in resonance with each other, they perceive themselves to be managers of a global ecoregime of moral authority. Ironically, at the national level political advantage derives from the totalizing, apparently apolitical, quality of their ontological vision.

In spite of their vast differences in geography, environment, and historical position, most indigenous American societies define authority in terms of some kind of systematized articulation of human and nonhuman agencies. Amazonian regimes articulate complex relations among human beings, animals, and plants, while in the Andes and Mesoamerica relations with places gain paramount importance. Yet environment is not all-determining. Even in relatively similar environments and historical circumstances, ontological assumptions play out differently. Although Wari' villages contrast dramatically with urban and ceremonial centers like Tiahuanaco or Tenochtitlan, there, too, the human being is intrinsically constituted as a complex of intra-relations with other-than-human beings; personhood is diffuse in the sense of extending beyond the boundaries of the individual body. Yet affective relations seem to play a larger role in the constitution of the Wari' ecoregime; authority is not vested in particular individuals, groups, or locations, but in relations of love and grief. In contrast, the Xinguano ecoregime bears more resemblance to the ecoregimes of the Andes and Mesoamerica. Strikingly reminiscent of Cuzco's *ceque* system, a "galactic system" of roads connects dispersed villages in a "ritual-economy of grandeur" (Fausto, this volume).

Reading about Kuikuro chiefs brought a Quechua word to mind: *kamachikuq*—literally, "the one who makes things happen." "Upper Xinguano chiefs are imagined as nurturing their people and making them increase, instantiating this growth not only in their own names and physical bodies, but also in all the other material bodies assigned to them" (Fausto, this volume). Building a chiefly house makes tangible the chief's authority. At different points in the life cycle, a chief shares personhood with other nonhuman denizens of the Xingu environment: jaguars and *humiria* trees. The Quarup mourning ritual reallocates the chief's personhood, subduing its jaguar aspects and entrapping it in the tree trunk.

A World of Synecdoches

As I round a curve in the path a vast expanse opens up. More snowcapped peaks loom up over the horizon; hills and valleys stretch away before me; streams course downhill and form into rivers or pool into lakes. I pause to reorient myself, reminded of the spectacular aerial photo in Janusek's chapter on Tiahuanaco as an ecoregime.

Ecoregime, as formulated by Janusek, is a useful way of thinking about animacy and authority in the precontact Andes and Mesoamerica (and perhaps the Amazon as well). It neatly reformulates Arturo Escobar's (1999) concept of *nature regime* in ontological contexts in which "nature" (as understood in Euro-American traditions) does not exist. Janusek defines the Tiahuanaco ecoregime as a cosmopolitical "field of articulations that assembled mountains, celestial movements, water flows, humans, and nonhuman lithic persons as a coherent, if shifting, master geopolitical cartography." This seems an apt characterization of other indigenous American urban ceremonial centers such as Tenochtitlan, Monte Albán, Cuzco, and possibly Chavín. "Cosmopolitical," in Janusek's terms, describes the participation of human, geomorphic, and other nonhuman entities in a network of relations calibrated hierarchically in terms of relative power and authority.[7] Humans do not control the system in the sense of acting *upon* a "natural" world of passive entities; rather they operate *within* it, articulating human agency with that of other-than-human beings like mountains and monoliths. Pilgrims traveling to Tiahuanaco's ceremonial center experienced their world's complex synecdoche by moving through a synesthetic sequence of enclosed spaces, vast vistas, and windy or watery soundscapes. Marco Curatola's chapter also emphasizes this kind of synesthesia. He points out that the aural aspect of archaeological sites needs to receive more attention, as a soundscape can "condense and encode a vast and coherent system of meanings, beliefs, and collective representations."

The ecoregime concept recasts our understanding of centralized systems in the Andes, for example, the radial system of *wak'as* that comprised the *ceque* system of Cuzco (e.g., Bauer 1992; Zuidema 1964; also McEwan 2014; Urton 1990). Although we do not have ethnohistorical records, archaeological evidence indicates that Tiahuanaco occupied a similar position as the lynchpin of an ecoregime extending, ideally, in all directions. The urban ceremonial complex at Tiahuanaco's conceptual center exerted a kind of centripetal force, drawing humans and other-than-human entities into its sphere of influence. Temples and monoliths were visually aligned with distant places from which they were quarried. *Part* (temple complex) and *whole* (ecoregime) played off each other in a synecdochal (or, following Descola, analogical) relationship. In other words, the temple complex was a fractal instantiation of the total ecoregime it articulated.

Blood and Stone

Moving ahead, I realize that I have not properly oriented myself to the living panorama of earth beings that is opening before me. I should at least pause, take out my coca bundle, and share the leaves' energizing aroma with these telluric presences. I am forcefully reminded of my omission as, at a bend in the path, my way is blocked by an immense boulder. What is going on? Penelope Harvey's (2001:198) caution comes to mind: "It is important to understand that the personhood of hills and pathways is not a metaphorical extension of human attributes. Personhood is literal. The reading of the signs that the landscape affords is less like reading a map and more akin to how one might try to interpret the feelings of others by looking at facial expressions and bodily postures." Is this boulder like the famous Tired Stone of the Incas, who balked en route to a construction site near Cuzco, sat down, and refused to move, weeping blood in exhaustion?

The Tired Stone asserted his own telluric agency by weeping blood and refusing to participate in wall-building. Earth beings, when tired and neglected, not only get hungry for blood but also may bleed in rage. Violent weather ensues, and blood may gush out in a *yawar paccha* ("bloody stream"; Allen 2002:198). This is one reason places need to be fed; if left to go hungry, they draw vitality—blood and fat—from human beings in their vicinity. Illness, weight loss, and lassitude provide immediate experiences of earth beings' agency. Human beings protect their own healthy blood and fat by offering other kinds of sustenance, particularly coca leaves and alcohol, supplemented periodically with more substantial meals (*despachos*) including special herbs, seeds, shells, and llama fetuses. Early chroniclers recorded that Incas fed the *wak'as* around Cuzco with similar offerings.

Ethnographic data from Central America and Mexico also record the importance of feeding powerful places, including buildings, and inform archaeological interpretations of offerings uncovered in Mesoamerican buildings and burials. As Arthur Joyce comments, "Sacrifice in Mesoamerica can also be considered a form of animating practice involving transactions of the vital force between humans and divinities, typically where it is released from one animate being to sustain, feed, or animate another." Mannheim's chapter argues that it is through such practices (rather than an abstract cosmology) that places are experienced as animate, that is, as having agency. However, we should keep in mind that such practices are not invented out of thin air, but develop over time within a particular ontological orientation.

Most of the societies explored in this book share underlying ontological assumptions about personhood, materiality, and authority that manifest themselves in various ways. In general, Mesoamerican sources are more explicit than Andean or Amazonian ones in emphasizing the importance of time and timekeeping in articulating regimes of authority among humans and other-than-human beings.[8] The *Codex Boturini* is a "dense, calendar glyph–filled band of migration history" (Hamann, this volume). Time itself, as expressed in complex calendrical systems, was intrinsically connected with authority. For Hutson and colleagues (this volume), the reed mat motif identifies Structure 92c-SubIV in Ucanha as a probable seat of governance because "reed mat" is a Maya calendar glyph that indexes authority. Timekeeping was a skilled and authoritative process of accommodation to incredibly complex temporal cycles.

An Endless Cycle of Mutual Consumption

Confronted by the stubborn boulder in my path, I place a small bouquet (k'intu) of coca leaves in its *crevices and proceed to blow coca's fortifying aroma to the panorama of earth beings around me, calling their names as I do so and asking that I may journey well. My words, gestures, and gaze draw the attention of the earth beings and emphasize our shared personhood. If I were traveling with other people, I would share with my companions as I shared with the earth and earth beings around me, and each of my companions would do the same. I recall how, years ago, as a graduate student steeped in Erving Goffman's symbolic interactionism, I realized that my analyses of the coca-sharing ceremony made no sense unless mountains were included as participants along with human beings. So I pause to consume coca leaves along with the* tirakuna, *enjoying our moment of commensality and meditating on the universal importance of food-sharing in human societies as a means of forging social bonds. Lost in these thoughts, I feel my feet begin to slide—I have stepped into yet another slippery space of equivocation.*

Is this ceremonial coca-sharing not the same kind of communion as that experienced by devout Christians as they partake of the bread-body and wine-blood of Christ during the Mass? My Quechua acquaintances frequently likened coca to *hostia* in an explicit analogy with Catholic Communion. The similarities are obvious, yet the differences are equally significant. Coca needs no transubstantiation—its substance does not change. What it needs is direction. The more directly and intently I can direct its *sami* (enlivening energy), the stronger my connection with its telluric recipients. Andean authority, like that deployed by Mariano Turpo (de la Cadena 2015:63), develops out of this ability to intervene in human and other-than-human relationships. Kogi/Arhuaco authority, too, derives from an ability to divine what the telluric mothers and fathers want to be fed.

Lawrence Sullivan (1988:69) comments in his study of native South American religions, "This world [is] an endless cycle of consumption in which all is food." In Andean contexts, kinship derives not so much from shared parentage as from the continuous sharing of food (Mannheim and Salas Carreño 2015; Weismantel 1995, [1988] 1998). Thus, "places may be kin" (Kosiba 2015; Salas Carreño 2016). To feed others puts one in a position of authority, as Carlos Fausto (this volume) emphasizes so clearly in his discussion of Xinguano chieftainship: "To sponsor a ritual means to provide food not only to the community and the human invitees, but also to nonhuman ones. This position of feeder is typically one of authority . . . [and] every ritual performance publicly marks and produces a chiefly status." Chief and community, part and whole, feed off each other. The Inka ruler similarly produced and maintained his authoritative status, as reflected in the title of Susan Ramírez's study of authority and identity in the Andes, *To Feed and Be Fed* (2005). The theme runs through Mesoamerican sources as well. Hamann, for example, emphasizes that pulque drinking, a sacred authoritative practice, was understood as "the absorption of one body by another."

Chips Off the Old Block (and Vice Versa)

Closing my coca bundle and turning my thoughts away from food, I edge my way around the boulder, aware of its looming presence, wondering how long it has been sitting on the path and where it came from before that. I am reminded of the Lanzón and of the Tiahuanaco monoliths.

The Lanzón may have gained fame as just such a boulder before being transported to Chavín, where its inner form was revealed and its stony surfaces were "modified to increase its ability to interact with other kinds of substances and bodies, whether liquid or mammalian" (Weismantel, this volume). The Tiahuanaco monoliths, as an organized group, contrast with the singularity of the Lanzón. While the Lanzón's original location is unknown, Janusek's research shows that Tiahuanaco's monoliths were quarried in the vicinities of powerful places (e.g., the Bennet presentation monolith in Mount Kimsachata and the Ponce in Mount Ccapia). It seems fair to presume that the mountains were consulted during this process. The stony personages were then set in relation to each other so as to reinstantiate the entire ecoregime in the ceremonial center. "Monolithic personages ordered space by gathering and condensing biophysical landscapes" (Janusek, this volume).

Janusek makes an interesting connection with certain miniatures in contemporary Andean communities. These *inqaychus* are small stone animals that powerful places bestow upon favored individuals (Allen 2016a, 2016b; Flores Ochoa 1977; Ricard Lanata 2007). They originate as beautiful animals (e.g., alpacas) that emerge from springs or highland lakes. A very lucky and quick-witted person may catch one, at which point the animal shrinks into a tiny stone to be taken home "still warm and palpitating" (Flores Ochoa 1977:221). They are kept carefully hidden in the interior of the family's house, brought out only at certain times of year to graze on a pasture of coca leaves and drink drops of liquor. At this point they exhale the mountain's powerful breath, infusing the family's herd with vitality and their specific characteristics or *anímu* (Ricard Lanata 2007:211).[9]

Given its powerful agency, it should be clear that the *inqaychu* is not a representation of an animal. It is simply a special kind of animal, an instantiation of the mountain, or, as de la Cadena (2015:107) puts it, "a piece of it, which is also all of it" (see also Allen 2016a, 2016b). This phrase, I think, sums up the ontological orientation we are exploring under the label of "animism" (or, following Stensrud's modification of Descola's terminology, "animic-analogism").

Similarly, Nahua bundles seem best understood as instantiations of powerful entities. Huitzilopochtli's bundle embodied Mexica authority by condensing geography and cosmic time. Hamann observes that the *Codex Boturini*, a book about a sacred bundle, was itself a sacred bundle with a key narrative in its center—the invention of pulque. The structure does not simply "symbolize" a sacred bundle: it actually creates a sacred bundle, "to be unfolded and unwrapped in the reader's hands" (Hamann, this volume). The small animate bodily objects discussed in Diana Loren's chapter may have derived their healing qualities from similar relationships.

Wind, Water, and the Interior of Things

As I edge my way around the rock a blast of wind nearly blows me off my feet. The vista has changed; I am peering into a canyon with a river at its bottom. In several places along its walls water emerges from springs and gushes down into the river. The canyon channels gusts of wind right into my path with such force that I am propelled back against the boulder. I had been resting in the leeward side of this massive rock, a comfortable, sunny spot. Now, as I shift position, it ceases to shield me from the force of the wind. Combined with the polyphonic reverberation of water—rushing, pouring, trickling—the effect is nearly overwhelming. I recall Mannheim's observation of "the ontic bind between mayu *[river] and* qaqa *[rock] as substances." Peering ahead, I spy a cave in the canyon wall, perhaps the mouth of one of those labyrinthine caverns that inspired such awe in my acquaintances in Sonqo. I am reminded of the Lanzón's subterranean temple home, which Weismantel in her chapter likens to "being inside the entrails of an enormous stony creature."*

Cummins (this volume) describes the Andean landscape as "replete with natural and built places where the underworld breaks open into the light and air." He emphasizes the significance of *emergence* in both indigenous American and medieval Christian religious experience. The Mesoamerican landscape is equally replete such points of emergence: caves are places of ancestral origin and sites for communication with interior aspects of the cosmos (e.g., Brady and Prufer 2005). In the *Codex Boturini*, Huitzilopochtli's journey from Aztlan begins in a cave where his bundle "awaits the Mexica ancestors, commanding them with speech scrolls rising above his hummingbird helmet" (Hamann, this volume). Inka mythology, too, tells us of founding ancestors emerging either from caves in Paqariqtambo or from Lake Titicaca. Curatola remarks on how the sun and other deities spoke to human beings through the sound of water emerging from springs and fountains.

Like a great house, the earth has many doors. I learned in Sonqo that springs are "water doors" to an interior landscape that includes lakes, underground rivers, and even cities. Springs, caves, glacial lakes, and marshes are openings to an inner existence, dark to us and hidden from our normal consciousness. Ancestral Inkas are said to have fled from Spanish invaders into the depths of the tropical forest, where they are hidden in a golden city, Paititi, "just as we are hidden in a house" (Allen 2002:92). Sonqueños laughed and told funny stories about adventurers and archaeologists who go searching for this golden legend: obviously they will never find it—not on the ground, not even from the air—because it is "inside" (*ukhupi*). It exists, but not in our own time and daylight. Occasionally, people referred to Paititi as located in a subterranean lake under Sonqo's guardian hill, Antaqaqa. The apparent inconsistency did not bother them; the important point was that Paititi has an interior existence (Allen 2014:75).

Throughout the Andes, lakes are said to contain cities that were submerged when the inhabitants refused to admit a beggar—actually Dios Tayta (Father God) in disguise—when he attempted to enter a wedding feast (Allen [1988] 2002:48; Mannheim and Van Vleet 1998; Morote Best 1988:241–282). Only one generous woman welcomed the wretched visitor. Before wreaking his vengeance, God sent this kind hostess away from the city with the command not to look back. But she stopped to urinate and, in the process, cast her gaze backward. At that very moment, she turned to stone and the city was swallowed up by the lake. "If only that woman hadn't urinated that city would have been Cuzco," Basilia told me mournfully. But eventually, she went on to tell me, that will change: there is a subterranean lake located right under Cuzco's cathedral and at some time—when the world turns inside out—the lake will rise up from within and swallow Cuzco while Lake Qesqay recedes to reveal the city within its depths. Contemplating this story, Erasmo commented, "It must be true [*chiqaq*], because you can go up there and see the lake and the stones."[10] Indeed, Sipas Qaqa (Girl Boulder) stands above the lake, urinating a trickle of water from her base. To rest by such a boulder connects one with the interior land- and timescapes it contains. As Tom Abercrombie (1998:119) observes in a Bolivian context, such resting places are "objects that in their invisible interiors still pulse with breath and life from signally important past events."

In my study of Andean narrative practice, I discovered that the high puna no-man's-land, far outside human habitation, is also conceived as a kind of interior; persons who get lost in the puna emerge fundamentally changed in some way, just as they do after being lost in a *chinkana* (cave). Deep interior and far exterior are the same when it comes to states of consciousness. "This equation of interior and exterior will feel intuitively right [to Quechua speakers] because they are in the habit of thinking in terms of a circulating world in which every motion eventually returns, via an interior route, to its place of origin" (Allen 2011:167).

Journey's End

Turning away from the wind, I work my way back around to the lee side of the boulder. It shields me from the wind, keeps me from going farther. The sound of rushing water is fainter here as well and has a pleasantly mesmerizing quality. I sit down and bring out my coca bundle again, realizing that my journey ends here, at the base of this boulder. I wonder about it—who is it, how did it get onto the spot, is it connected with one of the mountains here—"a piece of it, which is also all of it." As I rest comfortably out of the wind, I feel the boulder's presence, recognizing its agency in drawing my journey to a close. My mind turns again to the relationship between animism and authority.

The orientation we call animistic is neither mystical nor "prelogical."[11] To the contrary, by prioritizing relationships over discrete individuality, it is profoundly pragmatic. Harking back to Basilia and her *q'uncha*, if the stove smokes or cooks unevenly, Basilia addresses the problem as does a sensible person anywhere in the world: Is there an issue in its construction that can be fixed? Is the fire being laid correctly? Should she be more careful, perhaps use different utensils or manipulate them from a different angle? The ontological orientation is expressed in the attitude that informs her behavior, for all the time she would be examining her relationship with the *q'uncha*. That relationship is the context for her actions; her actions grow out of the relationship. Similarly, to take another mundane example, nights are cold in the high Andes, so Basilia sleeps under a blanket. She treats that blanket with respect by keeping it clean and whole; the blanket responds by keeping her warm. Her *behavior* with regard to the blanket is no different from yours or mine, but the attitude informing that behavior is culturally specific: she feels a sense of responsibility to the relationship. If it repeatedly slips off the bed at night, she will probably want to mentally review her treatment of the blanket. Life consists of a myriad of such relationships. One becomes acutely attuned to the nonverbal sign. If a rock rolls down a hillside and narrowly misses my foot, chances are that the hill is displeased and I have to figure out why—that is, to arrive at an interpretation of the sign.

During my first fieldwork in 1975, I asked don Erasmo, a fine storyteller, to record the story of Lake Qesqay's origin and of the city in its depths. He refused, saying that Qesqay might be angered. In 1984, after I had returned to Sonqo several times, he volunteered to record the narrative. I asked him what had changed, and he replied that by this time Qesqay knew me and would not mind having his history recorded. In other words, Erasmo's behavior toward me was inseparable from our entangled relationships with the places among whom we were dwelling.

Within this ontological orientation, one's own being is experienced as a collective condition, entailing relations among a multitude of human as well as other-than-human persons. As Fausto tells us regarding Xinguano chiefs, authority derives from an ability to coax this collective entanglement of relations into a prosperous state of well-being, like a weaver or house builder who coaxes living materials into new configurations. There is no acting upon the collective, there is only acting within and through it.

———————

I rest awhile longer, enjoying the boulder's protection and the warmth of our shared presence. But I know not to stay too long. This earth being is more powerful than I am; if I doze off or let my attention wander it may overwhelm me, draw me into its interior never to be seen again. I say my farewells, thank it for its attention (as I also thank you, my readers), and turn back the way I came.

Acknowledgments

This chapter looks back over forty years of research and writing during which I benefited from the support of many individuals and institutions, more than I can enumerate here. I owe the greatest debt of gratitude to the people of Sonqo who opened their homes and shared their lives with me, especially the late Luis Gutiérrez, his sister Basilia Gutiérrez, and Erasmo Hualla. Colleagues and friends in Cuzco and Lima have been unfailingly gracious and helpful as well. I particularly want to thank Colin McEwan, director of Pre-Columbian Studies at Dumbarton Oaks, and symposiarchs Steve Kosiba, John Janusek, and Tom Cummins for including me in the conference at Dumbarton Oaks that gave rise to this volume. This chapter has benefited especially from Steve Kosiba's astute comments and editorial feedback. As I have indicated in footnotes, some sections are adapted from previous publications (Allen 2016b, 2017). I am grateful for institutional support I have received from the George Washington University, as well as fellowship support from several institutions, including the Sainsbury Research Unit for the Arts of Africa, Oceania and the Americas (2015), the Fulbright Specialist Program (2011), the Guggenheim Foundation (2001–2002), the Center for the Advanced Study of the Visual Arts at the National Gallery of Art (2001), and the Dumbarton Oaks program in Pre-Columbian Studies (1994). Any errors of fact or interpretation are, of course, my own.

NOTES

1 Abercrombie (1998:119) makes a similar association between Aymara "pathways of memory and power" and his own research path.

2 Sonqo is located between 3200 and 3800 meters above sea level, in the province of Paucartambo, northeast of the city of Cuzco. I carried out research there for about a year in 1975–76 and have returned nine times, most recently in 2011, for stays ranging from two months to a few days. Sonqo's eighty-four households are devoted mainly to potato farming and the herding of sheep and camelids, supplemented by occasional wage labor in the city of Cuzco. The community has undergone many changes since 1975, due in part to completion of a road linking Sonqo with the city of Cuzco. Among these changes are a steep decline in pastoralism, the collapse of community-wide sectorial fallowing, and conversion of some families to a sect of evangelical Protestantism called Maranata (cf. Allen [1988] 2002:203–247).

3 Also cf. Strathern (2004) on "partial connections."

4 As *Católicos*, contemporary Andeans may also invoke blessings of the distant deity they call *Dyus* (God) without negating the house's material personhood.

5 The following section is adapted from my opinion piece in *Mundo de antes 11* (Allen 2017).

6 Gell's viewpoint differs from the one I outline here in that he does not ascribe life force to artifacts. See my discussion in Allen 2015.

7 Janusek deploys the term "cosmopolitical" in a somewhat different sense from that propounded by Isabel Stengers (2005), who refers to a politics of practices that bridge ontological divergence (also see de la Cadena 2015:180). Janusek uses *cosmopolitical* to describe a cosmos in which diverse entities, human and other-than-human, participate in a single political system.

8 The concept of the soul seems to be more complicated in Mesoamerica than in the Andes, possibly related to the greater emphasis on timekeeping.

9 The Quechua word *anímu* is derived from Spanish *anima* (spirit or soul). Unlike *sami*, which is a general enlivening force (Allen 2002a:33), *anímu* is inseparable from one's individuated corporeal being. One's *anímu* is sometimes likened to a halo surrounding the body, the shadow attached to the body, or a small in-dwelling double (La Riva 2004:78; Ricard 2007:85; also Arnold and Yapita 1998; Gose 1994; Robin 2008). Unlike Christian

concepts of the soul, the *anímu* has no eternal existence independent of the body. The two are distinct but mutually constitutive; neither can survive for long without the other. Xavier Ricard likens *anímu* to entelechy and glosses the word as "essence in action" (*esencia en acto*; Ricard 2007:83), suggesting

that the Spanish term replaced Quechua *kamaq* (Cummins, this volume; also Salomon 1991:16).

10 A synonym of *chiqaq* (true, straight) is *kunan* (now, in the present moment) (Allen 2011:44).

11 The following paragraphs are adapted from my discussion of animism in Allen 2016b.

REFERENCES CITED

Abercrombie, Thomas

  1998 *Pathways of Memory and Power: Ethnography and History among an Andean People.* University of Wisconsin Press, Madison.

Allen, Catherine J.

  1998 When Utensils Revolt: Mind, Matter, and Modes of Being in the Pre-Columbian Andes. *RES: Anthropology and Aesthetics* 33:18–27.

  [1988] 2002 *The Hold Life Has: Coca and Cultural Identity in an Andean Community.* 2nd ed. Smithsonian Institution Press, Washington, D.C.

  2002 The Incas Have Gone Inside: Pattern and Persistence in Andean Iconography. *RES: Anthropology and Aesthetics* 42:180–203.

  2011 *Foxboy: Intimacy and Aesthetics in Andean Stories.* University of Texas Press, Austin.

  2014 Ushnus and Interiority. In *Inca Sacred Space: Landscape, Site and Symbol in the Andes*, edited by F. Meddens, K. Willis, Colin McEwan, and N. Branch, pp. 71–78. Archetype, London.

  2015 The Whole World Is Watching: New Perspectives on Andean Animism. In *The Archaeology of Wak'as: Explorations of the Sacred in the Pre-Columbian Andes*, edited by Tamara Bray, pp. 23–46. University Press of Colorado, Boulder.

  2016a The Living Ones: Miniatures and Animation in the Andes. *Journal of Anthropological Research* 72(4):416–441.

  2016b Stones Who Love Me: Dimensionality, Enclosure, and Petrification in Andean Culture. *Archives de sciences sociales des religions* 174:327–346.

  2017 Ensayo de opinión: Pensamientos de una etnógrafa acerca de la interpretación en la arqueología andina [An ethnographer's thoughts about interpretation in the archaeology of the Andes]. *Mundo de antes* 11:13–68.

Arnold, Denise Y., and Juan de Dios Yapita

  1998 *Río de vellón, río de canto: Cantar a los animales, una poética andina de la creación.* ILCA/Hisbol, La Paz.

Barad, Karen

  2007 *Meeting the Universe Halfway: Quantum Physics and the Entanglement of Matter and Meaning.* Duke University Press, Durham, N.C.

Basso, Keith H.

  1996 *Wisdom Sits in Places: Landscape and Language among the Western Apache.* University of New Mexico Press, Albuquerque.

Bauer, Brian S.

  1992 *The Sacred Landscape of the Inca: The Cusco Ceque System.* University of Texas Press, Austin.

Brady, James E., and Keith M. Prufer (editors)

  2005 *In the Maw of the Earth Monster: Mesoamerican Ritual Cave Use.* University of Texas Press, Austin.

Dean, Carolyn

  2010 *A Culture of Stone: Inka Perspectives on Rock.* Duke University Press, Durham, N.C.

de la Cadena, Marisol

    2015   *Earth Beings: Ecologies of Practice across Andean Worlds*. Duke University Press, Durham, N.C.

Descola, Philippe

  [2005] 2013   *Beyond Nature and Culture*. University of Chicago Press, Chicago. Originally published as *Par-delà nature et culture*. Gallimard, Paris.

Escobar, Arturo

    1999   After Nature: Steps toward an Antiessentialist Political Ecology. *Current Anthropology* 40(1):1–20.

Flores Ochoa, Jorge

    1977   Aspectos mágicos del pastoreo: Enqa, enqaychu, illa y khuya rumi. In *Pastores de puna*, edited by Jorge Flores Ochoa, pp. 11–138. Instituto de Estudios Peruanos, Lima.

Gell, Alfred

    1998   *Art and Agency: An Anthropological Theory*. Oxford University Press, Oxford.

Gose, Peter

    1994   *Deathly Waters and Hungry Mountains: Agrarian Ritual and Class Formation in an Andean Town*. University of Toronto Press, Toronto.

Harris, Oliver J. T., and John Robb

    2010   Multiple Ontologies and the Problem of the Body in History. *American Anthropologist* 114(4):668–679.

Harvey, Penelope

    2001   Landscape and Commerce: Creating Contexts for the Exercise of Power. In *Contested Landscapes: Movement, Exile and Place*, edited by Barbara Bender and Margot Winer, pp. 197–210. Berg, Oxford.

Ingold, Tim

    2000   *The Perception of the Environment: Essays on Livelihood, Dwelling, and Skill*. Routledge, London.

    2011   *Being Alive: Essays on Movement, Knowledge and Description*. Routledge, London.

Kosiba, Steve

    2015   Of Blood and Soil: Tombs, Wak'as, and the Naturalization of Social Difference in the Inka Heartland. In *The Archaeology of Wak'as: Explorations of the Sacred in the Pre-Columbian Andes*, edited by Tamara Bray, pp. 167–212. University Press of Colorado, Boulder.

La Riva, Palmira

    2004   Las representaciones del *anímu* en los Andes de Sur Peruano. *Revista andina* 41:63–88.

Manga Qespi, Atuq Eusebio

    1994   *Pacha*: Un concepto andino de espacio y tiempo. *Revista española de antropología americana* 24:155–189.

Mannheim, Bruce, and Guillermo Salas Carreño

    2015   Wak'a: Entifications of the Andean Sacred. In *The Archaeology of Wak'as: Explorations of the Sacred in the Pre-Columbian Andes*, edited by Tamara Bray, pp. 46–72. University of Colorado Press, Boulder.

Mannheim, Bruce, and Dennis Tedlock

    1995   Introduction. In *The Dialogic Emergence of Culture*, edited by Dennis Tedlock and Bruce Mannheim, pp. 1–33. University of Illinois Press, Urbana.

Mannheim, Bruce, and Krista Van Vleet

    1998   The Dialogics of Southern Peruvian Quechua Narrative. *American Anthropologist* 100(2):309–325.

McEwan, Colin

    2014   Cognising and Marking the Andean Landscape: Radial, Concentric and Hierarchical Perspectives. In *Inca Sacred Space: Landscape, Site and Symbol in the Andes*, edited by F. Meddens, K. Willis, Colin McEwan, and N. Branch, pp. 29–48. Archetype, London.

Momaday, N. Scott

    1976   Native American Attitudes to the Environment. In *Seeing with a Native Eye: Essays on Native American Religion*, edited by Walter Holden Capps, pp. 79–85. Harper and Row, New York.

Morote Best, Efraín

    1988   *Aldeas sumeridas: Cultura popular y sociedad en los Andes*. Centro Bartolomé de las Casas, Cuzco.

Ramírez, Susan Elizabeth

    2005   *To Feed and Be Fed: The Cosmological Basis of Authority and Identity in the Andes.* Stanford University Press, Stanford.

Ricard Lanata, Xavier

    2007   *Ladrones de sombra: El universo religioso de los pastores del Ausangate.* Centro Bartolomé de las Casas, Cuzco.

Robin Azevedo, Valerie

    2008   *Miroirs de l'autre vie: Pratiques rituelles et discours sur les morts dans les Andes de Cuzco (Pérou).* Société d'Ethnologie, Nanterre.

Sahlins, Marshall

    2014   On the Ontological Scheme of *Beyond Nature and Culture. HAU: Journal of Ethnographic Theory* 4(1):281–290.

Salas Carreño, Guillermo

    2016   Places Are Kin: Food, Cohabitation, and Sociality in the Southern Peruvian Andes. *Anthropological Quarterly* 89(3):813–840.

Salomon, Frank

    1991   Introduction. In *The Huarochirí Manuscript*, edited and translated by Frank Salomon and George Urioste, pp. 1–38. University of Texas Press, Austin.

Stengers, Isabel

    2005   A Cosmopolitical Proposal. In *Making Things Public: Atmospheres of Democracy*, edited by B. Latour and P. Weibel, pp. 994–1003. MIT Press, Cambridge, Mass.

Stensrud, Astrid

    2010   Los peregrinos urbanos en Qoyllurit'i y el juego mimético de miniaturas. *Anthropologica* 28:39–65.

Strathern, Marilyn

    2004   *Partial Connections.* Altamira, New York.

Sullivan, Lawrence E.

    1988   *Icanchu's Drum: An Orientation to Meaning in South American Religions.* Macmillan, New York.

Urton, Gary

    1990   *The History of a Myth: Pacariqtambo and the Origin of the Incas.* University of Texas Press, Austin.

Viveiros de Castro, Eduardo

    2004   Perspectival Anthropology and the Method of Controlled Equivocation. *Tipití: Journal of the Society for the Anthropology of Lowland South America* 2(1):3–22.

Vogt, Evon Z.

    1976   *Tortillas for the Gods: A Symbolic Analysis of Zinacanteco Rituals.* Harvard University Press, Cambridge, Mass.

Weismantel, Mary

    1995   Making Kin: Kinship Theory and Zumbagua Adoptions. *American Ethnologist* 22(4):685–704.

  [1988] 1998   *Food, Gender, and Poverty in the Ecuadorian Andes.* Waveland Press, Prospect Heights, Ill.

Zuidema, R. Tom

    1964   *The Ceque System of Cuzco: The Social Organization of the Capital of the Inca.* E. J. Brill, Leiden.

CONTRIBUTORS

Catherine J. Allen (PhD 1978, University of Illinois) is a cultural anthropologist with an abiding interest in the connections—and disconnections—between the Andean present and the Pre-Columbian past. She is professor emerita of anthropology at George Washington University where, from 1978 to 2012, she taught courses on South American cultures, the anthropology of art, symbolic anthropology, and anthropological theory. Among her academic awards are research fellowships with the Guggenheim Foundation, Fulbright Specialist Program, the Sainsbury Centre for Visual Arts, Dumbarton Oaks, and the National Gallery's Center for the Advanced Study of the Visual Arts. She is the author of an ethnography, *The Hold Life Has: Coca and Cultural Identity in an Andean Community* (1998), based on her fieldwork in a Peruvian highland community. A long-standing commitment to humanistic writing led her to coauthor an ethnographic drama, *Condor Qatay: Anthropology in Performance* (1997, with Nathan Garner). Her latest book, *Foxboy: Intimacy and Aesthetics in Andean Stories* (2011), explores parallels between Andean textiles and oral narratives in terms of their compositional strategies. She has recently published several papers exploring ontological orientations expressed in Andean "animistic" practices.

Beth A. Conklin (PhD 1989, University of California, Berkeley and San Francisco) is associate professor and chair at Vanderbilt University. An ethnographer and medical anthropologist, she has worked with the Wari', a Chapakura-speaking population in western Rondônia, Brazil, since the 1980s. She is the author of *Consuming Grief: Compassionate Cannibalism in an Amazonian Society* (2001), as well as of numerous publications on the anthropology of the body, sociality, and emotion; ritual, cosmology, healing, and warfare in historical and comparative perspectives; and ecology, environmentalism, and the politics of indigenous rights.

Thomas B. F. Cummins (PhD 1988, University of California, Los Angeles) is Dumbarton Oaks Professor of the History of Pre-Columbian and Colonial Art in the Department of the History of Art and Architecture, Harvard University. He is the author of *Huellas del pasado: Los sellos de Jama-Coaque* (1996, with Julio Burgos Cabrera and Carlos Mora Hoyos), *Toasts with the Inca: Andean Abstraction and Colonial Images on Quero Vessels* (2002), *The Getty Murúa: Essays on the Making of Martín de Murúa's "Historia General del Piru" J. Paul Getty Museum Ms. XIII 16* (2008), and *Manuscript Cultures of Colonial Mexico and Peru: New Questions and Approaches* (2014). He has also published essays on New World town planning, the early images of the Inca, miraculous images in Colombia, on idolatry and the relationship between visual and alphabetic literacy in the conversion of Indians. His book *Beyond the Lettered City: Visual and Alphabetic Literacy in the New World* (2012, with Joanne Rappaport) was awarded the Katherine Singer Kovacs Prize for an outstanding book published in English or Spanish in the field of Latin American and Spanish literatures and cultures, awarded by the Modern Language Association, 2014, and the Bryce Wood Book Award to the outstanding book on Latin America in the social sciences and humanities published in English, awarded by the Latin American Studies Association, 2013.

Marco Curatola Petrocchi (PhD 1991, University of Genoa) is professor of history and director of the Andean Studies Program at the Pontificia Universidad Católica del Perú (PUCP), Lima. He is the director of the Andean Studies Series of the PUCP Press. He has been curator of South American Archaeology and Ethnology at the National Prehistoric and Ethnographic Museum, Rome; visiting scholar at the Center of Latin American Studies, University of Cambridge; fellow in Pre-Columbian Studies at Dumbarton Oaks; and Tinker Visiting Professor in Anthropology at the Center for Latin American Studies, University of Chicago. As a specialist in the history of Andean culture, he has focused his interests on native religion in prehispanic and colonial times. He has published the books *Il giardino d'oro del dio Sole: Dei, culti e messia delle Ande* (1997), *Adivinación y oráculos en el mundo andino antiguo* (2008, with Mariusz Ziólkowski), *El quipu colonial* (2013, with José Carlos de la Puente), *El Inca y la huaca: El poder de la religión y la religión del poder en el mundo andino antiguo* (2016, with Jan Szemiński), and *El estudio del mundo andino* (2019).

Diana DiPaolo Loren (PhD 1999, SUNY Binghamton) is director of Academic Partnerships and museum curator of North American Archaeology at the Peabody Museum of Archaeology and Ethnology, Harvard University. Loren specializes in the colonial-period southeast and northeast, with a focus on the body, health, dress, and adornment. She is the author of *In Contact: Bodies and Spaces in the sixteenth- and seventeenth-century Eastern Woodlands* (2007) and *The Archaeology of Clothing and Bodily Adornment in Colonial America* (2010). Since 2005, she has been codirector of the Harvard Yard Archaeology Project, which examines the lives of Native American and English students at Puritan Harvard College.

Carlos Fausto (PhD 1997, Universidade Federal do Rio de Janeiro) is professor of anthropology at the National Museum, Federal University of Rio de Janeiro, and senior researcher at the National Council for the Development of Science and Technology (CNPq). He is the author of *Os índios antes do Brasil* (2000), *Inimigos fiéis: História, Guerra e xamanismo na Amazônia* (2001) *Warfare and Shamanism in Amazonia* (2012), and *Art Effects: Image, Agency, and Ritual in Indigenous Amazonia* (in press). He coedited, among others, *Time and Memory in Indigenous Amazonia* (2007) and *Ownership and Nurture: Studies in Native Amazonian Property Relations* (2016).

Santiago Giraldo (PhD 2010, University of Chicago) is the director for Latin America Studies at the Fundación ProSierra Nevada de Santa Marta and for Latin America at the Global Heritage Fund; he previously worked for the Colombian Institute of Anthropology and History as a research archaeologist and as the director-in-charge of Teyuna Ciudad Perdida Archaeological Park. He is the author of the Teyuna-Ciudad Perdida Archaeological Park Guidebook, as well as other publications on the Tairona and the history of archaeology in the Sierra Nevada de Santa Marta. He has conducted archaeological research and fieldwork on the Tairona, as well as ethnographic fieldwork among the Kogi, Wiwa, and Arhuaco indigenous peoples.

Byron Ellsworth Hamann (PhD 2011, University of Chicago) is Hanna Kiel Fellow at I Tatti, The Harvard University Center for Italian Renaissance Studies in Florence. His research focuses on the art and writing of pre-Hispanic Mesoamerica, as well as on the connections linking the Americas and Europe in the early modern Mediterratlantic world.

He is an editor of *Grey Room* (www.greyroom .org); codirector (with Liza Bakewell) of *Mesolore: Exploring Mesoamerican Culture* (www.meso-lore.org); project manager (for Dana Leibsohn and Barbara Mundy) of *Vistas: Visual Culture in Spanish America, 1520–1820* (http://vistas-visual-culture.net); and author of *The Translations of Nebrija: Language, Culture, and Circulation in the Early Modern World* (2015) and *Bad Christians, New Spains: Muslims, Catholics, and Native Americans in a Mediterratlantic World* (2020).

Scott Hutson (PhD 2004, University of California, Berkeley) teaches archaeology at the University of Kentucky. After eight seasons of fieldwork at the ruin of Chunchucmil and two seasons of fieldwork at Yaxuna, he now directs the Uci-Cansahcab Regional Integration Project (UCRIP), located in Yucatan, Mexico. He has published on urbanism, household archaeology, commerce, settlement patterns, and other subjects.

John Wayne Janusek (PhD 1994, University of Chicago) was an associate professor of anthropology at Vanderbilt University. He worked in the Bolivian highlands throughout his career, conducting research on Tiwanaku and its formative precursors. In 2000–2010, he directed a large-scale research project at the sites of Khonkho Wankane and Iruhito in the southern Lake Titicaca Basin; he codirected a transdisciplinary project in the eastern Lake Titicaca basin and Andean valleys. His books include *Identity and Power in the Ancient Andes* (2004), *Ancient Tiwanaku* (2008), and *Archaeological Research at Khonkho Wankane, Bolivia* (2018).

Arthur A. Joyce (PhD 1991, Rutgers University) is a professor at the University of Colorado, Boulder. Since 1986, he has conducted interdisciplinary archaeological research in Oaxaca on issues of political dynamics, religion, materiality, landscape, and ecology. He is the author of *Mixtecs, Zapotecs, and Chatinos: Ancient Peoples of Southern Mexico* (2010) and *El Pueblo de la Tierra del Cielo: Arqueología de la mixteca de la Costa* (2014, with Jamie Forde), as well as the editor of *Polity and Ecology in Formative*

Period Coastal Oaxaca (2013). He has held research fellowships from the American Museum of Natural History, Fulbright Foundation, Dumbarton Oaks, and the American Council of Learned Societies.

Barry Kidder (PhD 2019, University of Kentucky) completed three field seasons with the Uci-Cansahcab Regional Integration Project (UCRIP); he has also conducted research in Quintana Roo and Belize.

Steve Kosiba (PhD 2010, University of Chicago) is an assistant professor in the Department of Anthropology at the University of Minnesota. As an archaeologist and historical anthropologist, he focuses on the practices that constituted social authority and positioned both people and things as political subjects in the ancient and early modern world, with a particular focus on the Andes under the Inca and Spanish empires. He is the author of multiple publications on politics, ecology, and identity in imperial Cuzco. He has also authored essays that address general theories regarding how people constituted social value in the precapitalist world and how material things contributed to political action in both ancient and modern contexts. His book *Becoming Inca: Landscape Construction and Subject Creation in Ancient Cuzco* details the processes by which the Incas founded and consolidated their imperial capital of Cuzco. He is now conducting two research projects in the Inca capital. One project investigates the rites by which people became Inca warriors at the shrine of Huanacauri; the other project examines the practices by which forcibly resettled workers formed communities at the Inca and Spanish labor colony of Rumiqolqa.

Bruce Mannheim (PhD 1983, University of Chicago) is professor of anthropology at the University of Michigan. A linguistic anthropologist, he studies the interrelations among language, culture, and history, particularly in Andean South America. His works span from a linguistic history of the Quechua language since the sixteenth century and its shifting social ecology, to narrative, ritual practices around places, and ontology. His publications span the disciplines of anthropology, linguistics, and colonial Latin American history, and include collaborations in psychology and history of art.

Patricia A. McAnany (PhD 1986, University of New Mexico) is Kenan Eminent Professor and Chair of Anthropology at the University of North Carolina–Chapel Hill and chair of the senior fellows of the Pre-Columbian Studies program at Dumbarton Oaks in Washington, D.C. She has been the recipient of research awards from the National Science Foundation and the Archaeological Institute of America, and of fellowships from the Guggenheim Foundation, the John Carter Brown Library, the National Endowment for the Humanities, the Radcliffe Center for Advanced Study at Harvard University, Dumbarton Oaks, and the Institute for the Arts and Humanities at the University of North Carolina–Chapel Hill. A Maya archaeologist, she is principal coinvestigator of Proyecto Arqueológico Colaborativo del Oriente de Yucatán, a community archaeology project focused on the Preclassic through colonial community of Tahcabo, Yucatan. As executive director of *InHerit: Indigenous Heritage Passed to Present* (www.in-herit.org), she works with local communities throughout the Maya region to provide opportunities to dialogue about cultural heritage and to participate in heritage conservation. She is the author and coeditor of many publications, including *Maya Cultural Heritage: How Archaeologists and Indigenous Communities Engage the Past* (2016), *Ancestral Maya Economies in Archaeological Perspective* (2010), *Questioning Collapse: Human Resilience, Ecological Vulnerability, and the Aftermath of Empire* (2010, with Norman Yoffee), and *Living with the Ancestors: Kinship and Kingship in Ancient Maya Society* (2014, revised edition).

Shannon Plank (PhD 2003, Boston University) is a lecturer in the Department of Anthropology at the University of Kentucky. She specializes in Maya glyphs and ceramics.

Mary Weismantel (PhD 1986, University of Illinois, Urbana-Champaign) is professor and chair of the Department of Anthropology at Northwestern University, as well as an adjunct curator at the Field Museum of Natural History. She has published articles on "slow seeing" at the site of Chavín de Huantar, on sexual themes in Moche ceramics, as well as on the Neolithic site of Çatalhöyük in Turkey. She is currently completing a monograph on Moche ceramics for the University of Texas Press. Additionally, she is the author of two books on her ethnographic work, *Food, Gender, and Poverty in the Ecuadorian Andes* (1989) and the award-winning *Cholas and Pishtacos: Tales of Race and Sex in the Andes* (2001). She has also published numerous articles based on her ethnographic fieldwork, notably "Making Kin: Kinship Theory and Zumbagua Adoptions."

Jacob Welch is a graduate student in the anthropology department at Yale University and has worked with Uci-Cansahcab Regional Integration Project (UCRIP) since 2011. He has also done fieldwork in the Copan River Valley in Honduras.

INDEX

Page numbers in *italics* indicate illustrations. Titles of works will normally be found under the name of the author.

A

Abercrombie, Tom, 432, 434n1

aburu, 402, 413, *416*

Acanceh, 309

Achuar, 11

acllacuna, 268, 270, 292n2

Acosta, José de, 181, 184; *Historia natural y moral de las Indias* (1590), 289–291

actor network theory, 360

Acuytapia, 268, 275, 284

ADE (Amazonian dark earth; *terra preta de índio*), 115–116, 124, 125n5

affective assemblages, 116–117

affordance, 389n3

Agamben, Giorgio, 16, 21n19

agency, 373, 384–386, 427–428

Agüero, Diego de, 277

Akapana *chachapuma,* Tiwanaku, 249, *250*

Alberti, Benjamin, 401

Allen, Catherine J., x, 4, 10, 18, 113, 134, 182, 229n7, 269, 270, 378, 421, 433, 439

allocentric versus egocentric frames of reference, 373, 377–380, 383, 384, 390n13, 390n16, 424

alqa, 421

Althusser, Louis, 21n19

Altitudo divini concilii (papal bull), 151

aluna, 402, 405, 406, 410, *411*, 418n15

Aluna (documentary film), 399–401

alunashiguaishi, 408–409

Amaru Marcahuasi, 276–277

Amaru Tupa, 276

Amatlan, 77, *79,* 81

Amazonian dark earth (ADE; *terra preta de índio*), 115–116, 124, 125n5

Amazonian perspectivism as model for Amerindian animism, 11–13, 20–21n16

amoxtli, 143

amulets, 363, 364–365, *366*

analogism, 20n15, 65n49, 158n4, 229n7, 242, 372, 387, 426–427, 429

Ancash Quechua, 378

don Andrés of Culhuacan, 139–140

Angrand Monolith, Tiwanaku, 250, *251*

animacy and authority in the Americas, 1–18, 421–433; agency and animism, 385; animism and Western/colonial assumptions about nature, x, 2, 4–7, 11; anthropology and ethnology, development of, x, 6–9; approaches to, 17–18; consciousness and natural reality, raising questions about relationship between, ix–xi; definitions of animacy and authority, 3, 14–17, 19n3, 213, 229n7; divergent models within cultures and social strata, 3, 19n4; ecoregime, concept of, 428–429; equivocation, progressing through, 423–426; food and feeding, importance of, 429–431 (*See also* food, feeding, and biosocial activity); health and spirituality, 357–367 (*See also* health and spirituality northeastern New Spain); of houses, 423, 425–246, 427–428 (*See also* houses); journey as metaphor for, 421–422; landscape and, 431–433; literal, nonmetaphorical nature of, 426, 429; misrecognition of nature, animacy/animism regarded as, 6–7, 301; monoliths and scaled monolithic embodiments, 431 (*See also* Lanzón, Chavín de Huantar; Tiwanaku; *specific named monolithic structures*); multiple pathways through, 426–427; ontological approach to, 10–13, 20nn14–15, 73, 133, 327–328, 371–372, 424 (*See also* ontologies); political questions raised by, 3–4, 13–17; power versus authority, 14, 19n3; radical alterity of animist viewpoint, 301–303; relationship between, 433; sonic-aural dimension of, 267–292 (*See also* sonic-aural dimension of Andean sacred spaces); Thupa Amaru, execution of, ix, 1–3, 6, 13, 19n6; visual

Catequil, 286

Catholicism: All Saints' Day and Day of the Dead, integration with, *79*; conversion rates in northeastern New Spain, *357*; Descartes' *Discourse on Method* and, 157; healing, relationship to, 357, 361; houses, animacy of, 425–426, 434n4; Maya rejuvenation of souls and, *94, 95,* 95–96; *nagualismo* as indigenous tradition opposing spread of, 13, 21n18; Nicene Creed, Quechua translation of, 202n24; Protestant Reformation and, 15–16, 153–155, 160–161n32, 301; rationality of Indians and fitness to receive Communion, 131, 149–153; small bodily objects (medals, crucifixes, and rosaries), 363, 364; transitional *keros* with Christian crosses, *176*; transubstantive concepts, visual representation of, 172–181, *173, 174, 175, 177, 179,* 426; Wari' funerary cannibalism, government/missionary halting of previous practice of, 105–106, *106*

causal structures in southern Quechua ontology, 373, 387

caves, serpents, and soul loss, *77, 78*

Cepek, Michael, 399

ceque system, Cuzco, 270, 276, 428, 429

cercacdos/cercados, 190, 192, 193

Cerro Churo, 261n2

Cerro de la Cruz, 343, *346,* 352

Cerro de la Virgen, 340–343, *342–343, 345, 347,* 350, 352

Cerro Jazmín, 350

Certeau, Michelle de, 201n20

Chachabamba, 271–275, *271–275,* 285, 291, 292nn10–11

chachapumas, 222, 228, 239, *248,* 248–252, *250, 253, 254, 256, 257,* 259–260, 261n3

Chalcatzingo, 9

Chan, Juan B., 96

Chanca, 276

charismatic authority, 21n21

Charles V (Holy Roman Emperor), 148, 153, 289

Chase, Diane, and Arlen Chase, 96

Chatino, 329, 331, 340

Chaumeil, Jean-Pierre, 118

Chaupi Ñamca, 257

Chavín de Huantar: as ecoregime, 429; Obelisk Tello, 213, 223; as pilgrimage site, 422; religion at, 7; site of, 211, *212*–213, *216,* 221; sonic-aural dimension of, 271, 286, 291, 292n13; Stela Raimundi, 213; visual imagery at, 192, 200n5. See also Lanzón, Chavín de Huantar

chicha, 113, 115, 196, 239, 242, 257, 260, 270

Chichen Itza, 305, 309, 312, 315, 317

chiefly status in Upper Xingu. See Upper Xingu

Chimaltenango, 305, 306

Chiminigagua, 186

Chimú pectoral, Dumbarton Oaks, 182

Chinchaysuyu, 268

Chinchilla Mazariego, Oswaldo, 95

Chorti, 316

Christianity: descent into darkness and emergence into light in, 186; *huacas* and Andeans revolting against, 20n2. See also Catholicism; Protestant Reformation

Chronicle of Calkini, 309

ch'ulel, 8, 9, 20nn10–11, 74–75, 77–78, 303, 329, 332

Chunhuayum, 306

Chuquillanto, 268, *269,* 270, 274–275, 284

Chuspiyoq, *276,* 277–285, *278, 280–284,* 291, 293n15

Cieza de León, Pedro de, 200n10

Classen, Constance, *Worlds of Sense,* 267

Cobo, Bernabé, 275; *Historia del Nuevo Mundo* (1653), 275

coca leaves, 110, *404,* 413, 417n10, 421, 427, 429–431, 433

codices: *Codex Aubin,* 134, 143, *144; Codex Badianus,* 145; *Codex Boturini,* 131, 134–137, *135, 136,* 140, 143–148, *144, 145, 146, 148,* 158n7, 430, 431, 432; *Florentine Codex, 77,* 140, 146; *Codex Mendoza,* 181; *Codex Vienna,* 144–145; *Codex Y,* 143

coessences, 9, 97

Colca Valley, 384

Collasuyu, 268

Columbus, Claudette, "Soundscapes in Andean Context," 267

Communion, rationality of Indians and fitness to receive, 131, 149–153

Comte, Auguste, 6

concept versus percept, x

Condenados, 427

Conklin, Beth A., 17, 18, 62n1, 64n31, 81, 99, 105, 439

Contisuyu, 268

Contreras, Daniel A., 226, 230n12

Copacabana, Virgin of, 235

Copan, 79, 87–90, *90, 91,* 96, 309, 312

Corbin, Jim, 360

Coricancha, 271, 290

corporate personhood, 169

Cortés, Hernán, 138

coscojos, 365

cosmopolitics and cosmopolitical order, 43, 63n11, 233, 256, 257, 402, 403, 417n7, 429, 434n7

Covarrubias, Sebastian de, 152

Cozumel, oracle of, 5–6

cross, representations of, 178–180, *179*

crucifixes, 363, 364, 367

Cuchavia, 186

Cuello, 316

Culhuacan, 133–137, *139,* 143, 158n8

Cummins, Thomas B. F., 17, 18, 63n23, 75, 134, 169, 202n24, 242, 426, 432, 439–440

curandería, 358, 362–363, 365–367

Curatola Petrocchi, Marco, 14, 17, 18, 134, 224, 226, 229n7, 267, 432, 440

el Cusqueño. See Molina, Cristóbal de

Cuzco: *amaru* and jaguar cave carvings, *185,* 185–186; *ceque* system of, 270, 276, 428, 429; Coricancha, 271, 290; Painted Temple, 291; shrines of, 421, 430; sonic-aural dimension of Andean sacred spaces and, 269–271, 275–276, 281, 290, 291; Sonqo and, 434n2; southern Quechua ontology and, 374, *376, 377,* 380, 381, *382,* 384, 390n19, 390n20; Thupa Amaru, execution of, 1, 2; Tiwanaku compared, 234, 242, 257

Gow, Peter, 126n7

Graeber, David, 20n10, 302, 319, 399, 402, 406–408

grammatical analysis of southern Quechua ontology. *See* southern Quechua ontology

Gregory, Hiram, 365

Gregory, Pete, 360

Gregory I the Great (saint and pope), featherwork mosaic of Mass of (1539), 131, 149–154, *150*, 159n20, 178

Grove, David, 9

Grube, Nikolai, 97

Guadelupe, Virgin of, 227

Guaman Poma de Ayala, Felipe, *El primer nueva corónica y buen gobierno* (1615), 268, 283, *285*, 373–374, *374*, 380

Guattari, Félix, 20n14, 117, 318

Gudemos, Mónica, 267, 270

Guedes, Marcelino, 123

Guerreiro, Antonio, 64n29

Guevara, Antonio de, *Book Called Clock of Princes* (1528), 152

Guss, David, 201n20

H

Haber, Alejandro, 302

Hallam, Elizabeth, 121

Hallowell, A. Irving, 10–11, 134, 260, 318, 372

Hamann, Byron Ellsworth, 17, 18, 131, 175, 426, 430, 431, 432, 440–441

Hanks, William, 317

Harris, Oliver, 360, 424

Harrison-Buck, Eleanor, 327

Harvey, Graham, 299

Harvey, Penelope, 429

hasina, 20n10

health and spirituality in northeastern New Spain (western Louisiana/eastern Texas), 357–367; Catholicism and healing, association between, 357, 361, 362–363; diseases impacting New Spain, 362; early eighteenth-century New Spain, 358–360, *359;* folk medicine *(curandería),* 358, 362–363, 365–367; humoral theory of medicine, 361–362; map, *359;* materiality, animacy, and the colonial body, 360–363; Native American healing practices, 357–358, 362; ontological ambivalence at intersection of magic, medicine, and religion, 358, 360–361, 367; small bodily objects associated with, 361, 363–365, *366,* 431

Hecht, Suzanna, 121

Heckenberger, Michael J., 62n5, 115

heisei, 405, 406

Heizer, Robert, 316

Henare, Amira, 302

Hendon, Julia, 81

Hermes Trismegistus, *Logos telios (Perfect Discourse),* 180

Hershey, 79

Hertz, Robert, 71

Heywood, Paolo, 133

higas, 364–365, *366*

Hill, Jonathan, 126n7

Hockey, Jenny, 121

Hofling, Charles, 77

Holbraad, Martin, 302, 399, 401

Hopewell mortuary practices, 79

Hornborg, Alf, 74

house society/*société a maison,* 378–380, 390nn19–20

houses: animacy of, 423, 425–426, 427–428, 434n4; ensoulment of, 305–306, 423, 427; Maya house dedication, 4; Upper Xingu *kuakutu* (flute's or men's house), 47; Upper Xingu *tajühe* (chiefly house), 47–49, *48,* 423

Houston, Stephen, 9, 73, 79, 81, 97, 302, 313

Huacaloma, 286

huacas: Christianity, revolt against, 20n12; as deity-shrines, 270; as epiphenomena, 199–200n2; *kamay,* as manifestation of, 182; as presence of the divine, 178. *See also* sonic-aural dimension of Andean sacred spaces

Huamelulpan, 350

Huanaco Pampa, 173–174

Huanitzin, don Diego de Alvarado, 149–150, 152, 153

Huánuco Pampa, 384

Huaorani, 127n7

Huari, 234

Huarochirí Manuscript, 169, 175, 184, 257, 259, 269–270

Huchuy Qosqo, 271

Huitzilopochtli's bundle, 131, 133–138, 140, 143, 146–149, 153, 158n8, 421, 422, 431, 432

Hull, Kerry, 305

Hume, David, 19n8

humoral theory of medicine, 361–362

hunting shrines, Lake Atitlan area, 78

Hutson, Scott R., 17, 18, 81, 299, 329, 364, 422, 423, 430, 441

Hvidtfeldt, Arild, 9

I

idolatry, Western/colonial concept of, ix, 2, 5–6, 19n7, 149, 153, 172, 176, 180, 187, 189, 200n8, 203n40, 270, 287, 363

iglesias de plumerías, 189–190

ihiyotl, 8, 329

implicature, 376, 390n12

Inca Huayna Capac, 286

Inca Viracocha, 276

Inca Yupanqui (Pachacuti), 275–277, 281, 284

Incallacta, 277, 279

Ingold, Tim, 74, 108, 116, 134, 318

Inka: *chicha* offering practices of, 242–243; descent into darkness and emergence into light for, 186, 187; on divine beings moving amongst living and dead, 182, 185–186; political understanding of animacy and, 13, 14; Thupa Amaru, execution of, 1–3, 6, 13; transubstantive concepts, visual representation of, 172–181, *173, 174, 175, 177, 179,* 201n14. *See* sonic-aural dimension of Andean sacred spaces; *specific sites*

Innocent X (pope), 155

Inomata, Takeshi, 16

inqaychus, 431

interactional lamination, 376, 390n12

Inti, 182

Intiwatana, 271

Machu Picchu, 271, *273*, *375*, 389n10
Makuna, 12
mal de ojo (evil eye), 358, 362, 365
Mam Maya, 76, 318
mamas. See Sierra Nevada de Santa Marta
mana, Polynesian concept of, 4, 6–7, 10, 17, 20n10, 21n21
Manco Capac, 182, *183*
mangrove, in Jama Coaque culture, *195–198, 196–197*
Mannheim, Bruce, 7, 17, 18, 94, 170, 199, 202n24, 371, 389n2, 390n18, 424, 425, 432, 441–442; *The Dialogical Emergence of Culture* (with Dennis Tedlock), 424
manuscripts: Cambridge, Mass., Harvard University, Houghton Library, MSTyp184 *Institución de la regla y hermandad de la cofradía del Sanctissimo Sacramento* (1502), *177*, 177–178, *179*; Galvin Manuscript (Martín de Murúa, *Historia del origen y genealogia real de los reyes del Piru,* ca. 1590), 182–184, *184*, 268, *269*, 270, 284, 292n5; Glasgow, University of Glasgow, Sp Coll MS Hunter 242, *Descripción de la provincia y ciudad de Tlaxcala,* 178, *179*, 180; *Huarochirí Manuscript,* 169, 175, 184, 257, 259, 269–270; Los Angeles, Getty Museum, Ms. Ludwig XIII 16, Murúa, Martín de, *Historia general de Piru* (1615), 182, *183. See also* codices
Maras, 377
Marcus Joyce, 332, 338
Marx, Karl, 6, 21n20, 199, 201n20; *Capital,* 169
mat motif, 309–310, *310,* 312, 313, 316, 317, 430
material artifacts, animacy and authority of. *See* animacy and authority in the Americas
Matipu, 41
Mattox, Christopher Wesley, 251
Mattox Monolith, Tiwanaku, 251, *253*
Maukallaqta (Pacarictambo), 281, 284
Mauss, Marcel, 242, 249
Maya: *ch'ulel,* 8, 9, 20nn10–11, 74–75, 77–78, 303, 329, 332; Cozumel, oracle of, 5–6; descent into darkness and emergence into light for, 186, *187*; god-pots (*u-läk-il k'uh*), 9; house dedication, 4; life/personhood, concepts of, 303–306; *naguals,* 9, 13; political understanding of animacy and, 14, 201n20; portrait statues, defacement of, 9. *See also specific Mayan groups, e.g., Tzotzil Maya; specific sites*
Maya ontologies of soul, 71–100; access to spiritual entities, ensuring, 79, 96, 96–97; All Saints' Day and Day of the Dead, integration with, 79; breath soul, 81, *84, 85,* 96; *ch'ulel,* 74–75, 77–78; deep time, managing spiritual entities in, 75, 79; ensoulment processes, 74–79, *75–78*; funerary practices, importance of, 76–77, *77,* 81, 99; *k'uh, 72,* 73–74, 96, 303; life/personhood, concepts of, 304, *305*; management of errant vital forces, 77, *78,* 79, 87, 97–98, *98*; map of sites, *80*; proprietary concerns, 98–99; protecting and nourishing souls, 79, 81–90, *82–86, 88–93*; rejuvenation of souls, promoting, 76–77, 79, *94,* 94–96, *95*; soul, concept of, 73–74; soul loss, 77, *78*; Wari' and Kuikuro compared to, 99

Mayo Chinchipe–Marañón spiral temples, 192
McAnany, Patricia A., 9, 17, 18, 71, 109, 157, 318, 331, 442
McCord, Robert, 79
McEwan, Colin, xi
McKenzie, Yaya, 379
medals, religious, 363, 364, 367
medicine. *See* health and spirituality in northeastern New Spain
Mehinaku, 41
Meira, Sergio, 65n41, 378
Meléndez, Juan, 187, 188
Melly, Alfredo, 286
Mendoza, Antonio de, 149
Codex Mendoza, 181
Menezes Bastos, Rafael José de, 42
Merleau-Ponty, Maurice, 21n17
Mexica, 133–136, 143, 146, 147, 201n17, 202n22, 422, 431, 432
Mexico City, 134, 135, 137, 143, 149, 152, 153, 357, 359
Miller, Virginia, 310
Mission Dolores (Nuestra Señora de Los Dolores de Los Ais), 358, 359–360, 364, 365, 367
Mission San Miguel (San Miguel de Linares de Los Adaes), 358, 359, 363
Mitla, Oaxaca, 317
Mixe, 329
Mixtecs, 340
Moche: authority and, 16; "revolt of the objects," 21n17, 175, 427; temples as serpents, 224; visual imagery of animacy and authority of, 175, 176, 181, 194, 199n2, 201n20; whistling serpent vessels, 287, *288,* 289, 291
Moctezuma, 138, 139, 148, 149, 158n8
Moguer, Pedro Martín de, 277
mojos (sacrificed children, in Muisca tradition), 189
Mol, Annemarie, 360–361
Molina, Alonso de, 140
Molina, Cristóbal de (el Cusqueno), 20n12, 275–276, 289–290; *Fábulas y ritos de los Incas* (1574), 276
Molina-Wong, Sam, 216, 227, 228
Momaday, Scott, 422
Monaghan, John, 327, 330, 351
Mondloch, James, 74–75
monoliths, 431. *See also* Lanzón; Tiwanaku; *specific named monolithic structures*
Montaigne, Michel de, 6, 155, 157n1
Monte Albán, 332–337, *334–337,* 339–340, *340–341,* 351–352, 428
Monte Grande, 192
Monte Negro, 350
Moore, Jeremy, 267
Morfí, Juan Agustín, 363
Motul de San José, 79, 97
movement, animation through, 134–138, *411*
Muisca, 170, 186–189, *188, 189,* 192–194, 199, 202–203nn33–34
Munn, Nancy, 255
Murphie, Andrew, 117

Murúa, Martín de: *Historia del origen y genealogia real de los reyes del Piru* (ca. 1590; Galvin Manuscript), 182–184, *184, 268, 269,* 270, 284, 292n5; *Historia general de Piru* (1613), 182, *183,* 268
music/sound and ritual, 201n20. *See also* sonic-aural dimension of Andean sacred spaces
Muslims and Islam, 152, 223
Mutuá Mehinaku, 65n40

N

naguals and *nagualismo,* 9, 13, 21n18, 330
Nahm, Werner, 97
Nahua, 74, 76–77, 81, 138, 140, 172, 181, 201n17, 202n21, 431
Nahuatl, 8, 140, 143, 172
Nahukwá, 41
naturalism and naturalists, 11, 20n15, 158n4, 161n34, 372, 373, 387, 404
Nazca, 286, 291
nebbi, 405
Neurath, Johannes, 73
Neves, Eduardo, 110, 115
New Archaeology, 170, 182
New Fire ceremony, 143–144, *145*
New Materialism, 99–100, 318, 319, 360
Nieves Zedeño, María, 329
Noboa, Bernardo de, 270
northeastern New Spain (western Louisiana/eastern Texas). *See* health and spirituality in northeastern New Spain
Novotny, Anna, 79
Ñudzavui, 145, 175
nuizhi, 411
Nuyoo, 351

O

Oaxaca, animating public buildings in, 327–352; class/status and, 351, 352; feeding and nurturing animated buildings, 330, 331, 340, 341–343; Formative period, focus on, 328; initial animation, 330, 331; in lower Río Verde Valley, 340–350, *342–49,* 351, 352; map, *328;* Mesoamerica, animating practices in, 329–332; in Mixteca, 328, 350, 351; political power, public buildings as sources of, 351–352; termination practices, 331–332, *347, 349,* 350; in Valley of Oaxaca, 332–340, *333–338, 340–341,* 350, 351–352; variability of practices, 328, 332, 350–351
Obelisk Tello, Chavín, 213, 223
Ocampo Conejeros, Baltasar de, 19n1
och k'ahk' (fire-entry) ritual, 85–87, 97
offerings. *See* sacrifices and offerings
Ojibwe (Anishaabe), 10–11, 13, 318
Oliver, José, *Caciques and Cemí Idols* (2009), ix–x
Olsen, Bjørnar, 100
Ondegardo, Polo de, *Relación de los adoratorios huacas del Cuzco* (1559), 276, 289
One Punch Man (Japanese animated television series), 228
O'Neil, Megan, 90

ontological approach, 10–13, 20nn14–15, 73, 133, 327–328, 371–372, 424
ontologies, 131–157, 424, 425; Cartesianism dualism and, xi, 11, 131, 154–157; *Codex Boturini,* ontology of, 131, 134–137, *135, 136,* 140, 143–148, *144, 145, 146, 148,* 158n7, 430, 431, 432; drowning of captive Spaniards by Indians to test their immortality, 131–133, *132;* of featherwork mosaic of Mass of Saint Gregory (1539), 131, 149–154, *150,* 159n20, 178; Huitzilopochtli's bundle, travels of, 131, 133–138, 140, 143, 146–149, 153, 158n8, 421, 422, 431, 432; movement, animation through, 134–138; northeastern New Spain, ontological ambivalence at intersection of magic, medicine, and religion in, 358, 360–361, 367; Portestant Reformation and Eucharistic Sacrament, 153–155, 160–161n32; pulque, origins of, 145–147, *148,* 431; rationality of Indians, papal bulls declaring, 131, 149–153; of Tiwanaku, 257–259; *tlacamecayotl* (genealogical connections) and, 138–143, *139, 141, 142. See also* Maya ontologies of soul; southern Quechua ontology
Orrantia, Juan, 415
Orsi, Robert, *History and Presence,* 211, 228
Ortiz, Diego, 19n6
Oviedo, Fernández de, 189
Oviedo, Gabriel de, 19n1
Oviedo y Valdés, Gonzalo Fernández de, *La historia general de las Indias* (1535), 157n3
Oxkutzcab, 317
Oyuela-Caycedo, Auguste, 401

P

Pacarictambo (Maukallaqta), 281, 284
pacha, 181–182, 186, 202n26, 427
Pachacamac, 5, 184, 192, 224, 226, 227, 255, 281, 289–291, *290,* 413
Pachacuti (Inca Yupanqui), 275–277, 281, 284
Pachakama Monolith, Tiwanaku, 244–245, *246,* 248, 250, 259
Pachayachachic (Viracocha-Pachacamac), 290
Paititi, 432
Paiva, Paulo, 123
Pakal 1 (K'inich Janaab' Pakal) of Palenque, 95, 96
Pakal Na, 79, 85–87, *86, 88, 89,* 96, 97
Palenque, 79, 94, 95, 96, 309
Panofsky, Erwin, 201n13
paqu, 427
Parakanã, 37, 62n2
Pariacaca, 257, 269
parrots and tropical birds, 188–190, 192, *193, 194*
Pauketat, Tim, 20n14, 329
Paul III (pope), 133, 149–153, 159n20, 160n23
Pauw, Cornelis de, *Philosophical Researches on the Americans* (1768), 150–151
Pensacola, 364
percept versus concept, x
Pérez de Perceval, José María, 152
perspectivism, Amazonian, 11–13, 20–21n16
Peter Lombard, 152
pets and pet-keeping, 43, 63n10

Piedras Negras, 79, 94; Stela 40, *96*, 96–97
Pitarch, Pedro, 74–76
Pizarro, Francisco, *Relación para Su Magestad* (1534), 277
Pizarro, Pedro, 14
Plank, Shannon, 299, 311–312, 442
Plato and Platonism, 15, 275
Plazas, Clemencia, 401
Ponce, Carlos, 239
Ponce Monolith, Tiwanaku, *238, 239*, 240–241, *242, 243*, 248, 250, 260
popol nah, 309, 310
Popol Vuh, 21n17, 309, 310
poporo, 402, 417n10
portrait statues, defacement of, 9
Posey, Darryl, 115, 121
Posnansky, Arthur, 248, 249
potlatch, 113
power versus authority, 14, 19n3
Prechtel, Martin, 74, 76
Presidio Los Adaes, 358, 359–360, 364, 365–367
presupposition, 376, 390nn11–12
"Primitivism," Western concept of, 199n1, 301
properties of the world in southern Quechua ontology, 373–377, *374–376*
Protestant Reformation, 15–16, 153–155, 160–161n32, 301
Proulx, Donald, 286
Pucapucara, 276–277
Pueblito Archaeological Site, *408, 412*
pulque, origins of, 145–147, *148*, 431
Puma Urqu, 186
Pumapunku Monolith, Tiwanaku, 239, 240, 241, 261n1
Punchao, 1–2
Punchao (Young Sun), 290
Putuni Monolith, Tiwanaku, 250, *251*

Q

Q'eqchi' Maya, 77, 78, 304, 318
Qoyllur Rit'i, 10
Quechua: *alqa*, 421; *cama/camay/camaquen*, 8, 19n10; *Huarochiri Manuscript*, 169, 175, 184, 257, 259, 269–270; Maya soul rejuvenation compared, 94; Nicene Creed, Quechua translation of, 202n24; *pacha*, 427; woven objects for, 187. *See also* southern Quechua ontology
Quesada, J(X)imenez de, 202n28
quetzallalpiloni, 181
Quíchua, 42
Quine, W. V. O., 389n5
Quintana Roo, 318
Quinuapuquio, 276
quipus, 275, 380, 381
q'uncha, 425, 433

R

Radin, Paul, 7, 12
Rain God, 339, 350, 351
Ramirez, Henri, 124
Ramírez, Susan, *To Feed and Be Fed*, 431

Ramos Gavilán, Alonso, *Historia del célebre santuario de Nuestra Señora de Copacabana* (1621), 290
ranti, 384
Rappaport, Roy, 116
rationality of Indians, papal bulls declaring, 131, 149–153
reciprocal appropriation, 422
Redfield, Robert
Reichel-Dolmatoff, Gerardo, 401, 409
relational typologies, 372, 390n16
religion, critiques of, 201n20
repaired objects, 200n5
representation, as term, 371–372
"revolt of the objects," 21n17, 175, 427
Ricard Lanata, Xavier, 270, 435n9
Rimay Puquio, 270
Río Viejo, 340, 345, 347–349, *348, 349*, 352
Rival, Laura, 126n7
Rob, John, 360, 424
Rodríguez, Daniel, 410
Roman Catholicism. *See* Catholicism
Rosalila structure, Temple 16, Copan, 87–90, *90, 91*, 312
rosaries, 364
Rosario Ferro, Maria del, 401
Rowe, John, 213
Rubí, Marqués de, 359
Rybka, Konrad, 378

S

sacred matter, animacy and authority of. *See* animacy and authority in the Americas
sacrifices and offerings: as animating practice, 330–331; burials as form of, 343; *chicha* offering practices of Inka, 242–243; *mojos* (sacrificed children, in Muisca tradition), 189; in Oaxaca animating practices, 339–345, 350, 352; in Sierra Nevada de Santa Marta cultures, *400, 403, 404, 408*, 410–413, *412, 416*; subfloor offerings, 306, 331. *See also* food, feeding, and biosocial activity
Sahagún, Bernardino de, *Historia general*, 172, *173*, 180, 200n8, 201n19
Sahlins, Marshall D., 390n21, 426
Saint Augustine (Florida), 364
Salas, Guillermo, 386
Salazar, Antonio Bautista de, 19n1
Salomon, Frank, 182, 269
sami, 269–270, 430
San Francisco de Arriba, 340, 347, 350
San Isidro, 192
San José Mogote, 332–334, *333*, 337–339, *338*
San Juan de Pariachi, *kero* burial, *174*
San Lucas, 78–79
Sancho, Pedro, 277
Sandstrom, Alan, 10, 77, 81
Santa Ana–La Florida, 192
Santa Cruz, Alonzo de, 202n28
Santa Cruz Pachacuti Yamqui, Juan, 276
Santiago Imán, 1838 Rebellion of, 95, 96
Santiago of Chimaltenango, 305, 306
Santos, Gelsama Maria Ferreira dos, 64n40

concept of, 59, 65n48; Wari' compared, 64n31, 113, 118, 124; wrestling contests, 45, *46, 50,* 57–58, 59
Urcid, Javier, 338–339
Urton, Gary, *At the Crossroads of the Earth and Sky,* 377
Usaca, 286
ushnu, 280

V

Velásquez García, Erik, 97
Veritas ipsa (papal bull), 151
vibrant matter, concept of, 71
Vicús, 287
Codex Vienna, 144–145
Vilaça, Aparecida, 105
Vilcashuamán, 384
Villa Rojas, Alfonso, 7
Villafañe, Amado, 417n12
Viracocha, 291
Virgin of Copacabana, 235
Virgin of Guadalupe, 227
Virú-Gallinazo, 287
visual imagery of animacy and authority, 169–199; cultural variations within universal ecologies, 169–170; divine personages moving amongst living and dead, 181–186, *183–185;* as epiphenomena, 199–200n2; in Jama Coaque culture, 170, *191–198,* 193–197, 199, 200n5, 203n43; light/darkness, 186–197, *188–198,* 202n23; in Muisca culture, 170, 186–189, *188, 189,* 192–194, 199, 202–203nn33–34; rational functionalist/materialist paradigm, moving beyond, 170–172; repaired objects, significance of, 200n5; transubstantive concepts, 172–181, *173, 174, 175, 177, 179,* 425
Viveiros de Castro, Eduardo, 11–12, 21n17, 108, 117, 131, 133, 172, 178, 200n4, 224, 302, 360, 404, 424
Vogt, Evon Z., 8, 74, 76, 77–78, 305
Voltaire, 6
von der Steinen, Karl, 40–41
Vranich, Alex, 286

W

Wagner, Elisabeth, 312
wak'as. See huacas
Waldron, Jeremy, 21n20
Walker, John, 110, 115
Wankane, 256
War of Quadruple Alliances (1717–1720), 358
Wari' death rituals, 105–124; affective assemblages, concept of, 116–117; animacy versus animism of, 108–109; authority/power in Wari' culture and, 109, 111–113, *112,* 114, 125n4; burning/destruction/giving away possessions of deceased, 106–107, *107,* 109, 113, 125n3, 423; disruptiveness of, 113, *114;* as ecological acts, 110, 116, 121–124, *122, 123,* 428; food, feeding, and biosocial activity, 118–20, *119;* funerary cannibalism, previous practice of, 105–106, *106; iri' makan* (dark earth) agricultural practices and, 109–110, 114–116, 124, 125n5; maize, special status of, 109, 113; Maya compared

to, 99; other Amazonia death practices compared to, 117–118; outsiders, precontact mistrust and avoidance of, 109, 111; precontact versus current situation, 105–106, *106,* 109, 110–114; *ton ho'* ritual for places/trees associated with deceased, 107–108, 109, 110, 115, 120–121, 122; Towira Towira and underworld of, 119–120; Upper Xinguaro compared to, 64n31, 113, 118, 124
Wari *keros,* 175
wasichayay, 423
wasitira, 423, 425, 427, 428
Wastell, Sari, 302
Watanabe, John, 76
Watunna, 176
Wauja, 41, 63n20, 63nn11–12
way glyph, 97, *98*
Weber, Max, 16, 21n21, 199n1
Weismantel, Mary, 17, 18, 63n23, 170, 211, 255, 319, 431, 442
Welch, Jacob, 299, 442
Westphalia, Peace of (1648), 155
whistling serpent vessels, 287–291, *288–290*
Whitehead, Neil, 126n7
Whorf, Benjamin Lee, 372
Wiersema, Juliet, 287
Williams, Caroline, 227
WinklerPrins, Antoinette M. G. A., 121
witchcraft, 20n10, 55, 77, 79, 97, 362, 363
Wiwa, 401, 417n11, 418n15. *See also* Sierra Nevada de Santa Marta
Wolf, Eric, 19n4
women of Upper Xingu, chiefly status of, 44, *45,* 64n33
Workers' Monolith, Tiwanaku, 259

X

Xcalumkin, 312, 317
Xinguaro. *See* Upper Xingu

Y

Codex Y, 143
Yawalapiti, 41, 62n6, 63n12
Yaxchilan, 79, 305, 312, 317
Yaxchilan Stela 31, *72, 73*
Yaxuna Structure 5E-52, 312
Yekuana, 176
Yucatan Maya, 5. *See also* Ucanha Structure 92c-SubIV
Yucatec Maya, 5, 81, 306, 309, 317, 421, 422
Yugüe, *344, 345, 347*
yúuntun, 87–90, 92

Z

Zamora, Alonso de, 190
Zender, Marc, 87, 310, 312
Zinacanteco Maya, 76, 78
Zincateco Maya, 8
Ziólkowski, Mariusz, 271
ziqi lines, 381, *382,* 384
Zuidema, Tom, 276, 371

DUMBARTON OAKS PRE-COLUMBIAN
SYMPOSIA AND COLLOQUIA

PUBLISHED BY DUMBARTON OAKS RESEARCH LIBRARY
AND COLLECTION, WASHINGTON, D.C.

The Dumbarton Oaks Pre-Columbian Symposia and Colloquia series volumes are based on papers presented at scholarly meetings sponsored by the Pre-Columbian Studies program at Dumbarton Oaks. Inaugurated in 1967, these meetings provide a forum for the presentation of advanced research and the exchange of ideas on the art and archaeology of the ancient Americas.

Further information on Dumbarton Oaks Pre-Columbian series and publications can be found at www.doaks.org/publications.

Dumbarton Oaks Conference on the Olmec, edited by Elizabeth P. Benson, 1968

Dumbarton Oaks Conference on Chavín, edited by Elizabeth P. Benson, 1971

The Cult of the Feline, edited by Elizabeth P. Benson, 1972

Mesoamerican Writing Systems, edited by Elizabeth P. Benson, 1973

Death and the Afterlife in Pre-Columbian America, edited by Elizabeth P. Benson, 1975

The Sea in the Pre-Columbian World, edited by Elizabeth P. Benson, 1977

The Junius B. Bird Pre-Columbian Textile Conference, edited by Ann Pollard Rowe, Elizabeth P. Benson, and Anne-Louise Schaffer, 1979

Pre-Columbian Metallurgy of South America, edited by Elizabeth P. Benson, 1979

Mesoamerican Sites and World-Views, edited by Elizabeth P. Benson, 1981

The Art and Iconography of Late Post-Classic Central Mexico, edited by Elizabeth Hill Boone, 1982

Falsifications and Misreconstructions of Pre-Columbian Art, edited by Elizabeth Hill Boone, 1982

Highland-Lowland Interaction in Mesoamerica: Interdisciplinary Approaches, edited by Arthur G. Miller, 1983

Ritual Human Sacrifice in Mesoamerica, edited by Elizabeth Hill Boone, 1984

Painted Architecture and Polychrome Monumental Sculpture in Mesoamerica, edited by Elizabeth Hill Boone, 1985

Early Ceremonial Architecture in the Andes, edited by Christopher B. Donnan, 1985

The Aztec Templo Mayor, edited by Elizabeth Hill Boone, 1986

The Southeast Classic Maya Zone, edited by Elizabeth Hill Boone and Gordon R. Willey, 1988

The Northern Dynasties: Kingship and Statecraft in Chimor, edited by Michael E. Moseley and Alana Cordy-Collins, 1990

Wealth and Hierarchy in the Intermediate Area, edited by Frederick W. Lange, 1992

Art, Ideology, and the City of Teotihuacan, edited by Janet Catherine Berlo, 1992

Latin American Horizons, edited by Don Stephen Rice, 1993

Lowland Maya Civilization in the Eighth Century AD, edited by Jeremy A. Sabloff and John S. Henderson, 1993

Collecting the Pre-Columbian Past, edited by Elizabeth Hill Boone, 1993

Tombs for the Living: Andean Mortuary Practices, edited by Tom D. Dillehay, 1995

Native Traditions in the Postconquest World, edited by Elizabeth Hill Boone and Tom Cummins, 1998

Function and Meaning in Classic Maya Architecture, edited by Stephen D. Houston, 1998

Social Patterns in Pre-Classic Mesoamerica, edited by David C. Grove and Rosemary A. Joyce, 1999

Gender in Pre-Hispanic America, edited by Cecelia F. Klein, 2001

Archaeology of Formative Ecuador, edited by J. Scott Raymond and Richard L. Burger, 2003

Gold and Power in Ancient Costa Rica, Panama, and Colombia, edited by Jeffrey Quilter and John W. Hoopes, 2003

Palaces of the Ancient New World, edited by Susan Toby Evans and Joanne Pillsbury, 2004

A Pre-Columbian World, edited by Jeffrey Quilter and Mary Ellen Miller, 2006

Twin Tollans: Chichén Itzá, Tula, and the Epiclassic to Early Postclassic Mesoamerican World, edited by Jeff Karl Kowalski and Cynthia Kristan-Graham, 2007

Variations in the Expression of Inka Power, edited by Richard L. Burger, Craig Morris, and Ramiro Matos Mendieta, 2007

El Niño, Catastrophism, and Culture Change in Ancient America, edited by Daniel H. Sandweiss and Jeffrey Quilter, 2008

Classic-Period Cultural Currents in Southern and Central Veracruz, edited by Philip J. Arnold III and Christopher A. Pool, 2008

The Art of Urbanism: How Mesoamerican Kingdoms Represented Themselves in Architecture and Imagery, edited by William L. Fash and Leonardo López Luján, 2009

New Perspectives on Moche Political Organization, edited by Jeffrey Quilter and Luis Jaime Castillo B., 2010

Astronomers, Scribes, and Priests: Intellectual Interchange between the Northern Maya Lowlands and Highland Mexico in the Late Postclassic Period, edited by Gabrielle Vail and Christine Hernández, 2010

The Place of Stone Monuments: Context, Use, and Meaning in Mesoamerica's Preclassic Transition, edited by Julia Guernsey, John E. Clark, and Barbara Arroyo, 2010

Their Way of Writing: Scripts, Signs, and Pictographies in Pre-Columbian America, edited by Elizabeth Hill Boone and Gary Urton, 2011

Past Presented: Archaeological Illustration and the Ancient Americas, edited by Joanne Pillsbury, 2012

Merchants, Markets, and Exchange in the Pre-Columbian World, edited by Kenneth G. Hirth and Joanne Pillsbury, 2013

Embattled Bodies, Embattled Places: War in Pre-Columbian Mesoamerica and the Andes, edited by Andrew K. Scherer and John W. Verano, 2014

The Measure and Meaning of Time in Mesoamerica and the Andes, edited by Anthony F. Aveni, 2015

Making Value, Making Meaning: Techné in the Pre-Columbian World, edited by Cathy Lynne Costin, 2016

Smoke, Flames, and the Human Body in Meso-american Ritual Practice, edited by Vera Tiesler and Andrew K. Scherer, 2018

Sacred Matter: Animacy and Authority in the Americas, edited by Steve Kosiba, John Wayne Janusek, and Thomas B. F. Cummins, 2020